INTEGRATED TRANSFORMATION OF AGRICULTURE

NIPA® GENX ELECTRONIC RESOURCES & SOLUTIONS P. LTD.
New Delhi-110 034

About the Editor

Dr Jag Paul Sharma is presently Director Research, Sher-e-Kashmir University of Agricultural Sciences and Technology of Jammu. His previous assignments have been, Dean Faculty of Agriculture, Associate Director Research and Head Division of Vegetable Science and Floriculture, SKUAST-Jammu. As plant breeder to his credit are 13 crop varieties, six of cereals, six of vegetables and one of pulses. As an academician contributed 11 books to the field of agriculture, two on cold arid agriculture, three each on vegetable science, organic agriculture and general agriculture. He has published more than 100 research papers and technical communications. As Director of Research he has been instrumental in establishing Organic Farming Research Centre, Basmati Rice Research Centre and Mushroom Research Centre at Main Campus of SKUAST Jammu, Chatha. He could also mobilize funds to the tune of more than 100 crores to the University during his tenure through *ad hoc* research projects from more than 24 funding agencies. He is member of various national committees of ICAR and DST, Govt of India. He is the founder president of a non-profit professional society SIDAVES (Society for Integrated Development of Agriculture, Veterinary and Ecological Sciences, India) and Editor-in-Chief of SIDAVES Journal of Safe Agriculture. He envisions agripreneurship and agri-business as tools for women empowerment in India.

INTEGRATED TRANSFORMATION OF AGRICULTURE

Jag Paul Sharma

Director Research & President SIDAVES
Directorate of Research
Sher-e-Kashmir University of Agricultural Sciences and Technology- J
Chatha, Jammu-180 009, J&K, India

NIPA® GENX ELECTRONIC RESOURCES & SOLUTIONS P. LTD.

New Delhi-110 034

NIPA® GENX ELECTRONIC
RESOURCES & SOLUTIONS P. LTD.

101,103, Vikas Surya Plaza, CU Block
L.S.C. Market, Pitam Pura, New Delhi-110 034
Ph : +91 11 27341616, 27341717, 27341718
E-mail: newindiapublishingagency@gmail.com
web: www.nipabooks.com

For customer assistance, please contact
Phone: + 91-11-27 34 17 17
Fax: + 91-11- 27 34 16 16
E-Mail: feedbacks@nipabooks.com

ISBN: 978-81-19215-79-9

Composed and Designed by NIPA®.

Dedication

To my
Mother Prakasho Devi
&
Father Mansa Ram
who brought me to
the world of wonders

Preface

Agriculture is the lifeline of India as being central to food security, nutritional security, poverty alleviation, socio-economic stability and sustainable development. Though contribution to nation's GDP is 18% yet agriculture is the major profession providing employment to more than 58% households in rural India. Indian agriculture is vibrant, responding and gigantic enterprise with annual production of 285 million tons of food grains, 181 million tons of vegetables, 115 million tons of fruits, 25.3 million tons of pulses, 174 million tons of fresh milk, 74 billion of poultry eggs and 11.5 million tons of fish. Inspite of this, nutritional security to many and food security to 115 millions, targets of higher livestock and crop productivity, consumers' demand for innovative agri-products and export orientation are yet to be achieved. This advocates factorial analysis of agriculture and renovations and reforms in earlier and present recommendations. Major factors impacting Indian agriculture comprise weather parameters, monsoon, irrigation patterns, crop and livestock nutrition, government policy (federal as well as state), commodity prices (global, national as well as local) and consumers' preferences. The predictability as well as modeling of risks on abovementioned factors, is a herculean task. In fact, the number of factors impacting the viability of agriculture sector, as well as the volatility in the magnitude of these factors is increasing and thus, the sector requires integrated transformation for sustainable development and stable food security.

The Indian agriculture sector is witnessing a massive transformation because of technological interventions and governmental initiatives. In the past three consecutive budgets, the agriculture sector has received special attention but this time the focus of the Indian Union Budget is on agribusiness and "agri-value" addition. In the Indian Union Budget 2018-19, the government has allocated Rs. 14.5 lakh crores ($222.4 billion) for the rural development and agriculture sector. Indian government has set a target to double farmers' income by 2022. Indian finance minister has announced a number of initiatives, keeping the recommendations of the Doubling Farmers' Income committee in mind, for example the decision to keep MSP (Minimum Support Price) for crops at least at one and- half times of their production cost. For those farmers who are not in a position to directly transact at APMCs (Agriculture Produce Market Committees) and other wholesale markets, the government has decided to develop and upgrade existing 22,000 rural haats into Gramin Agricultural Markets (GrAMs). These GrAMs will be electronically linked to e-NAM (Electronic National Agricultural Market, an online platform) to provide farmers with a facility to sell their produce directly to consumers. The government has launched with allocation Rs. 2600 crore ($360.8m.) Pradhan Mantri Krishi Sinchai Yojana, a national mission to improve farm productivity and ensure better utilization of the resources in the country, in 96 irrigation- deprived districts.

In words of Indian Finance Minister "We consider agriculture to be an enterprise and want to help farmers produce more from the same land parcel at less cost, and simultaneously to realize higher prices for their produce". To address the challenge of price volatility of perishable agricultural commodities, the finance minister has proposed launching a scheme called "Operation Greens." This scheme will help bring farmers closer to the marketplace through better logistics, processing facilities and professional management. A sum of Rs. 500 crore ($75.2 million) is allocated for this purpose.

Hence, a shift from agriculture to agripreneurship and agribusiness is the focus to revitalize Indian agriculture so that it becomes more receptive and remunerative venture for youths that has the potential to contribute to a range of social and economic developments such as employment generation, women empowerment, income generation, poverty reduction and improvements in nutrition, health and overall food security in the national economy. Nearly 40 crore women out of the total of 60 crore female population depend upon crop and animal husbandry, fisheries, forestry, agro-processing and agri-business for their livelihood. Moreover, agripreneurship ventures are seen to have a potential to promote job-led economic growth in rural areas by harnessing technologies for environmentally sustainable and socially equitable development which can provide a decent livelihood to women as well.

Considering the existing scenario that two-thirds of the Indian population is employed in agriculture sector, agripreneurship and agribusiness stand out as imperatives for sustainable development and employment generation in the country. With this contention in mind, an attempt has been made through this volume entitled "Integrated Transformation of Agriculture with Special reference to India" to narrow down on the challenges related to agricultural transformation in India. Technological amalgamations required to upgrade agriculture to commercial form. Strategical deployment of innovations to transform agriculture into an attractive and profitable venture. In all, there are 23 chapters first one describes the bottlenecks and gaps in the form of challenges that one needs to know while thinking of futuristic plans. Chapter 2nd elaborates technologies that brought green revolution while third one focuses on technologies that deserve priority if transformation in agriculture is desired. In view of small holdings, contract farming is important which is enumerated in chapter 4. Due emphasis is placed on livestock farming through zoonotic diseases control, strategic parasite management and dairying at chapters 5, 8 and 15. Innovative approaches like ICTs interventions, climate smart agriculture, seed priming, biochar, organic agriculture and integrated farming system are appropriately dealt in chapter no 6, 7, 10, 13, 14 and 17. Horticulture and marketing aspects are covered in chapter no 11, 12 and 9 and hi-tech agronomy in chapter no 22. Weather forecasting, remote sensing and agro-advisory relevance is discussed in chapter no 16 and 18. Last chapter but not the least, is on organic agriculture as an entrepreneurship for women empowerment and socio-economic transformation which discusses the compatibility and suitability of organic agriculture to women entrepreneurs.

I am thankful to the scientists, teachers and my professional colleagues who took pain to contribute to this volume and solicit their cooperation in future, too. From the core of my heart, I acknowledge the various internet sites, international and national institutes, Govt. organizations, social sites, scholars and farmers whose information has been used to develop this volume. The sole purpose of this task has been academic, social and reference book for policy makers. I don't claim the exclusiveness of the information but surely way and form of the compilation and presentation is maiden. This will be useful to scientists, teachers and scholars as a reference book on Indian Agriculture while it will act as a source book for field functionaries for plethora of new technologies fit for project development and field implementation.

I am obliged to the Executive Body of SIDAVES (Society for Integrated Development of Agriculture, Veterinary and Ecological Sciences, J&K, India), Dr Vikas Sharma, Dr Narinder Panotra, Dr AP Singh and Dr Neelesh Sharma for entrusting me the responsibility of editing this volume. I owe thanks to my wife Mrs Kusam Lata for her support and inspire me to take this kind of venture. A word of appreciation is must for my son Vishaw Vikas, daughter Sabhyata Sharma and daughter-in-law Aarushi Singh Sharma who have been always amicable, cooperative and supportive to me during long busy hours with this assignment. Special thanks and gratitude my gurus Sh OP Pushap, Jammu, Prof HS Chawla, Pantnagar, Prof SC Mani, Pantnagar, Prof BB Mukerjee, Bose Institute, Kolkatta who motivated and instilled in me the sentiments for service to the social and academic societies.

Last but not the least, I acknowledge whole heartedly M/S New India Publishing Agency, New Delhi for accepting my request to publish this book and appreciate the keen interest shown by NIPA for fast track preparation of this volume for the benefit of agricultural fraternity.

February, 2019 **Jag Paul Sharma**

Contents

List of Contributors

Aarushi Singh
School of Biotechnology
SKUAST-J Chatha, Jammu, J&K, India

Akash Sharma
Organic Farming Research Centre
SKUAST-J Chatha, Jammu, J&K, India

Akhil Verma
Maize Research Centre
SKUAST-J, Udhampurm Jammu
J&K, India

Ametesh Sharma
Organic farming Research Centre
SKUAST-J Chatha, Jammu, J&K, India

Anil Bhat
Division of Agricultural Economics
SKUAST-J Chatha, Jammu, J&K, India

Anil Bhushan
Organic farming Research Centre
SKUAST-J Chatha, Jammu, J&K, India

Anish Yadav
Division of veterinary Parasitology
FVSc, SKUAST-J, RS Pura, J&K, India

Ashwani Kumar
VAEA
Department of Agriculture
Jammu, J&K, India

Arshad Bhat
Division of Agricultural Economics
SKUAST-K, Shalimar, Srinagar, J&K, India

Ajaz Ahmad Malik
Division of Vegetable Science
SKUAST-K, Shalimar, Srinagar, J&K, India

BC Sharma
Division of Agronomy
SKUAST-J Chatha, Jammu, J&K, India

Banarsi Lal
KVK, SKUAST-J
Reasi, Jammu, , J&K, India

Bharat Bhushan
Joint Registrar (Acad)
SKUAST-J, Chatha, Jammu, J&K, India

Bharat Singh Ghanghas
CCS, HAU, Hisar
Haryana, India

Charu Sharma
Agro-Met. Section, Division of Agronomy
SKUAST-J Chatha, Jammu, J&K, India

DB Singh
ICAR- CITH, Old Air field, Rangreth
Srinagar, J&K, India

Dileep Kachroo
AICRP on IFS, Division of Agronomy
SKUAST-J Chatha, Jammu, J&K, India

FA Khan
Division of Basic Sciences and Humanities
SKUAST-K, Shalimar, Srinagar
J&K, India

Imtiyaz Murtaza
Division of Basic Sciences and Humanities
SKUAST-K, Shalimar, Srinagar, J&K, India

JP Saini
CSK, HPKV, Palampur
Himachal Pradesh, India

JI Mir
ICAR- CITH, Old Air field, Rangreth
Srinagar, J&K, India

Jag Paul Sharma
Directorate of research,
SKUAST-J Chatha, Jammu, J&K, India

K Stephen
Division of Basic Sciences and Humanities
SKUAST-K, Shalimar, Srinagar, J&K, India

M Amir
NDUAT, Kumarganj, Faizabad
Uttar Pradesh, India

MH Wani
Rajiv Gandhi Chair
SKUAST-K, Shalimar, Srinagar, J&K, India

MY Zargar
Directorate of Research
SKUAST-K, Shalimar, Srinagar, J&K, India

Mahender Singh
Agro-Met. Section, Division of Agronomy
SKUAST-J Chatha, Jammu, J&K, India

Manmohan Sharma
School of Biotechnology
SKUAST-J Chatha, Jammu, J&K, India

Mansah Gul
Division of Basic Sciences and Humanities
SKUAST-K, Shalimar, Srinagar, J&K, India

Manish Sharma
Organic Farming Research Centre
SKUAST-J Chatha, Jammu, J&K, India

Mohd Rashid
Division of Veterinary Public Health
FVSc, SKUAST-J RS Pura, Jammu
J&K, India

Nallamilli Siddardha
Division of Agricultural Economics
SKUAST-K, Shalimar
Srinagar, J&K, India

Narinder Panotra
Organic Farming Research Centre
SKUAST-J Chatha, Jammu, J&K, India

Neelesh Sharma
Division of Veterinary medicine
FVSc, SKUAST-J, RS Pura
Jammu, India

Neetu Sharma
Division of Agronomy
SKUAST-J Chatha, Jammu, India

Pallivi Khajuria
Division of Veterinary Parasitology
FVSc, SKUAST-J, RS Pura, Jammu, India

Pradeep K Sharma
Vice Chancellor
SKUAST-J Chatha, Jammu, J&K, India

Pranav Kumar
Division of VAHEE, FVSc
SKUAST-J, RS Pura, Jammu, J&K, India

Peeyush Sharma
Division of Soil Science
SKUAST-J Chatha, Jammu, J&K, India

R Godara
Division of Veterinary Parasitology
FVSc, SKUAST-J, RS Pura, Jammu
J&K, India

RK Salgotra
School of Biotechnology,
SKUAST-J Chatha, Jammu, J&K, India

Rajesh Katoch
Division of Veterinary Parasitology
FVSc, SKUAST-J, RS Pura, Jammu
J&K, India

Ravikant Avasthe
ICAR-National Organic Farming Research
Institute, Tadong, Gangtok, Sikkim

Rohit Sharma
GKMS, AMFU, RARS,
SKUAST-J, Rajouri, J&K, India

SK Gupta
Division of Veterinary Medicine
FVSc, SKUAST-J, RS Pura
Jammu, India

SK Singh
Organic Farming Research Centre
SKUAST-J Chatha, Jammu, J&K, India

Satesh Sharma
Organic Farming Research Centre
SKUAST-J Chatha, Jammu, J&K, India

Sabhyata Sharma
Department of Veterinary Parasitology
NVC, MAHFSU, Nagpur
Maharashtra, India

Santosh Sethi
Department of Sociology
RSD College, Ferozpur
Punjab, India

Sandeep Sharma
Division of Soil Science
PAU, Ludhiana, Punjab

Satish Kumar Sharma
Seed Production Farm
SKUAST-J Chatha, Jammu, J&K, India

Shafiya Imitiaz Rafiqi
Division of Veterinary Parasitology
FVSc, SKUAST-J, RS Pura, Jammu
J&K, India

Shahid Ahamad
PME Cell, Directorate of Research
SKUAST-J Chatha, Jammu, J&K, India

SW Kolte
Department of Veterinary Parasitology
NVC, MAHFSU, Nagpur
Maharashtra, India

Sumiti Narayan
Division of Vegetable Science,
SKUAST-K, Shalimar, Srinagar, J&K, India

Veena Sharma
Agro-Met. Section
Division of Agronomy
SKUAST-J Chatha, Jammu, K&K, India

Vikas Abrol
Advanced Centre on Rainfed Agriculture
SKUAST-J, Dhiansar, Samba, Jammu
J&K, India

Vikas Sharma
Organic Farming Research Centre
SKUAST-J Chatha, Jammu, J&K, India

Vishaw Vikas
Division of Soil Science and Agricultural
Chemistry, FoA, SKUAST-J Chatha, Jammu
J&K, India

Zul-I-Huma
Division of Veterinary Medicine
FVSc, SKUAST-J, RS Pura, Jammu
J&K, India

1

Challenges Before the Indian Agriculture: Lessons from Past and Strategies for Future

Jag Paul Sharma

Directorate of Research, SKUAST Jammu, Jammu and Kashmir, India

1. Introduction
2. Land fragmentation
3. Marginalization of holding size
4. Obscure marketing prospects
5. Low water and inputs use efficiencies
6. Modest level of farm mechanization
7. Un-organization in agriculture
8. Low level of food processing
9. Predominance of rainfed agro-ecosystem
10. Inadequate cold chain and storage infrastructure
11. Meagre investments
12. Sublimation
13. *References*

Abstract

India today has 1.30 billion people and would be the world's most populous country by 2025. The challenge is how to feed India's growing population with rising income, but limited land and water resources. Whereas area under crop cultivation has come down from 142 million ha to 138 million ha, asking for protecting the arable lands from mass urbanization and more productivity per unit area. The agricultural production systems are still operating at low productivity and high uncertainty in the country. There is little or no alignment between production, the growth of agricultural commodities in the market and the supply of these commodities. All this leading to considerable farm produce wastage, mounting tremendous pressure on natural resources and would pose a challenge to the country in providing food, water, health, shelter, sanitation and jobs to all.

While industry and services have grown, agricultural sector has lagged behind. Information technology sector is growing consistently at 30 per cent every year but agriculture has not even achieved 4 per cent growth. The contribution of agricultural sector to national Gross Domestic Product (GDP) has continued to decline over the years; has shrunk from 55 per cent in 1951-52 to 14.6 per cent in 2015-16. Land fragmentation, reducing holding size, obscure marketing prospects, low water and inputs use efficiencies, modest level of mechanization, unorganization, unreliable returns from rainfed areas, inadequate storage infrastructure, weak processing sector and meagre investments continue to leave visible impressions on Indian agriculture. Nonetheless, agriculture remains a major source of employment, absorbing about 52 per cent of the total national workforce. Higher levels of investments in agriculture, both by the public and private sector can yield much better results if the reforms are undertaken to streamline not only the incentive structures for the farmers, but also the institutional framework to address the issues of integration, export orientation, infrastructure development, and information technology and management to achieve the objective of a innovative agricultural sector capable of providing food security to all. Farmer insecurity about crop failure also prevents them from adopting changes. A balance between risk and reward is considered to be an important economic factor for enhancing relationships. Trust among channel partners, power share and interdependence are other important factors for enhancing relationships in the supply chain system.

Private organizations investment in the agribusiness sector is low due to the high level of government regulations including procurement and movement, storage, warehousing and marketing of major commodities, plant-scale restriction in food processing, and restriction on contract farming and land leasing. Agricultural growth and modernization need to be underpinned by an efficient credit system capable of providing an expanding flow of credit for both investment and working capital. Input subsidies in agriculture show sustainable benefits only up to a point, beyond which they lead to considerable inefficiencies. If we reduce non-essential input subsidies, it will enhance production, productivity, return and public investment in agriculture.

The food consumption basket is getting diversified none the less cereals still dominate, this dominance is being successively eroded by rising expenditure on fruits, vegetables, milk, eggs, meat and fish which together is sometimes referred to as the "high value" segment. It speaks of future in farming system approach which fetches different commodities and products. Indicating success is close when integrated farming is adopted by the farmers where diversification is the rule. Although rural incomes have increased and rural poverty has reduced over the years, the gap between urban and rural incomes has widened sharply because agriculture has grown slower than the other sectors. Moreover, employment growth in non-agriculture sectors has not been enough to sufficiently reduce the population dependent on agriculture. So there is urgent need to shift from commodity to product development approach that is, maintaining the growth of primary agriculture with focus on secondary agriculture. This will open avenue for innovative products, more job opportunities, more investors, successful contract farming, strong production and market linkage, diverse entrepreneurial environment, less postharvest wastage, increased input use efficiency, lower cost of production and higher benefit cost ratio.

Keywords: Indian agriculture, challenges, land fragmentation, low mechanization, meagre investment

1. Introduction

India experienced remarkable growth in the production of various agricultural commodities over the last four decades, because of technological interventions, bringing the country from a deficit to a surplus stage in food grain production. With approximately 195 m ha area under cultivation of which 63 percent is rainfed (roughly 125m ha) while 37 percent is irrigated (70m ha), India has forests cover of some 65m ha. Being the world's largest producer of milk, pulses, and spices, India has the world's largest cattle herd (buffaloes) as well as the largest area under wheat, rice and cotton. It is the second largest producer of rice, wheat, cotton, sugarcane, farmed fish, sheep & goat meat, fruit, vegetables and tea. In spite of self sufficiency in food grain production, food insecurity continues to haunt the Indian majority even today. Rising inputs prices and proportionately diminishing market returns cast shadow on creditability of agriculture as a viable commercial profession in India. Cobweb effect is still the characteristic feature of Indian agriculture. Agriculture policy is inflicted with vested political interests. It is developed, renovated and implemented under the fear of vote banks perhaps least caring for the plight of farms and farming community. Serving to short term fixes and overlooking issues of lasting growth in agriculture, politicians are illogically pandering farm voters.

In words of Malone (2010) India was once at the apex of international achievement in agricultural innovation. Drawing on a wide variety of international grain types, notably MS Swaminathan, was able to achieve in the 1960s and 1970s a real "green revolution" in India, boosting agricultural productivity impressively and making the country fully self-sufficient in its main food requirements for the first time in modern history. Scientific innovation was supported by energetic policy at the Union and State levels to achieve one of the world's most striking agricultural successes of the 20th century. But then, as so often with success, a purposeful policy dissolved into politicking and piece meal implementation.

India suffers from higher levels of child malnutrition than Sub-Saharan Africa. This is not because basic Indian foodstuffs are less nutritious than Africa's. Canada's global micro-nutrient initiative, co-funded by U.N. agencies and the World Bank, while making a significant contribution to fighting against malnourishment, stunting and wasting in India (all at heart breaking levels, all with life-long effects) is not as successful as it should be. Why? Because of poor rural health, education and physical infrastructure (the latter inhibiting the free flow of foodstuffs that would naturally alleviate nutrition problems).

Food security relates to much more than agricultural incentives and disincentives. Wider national policies and programs are at least as important. And yet, in spite (or perhaps because) of India's vibrant democracy, admirably free and crusading press and dynamic civil society inconstant contention with each other, little has been achieved in recent years.India should learn from the success of the U.S. and Canadian rural development models of creating non-farm rural jobs so that sub-division of farms and unemployment could be avoided. These jobs mostly related to servicing, a growing agricultural sector and processing food, in order to get as much of it as possible to distant markets intact (a major challenge for India today with respect to fresh produce). Rather than misguided attempts to force rural migrants from urban settings they have reached in search of livelihoods, coherent government policies need to encourage good non-farm jobs in rural areas.

Land fragmentation, reducing holding size, obscure marketing prospects, low water and inputs use efficiencies, modest level of mechanization, unorganization, unreliable returns from rainfed areas, inadequate storage infrastructure, weak processing sector and meagre investments continue to leave visible impressions on Indian agriculture.

2. Land fragmentation

Land fragmentation is a situation where a farming household spreads over several non-contiguous land plots. It is an observed phenomenon in many countries around the world including India. This is an obstacle to commercialization and modernization of agriculture particularly when holding size falls below two hectares. Anthropologists, on the other hand, see land fragmentation as a positive situation under which farmers can cultivate many environmental zones, minimize production risk and optimize the schedule for cropping activities. Many environmentalists consider that any intervention to land tenure structure to remove land fragmentation may have serious environmental effects in nature and even social effects on land owners.

Various studies have disclosed that consolidation, land ownership and crop diversity have positive association with input use efficiencies and profit at the farm. Increased fragmentation is continuing feature of Indian agriculture weakening its commercial strength because land holding size is falling below the viable threshold limit.

Reasons

- Disintegration of joint family system
- Limited off-farm employment opportunities in rural areas
- Selling of agricultural lands
- Conversion of agricultural lands for non-agricultural purposes

Effects

- Impediment to mechanization,
- Hurdle to export orientation
- Obstacle to input accessibility

3. Marginalization of holding size

The average size of holdings was 2.28 hectares in 1970-71 which was reduced to 1.82 hectares in 1980-81 and 1.50 hectares in 1995-96. The size of the holdings will further decrease with the infinite Sub-division of the land holdings. More than 85% farmers fall in marginal category. Holdings are of four types.

Economic holding indicates that particular size of holding which will provide necessary support to the farmer's family. It allows a grower of producing sufficient to support himself and his family in reasonable comfort after paying his necessary expenses. 10 acres of holding size is economical under Indian conditions provided soil quality is good and irrigation facility exists. If well managed, economic holding can yield net income of Rs 25,000 per month to a farming family.

- **Basic holding** is smaller than economic holding and it offers only subsistence living to farmers.
- **Optimum holding** is defined by the Agrarian Committee as three times of economic holding.

- **Family holding** (introduced by Five Year Plan) implies an area which is equivalent to either a plough unit or a unit of average family having a pair of bullocks. Land reforms panel observed that a family holding should provide an annual income worth Rs. 12000 to an average farmer family.

Causes

With the growth of the size of families, the agricultural holdings in India are gradually being sub-divided among the heirs on the death of the owner of the land. In this way generation after generation the land is being subdivided and fragmented as well.

The following are some of the important causes of growing sub-division and fragmentation of agricultural holding in India:

i) Proliferation of human dwellings

With the rapid growth of population, in the country, the pressure of population on land is increasing. Much of agricultural land nearer to cities and metros is being converted to human settlements.

ii) Laws of Inheritance

In India, the laws of inheritance made provision for equal share of the ancestral property including agricultural land among the children. Due to the application of this law there is a continuous split in the size of farms with every new generation.

iii) Fall of joint family system

Under the system of joint family there was no need to sub-divide the size of agricultural holding. With emergence of nucleus family system, the joint family system is breaking up rapidly leading to a sub-division of agricultural holding in the country.

iv) Decline of village handicrafts and industries

Village handicrafts and industries are facing threat of closure due declination of choice of the products in market. Artisans are being forced to leave their ancestral occupations and started to depend on agriculture.

v) Rural indebtedness

Village moneylenders are charging exorbitant rate of interest and adopting unfair practices and in the process gradually grab the land of the poor cultivators. In this way a part of a land is passing away into the hands of money lenders leading to sub-divisions of land holding.

vi) Psychological attachment to a field

Indians are psychologically attached to land or a piece of land and want a chunk of land piece from each and every field. The type of psychology results into sub-division and fragmentation of each and every field. Sub-division and fragmentation of the holdings is one of the main causes of our low agricultural productivity and backward state of our agriculture.

A lot of time and labour is wasted in moving seeds, manure, implements and cattle from one piece of land to another

- Per unit energy consumption increases
- Irrigation becomes difficult on such small and fragmented fields
- Marginal holdings are generally commercial non-viable units
- A lot of fertile agricultural land is wasted in providing boundaries
- Under such circumstances, the farmer is unable to adopt latest innovations

The only answer to this ticklish problem is the consolidation of holdings which means the reallocation of holdings which are fragmented, the creation of farms which comprise only one or a few parcels in place of multitude of patches formerly in the possession of each peasant. But unfortunately, this plan has not succeeded much. Although legislation for consolidation of holdings has been enacted by almost all the states, it has been implemented only in Punjab, Haryana and in some parts of Uttar Pradesh.

Consolidation of about 45 million holdings has been done till 1990-91 in Punjab, Haryana and western Uttar Pradesh. The other solution to this problem is cooperative farming or contract farming in which the farmers pool their resources and share the profit.

4. Obscure marketing perspective

Agriculture and allied sectors (including agriculture, livestock, forestry and fishery) contribute 16 per cent in GDP and employs over 58 per cent of the workforce in the country. India is the largest producer, consumer and exporter (15% of the world exports) of spices and spice products. In production of fruits, India got the second position in the world. India's horticulture output (fruits, vegetables and spices) reached to third position with the help of producing 283.5 million tons (MT) in 2014-15. Agriculture also contributes in export which is 10 per cent of the total country's export. India is the largest producer of milk with annual output of 146.31 MT which is 18.5 per cent of the total world production. Along with this, India is the second largest producer (14 % of the world output) and sixth largest exporter (2.76% of the world exports) of sugar.

In spite this, marketing prospects are obscure and did not assure expected profit of the produce to Indian farmers.

Lack of assured marketing with reasonable profit is the biggest drawback that makes agriculture a business of uncertainty and unreliability in India. Factors responsible for this are as below:

1. Small size fields and scattered holding: it makes collection and transportation cumbersome. A farmer produces varieties of commodities and products in small quantity for small period, thus unable to fulfill traders demand.
2. Storage infrastructure: it is inadequate with the farmers or with the agencies to keep the produce safe after harvest or till the market demand arises. Consequently in peak period prices shot down and returns turn poor.
3. Problems of transportation: Roads are either in shabby conditions or not available. Specialized vehicles required as per nature of the produce are the limitations.
4. Middlemen: Along chain of middlemen from the village to storage to market to retailers is there. A proper orientation of the system has to be put in place by the Govt agencies to shorten the chain.
5. Lack of grading and standardization fetch either no price or poor price to the farmers. Often packing poor quality produce at the bottom layers has given bad name to the producers.
6. Poor post harvest handling practices: packaging and processing are either absent or of below acceptable standards.
7. Demand and supply not connected with production: very often farmers are producing crops or variety of a crop as per their choice which doesn't match either market requirements or consumer preference.
8. Credit facilities available but investments are scanty because of un-assured profitability.
9. Un-organization: mainly because of marginal holding size and low quantity and quality produce. It results in poor investments on modern amenities in agriculture.
10. Government interventions are ineffective because of wrong research inferences.

What is required to be done?

1. Production must match with demand, supply and consumption
2. Consumer preference must be given due consideration when intending for commercial farming.
3. Development of infrastructure for post harvest handling, processing, storage and transportation in rural areas.
4. Export orientation through awareness on grading and packing.
5. Promotion of contract /cooperative farming to match production with market demand.
6. ICTs interventions to identify and maintain balance between producing locations and consuming sites.
7. Zonalization of entrepreneurships in agriculture.
8. Special regulated markets for small and marginal farmers: it should have some extra incentives to small holders.

5. Low water and in-puts use efficiencies

B:C ratio is low in crop production systems as majority of the farmers do not know how much seed, fertilizers, water or pesticides are to be used. Being fact that input applications vary with field, crop, crop stage, variety, quality, climate and purpose for which raised etc. Water and fertilizers need particular attention as efficiencies are below 25% in these cases.

5.1. Water management

The agricultural sector consumes approximately 80 percent of the available water in India. It continues to be the major water-consuming sector due to the intensification of agriculture. India has the largest irrigated area in the world, but with coverage of irrigation is only 40 percent of the gross cropped area. One of the main reasons for the low coverage of irrigation is the predominance of flood method of irrigation, where water use efficiency is very low due to conveyance, seepage and distribution losses. One of the strategies to high up water use efficiency and expand area under irrigation in Indian agriculture is micro-irrigation, which includes mainly drip and sprinkler irrigation methods. The conveyance and distribution losses are reduced completely consequently resultis higher water use efficiency.

Micro-irrigation techniques can save water 40% to 80% and water use efficiency (WUE) can be enhanced up to 100% as compared to 30-40% under conventional practice (INCID 1994; Suresh Kumar 2008). It can save fertilizer 25 to 30 per cent when applied through micro-irrigation and 15 to 30 per cent increase in yield depending on crop (Table 1). Thus, micro-irrigation can be one of the viable options for expanding area under cultivation. The coverage of area under micro-irrigation is not appreciable in India, except for a few states. The area under drip irrigation has increased from meager 1500 ha in 1985 to 70,859 ha in 1991-92 and further to 0.5 Mha in 2003 (GoI, 2004). Similarly, the area under sprinkler irrigation has increased from 0.23 Mha in 1985-86 to 0.67 Mha in 1997-98 and further to 1.63 Mha in 2004-05.

Micro-irrigation has several advantages and one is saving of water was up to 84 per cent over surface method of irrigation. India has enormous potential for drip as well as sprinkler irrigation methods. Drip irrigation is more suitable for wide spaced and high value commercial crops. It is also being used for cultivating oilseeds, pulses, cotton, and even for sugarcane and wheat crop. Sprinkler irrigation suits to closely grown crops such as millets, pulses, wheat, sugarcane, groundnut, cotton, vegetables, fruits, flowers, spices and condiments in environments where evaporation losses are minimum.

In rainfed areas emphasis has to be on water and soil moisture conservation where interventions like mulching technology to arrest water evaporation and use of anti-transpirants to withhold transpiration at optimal rate, are desired. Plastic, dry grasses, crop stubbles and FYM can be used as source for mulching. In vegetables like cucurbits mulches are used to protect fruit damage from sun scorching heat while in cole crops they conserve water, result early and big curd or knob size with yield increase of 10-15% and water use efficiency up by 15%.

5.2. Nutrient use efficiency

Six crops (rice, wheat, cotton, sugar cane, rapeseed and mustard) consume about two-thirds of the fertilizer applied. The irrigated area, accounting for 40 percent of the total agricultural area, receives 60 percent of the fertilizer applied. there is plenty of scope for increasing nutrient use efficiency by the facts that in India average response of cereals is only about 9 kg grain per kg of fertilizer nutrient while the figure for Punjab is about 15 kg and, in experiments, response is of the order of 25 kg grain per kg of nutrient applied. Nitrogen recovery in crops grown by farmers rarely exceeds 50% and is often much lower. A review of research on fertilizer applications reports that average N recovery efficiency for cereal crops from researcher managed experimental plots averaged 65 % for corn, 57 % for wheat, and 46 % for rice (Ladha *et al.* 2005) and fields managed by farmers ranged from about 20% to 30% under rainfed conditions and 30% to 40% under irrigated conditions.

Table1: Water requirement, yield and water use efficiency for different Crops under drip and surface irrigation methods

Crop	Water Consumption (mm/ha)		Yield (ton/ha)		Water Saving over Surface (%)	Yield Increase over Surface (%)	Water Use Efficiency (kg/ ha-mm)	
	Surface	Drip	Surface	Drip			Surface	Drip
Vegetables								
Ash gourd	840	740	10.84	12.03	12	12	12.90	16.26
Bottle gourd	840	740	38.01	55.79	12	47	45.25	75.39
Brinjal	900	420	28.00	32.00	53	14	31.11	76.19
Beet root	857	177	4.57	4.89	79	7	5.33	27.63
Sweet potato	631	252	4.24	5.89	61	40	6.72	23.37
Potato	200	200	23.57	34.42	Nil	46	117.85	172.10
Lady finger	535	86	10.00	11.31	84	13	18.69	131.51
Onion	602	451	9.30	12.20	25	31	15.45	27.05
Radish	464	108	1.05	1.19	77	13	2.26	11.02
Tomato	498	107	6.18	8.87	79	43	12.41	82.90
Chillies	1097	417	4.23	6.09	62	44	3.86	14.60
Ridge gourd	420	172	17.13	20.00	59	17	40.79	116.28
Cabbage	660	267	19.58	20.00	60	2	29.67	74.91
Cauliflower	389	255	8.33	11.59	34	39	21.41	45.45
Fruit Crops								
Papaya	2285	734	13.00	23.00	68	77	5.69	31.34
Banana	1760	970	57.50	87.50	45	52	32.67	90.21
Grapes	532	278	26.40	32.50	48	23	49.62	116.91
Lemon	42	8	1.88	2.52	81	35	44.76	315.00
Watermelon	800	800	29.47	88.23	Nil	179	36.84	110.29
Other Crops								
Sugarcane	2150	940	128.00	170.00	65	33	59.53	180.85
Cotton	856	302	2.60	3.26	60	25	3.04	10.79
Groundnut	500	300	1.71	2.84	40	66	3.42	9.47

India's National Agricultural Policy lays much emphasis on enhancing use efficiency of agricultural inputs of which fertilizers represent an important and expensive component. Inefficient use of fertilizers means increase in cost of cultivation and more threat for biosphere pollution. Thus, economic and ecological considerations highlight imperative need for more efficient use of nutrients in crop production.

Consumption of chemical fertilizers in India has increased steadily over the years, the use efficiency of nutrients applied as fertilizers continues to remain considerably low (40-50% for N, 20-25% for P and 2-5% for Zn, Fe & Cu) owing to nutrient losses from the soils or conversion of nutrients into slowly cycling/recalcitrant pools within the soil. Further, at national level the partial factor productivity (PFPf) and incremental use efficiency (IUEf) of fertilizers used in food grain production have been gradually declining over the years revealing it a matter of great concern and a challenge to be addressed on priority.

Fertilizer nutrients are expensive and used in large quantities at national level, any increase in use efficiency will lead to a substantial cut in nutrient requirement and huge economic benefit at national level. For example, At the present level of fertilizer consumption (14.05 M t N and 5.66 M t P2O5 in 2006-07) and with use efficiency of 50% for N and 20% for P, increase in the efficiency of N and P use by just 2 percentage units would lead to a saving of 5.38 lakh tons of N and 5.15 lakh tons of P, which together translate to a saving of Rs.14,920 million annually. This amply highlights the importance of enhancing nutrient use efficiency. This staggering annual economic benefit is in addition to reduced risk of environmental pollution.

Nutrient use efficiency goes on decreasing as the yield target goes on increasing. Best management practices are the solution to fertilizer use efficiency such as site specific nutrient management (customized nutrient recommendations), balanced fertilization, right type of application (broadcasting, drilling, fertigation,top dressing or foliar spray), right dose (single or split), right time (application should correspond with nutrient requiring stage of the crop). Implementation will vary with soil type and soil test reports.

Some management interventions for increased NUE and consequently crop productivity enhancement are listed hereunder:

- Identify management interventions with high carbon sequestration potential to promote SOC storage critical for optimum soil processes.
- Climate resilient varieties with high yield potential and adaptability
- Soil and water conservation to minimize nutrient losses

- Customized fertilizers and fertilization for enhanced NUE
- Fertilization practices in moisture stressed production systems must be tailored to moisture availability so that the added nutrients are utilized more efficiently.
- Exploit water-nutrient synergy for greater productivity and use efficiency
- Integrated nutrient management and balanced fertilization including secondary & micronutrients for improving soil fertility and productivity
- Strategic interventions for abiotic and biotic stress management

6. Modest level of mechanization

Farm mechanization has been known to provide a number of economic and social benefits to farmers. Primary among the economic benefits is the improved yield that comes as a result of greater level of mechanization. Looming water scarcity crisis along with the need to ensure food security in the country, the benefits of farm mechanization makes it a crucial component of shaping the future of Indian agriculture.It is estimated that farm mechanization can help reduce time by approximately 15-20 percent. Additionally, it helps in improving the harvest and reducing the post-harvest losses and improving the quality of cultivation. Mechanization of agriculture and farming process connotes application of machine power to work on farm for crop production, post harvest management, value addition, marketing and other operations which are otherwise performed by bullocks, horses and other draught animals or by human labour.

Mechanization level in India is about 40-45 percent with states such as UP, Haryana and Punjab having very high mechanization levels but north-eastern states having negligible mechanization. Govt.'s interventions through centrally sponsored schemes such as custom hiring centres for agro-machines could not become successful because of bleak response from the farming community.

6.1. Hurdles in promotion of mechanization

Mechanization of agriculture in India is required but constrained by social, economical and topographical factors.

1) 60% of the country's population is directly involved in agriculture which is more than its carrying capacity. Mechanization would further reduce mandays requirement enhancing unemployment.
2) Small holding size and at the same time, unconsolidated holdings are major obstacle in application of farm machineries.

3) 70% farmers fall in small and marginal category where machines cannot be used economically and effectively.
4) Indian cultivators are economically are not well off to purchase the machines or hire on rental basis.
5) Lack of facility for spare parts and servicing of machines at accessible place and with affordable price.
6) Low cost small and simple machines are not available
7) Machines for hilly terrains are either scanty or not available

Recommendations

1) Provide credit facilities to those farmers who are willing to purchase the machinery individually.
2) FPOs may be developed to serve as machinery co-operatives in the different States.
3) Small machines suitable for Indian conditions should be developed to meet the topographical requirements.
4) Government should extend the scheme gradually on the following lines:
    i) Mechanization be made mandatory to the state farms and SAUs farms,
    ii) Reclaimed areas need and should be brought under mechanization on priority.
    iii) Mechanization be extended over to such lands where co-operative joint farming societies or contract farming systems are in vogue.
    iv) Private big farmers should be motivated to adopt mechanization.

7. Un-organization in agriculture

Indian economy has preponderance of informal and unorganized sector both in terms of number of workers and enterprises. Unorganized or informal sector constitutes a pivotal part of the Indian economy. More than 90 per cent of workforce and about 50 per cent of the national products are accounted for by the informal economy. The high level of growth of the Indian economy during the past two decades has been accompanied by increasing informalization. A high proportion of socially and economically underprivileged sections of society are concentrated in the informal economic activities. This segment of economy has inbuilt vulnerabilities.

Table 4.2: Share of Labour Input in Unorganized Sector (%) 2004-05

Tabulation category/Description	Share of Unorganized Sector
A: Agriculture and forestry	99.9
Fishing	98.7
Mining	64.4
Manufacturing	87.7
Electricity, Gas, Water supply	12.4
Construction	92.4
Wholesale and Retail Trade	98.3
Hotel & Restaurants	96.7
Transport, Storage & Communication	82.2

7.1. Dairy

India with 134 Million metric tons of production is world's largest liquid milk producer, which accounts for 18 per cent of total global milk production. Most of the milk produced is consumed domestically. Ironical fact, Indian dairy industry is still predominantly unorganized. Of the total milk produced in India, only 18-20 per cent is channelized through the organized segment. Milk production takes place in millions of rural households scattered across the country. A large share of the marketable surplus of milk (70-85 per cent in different regions) is marketed through the unorganized sector comprising of milk vendors, traders and small private dairies (GCMMF, 2009). India's dairy sector is expected to triple its production in the next 10 years in view of expanding potential for export to Europe and the West. Moreover, with WTO regulations expected to come into force in coming years, all the developed countries which are among big exporters today would have to withdraw the support and subsidy to their domestic milk products sector. India today is the lowest cost producer of per liter of milk in the world, at 27 cents, compared with the U.S' 63 cents, and Japan's $2.8 dollars. Also to take advantage of this lowest cost of milk production and increasing production in the country, multinational companies are planning to expand their activities here. Domestic dairy sector is characterized by a large share (around 85%) of small local players operating in the unorganized sector. The organized dairy sector comprises co-operative societies and large private players with established supply chain. A positive development is that there is a clear shift towards the share of organized segment, increasing from 13 per cent in 2005 to 20 per cent currently.

Liquid milk constitutes around 65% of the total dairy output in India. Value-added dairy products are the second major category with 22% share. Hence it is evident that the unorganized segment has not yet participated into modern processing infrastructurc in India.

While the liquid milk segment is growing at a rate of 6-8%, the market for value added dairy products is growing at a faster clip of rate of 15-18%. The dairy sector plays a significant role in rural economic development generating employment to over 72 million people providing supplementary income and nutrition to millions of rural households. Organization in dairy sector will assure marketing and more income, building confidence among the people involved in this entrepreneurship.

Growth of organized retailing has increased the demand for value-added dairy products in the recent years, a fast growth in value-added dairy products is anticipated.

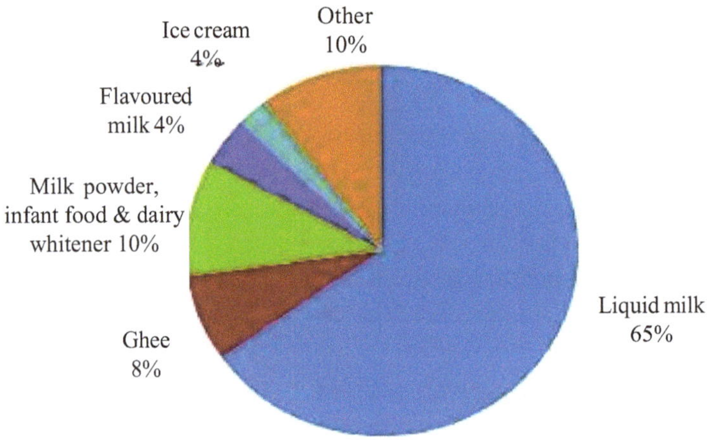

Source: Secondary research

Other include Cheese, UHT, Paneer, Butter and Yoghurt

Fig.1: Dairy Output: Organized sector, Break-up by Segments, %, 2012-13 (*Source:* consultmcg.com)

7.2. Poultry

Poultry is relatively organized sector with export of 6.6 lac tons products. Nearly 70 per cent of the total output of poultry industry is contributed by organized sector and remaining 30 per cent by unorganized sector but as per 2015-16 estimates Poultry sector in India is valued at about Rs. 80,000 crore, one with a highly organized commercial sector with about 80% of the total market share (say, Rs. 64,000 crore) and the other being unorganized with about 20% of the total market share of Rs. 16,000 Crore indicating shift towards organization. The unorganized sector also referred to as backyard poultry plays a key role in supplementary income generation and family nutrition to the poorest of the poor. It is estimated that with a poultry population of 729 million [30% layers at around 215 million and 40% broilers at around 480 million] small and medium farmers are mostly engaged in contract farming system under larger integrators and there are around 30 million farmers engaged in backyard poultry as per 19th Livestock Census. The unorganized sector is very dispersed and micro-fragmented needs conducive environment to grow for which policy support & intervention is required mainly for marketing, disease surveillance, drug residue and drug/ vaccine quality control, standardization & quality control of poultry feed, eggs & meat. Much potential of this sector can be exploited by value addition and product development.

7.3. Mushroom

Mushroom production in the country started in the 70s but growth rate, both in terms of productivity as well as production has been phenomenal. In seventies and eighties button mushroom was grown as a seasonal crop in hills, but with the development of the technologies for environmental controls and increased understanding of the cropping systems, mushroom production shot up from mere 5000 tons in 1990 to over 1,00,000 tons in 2010. However in global context this is just 1%. China with its meagre production of 60,000 tons in 1978 became leading producing in 2006 with 14 million tons production of edible mushroom providing employment to 30 million people. India's production is far below that is 1.2 lakh tons with low productivity of 20kg per 100 kg of compost. India produces about 600 million tons of agricultural waste per annum and a major part of it is left out to decompose naturally or burnt *in situ*. This can effectively be utilized to produce highly nutritive food such as mushrooms and spent mushroom substrate can be converted into organic manure/vermi-compost. By just diverting 1% of agro-wastes towards mushroom production, India can produce 3 million tons of mushroom and about 15 million tons of compost.

The per capita consumption of mushroom in India is a dismal 30-40 g as compared to 2-3 kg in USA and Europe. India itself is a big market and increase of per capita consumption even up to 100 g from present figure will help growers to market over 1.00 lakh ton mushroom within the country. Being an indoor crop, the commodity provides immense opportunities for empowerment of rural and urban women, landless farmers through cultivation and also the production of value-added products. Mushrooms cultivation not only imparts diversification but also helps in farm waste management. As an enterprise quite competent to promote nutrient recycling and to address very well problem of unemployment, malnutrition and environment health so needs focus in country like India congenial situation prevails. Where training and skill development on cultivation and value addition on mushrooms remain priority, unorganization in this sector continues to haunt the enterprise amid obscure marketing and trading prospective. Almost the whole production comes from informal sector where production and supply hardly match with the demand scenario.

8. Low level of Food Processing

Indian food market was worth $193 billion in 2016 and is expected to cross $540 billion in 2020. The sector has been growing at the rate of 12 per cent annually. Second largest food producer, India has attained self-sufficiency in food, despite its strong agricultural production base, a significant amount of food produce gets wasted due to inadequate infrastructure such as packaging facilities, storage, transportation, cold chain, and low levels of processing. According to the Ministry of Food Processing Industry (MoFPI), only post-harvest losses account for US$1.5 billion (Rs 92,000 crore) annually. Overall, less than 10 percent of the total food produced is processed into value added products in India (Table1). Currently, food processing accounts for almost one-third of the total food market in India. The food processing industry is valued at US$258 billion, and is the fifth largest industry domestically in terms of production, consumption, export, and expected growth in the country. It contributes to around 14 percent of manufacturing Gross Domestic Product (GDP) and 13 percent of India's total food exports.

Table 1: Food processing industry in india

Sector	Level of processing (%)
Dairy	35
Meat buffalo	20
Poultry	6
Fisheries	8
Fruit and vegetables	2
Consumers foods (packaged foods, aerated soft drinks, packaged drinking water, alcoholic beverages)	NA
Grain and cereals (flour, bakeries, starch glucose, corn flakes, vermicelli, beer, malted extracted, grain based alcohol)	NA

India's vast agricultural resources alone create huge potential for investments in its food processing and equipment industry. Major areas holding scope for value added processing are in the canning, packaging, dairy and food processing, frozen food, and thermo-processing industries. US and China process 65 percent and 23 percent of their produce, respectively. Developing countries such as Thailand, Philippines, and Brazil process as high as 30, 78, and 70 percent of their produce, respectively. Similar potential exists for India also. According to a 2017 report by the Associated Chambers of Commerce and Industry of India (ASSOCHAM), the country's food processing industry is expected to reach US$482 billion by 2020, driven by growth in organized retail, changing consumer behavior, and increasing consumerism in tier II and tier III cities.

Food processing is going to be one of the principal industries of India in future owing change in consumers' preference.

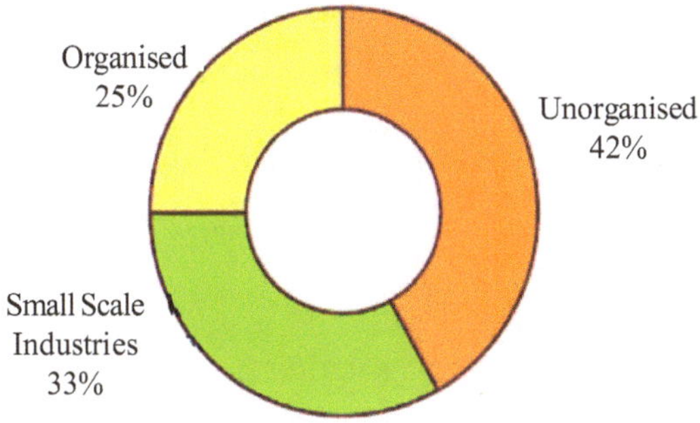

Fig. 2: Status of Indian processing industry

The food processing sector in India faces challenges of:

Inadequate cultivation of varieties suited for processing

All varieties are not suited for processing. Processing requires identification, development and cultivation of varieties endowed with processing characters. Table purpose varieties if used may develop poor quality processed products.

Poor market linkages

India's agriculture market has a long and fragmented supply chain that results in high wastage and high costs, especially due to seasonality, perishability, and variability of produce.

Infrastructure bottlenecks

The export related infrastructure for agri-produce is grossly inadequate, especially at sea ports and airports. More than 30 percent of the produce from the fields gets spoilt due to poor post-harvesting facilities and lack of adequate storage infrastructure.

Lack of skilled manpower

The agricultural workforce is inadequately skilled across different levels of food processing.

Non-adherence to international quality standards

India lacks basic standardization and certification infrastructure. Given the size of the food processing industry, there is a huge gap in the availability of laboratories, trained manpower, and certification agencies.

The food processing sector is highly fragmented industry, it widely comprises of the following sub-segments: fruits and vegetables, milk and milk products, beer and alcoholic beverages, meat and poultry, marine products, grain processing, packaged or convenience food and packaged drinks. A huge number of entrepreneurs in this industry are small in terms of their production and operations, and are largely concentrated in the unorganized segment. The informal or unorganized sector accounts for more than 70% of the output in terms of volume and 50% in terms of value (Fig.2).

9. Rainfed agro-ecosystem

India ranks first among the rainfed agricultural countries of the world in terms of both extent and value of produce. The Rainfed agriculture plays an important role in Indian economy covering 68 per cent of the total net sown area (86 Mha) spread over 177 districts. It contributes to nearly 40 per cent of the national food basket. Even after achieving the full irrigation potential, nearly 50% of the net cultivated area still remains dependent on rainfall. Rain-fed agriculture supports nearly 40% of India's estimated population. In the Indian context, rainfed agriculture productions systems accounts 55 per cent production of rice, 91 per cent coarse grains, 90 per cent pulses, 85 per cent oilseeds and 65 per cent cotton thereby demonstrating the importance of rainfed agriculture in the country. These regions also account for nearly 50 percent of the total rural workforce and 60 percent of livestock in the country. In these rainfed systems the annual rainfal varies for 400 mm to 1000 mm and given their uneven distribution and highly uncertain and erratic nature a significant fall in food production is often noticed. Spanning several agro-ecological regions and spread across the length and breadth of the country, the rainfed areas represent areas with largest concentration of poverty and backwardness.

Several efforts have been made during the past years employing science and technology as well as policy interventions with an effort to extend sustainable and appropriate technologies to these areas to enhance productivity of the rainfed farming systems. However, achievements to these efforts are not significant. At the same time resource degradation problems, such as loss in soil fertility, groundwater depletion, loss of biodiversity and increase in climate associated vulnerabilities have continued to rise in view of climate change. Uncertainty in production due to fluctuations in total rainfall and changes in its distribution, decrease in relative productivity in rainfed lands etc. affect the livelihoods of many poor and marginalized farmers. Inadequate support for rainfed agriculture in terms of support price, availability of appropriate inputs, credit, market access and agricultural research and extension has compounded to these problems and has caused widespread desperation among farmers.

Hence, straightway challenge is to infuse characters of stability and sustainability in rainfed agriculture. Multiple problems are encountered in rainfed agriculture as enumerated below:

Climatic problems

- Variable rain fall with respect to intensity and distribution
- Higher thermal values often leading to heat stress
- Higher evapo-transpirational rates (3650 mm annually á 300 -1400 mm ppt)
- High solar incidence (450-500 cal cmÉ^{2} day É^{1})
- Low relative humidity
- High wind velocity
- Desiccating winds
- More water and wind erosion
- Weather aberrations
- Frequent droughts
- Frost

Edaphic factors

- Poor marginal lands
- Uneven topography
- Low moisture storage
- Presence of dissolved salts in spread water
- Problem with respect to pH and high concentration of soluble solids in the surface soil
- High surface crusting
- Low productivity

Technological Problems

- Limited choice of crop varieties matching the short period suitable for cropping e.g. 60% of the area has 2-4.5 months and 19% of the area has <2 wet months/year.

- Difficult to design a suitable cropping system, crop mixtures and crop geometry considering soil type and other flexible components such as moisture availability index (MAI) and duration of Monsoon.
- Difficulty in evolving static and adaptable technology putting into the prevailing and anticipating rainfall conditions on region basis.
- Response to fertilizers and biofertilizers very low
- Mechanization has limited scope because of peculiar soil topography
- Land capacity poor and the scope to improve it is very limited.
- Difficulty in conserving moisture for proper and timely use by crop
- Unpredicted heavy showers erode fertility
- Soil amendments scope limited
- Water harvesting and recycling is the high investment preposition at the initial level.
- Water damage (18000-20000 acre commonly) and run off 50% of the incident rainfall causing loss of soil (7-10 ton/ha) and causing degradation.

Socio-economic problems

- Fragile ecological and socioeconomic status
- Unstable production because of frequent failure of crops
- Low cropping intensity so low farm returns
- Malnutrition
- Poor quality of produce fetching low price
- Poor means of communication and transport
- Lack of marketing facilities and market incentives
- Low level of literacy and poor resource base of the farmers
- Unemployment for most of the period of year
- Dependency on the Monsoon
- Innovations, incentives, inspirations and initiatives have limited scope.

Challenges to Research

- With 68% area under rainfed agriculture only 20% scientific manpower is involved

- Whereas irrigated agriculture is 32% area draws upon 80% scientific manpower
- 85% publications come from either laboratories based or irrigated agriculture
- Averaging of three years observations hardly provides logical inferences in rainfed situations
- Findings of research from rainfed areas are mostly made logical after significant manipulations with the result that validation of such recommendations fails when implemented at field level.
- Most of the institutions working on rainfed agriculture carry experimentation under-irrigation system so reproducibility of results is very low
- Breeding programs are either meagre or missing in rainfed research stations

10. Cold chain and storage infrastructure

Cold Chain Management deals with efficient control and organization of production and logistic regarding thermal environment. Cold chain involves the transportation of temperature-sensitive products along a supply chain through thermal and refrigerated packaging methods to protect the integrity of products during shipment. The principal aims of Cold Chain Management are optimization of product quality and product safety and minimization of wastage. It comprises planning and implementation of processes and process steps as well as implementation of instruments and methods of process monitoring and control. Cold chain which is the fulcrum of an effective supply chain infrastructure in dealing with fruits and vegetables remains a grossly ignored area in India. What could have turned out to be a huge asset for national economy keeps on lingering as a serious weak spot. Major contribution again comes from unorganized sector. Around 40% of our produce is wasted due to inadequate cold chain infrastructure, and one third of losses incur during storage and transit. Experts opine that India has less than half the capacity to meet its current cold chain needs.

India has seen a dramatic increase in the production of perishable products including fruits, vegetables, meat, poultry and dairy. It ranks first in global milk production with an annual rate of 138 million tons and hosts more than 50% of milk product processing. With vegetable production of 280.4 million tons, it ranks second globally and only hosts 6% of total processing.

There has also been steady growth in the fish and meat industries due to export potential. Current cold storage capacity in India totals 31.8 million tons. Growth has averaged 3 to 4% over the past 10 years, and 10.5 million tons of space was created in the last seven years. Ownership is mainly in the private sector, with the public and cooperative sectors only comprising 10% of capacity. With around 3500 companies operating currently, the industry is quite fragmented and unorganized in nature. The cold chain supply base only comprises 8-10 percent organized players. India has a total of 6300 cold chain storages with 95 percent storage capacity under private players. Out of these cold chain storages, 36 percent have a capacity of below 1,000 MT. The current capacity allows only 11 percent of the total produce to be stored. The sector's value is estimated at $6.5 billion (USD) and market growth has averaged between 15 to 20%. This pace is expected to be consistent over the next five years.

Currently, India has 6,300 cold storage facilities unevenly spread across the country, with an installed capacity of 30.11 million metric ton. These are mostly used for storing potatoes. However, the market is gradually getting organized and focus towards multi-purpose cold storages is rising. More than 50% of the cold storage facilities in India are currently concentrated in Uttar Pradesh and West Bengal, while other states still face a challenge with investments from the government and private operators. Some facts about Indian cold chain industry:

- Organized players contribute only 8 to 10% of the cold chain industry market
- 36% of these cold storages in India have capacity below 1,000 MT
- 65% of India's cold chain storage capacity is contributed by the states of Uttar Pradesh and West Bengal
- At the current capacity only less than 11% of what is produced can be stored.

In 2012, Indian farmers produced 240 million metric ton of horticultural produce, almost equal to its grain and cereals production. The farmers, at times, do not have the requisite infrastructure, technical know-how or capital investment to channelize into cold storage and supply chain development. Add to that, the fragmented infrastructure of cold warehouses, transportation and associated services. This is a major reason why we require integrated logistical support, and in particular, cold chain solutions to enable easy accessibility and smooth flow of produce from farms to table, fresh and safe. It would also enable farmers to extend the life cycle of perishable products, traverse long distances, reach wider market segments and larger consumer base.

Various studies indicate that 18 to 40% of this produce was lost due to supply chain inefficiencies, concluding that a focused effort was required to promote the development of the cold chain in the country.

Globally cold chains have now become an integral part of supply chain management for the storage and transportation of temperature-sensitive goods. The focus has now shifted from increasing production to better cold storages and transportation of food produce. The utilization of cold chain logistics includes both cold storages and refrigerated transportation and is used to increase the shelf life of food produce. With 35 to 40% of agricultural produce in India being wasted due to lack of proper cold storage facilities, organized growth of this sector is mandatory for sustainable transformation in Indian agriculture.

Key challenges

Lack of quality cold warehousing infrastructure

There is a severe shortage of cold chain warehousing capacity as only 25% of the capacity is available for fruits, vegetables, processed foods and pharmaceuticals, whereas 75% of the capacity is dedicated to potatoes.

Lack of standards and protocols in construction and operation of facilities

Technical standards followed in India are mostly unsuitable for Indian conditions, which results in lower performance of standard refrigerated systems.

Low awareness in handling temperature-sensitive products

In India, the supply chain of most products is long and fragmented. A product passes on many hands from source to delivery point. Most workers involved in this are not properly trained in handling temperature-sensitive products resulting in deterioration of product quality before reaching the consumer.

High fuel cost and power cuts

Fuel costs in India constitute around 30% of operating expenses of cold storage in India as compared to 10% in the West. Further, cold storages are dependent on steady supply of power. Most Indian regions face power cuts. Hence, these companies have to invest in power back-ups, which push up the capital investment requirement.

11. Meagre investments

India's investment in agricultural research is still very low. China spends three to four times more than India. India has to invest more on research if it wants to catch up sustainable food and nutritional security for all its citizens. "It is seen that for every dollar we spend in agricultural research, there is a return of 10 dollars, Shenggen Fan, Director General of the Washington DC-based

International Food Policy Research Institute (IFPRI) said on the sidelines of a two-day conference on 'Achieving the Sustainable Development Goals (SDGs) through Agriculture in India'. Commenting on India's efforts to double farmers' income by 2022, the IFPRI chief said: "This is not possible if we focus just on rice, wheat or maize. It should encourage farmers to grow more vegetables and fruits and diversify into areas like dairy farming for additional income generation," he said.

Agriculture is key to meeting half of the 17 SDG (sustainable development goals) targets set for 2030, which includes eliminating poverty and hunger and reducing inequalities. The agriculture R&D share is less than 10% in HIS and much lower in other groups at 6%. This is worrisome given a deceleration in productivity growth of many crops and also the fact that R&D activity in agriculture is hardly undertaken by the private sector in the country. As share of agricultural GDP, India spends 1% on agri-R&D which is fairly low in comparison with its 3% share in the developed countries. Even if agricultural R&D is expanded by taking expenditure on soil conservation, crop and animal husbandry, its share in GSDP agriculture reaches to maximum 2%. This may have serious implications for agriculture and food production in the future

India needs to double or triple its investment in agricultural research if it has to reach to anywhere close to what China has achieved on the farm front. Ramesh Chand, member of NITI Aayog, during an interview in New Delhi had also stated that India should relax rules, give incentives and remove hurdles for companies investing in contract farming, transport, marketing, warehouses and food processing. He said for any improvement in farmers' income, private corporate investments in farming should at least double from the current 2 percent of total annual investments in agriculture.

Economic growth, structural transformation and wide-scale poverty reduction all require productivity gains in agriculture. Key investments are required in technological research, rural infrastructure and market standards, organization and enforcement to accelerate agricultural growth. These areas fall under public goods where Govts. Need to invest as the private sector cannot capture gains from these investments, they will not invest in amounts sufficient to ensure broad-based agricultural growth. Therefore, **the public sector needs to provide the necessary research, transport and market infrastructure necessary to stimulate agricultural growth**. The government has planned to set up a Rs. 20 billion fund to develop, and upgrade, agricultural market infrastructure. Another Rs. 5 billion would be allocated to promote farmer producer organizations, agriculture logistics, processing facilities and professional management. India also planned to loosen restrictions on the export of agricultural commodities to realize a market potential as high as $100 billion. Apart from raising the minimum support price for all crops, the government proposed raising credit for the agricultural sector to 11 trillion rupees ($172.3 billion) for the upcoming fiscal year.

The ailing agricultural pricing mechanism, India has to map the needs of its growing demographics with the entrepreneurial spirit of farmers across India to produce crops that will maximize their profits. Currently, as a result of the Essential Commodities Act (1956) and the National Food Security Act (2013), excessive government intervention and over-subsidization have worsened agri-performance and affected production patterns.

A dual-track market liberalization approach may allow farmers to get both a minimum price for their products from government agencies (in return for a minimum sell) and a market price i.e. on selling over and above a fixed quantity of agricultural produce (beyond government procurement). China followed a similar strategy at a local level across most agrarian provinces in the early 1980's. This allowed farmers to maximize efficiency in their production patterns to get the best price for their produce while the government was able to secure a minimum procurement of crops for redistribution purposes among people who were marked below the income poverty line.

Mohan (2017) suggested a package of reforms devised under the 5P framework would insert new life into India's most beleaguered agriculture sector. While crop loan waivers may temporarily relieve farmers' debt, they will have a harmful impact on the financial health of states while doing little to address the real problems afflicting farmers across the country. Instead, a cohesive policy approach that addresses each of the 5P's will be a vital step towards a strong and stable India.

Access to technology is already beginning to change the landscape of agriculture in India. ICTs interventions provide better access to market and ensure better selling price. More than half of farmers who provide food to Delhi use cell phones to directly negotiate prices for crops. Leveraging the power of technology can help connect farmers to markets, optimize agricultural output, and improve livelihoods." In the fiscal year 2014, INR 7.3 lakh crores was disbursed as credit to farmers. 2015 saw an increase to INR 9 lakh crores. In the new budget announced on February 2017, this number has been further hiked to INR 10 lakh crores. India also has the second highest spending on agricultural related R&D by a developing country, second only to China. But such enormous allocations to the sector have not yielded returns of the same magnitude with the consequences investors from private sectors show hitch to go for financial ventures in agriculture.

Research and Development investment crop focused

R&D investment in agriculture in India is primarily focused on crops (Fig.3) which cannot address food security. As food and nutritional security comprise food production, accessibility, affordability and consumption. Hence production has to be supported by post harvest management, transportation, storage, and distribution system and employment generation. Relatively more importance must be given to sectors such as livestock farming, landless enterprises, and forests. In view of climate change areas like forests, organic farming, biological resources management and biotechnology should be on priority. While the U.S. has an exclusive organization set up for R&D on forestry, India barely employs one percent of its total research staff in this sector!

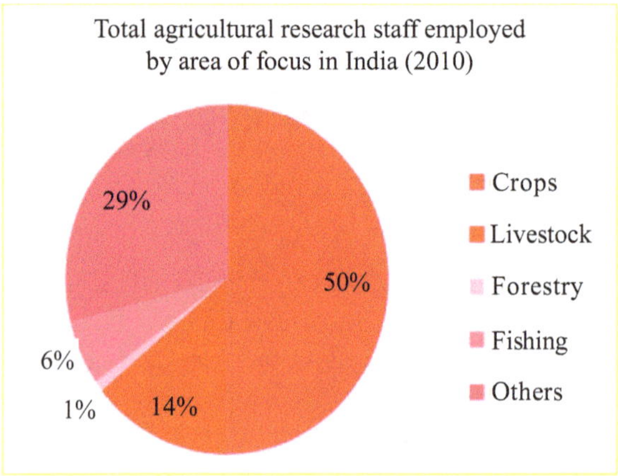

Fig. 3: Research staff distribution in India

Disbursed credit not reaching its target

Almost three-fourths of the total farmer population has no access to credit through formal channels. Of the remaining one-fourth, almost half of the credit is disbursed to large farmers who make up only one percent of the total farmer population. Small and marginal farmers are excluded from their share of government credit and are, in effect, forced to rely on their savings. Consequently, 84 percent of the total farmer population makes private investment in their farms and farming practices.

Infrastructural limitations

India has around 6500 cold storage facilities with a capacity of 30 million MT. Yet, a mere 4 million MT of the 104 million MT of fresh produce is transported through a cold chain. To fill the gap in India's cold chain, a total investment of approximately USD six to ten billion is required in the next five to ten years making the government's role in this area of paramount importance.

Focus on subsidies

Input subsidies – government sponsored subsidies to farmers for fertilizers, irrigation, electricity, and food are the most expensive aspect of India's agricultural policies. India has witnessed an increasing subsidy budget each year. This has resulted in our agriculture sector being more dependent on input subsidies when compared with other large emerging economies as seen in the graph below.

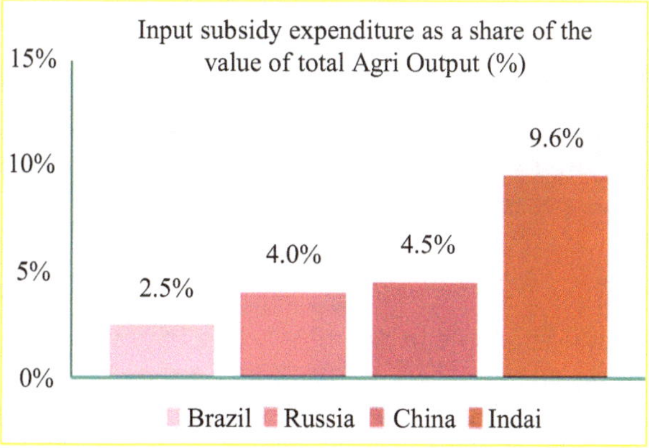

Fig. 3: Input subsidy scenario

Developing economies such as Brazil and China have made a conscious move away from subsidies towards investment on the understanding that subsidies add little value to the sector. Rather, they are one-sided transactions that do not provide long-term benefits of real development. However, India is yet to realize this. Of the total planned revenue expenditure, 35% of it is spent on subsidies while a mere 9% is earmarked for capital investment in agriculture.

Parting thoughts

The reality is that the government is putting enough funds in the sector. However, the resulting inefficiency is caused by the improper or low utilization of the allocated funds. There is need to examine other areas in which the government should invest such as infrastructure and R&D. The economy will only accelerate if we invest in development and not on unilateral subsidy schemes.

12. Sublimation

Research clearly shows that marginal returns on agri-investments are 5 to 10 times higher than from agri-input subsidies. Economics is quite clear on this.

But why then our policy making leans heavily towards subsidies and not towards investments? Is it the short-term political returns that are higher in doing out subsidies than in investments is a matter for political interest to probe? Investments take time to fructify, but they are more sustainable to give benefits. Almost 80% of the public expenditure going to agriculture is in the form of input subsidies (fertilizers, power and irrigation) and only 20% as investments in agriculture.

India is among those countries where both under-nutrition and over-nutrition co-exist equally. Studies have shown that between 2008 and 2014, the number of obese and overweight people in India doubled to 22 per cent of the population. Ironically, the number of people living below the poverty line is also close to 20 per cent. Food insecurity still haunts majority particularly to small and marginal farmers, daily paid laborers and work force associated with agriculture and allied activities. To accomplish the SDGs, it is imperative that policymakers support transformations in the food system, and some of the greatest changes to India's food system are coming from rapid urbanization. Equal investment and participation is urgently needed from private sector for environment of food security, peace and prosperity.

More than 300 million people in South Asia live in poverty, with up to 71 per cent of them living in India so improving the country's agricultural sector means an opportunity to address both urban and rural development needs. There is need to re-visit the investment policy to get the tangible results that will also create confidence among the private investors.

13. References

Bathla S .2014. Public and private capital formation and agricultural growth in India: state level analysis of inter-linkages during pre- and post-reform periods. *Agric Econ Res Rev* 27(1):19

Bathla S, Thorat SK, Joshi PK and Bingxin Y .2017. Where to invest to accelerate agricultural growth and poverty reduction? *Econ Pol Weekly* 52(39):36–45

Blundell R and Bond S .1998. Initial conditions and moment restrictions in dynamic panel data models. *J Econometrics* 87:11–143

Dalwai Ashok. 2012. Dynamics of Agricultural Growth in India. Ind. Jn. of Agri.Econ. Vol.67, No.1, 27-45

Mohan Deepanshu .2017. India's Failing Enterprise: The Agriculture Sector. South Asian Voices. http://jgu.edu.in

Fan S, Gulati A and Thorat SK .2008. Investment, subsidies and pro-poor growth in rural India. *Agric Econ* 39:163–170

Haque T .2016. (ed) Agrarian distress in India: causes and remedies. Concept Publishing Company (P) Ltd., New Delhi

Chand R and Kumar P .2004. Determinants of capital formation and agricultural growth: some new explorations. *Econ Pol Weekly* 39(52):5611–5616

Ladha JK, Pathak H, Krupnik TJ, Six J and Kessel CV .2005. Efficiency of fertilizer nitrogen in cereal production: Retrospects and prospects. *Adv Agron.* 87:85–156.

Reddy DD. 2010. Nutrient Use Efficiency in Rainfed Agro–ecosystems: Concepts, Computations and Improvement Interventions. Indian Institute of Soil Science, Berasia Road, Nabibagh, Bhopal - 462 038 (M.P.)

Roberts Terry L. 2008. Improving nutrient use efficiency. *Turk J Agric For*. 32: 177-182.

Parwez Sazzad. 2014. Supply chain dynamics of Indian agriculture: reference to information technology and knowledge management. *Stewart Postharvest Review* 1:3 www.stewartpostharvest.com

2

Ten Technologies that Changed the Scenario of Indian Agriculture

Jag Paul Sharma

Directorate of Research, SKUAST Jammu, Jammu and Kashmir, India

Abstract

Indian agriculture witnessed a transformation in early seventies with green revolution in cereals. The Green Revolution resulted in a record grain output of 131 million tons in 1978-79. Yield per unit of farmland improved by more than 30 per cent between 1947 and 1979. This was because of introduction of high yielding varieties and use of agro-chemicals, particularly synthetic fertilizers. Farmers realized 3-4 times increment in their profit when high yielding varieties and chemical fertilizers were used in integration.

Agriculture is the primary source of livelihood for about 58 per cent of India's population. Gross Value Added by agriculture, forestry and fishing is estimated at Rs 17.67 trillion (US$ 274.23 billion) in FY18. The Indian food industry is poised for huge growth, increasing its contribution to world food trade every year due to its immense potential for value addition, particularly within the food processing industry. Food & Grocery retail market in India was worth US$ 380 billion in 2017, is the world's sixth largest, with retail contributing 70 per cent of the sales. The Indian food processing industry accounts for 32 per cent of the country's total food market, one of the largest industries in India and is ranked fifth in terms of production, consumption, export and expected growth. It contributes around 8.80 and 8.39 per cent of Gross Value Added (GVA) in Manufacturing and Agriculture respectively, 13 per cent of India's exports and six per cent of total industrial investment. During 2017-18, food grain production is estimated at 279.51 million tons, with rice and wheat production in the country at 111.52 MT and 98.61 MT, respectively in the same period. Milk production stands at 165.4 million tons during FY17, while meat production is 7.4 million tons. India is the second largest fruit producer in the world. Production of horticulture crops is estimated at record 307.16 million tons (mt) in 2017-18 as per second advance estimates. Total agricultural exports from India grew at a CAGR of 16.45 per cent over FY10-18 to reach US$ 38.21 billion in FY18. In April-May 2018 agriculture exports were US$ 6.43 billion. India is the largest producer, consumer and exporter of spices and spice products. Spice exports from India reached US$ 3.1 billion in 2017-18. Tea exports from India reached a 36 year high of 240.68 million kgs in CY 2017 while coffee exports reached record 395,000 tons in 2017-18.

Thus Indian agriculture experienced transformation by way of technological interventions in the field of agro-chemicals, high yielding varieties, off-season cultivation, high yielding breeds, export orientation and entrepreneurship development in food processing, mushroom production, dairying and poultry. More or less 15 revolutions supported the transformation. With the result, India emerged as top producer of milk, millets, pomegranate, banana, mango, jute, pulses, okra, safflower etc and second top producer of wheat, rice, tea, tomato, potato, onion etc and third in egg production and fourth in poultry meat. Consequence was evolution of commercial farming from subsistence farming. Nonetheless, net income increase at the farm is amalgamation of technologies, tactics and government policies. Technologies that contributed to agriculture to emerge from area of deficiency to self sufficiency are described.

Keywords: Agro-chemicals, high yielding varieties, dairying, poultry and food processing.

1. Introduction

Origin of agriculture is associated with the beginning of human settlements that dates back to more than 10,000 years. From the initial character of hunting and gathering, domestication of useful animals and plants around the human settlements marked the initiation of earlier agriculture. This was characterized by taming of wild animals and plants in form of animal husbandry and crop plant management what was later defined as agriculture. Consequence was ease of availability of food and food products needed by them. This promoted human interest to demark the land and develop area for regular agricultural activities. Water observed to be the most important input, agriculture and civilizations developed on the shore or on the areas fed by the rivers. Further, human being's observations on management of wild plants and animals that some of them are doing better than others led to the intervention of selection process where inferiors were culled or eliminated from the activity of domestication. Identification of superior types during the process of gathering and hunting led to the evolution of permanent farming or modern agriculture over natural, shifting or temporary farming. Later, domestic and international trades of agricultural commodities favored introduction of superior types across the different regions of the world. India under the aegis of monsoon was the home of diverse flora and fauna since time immemorial and remained attraction to foreign invaders because of prosperity which stemmed from assured food and nutritional security to the dwellers.

Domestication, selection and introduction which predominated earlier agricultural developments were reinforced by several technological interventions that transformed the traditional agriculture into modern intensive agriculture. Production, productivity and products development touched new heights in early seventies keeping away the hunger in many regions of the world including Asia, particularly India, the most populated part of the world. This opened the new era of socio-economic development for many developing countries including India which was characterized revolutions in several areas (Table 1).

Table 1: Revolutions in India

S.No.	Designation	Area of socio-economic development
1.	Black Revolution	Petroleum Production
2.	Blue Revolution	Fish Production
3.	Brown Revolution	Leather Production
4.	Evergreen Revolution	Overall development of Agriculture
5.	Golden fibre Revolution	Cotton Production
6.	Green Revolution	Food grain Production
7.	Grey Revolution	Fertilizer Production

Contd.

8.	Pink Revolution	Onion /Pharmaceutical Production
9.	Red Revolution	Meat / Tomato Production
10.	Round Revolution	Potato Production
11.	Sliver Revolution	Egg/ Poultry Production
12.	Silver fibre Revolution	Cotton Production
13.	White Revolution	Milk / Dairy Production
14	Yellow Revolution	Oil seeds Production
15	IT Revolution	Information and communication Technologies

Even today Indian agriculture is the core sector and characterized by 17% of the world's population, 11% livestock, 4.2% of the world's water, 2.4% of the world's area, 51% arable land, 142% cropping intensity, 140±2 m ha cultivated area with only 68 m ha irrigated, <18% contribution to GDP but >52 % of workforce in agriculture. Nonetheless, it supports country's socio-economic growth and controls political stability via food security, nutritional security, employment generation and poverty alleviation.

The Agriculture and Allied sector contributes merely 17.0% to India's Gross Value Added (GVA) at current prices during 2015-16.The Agriculture and Allied sector witnessed a growth of 1.5 per cent in 2012- 13, 4.2 per cent in 2013-14, -0.2 per cent in 2014-15 and 1.2 in 2015-16 at 2011-12 basic prices. Though the growth has been slow yet peace and prosperity of the nation rest with agriculture whose milestones are adjudged to be green revolution, blue revolution, white revolution, golden revolution, evergreen revolution and ICT (information and communication technology) revolution. Indian agriculture after green revolution has been able to feed 1.24 billion population of the country and this is attributed to 10 technologies which brought revolutionary changes in agriculture. Impact was, India became a food surplus from food deficit country. Some of the forefront technologies that played pivotal role are enumerated here.

2. Technologies that changed the scenario of Indian agriculture

2.1. Chemical Fertilizers

About 50 % of the increase in agricultural produce during the twentieth century was achieved by application of chemical fertilizers to crop plants. Fertilizer application is still an important farm input that is required to achieve challenging yield targets of the twenty-first century. In India, Fertilizer production dates back to 1906, when the first fertilizer factory became operational at Ranipet (Tamil Nadu). India produces a large number of grades of NP / NPK complex fertilizer. The total indigenous capacity of N and P2O5 increased from 17,000 and 21,000 tons in 1950/51 to 12,276 million and 5,547 million tons in 2004/05. The total production of N and P2O5 rose from 1.51 million and 0.32 million tons respectively in 1975/76 to 7.30 million and 2.56 million tons in 1991/92. In 1992/93, phosphatic and potassic fertilizers were decontrolled. As a consequence, the rate of growth in the demand for these products dropped down. There has been a shift in the product pattern over the years. SSP and AS dominated fertilizer production before the 1960s whereas urea and DAP dominate production and consumption at present. In 2003/04, urea accounted for 84.6 percent of total N production and di-ammonium phosphate (DAP) accounted for 59.9 percent of total P_2O_5 production.

India imports urea, DAP and potassium chloride (MOP) but has almost reached self-sufficiency in urea production. As regards DAP, the level of imports was between 1.5 and 2 million tons in the 1980s and 1990s. A great deal of DAP capacity came on stream in the early 2000s. Consequently, the importation of DAP fell to less than 1 million tons after 2000/01. In 2003/04, DAP imports were 0.73 million tons. Imports meet the entire MOP requirement as there are no known natural potash deposits in the country. In 2003/04, MOP imports were 2.58 million tons In addition, India also imports a small quantity of mono-ammonium phosphate (MAP) and potassium sulphate (SOP) (65 000 and 10 500 tons, respectively, in 2003/04). Urea accounts for 82 percent of the total consumption of straight N fertilizers. Other straight N fertilizers, such AS, CAN and ammonium chloride account for only 2 percent. The share of N through DAP and other complex fertilizers is about 16 percent. DAP accounts for 63 percent of total P_2O_5 consumption and other complex fertilizers for 27 percent. Single superphosphate (SSP) accounts for 10 percent of total P_2O_5 consumption.

India is deficient in primary sources of fertilizer inputs (such as natural gas, rock phosphate, potash) and is dependent for import of the intermediates like phosphoric acid and ammonia.

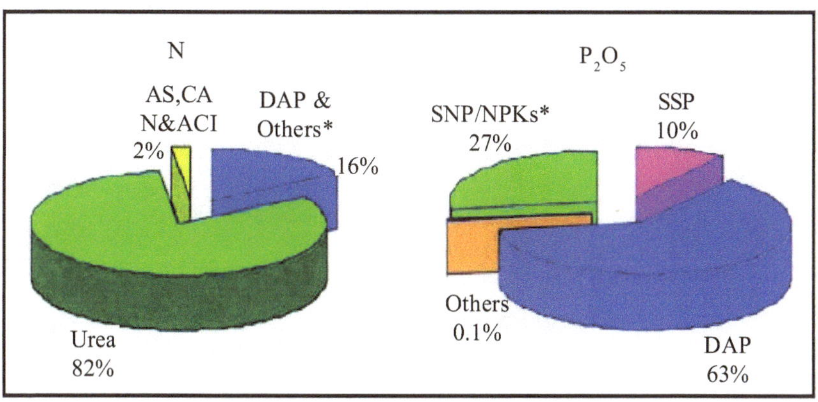

Fig. 1: N and P source for Indian soils

All India consumption of total fertilizer nutrients ($N+P_2O_5$ $+K_2O$) increased by 5.6%, from a total of 25.58 million metric tons (MMT) during 2014-15 to 27 MMT during 2015-16. N consumption at 17.60 MMT recorded growth of 3.8% and P_2O_5 at 7.07 MMT showed an increase of 15.9% during 2015-16 over the previous year. However, K_2O consumption at 2.33 MMT fell by 7.9% during the period. On average per hectare use of total nutrients increased from 131.6 kg in 2014- 15 to 138.9 kg in 2015-16 but only a few states are above 100kg consumption of nutrients per ha such as Punjab(184 kg), Haryana (167 kg) Andhra Pradesh (138 kg)Uttar Pradesh (127 kg), West Bengal (122 kg) Tamil Nadu(112 kg). This value is still low in comparison to some of the developed countries such as South Korea (400 kgs), Netherlands (275 kgs), Belgium (225 kgs), Japan (340 kgs). The main reason of low per hectare consumption of chemical fertilizers is low nutrient efficiency in absence of assured water supply.

All India NPK use ratio changed from 6.7:2.4:1 during 2014-15 to 7.5:3.0:1 during 2015-16 that is more inclination towards nitrogen (urea). Increased fertilizers consumption has been able to enhance food grain production (Table 2). This indicates that chemical fertilizers have been dominant factors in higher crop yields. However this association weakened over time as evident from Fig 2. Correlation coefficient was 0.88 during the period of the Green Revolution (1965–1966 to 1970–1971) to 0.95 in the second phase (1980s) and later declined during the 1990s (0.86) and 2000s (0.83). The major reasons for that in India are relatively low rate of application and the imbalanced use of plant nutrients per hectare. The NPK ratio, which is a measure of balanced use of fertilizer, reveals wider variation at interregional and interstate levels. While existing variation from the ideal ratio (4:2:1) was nominal in the south (3.9:2.2:1) and eastern regions (4.2:1.8:1), it was very wide in the north (20.4:6.8:1) and western regions (7.3:4.0:1). The state-wise consumption ratio of N and P in relation to K shows that the greatest degree of N:P:K imbalance was seen in Rajasthan (34.9:15.9:1), followed by Haryana (27.2:9.8:1) and Punjab (26.8:8.5:1) in 2011–12. Matter of concern to note is that the NPK ratio has deteriorated in almost all states in the post-NBS (nutrient based subsidy) period.

Table 2: Trends in Fertilizer consumption (lakh tons) and Food grain Production (Million tons)* in India

Year	Fertilizer Consumption	Food Grain Production	Year	Fertilizer Consumption	Food Grain Production
1986-87	86.45	143.42	2000-01	167.02	196.81
1987-88	87.84	140.35	2001-02	175.39	212.85
1988-89	110.40	169.92	2002-03	160.94	174.78
1989-90	115.68	171.04	2003-04	167.98	213.19
1990-91	125.46	176.39	2004-05	183.99	198.36
1991-92	127.28	168.38	2005-06	203.4	208.59
1992-93	121.55	179.48	2006-07	216.51	217.28
1993-94	123.66	184.26	2007-08	225.70	230.78
1994-95	135.63	191.5	2008-09	249.09	234.47
1995-96	138.77	180.42	2009-10	264.86	218.11
1996-97	143.77	199.43	2010-11	281.22	244.49
1997-98	161.88	193.12	2011-12	277.90	259.29
1998-99	167.98	203.61	2012-13	258.04	257.13
1999-00	180.69	209.8	2013-14	239.59	264.77
CAGR	5.83	2.95	CAGR	2.79	2.34

Source: Reserve bank of India, Ministry of consumer affairs, food and public distribution government of India, www. Indiastat.com.

*Total food grains include Rice, wheat, coarse cereals, and pulses. Total fertilizer consumption include N, P, K fertilizers

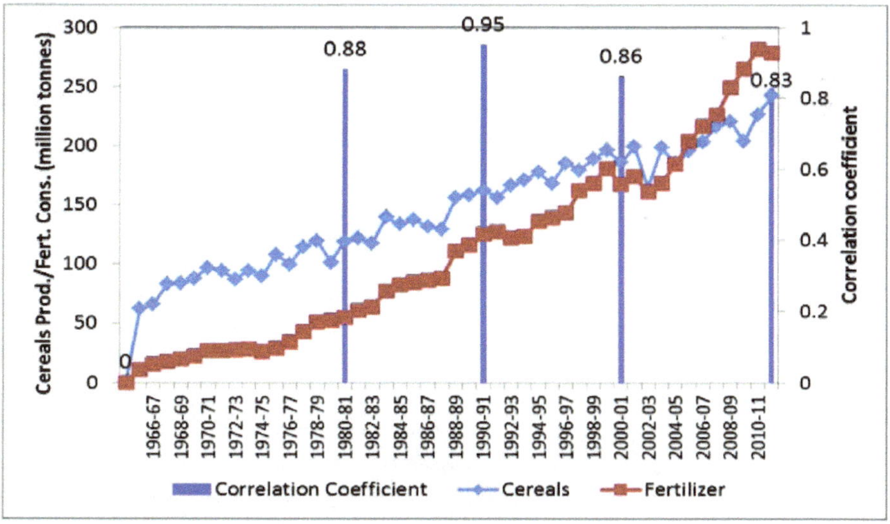

Fig. 2: Cereals production vs fertilizer consumption trends in India: 1965–1966 to 2011–2012

Source: FAI 2012

There exists a gap of about 10 million tons of nutrients (NPK) between the removal of nutrients by crops and their addition through fertilizers. It will have serious implications on sustaining the growth of agriculture so needs attention by policymakers. Fertilizer policy does not address balanced fertilization, Eutrophication (process by which a water body becomes enriched in dissolved compounds containing nitrogen, phosphorus, or both such as nitrates, phosphates) that stimulate the growth of aquatic plant life usually resulting in the depletion of dissolved oxygen, ground water pollution and low fertilizer use efficiency and these issues continue to haunt agro-ecosystems of India. Issues need attention and have to be resolved as chemical fertilizers will continue as the essential and major input of future agriculture.

2.1. Pesticides

Pest is an entity ranging from viral micromolecule, microbe, insect, unwanted plant to animal that attacks crops, food materials and livestock etc. According to FAO any substance or mixture of substances intended for preventing, destroying, or controlling any pest, including vectors of human or animal disease, unwanted species of plants or animals, causing harm during or otherwise interfering with the production, processing, storage, transport, or marketing of food, agricultural commodities, wood and wood products or animal feedstuffs is known as pesticide. On an average 35 % of potential crop yield is lost to pre-harvest pests (Oerke 2005). Prior to the introduction of pesticides, crop yields were lowered to the extent of 20-100% by uncontrolled diseases caused by pathogens and weeds. Popp et al (2013) reported that among crops, the total global potential loss due to pests varied from about 50% in wheat to more than 80 % in cotton production. The responses estimated as losses are 26–29 % for soybean, wheat and cotton, and 31%, 37% and 40% for maize, rice and potatoes, respectively. The reduction of potential yield losses caused by pests is a major challenge to agricultural production.

Pesticides are used to control pests through a preventing, destroying, repelling, or mitigating strategy. Introduction of synthetic insecticides–organophosphate (OP) in the 1960s, carbamates in 1970s and pyrethroids in 1980s and the introduction of herbicides and fungicides in the 1970s–1980s contributed significantly to pest control and agricultural output. Ideally a pesticide must be lethal to the targeted pests and which is not the case with most of them. Exposure to pesticides both occupationally and environmentally results in a range of human health problems causing genetic mutations, mutagenicity and carcinogenicity, reproductive damages as well as disturbances behavioral (depression and suicides). Further, toxic effects of pesticides have caused a large reduction in biodiversity (microbes as well as insects pollinators). The pesticides exposures have been linked to gastro-intestinal disorders, respiratory problems, immune suppression, hormone disruption, diminished intelligence, reproductive abnormalities, miosis, salivation, sweating, tearing, rhinorrhea, behavioral change, abdominal pain, vomiting, diarrhea, urinary incontinence, bronchospasm, dyspnea, hypoxemia, bradycardia, bronchial secretions, pulmonary edema, respiratory failure, drop in body temperature, incoordination, lip tingling, tremors, and seizures and cancer (Bernardes *et al.* 2015).

Studies show that less than 1% of the total amount of pesticides applied for weed and pest control reach the target pests. A large quantity of pesticides is lost via spray drift, off-target deposition, run-off, and photo-degradation and it contaminates soil, water, turf, and other vegetation including the users.

Developing countries use only 20% of the world's agrochemicals, yet they suffer 99% of deaths from pesticide poisoning. Hence pesticide poisoning is a significant problem in developing countries primarily because of unsafe pesticide application and handling practices. Safety is further exacerbated by the illiteracy and poverty that prevails in most farming communities of developing countries. Pesticides classified as being extremely or highly hazardous by FAO and WHO, including those banned by other countries, continue to be used in developing countries. Many farmers in developing countries continue to be exposed to pesticides from either storing them in or near their residences, or from inadequate or unsafe application or handling practices. Farming populations exposed to pesticides suffer from several health problems, primarily neurological abnormalities, respiratory ailments, and reproductive, endocrinological, and dermal problems.

Chemical group	WHO hazard classification
Dichlorvos	I highly hazardous
Methomyl (Carbamate)	I highly hazardous
Profenofos, Cypermethrin	II moderately hazardous
Chlorpyriphos	II moderately hazardous
Dimethomate	II moderately hazardous
Imidacloprid	II moderately hazardous
Thiodicarb	II moderately hazardous
Flubendiamide	II moderately hazardous
Fenvalerate	II moderately hazardous

Table 3: Toxicity labels of common pesticides

Label color	Pesticides
Red	Brom adiolone, carbofuran, ethyl mercury acetate, methyl parathion, Monocrotophos, phorate, zinc phosphide etc.
Yellow	Endosulfan, chlorpyriphos, quinalphos, fenthion, cypermethrin, fenvalerate, paraquat etc.
Blue	Malathion, carbaryl, dicofol, thiamethoxam, carbendazim, dodine, copper oxychloride, metalaxyl, tridimefon, glyphosate etc.
Green	Mancozeb, sulphur, benomyl, bitertanol, chlorthalonil, captan, Bt(Dipel, Halt, Hil Btk), oxyfluorofen, streptocycline, neem based formulations, etc.

India is the largest producer of pesticides in Asia and ranks twelfth in the world for the use of pesticides. Although Indian average consumption of pesticide is far lower than many other developed economies, the problem of pesticide residue is very high in India. Pesticide residue in several crops has also affected the export of agricultural commodities in the last few years. In this context, pesticide safety, regulation of pesticide use, proper application technologies, and integrated pest management are some of the key strategies for minimizing human exposure to pesticides. There is a dearth of studies related to these issues in India.

Pesticides in IndianAgriculture

Organophosphates (OP) in the 1960s carbamates in 1970s and pyrethroids in 1980s and the introduction of herbicides and fungicides in the 1970s-1980 contributred significantely to pest control and agricultural output

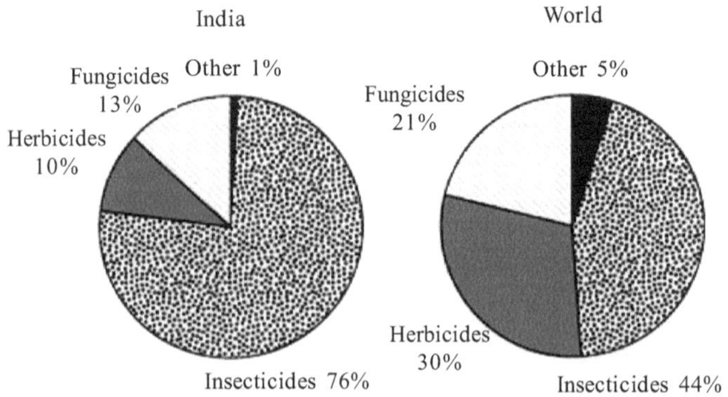

Fig. 3: Pesticides consumption of India compared with world

There are 234 pesticides registered in India. Out of these, 4 are WHO Class Ia pesticides, 15 are WHO Class Ib pesticides and 76 are WHO Class II pesticides, together constituting 40% of the registered pesticides in India. In terms of consumption too, the greatest volumes consumed are of these poisons. The following is a broad picture of the top pesticide-consuming states in India (total pesticides consumed, in metric tonnes of technical grade material, during 2005-06 to 2009-10, as per official data of the Directorate of Plant Protection, Quarantine and Storage, Govt of India).

Table 4: Most consumed pesticides in the country (during 2005-06 to 2009-10)

S. No.	Pesticide (Technical Grade)	Quantity consumed (metric tons)
1.	Sulphur (fungicide)	16424
2.	Endosulfan (insecticide)	15537
3.	Mancozeb (fungicide)	11067
4.	Phorate (insecticide)	10763
5.	Methyl Parathion (insecticide)	08408
6.	Monocrotophos (insecticide)	08209
7.	Cypermethrin (insecticide)	07309
8.	Isoproturon (herbicide)	07163
9.	Chlorpyrifos (insecticide)	07163
10.	Malathion (insecticide)	07103
11.	Carbendazim (fungicide)	06767
12.	Butachlor (herbicide)	06750
13.	Quinalphos (insecticide)	06329
14.	Copper oxychloride	06055
15.	Dichlorvos (insecticide)	05833

Carcinogenic pesticides in Indian agriculture

The following is a list of 24 pesticides registered and used in India, classified as Potential Carcinogens by the US EPA: acephate (C), alachlor (B), atrazine (C), benomyl (C), bifenthrin (C), captan (B), chlorothalonil (B), cypermethrin (C), dichlorovos (C), diclofop-methyl (C), dicofol (C), mancozeb (B), methomyl (C), metolachor (C), oxadiazon (C), oxyflourfen(C), permethrin(C), phosphamidon(C), propiconazole(C), propoxur (B) , thiodicarb(C), thiophanate methyl (C), triadimefon(C), trifluralin(C).

The benefits of Chemical pesticides use are high to farmers relative to risks so will continue to play a pivotal role in pest management until competitive alternatives are not available. One of the major benefits is protection of crop quality and yield, thus raising agricultural output and farm income. Pesticides are quick and effective in preventing large crop losses. Non-target effects of exposure of humans and the environment to pesticide residues however are a continuing concern. The correct application methodology of pesticides can deliver significant socio-economic and environmental benefits. Innovations in pesticide-delivery systems in plants are required to reduce adverse environmental affects but are not expected to eliminate them.

2.3. High yielding varieties

High yielding varieties are equipped with special features which enable them to perform better and stable under wide range of agro-climatic situations. Such varieties are generally semi-dwarf, have genetic in-built capacity to respond to higher doses of fertilizers and water, possess resistance to diseases, insect-pests and abiotic factors. Green revolution in India in early seventies which marked the spectacular production of wheat and rice was the consequence of introduction of these varieties. However, green revolution in seventies should not only be attributed to high yielding varieties but also to availability their quality seed, sufficient chemical fertilizers, promotion of irrigation facilities and pesticides.

Sonara, Sonara 64, Sharbati Sonara, Kalyan Sona and sonalika in wheat and China 1004, IR8, Jaya and Ratna in rice were the lead varieties in era of green revolution. Later on breeding through hybridization and selection continued to add more and more varieties with broader genetic base and better quality parameters. With the result that cultivation range and acceptability of these noble varieties increased among the Indian farmers. Ultimately India became a food self reliant country from food deficient country. Development of high yielding varieties is still the dominant feature of Indian agriculture. For instance, from 1999 to 2009, 220 varieties of rice, 146 of wheat and 290 of pulses (71 of chickpea, 19 of pigeon pea, 56 of moongbean, 39 of urdbean, 19 of lentil, 36 of field pea and 50 of minor pulses which include cowpea, moth bean, horse gram, Lathyrus and rajma) have been recommended for NFSM states. In rice, since1968 as a result of concerted efforts more than 850 rice varieties and 46 hybrids have been released for commercial cultivation in the country. India is the second largest wheat producing country with the production reaching 93.9 million metric tons in 2011-12. This feat was achieved as a result of development of improved high yielding varieties of wheat. More than 260 high yielding, disease resistant varieties of wheat are released.

Past three years of 2013-17, marked the development of 612 high yielding climate resilient varieties/ hybrids comprising 593 of field crops and 30 of horticultural crops for cultivation in different agro-ecological zones of the country. Nutrient rich (zinc, iron, protein) varieties viz., DRR Dhan 45 (18.18 ppm Zinc) and CRR Dhan 310 (10.3% protein) of rice; WB-2 (42 PPM Zinc and 40 PPM Fe) and HPBW-01 (40.6 PPM Zinc and 40.6 Fe) of wheat, Pusa Mustard 30 (zero erucic acid) and Pusa Mustard 31 (Double zero) of Indian mustard have been developed. Rice variety IR-64 Drt-1 (DRR Dhan 42) resistant to drought and Samba Sub-1 tolerant to submergence has been developed. IPM 205-7 (Virat), an extra-early (52-55 days) maturing summer mungbean variety, first-of-its-kind globally, developed. Being short duration variety, it will help in increasing the cropping intensity and diversify the rice-wheat cropping system. Jammu Basmati 129, Pusa Basmati 1609, Pusa Basmati 1509, Pusa Basmati 1637 and Pusa Basmati 1728 have been developed by using new biotechnological tools taking India's grain production to 274 million tons. Similarly more than 550 high yielding varieties have brought production revolution in vegetables to the tune of 180 million ton from an area of 9.2 million ha.

2.4. Entrepreneurship in Off-season crop cultivation

India is bestowed with large agro-climatic diversity recognized in the form of 20 agro-ecological zones and of cousre these can be further subdivided into 60 subzones because of altitude and soil variations (ICAR, National Bureau of Soil Survey and land use planning, Nagpur). For planning and development of agriculture, Ministry of Agriculture and Farmers Welfare, Govt of India divided the country into 15 agro-climatic zones with 124 sub-zones whereas based on variations in topography, rainfall, temperature and croppig pattern ICAR divided the country into 129 agro-climatic zones to have effective location specific crop improvement programs. This diversity has been used by farmers to increase their farm income.

Kharif season crops like urd bean, moong bean and arhar finds cultivation in southern part of India during the rabi season. Many vegetables like tomato, brinjal, chilli, cucurbits and okra are grown in rabi in southern states and fetch good price to the farmers. Whileas cooler climate of higher Himalaya allows the cultivation of many rabi vegetables such as cauliflower, cabbage, broccoli, potato, radish, carrot, french bean, onion and peas in summer. This feature enables our countrymen to have access to fresh vegetables round the year. Moreover farmers get premium price for off-season vegetables. Added advantages are less pests and diseases attack which reduces the cost of cultivation and healthier vegetables. Thus, agro-climatic diversity provides good off-season entrepreurship and has commerical viability at the national level if policy for institutional and investment support exists.

Vegetables are the primary candidates which qualify for off-season venture as demand exists in large quantity round the year but supply is affected because of their relatively short shelf life and perishable nature. Production of vegetable after or before their normal season is called off-season vegetable production. For this vegetable forcing, a technique that enables farmers to grow vegetables and sell the produce before the onset of their normal season.The objective is to supply vegetables to the market to meet their demand during their lean period.

Off season crop-cultivation in India	Crops	Areas where popular
Off season production of vegetables	Radish, knol khol, cauliflower, peas	North Himalayan temperate region growing several rabi vegetables in summer season
Offseason production of pulses	Urdbean, mungbean	Southern states growing kharif pulses in rabi season
Off season production of cereals	wheat, oat, barley	Cold arid region of J&K and Himachal growing rabi crops in summer season
Off season production in protected structures	Leafy vegetables, Cucurbits, tomato, brinjal, chilli	Ladakh region of J&K and Lahual Spiti of Himachal growing
Off season production of tuber crops	Potato	Cold arid region of J&K and Himachal

Advantages

1. Round the year production and supply of vegetables from farm makes it an employment entrepreneurship
2. Fresh vegetables ensure food and nutritional security to the society
3. Farmers develop confidence to adopt vegetable production as their main profession
4. Higher profits from off-season production
5. Consumers can get fresh vegetables during off-season
6. Possible to export fresh vegetables
7. Creates employment for farm laborers round the year

2.5. Processing and Value addition

Value-added agriculture means changing a raw agricultural product into a new one through packaging, processing, cooling, drying, extracting or any other type of process that differentiates the product from the original raw commodity namely changing wheat into flour, retail packing of pulses and bagged salad mix are simple examples of value addition. Value-added products are gaining popularity in the local market and producers can take advantage of high-demand product niches. This is the key to success in value added agriculture—niche markets are where smaller producers can be most successful in creating value and establishing a profitable business. Indian agriculture needs to move up the value chain if it has to benefit both the farmer and the consumer.

India is the number one producer for many fruits: banana, mango, lime, guava, papaya and pomegranate, and among the top five in several others. Yet, for many of these fruits, we do not have global scale processing facilities. In India, only four per cent of the fruits are processed compared to other benchmark countries, such as 23 per cent in China, 50 per cent in Indonesia and 70 per cent in Brazil. Fruit provides far higher incomes to farmers (as much as 2-4 times of cereals and sugarcane) and uses 40-80 per cent less water per hectare compared to cereals. Increasing the share of horticulture would have a meaningful impact on the livelihood of farmers and also help raising production per drop of water. India is one major the producer of the world but turnover of the total Indian food market is 2,50,000 crores per year contributing 1.5 percent to the global processed food trade. Annual consumption of value added foods alone has grown to Rs.2,25,000 crores larger than manufacturing sector.

Agro-Food Processing industries can reduce losses to the tune of Rs.8000 crores by increasing value addition from current level of 7 percent to 35 percent. It creates additional employment directly for 77 lakh people and indirectly for 3 crores people. Value addition coupled with marketing has thus the potentials of solving the basic problems of agricultural surplus or wastage and providing rural jobs, ensuring better prices to the growers, The most important problem facing the country today perhaps is providing remunerative price to the farmers for their produce without incurring additional burden of subsidy through minimum support price or some such measures. This problem could be solved largely in the surplus production of cereals, vegetables, fruits, milk, fish, meat, poultry, etc., which are processed and marketed aggressively both inside and outside the country.

Starting a value-added agricultural business is an exciting opportunity for the small farmer interested in diversifying and exploring new markets, but starting small and finding niche is key to long-term success. But challenges to the small holders are quality and to match supply with demand, should have license and some investment to sustain in the market.

2.6. Mushroom production

Mushrooms are very nutritious products rich in crude fibre and protein but make use of left tover materials such as, wheat bhusa, paddy straw, cotton wastes, coffee waste, water hyacinth, tree saw dust, sugar cane bagasse, wild grasses and various categories of refuse and lignocellulosic wastes. Mushroom cultivation has socio-economic and ecological perspectives. It is an effective regular income generating enterprise for landless farmers and helping in ecological maintenance through recycling of agro-solid wastes. Of the 1151 million tons agricultural residues available globally only 34.5 million tons finds application in mushroom production and much of it is creating ecological hazards, one such example is burning of paddy straw and crop stubbles.

US, UK, Spain, Netherlands, South Korea and China are major mushroom producing countries. However, India and some of other developing countries has commercial potential for mushroom production and related entrepreneurial areas because of the cheap and easily available raw materials needed for this activity, coupled with growing local market demand for fresh produce and value added products. China with its meagre production of 60,000 tons in 1978 became leading producing in 2006 with 14 million tons production of edible mushroom providing employment to 30 million people. India is production is far below 1.2 lakh tons in global context with productivity of 20kg per 100 kg of compost.

In Indian perspective, mushroom cultivation could be:

- A very important cottage industry activity in the integrated rural development programs
- An activity of economic betterment for marginal farmers, landless labourers and other weak sections of communities.
- Agro-wastes management enterprise utilizing cereal straws are largely burnt by the farmers, which causes air pollution, can actually be used for the cultivation of mushrooms
- Means of generating employment, particularly for rural women and youths. Provides additional work for the farmers during winter months when the farming activities are at low ebb.
- A cash crop for selling in local markets or exported for additional family income that will improve the economic standards of the people.
- Source of nutraceuticals which can be of direct benefit to the human health and fitness, another area of entrepreneurship. The extractable bioactive compounds from medicinal mushrooms would enhance human's immune systems and improve their quality of life.
- High cropping intensity enterprise by adopting relatively fast growing strains. Some tropical mushrooms can beharvested and consumed within 10-20 days after spawning, namely *Volvariella volvacea* (Straw mushrooms) and *Pleurotus, sajor-caju* (Oyster mushrooms) and these can be harvested in 3 to 4 weeks after spawning.
- Source of several value added products such as Mushroom pickle • Mushroom nuggets • Mushroom cookies • Mushroom soup powder • Mushroom ketchup • Mushroom candy • Mushroom papad • Mushroom powder

2.7. Dairying

Milk Production: India continues to be the largest producer of milk in world. Several measures have been initiated by the Government to increase the productivity of livestock, which has resulted in increasing the milk production significantly from the level of 102.6 million tons at the end of the Tenth Plan (2006-07) to 127.9 million tons at the end of the Eleventh Plan (2011-12). Milk production during 2014-15 and 2015-16 is 146.3 million tons and 155.5 million tons respectively showing an annual growth of 6.27%. The per capita availability of milk is around 337 grams per day in 2015-16.

India ranks first among the world's milk producing nations since 1998 and has the largest bovine population in the World. Milk production in India during the period 1950-51 to 2014-15, has increased from 17 million tons to 146.3 million tons as compared to 137.7 million tons during 2013-14 recording a growth of 6.26 %. FAO reported 3.1% increase in world milk Production from 765 million tons in 2013 to 789 million tons in 2014.The per capita availability of milk in the country which was 130 gram per day during 1950-51 has increased to 322 gram per day in 2014-15 as against the world average of 293.7 grams per day during 2013.

Operation Flood is a program designed to develop dairying by replicating the Anand Model for dairy development, which has stood the test of time for almost half a century. The first phase of Operation Flood was launched in 1970 following an agreement with the World Food Program, which undertook to provide as aid 126000 tons of skim milk powder and 42000 tons of butter oil to finance the program.

In order to meet the growing demand for milk with a focus to improve milch animal productivity and increase milk production, the Government approved National Dairy Plan Phase-I (NDP-I) in February, 2012 with a total investment of about Rs.2242 crores to be implemented from 2011-12 to 2016-17. NDP-I will help to meet the projected national demand of 150 million tons of milk by 2016-17 from domestic production through productivity enhancement, strengthening and expanding village level infrastructure for milk procurement and provide producers with greater access to markets. The strategy involves improving genetic potential of bovines, producing required number of quality bulls, and superior quality frozen semen and adopting adequate bio-security measures etc. The scheme is implemented by NDDB through end implementing agencies like state Dairy Cooperative Federations/Unions/Milk Producers Companies. NDP-I would focus on 15 major milk producing States - Uttar Pradesh, Punjab, Haryana, Gujarat, Rajasthan, Madhya Pradesh, Bihar, West Bengal, Maharashtra, Karnataka, Tamil Nadu, Andhra Pradesh, Telangana,

Orissa and Kerala which account for over 90% of the country's milk production. Now the area of Operation of NDP-I has been extended to three more states i.e.Uttarakhand, Chhattisgarh and Jharkhand. Coverage of NDP- I will however be across the country in terms of benefits accruing from the scheme.

Milk is India's single largest agricultural commodity in value terms and is more than the combined value of paddy and wheat put together. Milk producing households are predominantly small farmers with less than 2 ha of land and 1 to 2 animals. Ownership of dairy animals is more evenly distributed in India as compared to operational land holdings. India's model of milk production is based on feeding crops residues and agricultural byproducts and using family labour to add value to resources which otherwise have limited alternative economic value. As per market research reports, the value of the Indian market for milk and milk products is expected to grow at 15% annually of which the contribution of milk products like cheese, paneer, fermented milk products, butter and ghee would be significant which represents both an opportunity and challenge to our dairy industry.

Shri Rath, Director said that NDDB's wholly owned subsidiary has helped promote five large producer companies in five states. In a short period of five years till March 2016, these five producer companies have enrolled about 3.26 lakh milk producers of whom about 62 percent are small holders and 40 percent are women. These five companies collectively procured about 19.3 lakh kg of milk per day during 2015-16.

While the organized dairy sector is the only source for milk powder and condensed milk due to the requirement for specialized equipment at a certain scale, it has managed to gradually increase its market share for items such as liquid milk, ice cream, ghee, curd, milk based beverages, cheese, paneer etc even though the unorganized small scale operators continue to account for a major share, particularly in unpasteurized liquid milk and indigenous dairy based sweets. In case of many traditional indigenous products, a large proportion is still being produced and retailed by the unorganized sector. As widely prevalent nutritional deficiency disorders can be prevented or even reversed with fortification of foods with Vitamin A & D, it represents an opportunity to address health conditions that affect the lives of millions. Dairy sector provides huge opportunity for growth of organized dairy industry in future for which focused and continuous R&D and product development efforts need to be undertaken keeping in mind the fast changing consumer preferences. Similarly, development of longer shelf life dairy products, specialized dairy based nutraceuticals & functional products, probiotics catering to different classes of consumers and niche markets needs to be undertaken by the dairy industry particularly by cooperatives to increase realization and for market diversification.

2.8. Poultry production

Poultry in India roots to some 5000 years back but has undergone a paradigm shift in structure and operation recently. During the last four decades, poultry production in India has taken a quantum jump, emerging from an unscientific farming practice to commercial production system with state-of-the-art technological interventions. This transformation has been owing to sizeable investments in breeding, hatching, rearing, low cost equipments and processing by public and private sectors. Farmers in India have moved from rearing non-descript birds to rearing hybrids such as Hyaline, Shaver, and Babcock, which ensure faster growth, good livability, excellent feed conversion and high profits to the rearers. Egg production at the end of the Tenth Plan (2006-07) was 50.70 billion as compared to 66.45 billion at the end of the Eleventh Plan (2011-12). Currently the total Poultry population in our country is 729.21 million (as per 19th Livestock Census) and egg production is around 82.93 billion during 2015-16. The poultry meat production is estimated to be 3.26 million tons.

The current scenario of poultry production in India indicates its fast growth of 6-8% in layers and 10-12% in broilers per year against the growth of agriculture as a whole which is around 2.5%. India is the third-largest egg producer after China and USA and the fourth-largest chicken producer after China, Brazil and USA. The per capita eggs consumption has gone up from 30 to 68 and the chicken from 400 gm to 2.5 kg. Production is getting more organized and moving ahead of consumption resulting in optimum prices and with minimum profits. Human nutritionists recommend 180 eggs & 10 kg chicken per year while as most of the countries consume over 240 eggs and 20 kg of chicken indicating potential scope and opportunities of poultry production in India. At present, four states, Andhra Pradesh, Maharashtra, Punjab and Tamil Nadu account for more than 50 per cent of the total output of eggs and broilers in the country. Indian Poultry Industry provides employment to 1.5 million people directly and to 1.5 million indirectly through feed formulations, equipments, processing and retailing etc.

Short duration breeds, feed efficient breeds, dual purpose breeds are some of the factors adding to economics of poultry profession. The low technology input birds are mostly dual purpose. The broiler growing period has come down to less than 40 days from 50. The birds grow faster than native chicken reaching 1.5 kg weight in 45 days and can withstand variable feed qualities. Clustering farming approach, contract farming, organic poultry farming with branding can help more profitability and quality assurance to the consumers. Poultry has attracted larger investments in southern states of India where units with one million birds have become the icon of poultry business in India (Table 1).

Table 1: Growth of layer sector in poultry

Parameter	1990	2015
Layer birds (crore)	10	24
Layer feed price (Rs)	12	22
Egg price (Rs)	1.5	2.90
Eggs per head/ year	20	68
Eggs per hen	260	310
Average layer farm size	20000	200000
Separate brooding	10%	80%
Feed automation	10%	80%
Small eggs discount	Nil	Discounted
Eggs cleaning & packing	No	Imp

Table 2: Growth of broiler sector in poultry

Parameters	1990	2015
Broiler parents housed (cr)	0.7	3.5
Broilers/month (crore)	5.0	25.0
Broiler feed price (Rs/kg)	20.0	30.0
Chicken per head (kg)	0.4	2.5
Broiler price/kg live (Rs)	25.0	65.0
Broiler integration	0%	60%
Broiler FCR	02.2	1.65
Days to slaughter (2 kg)	48.0	38.0
Multi-age group farms	90%	10%
Chicken processing	1%	7%
Antibiotics issue	Nil	50%

India's share in the poultry exports is very low, accounts for only 2% of the world market.

Live poultry: Sri Lanka (50%), Bangladesh (32.5%), Nepal (8.2%)

Hatching eggs: UAE (38%), Oman (26.8%), Kuwait (5.4%)

Table eggs: UAE (72.8%), Kuwait (8.3%), Oman (8.3%)

Egg powder: Japan (16%), Poland (14.5%), UAE (8.9%), Belgium (5.54%)

Frozen eggs: UAE (83%), Oman (5%), Kuwait (3.9%)

India has a great opportunity to export many things in poultry to Africa. India has developed birds (breeds) suitable for open houses, which can take lower quality feed and resist higher level infections. They can prove better for Africa.

India produces the best quality hatching eggs which can be exported to the Middle-East and Africa. Hatchery is a better option to start with, before going in for breeding stocks. This involves mostly airlifting of eggs and liasoning.

Production technology adopted in India involves fewer investments on low-cost housing, encourages more manual labour, and less dependence on consistent power supply are valuable for developing African nations.

Poultry equipment, feed additives, vaccines & pharmaceuticals have a good potential for exports. India's export is low, as per Agriculture and Processed Foods Products Export Development Authority (APEDA), India exported 659,304 MT of poultry products for the worth of INR 7,680 million during 2015-16.

India could not find market in European countries because of low quality standards. DOL 53 sensor developed by Drager and marketed by Big Dutchman helps in controlling poultry house climate precisely. Farmers can use this sensor to measure and monitor the ammonia concentration in their poultry houses. The data provided by the sensor guides towards the ideal regulation of climate, manure removal and feed management in the barn. This results in a significant reduction of the ammonia content in the air. Bird health improves significantly because of low respiratory diseases or footpad infections. As proven by long-term studies conducted both in the laboratory and in the field, the innovation remains unaffected by temperature fluctuations and humidity changes and is not influenced by other gases such as methane or CO2. The DOL 53 sensor can additionally be used in manure drying both in the poultry house and in a connected manure drying tunnel.

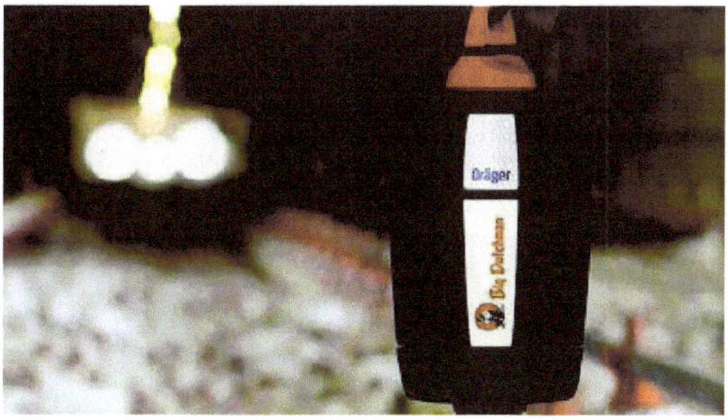

Fig. 3: Poultry climate control device DOL 53 sensor

Entrepreneurship

- Poultry
- Hatchery
- Low cost feed and housing equipments
- Processing and value addition

2.9. High yielding breeds

800 cattle breeds have been identified as milk producing while there are many breeds suited for beef production and many of breeds are dual purpose i.e., equally good for milk and beef production. High milk yielding top cattle breeds are enumerated below:

Holstein Cattle Breed

Holstein also known as Holstein-Friesian Cattle or Friesian Cattle has amazing milk production and is the highest milk producing dairy farm animal in the world. This dairy cattle produces 11000 kg milk in a year. The current National Holstein milk production leader is Ever-Green-View My 1326-ET EX-92. This amazing milk producing or dairy cattle produced 32,740 kg of milk in 365 days attaining her world record in February 2010.

Norwegian Red Cattle Breed

Norwegian Red is well known as NRF and also well known for the fortune of its milk. NRF provides 10,000 kilogram milk per year.

Kostroma Cattle Type

Kostroma has relatively more life span. This breed survives for duration of 25 years. This produces 10,000 kilograms of milk every year.

Brown Swiss Cattle Breed

Brown Swiss is famous cattle breed whose milk is more suited for cheese production. Brown Swiss yields 9,000 kilogram of Milk per year.

Swedish Red Cattle Breed

Swedish Red Cattle is well-known as Swedish Red and White Cattle. This cattle breed is famous for its healthy structure and long life. The cattle breed produce milk 8000 kilograms per year. The height of this cattle breed is 140cm and weight is 600 kg.

Ayrshire Cattle Breed

Ayrshire Cattle Breed is well-known as Dunlop Cattle. It is a healthy and strong breed with body weight upto the 600 kg and simple to rear. The cattle breed produces 7,831 kilograms of milk a year.

Angeln Cattle Breed

This dairy cow is famous for the higher milk fat percentage in its milk. It provides milk production 7570 kg per year. Milk of the cattle is more suited for processing.

Guernsey Cattle Breed

This Cattle Breed produces the top percentage of A2 milk. The Milk Production of this cattle breed is 7363 kilogram.

Milking Shorthorn Cattle Breed

Milking Shorthorn is also well known as Dairy Shorthorn type of cattle breed which is red cattle with white markings, all white or red roan. This cattle produce milk 7,000 kilograms every year. The Height of Milking Shorthorn 140 cm and Weight is 680 kilogram.

Pie Rouge des Plaines Cattle Breed

It is well known as Lowland Red Pied Cattle that meat is improved in value and amount than Holstein cattle. The Milk Production is 6900 kg per year and Height is 138cm and Weight is 700 kilograms.

Poultry breeds

Dual purpose poultry breeds are the classic backyard chickens. These breeds are hardy, self-reliant and fairly large-bodied. Most lay large brown shelled eggs. Some popular examples include Rhode Island Red and New Hamshire breeds. India also has its own local breeds like Aseel, Naked Neck, Kadaknath and few more which are robust and have survived harsh climates.These breeds produce anywhere between 92 -110 eggs annually on maturity. Some important egg production breeds are tabulated below:

Table 3: Egg lying breed of poultry

S. No.	Breed	Number of eggs per year
1.	White Leghorns	280
2.	Rhode Island Red (Dual purpose)	260
3.	Golden Comet	250-300
4.	Ameraucana (Dual purpose)	250
5.	Barred Plymouth Rock	280
6.	Golden Laced Wyandottes	200
7.	New Hampshire Red	200
8.	Buff Orpington	150-200
9.	Australop (Dual purpose)	250-300
10.	Speckeled Sussex (Dual Purpose)	250-300

2.10. Export orientation / world trade liberalization through WTO

Today the world is a global village. Various factors like global accessibility, telecommunication revolution, information metamorphosis, media transformation and redefined living standards have led to the integration of the world economy. In order to give export orientation to agri-products, The Agricultural and Processed Food Products Export Development Authority (APEDA) was established by the Government of India under the Agricultural and Processed Food Products Export Development Authority Act passed by the Parliament in December, 1985. It is mandated to develop and promote export of Agricultural and processed food products from India. In 2016–17, export of agri-products such as cereals, processed fruit and vegetables, processed foods, and animal products was around USD 16.27 billion, according to APEDA.

India's agricultural exports increased at a brisk pace for more than two decades after the economy was opened up in 1991. Although imports also increased, they were more than compensated for by exports. The concept of AEZs (Agri-Export Zones) was first introduced in India under the EXIM policy 2001 to strengthen of production linkages with a market-oriented approach, product acceptability and its competitiveness abroad as well as in the domestic market, value addition to basic agricultural produce, bring down cost of production through economy of scale, better price for agricultural produce, Improvement in product quality and packaging, promote trade related research and development and generating employment opportunities. APEDA set up 60 AEZs spread over 230 districts in 20 states. The crops covered include fruits, vegetables, spices, cashew, tea, basmati rice, medicinal plants, and pulses. In all, 35 crops were identified for promotion in these zones.

India's agricultural trade surplus recorded a more than ten-fold increase between 1991-92 and 2013-14. Three years later, the picture is vastly different. Between 2013-14 and 2016-17, agricultural exports fell by 22% while imports increased by 62%. As a result, the trade surplus has fallen by 70%. US agricultural exports to India totaled nearly USD 1.3 billion in 2016, with tree nuts, cotton, pulses, fresh and processed fruits, and prepared foods and a senior officer remarks that during the last decade US agricultural exports to India have grown nearly 250 per cent. However US continue to impede barriers to imports of many of India's products which needs serious considerations.

The Govt of India has revamped the export subsidy regime and indicated its intention to phase out subsidies for overseas shipments in compliance with rules of the World Trade Organization (WTO) while setting an ambitious export target of $900 billion to be met by 2019-20. WTO that originated from the Uruguay round of GATT (1986-94). It was officially constituted on January 1, 1995 which took the place of GATT. Based in Geneva, The WTO has nearly 164 countries as its members accounting for over 97% of world trade. Around 20 others are negotiating membership. It is not an agency of the United Nations Organization (UNO). The World Trade Organization (WTO) is the most powerful legislative and judicial body in the world. By promoting the free trade agenda of multinational corporations above the interests of local communities, working families, and the environment, the WTO has systematically undermined democracy around the world. Unlike United Nations treaties, WTO rules can be enforced through sanctions. This gives the WTO more power than any other international body. The WTO was born out of negotiations, and everything the WTO does is the result of negotiations. The bulk of the WTO's current work comes from the 1986–94 negotiations called the Uruguay Round and earlier negotiations under the General Agreement on Tariffs and Trade (GATT).

The WTO is currently the host to new negotiations, under the 'Doha Development Agenda' launched in 2001. It administers agreements, handles trade disputes and monitors country-specific trade policies while training and cooperating with developing nations and other international organizations.

Objective

1. To improve the standard of living of people in the member countries
2. To ensure full employment and broad increase in effective demand
3. To enlarge production and trade of goods
4. To increase the trade of services
5. To ensure optimum utilization of world resources
6. To protect the environment
7. To accept the concept of sustainable development

Functions

1. To implement rules and provisions related to trade policy review mechanism
2. To provide a platform to member countries to decide future strategies related to trade and tariff
3. To provide facilities for implementation, administration and operation of multilateral and bilateral agreements of the world trade
4. To administer the rules and processes related to dispute settlement
5. To ensure the optimum use of world resources
6. To assist international organizations such as, IMF and IBRD for establishing coherence in Universal Economic Policy determination

Notes of contention

- WTO has emerged as a strong institution that is successfully promoting trade developments across the nations in terms of volume, value, countries and companies.
- Closer economic ties and few disputes in comparison to magnitude of trade expansion is sign of reduced tension in international trade.
- WTO members are now reducing the subsidies and the trade barriers which provides a broader range of choices for product qualities to consumers.
- WTO has broadened the scope of investment and intellectual property rights

Notes of attention

- Leading principle in the WTO's Agreement on Agriculture is that market forces should control agricultural policies rather than a national commitment to guarantee food security and maintain decent family farmer incomes. WTO policies have allowed dumping of heavily subsidized industrially produced food into poor countries, undermining local production and increasing hunger.
- WTO is seeking to privatize essential public services such as education, health care, energy and water.
- The policies of the WTO impact all aspects of society and the planet, but it is not a democratic and transparent institution.

2. Conclusion

India with its second largest arable land in the world, approx. 160 million hectares, is the second largest producer of food after China. India is one of the largest producers of fruits (mangoes, papaya), vegetables (potatoes, onions, ginger), pulses (chickpea) cereals (wheat and rice), sugarcanes, tea and live stock products (milk and eggs). Indian agriculture caters to around 60 percent of the population for their livelihood and contributes to 17 percent of GDP. There have been evolutionary changes in production and productivity of food grain crops, horticultural crops, dairy, poultry and mushroom while considerable livelihood was provided to farmers by infusion of export orientation and promotion of food processing industry in agriculture. During the course of compilation author came across with the fact none of the ten technologies could be judiciously utilized or integrated to reap their full economic potential, for instance, owing to massive production India has a strong raw material base for the food processing industry but degree of processing remained low in range of 2 to 35 percent for different commodities. Challenges also continued to grow with opportunities in Indian agriculture. This seeks for more scientific interventions to change challenges into opportunities and transform agriculture into viable commercial industry with global competitiveness. Subsequent chapter will enumerate some of the latest developments in the field of science and technology to counter the challenges which the present agriculture is facing.

3. References

Bernardes MFF, Pazin M, Pereira LC and Dorta DJ .2015.Impact of Pesticides on Environmental and Human Health, In book edited by Ana Cristina Andreazza and Gustavo Scola entitled "Pharmacology, Toxicology and Pharmaceutical Science » Toxicology » "Toxicology Studies - Cells, Drugs and Environment" ISBN 978-953-51-2140-4, Published: July 8, 2015 under CC BY 3.0 license.

Oerke EC.2005. Centenary review; Crop losses to pests. Journal of Agricultural Science (2006), 144, 31–43.

Popp Jozef, Peto Karoly and Nagy Janos. 2013. Pesticide productivity and food security: A review. Agronomy for Sustainable Development, 33(1): 243–255.

Punith Kumar LM and Indira M. 2017. Trends in Fertilizer Consumption and Food grain Production in India: A Co-integration Analysis. SDMIMD Journal of Management, 8 (2): 45-50.

Sharma Vijay Paul .2014. The Role of Fertilizer in Transforming Agriculture in Asia. A case study of the Indian fertilizer sector. Working paper 06 | November 2014. ifpri-copyright@cgiar.org.

Sidhu DS and Sidhu JS. 1993. "Demand for Fertiliser and Foodgrains Production in India." In *Fertiliser Pricing: Issues Related to Sub-sidies*, edited by Vidya Sagar, 115–130. Jaipur, India: Concept Publishing House.

Singh Maha V. 2008. "Micronutrient Deficiencies in Crops and Soils in India." In *Micronutrient Deficiencies in Global Crop Production*, edited by Brian J. Alloway, 93–125. Dordrecht, The Netherlands: Springer.

Subramanian G and Nirmala V. 1991. "A Macro Analysis of Fertiliser Demand in India (1966–67 to 1985–86)." *Indian Journal of Agri-cultural Economics* 46 (1): 12–19.

3

Ten Technologies that can Transform Indian Agriculture

Jag Paul Sharma

Directorate of Research, SKUAST Jammu,Jammu and Kashmir, India

Abstract

With its core intention to raise economic status of farmers, Govt of India vows for transformation in agriculture and sets goal to double farmers' income by 2022. Nonetheless, net income increase at the farm is amalgamation of technologies, tactics and government policies. Farmers realized 3-4 times increment in their profit during era of green revolution when high yielding varieties and chemical fertilizers were introduced in early seventies. Subsequently income enhancement of the farmers continued through raising of farm productivity per unit area and entrepreneurship. Thus Indian agriculture experienced transformation through chemical fertilizers, high yielding varieties, synthetic pesticides, off-season cultivation, high yielding breeds, export orientation and entrepreneurship development in food processing, mushroom production, dairying and poultry. With the result, India emerged as top producer of milk, millets, pomegranate, banana, mango, jute, pulses, okra, safflower etc and second top producer of wheat, rice, tea, tomato, potato, onion etc and third in egg production and fourth in poultry meat. Consequence was evolution of commercial farming from subsistence farming. In era of globalization and increased purchase power of consumers, profitability at the farm has become subject of competitiveness, quality and consumer preference. Price shoot-up and market crashing of commodities in the country has made agriculture, a profession of risk, uncertainties and unpredictability. It has thus, lost creditability of socio-economic security. To make it remunerative and attractive, a combo plan of transformational technologies that has the competence to break production and productivity barriers and can also address market needs as well as consumer preferences is highly wanted. There is urgent need to infuse characteristic of market orientation in agriculture through marketing information system and promoting demand driven production system with focus on zonalization of crops taking advantage of niche area or geographical indications. Commodity supply must remain high through promotion of climate resilient varieties or breeds, mechanization, adoption of hi-tech crop and livestock management practices. All this has to be made sustainable by way of produce and product diversification through integrated farming system, organic agriculture and secondary agriculture. Considering future vision, research initiatives must continue on noble areas like vertical farming and in vitro *farming. Information and communication technologies will open avenue for assured marketing by linking production to consumption system via proper marketing and distribution leading to increased farm profitability. This as a whole will make transformation in agriculture a reality.*

Keywords: integrated entrepreneurship, secondary agriculture, ICTs, globalization

1. Introduction

Indian agriculture is the core sector and characterized by 17% of the world's population, 11% livestock, 4.2% of the world's water, 2.4% of the world's area, 51% arable land, 142% cropping intensity, 140±2 m ha cultivated area with only 68 m ha irrigated, <18% contribution to GDP but >55 % of workforce in agriculture. Nonetheless, it supports country's socio-economic growth and controls political stability via food security, nutritional security, employment generation and poverty alleviation. India is the world's largest producer of many fresh fruits and vegetables, milk, major spices, select fibrous crops such as jute, staples such as millets and castor oil seed. India's milk production is estimated to have increased by 6.6 per cent to 176.35 million tons during the financial year 2017-18. India is the second largest producer of wheat and rice and ranked in the world's five largest producers of over 80% of agricultural produce items, including many cash crops such as coffee and cotton, in 2010. India is one of the world's five largest producers of livestock and poultry meat, with one of the fastest growth rates (Wikipedia).

Indian agriculture after green revolution has been able to feed 1.24 billion population of the country but unable to attract human preference for entrepreneurship and investment. The reasons being that agriculture under present system of reforms is not competent to address production market linkage, marginalization of land holdings, transport and storage losses, poor public distribution system. The cobweb effect haunts Indian agriculture (cobweb effect means that higher cultivation leads to lower prices, which in turn leads to lower cultivation in the next period). The problem of bumper crops leading to a price crash can be taken care of by policies such as minimum support prices and increased warehousing capacity. India's warehousing capacity for perishables is disproportionately concentrated in a few regions. Almost 50% of cold-storage capacity is concentrated in the states of Uttar Pradesh and Punjab.

To attract investment and entrepreneurs in agriculture, transformation is required. Agricultural transformation is the process by which individual farms shift from highly diversified, subsistence-oriented production to more specialized production oriented towards the market. There is need to revisit the technologies that transformed the agriculture and the innovations that have the competency to transform the present agriculture into entrepreneurial industry with commercial viability at national and international levels.

2. Technologies that can change the scenario of Indian agriculture

Targeted activities in focused areas of proven commercial viability are likely to increase the production and productivity of agricultural crops and allied enterprises, add value to the produce, reduce cost of production and increase profit margins for the farmers. However profit and pricing in agriculture is not simply a production and productivity relationship but has to be linked with demand and supply. Indian situation where size of land holding is continuously falling, knowledge gaps are increasing, farmer's wills are poor and non-strategic, requires technological and administrative interventions to be applied in innovative way. Strategies have to vary from village to village, region to region, agro-climate to agro-climate and class to class, namely

- Landless farmers
- Marginal farmers
- Small farmers
- Medium to large farmers

Special attention required for exclusive programs designed for landless and marginal farmers where direct governmental interventions are required so they also become part of commerce and trade in agriculture. ICAR, the largest body on agricultural R and D in the country has set for diverse targets to bring socio-economic transformation among farming community namely focus on farming system approach, soil inventory and capability classification, designing and developing of organic farming package of practices, designing, developing and demonstration of climate resilient technologies, designing and developing technologies for managing soil health and designing, developing and testing of 3 technologies for Irrigation water Management. Separate targets have been set for animal sciences, fisheries sciences, agricultural engineering, agricultural education and agricultural extension also. Some of the relevant technological interventions where research outcomes of aforesaid activities can be converged are described here under:

2.1. Zonalization /niche area expolitation/ promotion of geographical indicators

Zonalization is area specific demarcation based on agro-climatic feasibility and socio-economic status for promotion of one or more activities/ products / commodities with an aim of strong visible socio-economic impact.

Zonalization delivers to:

a. Better quality produce /product
b. More profitability
c. More productivity
d. Economic security through planned marketing

e. Effective implementation

f. Growth oriented nature

g. Sustainable development

h. Minimum surplus wastage

Table 1: Agri-horti zonalization of Jammu province for commercial venture

Entrepreneurship	Suggested areas	Justification
Organic vegetables crop zone	Irrigated vegetable belt of Jammu, Samba and Kathua districts	• Ground water available • Inputs available • Market avenues exist
Apple/ pear zone	Doda, Bhaderwah, Batote, Kud	• Earlier harvest than Kashmir • Good quality varieties available • Market avenues exist
Walnut zone	Kishtwar, Doda, Reasi (Arnas, pouni), poonch	• Niche area excellence • Agro-climatic specificity • Export quality varieties available
Anardana zone	Ramban, Reasi, batote, kud, Rajouri, poonch	• Naturally established habitat (niche area) • Promotional potential exist • Market avenues exist
Rajmash zone	Bhaderwah, Chinchora, Mandwah, podder,	• Niche area crop • Known for quality and liking • Market avenues exist
Basmati zone	RS Pura, Arnia, Bishnah, Mishriwala, Akhnoor	• Niche area crop • Known for world quality basmati • Market avenues exist

Benefits

- Easy to generate post harvest management, transportation, marketing facilities
- Because of integrated and convergent efforts vertical progress is much assured
- Skill up gradation and capacity building are regularly possible
- Threats are reduced because of enhanced opportunities
- Benefit cost ratio are higher as inputs efficiencies are increased

Role of SAU

- Technological demonstrations through field schools
- On-farm technological refinement program
- Participatory variety evaluation and development program
- Technical backstopping support to developmental departments

With a view to promoting agricultural exports from India and remunerative returns to the growers in a sustained manner, the concept of the agri export zones (AEZ) was floated. These zones have been set up for end to end development for export of specific products from a geographically contiguous area. AEZ have to be identified by the State Government, who would evolve a comprehensive package of services provided by all State Government agencies, State agriculture universities and all institutions and agencies of the Union Government for intensive delivery in these zones. Corporate sector with proven credentials would be encouraged to sponsor new agri-export zone or take over already notified agri export zone or part of such zones for boosting agri-export from the zones. Now the country has 60 AEZ spread across the 22 states (Table 2). Much could not achieved because of vested political interests and non-integration of among the identified agencies.

Table 2: Agri-export zones in India

State	AEZ	Crops
West Bengal	6	Pineapple, litchi, potatoes, mangoes, vegetables, Darjeeling tea
Karnataka	4	Gherkins, rose onion, flowers, vanila
Uttarkhand	4	Litchi, flowers, basmati rice, medicinal and aromatics plants
Punjab	3	Vegetables, potatoes, basmati rice
Uatter Pradesh	4	Potatoes, mangoes, vegetables, basmati
Maharashtra	8	Grapes, grapewine, mangoes, kesar mango, flowers, onion, pomegranate, banana, oranges
Andhra Pradesh	5	Mango pulp, vegetables, grapes, mangoes, gherkins, chilli
Jammu & Kashmir	2	Apples and walnut
Tripura	1	Pineapple
Madhya Pradesh	5	Potatoes, onion, garlic, seed spices, wheat, lentil, grams, oranges
Tamil Naidu	4	Cut flowers, flowers, mangoes, cashewnut
Bihar	1	Litchi, vegetables, honey
Gujarat	3	Mangoes, vegetables, value added onion, sesame seeds
Sikkim	2	Flowers, ginger
Himachal Pradesh	1	apples
Orissa	1	Ginger and turmeric
Jharkhand	1	Vegetables
Kerala	2	Horticultural products, medicinal plants
Assam	1	Fresh and processed ginger
Rajasthan	2	Coriander, cumin

Objectives

- Strengthening of backward linkages with a market oriented approach.
- Product acceptability and its competitiveness abroad as well as in the domestic market
- Value addition to basic agricultural produce
- Bring down cost of production through economy of scale.
- Better price for agricultural produce.
- Improvement in product quality and packaging.
- Promote trade related research and development.
- Increase employment opportunities.

Causes of failure

- Lack of political will
- Incorrect area identification either because of incompetent field agency or political interference
- Inadequate funding probably due to diversion to non-demarcked areas
- Demand supply chain not well studied
- Integration of different agencies is lacking
- Poor technical backstopping to the farmers and field functionaries

2.2. Marketing linkages/ market intelligence and market assurance

Today's marketing is dynamic, and manager has to undergo necessary changes to cope with the pace of changing marketing environment. Information is a basic input to know what is happening and what is going to happen. A company needs information on a continuous basis to be aware of marketing developments taking place in the market. In order to learn about changing needs of customers, new competitors' initiatives, changing distribution practices, recent trends in promotion practices, etc., a manager requires the permanent arrangement to get the needed information on a regular basis. Information is like a life-blood of business. Circulation of needed information is as important as the circulation of blood in human being. If a firm is unable to manage information will fail to achieve the goals.

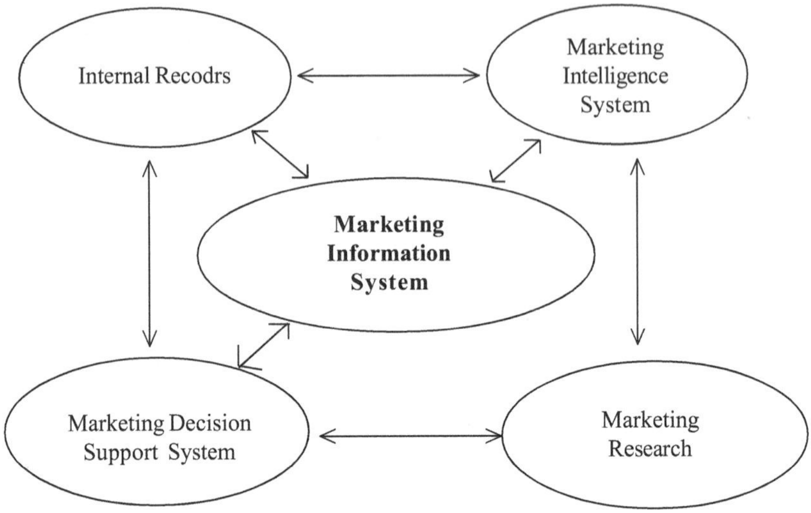

Fig. 1: MIS in balancing production and supply relationship (*Courtesy:* Google)

The system or arrangement that deals with providing the information regularly is known as marketing information system (MIS). **A marketing information system (MIS)** is a set of procedures and methods designed to generate marketing data, analyze it, disseminate to managers and store anticipated marketing decision information on a regular, continuous basis. MIS can be used operationally, managerially, and strategically for successful marketing and timely harvest of business opportunities. In simple words, *Marketing Information System (MIS) is a permanent arrangement (system or setup) for provision of regular availability of relevant, reliable, adequate, and timely information for making marketing decisions.*

2.2.1. Contract farming

One such system utilizing the MIS in agri-business management is Contract Farming. It is a system for the production and supply of agricultural and horticultural produce by farmers/primary producers under advance contracts, the essence of such arrangements being a commitment to provide an agricultural commodity of a type, at a specified time, price, and in specified quantity to a known buyer.

Contract farming is defined as agricultural production system carried out according to an agreement between a buyer and farmers, which establishes conditions for the production and marketing of a farm product or products. Typically, the farmers agree to provide committed quantity of a specific agricultural product. This way farmer gets assured market through the contract system.

The buyer specifies the quality required and the price offered, and the farmer commits to deliver at a future date. Commonly, however, contract farming implies more than a farmer just having a contract to supply a buyer. The important feature is that the buyer has some say in how, when and where a product is produced and harvested. For example, a farmer who is growing certified seeds at an agreed price, using the foundation seed supplied by a seed company, using inputs either supplied by or recommended by the company and following all recommended production practices is doing contract farming.

Benefits of Contract farming

- Provides assured market access to the produce.
- Contract farming gives access to additional sources of capital, and a more certain price by shifting part of the risk of adverse price movement to the buyer.
- Farmers also get an access to new technology and inputs, including credit, through contracts which otherwise may be beyond their reach.
- For a processor or distributor, contracts are more flexible in the face of market uncertainty, make smaller demands on scarce capital resources, and impose less of an additional burden of labour relations, ownership of land, and production activities, on management.
- The firm even gets an access to unpaid family labour and can make use of state funds indirectly through agricultural production sector which are directed at farmers by development agencies.
- Food processors can minimize their overhead costs per unit of production by operating their plants at or near full capacity as contracting gives assured and stable raw material supplies from farms.
- The firm can also project an image of working with local producers as a partner when it undertakes CF and may even obtain state and international agency incentives for its activities as developmental projects, instead of corporate farming.
- Contracts also help improve product quality by directly introducing incentives and penalties as there are problems of adverse selection and moral hazard in any contractual arrangement resulting in underinvestment or shirking by any of the parties.
- Contracting can help to remove market imperfections in produce, capital (credit), land, labour, information and insurance markets; facilitate better coordination of local production activities which often involve initial

investment in processing, extension etc.; and can help in reducing transaction costs

- CF can help to reduce costs of cultivation as it can provide access to better inputs and more efficient production methods. The increasing cost of cultivation was the reason for the emergence of CF in Japan and Spain in the 1950s and in the Indian Punjab in the early 1990s.
- Contract farming also lowers transaction costs for the farmers as many of the transactions are internalized by the procuring firm.
- CF is also an alternative to corporate farming which may be costly, risky, and difficult to manage and still not viable.

2.2.2. Demand driven production system (production to consumption linkage)

A market economy is an economic system where decisions regarding investment, production, and distribution are based on the interplay of supply and demand, which determines the prices of goods and services which the Indian agriculture lacks totally and consequence is *cobweb effect*. To be market oriented farmers will need to produce what the market wants and what satisfies the consumer. Scientists need to develop strategies and technological packages to have a shift from production-driven agriculture to market-driven agriculture. Farming as a business means replacing the multiple goals of traditional farming with the single goal of profit. Market-oriented farming calls for farmers to be aware of the different market channels and input suppliers, the differences in prices and costs, and other conditions of buying and selling. A farm business is an enterprise with linkages to input suppliers and output markets. It consists of activities which, if operating together efficiently and effectively, create value and, at the end of the process, create more profit. Market-oriented farmers have to make decisions relating to the purchase of inputs and the sale of final produce.

Making agriculture remunerative and attractive to youth by underlining the agri-preneurial areas. Transforming the way youth view and engage in the agricultural sector is key for significantly increasing employment, improving livelihoods, and in the long run building rural economies that expand in step with fast-growing urban centres. Often, rural youths do not see agriculture as a viable career option, having grown up witnessing small-holder farms struggle against unfavorable market and environmental factors for precious little profit after hard physical toil. Constraints that youth face engaging in the sector reinforce these perceptions. Approaches that leverage technology, education, land-rights reform, access to financial and information resources, and creation of entrepreneur networks can make agribusiness profitable and scalable for youth, making the sector more attractive. Integration of these approaches can enhance their impact and sustainability.

The global changes of rapid population growth, urbanization and market liberalization impact directly on farming, making it more market-oriented and thus more competitive. These trends have an effect on farmers who need to develop stronger management skills and competencies to cope with the ever changing farming environment and take appropriate marketing decisions. **MIS** will facilitate them in taking appropriate decision.

Marketing Decisions

- Deciding on what inputs to use and where to get them.
- Deciding what quantities to sell and when.
- Deciding where and to whom to sell the products and at what prices.
- Deciding how to get premium prices.
- Deciding which marketing channel to use

Market liberalization, globalization, changes in demography and income, urbanization, information technology, climate change and the global financial crisis are all affecting small-scale farmers around the world. Some of these changes create challenges and some create opportunities. Farmers need to be not only good managers but 'entrepreneurial' by being innovative, taking risks and having a longer term perspective of their business. They need to be active and able to respond to the threats that they face in the future. To prosper in this ever-changing environment, farmers must be able to respond to change.

Record-keeping is a vital part of generating and collecting data. Some farmers are reluctant to keep records for all their enterprises on a regular basis. But entrepreneurial, market-oriented farmers soon see the benefits of recording data, especially as they diversify their system and introduce higher value commercial enterprises. It helps the entrepreneurs calculating profits and efficiency of the approach they are following.

2.3. Hi-tech agronomic-management (High cropping intensity/high density horticulture)

Cropping intensity refers to raising of number of crops from the same field during one agricultural year. it can be expressed through a formula.

Cropping Intensity = Gross Cropped Area /Net Sown Area x 100

As per the land use statistics 2013-14, the total geographical area of the country is 328.7 million hectares, of which 141.4 million hectares is the reported net sown area and 200.9 million hectares is the gross cropped area. The net sown area works out to be 43% of the total geographical area. The net irrigated area is 68.2 million hectares. Cropping intensity on the net sown area is142%. Cropping intensity is the number of times a crop is planted per year in a given agricultural area. It is the ratio of effective crop area harvested to the physical area. The net sown area of the country has risen by about 20 per cent since independence and has reached a point where it is not possible to make any appreciable increase. Only option available to increase productivity per unit area is the higher cropping intensity.

Box 1: Land Use in India

- Forest area: 70 mha (21.30per cent)
- Non-agricultural uses: 26.5 mha (8.05per cent)
- Barren & uncultivable: 17.3 mha (5.26per cent)
- Culturable waste: 12.6 mha (3.83per cent),
- Permanent pastures:10.2 mha (3.1 2per cent)
- Miscellaneous tree crops: 3.2 mha (0.96per cent)
- Fallow land: 26.3 mha (8per cent),
- Agricultural land: 181.95 mha (55.3per cent)
- Net Sown Area: 139.9 mha (42_57per cent)

Source: Land Use Statistics (2012-13), Ministry of Agriculture & Farmers Welfare

Higher cropping intensity means that a higher portion of the net area is being cropped more than once during one agricultural year. This also implies higher productivity per unit of arable land during one agricultural year.

According to the data of 1990-91, 2014-15, 2015-16 (latest available), the index of intensity of cropping for the country as a whole was 130, 139, 142 per cent. Cropping intensity varies from 100 per cent in Mizoram to 194.43 percent in Punjab (1999-2000). Next to Punjab is West Bengal (174%), Himachal Pradesh(173%), followed by Haryana (169%), and Uttar Pradesh (151%). It is higher than the national average in Jammu and Kashmir, Assam, Manipur, Sikkim, Bihar and Orissa. It is low and very low in the states of peninsular plateau and dry, rainfed regions of Rajasthan, Gujarat, Maharashtra and Karnataka (110-125 per cent). This indicates that none of the states has been able to grow two or more crops on a field in an agricultural year.

Eight measures need consideration on priority when intending for high cropping intensity namely assured irrigation, short duration varieties, appropriate crop rotations, relaying cropping, mixed cropping, mechanization, integrated nutrient management and integrated pest management.

The following factors determine the cropping pattern, yield of crops and overall agricultural development:

Physical factors – Topography, Climate and Soil

Institutional factors – Land holding size, land tenure

Infrastructural factors – Irrigation, Electricity, Credit, Roads, Storage, Marketing

Technological factors – short duration high yielding varieties (HYV), seeds, seed priming, zero till, fertilizers, insecticides, pesticides, growth promoting substances and farm machinery

Following relay cropping pattern, 400% cropping intensity has been well documented at the national level while with the same system when short duration varieties are included higher cropping intensity should be possible. At SKUAST Jammu, experimentation with 600% cropping intensity is in progress and results are indicating that with specified production package it is possible. These findings if promoted at national level will enhance the net cropped area 2 to 3 times. This speculation if becomes true will have evolutionary impact on Indian agriculture.

The prerequisites for high cropping intensity agriculture are:

1. Short duration varieties
2. Agrochemicals like fertilizers, biofertilizers and growth promoting substances are available
3. Relay cropping concept is well understood
4. Mechanization followed
5. Full knowledge of special techniques like seed priming, zero-till, protected vegetable nursery etc
6. Assured marketing *via* ICTs application

Horticulture, the fastest growing sector within agriculture, presently contributes 30.4 per cent of agricultural GDP. It has received considerable attention in recent years as it is recognized a potentially important source of growth, employment generation, nutritional security and foreign exchange earnings. Technological interventions like early fruiting varieties, micro-irrigation, precision farming, greenhouse cultivation, and improved post harvest management have shown the impact. Therefore, horticulture has moved from rural confines to commercial production. In changing scenario, private sector investment has increased several folds in production, post harvesting handling, processing and value addition. Consequently, India has emerged as the largest producer of mango, banana and cashew and second largest producer of many other fruits & vegetables in the world. However, low productivity and poor quality produce continue to affect the prospects of Indian horticulture.

High density plantations (HDP) in fruit crops (orchards) appears to be the most appropriate answer to overcome low productivity and long gestation period for early returns and export quality fruits. High density orchard development is gaining popularity among the farmers with advancing knowledge in tree architecture, growth physiology, availability of dwarfing root stock, possibility of using growth retardants. High density planting technique is a modern method of fruit crop cultivation involving planting of trees densely, allowing small or dwarf trees with modified canopy for better light interception and distribution and ease of mechanized field operations. This has enabled farmers to adopt closer planting and maintaining reachable canopy following improved farm management practices, leading to higher productivity and more profitable cropping.

HDP would prove evolutionary in transforming horticulture provided suitable scion and rootstock varieties are bred, fast propagation techniques, relevant cultural practices, handling and marketing are integrated. The changes are required to design HDP to produce quality fruits with ease and sustain. In India more focus is needed on HDP of tropical and sub-tropical fruits with regards to agro-climatic zone and crop specific strategies and demand and supply scenario.

Latest technical skills in tree architecture and canopy management have to be imparted to fruit growers through on farm demonstrations and hands-on-trainings so that technology sustains in the farmers orchards.

There is need for greater attention on utilization of available wastelands against the background of dwindling water and energy resources along with focus on dry land, arid and semi-arid tracts and to horticultural crops which have lesser demands on water and other inputs besides being 3 to 4 times more remunerative than field crops.

Hi-tech agronomic/ horticultural technologies are full time jobs generating enough profits at the farms round the year and qualify as the employment sources where growers can show the competence of not only as job seeker but also as a job provider.

2.4. Integrated entrepreneurship (Integrated Farming system)

Food security, livelihood security, water security as well as natural resources conservation and environment protection have emerged as major issues worldwide. Integrated farming system addresses all these issues in its im plem entation at the farm . integrated Farm ing means to integrate crop production with livestock management in a way that they function in complementation more or less in a nice symbiotic relationship proving economically viable and profitable, environmentally suitable, and encompassing the natural principles of diversification, nutrient recycling and resource conservation.

The operational farm holding in India is declining and over 85 million out of 105 million are below the size of 1 ha. Due to ever increasing population and decline in per capita availability of land in the country, practically there is no scope for horizontal expansion of land for agriculture. Only vertical expansion is possible by integrating farming components requiring lesser space and time and ensuring reasonable returns to farm families. Farming system approach (IFA) therefore assumes greater importance for sound management of farm resources to enhance the farm productivity, reduce the environmental degradation, improve the quality of life of resource poor farmers and maintain sustainability. SAUs in coordination with AICRP on IFS are thriving hard to empower farmers towards entrepreneurship through a combination of technological interventions for their betterment at macro- and micro-level trade, economy, health and prosperity through promotion of integrated farming approach. J&K Govt. in its resolution of 2016 intended to establish one such IFS model of one hectare at block level in all districts with the help of SKUAST- Jammu.

Objectives

- Maximization of yield of all component enterprises to provide steady and stable income.
- Rejuvenation / amelioration of system's productivity and achieve agro-ecological equilibrium.
- Avoid build-up of insect-pests, diseases and weed population through natural cropping system management and keep them at low level of intensity.
- Reducing the use of chemicals (fertilizers and pesticides) to provide chemical free healthy produce and environment to the society.

Table 2: Enterprises in integrated farming system under different agro-ecosystems (Crop husbandry is basic supporting enterprise in all the three systems)

Rainfed agro-ecosystem	Irrigated agro-ecosystem	Wetland agro-ecosystem
Poultry	Dairy	Fisheries
Goatry/ Sheep husbandry	Vegetable production	Mushroom production
Fruit crop orchard	Poultry	Duckery
Agro-forestry	Vermicomposting	Dairy
Sericulture	Piggery	High quality basmati production
Apiary	Fisheries	Vermicomposting
Mushroom	Horticulture/Floriculture	

Benefits

- Increased productivity through increased economic yield per unit area per time by virtue of intensification of crop and allied enterprises.
- Improved profitability achieved mainly by way of reduced costs due to recycling of wastes of one enterprise as energy inputs for other systems.
- Greater sustainability in production on farm due to integration of diverse enterprises of different economic importance. Recycling of wastes being in built in the system, this helps to reduce dependence on external high-energy inputs thus conserving natural and scarce resources.
- Integration of different production systems provides an opportunity to solve malnutrition problem due to production of variety of food products.
- The recycling of wastes for production helps to avoid piling of wastes and consequent pollution.
- The farming system provides flow of money to the farmer round the year by way of disposal of eggs, milk, edible mushroom, honey, silkworm cocoons etc. This will help resource poor farmer to get out from the clutches of moneylenders/agencies.
- Because of the linkage of dairy/mushrooms/sericulture/fruit crops/ vegetable crops/flower cultivation etc. cash available round the year could induce small and marginal farmers adopt new technologies such as fertilizer, mechanization, pesticides etc.
- Recycling of organic wastes reduces requirement of chemical fertilizers. Further, biogas production can meet household energy requirement. Thus, IFS, goes a long way in solving energy crises.
- Fodder/pasture/tree species included in the system help to get more fodder and thus solve fodder crises to some extent.

- Silvi component used in the system provides fuel and timber wood.
- Inclusion of timber component in the farming system reduces pressure on forests.
- Diverse components integrated can provide enough scope to employ farm labour round the year.
- Integrated farming system forces the entrepreneur to know more things and hence improves the literacy level.
- IFS provide opportunity for the growth of agri-oriented industries.
- There is also advantage of increased input use efficiency.
- Overall benefit of IFS is improved standard of living of the farmer because of the products like edible mushroom, fruits, eggs, milk, honey, vegetables etc.

Some examples of success stories (Srivastava, 2018)

1. Integrated rice–fish–poultry farming system

Annamalai University demonstrated integrated rice–fish poultry farming system on 430 farm holdings in 12 villages of Cuddalore, Villupuram, Nagapattinam and Thiruvannamalai districts of Tamil Selected integrated farming system models for enhanced income A. P. Srivastava1 Former National Co-ordinator (NAIP), Krishi Anusandhan Bhavan II, New Delhi 110 012 Under National Agricultural Innovation Project (NAIP), supported by The World Bank and implemented by the Indian Council of Agricultural Research (2006-14), an effort was made to enhance income of the rural people living in selected disadvantaged regions through technology led innovation systems. Very often emphasis on one component in rural areas, particularly among those people whose livelihood is threatened cannot lead to overall livelihood improvement of a household. Accordingly, interventions in IFS mode (crop-livestock-aquaculture) were planned and demonstrated, keeping in view the overall need of the area, available technological options, market accessibility both for input and produce etc. The interventions included transplanted rice in 200 m2 area, 20 poultry birds kept in cages of size 1.8 m × 1.2 m × 1 m and 100 fingerlings (Rohu, Mrigal, Catla, Common Carp) in trench of 20 m2 area. The results indicated annual increase in net return per household by ‘ 33,000/- to ‘ 50,500/ha/year for two and three crops, respectively. Poultry manure addition due to poultry dropping was 11.4 to 19.6 ton/ha and also pest suppression ranged from 17 to 27%.

2. Enhanced income through high value poultry race 'Kadaknath'

An Indian poultry breed, 'Kadaknath' is native to Jhabua district of Madhya Pradesh. This breed is famous for its meat quality, texture, and flavour and has special medicinal value in homeopathy. Due to its meat and alleged medicinal properties, it fetches high price and is in high demand in Madhya Pradesh and adjoining states. However, it was observed that the population of this bird was declining rapidly and it was under threat of extinction and genetic erosion. An attempt was therefore made for conservation and promotion of this high value Indian poultry race under NAIP by RVSKVV, Gwalior. A suitably designed low cost shed and one hundred poultry chicks of ten days old were made available to each. The farmers were educated on technologies for scientific poultry production, balance feeding, handling of feeder and drinkers, health management and marketing. This new Kadaknath production technology reduced the mortality rate from more than 50% to 10-12%. The birds gained the body weight in faster way and attained saleable weight of 1.10 kg in 105-120 days. On an average, an individual beneficiary got the net income of ` 90,000 to 1,00,000 / beneficiary/ year. Due to success of this intervention, number of low cost poultry sheds have increased to 162 and are further increasing. A hatchery was further supported by NAIP to ensure supply of chicks.

2.5. Organic farming/ quality assurance

Organic farming as it literary conveys that raising of crops with organic manures and no use of synthetic chemicals. Organic agriculture considers the medium- and long-term effect of agricultural interventions on the agro-ecosystem. It aims to produce food while establishing an ecological balance to prevent soil fertility or pest problems. Soil building practices such as crop rotations, inter-cropping, symbiotic associations, cover crops, organic fertilizers and minimum tillage are central to organic practices. organic agriculture or organic farming aims to optimize the health and productivity of interdependent communities of soil life, plant, animals and people, it comprises all technologies that maintain the integrity of organic agricultural products namely production, handling, processing, transport, storage and retailing etc. In context of commercial perspectives keeping the IFOAM principles intact it may be defined as, "A safe agricultural production management system that has competence to yield better qualitatively and quantitatively avoiding the application of synthetic fertilizers and pesticides". Organic farming scope has increased in view of growing health consciousness among the society as it assures quality through certification or participatory gaurantee system. It is fastest growing commercial enterprise with annual turnover of 80 billion USD.

Export/Commercial dimension

Organic agriculture movement has gained momentum globally encompassing 174 countries with 73 organic production systems recognized worldwide. The global market for organically produced foods in 2005 was US$ 30 billion and is estimated to grow to 102 billion US$ by 2020. It is growing with a pace of 20-30% annually revealing its commercial dimensions in international trade.

Table 3: Global Organic Food Market (USD)

2020: 102.0 billion US dollars (projected)
2012: 69.0 billion US Dollars
2010 : 59.1 billion US dollars
2009 : 54.1 billion US dollars
1999 : 15.2 billion US dollars

Entrepreneurship in organic agriculture

Organic agriculture offers much more entrepreneur opportunities than the conventional being a certified and guaranteed system. In the era of health consciousness, people want product of authenticity with traceability, the conditions which are met by organic agriculture. Right from the soil, seed to crop management and post harvest handling, organic agriculture has its own specific production package which involves many enterprises. Thus the approach has more income generating avenues than conventional one.

Table 4: Entrepreneurship in organic agriculture

Organic crop production
Organic seed /planting material production
Organic composts
Biofertilizers
Bio-pesticides
Organic dairying/ poultry
Organic mushrooms
Processing and value addition
Organic grocery store
Organic inputs enterprise
Vermicomposting
Consultancy, inspection and certification services

Employment generation

In two ways organic agriculture provides greater opportunities for employment. One it requires more man days per unit of working area. Many farm operations and post harvest management of produce involve manual handling. Organic agriculture enterprises often require more labor input than conventional farming in order to replace external energy and capital inputs such as fertilizers and herbicides.

Crop diversification on organic farms, and related different planting and harvesting schedules, distributes labor demand throughout the season. This stabilizes employment, reduces turnover, alleviates problems related to labor migration, and helps to spread the overhead payroll costs per employee. For small and marginal organic farmers it is whole of the family employment source rather essential to make the organic farming more economical. Secondly being a specialized area, it opens avenue for a number of entrepreneurships (table 7) wherein one can establish income generating units.

Organic agriculture and climate change

Climate change which is mainly due to the emission of greenhouse gases (CO_2, CH_4, N_2O) has a direct impact on agriculture. Agriculture contributes to over 20 percent of global anthropogenic greenhouse gas emissions. This seeks for development and implementation of environmentally sound farming methods. Organic agriculture not only enables ecosystems to better adjust to the effects of climate change but also offers a major potential to reduce the emissions of agricultural greenhouse gases. CO_2 emissions per hectare of organic agriculture systems are 48 to 66 percent lower than in conventional systems.

Globally, agriculture contributes to 65-80 percent of total N_2O, mainly from nitrogenous fertilizers on cultivated soils, cattle and feedlots. The ban on synthetically-produced mineral nitrogen in organic agriculture confines the productivity to the natural system limits (i.e. N-fixation) or the limits defined by the annual nutrient balance of the farm, including imported fodder and organic fertilizers. Organic agriculture therefore is likely to emit less N_2O due to restricted intensity.

Scope

India with its contingent of more than 4 lakh organic farmers, highest in the world indicates the liking and preference of the Indian farmers for organic farming. Now the need is to translate the interest of farmers into socio-economic venture benefitting both the country and countrymen.

2.6. Mechanization of farming

With shortage of labour for agricultural operations owing to rural urban migration, shift from agriculture to services and rise in demand for labour in non-farm activities, there is need to use labour for agricultural operations judiciously, which makes a strong case for mechanization of farming. Farm mechanization in India requires promotion in terms of introduction of better equipments for each farming operation in order to facilitate timely, precise and scientific farm operations, increasing farm input and labor use efficiency, reducing drudgery, improve productivity, minimize wastage and reduce labour costs for each operation. Innovation in farm machinery sector will drive the next phase of agricultural growth in the country. Further there are high proportion of female workforce in both the cultivation and processing stages of farming. Therefore, agronomically designed tools and equipment for reducing drudgery, enhancing safety and comfort and also to suit the needs of women workers would help in better adoption of technologies in agriculture. Moreover, to sustain an overall growth rate of 9 per cent it is essential for the agricultural sector to grow at 4 per cent. Introduction of high yielding varieties and expansion of irrigated area have played a crucial role in achieving the goal of food self sufficiency in the past. It is now imperative to focus on improving the intensity of farm mechanization in the country.

The Government of India has been encouraging mechanization through different policy interventions, Such as sub-mission on Agricultural Mechanization with focus on establishing custom hiring centres and Kisan Credit Card scheme to facilitate purchase of farm machinery by the farmers. The technologies that have evolved in the farm machinery sector in last few years have enormous potential to realize the vision of 'Make in India' initiative which promotes innovation and investment. It is estimated that the global demand for agricultural equipments will reach nearly US$ 200 billion by 2018, with Asia contributing more than 60 percent to the total.

Countries with higher levels of farm mechanization are able to increase their productivity and therefore, are better equipped to meet their demand factors. Over 95 percent of agricultural activities are have been mechanized in Canada similarly, in the US, 95 percent of the farming is mechanized. France indicates a 99 percent level of mechanization, with 54 percent of the metropolitan France under agriculture comprising of total 680,000 highly mechanized farms. China has around 60 percent of farm activities mechanized. Main agricultural equipments used include tractors, combine harvesters (self-propelled and tractor-mounted), rice transplanters and cotton processing machinery. Level of mechanization for various activities such as ploughing, planting and harvesting levels are 76.1 percent, 49.2 percent and 46.9 percent, respectively. Japan is one of the most agriculturally mechanized nations in Asia Pacific region touching figure of 95% mechanization.

Operations in farming	Percentage of mechanization
Soil working and seed-bed preparation	40
Seeding and planting	29
Plant protection	34
Irrigation	37
Harvesting and threshing	60 to 70 per cent for wheat and rice; less than 5 for others

Farm mechanization in India stands at about 40-45 percent. As there is direct relationship between the productivity level and farm mechanization so there is a need to enhance the level of farm mechanization in the country strategically.

Benefits

- Increase in crop intensity and yield thus ensuring better returns to the farmer
- Reduction of weather risk
- Less risk of non-availability of labor thus minimizing post harvest wastages
- Improved working conditions and enhanced safety for the farmers
- Conversion of uncultivable land to agricultural land through advanced tilling technologies
- Shifting land used for feed and fodder cultivation for draught animals towards food grain production
- Increased rural employment

Way Forward

Increased farm mechanization is a key step towards better rural prosperity. However, farm mechanization in India is in the initial stages of development and dominated by use of tractors and tractor mounted implements. While the Indian tractor market is highly organized and among the largest in the world, the farm equipment market is dominated by unorganized players accounting for more than 50 per cent of market share. Policy makers have initiated preliminary support to farm mechanization by including it as focus area in broader schemes such as in Rashtrya Krishi Vikas Yojna, Mission for Integrated Development of Horticulture and Sub Mission on Agricultural Mechanization. Concerted focus on this sector is still lacking.

- Focus is needed to enhance the growth of this sector and tap the immense potential it offers for transforming agriculture.

- Develop a legislative and structural framework that encourages custom hiring (renting) services so as to facilitate better capacity utilization of farm equipment.
- Enabling framework to encourage land consolidation and development of land lease market to make efficient use of farm machinery.
- Need to focus research efforts towards design and development of farm machinery suitable for different types of soils, farm sizes and diverse crops.
- Increased focus on commercialization of research done by various university especially in the farm equipment space.

2.7. Climate smart varieties/ planting material

India is characterised by varied agro-climatic conditions and climate change is expected to significantly affect agriculture, horticulture and livestock farming. Climate change has led to increased incidences of drought, heat and extreme weather events as well as crop pests and diseases, all of which can severely limit the growth of staple crops such as maize, wheat, rice and potato. Right choice of breeds and varieties has to remain the focussed area to stabilize the productivity. Appropriate variety for right type of agro-climatic situation gives climate resilience to the crop production system. Climate resilient varieties tide over various abiotic and biotic stresses because in-built genetic resistance or they may be of short duration so suited for late sowing in case of delayed monsoon showers. Moreover, early maturity enables the varieties many a times to escape natural calamity. The increase in frequency of heavy rainfall events in last 50 years over Central India points towards a significant change in climate pattern in India (Goswami, 2006). Delayed monsoon has brought shift in paddy planting and sowing of maize and pulses in kharif season in north west India while reduced number of rainy days has been observed in beginning of rabi season creating water deficit situation in October and November and while terminal moisture stress is witnessed in rabi crops because of few rainy days in March. Adoption of climate resilient crop varieties is the best economical options to tackle the problem and has been exercised as a first priority (Khatri-Chhetri et al 2016).

International plant breeders at CIAT have developed 30 new heat-resistant bean varieties for rising temperatures in Africa and other developing countries to help overcome predictions that, by 2050, climate change could reduce areas suitable for growing beans by 50%. Generally, bean yields start to fall when temperatures exceed 19°C while the new varieties remain productive even when night-time temperatures exceed 22°C. Similarly to help overcome climate-related challenges in rice growing ecosystems, the International Rice Research

Institute and partners also announced in early 2015 the release of 28 new rice varieties with high-yielding and stress-tolerance traits to help farmers maintain yields. New varieties include salinity-tolerant rice for Gambia, cold-tolerant rice for Mali and Senegal, and iron-tolerant rice for Burkina Faso, Ghana and Guinea.

According to recent findings by the International Crops Research for Semi-Arid Tropics, hybrid crop varieties perform two times better under heat and water stress than ordinary crops. In an effort to increase income at the farm, a report from ICAR (July, 2017) says that past three years of 2013-17 marked the development of 596 high yielding climate resilient crop varieties/ hybrids of field crops for cultivation in different agro-ecologies of the country. Alone 2016-17 recorded release of 313 field crop varieties, 51 horticultural crop varieties, 51 new farm implements, 3 vaccines, 15 diagnostic kits and breeding technology for two new fish species developed. Nutrient rich (zinc, iron, protein) varieties viz., DRR Dhan 45 (18.18 ppm Zinc) and CRR Dhan 310 (10.3% protein) of rice; WB-2 (42 PPM Zinc and 40 PPM Fe) and HPBW-01 (40.6 PPM Zinc and 40.6 Fe) of wheat, Pusa Mustard 30 (zero erucic acid) and Pusa Mustard 31 (Double zero) of Indian mustard have been developed. Rice variety IR-64 Drt-1 (DRR Dhan 42) resistant to drought and Samba Sub-1 tolerant to submergence has been developed. IPM 205-7 (Virat), an extra-early (52-55 days) maturing summer mungbean variety. Being short duration variety, it will help in increasing the cropping intensity and diversify the rice-wheat cropping system. Pusa Basmati 1609, Pusa Basmati 1509, Pusa Basmati 1637 and Pusa Basmati 1728 have been developed by using new biotechnological tools. Developed 51 new equipment/technologies/products and processes; 219 new prototypes for farm machinery/new farm implements; established 51 agro processing centres; and supplied 16500 units of multiplied prototypes, in the frontier areas of agricultural engineering with great potential to increase productivity, reduce cost of cultivation, reduce drudgery, improve value addition, conserve resources, provide alternate means for energy generation. Demonstrated production potential of new technologies of pulses, oilseed and other crops through 3.21 lakh frontline demonstrations in farmers' field. Skill development of 40.9 lakh farmers and rural youth. Produced and provided 8.79 lakh quintal seed, 12.52 crore planting material and 9.09 crores livestock strains and fingerlings to farmers. Provided agro mobile advisory to 3.95 crores farmers for improved decision-making. Established 150 pulses seed hubs to produce quality seeds of important pulse crops and production of additional quantity of breeder seed of different pulses was undertaken to attain self-sufficiency in pulses. Established 38 on-station Integrated Farming System (IFS) models and refined 63 existing IFS in 14 agro-climatic regions. All these efforts complement the Government's efforts to double the farmers' income by 2022.

ICAR has set targets, both for short and long term for complementing the efforts of the Govt. by providing technology back up for achieving the goal of doubling farmer's income. Targets for next 2 years include, evaluation of 20000 germplasm and breeding lines and conservation of 4000 Germplasm for long term storage, conservation of 200 microbial genetic resources, to identify 30 genotypes and register for unique traits, clone and characterize 10 genes, testing 2000 entries in AICRP multi-location trials, identification of 40 varieties including pulses and oilseeds by AICRP varietal identification committees, production of 56000 quintal Breeder seed, developing and testing 25 new technologies, conducting 10000 front line demonstrations and organizing 220 farmers' trainings.

In horticulture sciences targets for next 2 years include, collection of 400 germplasms and characterization of 500 germplasms, development of 100 pre-breeding lines, Identification of 60 promising/elite breeding lines, release of 30 varieties/hybrids, standardization of 50 production technologies, organization of 155 frontline demonstrations, developing 167 modules for capacity building of farmers and other stakeholders, production of 2261 kg breeders / truthfully labeled seed, production of 2250 tons breeder seed of tuber crops and production of 12.5 lakh quality planting materials and 5 lakh rooted cuttings.

Table 5: Climate resilient varieties in use in Jammu region

S.No.	Crop	Variety	Maturity duration (days)	Remarks
1.	Rice	Pusa 1509	75-80	Fine grained variety
		Sharbati	70-80	Fine grained variety
		Jammu Basmati 129	90-100	has medium aroma
2.	Wheat	Raj 3765	120-140	Resistance to yellow rust,
		PBW 175	130-150	Suited for late sown conditions, Suited for rainfed conditions
3.	Toria	RSPT-01, RSPT-02	60-6565-70	Both are short duration, aphid tolerant & Suitable for autumn season
4.	Knolkhol	G -40	30-35	Early, No disease and pest attack
5.	Radish	CR 45	40-45	Early, No disease and pest attack
6.	Mungbean	PDM 54S ML668	60-70	Suited for spring season cultivation and green manuring
7.	Okra	Seli special (Jammu Okra 07)	100	High ratooning ability, Export quality, Resistance to YVMV

Climate resilience characters and benefits to users

- Drought resistance
- Heat tolerance
- Disease and pest resistance
- Short duration
- Submergence tolerance
- Salinity tolerance
- Response to agro-chemical applications

2.8. Secondary Agriculture

Value addition is a process of increasing the economic value and consumer appeal for a commodity. It is a process in which for the same volume of a primary product, a high price is realized by means of processing, packing, upgrading the quality or other such methods. Value-added agriculture or secondary agriculture may also refer to increasing the economic value of a commodity through particular production process, e.g., organic produce, or through regionally branded products that increase consumer appeal and willingness to pay a premium over similar but differentiated products. In the present agricultural scenario when the world has become a single market, agriculture has to be dynamic and competitive through, product diversification, quality enhancement and branding. Agri-business has to be a production/ marketing strategy driven by customer needs and preferences. Produce is changed, modified or blended from its original form to a product having demand in the market.

During the peak period of production, huge volumes of surplus fruits, vegetables, milk, poultry and mushroom etc results in glut in the market. Being time bound operation with limited shelf life of product, forced harvest and translocation to market leads to price crash of agricultural commodities causing unbearable losses to farmers. Potato prices vary from Rs 5.0 to 25, that of tomato from Rs 8.0 to 80, that of green peas from Rs10 to 120. Similar case applies to many fruit and livestock products. This makes the agriculture a risky and unreliable enterprise and at the same time agriculture involves more climatic uncertainties and man power. Economic interests of the farmers are needed to be protected by policy interventions particularly with respect to market assurance if the agriculture has to be made youth attractive.

The post-harvest losses of fruits and vegetables are estimated to be 25 to 40 %, amounting to more than Rs. 44,000 crore. Yet less than 2 % is processed as compared to 30 and 80% in Thailand and Malaysia whereas value addition to agricultural products is less than 7% as against 23, 45 and 188% in China, Philippines, UK. Marketing trends are now- a-days are guided by consumer preferences which hover around below listed points

- Provide health benefits
- Weight control
- No chemical additives
- Fresh
- Long shelf life
- Safe food
- Require minimal preparation
- Ready-to-eat form
- Functional foods
- –Omega 3 fatty acids
- –Anti-oxidants
- –Flavonoids
- Probiotics and pre-biotics
- Glycemic Index (GI)
- Low carbohydrate diets
- Low trans fats
- Free from food allergens
- Acrylamide low or free

Notable trends in the Indian food processing sector (*Source*: IBEF Website)

a. Changing consumer tastes

- Wide array of products, coupled with increasing global connectivity, has led to a change in the tastes and preference of domestic consumers
- This trend has been bolstered by rising incomes, increasing urbanization, a young population, and the emergence of nuclear families.
- Consumer preference is moving towards healthier snacks

b. Entry of international companies

- Liberalization and growth of organized retail have made the Indian market more attractive for global players
- With a large agriculture sector, abundant livestock, and cost competitiveness, India is fast emerging as a sourcing hub of processed food. McDonald, Nestle, Kraft Foods, Mondelez International, Heinz are the international players in food processing market in India

c. Rising demand on Indian product in international market

- Strategic geographic location and continuous increase in raw material production help India to supply cheaper products to other countries
- India's exports of processed food and related items rose at a CAGR of 21.5 percent, accounting for US$ 19,337.4 mn in FY16(1)
- Companies like Haldiram's and Bikanervala have a presence in over 70 countries, where they provide Indian snacks

d. Higher consumption of horticulture crop

- There is a surge in demand for fruits & vegetables as a result of a shift in consumption.
- Accordingly, Indian farmers are also shifting production towards horticulture crops to cash in on the growing demand.

e. Emphasis on healthier ingredient

- Food processing companies are serving health and wellness as a new ingredient in processed food, given that health conscious consumers prefer food products with lower carbohydrate content and with low cholesterol edible oils. e.g. zero-percent trans fat snacks and biscuits, slim milk, whole wheat products, etc. ITC is planning to launch multi-grain Bingo to increase its share in healthy snacks market.

f. Packaging as purchase influencer and communicator

- Food packaging provides various options to purchasers to look for varieties of a product
- Packaging enhances 'carry ability' of products
- Increase shelf life of products

g. Frozen and processed goodness

- Frozen processed foods offer both convenience and nutrition
- The increase in spending capacities and the concurrent time-paucity has led to the continuous development of such frozen processed food products as frozen vegetables (e.g. peas, potato, corn, etc.) and such non-vegetarian products as chicken, fish, and meat products.

h. Product innovation as the key to expansion

- It is now the norm for food processing companies to offer value-addition; those who hitherto offered solely milk have now added other dairy products.
- This helps the processors to not only reduce wastage, but also expand uses and realise higher returns. In 2015, Bonhomia has announced to launch 'Boho' coffee machines, the company is the first one to manufacture coffee and tea capsule in India.
- In FY16, Ministry of Food Processing Industries has granted fund of US$ 18.81 mn for the ongoing Mega Food Park projects. As on September 2016, a Mega Food Park has been setup by the government in Ludhiana.

i. Strengthening procurement vis direct farmer-firm linkages

- Contract farming has been operational in India for a long time however, the experience of the private sector players involved therein has been a mixed bag of successes and failures
- Largely, it has helped both the processing companies, via increasing sales and therefore augmenting their incomes, as well as providing access to better technology and fetching better prices by securing an assured market for Indian farmers. Examples include Nestlé, PepsiCo, Venky's, Milkfed, and Mahagrapes, among others.

Hence to drive the growth of primary agriculture, secondary sector interventions are imperative not only to generate employment but also to boost net income of the farmers. Appropriately defined as Secondary agriculture comprises all practices, processes and technologies which add value to primary agricultural commodities by using, market information and consumer preference. The focus on development of secondary agriculture is due to consumers demand for value added goods like ready-to-eat, ready-to-serve, convenience food, functional food and nutraceuticals in both domestic and international markets. Secondary agriculture is competent to enhance two to three fold value of primary agriculture so there are significant opportunities to strengthen rural economy. Food processing is a key contributor to employment generation in India by 2024, food processing sector is expected to employ 9 million people in India.

The Indian food processing industry values close to US$ 121 bn to US$ 130 bn. With the second largest arable land in the world, India is the largest producer of milk, pulses, sugarcane and tea in the world and the second largest producer of wheat, rice, fruits and vegetables. Indian agriculture being the primary supporter caters to around 60 percent of the population for their livelihood and contributes to 17 percent of GDP. Despite the massive production, the degree of processing is low and ranges between 2 to 35 percent for different produce (Source: IBEF Website).

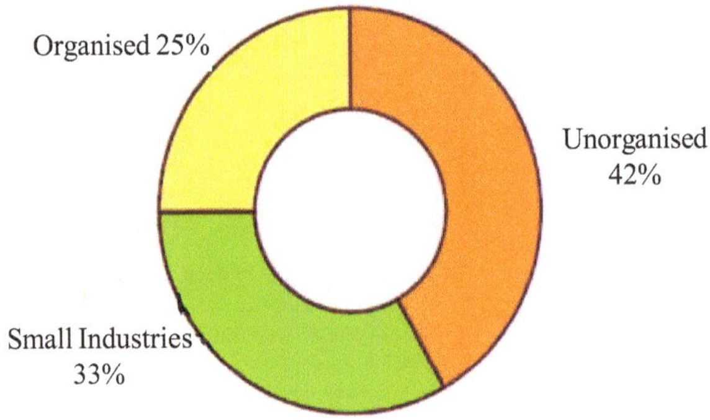

Fig. 2: Status of Indian food processing industry

It has scope for Complete vertical integration means to align and control all of the segments of a production and marketing system under single ownership. The factors aligned and controlled are price, quantity, quality and transactional terms of exchange. Producers who invest in value-added projects past the farm gate cause the market to become more vertically integrated. A totally integrated system can provide consistent quality from the field to the shelf, eliminating middlemen and even saving money for consumers.

The secondary agriculture is transformational sector for the Indian farmers' economy, owing to its untapped potential but needs administrative as well as technical interventions such as:

- Innovative initiatives in R&D programs be invigorated and refocused on high value crops
- Planned withdrawal of working force from primary sector by establishing appropriate linkages with secondary agricultural sector.

- Encash the changing demand towards value added products by promoting diversification of primary agriculture so that farmers improve their production base.
- Building strong demand through value addition and promotion for underutilized crops such as minor millets, medicinal and aromatic plants and crop by-products so that farmers realize higher returns.
- Encouraging rural industrialization so that the demand for primary produce is increased as they are used as raw material by the industry and the required quality inputs are made available to improve primary agriculture.
- Improve the supply chain management so that the transaction cost is reduced and market is expanded for primary agricultural commodities.
- Develop human resource to undertake research and extension relating to secondary agriculture so that its expansion and increased efficiency will benefit the primary sector.

2.9. Information and Communication Technologies (ICTs)

With rising food prices that have pushed over 40 million people into poverty since 2010, more effective interventions are essential in agriculture (World Bank 2011). Agriculture accounts for the vast majority of the poor's livelihood activities; it is also the sector that holds the most promise for pro-poor economic growth. In fact, agriculture is around four times more effective at raising incomes among the poor than other sectors (World Bank 2008). For more efficient food chain management, ICT is highly effective in strengthening backward and forward linkages, reducing wastage, tackling glut situation and judicious public distribution. The smallholders, who still provide a significant portion of the world's food, need information to advance their work just as much as industrial scale producers. ICT has found a foothold even in poor small holder farms and in their activities so ICTs can be used effectively to address both the long- and short-term challenges in agriculture, including how to answer the abundant information needs of farmers. It is in the context of globalizing agriculture where the need for information becomes most essential, requires the implementation of a complex set of policy, investment, innovation, and capacity-building measures, in concern with beneficiaries and other partners, which will encourage the growth of locally appropriate, affordable, and sustainable ICT infrastructure, tools, applications, and services for the rural economy.

- To empower poor farmers with information and communication assets and services that will increase their productivity and incomes as well as protect their food security and livelihoods,

- to harness ICTs effectively to compete in complex, rapidly growing global markets

> Mobile phones are in the vanguard of ICTs in agriculture. By the end of 2011, over 6 billion mobile phone subscriptions were there globally covering 90 percent of the population. 143 countries offered commercial 3G services, providing at least 256 kilobits per second of bandwidth and supplying voice and data simultaneously.
>
> (*Source:* International Telecommunications Union)

Five main trends have been the key drivers of the use of ICT in agriculture, particularly for poor producers: (1) low-cost and pervasive connectivity, (2) adaptable and more affordable tools, (3) advances in data storage and exchange, (4) innovative business models and partnerships, and (5) the democratization of information, including the open access movement and social media. These drivers are expected to continue shaping the prospects for using ICT effectively in developing country agriculture.

The entrepreneurial nature of ICTs attracts new partnerships and forms of investment. Mobile phone applications, software design, local language customization, and remote transaction services represent only a fraction of the opportunities for continued innovation. Private companies that have invested in technology and applications are often interested in working with the public sector to provide their products and services to smallholders.

Central, state governments and private organizations have taken ICT measures for agriculture extension which include ITC- e-choupal, Kisan Kerala, Aaqua, Rice knowledge management portal , e-krishi, Mahindra Kisan Mitra, IFFCO Agri-portal, Village knowledge centers (VKCs)- MS Swaminathan research foundation (MSSRF), village resource centres (VRCs)- Indian Space research organization, etc.

2.10. Vertical farming (soilless farming, hydroponics, rooftop farming, aeroponics)

Vertical farming has been in vogue since ancient times as evidenced by the Hanging Gardens of Babylon. In the year 2010, an American scientist Dickson Despommier, published a book, *The Vertical Farm: Feeding the World in the 21st Century*, wherein he laid down the principles and practices of modern vertical farming or urban agriculture around cities, and inside buildings, instead of horizontal expansion on the ground. Over the last few years, multi-storeyed vertical farms have been established in Japan, Singapore, Taiwan, China, Korea and the United States of America. A vertical farm is well-designed farm that utilizes space vertically rather than horizontally, multi-storeyed structure facilitating round the cultivation of vegetables. Thus, modern concept of vertical farming involves the union of plant biology and engineering know-how and can be considered as an extension of indoor farming. It could solve the double-edged problem of shrinking arable land and providing food to an ever-increasing population.

Vertical farming or urban agriculture is blooming around cities of the developed world as a response to the increasing urban population, the growing environmental awareness of the industrial food system and the need of addressing social gaps. These new local food systems aim to develop sustainable pathways that re-establish the relations between producers and consumers. It is a relatively new concept, and is expected to help raise production without occupying space. If a building stood on a one-hectare plot of land but had five stories, it would result in production from five hectare of land. Vertical aeroponic farm of 400 sq ft area has the distinct advantage of producing the same quantum of better-quality produce than a 1600 sq ft soil-based farm. The new farming technique envisages production of crops hydroponically (nutrient-enriched water) or aeroponically (nutrient-enriched air), without using soil or compost. The plants can get the required sunlight through glass windows. It is nothing but crop farms stacked on top of each other instead of spanning out horizontally. These high-rises are often called "Farmscrapers". It is predicted that vertical farming is scientifically viable in 2023 and mainstream and financially viable in 2027.

Vertical urban agriculture is essentially made up of growing all kinds of fruits, vegetables, and flowers high-rise towers 20–30 stories tall or taller that provide a temperature-controlled environment. Plants are fertilized with compost and irrigated with nutrient-rich water provided through soil-less conditions known as "Hydroponics" or growing plant in air and nutrient supplied through mist spray (Aeroponics).

The idea of vertical farming has been adopted mainly developed nations such as Singapore, Japan, the US, etc. However, India is not far behind too, many experiments are being conducted in agricultural institutions. Leafy vegetables, especially the high-value ones like lettuce, celery, and cucurbits with export potential, tomato, capsicum, bottle gourd, brinjal, fruits like strawberry, and flowers like gerbera, carnation and anthurium were considered to be more relevant in the Indian context. There are limitations with the present system which need to be addressed through research (Aswath and Selvakumar 2016).

- Limited vegetable crops have been identified for the purpose. However, vegetable crops in vogue are being grown without any scientific validation.

- No varieties/hybrids have been exclusively bred for the purpose of vertical farming. As a result, yield and quality of the produce cannot be guaranteed.
- Production technologies and Good Agricultural Practices for these crops have not been standardized.
- Presently, the high-rise inclined buildings are not built to suit vertical farming. There is a need to re-engineer the existing buildings by providing additional structures to suit the purpose.

Small-scale adaptations of vertical farming have been seen in Nadia, West Bengal and in Punjab. Bidhan Chandra Krishi Vishwavidhalaya in Nadia has found initial success in growing brinjal and tomato. Punjab also has succeeded in producing potato tubers through vertical farming. However, the huge cost of infrastructure for a large-scale farm is a major hurdle for implementing vertical farming in India

The advantages of vertical farming as envisioned by Despomier, include:

- Year round crop production
- Elimination of agricultural run-off
- Significant reduction in the use of fossil fuels for operation of farm machines
- Low cost on transport of crops
- Utilization of abandoned or unused properties
- Reduction in weather-related crop failures
- Sustainable food supply for all urban centres
- Conversion of black and grey-water to drinking water
- Addition of energy back to the grid via methane generation or plasma arc gasification,
- Creation of new urban employment opportunities,
- Reduction of the risk of infection from agents transmitted at the human agricultural interface Return of farmland to nature, thereby helping restore ecosystem functions and services.
- Using techniques similar to glass houses, vertical farms could augment natural light using energy-efficient lighting.

3. References

Aswath C and Selvakumar G .2016. Utilization of vertical spaces for horticultural crop production in urban and peri-urban areas (News). *Current Science*, 110(11): 2048-2049.

Boland M .2009. How is Value-added Agriculture Explained? *mboland@agecon.ksu.edu*

Chang ST. 2006a. The need for scientific validation of culinary –medicinal mushroom products. *Intl. J. Med. Mush*, 8:187-195.

Chang ST. 2006b. The world mushroom industry: Trends and technological development. *Intl,J. Med. Mush.* 8:297-314.

Chang ST .2007. Mushroom cultivation using the "ZERI" principle: potential for application in *Brazil.Micol. Apl. Int.*, 19:33-34.

Chengappa PG .2013. Secondary Agriculture: A Driver for Growth of Primary Agriculture in India. *Ind. Jn. of Agri. Econ.*Vol.68 (1): 1-19.

Gill MS, Singh JP, Gangwar KS .2009. Integrated farming system and agriculture sustainability. *Indian J Agron*. 54(2):128-139.

Khatri-Chhetri A, Aryal JP, Sapkota TB and Khurana R .2016. Economic benefits of climate-smart agricultural practices to smallholder farmers in the Indo-Gangetic Plains of India. *Current Science,* 110 (7), 1251-56.

Maheswari M, Sarkar B, Vanaja M, Srinivasa Rao M, Srinivasa Rao Ch,Venkateswarlu B, Sikka AK .2015. Climate Resilient Crop Varieties for Sustainable FoodProduction under Aberrant Weather Conditions. Central Research Institute for Dryland Agriculture (ICAR), Hyderabad. P47.

Oerke EC .2005. Crop losses to pests. *J. Agr. Sci.* 144:31–43.

Popp J, Petõ Károly and Nagy János .2013. Pesticide productivity and food security. A review article. *Agron. Sustain. Dev*.33:243–255.

The International Bank for Reconstruction and Development / The World Bank (*Info*Dev & ARD) .2011. ICT in agriculture. The World Bank Report No. 64605, 1818 H Street, Washington DC 20433

Srivastava AP .2018. Selected integrated farming system models for enhanced income. *Indian Farming*. 68(01): 13–16.

4

Contract Farming: A Boon for Agri-Business Farming in India

Narinder Panotra*, Rohit Sharma[1] Ashwani Kumar[2] and Vishaw Vikas[3]

Directorate of Research, SKUAST- Jammu, Chatha, Jammu & Kashmir, India
[1]RARS-Rajouri, SKUAST- Jammu, Jammu & Kashmir, India
[2]VAEA, Department of Agriculture, Jammu, Jammu & Kashmir, India
[3]Division of Soil Science, SKUAST- Jammu, Chatha, Jammu & Kashmir, India
**Corresponding author: Email: drpanotra@gmail.com*

1. Introduction
2. Relevance of contract farming in India
3. Need for contract farming
4. Crop diversification and contract farming
5. Contract farming attracts private sector involvement
6. Price fixation models
7. Strengths and advantages of contract farming
8. Problems confronted by contract farming
9. Some successful cases of contract farming
10. Model Contract Farming Act 2018
11. Conclusion
12. *References*

Abstract

Indian agriculture is undergoing rapid transformation and agricultural-based food industry in India requires timely and adequate supply of good quality raw material for processing, value addition and export. The recent growth and diversification of consumer demand and the expansion of organized agricultural processing and marketing ventures in India has the potential to boost the market opportunities, productivity, and incomes of farmers, including that of marginal and small holders. However, achieving these goals will likely require creation of new institutions and innovations to develop supply chains and facilitate linkages between farmers, wholesalers, processors, and retailers. Among these institutions and innovations are various models of contract farming, including those led by cooperatives, by farmer groups, and by various types of private sector resource intermediation that develop backward linkages to growers. Contract farming is a system where agricultural production is carried out according to an agreement between a buyer and farmers, which establishes conditions for the production and marketing of a farm product or products. In other words Contract Farming is a system of production and supply of agricultural/horticultural produce under forward contracts between producers/ suppliers and buyers. The essence of such an arrangement is the commitment of the producer to provide an agricultural commodity of a certain type, at a time and a price, and in a quantity required by a known and committed buyer. Well-managed contract farming is an effective approach to help solve many of the market linkage and access problems of small and marginal farmers which constitute 86% of the farming households in India. This chapter examines growth and status including the performance of different models of contract farming based on empirical studies. It concludes that by entering into the contractual arrangement, the income level of the farmer and employment level in the rural economy has increased despite certain problems faced by the farmers like delayed payment, delay in procurement and low supply of agricultural inputs to them.

Keywords: Contract farming, concept, Indian relevance, private sector models, marketing.

1. Introduction

The small size of farms has brought in challenges of farm viability. In an age of market liberalization, globalization and expanding agribusiness, there is a danger that small-scale farmers will find difficulty in fully participating in the market economy. The combined impact of inelastic nature of land, steadily increasing population density and continued dependence of a vast majority for their livelihood on agriculture and prevailing laws of inheritance has been causing division and fragmentation of arable land in India. More than 86 percent of close to 120 million agricultural households are small (less than or equal to 2 ha. of cultivable land) and marginal (less than or equal to 1 ha. of cultivable land). As per census 2011, the average size of landholdings in India was 1.1 ha. Contract farming which in essence is a pre-production season agreement between farmers (either individually or collectively) and sponsor(s), transfers the risk of post-harvest market unpredictability from the former to the latter. It can be defined as a system for the production and supply of agricultural produce under forward contracts, the essence of such contracts being a commitment to provide an agricultural commodities of a type, at a time and a price and in the quality required by known buyers, it basically involves four things: pre-agreed price, quality, quantity or acreage and time. In this contract exists between a farmer and a cooperative or processing organization, for example, to grow seeds, potatoes or vegetables etc as per terms and conditions mutually agreed upon. These are mostly the commodities, often brought in advance, and with certain level quality.

Contract farming represents an expanding and much suggested method of agro-industrial integration for developing economics. Agribusiness investment has grown through integrating the independent growers and farm families into new production complexes of the wide national and global economy by separating land ownership from the power to make land use decisions. Thus business firms control large number of growers to produce the desired crops. The grower provides land and labour whereas the agribusiness firms control quantity, quality, credit, inputs, production methods, price, market access and timing of delivery. The global change towards the relationship between agriculture and industry, urban and rural areas are inextricably linked. Contract farming is that it facilitates backward and forward market linkages that are the corner stone of market-led, commercial agriculture. Well-managed contract farming is considered as an effective approach to help solve many of the market linkage and access problems for small farmers. Dynamics of forward and backward linkages of contractual services for a wider range of field operations between growers and company form a crucial part of the process of globalization.

There are three major players in the system of contract farming i.e. producers along with its agro climatic environments; consumers demand a particular/ specialized product and the company with its technology and management. Assured marked for the farm produce motivates a farmer to enter into contract with company thus producers should be benefited, product of the company should be successful both in domestic and international markets and ultimately the demand of the consumers should be fully met and satisfied. Contact farming acts as a vehicle for the transfer of technology because it intends on changing land and crop rights induced by it. Contract farming is generally successful in supplying credit, inputs, technology and market information to growers. It transfers production technology to growers and provides a more secure market outlet. Apart from production of desired raw produce directly linked to processing, the agribusiness firms wish to become the main supplier of seed and other inputs. They are developing weedicides that are specific to a particular seed variety that it would not harm. The farmers thus, depend exclusively on a package of seed, chemicals and fertilizers suggested by a particular agribusinesses multinational company. Over the time, the concerned MNCs, by investing an enormous amount on R & D may do everything to make the peasants perpetually dependent on by producing new package of practices every few years where Governmental interventions are necessary to protect the interest of farmers. Food manufacturers need the detailed information like price, quality, timing of delivery etc. to meet the retailers requirements especially for own brands lines which are popular. Thus firms make contracts direct with producers cutting out the middlemen and they control a critical step from production to consumption. Such new demand driven technologies are turning bulk commodities into tailor-made products of consumer requirements. As consumers become better informed and more demanding, companies are consolidating in pursuit of new efficiencies and economics of sale.

2. Relevance of contract farming in India?

In our country the farmers face the problems of traditional technology and management practices, little bargaining power with input suppliers and un-assured marketing of produce, inadequate infrastructure and meagre market information, inadequate of post-harvest facilities. Management expertise, poor package of produce and inadequate capital to grow a quality crop. They are waiting for change for better living standards.

Contract farming helps small farmers to participate in the production of high value crops like vegetables, flowers, fruits etc and benefit from market led growth. Extensive areas are required by the Agroprocessors for an intensive cultivation to build a uniform method of cultivation that would reduce their production and transaction costs with the growers. Effective & efficient monitoring of production operations, extension activities and credit delivery in a conjugal area is easy in Contract farming.

Contract farming will maximize the profits to the farmers and minimize risk in farming like production related risks, transfer price risk and produce risk. There is a tendency amongst the users to go in for environmental friendly, value added quality agro products in their daily life. The farmers find it easy to get under one roof inputs, technological & extension services, postharvest processing facilities and more importantly, the marketing of their produce with assured cash returns.

There is a tendency amongst farmers to go in for an alternate cropping system for better monetary returns. Contract farming facilitates more and more private Companies to develop backward linkages with the farmers. Access to crop loans at attractive terms through tie-ups with Banks is facilitated through contract farming.

3. Need for Contract Farming

- Inadequate linkages with markets
- Problems of fragmented land holdings
- Lack of capital
- Poor infrastructure
- Inadequate information dissemination
- Loss/wastage of large quantities of fruits and vegetables
- Agri-based and food industry's inability to acquire timely and adequate good quality agricultural produce
- Closing down of marketing boards
- Changes in consumption habit
- Increasing number of fast-food outlets
- The growing role played by supermarkets
- Continued expansion of world trade in fresh and processed products

4. Crop diversification and contract farming

Agronomic and climatic factors favor wheat-rice crops over others. Production of rice-wheat cropping sequence has reached plateau and has done immense harm to ecology of North-west region of the country, Effecting soil health, depleting water table and having negative impact on the economy of the farmers as well. Farmer is always price responsive and is assured of better returns in market of his crop in contract farming. That is why farmer gets encouraged and enter into a contract production. Diversification of agriculture aimed to reduce area under rice –wheat rotation contract farming needs to be encouraged. Similar changes can be expected in different parts of the country for better returns with crop diversification

5. Contract farming encourages private sector involvement

The farmers would grow the crop and sell it to concerned State Agro Food Grain Corporation at a pre-determined contract rate and the latter will supply the same to that firm concerned. The Punjab Agro Food Grains Corporation Ltd. not only purchased seeds from reputed MNCs to contract farmers, but also will buy back the entire produce at pre-agreed price. This would enhance the high degree of private sector involvement in contract farming and concentration of foreign direct investment in agriculture and agro-industry. The role of concerned state Agro Food grains Corporation Ltd. is that of an integrated farming solutions provider and could play the role of nodal agency to ensure timely and remunerative price to farmers and assured supply of quality produce to the units. Corporates are forging alliances with state government for contract farming. New incentives from sector in precision farming and contract management of farm which must be linked to both domestic and external market through agro-processing zones, stimulating floriculture and horticulture. Hence the state government can shift some area under paddy wheat rotation to either cash crops like oilseeds, pulses etc by adopting contract farming and right mix of price incentives.

6. Price fixation models

Incentive price is given to farmers to meet extra cost incurred in producing the requisite quality of produce. Since the farmer has to take extra care to maintain the quality. Generally three types of price fixation models are observed in contract farming in the country are:

Pepsi model

Pepsi model of price fixation is decided between producers under company. Farmer entered into contract production due to incentive price and assured market. The individual farmer is not able to bargain with company on equal footing. There are instances of breach of contract and end up in the court of law, since there is no arbitration agreement. This is the most exploitative model prevailing.

Tripartite model

Tripartite price model is generally followed for procuring quality raw material in agri-export zones for exporting the finished products. The procuring /processing firms make contracts with producer and price is decided by government agency after consultation with both the parties. None of the party can breach the contract and is liable to penalty in case of non-compliance. Contract is enforced by government agency.

Tamil Nadu (TN)Model

Tamil Nadu (TN) is the only state in the country that has enacted Act on contract farming. In TN model the producer and company are free to set price as they mutually agree upon. Once the price is discovered has to submit to enforcement officer of the government. Arbitration is a method of settling, out of court through independent party/person. Both parties are liable to comply with the final award of arbitrator.

7. Advantages and weaknesses of contract farming

The contract farming open avenues for:

- One option for creating a role for price sector in agricultural development and extension
- Acceleration of technology transfer,
- Increased private capital flows in agriculture,
- Assured markets for crops such as oilseeds, cotton, horticulture etc
- Spot market purchases are fraught with certainties vis-à-vis quality, quantity and price.
- Advantage to farmer in terms of access to technology, supply of inputs and extension service thus modernizing the contract farming,
- Quality and health consciousness among consumers has increased who demand food products of certain specification.
- Contractors get guaranteed and steady source of supply, which allows investment at large scale.
- Contract farming is essential for entrepreneurial development.
- The small farmers can effectively participate
- Farmers get exposed to world class technology i.e, seed, inputs, monitoring etc
- Long term planning and investment is promoted.

7.1. Weaknesses

Monopsony: Typically, contract firms enter into an agreement with farmers to grow differentiated crops. This turns the firm into a sole buyer and farmers into price-takers. Contracting firms can exploit this situation to their advantage by offering lower prices to farmers.

Information asymmetry: Contracting firms do not have complete information on productivity and land quality. This can lead to a situation where farmers produce below-quality crops. On the other hand, farmers sometimes do not understand contract specifications like the quantity and quality to be produced, or the effect of price change. These market failures lead to suboptimal outcomes. Buyers may penalize farmers.

Legal binding counterproductive: Registration imposes additional procedures and costs on the parties, and small and medium farmers cannot easily afford these costs. The Act also proposes price protection for farmers by determining a pre-agreed price. This will be counterproductive. How would the sponsors incentivize the farmers to perform if the state provides farmers a perverse incentive to not perform? The entire premise of the model contract Act seems to be aimed at creating a legal infrastructure to ensure that both parties honour the contract. This approach is flawed.

8. Problems confronted by contract farming

- Contract farming is basically a way of allocation of risk between the firm and its farmers. This depends on bargaining power, availability of alternatives and access to information which are generally lacking with farmers.
- Small size of farmers land holding.
- Sometimes farmers tend to divert the produce to open market rather than supplying to processing firm when prices are high.
- The cost calculations of firm crumble.
- Similarly in long duration plantation crops firms often fail to honour the contracts they know that farmers have no alternative but to sell the products to them.
- Normally firms select established rich farmers.
- Monoculture is encouraged.
- There is no uniform regulatory authority to ensure check unintended problems.
- Lack of comprehensive crop insurance scheme to protection against natural calamity.
- Less generation of employment, labour-saving farm practices, low level of commitment of corporate over rural development, lack of transparency and communication etc.
- Enforceability of the agreement, and standardization and operationalization of contract farming agreements are the major bottlenecks plaguing contract farming ventures in India.

9. Some successful cases of contract farming in India:

Green revolution

Government of India has run the largest contract farming model the "Green revolution". It included the supply of improved wheat varieties and hybrids of other crops. Subsidized fertilizer was made available and procurement of produce was guaranteed with minimum support price. Extension service was provided by ICAR and agricultural Universities. This was one sided contract and a farmer got used to it. Although food security was achieved but monoculture, over-fertilization soil degradation was outcome over the period.

McDonald and McCainn Foods

McDonald's is famous for French Fries or wedges. The right type of potatoes was found in traditional area of Gujarat State. Though India grows a lot of potatoes, these are not suitable for making wedges because they have high moisture content. They go limp very soon. The agro-climatic conditions like right soil, water availability, sunshine and other climatic conditions have been found suitable for growing the right size of tasty potatoes having low moisture content required for the French Fries. The farmers so far, were using age old techniques and low quality seed. The farmers were gently nudged into accepting modern cultivation practices by demonstration and training to achieve better yield at lower costs. McDonald got the kind of potato it wanted. McCainn Foods, the world's largest French Fries Company, which has partnered with McDonald's to work with farmers in the state. It has started picking up the Gujarat potato to make its 'Chatpatey' potato wedges. This is the first time to MNC starts procuring potato from India. There was potential for exports particularly to the Middle-East and Far East.

Hindustan Lever Ltd (HLL) Rallis and ICICI

Contract farming in wheat is being practiced in Madhya Pradesh by Hindustan Lever Ltd (HLL), Rallis and ICICI. Under the system, Rallis supplies agri-inputs and know-how, and ICICI finances (farm credit) the farmers. HLL, the processing company, which requires the farm produce as raw material for its food processing industry, provides the buyback arrangement for the farm output. In this arrangement, farmers benefit through the assured market for their produce in addition to timely, adequate and quality input supply including free technical know-how; HLL benefits through supply-chain efficiency; while Rallis and ICICI benefit through assured clientele for their products and services. The consortium is also planning to rope in other specialist partners including insurance, equipment and storage companies.

Pepsi Foods Ltd.

Launching its agro-business in India with special focus on exports of value-added processed foods, Pepsi Foods Ltd. ('PepsiCo' hereafter) entered India in 1989 by installing an Rs. 22 crore state of- the-art tomato processing plant at Zahura in Hoshiarpur district. The PepsiCo model of contract farming, measured in terms of new options for farmers, productivity increases, and the introduction of modern technology, has been an unparalleled success. The company focused on developing region- and desired produce-specific research, and extensive extension services. It was thus successful in bringing about a drastic change in the Punjab farmers' production system towards its objective of ensuring supply of right produce at the right time in required quantities to its processing plant. Another important factor in PepsiCo's success is the strategic partnership of the company with local bodies like the Punjab Agricultural University (PAU) and Punjab Agro Industries Corporation Ltd. (PAIC). Right from the beginning, PepsiCo knew that changing the mindset and winning the confidence of farmers would not be an easy task for outsiders. The company's unique partnership with PAU and PAIC fuelled its growth in Punjab. Encouraged by the sweeping success of contract farming in tomato in several districts of Punjab, PepsiCo has been successfully emulating the model in food grains (Basmati rice), spices (chillies) and oilseeds (groundnut) as well, apart from other vegetable crops like potato.

Similarly, PepsiCo planned a foray into contract farming in groundnut with the farmers of Punjab with the objective of producing export-quality, value-added groundnut such as roasted and salted peanuts, flavoured and coated peanuts, and peanut butter. Using plastic mulch groundnut (PMG) technology sourced from China has enabled PepsiCo to take up two crops in a year - one in the *kharif* and the other in the *rabi* season. The company has demonstrated yields of 3.0 and 4.0 tons per hectare on field trials for *kharif* and *rabi* crops respectively, much above the national average of 1.0 ton/ha.

Key elements of PepsiCo's success

- Core R&D team
- Unique partnership with local agencies including a public sector enterprise
- Execution of technology transfer through well-trained extension personnel
- Supply of all kinds of agricultural implements free of cost to contracted farmers
- Supply of timely and quality farm inputs on credit
- Prompt dispatch/delivery/procurement of the mature produce from every individual contracted farmer through the system of 'Quota Slips'
- Effective adoption/use of modern communication technology like pagers for communication with field executives
- Regular and timely payment to contracted farmers through computerized receipts and transparent system
- Maintenance of perfect logistics system and global marketing standards

Appachi's Integrated Cotton Cultivation

Appachi Cotton Company (ACC), the ginning and trading house from Pollachi (Coimbatore district of Tamil Nadu, India) hit the headlines in May 2002 for the street play it employed to encourage farmers in the Nachipalayam village in Kinathukadavu block of Coimbatore to sow cotton seeds in their fields. ACC caters to top-bracket, quality-conscious clients from the textile industry in India and abroad, and their client specific operation has won them laurels. ACC is the only private ginner in the country to have successfully entered backward and forward integration between the 'grower' (farmer) and the 'consumer' (textile units). The Appachi formula ensured that its farmer members never went short of money and materials during the crucial 100 days of the crop cycle. The contract assured the farmers easy availability of quality seeds, farm finance at an interest rate of 12% per annum, door delivery of unadulterated fertilizers and pesticides at discounted rates, expert advice and field supervision every alternate week, and a unique selling option through a MoU with the coordinating agency (ACC)

Key principles of the ACC model

- One village, one group (SHG)
- One village, one variety/hybrid of cotton seed
- Crop loan at 12% per annum on Group's guarantee
- Door delivery of quality inputs at discounted rates
- Cotton crop insurance
- Synchronized sowing
- Integrated crop management through competent Farm Service Centres
- Contamination control measures from farm to factory Assured buyback of final produce from farmers' doorsteps
- The sponsor (ACC) plays the role of a perfect coordinator/ facilitator between the producer and the consumer

Ugar Sugar's experience with barley

The story of the Belgaum (Karnataka)-based Ugar Sugar Works Ltd., which established a successful backward linkage with farmers of Northern Karnataka for supply of barley for its malt unit, is quite interesting and insightful. Farmers surrounding Ugar Sugar in Belgaum, who had been cultivating sugar under intensive irrigation found themselves with the problem of salinity in soils. Ugar Sugar took this opportunity to begin creating awareness among the farming community about alternative crops suitable for saline soils. Of these, barley was known to give economic yields of good quality in saline soils. The company assured the farmers of a market for their produce if they agreed to grow barley, as well as the required technical and input support. All this happened way back in 1997, when the company required 5000 tons of barley annually for its malt unit. At that point of time, barley was cultivated on a commercial scale only in the northern parts of India, which meant huge transportation costs for the company to source from there. Furthermore, such lots carried a mixture of feed and malt grade barley, which meant no surety of consistent quality raw material. The company had no land of its own to start barley production near its malt plant. This led to the birth of Ugar Sugar's unique contract farming system for barley production.

Ugar's barley contract farming model: Key elements

- The company supplies genetically pure seed on credit to the contracted farmers without interest.
- The price of barley seeds supplied for sowing and the final produce that is procured by the company is the same i.e. cost of the seed is same as that of the pre-agreed price of barley. Hence, the quantity of seed supplied for sowing is recovered at the time of procurement of the produce.
- A technical person from the company visits the farmers' fields at least four times in a crop cycle, giving free technical assistance.
- The company supplies seed at the sowing points in farmers' fields, and the final produce is procured from the fields at the company's transportation cost.Under the contract, it is obligatory on part of both the contracting farmer and the company to sell and buy respectively the entire contracted quantity at the Pre-agreed price.

10. Model Contract Farming Act 2018

As continuing of reforms in the agriculture sector, with natural corollary to GoI for commitment to doubling the farmers' income by 2022, the Union Government in its budget, 2017-18 announced the for draft of "Model Contract Farming Act". The Act lays special emphasis on protecting the interests of the farmers, considering them as weaker of the two parties entering into a contract. In addition to contract farming, services contracts all along the value chain including pre-production, production and post-production have been included. The salient features of this Model Contract Farming Act 2018 are as follows:

(i) Setting up of an appropriate and unbiased state level agency called " The— State/UT Agricultural Produce & Livestock Contract Farming and Services (Promotion & Facilitation) Board" to carry out the assigned mandates under the provisions relating to contract farming, services contracts and such other contracts and popularize it among the stakeholders. Alternately, existing organization/ institution in the State/UT deemed appropriate to take on such a role to be recognized.

(ii) Constitution of a "Registering and Agreement Recording Committee" or alternatively designation of "Registering and Agreement Recording Officer" at district/block/taluka level for registration of contract farming sponsor, services contract sponsor & such other sponsors and recording of contract thereof, so as to implement the same effectively.

(iii) Enables production support, including extension services to the contracting farmers or group of farmers through supply of quality inputs, scientific agronomic package of practices, technology, managerial skills and necessary v credit. Contracted produce is to be covered under crop / livestock insurance in operation.

(iv) Contract farming, services contract and such other contract under this Act to remain outside the ambit of respective Agricultural Produce Marketing Act of the states. The additional benefit in consequence to the buyers is freedom from market fee and commission charges, resulting in a saving of 5 – 10 per cent to their transaction costs.

(v) Prohibiting contract farming sponsor from raising permanent structure on contract farming producers' land and premises.

(vi) Promoting Farmer Producer Organization (FPOs) / Farmer Producer Companies (FPCs) to mobilize small and marginal farmers to benefit from scales of economy in production and post-production activities. FPO/FPC can be a contracting party if so authorized by the farmers.

(vii) No rights, title ownership or possession to be transferred or alienated or vested in the contract farming sponsor etc.

(viii) Ensuring buying of entire pre-agreed quantity of one or more of agricultural produce, livestock or its product of contract farming producer as per contract, consistent with the provisions of this Act and Rules made there under.

(ix) Making provision to guide the contracting parties to fix pre-agreed price and also to decide sale-purchase price in case of violent movement (upswing or downswing) of market price vis-à-vis pre-agreed price as a win-win framework.

(x) Providing Contract Farming Facilitation Group (CFFG) at village /panchayat level to take quick and need based decision relating to production and post production activities of contracted agricultural produce, livestock and/or its product.

(xi) Purchasing of agricultural produce, livestock and/or its product based on quality parameters as per contract farming agreement.

(xii) Catering to a dispute settlement mechanism at the lowest level possible for quick disposal of disputes arising out of the breach of contract or contravention of any provision of the Act. 8.

The Act falls under Entry 7- "Contracts, including partnership, agency, contracts of carriage , and other special forms of contracts , but not including contracts relating to agricultural land" of the List-III (Concurrent List) of the Seventh Schedule (Article 246) of the Constitution.

Hence, the State Legislature, in accordance with Article 246 (2), is competent to enact the law on farming contract. 1 The ------------- State /UT Agricultural Produce & Livestock Contract Farming and Services (Promotion & Facilitation) Act, 2018 An Act to provide for improved production and marketing of agricultural produce and/or livestock and/or its product through holistic contract farming and to facilitate the contracting parties to develop mutually beneficial and efficient contract farming system, and also promote services contract, by putting in place a friendly and effective institutional mechanism and conducive regulatory and policy framework for contract farming and services contract or such other contracts and lay down procedures and systems and the matters connected therewith and incidental thereto.

11. Conclusion

Contractual arrangements can provide farmers with the access to production services and credit as well as knowledge of new technology, reduction of risk and uncertainty by pricing arrangements, and the farmers would have the opportunity to diversify into new crops that not possible without the processing and/or marketing facilities provided by the sponsor (firm).To ensure food and nutrition security to a population of over a billion, raw material for its expanding industrial base, surpluses for exports, and a fair and equitable rewarding system for the farming community, 'commitment driven' contract farming is no doubt a viable alternative farming model, which provides assured and reliable input service to farmers and desired farm produce to the contracting firms. Several Indian and multinational companies have already begun such initiatives in India and have demonstrated repeated success. The successful cases should encourage the rest of the producing and the consuming enterprises to emulate them for mutual benefits in specific and Indian agriculture in general. For successful implementation of contract farming, Government attitudes and incentives are important aspects. The present need for transforming Indian agriculture is that Government must promote contract farming by developing the necessary legislation as that of MCFA-2018 and provide financial support – engage consultant and Research to investigate the suitability of various raw commodities for contract farming and to develop small-scale technologies. It is essential need for identification of key players in coordinating contract farming and to investigate the potential of contract farming as a possibility of promoting and increasing productivity through the inclusion of small-scale farmers in the agri-business demand and supply chains.

12. References

Aboi A .2002. Contract Farming: A Short Case Study of Silk Worm Production in Lundu District. M.Sc. Thesis. Faculty of Economic and Business, University Malaysia Sarawak.

Anonymous .2008. Contract Farming Resource Centre, FAO, Rome

Eaton C .1998. Adaptation Performance and Production Constrains of Contract Farming in China. (Unpublished Ph.D. Thesis). Department of Geography, University of Western Australia, Perth.

Eaton C and Shepherd AW .2001. "Contract Farming: Partnership for Growth."Rome: Food and Agriculture Organization. Agricultural Services Bulletin, No.145.

Farmer's Association Board .2003. Laporan Hasil Projek Kelompok Padi Komersil. Kota Kinabalu: Lembaga Pertubuhan Peladang

Key N and Runsten D .1999. Contract Farming, Smallholders, and Rural Development in Latin America: The Organization of Agro processing Firms and the Scale of Out grower Production. *World Development*. 27(2): 381-401.

Mugerwa WK .2005. "Emerging Role of Farmer Groups in Contract Farming in Uganda." Working Paper, Addis Ababa, International Food Policy Research Institute.

Porter G and Howard KP .1997. Comparing Contracts: An Evaluation of Contract Farming Schemes in Africa. *World Development*: 25, (2): 227-238.

Singh, Sukhpal .2002. Multi-national corporations and agricultural development: a study of contract farming in the Indian Punjab. *Journal of International Development*: 14:181–194.

Subrahmanyam KV .2000. Linkages Between Farm and Non-Farm Sector: Role of Processing of Horticultural Products', NABARD Occasional Paper No. 16, National Bank for Agriculture and Rural Development (NABARD), Mumbai.

White B .1997. Agro-industry and Contract Farming in Upland Java. *The Journal of Peasant Studies* 24(3):100-136.

5

Zoonotic Diseases: A Challenge to Livestock and Human Health Transformation

M Rashid and Sabhyata Sharma*

Division of Veterinary Public Health, FVSc, SKUAST-Jammu, Jammu, India
**Department of Parasitology, Nagpur Veterinary College, MAFSU, Nagpur India*

Abstract

The global economic burden due to zoonotic diseases is very high. According to a recent World Bank estimate, the economic burden due to six of the zoonotic diseases that have occurred in specific countries between 1997 and 2009 is estimated to be US$80 billion. In a worst-case scenario, potential losses from a pandemic influenza outbreak could be US$3 trillion, which is equivalent to 5% of the global GDP. Zoonotic diseases continue to represent an important health hazard in most parts of the world. More than 200 zoonotic diseases have been described, caused by bacteria, parasites, viruses, fungi and unconventional agents (e.g. prions). About 75 percent of the new diseases that have affected humans over the past ten years are caused by pathogens originating from animals or from products of animal origin. Many of these diseases have the potential to spread by various means over long distances and to become global problems. India contributes to substantial *portion of the global burden of endemic zoonoses and is one of the several 'EID hotspots'. The quality and safety of food supplies are put at risk by demands for more, cheaper food, driven by growing population and increasing urbanization, combined with a lack of resources to deal with issues related to food safety and lower or less rigorously enforced regulatory standards add to spread of zoonotic diseases. Human and financial resources that are dedicated by national authorities to the support of regulatory and non-regulatory food safety programs generally fall well short of needs. Commonly, many of the resources available are used for quality control of food for export, rather than products for domestic consumption, leaving the domestic market more vulnerable to unacceptable levels of food safety hazards, thus adding to the problem. In many developing countries, there is a substantial informal market that generally escapes any food safety controls. The successful control of zoonoses is possible if acceptable standards of life and social welfare are observed in developing country like India. Close cooperation and interaction between veterinarians, health physicians and public health operators, agriculturists and ecologists is thus necessary via one health approach strategy facilitating interdisciplinary collaborations and communications in all aspects of health care for humans, animals and the environment.*

Keywords: zoonoses, global perspective, challenges, strategies.

1. Introduction

Zoonoses, diseases and infections that are naturally transmitted between humans and other vertebrate animals, have been recognized since the beginning of history, but their public health importance has assumed more socio-economic significance in the last few decades as global analyses of emerging infectious diseases (EIDs) between 1940 and 2004 identified that 60.3% of them were zoonotic and were increasing rapidly over time Chatterjee et al (2017). India is experiencing rapid urbanization, industrialization, increasing incomes and changing food preferences raising demands for animal source proteins, leading to a larger section of the workforce being in close contact with livestock, including poultry, making a wider section of the population extremely susceptible to zoonotic diseases. Therefore India contributes to substantial portion of the global burden of endemic zoonoses and is one of the several 'EID hotspots'. Owing to the public health importance of zoonotic diseases in India, a National Standing Committee on Zoonoses was formed in 2007. Lately, a Centre for Zoonoses Research has been proposed to be set up to harness intersectoral collaborative research using the One Health approach. 'One Health' is holistic multidisciplinary approach to address human, animal, and ecosystem health. It encompasses many disciplines, professions, and areas of interest that includes the protection of animal health, the relief of animal suffering, the conservation of livestock and other natural resources, the promotion of public health, and the advancement of medical knowledge and aims to enhance global efforts to mitigate and counter the emergence of zoonoses and other diseases. Thus, a worldwide strategy to expand interdisciplinary collaborations and communications in all aspects of health care for humans, animals and the environment is essential to check the spread of zoonotic diseases.

Various anthropogenic factors, led to the emerging and reemerging infectious diseases and these factors are: genetic and biological factors, such as microbial adaptation to macro- and micro environmental changes along with changes in host susceptibility to infection; environmental factors, including climate change, changes in ecosystems, and changes in human and animal population densities; and socioeconomic and political factors, such as increasing international travel and commerce, social inequality, poverty, conflict, famine, lack of political will, and changes in economic development and land use.

Over the last 15 years, our planet has faced more than 15 deadly zoonotic or vector-borne global outbreaks, both viral (e.g., Hanta, Ebola, highly pathogenic avian influenza [H5N1 and recently H7N9], West Nile, Rift Valley fever, norovirus, severe acute respiratory syndrome [SARS], Marburg, influenza A [H1N1]) recent emerging outbreak of Nipavirus in May 2018 in Kerala of India and bacterial (e.g., *Escherichia coli* O157:H7, *Listeria monocytogens Yersinia pestis* and *Bacillus anthracis*. Since 1980, more than 87 new zoonotic and/or vector-borne EIDs have been discovered. Some parasitic zoonotic diseases such as taeniasis (cysticercosis), echinococcosis, toxoplasmosis trichinellosis and water-borne parasitosis, the protozoa *Giardia*, *Cryptosporidium* and *Toxoplasma* are the most significant ones (Gebreyes, *et al,* 2014). Diseases like plague, Japanese encephalitis, leishmaniasis, rabies, leptospirosis, Nipah virus and dengue fever etc. have been major public health concerns in India.

The global economic burden due to zoonotic diseases is very high. According to a recent World Bank estimate, the economic burden due to six of the zoonotic diseases that have occurred in specific countries between 1997 and 2009 is estimated to be US$80 billion. In a worst-case scenario, potential losses from a pandemic influenza outbreak could be US$3 trillion, which is equivalent to 5% of the global GDP. A recent report from the International Livestock Research Institute highlighted zoonoses as major obstacles to poverty alleviation, affecting 1,000,000,000 livestock keepers. The report estimated that there are over 2,500,000,000 cases of human illness and 2.7 million deaths annually due to the top 56 zoonoses. In addition, the report estimated this group of diseases infected more than one in seven of the livestock found in less developed countries (Gebreyes *et al* 2014).

Animal health and food safety systems are facing new and additional challenges as a result of the lengthening and increasing complexity of supply chains in the livestock sector that have been facilitated by globalization and trade liberalization. At the same time, increasingly stringent food safety and animal health regulations and private standards aimed at promoting consumer welfare are creating challenges for producers, especially small holders who have less technical and financial capacity to comply with them.

2. Challenges of zoonoses in Livestock and Human Health

Zoonotic diseases pose two types of problem for humans: socio-economic and health problems. Economic threats from zoonotic diseases come on account of three reasons, namely Losses in production, productivity and profitability caused by disease agents and the cost of their treatment.

Disruptions to local markets, international trade and rural economies arising from disease outbreaks and the control measures aimed at controlling their spread, such as culling, quarantines and travel bans. The circumstances also lead to threats to the livelihood security of the poors. Livelihood threats arise from the first two categories of threat. Because livestock serve multiple functions in the livelihoods of poor people, livestock diseases affect poor livestock producers differently from commercial producers. The poors face diverse type of socio-economic problems and have different capacities to respond to disease outbreaks. An economic problem for some producers can destroy the livelihoods of others.

Threats to Human health

I) From Zoonotic Diseases

II) From Food Borne Illnesses

Threats to human health from zoonotic diseases arise mainly from existing and emerging zoonotic diseases (those that are shared between animals and humans-Zooanthroponoses and amphixenoses), that arise in animals but can be transmitted to humans. Potentially pandemic viruses, such as influenza, Ebola, Dengue, J.E., Nipavirus are the some problems of these days, but many others exist, including rabies, brucellosis and anthrax from food borne illnesses and from residues left by the improper use of veterinary medicines (e.g. antibiotics), hormones and toxic substances. During the early stages of intensification of livestock production, large scale livestock production units tend to be established near to growing urban population. This can foster the emergence and spread of diseases affecting both animals and humans (Fiona, *et al,* 2009).

Food-borne illness can come from disease agents such as *salmonella* and *E. coli, listeria monocytogens, campylobacter species* or contaminants that enter the food chain during the production and processing of animal based foods. These illnesses and the way they are managed create problems for everyone, but small holders are often particularly vulnerable because they are more exposed to the risk and have less capacity to respond and recover. At the global level new pathogens are emerging at the human–animal–ecosystem interface (WHO, 1982, FAO 2008a and OIE 2008b).

Challenges to Economy

Zoonotic Diseases affecting the livestock and poultry reduce production and productivity, disrupt trade and cause losses in local and regional economies and there by exacerbate poverty. A sick animal produces less meat, less milk or fewer eggs. It provides less draught power and poorer quality food and fibre. In economic terms, output declines, costs rise and profits fall. Productivity losses occurs due to death of the animal or illness leading to condemnation of meat at slaughter, as well as reduction in weight gain, milk yield, feed conversion, reproductive capacity and work capacity for ploughing and transport. Treatment costs include direct financial costs and indirect costs of time taken up by seeking or providing treatment. Livestock in developing countries are exposed to a range of diseases that affect productivity. For example, in J & K state, sheep goat pox, FMD and enterotoxaemia etc affect sheep and goats. Foot-and-mouth disease in India and elsewhere in Asia causes considerable loss of production; it is a particular problem when it infects draught animals during the ploughing season, limiting their ability to work. This reduces farmers' incomes from renting out draught animals and causes a reduction in the area of land that can be planted to staple food crops (WHO, 1982, FAO 2008a and OIE 2008b). The transboundary and emerging diseases can be vectored by birds, rodents and insects and carried by live animals and animal products or through fomites such as on the clothes, shoes and vehicle tyres of people moving through an affected area. The emergence of new diseases that are not understood or for which control technology is not available are of particular concern. Because of their dramatic effects on animal mortality and their high economic costs, they tend to attract the greatest attention from public animal health programs and national and international regulations.

The main strategy used to reduce the impact of transboundary and emerging diseases involves eliminating them from a population and then preventing their reintroduction, for example, through vaccination and sanitary measures aimed at protecting susceptible species from exposure from infected populations. The international institutions most directly involved are the Agreement on the

Application of Sanitary and Phytosanitary Measures (SPS) of the World Trade Organization (WTO) and the OIE. The framework for international trade in livestock and livestock products allows countries that are free of a given notifiable disease to require their trading partners to have equivalent disease free status (WHO, 1982, FAO 2008a and OIE 2008b).

Challenges in Disruption of Markets, Trade and Rural Economies

Zoonotic diseases that cause high mortality in animals and spread rapidly nationally and internationally into disease free areas can cause high economic losses. They disrupt the market, trade and their by posing economic losses. However, they can also carry costs in the form of investment for welfare friendly animal housing and training of staff, longer time periods to produce outputs or less output per unit space allocated to animals. An approach to animal welfare that focuses on benefits to people, rather than to the animals, is more likely to succeed, especially in parts of the world where many people suffer from poverty and starvation (WHO, 1982, FAO 2008a and OIE 2008b).

Challenges to Livelihoods

Zoonotic diseases affect all livestock and pose economic losses. For many families in the poorest strata, livestock diseases consume asset that they use, for dealing with livelihood. They also affect people who are employed by livestock owners, small scale traders of livestock and poor consumers. The measures used by veterinary authorities to combat disease can have severe consequences for people living in poverty, including depriving poor producers of their livelihoods, in the case of culls and driving up costs of livestock products to poor consumers.

Some diseases that can be prevented or controlled by wealthier farmers are a continuing problem in the flocks and herds of poor households. For example, brucellosis is often present in sheep and goat flocks under extensive management in many parts of the world, but vaccination is not widely practiced by extensive herders because of the high cost. This disease has step down in our nomadic flocks in J&K state as evident from our some findings. Likewise, Newcastle disease in poultry is kept under control by segregation and vaccination in commercial flocks but no economically viable control system has yet been found for scavenging flocks. Other diseases affect rich and poor alike but have very particular effects on the poor. For example, FMD, a disease that disrupts international trade, usually a major cause for concern among milch animal and in traction animals during land preparation (WHO, 1982).

In recent years, the scientific community has developed a variety of animal health technologies and interventions that can reduce the threat of disease. But because of financial and institutional constraints the delivery of new technology to small scale producers is difficult. Despite the global shift towards intensive livestock production, the many poor people who will continue to rely on small numbers of poultry or other livestock for income diversity and security still require better animal-health services than those available at present. One of the greatest challenges will be to find ways to provide and sustain these services in countries where investment in such services has been falling for many years (WHO, 1982, FAO 2008a and OIE 2008b).

Zoonotic diseases and Pandemic threats

Emerging zoonotic diseases (from wild or domestic animals) can spread out of their natural ecosystem due to many reasons, such as human and animal demographic changes, ecosystem encroachment, climate fluctuations and trade flows. These diseases cause sickness and death in humans and are an issue of growing importance to medical and veterinary authorities. A very large number of new diseases in animals are able to infect and affect humans. At least half of the 1700 known causes of infectious disease in humans have a reservoir in animals, and many new infections are zoonotic diseases. More than 200 zoonotic diseases have been described, caused by bacteria, parasites, viruses, fungi and unconventional agents (e.g. prions). About 75 percent of the new diseases that have affected humans over the past ten years are caused by pathogens originating from animals or from products of animal origin.

Many of these diseases have the potential to spread by various means over long distances and to become global problems. In recent years, the world has experienced the emergence of severe acute respiratory syndrome (SARS), HPAI (caused by type A [H5N1] virus) and an influenza caused by the A (H1N1) virus, all causing considerable concern about the risk of a major global pandemic. The end of 2008 marked the detection of the Ebola Reston virus circulating in pigs and pig workers in the Philippines. In addition, outbreaks of the Ebola virus flare up occasionally in the Democratic Republic of the Congo, Uganda and other countries in Africa, killing humans and large numbers of great apes. Some neglected endemic zoonotic diseases such as *cysticerocosis, echinococcosis and brucellosis* persist in the poorest and most vulnerable populations.

Zoonotic diseases and Food borne illnesses

Although several of the diseases previously mentioned can be transmitted through food. so food borne diseases are considered as a specific group. Organisms such as salmonella (particularly *S. enteritidis* and *S. typhimurium*), *Campylobacter, listeria monocytogens* and *E. coli* O157:H7 are major food borne threats, causing illness in millions of people worldwide every year. The major food safety hazards in livestock products are biological and chemical contaminants. These contaminants can originate from air, soil, water, feedstuffs, fertilizers (including natural fertilizers), pesticides, veterinary drugs or any other agent used in primary production, or from diseased animals.

Biological contaminants in livestock products include: abnormal proteins, such as those associated with BSE; bacteria, such as *Salmonella* and *Brucella* species and some types of *E. coli*; and parasites, such as *Echinococcus* species. Chemical and biological contaminants include: veterinary drug residues, such as antimicrobials, and pesticides; chemicals; heavy metals; and naturally occurring mycotoxins and bacterial toxins.

In developing countries, the quality and safety of food supplies are put at risk by demands for more, cheaper food, driven by growing population and increasing urbanization, combined with a lack of resources to deal with issues related to food safety and lower or less rigorously enforced regulatory standards. Human and financial resources that are dedicated by national authorities to the support of regulatory and non-regulatory food safety programs generally fall well short of needs. Commonly, many of the resources available are used for quality control of food for export, rather than products for domestic consumption, leaving the domestic market more vulnerable to unacceptable levels of food safety hazards. In many developing countries, there is a substantial informal market that generally escapes any food safety controls.

Informal food production systems, such as unregulated slaughter in developing countries, make available food that has not met food safety standards. Many rural and urban poor people buy food in informal and uncontrolled markets and, therefore, face a higher chance of contracting zoonotic and food borne diseases, resulting in illness and wage loss as well as medical expenses to treat the illnesses (FAO, 2005). Moreover, food borne illnesses often affect aged, young and malnourished people most severely.

3. Genesis of Human, animal and ecological interface

NiV was discovered when it caused a serious outbreak of viral encephalitis among pig farmers in Malaysia in 1998. The disease was named after the village Kampung Sungai Nipah, where the outbreak took place. Since then, the virus has returned several times in Bangladesh and several parts of India. 11 deaths in Kerala were confirmed because of Nipah virus outbreak. The sudden spurt of zoonotic diseases in the last few years has caught the world unprepared. It includes Ebola hemorrhagic fever and microcephaly caused by Zika virus. WHO (2015) highlighted that 75 per cent of new diseases that have affected humans over the last decade have been caused by pathogens originating from an animal or from products of animal origin. Many of the diseases have potential to cover long distance and affect the world. The apex body claims to engage in cross-sectoral activities to address health threats at the human-animal ecosystem interface.

KFD is not a new disease in the district. The first outbreak was reported in March 1957 after a number of monkeys died unnatural deaths and a mysterious fever engulfed the residents of Kyasanur, a forest village in Soraba taluk that gives the disease its name. Since then the state has seen frequent outbreaks, but the disease had been restricted to just five districts in the Western Ghats. NIV has in the past found the antibodies against this pathogen in samples collected from Gujarat, Rajasthan, Maharashtra, West Bengal, Tamil Nadu, and Andaman and Nicobar Islands. Mourya's fears have been proven right as cases of KFD have recently been reported in new areas. Little is known about the reasons behind the spread of the disease because there is hardly any research on it. But it is established that deforestation could be the primary reason as it increases the contact between humans and wild animals. Shivamogga district alone lost 4,000 hectares of forest between 2001 and 2007. There is evidence that global warming that increases population of insects like ticks that harbour the virus could also lead to the spread of the disease. Monkeys are the primary carrier of the disease. Ticks (Hemaphysalis spinigera) that live on them harbour the pathogen and pass it among the monkey population (see 'How humans contract Kyasanur forest disease',). "Monkeys are sure to die once infected," says Prakash K S, health officer of Thirthahalli. When infected monkeys die ticks drop from their bodies to the ground, thereby generating hot spots of ticks that spread the virus. It is transmitted to humans through the bite of a tick or when humans come in contact with an infected animal. The outbreak of the disease in humans generally occurs in the dry months, from January to May.

The devastating 2014 Ebola outbreak in West Africa can be traced back to a two-year-old boy from a small village in Guinea. Emile Ouamouno, known to the world as "patient zero", who died on December 6, 2013, was the first casualty of the deadly virus. Within a month, Emile's mother, sister and grandmother all succumbed to the virus. Since the beginning of 2014, Ebola has killed more than 11,312 (till October 11, 2015) people in Guinea, Senegal and Liberia, and the epidemic is yet to be conclusively thwarted. The origin of the scourge and how Emile came to be infected is still a mystery. What is known for certain is that the disease was contracted from an animal. Fruit bats, being natural reservoirs of the Ebola virus, have been zeroed in on as prime suspects.

This is not the first time that a disease has been contracted from animals and it shall not be the last either. For millennia, humans have feared the inevitable but unpredictable devastation wrought by infectious diseases emerging from forests and transmitted through wild animals. But there has been a stark increase in the incidence of emerging infectious diseases (EIDs) among both humans and domesticated animals in the recent past. Over the past 70 years, more than 300 zoonotic diseases have been observed. Notably, between 60 per cent of all human diseases and 75 per cent of all EIDs among humans originate in animals. According to a 2012 report of the Department for International Development, UK, that mapped zoonotic diseases, zoonoses are responsible for over 2.7 million deaths and over 2.5 billion cases of human illness every year.

Zoonoses are increasingly being considered a threat to the stability of human societies. The increase in the incidence of zoonoses, to a significant extent, is a reflection of the change in our interactions with our forest ecosystems. The development of agriculture brought an end to an exclusive hunter-gatherer way of life. Despite the fact that today there are no known populations that live purely as hunter-gatherers, it is reported that in 62 developing countries, people obtain more than 20 per cent of their nutrition through wild meat and fish. Populations living in and around forests also depend to a great extent on the forests as a source of livelihood. Nevertheless, the need for food drove the development of agriculture, which altered landscapes and populations. This changed the nature of human contact with forests.

India is particularly vulnerable to many forest-originated diseases. Some 2,474 villages are inside India's forests, while some 170,000 villages are around forest areas. More to it, 220 million people depend on forestry for survival. This means a significant number of people interact with forest in their day to day lives. India's poorest also reside in the forested areas thus having less economic capacity to fight disease outbreaks. In these areas, public health facilities are sparse and most of the residents have to travel long to access them. Research shows that changes in land use, including deforestation and forest fragmentation, urbanisation and intensification of agriculture, have contributed greatly to the rise in the incidence of infectious diseases. "Indeed the current increase coincides with accelerating rates of tropical deforestation in the past several decades. Today, both deforestation and emerging infectious diseases remain largely associated with tropical regions but have impacts that extend globally.

There are about 250 EIDs, about 15 per cent of which currently show a direct association with forests. Some EIDs were originally transmitted from animals to humans but have now escaped the sylvatic cycle, where the pathogen spends some time in an animal before being transmitted. These diseases have adapted to a human-sustained cycle independent of forests.

While speaking of pathogens escaping the forests, the foremost microbe that springs to mind is HIV, which causes the devastating AIDS. The disease is said to have emerged from chimpanzees and gorillas in Central and Western Africa.

Before adapting to human-to-human transmission a little over 30 years ago, HIV's transmission cycle involved a primate. According to the WHO, an estimated 39 million people have died worldwide of AIDS-related causes between 1981 and 2013. By the end of 2013, some 35 million people were still infected with HIV and over 2 million people were getting infected every year. According to the National AIDS Control Organisation, more than 2 million people in India were suffering from HIV/AIDS in 2014.

What makes HIV a striking example of EIDs is the global scale at which it proliferated. AIDS, in many ways, is the world's first truly global epidemic with an unprecedented rate and scale of incidence. The scope and speed of HIV transmission highlights the potential of EIDs to spread beyond borders and become a significant threat to human health and wildlife.

Multiple studies have pointed to habitat fragmentation and biodiversity loss to explain the emergence and transmission of novel diseases, such as Lyme disease in the US and Europe, to humans. The disease is caused by a bacterial pathogen, *Borrelia burgdorferi*. White footed mice and white tailed deer have been identified as natural reservoir species for the bacterium, which is transmitted by tick bites. Diminishing biodiversity and the lack of large predators have helped Lyme disease to become the most prevalent vector-borne disease in US.

Habitat destruction can also force species to venture into urban locales in search of food. In the first outbreak of encephalitis in Malaysia in 1998, fruit bats, which act as vectors for the Nipah virus, were displaced from their natural forested habitat due to severe deforestation and fires associated with the 1998 El Niño event.

An estimated 165.4 million people in 54 districts in the states of Bihar, Jharkhand, Uttar Pradesh and West Bengal that are deemed endemic are at the risk of contracting kala azar. A related disease of visceral leishmaniasis that is also making its presence felt is cutaneous leishmaniasis spread by P salehi and P papatasi. Desert rodents in rural areas of Rajasthan and dogs in urban areas act as reservoirs of the parasite.

However, in recent years the menace of leishmania has found its way to other states such as Himachal Pradesh, Uttarakhand and Assam and Kerala, where the disease has traditionally not been observed. This has led to postulations about possible diversification of disease reservoirs. The role of deforestation and increased contact between humans and forests due to construction in erstwhile forested lands have also been hypothesised as possible reasons for the emergence of the disease in new regions in recent years although there has still been no conclusive findings in this regard.

Migratory impacts on proliferation and adaptation of pathogens can be much more severe. Consider avian influenza, commonly known as bird flu. It is caused by diverse variants of the H5N1 virus. The primary mode of transmission is bird to bird, although bird flu has adapted to humans with increased human-bird contact since the advent of large-scale poultry farming.

Since birds do not obey geographic borders, the virus has caused flu globally. In 2014 alone, bird flu outbreaks were recorded in over 35 countries. The virus is notoriously difficult to track owing to its adept adaption. Different strains of the virus can interact with each other and exchange (Contd. on p48) chromosomes to create new stable variants that can be fatal to humans. One such strain, H5N1, has caused over 143 cases and 42 deaths worldwide between January and October 2015. In total, there have been at least 844 confirmed cases and 449 deaths among humans due to the H5N1 strain of avian influenza since 2003 when the disease was first identified in human beings.

As much as the pathogen and vector ecology is responsible for zoonotic diseases, changes in human ecology are responsible for the speed of transmission and the global scope many diseases have recently acquired.

Chikungunya is thought to have originated in Africa, where the virus is maintained in a sylvatic cycle between forest-dwelling mosquitoes and non-human primates. Outbreaks among humans have been observed to be sporadic and short-lived. In urban centres across Africa and Asia, though, the virus is sustained by immunologically naïve human hosts.

The most recent outbreak of chikungunya happened in Kenya in 2004 and spread to several Indian Ocean islands, India and Southeast Asia. The outbreak in India started in 2006 and has affected several million people since then. In India large populations of immunologically naïve humans have helped sustain the virus cycle. In 2015 Karnataka saw 16,235 cases of clinically suspected chikungunya. Telangana has seen nearly 1,500 cases. This is in contrast to outbreaks in other affected countries and islands with a limited pool of human hosts. These areas did not report cases once the epidemic was over.

During the epidemic in India, the virus spread from India to Italy through a traveller and was introduced into the local species of Aedes mosquitoes. It was then sustained in a mosquito-human-mosquito transmission cycle in the Mediterranean country.

Increased speed and scope of mobility due to globalisation has amplified the extent of zoonoses. Proximity to forests or close contact with animal vectors or reservoirs is no longer a limiting constraint on the reach of a pathogen. The case of severe acute respiratory syndrome (SARS) exemplifies the situation.

The SARS virus originated in wild animals in southern China. The virus mutated to adapt to nearby human settlements and jumped to humans in a few closely located towns and villages and then spread to the urban area Guangzhou. The crowded region facilitated development of the disease into an epidemic in late 2002. Early next year, the virus spread to Hong Kong through a doctor from Guangzhou. The island city served as the hub for what would become a global pandemic. The SARS pandemic started in February 2003 and within a few months it had spread to over 20 countries across the Americas, Europe and Asia. By the time it was contained, 8,000 cases and 774 deaths had been reported. The total losses related to the global outbreak were estimated to run into billions of dollars.

4. Spread and transmission of zoonotic diseases

Kumar et al (2015) observed that the major factor involved in the increase in zoonoses, include population shifts and growth; changes in behavior; group urbanization, poverty and crowding; changes in ecology and climate; evolution of new strains of microbes; inadequacy of the public health infrastructure, modern tourism and liberalized trade. Natural animal habitats like national park and sanctuaries are also frequent sources of disease transmission. They reported that at least 11 pathogens have emerged or re-emerged in India during 1992-2009, majority of which were of animal origin. In India, agriculture and animal husbandry workers such as farmers, livestock owners, animal handlers, veterinary extension workers and veterinarians had been found to commonly contract approximately 40 zoonotic diseases. Similarly, people engaged in production and processing of livestock products such as personnel working in abattoir, dairy, poultry enterprises and piggery suffer frequently with about 22 zoonotic diseases including rabies, JE, Kyasanur forest disease (KFD), anthrax, brucellosis, plague, TB, Leptospirosis, Salmonellosis, Campylobacteriosis, listeriosis, verotoxic E. coli and Clostridial infections. Kumar et al (2015) observations on emergence or re-emergence of bacterial zoonotic diseases are enlisted below:

- Etiological changes in man's environment and agricultural operations e.g. Leptospirosis, plague, Rift Valley fever, Kyasanur Forest Disease etc.
- Increased movement or traveling of man e.g. amoebiasis, giardiasis, colibacillosis, slmonellosis, SAARS, Yellow fever etc.
- Handling animal byproducts and waste e.g. anthrax, chlamydiosis, dermatophytosis, tularaemia
- Culture anthropological norms e.g. dermatophytosis, food borne infections, brucellosis etc.

- Increased in density of animal population e.g. dermatophytosis, tuberculosis etc.
- Increased trade in animal products e.g. anthrax, brucellosis, salmonellosis, Hantaan virus, Bird flu etc.
- Drug resistant organisms e.g. E.coli, Staphylococcus aureusetc.
- Changing livestock farming practices e.g. E.coli O157:H7, Salmonellosis, Listeriosis etc. Changing environmental conditions including climate and disaster e.g. plague, Leptospirosis etc.
- Pathogen changes like genetic shift and drift e.g. Influenza, E.coli, Staphylococcus aureus etc.

5. Management of Zoonoses and Food borne diseases

Management of Zoonoses and Food borne diseases requires action on several fronts that are based on five pillars such as: (WHO, 1982)

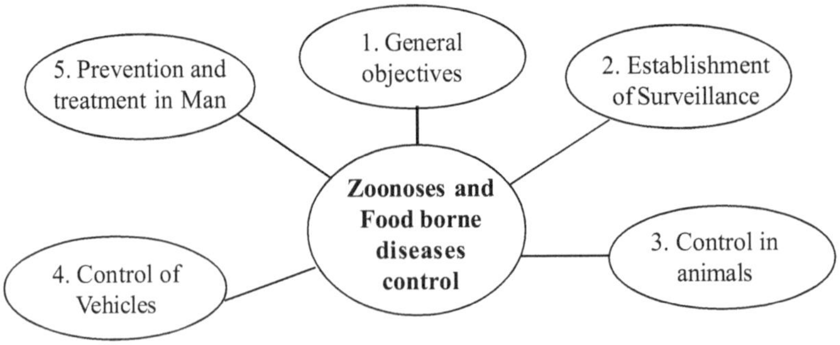

General objectives

The general objectives of zoonoses control program are:

Establishing cooperation- with a goal of one health concept by establishing co-operation internationally, regionally, intersectorally and with the public for effective retrieval of data about the diseases, education, awareness and effective implementation of strategies with active participation of common masses.

Efforts to control zoonotic diseases and food-safety problems related to the livestock sector must involve both human and animal health sectors. There is also a need to collaborate with wildlife or environmental experts in order to understand the origins and reservoirs of diseases. For this reason, many current efforts are focused on improving collaborative arrangements at the national, regional and international levels. "One World, One Health" is an interdisciplinary and cross sectoral approach to dealing with emerging infectious diseases, developed by the Wildlife Conservation Society. It has been adopted by a number of recent initiatives against zoonotic disease that bring together a wide range of stakeholders from human and animal health sectors, medical and veterinary communities, wildlife and environmental organizations, the private sector and advanced research institutions at the country, regional and international levels.

Significant progress in cross sectoral collaboration has been achieved regionally and at the international level. Internationally, collaboration exists among many organizations or institutions, such as WHO, FAO, UNICEF, OIE, WWF, WCS and IUCN6 and advanced research organizations and laboratories, including those of the Consultative Group on International Agriculture Research (CGIAR) system. FAO, the International Atomic Energy Agency (IAEA) and OIE reference laboratories and collaborating centres support diagnostic services, research in epidemiology and development of vaccines. OIE and FAO promoted joint Regional Animal Health Centres to support harmonized strategies and approaches for transboundary animal diseases and emerging infectious diseases across countries in regions with similar problems and challenges.

A risk management approach to food safety risks from animal products is essential to allocate efficiently the limited funds available for food-safety systems. Involvement of all members of the food supply chain in understanding risks and identifying priority areas for controls and mitigations will go a long way to ensuring social acceptance of and responsibility for, food safety along the food supply chain. This cross sector involvement helps to deal with business practices that may threaten food safety (WHO, 1982).

Influencing basic conditions-Ensuring awareness of high risk groups, altering agriculture practices by improving hygiene in animal production, proper disposal and recycling of animal wastes, hygienic supply of water, feed and fodder are the important considerations in controlling zoonoses.

Consider other basic factors- the two important basic factors such as Epidemiological conditions and Human factors must be taken care. The human factors include - population density, land use, urbanization, literacy rate social norms, customs, economic values of animals, social values of animals play a significant role in disease spread. Similarly epidemiological factors like incidence/ prevalence rate of diseases, routes of transmission, carriers, reservoirs and subclinical infections also play a significant role in disease transmission. All these factors must be decreased in disease prevention and control strategies.

Meeting project requirements – in this consideration, procurement of personnel, facilities, equipments, material is first carried out and then capacity building through training, education is carried out. So that farming community get involved in disease control program (WHO, 1982).

Establishment of Surveillance

For effective control of zoonoses two strategies are established

Establishment of diagnostic services

Establishment of epidemiological intelligence services

In diagnostic services clinical/pathological diagnostic tools, field test, laboratory tests are applied to find out the disease burden for implementation of control strategies. In epidemiological services data is collected from different sources, processed, analysed and feed back to the agencies who required or strategies for control are formulated and implemented by concerned authorities are sorted out.

Control in animals

The control of zoonotic diseases in animal population is based on

Control of animal populations,

Reduction of susceptible hosts and

Maintenance of ZFD free status.

Those animals that are either infected or remained in contact with infected ones, may be quarantined, or treated or destroyed according to the situation aroused. Stray susceptible animals are captured or destroyed where as wild animals reservoirs are hunt, trapped, poisoned, predated, or antifertility agents are applied. The attempts are made to control vectors of diseases in environment by applying different techniques such as chemicals, biological, modification of living environment or by control of fertility whatever is applicable.

Reduction of susceptible hosts is carried out by immunization, chemotherapy, changing of husbandry practices and altering of disease favoring environment.

Maintenance of zoonotic free disease (ZFD) free status is achieved by quarantine of animals/products/feeds in disease free areas to restrict entry of zoonotic diseases. Animal movement is restricted, environmental factors favoring spread of diseases are controlled and chemoprophylactic or immunization control techniques are utilized to overcome disease spread (WHO 1982).

Control of Vehicles

The vehicles transmitting the zoonoses are several and can be controlled on many fronts –

Establishing Food Hygiene: the food hygiene can be achieved by maintaining hygiene in animal production, in slaughter houses, and while handling and processing of food stuffs of animal origin.

Ensuring safety of other animal products (wool, hide, horn, bones, fat etc): all the way during collection, storage, processing and transport hygiene is maintained to avoid contamination and spread of diseases.

Dispose safely or use animal carcasses and wastes: the animal carcasses wastes or excreta must be rendered safe for recycling socioeconomically in the form of compost or generating energy resources. All efforts be considered to avoid soil, water or air pollution.

Decontaminate/Disinfect sites, vehicles, persons wherever there is apprehension of infection.

Prevention and treatment in Man

The zoonoses can be controlled in man by:

By preventing infection among susceptible animals and man: the human beings are educated by conducting awareness camps and imparting the knowledge of disease transmission by different routes so that they can protect themselves and their livestock. Risk group (occupationally exposed) are either immunized, or chemoprophylaxis is provided.

By Diagnosis of diseases in animals and man: diagnostic services are improved so that disease is early diagnosed and controlled.

By treating the diseased ones: after diagnoses treatment be carried out as early as possible, so that further spread of infection be controlled and minimized (WHO 1982).

Some additional measures for control of zoonoses

Location of production

The geographic concentration of production units near urban centres increases the risks of epidemic disease outbreaks in the livestock population, especially when people and animals move between traditional and intensive production systems, and increases the exposure of the urban population to livestock diseases. Animal health protection in large, clustered livestock production units is straight forward in some respects. It may be necessary, however, to encourage the relocation of these units away from urban centres in the interests of human health.

Meanwhile, backyard livestock production continues in many urban and peri-urban areas. There have been instances where governments have tried to ban such enterprises in light of human health concerns. This has been the case, for example, in recent efforts to control HPAI (ICASEPS, 2008). Where implemented without careful consultation with producers, this approach has damaged livelihoods and resulted in non compliance. Some governments have modified or removed these restrictions and are trying instead to provide incentives to encourage safer production practices (WHO, 1982, FAO 2008a and OIE 2008b).

Animal health, food safety and early-warning systems

Many developing countries lack mechanisms for gathering information about the incidence of animal health and food safety problems or any form of early-warning system for disease outbreaks. This limits their ability to diagnose and prioritize animal health problems and deliver appropriate interventions.

Many of the basic elements for a global information system already exist. Regional organizations in Southeast Asia and South America for instance, have played an important role in promoting cross border and regional animal health surveillance programmes. The Global Early Warning System (GLEWS), operated by FAO, OIE and WHO, provides warnings based on the most up to-date scientific information available; these permit national decision makers and the international scientific community to make more accurate assessments of risks of disease outbreaks. Global and regional networks of laboratories and epidemiologists – for example, the OIE/FAO Network of Expertise on Animal Influenza (OFFLU) and regional laboratory and epidemiology networks in Africa and Asia – have also been set up to facilitate the sharing of information and samples (WHO, 1982, FAO 2008a and OIE 2008b)..

However, these systems function where reliable local information is available. Gathering such information requires an effective surveillance system based on a sensitized, alert and engaged community, suitably trained and equipped staff and well-equipped laboratories. Regrettably, few developing countries have such systems in place. Some developing countries have had successful experiences with participatory disease surveillance involving villagers or community animal-health workers, for example in Africa during the 1990s to detect residual pockets of rinderpest (Mariner and Roeder, 2003) and in Indonesia in 2004–05 to discover the extent of H5N1 HPAI infection (Alders *et al.*, in press). However, sustained investment and government commitment are needed to create such systems, and given the contribution that good disease intelligence makes to global public goods, at least part of the investment should come from the international community.

Strengthening animal health and food safety systems requires consistent, sustained funding. This will have to be provided at the local and national levels as well as by the international community. Stronger planning, advocacy and monitoring of impacts of the systems will be important, together with closer engagement between public and private sectors in countries where the private sector is sufficiently robust.

There are a few examples of combined public and private animal health funds, but none are in developing countries. The best known example is in Australia, where a not-for-profit public company has been established by the federal government, state and territory governments and major national livestock industry organizations to manage national animal-health programs on behalf of its members (FAO, 2008a)

Private actions taken by livestock owners to preserve their own herds and flocks, such as voluntary vaccination, or the application of biosecurity measures can also create a public benefit by limiting disease spread to animals or people. So creation of awareness among rural masses has strong has strong footing in this aspect.

Engaging the poor in animal-health programs

Efforts to reduce the impacts of livestock disease on people living in poverty must take into account the wide range of diseases that affect the lives of poor people, including currently neglected diseases. They must also aim to minimize damage done by control measure used to deal with outbreaks of emerging zoonotics and trans-boundary diseases. Achieving these goals will require the close engagement of poor people and their representatives in planning and delivery of disease prevention and control measures; this will help ensure that more of the solutions proposed will be appropriate to, and wanted by, local communities.

This approach is essential both to protect the livelihoods of poor people and to increase the likelihood of disease-control efforts succeeding.

Measures that will help poor livestock keepers include: reducing the shock of control measures, e.g. avoiding extensive culls where possible; compensating those affected; and investing more heavily in local institutions that will help to provide better coping mechanisms. Public–private partnerships need to create space for the poor to become more engaged in order to capture local knowledge about prevailing diseases and impacts, and, where possible, to encourage them to develop their own measures to prevent and control livestock disease outbreaks.

Developing animal health protection tailored to local circumstances

Animal health protection should be tailored to specific local circumstances. Blanket solutions work well for some but not for others. Vaccination, is simple to apply in large, intensively managed flocks and herds, but tends to be much less cost effective in small scale systems because of the costs of delivering it to many small production units.

Small holders may be reluctant to participate in vaccination programs when they perceive little immediate benefit. More concentrated efforts are needed that takes account of the needs and strengths of small, medium and large scale producers in different types of production and marketing chains. Animal health solutions need to be developed in and for local situations and they must be seen in the context of wider developments in the livestock sector and beyond. Experience also underlines the need for those involved in animal health systems to be constantly evaluating and learning from experience. In all of these efforts, two-way communication is essential. Communication strategies to promote behaviours at the community and household levels aimed at preventing and controlling outbreaks of livestock disease include: informing communities of new or emerging health threats and how to recognize them; engaging local people in responding to such threats and in developing preventive practices for new diseases; and national public education campaigns to promote awareness of the impact of livestock diseases and what the public can do to help prevent and control outbreaks (WHO, 1982, FAO 2008a and OIE 2008b).

6. References

Chatterjee Pranab , Bhaumik Soumyadeep , Chauhan Abhimanyu Singh, and Kakkar Manish . 2017. Protocol for developing a Database of Zoonotic disease Research in India (DoZooRI). BMJ Open, 7(12): e017825

FAO (2008a) and OIE (2008b). Livestock in the balance. In: Livestock and human and animal health pages 75-93.

Fiona M. Tomley* and Martin W. Shirley. (2009). Introduction Livestock infectious diseases and zoonoses. *Phil. Trans. R. Soc. B* (2009) 364, 2637–2642.

Gebreyes WA, Dupouy-Camet J, Newport MJ, Oliveira CJB, Schlesinger LS, *et al.* (2014) The Global One Health Paradigm: Challenges and Opportunities for Tackling Infectious Diseases at the Human, Animal, and Environment Interface in Low-Resource Settings. PLoS Negl Trop Dis 8(11): e3257. doi:10.1371/journal.

Hubálek Z. 2003. Emerging human infectious diseases: anthroponoses, zoonoses, and sapronoses. Emerg Infect Dis ;9:403–4. doi:10.3201/eid0903.020208 [PMC free article] [PubMed]

Jones KE, Patel NG, Levy MA, et al. 2008. Global trends in emerging infectious diseases. Nature, 451:990–3. doi:10.1038/nature 06536 [PMC free article] [PubMed]

King L. 2011. Neglected Zoonotic diseases: Institute of Medicine (US), Forum on Microbial Threats, The causes and impacts of neglected tropical and Zoonotic diseases: opportunities for integrated intervention strategies. Washington: National Academies Press,. [PubMed]

Kumar, Vipan, Pal Heigo, Singh Bikram, Sharma Hanish, Kaur Parvinder and Wadhawan, V.M. 2015. Zoonoses in India: A review. *International Journal of Information Research and Review*, 2, (03): 562-564.

OIE Technical bulletin for control of zoonotic diseases.Wikipedia encyclopedia.

Shreeshan Venkatesh, Kundan Pandey. 2018. Why zoonotic diseases are fast spreading to humans. *Down to Earth*. Last Updated: Friday 08 June 2018

Taylor LH, Latham SM, Woolhouse ME (2001) Risk factors for disease emergence. *Philos Trans R Soc Lond B Biol Sci* 356: 983–989.

WHO (1982). Technical Report Series 682, "Bacterial and Viral Zoonoses"pp.1-145.

Woolhouse ME. 2008. Epidemiology: emerging diseases go global. *Nature*; 451:898–9. doi:10.1038/451898a [PubMed]

6

ICTs Interventions to Augment Agricultural Transformation in India

Bharat Bhushan, Pranav Kumar[1] and Santosh Sethi[2]

**Deputy Registrar (Acad.) SKUAST-J, Chatha, Jammu, Jammu and Kashmir India*
[1]Assistant Professor (VAHEE) SKUAST-Jammu, Jammu and Kashmir, India
[2]Assistant Professor (Sociology) RSD College, Ferozpur Punjab, India

1. Introduction
2. Priority areas of ICTs intervention
3. National and international IT enabled web tools for technology dissemination
4. Farmer call centre (Kissan call centre)
5. DHAN foundation
6. ISAP – community technology learning centres
7. Initiatives for Jammu and Kashmir
8. *References*

Abstract

ICT is contributing in every sphere of human society and agriculture cannot be an exception. It can bring revolutionary changes in farmers' life by improving accessibility to information and knowledge. Farmers certainly feel empowered and with confidence can opt for innovative approaches in business farming. Nearly 70 percent of the bottom fifth of the population in developing countries own a mobile phone. The number of internet users has more than tripled in a decade, from 1 billion in 2005 to an estimated 3.2 billion at the end of 2015. Thus, ICTs provide faster and newer ways of delivering and accessing information to many and are potential tools for poverty alleviation, health, education, judiciary, agricultural marketing and sustainable development. As per an ICAR report 80 per cent of the technologies generated by the researchers in agricultural sector are either not transferred to the ultimate users or they do not find applicability in the farmer's field. Out of the remaining 20 per cent of the technologies, around 50 per cent do not impress the farmers due to mainly its ineffective technology transfer that range from language to effective demonstration using the available tools. Information and communication technology revolution is the latest milestone in Indian agriculture that can usher an era of knowledge flow from institution to farmers field in much systematic and organized way and eliminate hurdles in technology transfer and adoption. From the perspective of agricultural knowledge and information systems (AKIS), ICTs can be seen as useful in improving linkages between the research, extension and the market sub systems. Real-time information and customized knowledge provided by 'e-Choupal' *enhance the ability of farmers to take decisions and align their farm output with market demand and secure quality and productivity. The* e-Krishi *project, Market driven Agricultural Initiative through IT enabled Agri-business Centres in Kerala, addresses the existing gap in agriculture information flow and transaction management. The touch screen kiosk with information on cattle health was tried and tested under a United Kingdom Department of International Development (DFID) – Animal Health Program (AHP) supported project on dissemination of animal health knowledge for development of landless dairy cattle owners in the peri-urban regions of Pondicherry. Being a global resource, and with billions of users, the Internet requires some degree of international cooperation on technical matters as well as on standards and norms that can ensure that it remains a global public good, facilitating information flows and contributing towards sustainable development.*

Keywords: ICTs, e-Choupal, e-Krishi, dairy toolbox, poultry expert system.

1. Introduction

ICTs are a diverse set of technological tools and resources to create, disseminate, store, bring value addition and manage information. In order to transform agriculture into information driven, modern and competitive sector, the role of information and communication technology (ICT) cannot be over-ruled. They provide faster and newer ways of delivering and accessing information. Thus, ICTs are potential tools for poverty alleviation, health, education, judiciary, agricultural marketing and sustainable development. Prior requisition for Sustainable Development is 'data revolution' to take advantage of new technologies, crowd sourcing, and improved connectivity to empower people with information on the progress towards the SDGs. Digital data provides an opportunity to gain a better insight in well-beings and emerging vulnerabilities, and to get real-time feedback on how well policy responses are working. Big Data initiatives already provide valuable information on land use changes around the world, crowd-sourcing facilitates the financial inclusion and market integration of small family farmers, but also provides real-time information on food price inflation. Global Pulse is a flagship innovation initiative of the United Nations Secretary-General working towards harnessing the potential of Big Data safely and responsibly for sustainable development and humanitarian action. Big Data creates unprecedented possibilities for informing decision-making, closing key gaps in access, transforming our society and protecting the environment. Increases in quality data and information will enable all stakeholders, governments, the private sector, the civil society and international organizations to identify problems, plan, monitor, and be held accountable for their actions (FAO, 2017). Thus, ICTs have become inevitable part of the programs initiated to achieve sustainable development goals (SDGs).

India is passing through the phase of communication revolution, which has brought about a significant growth of media in mass communication. ICTs that comprise communication devices or applications, encompassing cellular phones, computer, internet and network hardware and software, satellite systems and so on, as well as the various services and applications associated with them, such as video conferencing and distance learning find place in rural development programs. Information and communication technology revolution is the latest milestone in Indian agriculture to usher an era of knowledge flow from institution to farmers field in much systematic and organized way. It assists in implementation of precision crop farming, precision dairy farming, judicious applications of water, fertilizers and pesticides, matching production with demand, balancing distribution and availability, future projections and sustainability. It has become an important part of development initiatives in health, livestock farming, agriculture, family planning, education, and common man empowerment.

According to Selwyn (2002) information and communication Technology (ICT) is an umbrella term that includes computer hardware and software, digital broadcast and telecommunications technologies as well as digital information repositories online or offline and includes contemporary social networking aspects, read/write interfaces on the web besides file sharing systems online. It represents a broad and continually evolving range of elements that further includes the television (TV), radio, mobile phones and the policies and laws that govern the widespread use of these media and devices. The term is often used here in its plural sense (ICTs) to mean a range of technologies instead of a single technology. From the perspective of agricultural knowledge and information systems (AKIS), ICTs can be seen as useful in improving linkages between the research, extension and the market sub-systems. The experience of the rural tele centers in developing world shows that ICT can help in enabling rural development workers to gather, store, retrieve, adapt, localize and disseminate a broad range of information needed by rural families (Davison *et al.* 2005). The ICTs in extension can lead to the emergence of knowledge workers that will result in the realization of a bottom-up, demand-driven paradigm for technology generation, assessment, refinement and transfer (Meera, 2003; Meera *et al.* 2004).

According to the reports of the extension cell of ICAR, New Delhi, 80 per cent of the technologies generated by the researchers in agricultural sector are either not transferred to the ultimate users or they do not find applicability in the farmer's field. Out of the remaining 20 per cent of the technologies, around 50 per cent do not impress the farmers due to mainly its ineffective technology transfer that range from language to effective demonstration using the available tools. Now internet has emerged as the most powerful IT tool for storage and retrieval of information. It works around the clock and connects every nook and corner of the world. Information technology has connected the world globally and is now changing our lifestyle. There is no area of human life that has been untouched by IT sector. Agriculture and animal husbandry have also been influenced by IT in the present scenario of IT revolution although the share of IT in agriculture is only 1.3 per cent (Chargotra and Kanwat 2006).

ICTs are a diverse set of technological tools and resources to create, disseminate, store, bring value addition and manage information. In order to transform livestock sector into information driven, modern and competitive sector, the role of information and communication technology (ICT) cannot be over-ruled. They provide faster and newer ways of delivering and accessing information. The people working in the livestock sector are least equipped with proper tools to deal with rapidly changing livestock production scenario and international competitive environment. At present, the ratio of the farmers to extension workers is 1000:1 (Kumar, 2005), also existing transfer of technology mechanism and extension programs run by the government departments are slow and in many cases ineffective in view of the vast gaps between the research and farmers linkages. This is partly due to inadequate use of new areas of information dissemination in various development programmes. The introduction of ICT helps in upgrading the information at least cost.

Applications of IT in support of agricultural and rural development fall into five main areas, as outlined by Don Richardson (1996). These are:

- Economic development of agricultural producers
- Community development
- Research and education
- Small and medium enterprises development
- Media networks

Information and communication technologies are rapidly transforming the face of agriculture in industrialized countries. ICT infrastructures are very strong in such countries and e-commerce, e-business, e-procurement, e-auction activities have been in practice for past several years. High speed internet access in rural areas enables the farmers to access credit linkages, government programs and technical assistance to farmers through direct access. Many of the activities in the agricultural marketplace are nowadays mediated by web-linked to a database that specifies prices, qualities and quantities of essential agricultural commodities.

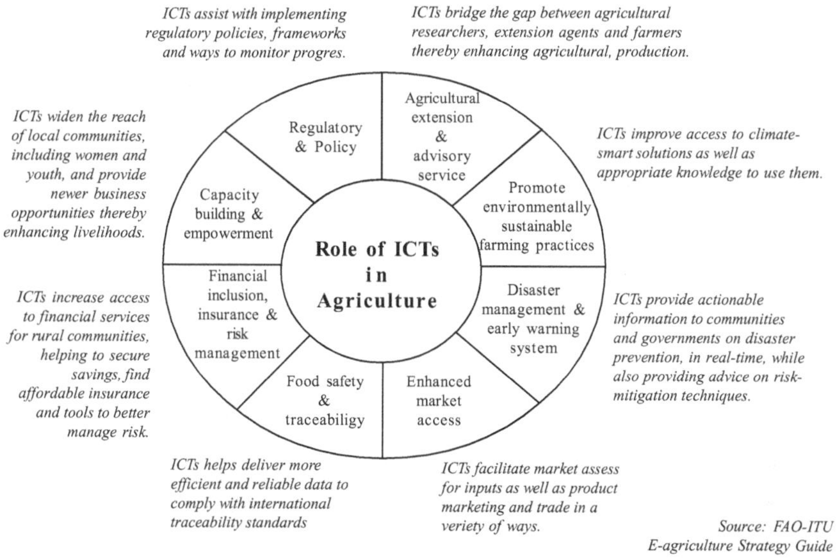

Fig. 1: Multi-prong role of ICTs in agric-transformation
Source: FAO-ITU E-agriculture Strategy Guide

The ICTs are potential tools for poverty alleviation, health, education, judiciary, agricultural marketing and sustainable development. The number of success stories in use of IT is growing. The Indian ICT initiatives and success stories are closely watched and appreciated world over. "India could lead the world in creating the grassroots social experiments that could teach both India and other nations how to use technology for the common good," says Kenneth Keniston (2004), a Professor at the Massachusetts Institute of Technology who follows such experiments globally. Unfortunately, grassroots ICT projects are not developed on sound principles and lack direction. Opportunities of IT in agriculture and rural development should be viewed as an investment rather than expenditure and focus on people's needs (Moni, 2004). Govt of India programs on use of ICTs are aimed at reducing the digital divide and empowering the rural people using this as yet one more policy instrument.

Before one can appreciate the importance of ICT's in livestock extension, it may be helpful to take a look at some of the limitations of traditional livestock extension techniques and processes. The traditional extension system costs a lot of money to produce and print materials. It involves a lot of time and efforts to deliver the message. The quality of extension messages gets heavily distorted and eroded when it ultimately reaches the end users. Most of the technical staff within the state departments of agriculture and animal husbandry lacks the capacity to effectively communicate with both the research system and the stakeholder group. On the other hand potential advantages of ICT's are that it saves money, time and effort. It cut steps involved in the dissemination of information among the farmers. The information is rich and interactive which creates a curiosity among farmers to know more about various innovations in agriculture and allied fields.

Zijp (1994) stated that there is a need for the dissemination of agricultural information through web based information and communication system to bring about sea change in the agricultural and rural development in terms of reduced costs, increased storage, easy use and speed. The important role of ICT is to provide two-way information flow between users and designers of the technology and to act as effective feedback mechanism (Roling 1995). With the millions of the internet subscribers using e-mail and World Wide Web (WWW), the internet is now considered a mass media. Individuals may soon consider such electronic connectivity as essential in daily living (James 1997)

The concept of village information shops is being discussed, debated and experimented at various places in India. Experiments include M S Swaminathan Research Foundation (MSSRF), Pondicherry, "information villages" of MANAGE in Ranga Reddy district in Andhra Pradesh. www.gyandoot.net initiative of district administration Dhar, Madhya Pradesh, EID-Parry's wireless in Local Loop based village kiosks in Cuddalore district of Tamilnadu and "Warna Wired Villages" of NIC in Kolhapur-Sangli districts of Maharashtra. The Wireless in Local Loop (WLL) technology developed by IIT Chennai has helped in providing the internet connectivity to 250 community kiosks that offers these services to over 700,000 people in rural India. To provide affordable computers in India, the Indian Institute of Science, Bangalore developed a low cost affordable personal computer named as 'Simputer'. In addition to the above, two interactive softwares, one for the Para Veterinarians and stockman entitled "Animal Health Information System" (AHIS) in English and another for the farmers of Maharashtra entitled "Health information system for dairy animals" in Marathi, have been developed at the Indian Veterinary Research Institute, Izatnagar, for animal health management and for animal disease diagnosis.

An information technology enabled 'Poultry Expert System'(PES) was developed using Visual Basic 6.0 and MS Access on selected dimensions of poultry farming. A total 29 items were considered for the measurement of applicability of PES, which were categorized into seven criteria: utility, complexity, compatibility, technicality, feasibility, design and other user attributes. This system had good technicality, feasibility and user friendly design and also brought improvement in the user attributes. In this way all these IT based projects are helping farmers in one or other way. Another major initiative in the corporate sector is Dairy Information System Kiosks (DISK) developed by Amul in Gujarat. DISK is a network of village milk societies.

2. Priority areas of ICTs intervention

a) Marketing networking

Transaction costs explain why markets are missing or do not function well. Small holders are not well integrated into markets due to high transport costs and their lack of ability to timely deliver consistent, quality and large volumes of produce. Consequence is emergence of false surpluses leading to wastage. With about one third of the food produced in the world for human consumption every year approximately 1.3 billion tons getting lost or wasted, there is need to improve awareness on the importance of sustainable consumption patterns, and information provided by ICT technologies, such as smart phone apps, can influence individuals and society to focus on the social, economic and environmental dimensions of food waste as now 50% of the world population is interconnected through mobile phones (FAO 2017).

b) Weather based agro-advisory

Climate change is a challenge to conventional, resource-intensive agricultural systems. Good agricultural practices, based on soil and water management and pest control, combined with improved access to markets, can lead to significant improvements in agricultural productivity, adapting to climate change. Sustainable production technologies are knowledge-intensive. Climate Smart Agriculture takes care of multiple objectives in agricultural growth and development under the specific constraints of climate change, building resilience and adaptive capacity in agricultural systems, while reducing and removing greenhouse gases to contribute to climate change mitigation. It requires knowledge on many aspects of farming including crop diversification, resource conservation, integrated farming system and sustainable cropping patterns etc. Weather extremities have become frequent events resulting in heavy crop and post harvest losses. Uncertainties in agriculture have increased over time. To large extent influence of climate change can be mitigated by providing weather based agro-advisory to farmers about timing of various crop operations so that wastage of agro-chemicals can be avoided. Similarly information about rain fall is necessary to undertake harvesting and and threshing operations.

3. National and international IT enabled Web tools for technology dissemination

3.1. Dairy Toolbox

The International Livestock Research Institute (ILRI) and International Crop Research Institute for Semi Arid Tropics (ICRISAT) developed **Dairy Toolbox**. It is an ICT based application with plenty of tools to carry out a job. It contain simple decision support tools as well as a broad range of modular information that can be easily accessed and compiled to form customized fact-sheets, or other extension materials, on a wide range of dairy related topics. The Dairy Toolbox was constructed with both web and CD interfaces so that it can be modified, expanded and updated. CDs allow distribution of updated information for those without access to the Internet. Many of the electronic tools of the toolbox can be used by the target institutions (extension workers, NGOs, producer groups, etc.) to produce customised paper-based tools for farmers /local extension workers where there is no access to either computers or the Internet. The Toolbox helps to overcome the constraints of poor access to appropriate information for a range of stakeholders including small-scale dairy farmers and extension delivery agents. In addition it supports the extension delivery agents or their clients to take a decision on whether particular practices are appropriate for their own circumstances (client's own objectives, management system, resource endowment or agro-climatic conditions).

3.2. Dairy Rationing System for the Tropics (DRASTIC)

This was developed with the objective of producing a genuinely usable, decision support tool for planning dairy feeding under tropical conditions. A major problem of rationing cows under these conditions is the lack of information on the nutritional quality of available feeds - particularly of the basal ration. This is compounded by a high degree of variation in feed quality that makes routine chemical analysis or reliance on "book values" for composition of little practical use. The following key requirements were addressed during the development of DRASTIC:

- It has a user-friendly design
- No expert knowledge of nutrition is needed to use it.

- Nutritional variables in the underlying model are assessed from simple indicators of feed quality allowing DRASTIC to cope with variable feed compositions in the absence of quantitative data (Adopted from: *http://www.stirlingthorne.com*)

3.3. Talking Pictures

It is a dynamic pictorial system used to represent the nutritional management of dairy cows in smallholder farming systems. This computer-based tool builds on the principles used in the development of DRASTIC, using the DRASTIC software to generate pictorial guides in hard copy. The hard copies consist of several separate pictorial layers that incorporate genotype, condition, stage of lactation and physiological status, calf rearing system, and quantity and quality of feed inputs (basal and supplements), which are dynamically linked and provide pictorial answers for the expected production outputs, costs and income. The A4 hard-copy guides are produced in such a way that users can choose one of three options, appropriate to each specific animal, for each of five pictorial input layers viz.,

- Lactation and physiological status
- Health condition
- Calf rearing system
- Quality of the basal diet
- Quantity of the basal diet

Each option is either colour-or pattern-coded, depending on whether colour or black-and-white printers are used to generate the hard-copy guides. The pattern or colour for each of the chosen input layer options is transferred with dry-wipe markers to a reusable laminated "credit card", leading to a unique sequence of five colours or patterns. This sequence is matched to the appropriate sequence out of 243 possibilities, supplied on three pages and linked to a pictorial representation of the expected production level for the animal in question. Based on this, users turn to the appropriate supplementation page, indicated by the picture of the expected production level. On these pages, users can select from different pictorial representations of supplementary feeds and different levels of supplementation, which are connected to a picture of the total milk production expected. Each of the supplementation choices also supplies pictorial data on the ratio between milk and concentrate prices at which supplementation of the chosen quantity becomes profitable (Adopted from: *http://www. stirlingthorne. com*).

3.4. RAGACOVAS touch screen based Information Kiosk

Ramkumar and Rao (2004) reported that for knowledge dissemination on Cattle health through information kiosks in veterinary centres the Rajiv Gandhi College of Veterinary and Animal Sciences has developed **Touch Screen-based Information kiosk** which has 17 inch Touch screen monitor and installed learning modules on dairy and goat farming made up of text, pictures, graphics and audio files. The learning modules can be accessed from kiosk through user-friendly interface. These touch screen based information kiosks was installed in various livestock related service centres (dispensaries, insemination centres and milk cooperative societies). In general when a farmer comes with animal for treatment or other services he / she need to wait for while for his / her turn. During this waiting time staffs of the service centres directs and helps the farmers to check what is available in Information Kiosk. Here the waiting time is converted to value added time. Once the farmers are familiarized with usage of interactive touch screen he helps his fellow colleagues to learn.

3.5. Poultry expert system from College of Veterinary Sciences, Hyderabad

Department of Veterinary & Animal Husbandry Extension Education and College of Veterinary & Animal Sciences, Hyderabad, developed **Poultry Expert System**. This expert system puts series of questions to end-users on the status of farm, feeding practices, egg yield, mortality pattern etc. From the answers of the end-users, the system identifies possible disease or condition. It has user-friendly interface, which helps the poultry farmers to diagnose disease.

3.6. Dairy Information System Kiosk (DISK) developed by AMUL, Anand

Dairy Information System Kiosk has been developed by Anand Milk Union Ltd, Gujarat with support of Indian Institute of Management, Ahmedabad. This DISK facilitates horizontal networking of all milk produces cooperative societies and vertical networking with district level milk union and state level federations with internet connectivity. DISK has dairy portal at district level serving transactional and information needs of co-operative staffs, members (farmers), and other stakeholders. Farmers have facilities to place orders for goods and services offered by different agencies in the co-operative sector and seek information on subjects of interest.

3.7. iKisan

iKisan is a comprehensive Agricultural Portal initiated by the Nagarjuna Fertilizers and chemicals Ltd., in South India. iKisan is addressing the Information,

Knowledge and Business requirements of various players in the Agriculture arena *viz.*, Farmers, Trade channel partners and Agri Input/Output companies. Leveraging Information Technology and extensive field presence, ikisan is positioned as an Information/ Knowledge exchange. Agriculture information; Crop Specific, Package of Practices of crops, Animal Husbandry, Aromatic and Medicinal Plants, Agricultural Machinery, Allied Agriculture, Sprayers, Rural Credit, Insurance iKisan crop solutions; farmers have a critical need to get timely solutions for protecting and nurturing their crops to get best yields. Addressing this key need, iKisan has developed easy to-use diagnostic packages for different crops which will be provided on demand. Further, it also provides local agri news, weather and market information to the farmers (*http://www.ikisan.com*).

3.8. e-Krishi

The *e-Krishi* project, Market driven Agricultural Initiative through IT enabled Agri Business Centres in Kerala, addresses the existing gap in agriculture information flow and transaction management. The project envisages facilitating and enabling farmers and other Stakeholders through Agri Business Centres to interact with Agricultural Service Providers in the Private, Government and Non Government sectors. The project provides a web based solution enabling the small and medium farmers as well as owners of large landholdings. Piloting was done in Malappuram with the participation of the existing *Akshaya e-Kendra* Entrepreneurs. The facilities and resources of *Akshaya e-Kendras* in terms of computers, printers, scanners, cameras, etc. and intranet/internet connectivity, already established throughout Malappuram District of Kerala (about 550 *e-Kendras*), can be leveraged to reach the masses of farming community and other stakeholders in Agriculture sector which can help the farmers in many ways. The *e-Krishi* portal also provides Farm Advisory Services (Crop Information, Fertiliser Recommendation, Planting Material Availability, Fertilizers and Pesticides, Weather Information), AgriMarket Information (Vegetable and Fruit Price, Daily Market Price, Market Analysis Report and Commodity Exchange), Resource Library: *e-Krishi* Eco-System, *e-Krishi* information centres, Photo Gallery, Model *e-Krishi* Project, KISSAN Video Channel. Further, *e-Krishi* news and online expert advisory, trade login and call centre support are the special features of the e-Krishi web portal (*http://www.e-krishi.org*).

3.9. Touch Screen Kiosk

The touch screen kiosk with information on cattle health was tried and tested under a United Kingdom Department of International Development (DFID) – Animal Health Programme (AHP) supported project on dissemination of animal health knowledge for development of landless dairy cattle owners in the peri-urban regions of Pondicherry, India (2002- 2004) by the Rajiv Gandhi College of Veterinary and Animal Sciences, Pondicherry, India in collaboration with the University of Reading, UK. The kiosks were installed in the veterinary centre and veterinary dispensary. The cattle owners bring their animals to the veterinary dispensary for treatment or Artificial Insemination (AI) and register the case. After that they will wait for their turn to come for service delivery. That waiting time is utilized for getting information from the kiosk.

e-Extension (e-Soil Health Card Program)

The Department of Agriculture, Gujarat State, India initiated office automation, networking and e-communication among department staff, digital data bank generation, management, storing and retrieving computerisation of farmer centric applications, web site, e-soil health card scheme. The crop estimation survey, online management and monitoring of Government schemes, online farmer accident insurance scheme applications and status, crop wise sowing area, crop and weather condition data will be ,entered online and state level weekly reports are generated automatically. It also provides online monitoring of individual beneficiary schemes and extension programmes (*Krishi Mahotsav*) and online applications for natural calamity, *etc.* The e-Soil Health Card Programme, an e-Agricultural extension service programme, is one of the ambitious programmes which aims to analyse the soil of all the villages of the state and proposes to provide online guidance to farmers on their soil health condition, fertilizer usage and alternate cropping pattern (*www.agri.gujarat.gov.in; www.shc.gujarat.gov.in*)

3.10. ITC e-Choupal

ITC's Agri Business Division, one of India's largest exporters of agricultural commodities, has conceived e-Choupal as a more efficient supply chain aimed at delivering value to its customers around the world on a sustainable basis. The e-Choupal model has been specifically designed to tackle the challenges posed by the unique features of Indian agriculture, characterized by fragmented farms, weak infrastructure and the involvement of numerous intermediaries, among others. e-Choupal also unshackles the potential of Indian farmer who has been trapped in a vicious cycle of low risk taking ability – low investment - low productivity – weak market orientation - low value addition - low margin - low risk taking ability. This made him and Indian agribusiness sector globally uncompetitive, despite rich and abundant natural resources. Such a market-led business model can enhance the competitiveness of Indian agriculture and trigger a virtuous cycle of higher productivity, higher income, enlarged capacity for farmer risk management, larger investments, higher quality and productivity.

Appreciating the imperative of intermediaries in the Indian context, 'e-Choupal' leverages Information Technology to virtually cluster all the value chain participants, delivering the same benefits as vertical integration. '*e-Choupal*' makes use of the physical transmission capabilities of current intermediaries – aggregation, logistics, counter-party risk and bridge financing -while disinter mediating them from the chain of information flow and market signals. With a judicious blend of click facility and user interactive mode and mortar capabilities, village internet kiosks managed by farmers – called sanchalaks – themselves, enable the agricultural community access ready information in their local language on the weather and market prices, disseminate knowledge on scientific farm practices and risk management, facilitate the sale of farm inputs and purchase farm produce from the farmers' doorsteps. Real-time information and customized knowledge provided by '*e-Choupal*' enhance the ability of farmers to take decisions and align their farm output with market demand and secure quality and productivity. The aggregation of the demand for farm inputs from individual farmers gives them access to high quality inputs from established and reputed manufacturers at fair prices. As a direct marketing channel, virtually linked to the 'mandi' system for price discovery, '*e-Choupal*' eliminates wasteful intermediation and multiple handling. Thereby it significantly reduces transaction costs. '*e-Choupal*' ensures world-class quality in delivering all these goods & services through several product / service specific partnerships with the leaders in the respective fields, in addition to ITC's own expertise. While the farmers benefit through enhanced farm productivity and higher farm gate prices, ITC benefits from the lower net cost of procurement (despite offering better prices to the farmer) having eliminated costs in the supply chain that do not add value. Launched in June 2000, '*e-Choupal*' has already become the largest initiative among all Internet-based interventions in rural India. '*e-Choupal*' services today reach out to more than 4 million farmers growing a range of crops - soyabean, coffee, wheat, rice, pulses, shrimp - in over 40,000 villages through 6450 kiosks across 8 states (Madhya Pradesh, Karnataka, Andhra Pradesh, Uttar Pradesh, Maharashtra, Rajasthan, Uttaranchal and Tamil Nadu). The problems encountered while setting up and managing these '*e-Choupals*' are primarily of infrastructural inadequacies, including power supply, telecom connectivity, internet, mobile internet, kiosk and bandwidth, apart from the challenge of imparting skills to the first Time internet users in remote and inaccessible areas of rural India (Source:*http://www.echoupal.com*).

4. Farmer Call Centre (Kissan Call Centre)

The Department of Agriculture & Cooperation (DoA&C), Ministry of Agriculture, Govt. of India launched *Kisan* Call Centres on January 21, 2004, across the country to deliver extension services to the farming community. The purpose of these call centres is to respond to issues raised by farmers, instantly, in the local language. There are call centres for every state which are expected to handle traffic from any part of the country. Queries related to agriculture and allied sectors are being addressed through these call centres. The *Kisan* Call Centre is a synthesis of two hitherto separate technologies namely, the Information and Communication Technology (ICT) and the Agricultural Technology. Both have their specialized domains and work cultures. To optimally utilize the strengths of both these systems, it was proposed to take full advantage of professionally managed Call Centre mechanism and dovetail it with the specialized Subject Matter Specialists knowledge of Agricultural Scientists and Extension Officers, so as to facilitate its reach to the farming community. It is accordingly proposed to make use of existing specialized infrastructure of Call Centres (which are normally industry driven and serve to high-end and many a times, mission critical service sector) and make this communication backbone available to the Subject Matter Specialists of Agriculture, Horticulture, Animal Husbandry, Marketing and other related areas. The *Kisan* Call Centre consists of three levels – namely Level-I (the basic Call Centre interface, with high quality bandwidth and local language proficient Agriculture Graduate), Level-II (Subject Matter Specialists on concerned important crops and enterprises, connected through good bandwidth telecom and computer connectivity) and Level-III (the Management Group to ensure ultimate answering and resolution of all the farmers' queries which are not resolved at Level-II, connected on off line mode).

5. DHAN Foundation

Development of Humane Action (DHAN) Foundation, a professional development organisation, was initiated on October 2, 1997. DHAN Foundation has taken up Information Technology for poor as a new theme with the following objectives: making information technology accessible to poor by developing relevant schemes through research and pilot activities and collaborating with research and academic institutions on e-governance and computer education at schools in rural areas. As part of the programme, internet kiosks in the rural areas as well as urban slums are set up through which services such as computer education, e-mail, ePost, agricultural market intelligence, *etc*., are rendered.(*http://www.dhan.org/themes/itforpoor.php*).

6. ISAP- Community Technology Learning Centres (CTLCs)

Indian Society of Agribusiness Professionals (ISAP), a non-governmental professional society- with support of Microsoft - Unlimited Potential Programme has established 'Community Technology Learning Centres (CTLCs)' in remote villages of Maharashtra to provide IT training to 450 00 farmers and unemployed youth. Under two-year programme, ISAP would be setting up 250 CTLCs at village level for imparting IT training to rural community and increase their income earning potential. ISAP is working on online weekly price monitoring system of herbal and medicinal plants with the funding support of National Medicinal Plant Board. ISAP gathers and manages authentic data about the weekly price and demand for 101 medicinal plants from 50-marketing centers in different states of the country. These data are weekly upgraded on the basis of prices and quantity offered for different medicinal plants (ISAP 2008).

7. Initiative for J&K

Major part of Jammu and Kashmir (J&K) is comprised of rural areas, which are under-developed and lack access to ICT tools as compared to their urban counterparts. The main reasons for this under-development are: low priority assigned by the government in developing the infrastructure and lack of interest of private sector to exploit the potential of rural sector. On an average, 2.9% population of Jammu and Kashmir has internet access (Internet Census Report, 2011). However, this is showing an ever increasing trend in the recent past. It is very important in context of the dissemination of the information via internet. State Agricultural Universities like SKUAST-J and SKUAST-K need to play an important role through its KVKs in motivating farmers for use of ICT to manage knowledge and undertake production and productivity by balancing activities in response to market demand, which will impart commercial sustainability to farming in J&K and raising the socio-economic status of farmers.

8. References

Chargotra M and Kanwat M .2006. Use of information technology in agriculture. *Agriculture Today* IX(7): 17-19.

FAO UN. 2017. Information and Communication Technology (ICT) in Agriculture. A Report to the G20 Agricultural Deputies. Pp 27.

James .1997. Opportunities for co-operative extension and local communities in the information age. *Journal of Extension* 35(5): 28-34.

Keniston K .2001. Grassroots ICT projects in India: A preliminary hypotheses. *E-Gateway*. (Online journal) 3(11).

Kumar S .2004. A study on management of dairy farming training programmes in MYRADA KVK in Tamil Nadu. M.Sc. Thesis, NDRI, Deemed University, Karnal (India).

Meera Shaik N. 2003. A critical analysis of information technology in agricultural development: impact and implications. Unpublished PhD. Thesis, IARI, New Delhi.

Meera Shaik N, Jhamtani A and Rao DUM .2004. Information and communication technology in agriculture, a comparative analysis from three projects of India. AgREN network paper No. 135, ODI, January 2004. Available at: *http://www.ejisdc.org/ojs2/index.php/ejisdc/article/view/90/90.*

Ramkumar S and Rao SVN .2004. Knowledge Dissemination on Cattle health through information kiosks in veterinary centres. Published by Rajiv Gandhi College of Veterinary and Animal Sciences Pondicherry, in collaboration with the University of Reading, UK and supported by the DFID animal health program.

Richardson D. 1996. The internet and rural development: recommendations for strategy and activity–Final Report. Rome: Sustainable Development Department of the Food and Agriculture Organisation of the United Nations. *http://www.fao.org/sd-dimensions*.

Roling .1995. What to think of extension? A comparison of three models of extension practices, *AERDDB Bulletin*.

Selwyn C .2002. Getting the organization to adopt e--learning from challenge to action. Technical report printed to Hathworne Associate White.

Zijp W .1994. Improving the transfer and use of agricultural information: a guide to information technology. World Bank discussion papers: 105 and 247.

Annexure

G20 Digital Economy Development and Cooperation Initiative

I. Overview: Global Economy in a Digitized World

1. During their meeting in Antalya in 2015, the G20 leaders recognized that we are living in an age of Internet economy that brings both opportunities and challenges to global growth. In 2016, the G20 will address ways to collectively leverage digital opportunities, cope with challenges, and promote the digital economy to drive inclusive economic growth and development.

2. The digital economy refers to a broad range of economic activities that include using digitized information and knowledge as the key factor of production, modern information networks as an important activity space, and the effective use of information and communication technology (ICT) as an important driver of productivity growth and economic structural optimization. Internet, cloud computing, big data, Internet of Things (IoT), fintech and other new digital technologies are used to collect, store, analyze, and share information digitally and transform social interactions. Digitized, networked and intelligent ICTs enable modern economic activities to be more flexible, agile and smart.

3. The digital economy is experiencing high growth, rapid innovation, and broad application to other economic sectors. It is an increasingly important driver of global economic growth and plays a significant role in accelerating economic development, enhancing productivity of existing industries, cultivating new markets and industries, and achieving inclusive, sustainable growth.

4. While recognizing existing national, regional, and global strategies on digital and internet issues between and among different stakeholders, the G20 Digital Economy Task Force (DETF) has taken the unique advantage of the G20 to help address both opportunities and challenges brought by ICTs, and propose some common understanding, principles and key areas for the development and cooperation of the digital economy. The G20 promotes communication and cooperation among its members and beyond to make sure strong, vibrant and connected ICTs will enable a thriving and dynamic digital economy, which drives global growth and benefits for all.

II. Guiding Principles: A Compass for Navigation

5. G20 members agree on the following common principles to promote the development of and cooperation in the digital economy:

Innovation

Technological innovation in ICTs as well as innovation in ICT-driven economic activities is among the key driving forces of inclusive economic growth and development.

Partnership

In order to improve cooperation, address common challenges, and advance the global digital economy, closer partnership among G20 members can help share knowledge, information and experiences, so that differences can be narrowed and various interests can be advanced through constructive dialogues. The G20 recognizes the Internet is an important part of modern information network that sustain digital economy. Internet governance should continue to follow the provisions set forth in outcomes of World Summit on the Information Society (WSIS). In particular, we affirm our commitment to a multi-stakeholder approach to Internet governance, which includes full and active participation by governments, private sector, civil society, the technical community, and 33 international organizations, in their respective roles and responsibilities. We support multi-stakeholder processes and initiatives which are inclusive, transparent and accountable to all stakeholders in achieving the digitally connected world.

Synergy

Since the digital economy touches almost all economic and social sectors and is closely related to other topics in the G20, particularly innovation and the new industrial revolution, it is the common aspiration of G20 members to create synergy among discussions of these topics in order to avoid duplication and ensure consistency.

Flexibility

The G20 recognizes the importance of flexibility given the different concerns and priorities of members.

Inclusion

The G20 members should work together with all stakeholders, to bridge all manner of digital divide and foster entrepreneurship, innovation, and economic activity, including further development of content and services in a variety of languages and formats that are accessible to all people, who also need the capabilities and capacities, including media, information and digital literacy skills, to make use of and further develop information and communications technologies. Accordingly, we recognize the vital importance of the principles of multilingualism to ensure the linguistic, cultural and historical diversity of all nations. Digital inclusion and the use of digital technology to enhance inclusion should remain key elements in promoting the digital economy to ensure that no one is left behind, regardless of their gender, region, age, disability or economic status. The G20 members recognize the potential of the digital economy to facilitate the implementation of the 2030 Agenda for Sustainable Development.

Open and enabling business environment

The G20 recognizes the critical importance of private sector on digital economy as well as of enabling and transparent legal, regulatory, and policy environments, and fostering open, competitive markets. Recognize the importance of enforcing competition and consumer protection laws in the digital economy, which are conducive to market access, technological innovation in ICTs and the growth of the digital economy.

Flow of Information for Economic Growth, Trust and Security

G20 members recognize that freedom of expression and the free flow of information, ideas, and knowledge, are essential for the digital economy and beneficial to development, as reaffirmed in paragraph 4 of the Tunis Commitment of WSIS. We support ICT policies that preserve the global nature of the Internet, promote the flow of information across borders and allow Internet users to lawfully access online information, knowledge and services of their choice. At the same time, the G20 recognizes that applicable frameworks for privacy and personal data protection, as well as intellectual property rights, have to be respected as they are essential to strengthening confidence and trust in the digital economy. The security of ICT enabled critical infrastructure needs to be enhanced, so that ICTs can continue to be a reliable driving force in accelerating economic development. 34

III. Key Areas: Unleash Greater Potential of Digital Economy

In line with the above principles, the DETF identifies priorities for cooperation in digital economy, to provide favorable conditions for its development, boost economic growth, and ensure digital inclusion. To this end, members are encouraged to:

6. Expand broadband access and improve quality

- Accelerate network infrastructure construction and facilitate interconnection. Promote the establishment of Internet Exchange Points (IXPs). Encourage all countries to make Internet access central to development and growth initiatives.
- Promote broadband network coverage, and improve service capacity and quality within a legally predictable competitive environment. In particular, explore ways to expand high-speed internet access and connectivity at affordable price.

7. Promote investment in the ICT Sector

- Improve the business environment through policy frameworks that facilitate research, development and innovation (RDI) as well as investment, including cross-border investment in the digital economy. Welcome Public Private Partnerships and commercial equity investment funds as well as social funds to invest in ICT infrastructure and ICT applications. Encourage development of open source technologies and other technologies.
- Encourage the organization of investment information exchange events among ICT companies and financial institutions, and mutual investment in the ICT sector among G20 members.

8. Support entrepreneurship and promote digital transformation

- Encourage internet-based RDI and entrepreneurship through an enabling, transparent legal framework, programs to support RDI and well-functioning capital markets for innovative enterprises. Support developing and emerging countries to build capacities in digital technology and internet-based entrepreneurship.
- Take advantage of the internet to promote innovation in products, services, processes, organizations and business models.
- Encourage the integration of digital technology and manufacturing, to build a more connected, networked, and intelligent manufacturing sector. Take advantage of ICTs to improve education, health and safety, environmental protection, urban plan, healthcare and other public services. Promote the continued development of service sectors such as e-commerce, e-government, e-logistics, online tourism, and Internet finance and the sharing economy. Promote digitization of agricultural production, operation, management, and networked transformation of agricultural products distribution.

- Create conditions for broadband providers to promote expansion, innovation, consumer protection, and competition, including examining the possibilities of introducing policies to prevent anti-competitive blocking, throttling, or prioritization of data by commercial broadband networks. We note the important regulatory and legislative processes in some members on the open Internet in the context of digital economy and the underlying drivers for it, and call for further information-sharing at the international level on the opportunities and challenges.

9. Encourage e-commerce cooperation

- Promote cross-border trade facilitation for e-commerce by using trusted digital means, such as paperless customs clearance, electronic transaction documents, mutual recognition of digital authentication, electronic payment and online payment. Meanwhile, strengthen cooperation to prevent barriers to market access and other barriers. Attention should be given to issues relating to taxation, such as ensuring the efficient payment of appropriate taxes for international e-commerce, taking into account in particular the Base Erosion and Profit Shifting (BEPS) issues. Improve international efforts to measure e-commerce, and the macroeconomic consequences of digital economy.
- Strengthen cooperation in protecting consumers' rights and develop dispute resolution approaches, ensuring options for consumers that are adapted to the characteristics of e-commerce within the national framework of laws and regulations provided that they are consistent with member's international legal obligations.
- Build confidence of users which is an essential element of the digital economy by ensuring the respect of privacy and protection of personal data.

10. Enhance digital inclusion

- Use a variety of policy measures and technical means to bridge the digital divides between and within countries, in particular between developed and developing countries, regions and groups, including between men and women, and promote universal access, including open access to the Internet with equal digital opportunities for all. Promote the broadband connectivity among the poorest citizens, especially the poorest 20 percent of citizens, and citizens from low-density areas and strive to provide universal and affordable access to the Internet in least developed countries. Reaffirm the goal of ensuring the next 1.5 billion people are connected and have meaningful access to the Internet by 2020 in accordance with the Connect 2020 agenda.

- Promote the use of technology in primary and secondary education as well as in non-formal education, including in libraries, museums, and other community-based organizations to reduce disparities between income levels and promote development of a workforce for the digital economy. Strive towards ensuring an increased number of primary and secondary students have lawful access to educational content, and broadband connectivity as well as digital tools in their classrooms.
- Promote digital technologies for societal benefits such as food distribution, education, health, subsidy distribution, governance.
- Recognizing that the digital economy may pose risks and challenges in terms of skills shortages and mismatches and rising inequality for those who might be left behind because they lack skills, it is important to promote the dissemination of digital skills and more competitive workforces through cooperation among academic institutions and technical schools, libraries, businesses and community organizations. Improve digital skills of all people, the youth as well as the elderly, women and men, persons with disabilities, the illiterate and vulnerable populations as well as those in low income and developing countries, to enable their participation in the digital economy to unleash the potential of creating opportunities for quality job creation, decent work provision as well as for income growth and improving welfare. Strengthen cooperation in protecting labor rights.

11. Promote development of MSMEs

- Promote policies that support micro, small and medium-sized enterprises (MSMEs) to use ICT technology for innovation, improved competitiveness, and new distribution channels in markets.
- Promote affordable digital infrastructures needed for the digitization of MSME operations.
- Encourage MSMEs to provide ICTs goods and services to the public sectors and to participate in global value chains.
- Encourage participation in efforts, such as the Global Enterprise Registration initiative, to make transparent and simple the business registration mechanisms.

IV. Policy Support: For an Open and Secure Environment

The G20 aims to encourage exchange of views, promote mutual understanding and strengthen cooperation in policy making and regulation. To this end, members are encouraged to:

12. Intellectual Property

Recognize the key role of adequate and effective protection and enforcement of intellectual property rights to the development of the digital economy, as reaffirmed by paragraph 26 of the G20 Antalya Communique.

13. Promote cooperation with respect to independent choice of development path

Encourage members engaging in international cooperation to reduce, eliminate, or prevent unnecessary differences in regulatory requirements to unleash the digital economy, recognizing that all members should chart development paths that are consistent with their international legal obligations and their development situations, historical and cultural traditions, national legal systems, and national development strategies.

14. Cultivate transparent digital economy policy-making

- Develop and maintain open, transparent, inclusive, evidence-based digital economy policy making which takes into account the full input of all public and private stakeholders. Solicit their comments publicly before laws, regulations, policies and other instruments are deliberated, developed and implemented.
- Encourage publishing of relevant, publicly available government data, recognizing the potential to boost new technology, products and services.
- Encourage intelligent public procurement schemes to support the production of innovative digital services and products by the private sector, whilst keeping the need to be market led.

15. Support the development and use of international standards

Support the development and their use of the international standards for technological products and services that are consistent with the international rules including WTO rules and principles.

16. Strengthen confidence and trust

- Promote the availability, integrity, confidentiality and authenticity of online transactions. Encourage the development of secure information infrastructure to promote trusted, stable, and reliable internet applications.
- As part of our efforts to address security risks, threats and vulnerabilities in the use of ICT, including those to ICT-enabled critical infrastructures, endeavor to strengthen international collaboration, capacity building and public-private partnerships, including through constructive discussions in relevant international fora. Support and encourage the use of risk-based

technical standards, guidelines, and best-practices to identify, assess, and manage security risk by both the public and private sectors.

- Jointly combat cybercrime and protect ICT environment by strengthening international cooperation on these issues in online transactions.

17. Manage radiofrequency spectrum to promote innovation

Recognize the importance of efficient management of radiofrequency spectrum to achieve the full potential of the mobile revolution in the time of digital economy.

V. Way Forward: Actions to Make a Difference

Recognizing that the digital shifts underway are reshaping economies and societies today and will continue to do so in the future, the G20 agrees to cooperate and continue to work closely on these matters. In this regard, the G20 will:

- Encourage multi-level exchanges, involving stakeholders such as governments, the private sector, civil society, international organizations, technical and academic communities as well as other parties such as industry organizations and worker organizations to share views and promote cooperation in digital economy.
- Encourage G20 members to exchange experience on policy making and legislation, and share best practices among members.
- Encourage training and research cooperation in digital economy issues to benefit the developing countries of the G20.
- Welcome and encourage efforts made by the United Nations, UNCTAD, UNIDO, ILO, IMF, ITU, OECD, World Bank Group and other international organizations to develop better metrics for important policy issues like trust in the digital economy, e-commerce, cross-border data flows, and the Internet of Things, as practical, relevant and appropriate.
- Look forward to IOs including the OECD and interested members, intensifying efforts to measure the digital economy in macroeconomic statistics through conducting a voluntary "good practices" survey of national statistical organizations, and organizing and hosting a workshop for statisticians and digital companies on source data to measure the digital economy.
- Interact actively with other engagement groups such as the B20, L20 and T20 to exchange views among industry, business, civil society, and academia to pool ideas on how to promote a sound digital economy.

(**Reproduced from ICT in Agriculture published by FAO, 2017 for the benefit of readers*)

7

Climate Smart Agriculture: More Returns at the Farm Through Climate Change Mitigation

Jag Paul Sharma

Directorate of Research, SKUAST Jammu, Chatha (J&K), Jammu & Kashmir, India

Abstract

Climate change is well acknowledged fact globally and in India has been witnessed with more frequent cloud bursts, highly variable frequency and distribution of rainfall, high seasonal thermal variations, receding glaciers and unstable agricultural production. Likely impact of climate change is expected to reduce agricultural productivity, production stability and incomes in some areas that already have high levels of food insecurity. However, Agriculture has the potential to retard the pace of climate change by capturing a significant part of the excess atmospheric carbon in the soil and plants in the form of organic matter and also competent to reduce emissions of nitrous oxide and methane if practiced in smart ways so developing climate-smart agriculture is thus crucial in achieving future food security and climate change goals. Transformations are needed in both commercial and subsistence agricultural systems, but with significant differences in priorities and capacity. Several climate smart agriculture practices such as cropping system improvement (e.g. crop rotation, diversification, improved varieties and integration of legumes), integrated nutrient management (e.g. green manure, compost and site specific nutrient management), resource conservation (e.g. minimum/zero tillage, keeping the land consistently covered with crop residues), precision water management (e.g. planting crops in bed, laser land leveling, mulching with crop residues) and agro-forestry have been proposed for adaptation to climate change and variability. However, their adoption decisions by the farmers are largely dependent on economic benefits associated with the interventions. It should be clearly understood that climate smart agriculture does not make use of different practices but certainly it uses them differently.

1. Introduction

Climate change is a change in the statistical distribution of weather patterns when it lasts for an extended period of time (i.e., decades to millions of years). It is perceived in significant changed pattern of GHGs, global warming and rainfall pattern. Two most important greenhouse gases are nitrous oxide from soils and methane from cattle, but carbon dioxide emission due to conversion of forests to crop land and due to fossil fuel consumption becomes the primary greenhouse gas that is largely contributing to recent climate change. Atmospheric CO_2 concentrations have increased by more than 40% since pre-industrial times, from approximately 280 parts per million by volume (ppmv) in the 18th century to over 400 ppmv in 2015(Fig.1). Climate models indicate that rising temperatures may have a beneficial effect on crops in the temperate areas. Tropical and subtropical areas, however, may experience significant reductions in crop productivity in a long-term perspective, i.e., towards 2080 (Fig. 2). Projections of future climate change anticipate an additional warming of 2.0 to 11.5°F (1.1 to 6.4°C) over the 21st century, on top of the 1.4°F already observed over the past 100 years. Warming is and will be greatest over land areas and higher latitudes. Climate change occurring, is largely caused by human activities, and poses significant risks for a broad range of human and natural systems. Projected impacts could be, more warmed atmosphere, sharp thermal fluctuations, low water availability, highly variable precipitation pattern associated with flood and drought, glaciers melting, coral reef bleaching as a result of increasing temperatures, rising sea levels, and ocean acidification, higher risk exposures to coastal ecosystems and threat to life in cold arid zone.

Climate change is also driving changes in the timing of seasonal biological activities. Many biological events, especially those in the spring and autumn, are based on seasonal cues. Studies have found that the seasonal behaviors of many species now happen 15–20 days earlier than several decades ago. Migrant birds are arriving earlier, butterflies are emerging sooner, and plants are budding and blooming earlier. Hence with regards to climate change it is now affirmed that

- That climate change is unequivocal
- Anthropogenic activities contribute significantly to climate change
- Climate change is being experienced in all regions of the world
- Warming of oceans and atmosphere is well acknowledged
- Volume of snow and ice has reduced significantly
- Glaciers have receded and are receding
- Sea level is rising
- Weather extremities have become more frequent
- Agriculture, horticulture, livestock and wild life affected

As decision makers respond to these risks, the global scientific community should contribute both by continuing to improve understanding of the causes and consequences of climate change, and by improving and expanding the options available to limit the magnitude of climate change and adapt to its impacts. There is need to have a comprehensive, integrated, and effective climate change research institutions that are closely linked with action-oriented programs at all levels.

Likely impact of climate change is expected to reduce agricultural productivity, production stability and incomes in some areas that already have high levels of food insecurity. Estimates show that world population will grow from the current 6.7 billion to 9 billion by 2050 with most of the increase occurring in South Asia and sub-Saharan Africa. Taking into account the changes in the composition and level of consumption associated with growing household incomes, FAO estimates that feeding the world population will require a 60 percent increase in total agricultural production (Bruinsma, 2009). With many of the resources needed for sustainable food security already stretched, the food security challenges are huge. At the same time climate change is already negatively impacting agricultural production globally and locally. Climate risks to cropping, livestock and fisheries are expected to increase in coming decades, particularly in low-income countries where adaptive capacity is weaker. Hence agriculture in developing countries must undergo a significant transformation in order to meet the challenges of achieving food security and responding to climate change.

International community adopted Green Climate Fund (GCF) as a financial mechanism of the UN Framework Convention on Climate Change (UNFCCC) at the end of 2011 to make an ambitious contribution to attaining the mitigation and adaptation goals at the global level. Thus, Green Climate Fund (GCF) is a fund within the framework of the UNFCCC founded as a mechanism to assist developing countries in adaptation and mitigation practices to counter climate change. The GCF became fully operational in 2015. The GCF is a legally independent institution with a fully independent secretariat headed by an Executive Secretary. The GCF is based in the New Songdo district of Incheon, South Korea. It is governed by a Board of 24 members and initially supported by a Secretariat. 'The Green Climate Fund will support projects, programs, policies and other activities in developing country parties using thematic funding windows. It is intended to be the centre piece of efforts to raise Climate Finance of $100 billion a year by 2020 (Wikipedia). The World Bank serves as the interim trustee of the GCF, and the Fund functions under the guidance of and remains accountable to the UNFCCC Conference of Parties.

The GCF will contribute to the achievement of the ultimate objective of the United Nations Framework Convention on Climate Change (UNFCCC). In the context of sustainable development, the Fund will promote the paradigm shift towards low-emission of GHGs and climate-resilient development pathways by providing support to developing countries particularly vulnerable to the adverse effects of climate change and to adapt to the impacts of climate change. The Fund will strive to maximize the impact of its funding for adaptation and mitigation, and seek a balance between the two, while promoting environmental, social, economic and development co-benefits and taking a gender-sensitive approach.

The Government of India has established the National Adaptation Fund on Climate Change (NAFCC) with a budget provision of Rs. 350 Crores for the year 2015-16 and 2016-17, with an estimated requirement of Rs. 181.5 Crores for financial year 2017-18. The National Bank for Agriculture and Rural Development (NABARD) has been appointed as National Implementing Entity (NIE) under the NAFCC. NABARD has been accredited by Green Climate Fund (GCF) Board as one of the National Implementing Entity (NIE) for GCF in India. According to the GCF Board document, NABARD as one of the NIEs of the Green Climate Fund is responsible for management and oversight of project implementation, which includes the origination and preparation of a funding proposal, the subsequent management of the necessary stages of the implementation process until its conclusion (project management) on behalf of GCF, and reporting obligations.

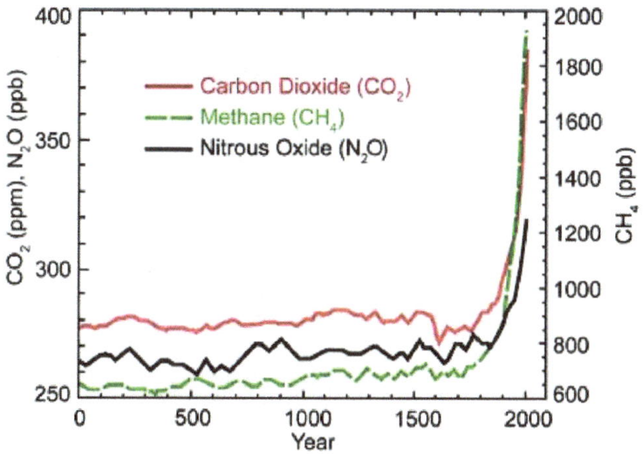

Fig. 1. Trends of Greenhouse gases (GHGs)
Source: U.S. National Climate Assessment (2014)

Agriculture has the potential to capture a significant part of the excess atmospheric carbon in the soil in the form of organic matter and also competent to reduce emissions of nitrous oxide and methane if practiced in smart ways so developing climate-smart agriculture is thus crucial in achieving future food security and climate change goals. Long term changes in the patterns of temperature and precipitation, that are part of climate change, are expected to shift production seasons, pest and disease patterns, and modify the set of feasible crops affecting production, prices, incomes and ultimately, livelihoods and lives.

More productive and resilient agriculture requires transformations in the management of natural resources (e.g. land, water, soil nutrients, and genetic resources) and higher efficiency in the use of these resources and inputs for production. Transitioning to such systems could also generate significant mitigation benefits by increasing carbon sinks, as well as reducing emissions per unit of agricultural product. Transformations are needed in both commercial and subsistence agricultural systems, but with significant differences in priorities and capacity. In commercial systems, increasing efficiency and reducing emissions, as well as other negative environmental impacts, are key concerns. In agriculture-based countries, where agriculture is critical for economic development (World Bank, 2008), transforming smallholder systems is not only important for food security but also for poverty reduction, as well as for aggregate growth and structural change. The sustainable intensification of production, especially in developing countries, can ensure food security and contribute to mitigating climate change by reducing deforestation and the encroachment of agriculture into natural ecosystems. The overall efficiency, resilience, adaptive capacity and mitigation potential of the production systems can be enhanced through smartly improving its various components.

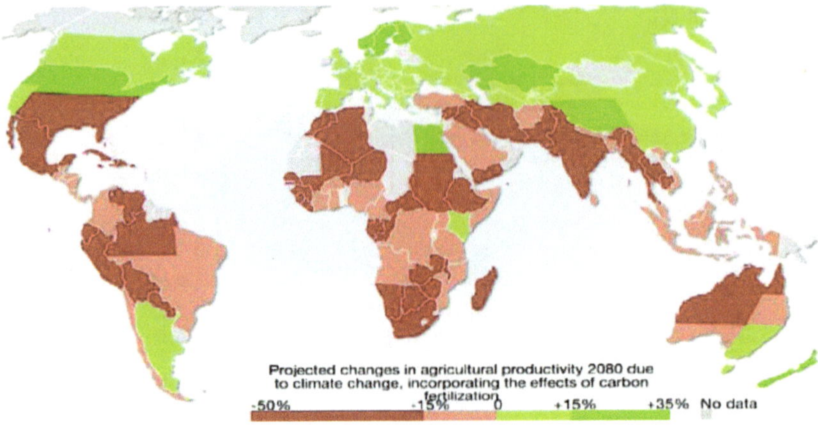

Fig. 2: Long-term projected changes in agricultural productivity from 2007 to 2080 (Cline, 2007)

A US expert panel group recommends that climate change research enterprise should be:

- Integrative and interdisciplinary including research across and among the physical, social, biological, health, and engineering sciences
- Focused on fundamental, use-inspired research that contributes to both improved understanding and more effective decision making
- Linked with action-oriented programs focused on limiting the magnitude of climate change, adapting to its impacts, and informing effective responses
- Flexible to respond to emerging needs and changing demands

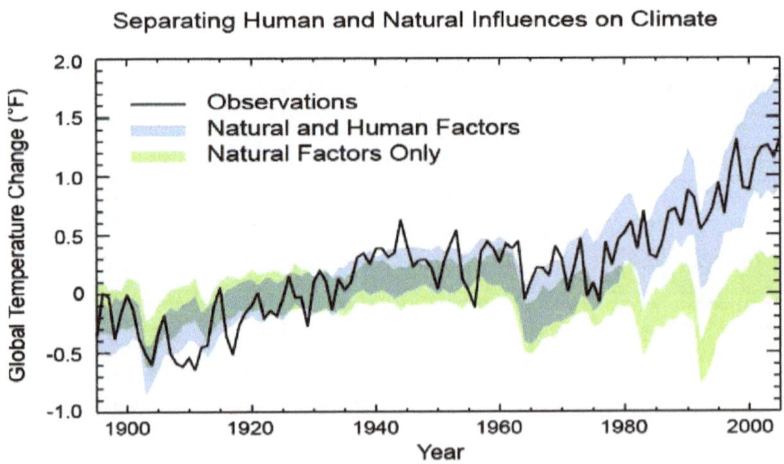

Fig. 3: Human activities effect on climate through the millennium

2. Understanding climate smart agriculture

Long term changes in the patterns of temperature and precipitation that are part of climate change, are expected to shift production seasons, pest and disease patterns, and modify the set of feasible crops affecting production, prices, incomes and ultimately, livelihoods and lives. Transformations are needed in both commercial and subsistence farming systems. Agricultural production systems must change in the direction of higher productivity and also, essentially, lower output variability in the face of climate risk and risks of an agro-ecological and socio-economic nature, in other words must be more capable of performing well in the face of disruptive climatic events. Such More productive and resilient agricultural systems requires transformations in the management of land, water, nutrients, plants and animals so that higher efficiency in use of these resources for production is achieved.

Climate change in India has been witnessed with more frequent cloud bursts, highly variable frequency and distribution of rainfall, high seasonal thermal variations, receding glaciers and unstable agricultural production. Impacts of climate change on agriculture threaten both food security and broad-based development. Also the agricultural sector, if emissions from land use change are also included, generates about one-quarter of global greenhouse gas emissions and needs to be appropriately addressed in *climate smart agriculture*. The term climate-smart agriculture (CSA) represent a set of strategies that can help to meet climate-change challenges by increasing resilience to weather extremes, adapting to climate change and decreasing agriculture's greenhouse gas (GHG) emissions that contribute to global warming. CSA also aims to support sustainable and equitable transitions for agricultural systems and livelihoods across scales, ranging from smallholders to transnational coalitions and forming a core part of the broader green development agenda for agriculture.

1st Global Conference on Food Security and Climate Change was held in The Hague, Netherlands in November 2010 with the themes:

1. Agriculture, food security and climate change: framing the issue and taking stock of innovations
2. Scaling up replicable models of climate change-smart agriculture: opportunities and challenges
3. Mobilizing investments from all sources for a transformational change to climate-smart agriculture
4. A road map for action

In The Hague conference, the term ***climate-smart agriculture*** was widely used to express agricultural practices that will (1) increase agricultural productivity and food security, (2) adapt agriculture to climate change, and (3) modify agriculture to mitigate climate change. FAO several publications describe climate-smart agriculture (CSA) as an integrative approach to address interlinked challenges of food security and climate change that explicitly aims for three objectives:

1. sustainably increasing agricultural productivity, to support equitable increases in farm incomes, food security and development;
2. adapting and building resilience of agricultural and food security systems to climate change at multiple levels; and
3. Reducing greenhouse gas emissions from agriculture (including crops, livestock and fisheries).

Climate Smart Agriculture (CSA) objectively focuses on increasing agricultural productivity in sustainable manner and incomes by adapting and building resilience to climate change and reducing and/or removing greenhouse gas emissions, where possible. *Climate-smart agriculture may be defined the agriculture that sustainably increases productivity, resilience (adaptation), reduces/removes GHGs (mitigation), and enhances achievement of national food security and development goals.* The concept is therefore a good way to unite the agendas of agriculture, development and climate change.

The conference in Addis Ababa was followed up by *The African Ministerial Conference on Climate-Smart Agriculture "Africa: A Call to Action"* held in Johannesburg, South Africa September 2011. In partnership with several international agencies, including the World Bank, FAO, IFAD and UNEP, the conference produced a policy brief proclaiming eight key messages:

- Food security, poverty and climate change are closely linked and should not be considered separately
- Without strong adaptation measures, and financing to support them, poverty alleviation and food security goals will not be reached
- Adaptation measures not only enhance food security but can potentially contribute to reducing greenhouse gas emissions from agriculture
- Climate-smart agriculture offers triple wins for food security, adaptation and mitigation
- COP 17 in Durban offers a unique opportunity for Africa to shape the global climate agenda and establish an agriculture work program that is informed by science and covers adaptation and mitigation

- Climate-smart agriculture needs heightened attention in African policy processes and strategies, from national to regional levels
- Early action is needed to identify and scale up best practice, to build capacity and experience, and to help clarify future choices
- Considerable public and private finance will be needed to rapidly implement climate-smart agriculture

In October 2011, the *Global Science Conference on Climate-Smart Agriculture* was hosted by Wageningen University which focused on three themes in its formulation of 'The Wageningen Statement: Climate-Smart Agriculture – Science for Action':

- Sustainable intensification and climate-smart solutions – enhancing food production while reducing greenhouse gas emissions
- Overcoming the barriers to climate-smart agriculture
- Managing volatility and risks – technical and social-economic options for climate-smart risk management

The *2nd Global Conference on Agriculture, Food Security and Climate Change,* "Hunger for Action", held at Hanoi, Vietnam in May 2012 made recommendations to:

- Call on developed countries and other partners, to support the implementation and scaling-up of early action programs, including best practice and technologies in climate-smart agriculture and food security, through regional, sub-regional and national programs and institutions as a matter of priority
- Emphasize the importance of government-led partnerships with non-state agencies in designing strategies, policies and appropriate market based approaches to promote climate-smart agriculture
- Encourage countries to leverage private sector investments through public private partnerships in support of climate-smart agriculture
- Urge countries to invest in research, technology and information dissemination to facilitate the adaptation and application of climate-smart agriculture.

A 10-year research program on Climate Change was launched in January 2011 by the Consultative Group on International Agricultural Research (CGIAR) and the Earth System Science Partnership (ESSP), to explore how agriculture can contribute to a reduction in atmospheric greenhouse gases and at the same time provide enough food for the global population. The program promotes six simple messages regarding food security and climate change:

1. Climate change has arrived
2. We need planned, accelerated and transformative adaptation
4. A "new" climate-smart agriculture is needed
5. A major push is needed for climate risk management
6. Farmers' efforts need to be supported by policies, incentives and knowledge.

The 2013 Global Science Conference on Climate-Smart Agriculture (Davis, CA, USA) focused on current gaps in knowledge, work within CSA, and agendas for interdisciplinary research and science-based actions and identified three themes: (1) farm and food systems,(2) landscape and regional issues and (3) institutional and policy aspects. The first two themes comprise crop physiology and genetics, mitigation and adaptation for livestock and agriculture, barriers to adoption of CSA practices, climate risk management and energy and biofuels (theme 1); and modelling adaptation and uncertainty, achieving multifunctionality, food and fishery systems, forest biodiversity and ecosystem services, rural migration from climate change and metrics (theme 2). Theme 3 comprises designing research that bridges disciplines, integrating stakeholder input to directly link science, action and governance.

Synnevåg and Lambrou (2012) claims that producing food in a more 'climate smart' way could be seen as having three advantages: 1) Providing food for an increasing population, 2) maintaining food production under a changing climate, and 3) reducing greenhouse gas emission from agriculture while absorbing carbon in vegetation and soil. However in certain areas efforts to restrict climate change may need focus on mitigation through forest protection (REDD+) and clean energy (Energy+). Interventions for climate change mitigation, adaptation and capacity building require huge funding from external sources encompassing governmental, public and private organizations but agricultural production systems due to low returns and high risk do not attract much private investors.

Terdoo and Adekol (2014) advocates that CSA is strong in aspects such as participation and sustainable use of resources but weak in aspects of compensation and equal distribution of benefits and costs. Many small-holder farmers have inadvertently practiced CSA as part of the traditional farming system. While the existence of CSA in current practice is a major element in its favour, the lack of a coherent climate mitigation approach and poor institutional structures are both detrimental. Sustainable agriculture will require a wider societal change towards appreciating the balance between agriculture and environmental change and suggest four main areas in need of urgent change: political commitment, human and financial investment, incentives and information.

Climate-smart agriculture (CSA) requires working across the forestry and agriculture divide and aims at achieving the triple win goals for food security, adaptation and mitigation.

The cross-cutting key issues in CSA, REDD+ and Energy+ to which universities can make a substantial contribution, include: i) building the human and institutional capacity required to respond to the challenges presented by a changing climate; ii) establishing and strengthening partnerships for designing, implementing, monitoring, reporting and evaluating outcomes in climate mitigation and adaptation efforts; and iii) providing information (e.g. publishing results in papers and policy briefs) from well-grounded research to guide policy and decision making. The scope of these studies and potential avenues for training could widen to investigate the interplay between REDD+, climate-smart agriculture (CSA) and Energy+ initiatives.

Universities may contribute to independent monitoring, reporting and verification of outcomes in REDD+, Energy+ or CSA projects through their various research (social and biophysical) and training activities. The information generated through independent research will enable policy makers and the various stakeholders to make better informed decisions related to food production, energy use and land use in a changing climate.

Gender disparities in the adoption, adaptation, allocation and utilization of various technologies in the production cycle also exist as evident from various FAO reports. Tasks performed by men, such as land preparation, harvesting and processing are the easiest to mechanize. Women's tasks, on the other hand, remain labour intensive and time consuming. Technological development is often modelled on western, pre-selected packages and implemented everywhere, irrespective of their appropriateness to the environmental, cultural, economic and social context. Despite their active and continuous interaction with the agricultural environment, women's technological knowledge on seed selection practices, pest and weed control measures, harvesting and food preservation technologies is insufficiently included in policy making and implementation. This omission limits the development of relevant techniques for rural farmers.

3. Climate smart agriculture: specific research

Reasons for low returns in agriculture are primarily attributed to failure to manage favorable environment around the crop mainly because of climatic uncertainties. Suitable climate is prerequisite for efficient use of various inputs right from variety, seed, sowing time, spacing, nutrient management, plant protection, harvesting and post harvest Handling. This infers that climate smart agriculture entails application of production practices in appropriate permutation and combination in context of existing climatic variations. It is package of tactics to act as catalyst for enhancement of inputs efficiency. It could be preplanned if a climate change is predicted well in advance or recommended through a long term research investigations. In case of seasonal climatic variation or short span climate variation it may require action on appearance of change, for instance in moisture deficit situation owing to delayed rain can be managed through use of rain gun or foliar application of anti-transpirants or mulching or their combinations. Research is needed for development of new CSA practices and also for refinements of already existing practices. Revalidation of such practices in different agro-climatic conditions is the next step which should follow large scale demonstrations in farmers' fields.

Scientists, field functionaries and farmers must act in coherence to develop an effective technological module to nullify the effect of climate change. Right from development of variety to its agronomic evaluation to demonstration in farmers' fields should be taken in participatory mode. India being place of several agro-ecological zones requires many such modules. In spite of this users must intelligent enough to add or drop a practice as per climate variation, thus unlike conventional agriculture CSA is knowledge intensive and demands for good connectivity between the experts and farmers. CSA modules comprises a set of practices touching all disciplines of agriculture but primarily plant breeding, agronomy, soil science, plant pathology, entomology and agri-engineering. Some of the major CSA practices and technologies will be enumerated subsequently.

Future research needs will include understanding how production, adaptation and mitigation objectives relate to local vulnerability, poverty and livelihoods. This may require understanding the significance of CSA for softer 'social'-based initiatives in addition to harder 'technocratic' interventions, potential conflicts of interest between mitigation, production and adaptation objectives and understanding limits to CSA in addressing these issues. Linkages to wider sustainability issues (social equity, justice and environmental integrity) and related terms such as sustainable adaptation and climate compatible development are required.

Climate-smart agriculture aims at achieving triple wins through higher productivity, adaption to climate change and mitigation of climate change. These objectives cannot be achieved without fundamental changes in how farming is practiced in India. Potential yield levels are not achieved in several field, vegetable and fruit crops because of poorly adoption of recommended package of practices. Below average fertilizer use, lack of location specific high yielding varieties, imbalanced fertilization, inappropriate use of pesticides and obscure marketing avenues still haunt the Indian agriculture.

Development of climate-smart agriculture (CSA) is dependent on appropriate technologies and input, market access, institutional development and favorable policies. India being region of diverse agro-climatic conditions, site-specific solutions have to be applied.

Knowledge base is well available in modern improved agricultural technologies as well as in indigenous practices sustained through ages. Results show that the yields realized by Indian farmers are far below the potential ones. Even the regions with high and stable crop yields are facing dwindle in agricultural production. Reasons for such disturbances in agriculture have been correlated with prolonged droughts, unusually high precipitation, shift in precipitation pattern, appearance of new races of pathogens and insect-pests and succumbing of high yielding varieties to pressure of climate change. Therefore, there is a need to:

- Continue research to evolve varieties and recommendations that are suitable for the diverse agro-ecological conditions and refine the ones those exist.
- Monitor and scientifically analyze the "when, why and where" of climate change particularly in context of entrepreneurial areas of agriculture.
- Continue research on integrated farming, diversified farming including agro-forestry and conservation agriculture aiming at more carbon sequestration.
- Research on improved livestock management as a part of CSA
- Ranking and prioritizing agro-technologies based on potential to mitigate GHGs emission (Global Warming Potential)

Improved livestock management practices have to be part of CSA. This includes improved grazing management, production of fodder of high quality and zero grazing systems. Such an approach will also allow intensification of livestock production. Less use of residues for fodder will reduce the emission from livestock because methane production is higher if fodder is of low quality. With more mechanical interventions at the farm better, change the composition of livestock from animals kept for traction purposes to livestock kept for milk and meat production. High yielding breeds with tolerance to biotic and abiotic stresses are essential component of climate smart livestock farming.

4. Capacity building and training

Even though many these practices exist in the region, they have not been integrated into the broader local and national strategies, policies and planning processes. This lack of an existing link of the approach with any government implementation plans translates to no budgetary allocation and, hence, the unavailability of funding for such initiatives. This is a potential weakness that has to be addressed in the adoption of climate smart agriculture. Another weakness towards the adoption of climate smart agriculture was revealed during the interaction with field functionaries and farmers and concerns the little or no knowledge of CSA and the fact that the approach is poorly understood even by extension officers, who are expected to champion the approach and explain it to the locals. This may be unrelated to another weakness, which is the lack of active non-governmental organizations in the region promoting sustainable agriculture. While there are few organizations promoting tree planting many have failed to address the main cause of desertification, thus treating the symptoms rather than addressing the cause. A further weakness is the limited opportunities for local managers to participate in the international policy which has led to the formulation of weak and ineffective implementation strategies.

Capacity building and awareness to farmers through training is must via continuous flow of knowledge from experimental fields to stakeholders and end users. Brainstorming sessions should proceed upward from ground level to scientists and policy makers and decision from downwards in the same fashion. There is a need to identify the types of interventions and measures that can effectively reduce vulnerability in different contexts. These may hover around type of variety, nutrient management, water management and energy management. Similarly climate change literacy is must for social and financial institutions to attract people's participation and private investments.

5. Climate smart agricultural practices and tactics

Development of appropriate adaptation strategy under smallholder production conditions is not only relevant to India but to the whole world to cope with the progressive climate change and variability as more than 80% farmers in India are small and marginal having less than two ha farm size. They contribute more than 50% of total agricultural output by cultivating 44% of agricultural land and support livelihood and food security of millions of people. Several CSA practices such as cropping system improvement (e.g. crop rotation, diversification, improved varieties and integration of legumes), integrated nutrient management(e.g. green manure, compost and site specific nutrient management), resource conservation (e.g. minimum/zero tillage, keeping the land consistently covered with crop residues), precision water management (e.g. planting crops in bed, laser land leveling, mulching with crop residues) and agro-forestry have been proposed for adaptation to climate change and variability. However, their adoption decisions by the farmers are largely dependent on economic benefits associated with the interventions. It should be clearly understood that climate smart agriculture does not make use of different practices but certainly it uses them differently.

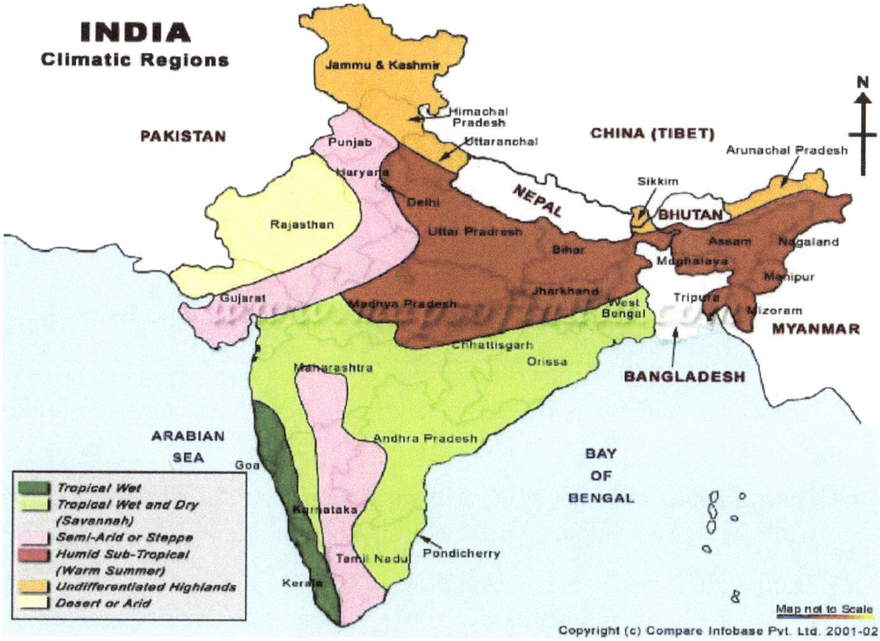

Fig. 4: Climatic zones of India

The sites selected for implementation and impact assessment of CSA have been often at the village level designated as climate smart village (CSV), a model of local actions for climate risk management through promotion of CSA practices and technologies. An effective association of research institutes, developmental organizations, farmers and policy makers is imperative to identify appropriate integrated package of practices to link government existing rural development schemes with environment and agricultural programs to build resilience to climate stresses and enhance food security in a sustainable way. CSVs are indicative of not only site of implementation of CSA programs but also farmers' literacy about climate and climate change.

CSA practices and technologies are of multidisciplinary nature sometimes across the faculty embracing social sciences and engineering etc. More commonly of them pertains to varietal development, crop management and plant protection.

5.1. Climate resilient varieties

Monsoon rainfall has become more erratic in India with heavy rainfall events and reduced number of rainy days during the latter half of the 20th century thus increasing the risk of drought and flood damage to crops like rice. Recently natural calamities have been witnessed in India as enlisted below (Mahashwari *et al.* 2015).

- The country witnessed drought in 2002 with 19% deficit rainfall.
- There was extreme cold wave in winter 2002-03 leading to frost damage of winter crops.
- The state of Andhra Pradesh faced three weeks of heat wave during May, 2003.
- The high temperatures during March 2004, adversely affected crops like wheat, apple and potato across northern India,
- There was a drought like situation in July, 2004 with overall deficit rainfall of 13%.
- Year 2005, witnessed destructive hurricanes/cyclones across the globe with some major floods in India (Venkateswarlu, 2013).
- During 2006, the states of Rajasthan, Andhra Pradesh witnessed floods while, it was a drought year for Northeastern States of the country.
- During 2012, wide spread drought was reported in the states of Punjab, Haryana, Gujrat and Karnataka while cyclone Neelam hit east coast of the country including severe flood in Andhra Pradesh.
- The year 2014 was also another year that witnessed number of natural calamities including hailstorms, early season dry spells; devastating floods in Kashmir and Hudhud cyclone in coastal Andhra Pradesh.
- Cyclone in Odhisa and Andhra Pradesh in the year 2018.

The increase in frequency of heavy rainfall events in last 50 years over Central India points towards a significant change in climate pattern in India (Goswami, 2006). Delayed monsoon has brought shift in paddy planting and sowing of maize and pulses in kharif season while reduced number of rainy days has been observed in beginning of rabi season creating water deficit situation and while terminal moisture stress is witnessed in rabi crops because of few rainy days in March. Adoption of climate resilient crop varieties is the best economical options to tackle the problem and has been exercised as a first priority (Khatri-Chhetri et al. 2016). Climate resilient varieties tide over various abiotic and biotic stresses because in-built genetic resistance or they may be of short duration so suited for late sowing in case of delayed monsoon showers. Moreover early maturity enables the varieties many a times to escape natural calamity. Some of the climate resilient varieties are enlisted the table 1.

S.No.	Crop	Variety	Maturity duration (days)	Remarks
1	Rice	Pusa 1509	75-80	Fine grained variety
		Sharbati	70-80	Fine grained variety
		SJR 129	90-100	SJR 129 has medium aroma
2	Wheat	Raj 3765	120-140	Suited for late sown conditions
		PBW 175	130-150	Suited for rainfed conditions
3	Toria	RSPT-01	60-65	Suitable for autumn season
		RSPT-02	65-70	
4	Konlkhol	G -40	30-35	Use of Azotobacter for seedlings treatment is recommended
5	Radish	CR 45	45	Responds to organic nutrient management
6	Mungbean	PDM 54S ML668	60-70	Suited for spring season cultivation and green manuring

5.2. Seed and Seed treatments

The modern agriculture strongly advocates use of high quality seeds with good genetic potential in terms of germination, emergence, canopy development and yield. Seed quality is indicator of good seed health, seed vigor, seedling vigor and early establishment. Such seed is fairly tolerant to adverse agro-climatic conditions. Growing of quality seed means a farmer is confident of following benefits

a) Better and rapid crop establishment

b) Better yield in less favorable crop seasons

c) Relatively efficient use of all inputs

d) More assured return

e) Quality produce of the crop from such seed

f) Easy marketing because of uniformity maturity and more consumer preference

g) Comparatively less needs of plant protection measures

So in areas of high vulnerability to climatic variation farmers must prioritize for use of certified seed only.

Ensuring quality seed availability of the resilient varieties in various crops at the appropriate time to the farmers is an important challenge and need to be addressed. Participatory approach to consolidate the involvement of village institutions will go a long way in ensuring the seed availability of resilient varieties locally. Seed village program and state seed corporations should be empowered to meet the challenge with strong third party monitoring system. Issues related to managing trade-off between risk and expected returns in vulnerable areas to weather aberrations including drought, flood, heat and cold waves etc., also need due consideration.

Seed treatment is carried with anti-microbial chemicals, water, biofertilizers, biological agents and other seed growth promoting formulations (beejoamrut, panchgavya etc) with the intention of enhancing seed capability to fight against early stage biotic and abiotic stresses. Seed treatment is most widely used among CSA practices by the Indian farmers. Seed priming has been also commonly used to reduce the time between seed sowing and seedling emergence and to synchronize emergence. Overnight soaking of seed of maize, rice, bajra, wheat, pulses, cucurbits and okra is also popular among farmers of Asian countries because of multi-beneficial effect on crop performance (Nawaz et al 2013). Some of the benefits of seed priming are enlisted below:

- Prevention disease and pests attack in storage or upon sowing in field
- Improvement in germination and seedling emergence
- Better crop growth
- Increased grain/ fruit yield
- Improving nitrogen fixing efficiency in legumes through Rhizobium culture seed treatment
- Resistance against abiotic stresses through Cycocel, gibbrellic acid and kinetin etc seed treatment
- Breaking of dormancy through physical or chemical treatment of seeds

Insufficient seedling emergence and inappropriate stand establishment are the main constraints in areas receiving less rainfall. Management of soil texture and soil structure is a big challenge in semi-arid regions. Poor farmers do not have sufficient resources to meet the requirements of fine seedbed preparation for sowing and they are at more risk as compared to progressive farmers. On-farm seed priming (Hydro-priming) can significantly be helpful in order to obtain good crop establishment in many crops of tropical region such as sorghum, rice, maize and pigeon pea. Inducing resistance against stresses like drought stress, heat stress etc. is one of the prominent advantages of seed priming in many important field crops.

Fifty three farmers tested maize seeds priming in the kharif season in 1996 in tribal areas of Rajasthan, Gujarat and Madhya Pradesh (Harris et al., 1999). Almost all farmers observed that primed crops grew more vigorously, tolerated dry spells better, flowered and matured earlier and produced bigger cobs and higher yield. Independent measurements on a subset of 35 trials showed a mean increase in cob weight of 6% (Harris et al., 2001). Polyethylene glycol and KNO_3 solutions increased the fresh and dry weight of roots in maize at 2% and 5% concentration primed for 12 h and 18 h. In addition they also increased the vigour index (Abdnadani and Ramezani, 2012). The increase in yield was 13% in case of hydro-priming alone and 26% when primed with $ZnSO_4$ solution.

Hydro-priming	Hydro-priming involves soaking the seeds in water before sowing
Halo-priming	Halo priming refers to soaking of seeds in solution of inorganic salts i.e. NaCl, KNO_3, $CaCl_2$, $CaSO_4$, etc.
Osmo-priming	Osmo-priming also known as osmo-conditioning or osmotic conditioning. seeds are soaked for a specified period in solutions of sugar, polyethylene glycol (PEG), glycerol, sorbitol, or mannitol followed by air drying before sowing.
Hormonal priming	Hormonal priming is the pre-seed treatment with different hormones i.e. cycocel, salicylic acid, ascorbate, kinetin, etc. which promote the growth and development of the seedlings.

5.3. Climate smart nutrient management

Nutrient management strives to balance the withdrawal of nutrients from soil by fields, crops, livestock, and natural processes with the addition of nutrients provided by crop residues, compost, manure or commercial fertilizers. The main objective of nutrient management is to optimize the yield and quality of crop production while minimizing costs and negative environmental impacts. Management practices that conserve soil organic matter and nitrogen (N) fertilizers generally also reduce losses of carbon dioxide and nitrous oxide. Reducing fertilizer costs while reducing GHGs through smart management presents a win-win proposition. Many environmental factors such as mineralization, nitrification and denitrification influence soil biological processes. These factors regulate availability of nitrogen for crop uptake, and nitrogen loss pathways such as leaching and gas emissions of nitrogen gas (N_2) and nitrous oxide. Farmers have always needed to account for timing, frequency and duration of drought and precipitation when planting, fertilizing or managing their crop.

Managing nitrogen application to minimize N_2O emissions requires attention to matching supply and demand. Timing of nitrogen fertilizer application should occur in synchrony with peak crop demand. Under high rainfall conditions, using multiple split applications is a particularly important strategy to conserve nitrogen by minimizing the size of the soil inorganic nitrogen pool at any point in time, reducing the potential for gaseous and leaching losses. Right placement or depth of nitrogen have an effect on overall N_2O emissions. Urea band applied below the seed row reduced N_2O emissions compared to urea broadcast across the soil surface of placed 8-12 inch deep. Newer technologies including controlled- and slow-release fertilizers may offer additional options concerning application timing. These products tend to either inhibit N transformations, require microbial decomposition or are coated with semi-permeable polymers to allow a controlled dissolution of fertilizer at a lower rate than conventional water-soluble fertilizers.

Table 1: Energy use and GHG emissions associated with use of nitrogen fertilizers

	Ammonia	Urea	Ammonium nitrate
		(per kg of N)	
Energy use (MJ)	45	53	65
CH_4 emission (g)	2.5	3.7	4.2
N_2O emission (g)	0.02	0.03	19.7
CO_2 emission (kg)	2.6	3.1	3.8
GWP (global warming potential) (kg CO_2 equiv.)	2.6	3.2	9.7

Management strategies are based on either nutrient removal by the crop/variety or response of the crop /variety to nutrient levels. These hardly take account of soil ecology whereas climate smartness lies in using permutations and combinations of following practices in a sustainable manner.

Management options

- Site-specific nutrient management: based on health card/ soil tests
- Integrated nutrient management: FYM / compost application /green manuring: Alone chemicals /combination with organic manures and or with biofertlizers
- Improving application methods: Single application /split over period with different growth stages: Broadcasting / drilled in soil: Top dressing / foliar application: fertigation
- Improving the fertilizer formulations:: Neem coated preparations, phospho-compost, zincated urea etc
- Integrated crop management

Tools and technologies

- Leaf colour chart
- Decision support system
- Remote-sensing

- Geographic information system
- Precision farming

5.4. Climate smart soil and water management

Population pressure on land showing no signs of diminishing and soil degrading processes for instance, the loss of topsoil by the action of water or wind, chemical deterioration such as nutrient depletion, physical degradation such as compaction, and biological deterioration of natural resources including the reduction of soil biodiversity have been accelerated. The expansion of agriculture into marginal areas, deforestation, the shortening or elimination of fallows, inappropriate farming practices, and low input inevitably have several environmental and economic impacts. Hence land use adjustment measures which contribute to a reduction in soil erosion rates, and at the same time increase land productivity, rural employment and income are imperative. Three aspects namely, agronomic measures, soil management strategies and mechanical or physical methods are pivotal to protect a watershed from climate change.

Agronomic Measures	Soil Management Strategies	Mechanical or Physical Methods
Mulching	Conservation Tillage	Terracing
Crop Management	Minimum tillage	Contour Bunds
Cover Crops	Improved fallows	Infiltration Galleries
Improved Fallows	No-till	Waterways
Intercropping	Contour Tillage	Gully Controls
Planting Pattern/Time	Strip farming	Stabilization structures
Crop rotation		Stone check dam
Agroforestry		Gabion baskets
		Reno Mattresses
		Stone lining

Source: REMA (2009)

Dependence on rainfall for food crops will leave rural populations increasingly food insecure in times of climate change so better water management will be essential for future food security in arid and semi-arid areas. Since the prospects for food security and reforestation are significant, research should focus on developing infrastructure for supplemental irrigation. As a first step, better use of plant nutrients on the best agricultural lands may increase yields three- to four-fold. This may facilitate conversion of marginal cropland in upland areas to forest/bush land and consequently increase the availability of groundwater and surface water for irrigation. Additional water supply may, in turn, facilitate better crop growth resulting in a total of five- to seven-fold yield increase.

Climate smart water management: technological options
Flood irrigation
Blocks/ strips
Check basin /drip irrigation
Rain gun
Foliar spray
Foliar spray with anti-transpirants
Mulching
Sowing with aqua-seed drill

1.1. Climate smart agronomic management

Zero tillage

Demonstrations of zero till drill sown wheat in farmers' fields were undertaken in several basmati growing villages of RS Pura and Bishnah tehsils. The zero till drill not only saves tillage costs and energy but also eliminates the need for seedbed preparation. Zero till drilled wheat yields were on par with conventionally sown wheat. There are reports of an average yield advantage in the range of 16 to 64% and benefit cost ratio was in the range of 2 to 3.2.

The machine operated with a 35 hp tractor can cover sowing of wheat in 4-5 ha/day. The cost of zero till drill is Rs.45,000 to 60,000. Zero till sowing of wheat could save 68% in time and 85% on the cost of operation compared to the conventional practice. Zero till drill was more efficient as the crop could be sown in large areas within a limited time of moisture availability. The main advantages include:

- Saves irrigation water up to 10-15% during first irrigation.
- Two days early and uniform germination and better plant stand than traditional.
- No crust formation after rains, hence no effect of rains on germination.
- Improvement in crop yield.
- Improvement in soil structure and fertility.
- No lodging of crops at the time of maturity in case of heavy rains.

Now the farmers are convinced about the performance and benefits of zero till drill in basmati villages. There is need to organize awareness programs on zero till. However, availability of zero seed drill remains the problem.

Direct seeded rice

It is estimated that flooded rice fields produce about 10% of global methane emissions. Also, injudicious use of nitrogenous fertilizers is a common feature in paddy cultivation which is a source of nitrous oxide emissions. Puddling and transplanting are common practices in rice cultivation. The current practice of excessive exploitation of ground water has led to a decline in the quality of natural resources i.e. land and water in rice growing areas. In direct seeded rice (DSR) cultivation, both puddling and raising of nursery for transplantation are skipped. Farmer can avoid the problem of labour shortage for transplanting. In case of delay in monsoon or shortage of water, DSR gives the farmer flexibility to take up direct sowing of paddy with a suitable duration variety to fit into the left over season. This allows timely sowing of the succeeding *rabi* wheat. Direct sown rice consumes relatively less water compared to transplanted flooded rice. Energy demand for pumping of irrigation water is also less and saving can be much higher during deficit rainfall situations compared to transplanted rice. Direct seeded rice with reduced tillage is an efficient resource conservation technology that holds great promise in era of climate change.

- Advantages of direct seeded rice cultivation
- Saving of water up to 25% in DSR
- Saving of energy up to 27% of diesel as pumping energy is saved for field preparation, nursery raising, puddling and reduced frequency of applying irrigation water
- Saving of 35 to 40 mandays / ha
- Enhanced fertilizer use efficiency due to placement of fertilizer in the root zone
- Early maturity of crops by 7-10 days helps in timely sowing of succeeding crops
- Reduction in methane emissions and global warming potential
- Little disturbance to soil structure
- Enhanced system productivity

In India

In India
Trials are being conducted In around 70 villages in Haryana, Bihar. Punjab, Odlsha and Karnataka out or wnich evidence has Pee- collected n a round 6C Locking at the success of the trials in 27 villages >.
Kama! district the Haryana government has decided to expand it to oOO more villages In the state
The Bihar government has also sought an action plan to take it across the state
There is a Similar homegrown project in India. Nations innovations in Climate Resilient Agriculture, also started in 2011. This project of the Indian Council of Agricultural Research %; CAR) covers 151 villages across the country
Source: CCAF5 and central Researm irstltut E lor Dryland Aer cu (lore

Impact of Climate-Smart Agriculture in Karnal, Haryana

Impact of Climate- Smart Agriculture in Karnal, Haryana
Zero tillage and line sowing instead of broadcasting of seeds increase rice and wheat yields by 10-15%
zero tillage cuts diesel use by 80-85% per hectare
Direct seeded rice, which involves the sowing of rice seeds directly, compared to the traditional method cf sprouting rice in a nursery and transferring the seediings to a field with standing water, reduces water use by 25% and methane emissions by 40%
Bed planting of maize and wheat, which is at a I eve raised from the soil cuts water use by 30-35%

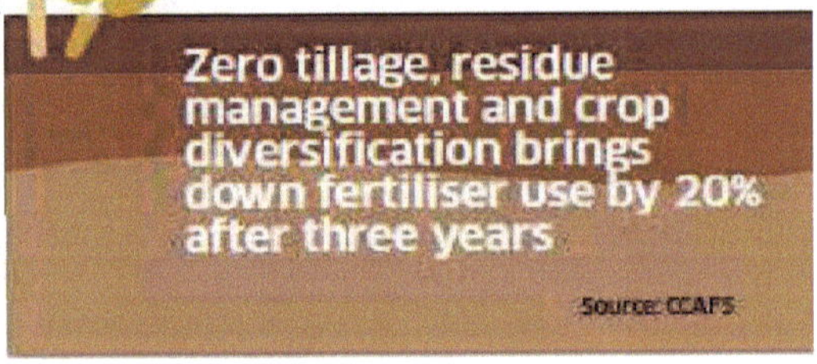

Other interventions of high consideration and relevance to climate smart agriculture are:

- High intensity cropping pattern /crop rotation
- Relay cropping
- Raised-sunken bed technology
- Integrated farming
- Organic agriculture
- Soilless farming
- Vertical gardening

- Vertical entrepreneurships
- Roof top cultivation
- Protected cultivation

2. Way forward

Enhancing the resilience of Indian agriculture to cope with climate change and variability is imperative to the livelihood security of millions of small and marginal farmers in the country. ICAR has responded to this challenge by launching National Initiative on Climate Resilient Agriculture (NICRA) in 2011 through Krishi Vigyan Kendras (KVKs) in 100 vulnerable districts of the country to the climate change with aim of evolving climate resilient agricultural technologies to address the concerns of projected climate change scenarios and also to demonstrate the climate smart modules that can help farmers cope with current climate change and variability (Ayyappan, 2014). Frequent cloudbursts, change in seasonal rainfall and temperature patterns associated with floods and droughts have been witnessed in India and anywhere in the world. Climate smart agriculture which recommends a practice or module of practices to be deployed tactfully to reduce or remove the abiotic and biotic stresses so that loss or damage to crop and climate is minimum, seems mandatory. Hence climate resilient technologies development, revalidation, refinement, and transfer should be prioritized and implementation in spirit of global climate agenda via flagship programs such as climate change agriculture and food security (CCAFS) and green climate fund (GCF). Research institutions, developmental departments, private organizations and farmer community must unite under the ambit of global initiatives and political will of respective country to take agenda of climate change and sustainable development ahead in the interest of future generations.

3. References

Abandani RR, Ramezani M. 2012.Thephysiological effects on some traits of osmopriming germ ination of m aize (*Zea mays* L.), rice (*Oryza sativa* L.) and cucumber (*Cucumis sativus* L). *Int. J. Agron*. 4132-148.

Aggarwal, P.K. 2008. Global climate change and Indian agriculture: Impacts, adaptation and mitigation. *Indian Journal of Agricultural Sciences*. 78:10-16.

Ayyappan, S. 2014. In, forward to Smart Practices & Technologies for Climate Resilient Agriculture, CRIDA Hyderabad.

Bruinsma, J. 2009. "The Resource Outlook to 2050", in *Expert Meeting on "How to Feed the World in 2050"*: FAO, Rome.

FAO, *Climate-Smart Agriculture Source Book*, Food and Agricultural Organization of the United Nations, Rome, Italy, 2013.

Harris D, Joshi A, Khan PA, Gothakar P, Sodhi S.1999. n-farm seed priming in semi-arid agriculture: Development and evaluation in corn, rice and chickpea in India using participatory methods. *Exp. Agric*. 35 15-29.

Harris D, Raghuwanshi BS, Gangwar JS, Singh SC, Joshi K, Rashid A, Hollington PA. 2001. Evaluation by Farmers of on-farm seed priming in Wheat in India, Nepal and Pakistan. *Expl Agric.* 37 403-415.

Hertel, TW. and Rosch, SD. 2010. *Climate change, agriculture and poverty.* Policy Research Working Paper 5468, The World Bank, Washington DC.

Khatri-Chhetri, A., Aryal, JP., Sapkota, TB. and Khurana, R. 2016. Economic benefits of climate-smart agricultural practices to smallholder farmers in the Indo-Gangetic Plains of India. *Current Science,* 110 (7), 1251-56.

Maheswari, M., Sarkar, B., Vanaja, M., Srinivasa Rao, M., Srinivasa Rao, Ch.,Venkateswarlu, B., Sikka, A.K. 2015. Climate Resilient Crop Varieties for Sustainable FoodProduction under Aberrant Weather Conditions. Central Research Institute for Dryland Agriculture (ICAR), Hyderabad. P47.

Morton, JF. 2007. The impact of climate change on smallholder and subsistence agriculture. *Proc. Natl. Acad. Sci.* 104(50), 19680–19685.

Nawaz J., Hussain M., Jabbar A., Nadeem GA., Sajid M., Subtain M. and Shabbir I. 2013. Seed Priming A Technique. *Intl J Agri Crop Sci.* Vol., 6 (20): 1373-1381.

REMA (2009): Rwanda State of Environment and Outlook Report, Rwanda Environment Management Authority, P.O. Box 7436 Kigali, Rwanda http://www.rema.gov.rw/soe/

Sapkota, TB., Jat, ML., Aryal, JP., Jat, RK. and Katri-Chhetri, A. 2015. Climate change adaptation, greenhouse gas mitigation and economic profitability of conservation agriculture: some examples from cereal systems of Indo-Gangetic Plains. *J. Integr.Agric.*, 14(8), 1524–1533.

Synnevåg, G. and Lambrou, Jayne. (Eds.) 2012. Climate-Smart Agriculture: Possible Roles of Agricultural Universities in a Strengthened Norwegian Climate Change Engagement in Africa. *Noragric Report No. 64* Department of International Environment and Development Studies, Noragric Norwegian University of Life Sciences (UMB) P.O. Box 5003 N-1432 Aas Norway

Terdoo, F. and Adekola O. 2014. Assessing the role of climate-smart agriculture in combating climate change, desertification and improving rural livelihood in Northern Nigeria. *African Journal of Agricultural Research* Vol. 9(15): 1180-1191.

8

Strategic Parasite Management for Transformation in Livestock Farming

Sabhyata Sharma* and SW Kolte

Department of Parasitology, Nagpur Veterinary College, MAFSU, Nagpur, India
**Corresponding Author: drsabhyatasharma@gmail.com*

1. Introduction
2. Impact of parasites on animal health
3. Impact of parasites on livestock productivity
4. External parasites
5. Internal parasites
6. Prevention and control
7. Conclusion
8. *References*

Abstract

Parasitic diseases are of great economic importance in livestock farming and are major obstacle in the health and productivity of animals. These may be due to endo-parasites that live inside the body or ecto-parasites such as ticks, mites, flies, fleas, midges, etc., which attack the body surface. Among ecto-parasites, ticks and mites are very important and harmful blood sucking external parasites of mammals. Blood sucking by large numbers of ticks causes reduction in body weight and anemia among domestic animals, while their bites also reduce the quality of hides. More than 250 species of mites can cause problems for humans and domestic animals because of their being vector for zoonotic diseases. Their attack may lead to problems of temporary irritation of the skin due to bites, persistent dermatitis due to mites invading skin or hair follicles, mite-induced allergies, transmission of pathogenic microbial agents, intermediate host of tapeworms, invading respiratory passages, ear canals and internal organs, fear of mites called acarophobia

The economic or medical importance of the Acari increases with their ability to be vector for viruses, rickettsiae, spirochaetes, phytoplasmas, mycoplasmas and protozoa, or to harbor and transport nematodes, bacteria and fungi pathogens that affect plants, domestic and wild animals and humans. Ectoparasites were not considered serious problem till the introduction of exotic animals or exotic semen in India as the indigenous breeds were considered resistant to parasites and the damages occurred by them were totally ignored. Much awareness was not there about the diseases caused by ectoparasites like anaplasmosis therefore dairy producers had to bear losses both, in milk production and proper animal growth. Ectoparasites may be causing death of animals in certain cases. Losses in dairy, poultry, goatry and other livestock farming can be considerably reduced through strategic management of parasites. This needs timely detection, identification and development of effective control measures. 10-30% production losses are estimated by parasitic infestation. If profitability is the goal in livestock entrepreneurship then target has to be the animal health, productivity and quality produce through strategic management and awareness campaign on economic importance of parasites.

Keywords: ectoparasites, endoparasites, economic significance, management

1. Introduction

Species of several animal-parasitic mite and tick families are moving daily from country to country, mostly due to international trade. As a consequence, native species are continuously expanding their range from their native geographical areas. Adventive ticks have also been spreading with some of them carrying very detrimental diseases to domestic animals, wild fauna and posing a threat to human health. Due to the dramatic increase in international movement of human and animal food products, baggage, ornamental plants, seeds, exotic pets, cattle and humans, mites from a wide range of hosts, habitats and countries are quickly transported across the globe. The detection of these species at the ports of entry has significantly increased our knowledge of the number and diversity of acarine species worldwide. The total number of mite species may be grossly underestimated possible the number may be between 3 and 5 million species. Thus, parasitic diseases are of great economic importance in livestock farming and are major obstacle in the health and productivity of animals.

Parasites are a major cause of poor animal health and productivity loss frequently resulting in significant economic loss in probable range of 10-30%. In addition to the adverse affects on animal health and production, some parasites promote susceptible of animals to various bacterial and viral infections increasing further loss of productivity. Many of helminth parasites like *Haemonchus contortus*, *Oesophagostomum* species suck blood from the abomasum and small intestine making animal debilitated and anaemic. *Fasciola gigantica* causes Hypoproteinemia, Bottle jaw and reduced growth rate especially in sheep and goat. Among the haemoprotozoans, Trypanosomiasis, Theleriosis, Babesiosis are most important causing heavy body weight loss and decrease in milk yield. The treatment and control measures are costly and often time-consuming. A major concern is the development of resistance by worms, lice and blow flies to many of the chemicals used to control them.

Planned preventive programs are necessary to minimise the risk of parasitic disease outbreaks and sub-clinical losses of animal production, and to ensure the most efficient use of chemicals. Integrated parasite management programs are necessary to provide optimal parasite control for the minimal use of chemicals by integrating pre-emptive treatments, parasite monitoring schedules and non-chemical strategies such as nutrition, genetics, and pasture management.

2. Impact of parasites on animal health

- Parasites can have a negative impact on the health and welfare of animals
- Parasites cause blood loss leading to anaemia and death
- Cause diarrhoea which, if severe, can lead to death
- Severe infestation can reduce the appetite of animals, resulting in debilitated animals that are more susceptible to other diseases
- Parasites can also act as vectors, transferring diseases from one animal to another
- External parasites like flies cause open sores on the skin of livestock while some can annoy the animals causing reduce in grazing behaviour and yield.

3. Impact of parasites on livestock productivity

- Reduction in growth rates
- Reduction in milk production
- Reduce in reproductive rates
- Condemnation of carcass parts at slaughter
- Reduced fleece weight, staple length and fibre diameter
- Damage to hides and fleeces

4. External parasites

External parasites/Ectoparasites live on the skin of cattle or visit them to feed. The most important groups of external parasites are ticks and flies. They cause skin and eye irritation and damage, which can lead to bacterial infection and fly maggot attack. Some of external parasites cause large wounds. Some cause diseases through poisonous bites. Some parasites cause disturbance while grazing leading to decrease in grazing efficiency. Some can spread from one animal to other through close contact. These all can lead to death of the animals.

4.1. Flies

Flies are characterised by one pair of wings having complete metamorphosis with egg, larva, pupa, and adult stages in their life. The most important characteristic of flies is their behaviour of very short contact with livestock.

Blood sucking flies

Horse and deer flies are called as Tabanids. These are strong fliers. They are daytime feeders and are vicious biters. Their bites often causes low weight gains and decrease milk production

These flies have anticoagulant in their bite causing blood to ooze which further leads to secondary invasion of other infections.

Sand flies and biting midges are also known as punkies. These flies breed in wet or aquatic habitats and are very difficult pest to control. These flies are major source of annoyance and irritation and also cause suffocation in large amounts. Culicoides, biting midge is a known vector of blue tongue virus in cattle and some are intermediate hosts of helminths.

Black Fliesare small, dark, stout-bodied flies with a humpbacked appearance. Adult females feed during daylight hours only. These hover about the eyes, ears and nostrils of animals, often puncturing the skin with an irritating bite

Stable Flies are also known as dog flies. Both male and female of the stable fly are vicious biters. These flies cause irritation and weakness in animal with severe wounds leading to secondary invasions. These flies are mechanical transmitters of anthrax and anaplasmosis. Dog flies can be easily interrupted while feeding.

Non-blood sucking flies

Cattle Grubs_lay its eggs on the hair of cattle, attaching 5 to 15 eggs to a single hair.

Eggs hatch within 4 days and the maggots burrow through the skin. The larvae produce two types of injury. First there is irritation caused by larval migrations in the body of the host and later by emergence from beneath the skin. Second, the escape of the larva from the warble leaves an open, running wound that is persistent and subject to secondary infection. Decrease in milk production up to 30-40% and drastic loss in body weight.

Myiasis: It is the parasitic infestation of the body of a live mammal by fly larvae (maggots) that grow inside the host while feeding on its tissue. Although flies are most commonly attracted to open wounds and urine or faeces soaked fur but some of the species like Botfly, Blowfly and Screw fly can create infestation even on unbroken skin using moist soils and non-myiatic agents as vectors for their parasitic larvae. Most commonly affected animal is Sheep.

Myiasis and their symptoms

Syndrome	Symptoms
Cutaneous myiasis	Painful, slow developing ulcers-(boil) like sores that can last for prolonged period
Nasal myiasis	Obstruction of nasal passage and severe irritation
Aural myiasis	Crawling sensations and buzzing noises. If larvae in middle ear, may reach upto brain
Opthalmomyiasis	Severe irritation, oedema and pain

Diagnosis

- Recent travel to an endemic area
- One or more non-healing lesions on the skin itchiness
- Discharge from a central punctum (tiny hole)
- Small, white structure protruding from the lesion

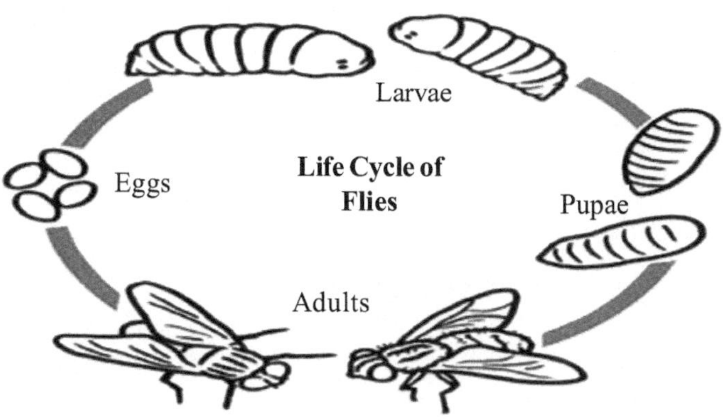

Flies	Diseases transmitted/vector of
Black fly	Onchocerca spp.
Sand fly	Leishmania spp.
Biting midges	Blue tongue virus and Onchocerca cervicalis
Mosquitoes	Equine encephalomyelitis, Japanese B encephalitis, Rift valley fever , African horse sickness
Horse fly	Equine infectious anaemia, African horse sickness, Anthrax, *Trypanosoma evansi*,T.vivax and Bovine leucosis virus
Stable fly	Anthrax, Surra, Anaplasmosis,Lumpy skin diseases,Equine infectious anaemia
Horn fly	Stephanofilaria stilesia
Tsetse fly	Trypanosome brucei
Louse fly	Haemoproteus spp.
Face fly	Moraxella bovis,Thelazia spp. and parafilaria bovicola

Treatment of Fly Strike

Treatment is only possible when infestation has taken place. Once the breathing hole is formed, cover it with petroleum jelly. Lack of oxygen will make the maggots to come on surface and can be easily dealt with. As the surgeons don't have time so they directly spray Topicure (herbal spray) and then removing the maggots with forceps.

Livestock may be treated prophylactically with slow release boluses containing ivermectin which can provide long-term protection against the development of the larvae.

Treat with antibiotics to prevent secondary bacterial infections.

Prevention and Control

- Practise good stable and kraal hygiene (clean regularly)
- Remove manure to large bins to restrict fly breeding and to make compost
- Drain damp areas to stop breeding of mosquitoes and biting midges
- Use dips, sprays and treat wounds to prevent fly and strike problems
- Immediately treat skin wounds so that strikes do not occur
- Keep the wounds clean
- Keep the animals in compound
- Avoid grazing of animals in susceptible areas
- Eradication of adult flies by spraying insecticides

- Sterile insect technique (SIT) where a significant number of artificially reared sterilized (usually through irradiation) male flies are introduced. The male flies compete with wild breed males for females in order to copulate and thus cause females to lay batches of unfertilized eggs which cannot develop into the larval stage.

4.2. Ticks

Ticks are small arachnids, part of order Parasitoformes. Ticks are ectoparasites (external parasites), living by feeding on blood of mammals, birds, reptiles and amphibians. Almost all ticks belong to one of two major families, the Ixodidae or hard ticks, which are difficult to crush and the Argasidae or soft tick. Adults have ovoid or pear-shaped bodies which become engorged with blood when they feed, and eight legs. As well as having a hard shield on their dorsal surfaces, hard ticks have a beak-like structure at the front containing the mouthparts whereas soft ticks have their mouthparts on the underside of the body. Both families locate a potential host by odour or from changes in the environment.

Important characteristics of Ticks

They are obligate hematophages, needing blood to survive and move from one stage of life to another. Some ticks attach quickly while others wonder around looking for thinner skin such as found on ears of mammals. They extract blood by cutting hole in the host's epidermis, into which they insert hypostome and keep the blood from clotting by excreting an anticoagulant or platelet aggregation inhibitor. Ticks when don't find their host, lie in wait and cling to leaves and grasses known as Questing. Ticks have 4 developmental stages: egg, 6-legged seed or larval stage, 8-legged nymphal stage, and 8-legged adult

Economic importance

Milk and meat production: there is reduction in both quality and quantity. Different reports have shown that ticks causes huge loss to cattle milk production conjugated with nutritional status and poor management pattern. Female tick is capable of ingesting 1.0 ml blood from the cow during its parasite phase which cause loss of body weight about 1gm and thus reducing and affecting the production of milk by 8.9 ml.

Skin and hide quality: Hide and skin accounts for 12-16% of the value of export. Ticks can affect the skin and hide through penetration of skin by piercing mouth parts makes holes which are defects in processing skin. While feeding, ticks can allow bacteria to pass through the skin leading to development of local abscessesion with damage skin quality more expensively than the hole caused by feeding.

Mortality and morbidity of livestock due to tick borne disease: Around billion of cattle mainly located in tropical regions have suffered significant loss in production system. Tick infestation is significantly higher in Zebu breed cattle as compare to crossbred cattle. This is due to currently animal husbandry practice where crossbred are kept most of time indoor with semi-intensive care, whereas Zebu cattle are kept under extensive farming system.

Effects of Ticks on Animals

Loss of blood: Ticks feed on blood. Each tick sucks not less than 30 drops of blood to complete its life cycle. Loss of blood results in retarded growth and loss of weight.

Tick worry: A tick bite leads to discomfort for animal. The animal gets irritated and doesnot graze well. This will in turn affect its weight gain and milk supply.

Wounds: When ticks attach themselves, their mouth pieces damage the skin and if they detach themselves thet leave wounds through which germs can gain access to the body, bloodstream and cause disease in various organs of the body

Screw worm strike: The wound that has been left behind by the ticks usually become an ideal site for screw worm infestation and is very difficult to cure.

Loss of distal end of tail: This results from clusters of ticks biting of tail brush. This loss deprives the animal of the swish with which it whisks off irritating flies and biting insects

Toxins: the saliva of ticks contains toxins which are released into the body of an animal. This will affect the general health and productivity of the animal.

Damage to the hide: The mouth of tick pierces through the skin and leaves permanent markings. These markings will affect the value of the hide when being processed for the manufacturing of leather goods.

Diseases: Many animal diseases are transmitted by ticks, e.g., Tick borne Theleriosis, Heartwater, Redwater, Gall sickness, Sweating disease in cattle.

Diseases	Animal or Humans Affected
Tick paralysis	Mainly Sheep and Goat
Spring lamb sickness	Lambs and sometimes calves
Sweating sickness	Cattle, especially calves
Tick borne diseases	Cattle, Sheep, Goat
Tick bite fever	Man
Tick paralysis	Man

Losses Due to Ticks

Tick Bite Paralysis: Characterised by acute ascending flaccid motor paralysis caused by injection of toxin by certain ticks like *Dermacentor andersoni*, sweating sickness by *Hyalomma truncatum*, Australian tick paralysis by Ixodes, tick toxicosis by *Rhipicephalus* species. Common in late winter and spring when the adult ticks are active.

Physical Damage: Ticks are attached to the body for a blood meal and may cause serious irritation and physical damage to livestock. Included are "tick worry" , irritation, unrest, weight loss due to tick infestation, direct injury to hides due to tick bites, blood loss due to feeding of ticks.

Vector of Pathogens: The major diseases like Babesiosis, Anaplasmosis, Theleriosis and Heart water, East coast fever where tick act as a carrier cause severe economic losses to livestock industry.

Public Health Importance

Ticks were the first arthropods to be established as vectors of pathogens and currently they are recognised, along with mosquitoes as the main arthropod vector of disease agents to humans and domestic animals globally. Moreover, the incidence of tick borne disease is increasing worldwide. For instance, more than 250,000 human cases of Lyme borreliosis were reported in US. Ixodes ticks can be infected with more than one agent and co-transmission and infection can occur. Alternatively, multiple infections can occur from multiple tick bites.

Table 1: Zoonotic bacteria transmitted by ticks around the world.

Zoonosis	"Transmittedpathogen	Tick Vector
Human granulocytic anaplasmosis	Anaplasmaphagocytopfrilum	Ixodes scapular is Ixodes padffeus, Ixodes persulcatus, Ixodes ricinus
	Ehrlichia chaffeectus	Ambiyomma americanum
Human monocytic ehrlichioses	E chaffeensts, E. ewingu	Rhiptcephalus sanguineus ?
	Ehdtchia canis	Rhtptcephalus sanguineus
Lyme disease	Borrelia burgdorferi sensu lato	Ixodes spp.(I. scapulads; I. padhcus; I. persulcatus; I. ridnus)
Tick-bome African fever	Rfckecrsja afncae	Ambiyomma hebraeum, Ambiyomma variegatum
Mediterranean spotted fever	Rickettsia cononi	Rhiptcephalus sanguineus
Rocky Mountain spotted fever Tobia Disease"	Rickettsia ridceasii	Ambiyomma cajennense, Dermacentor andersoni, Dermacentor variabitis, Rhiptcephalus sanguineus
Q Fever	Coxiella bumeoi	More than 40 species of different kinds. Haemaphysahs spp., and Zmodtes spp., (of highest prevalence in Europe), and Rhiptcephalus spp., Amb/yomma spp., and Dermacentor spp.. of highest prevalence in America.
Relapsing fever	BorrwMa spp.	Omithodorus spp.
Tularemia	Frandsellatvlarenus	Dermacentor andersorui, D. variabihs, D. occidentals, and Ambiyomma americanum

Control and Prevention of Ticks

The successful implementation of rational and sustainable tick control programs in grazing animals is dependent upon a sound knowledge of the ecology or epidemiology of the parasite as it interacts with the host in specific climate conditions.

Chemical control of Ticks: The main weapon for control of ticks at present is chemical control.

Chemical acaricides: Acaricides used to control ticks on livestock or in environment in the manner that the ticks are killed without harming livestock. Acaricides like arsenical, chlorinated hydrocarbons, organophosphates, pyrethroids are being used. The drawback is the presence of residues in the milk and meat and development of chemical resistant tick strains.

Application of chemicals: Various methods including dipping, spraying, ear tagging or pour on have been used to apply chemicals to protect livestock against ticks.

Dipping: In this method, animals are immersed in dipping tub containing solution of chemicals. A variety of tickicides including cotton seed oil, kerosene, soap. Infested cattle should be dipped in organophosphate acaricide. However, their immobility, high costs of construction and cost of acaricides may make dipping vats impractical for small operations. Also it should be prepared properly with proper concentration and the cattle are dipped carefully.

Spray: Spraying is highly portable and only small amount of acaricides need to be mixed for single application.

Biological control: It is a component of an integrated pest management. It is an introduction of one microorganism into the environment of other to obtain control of target parasite. Thereby it reduces the population growth of the latter below the threshold, above which causes clinical diseases and economic losses.

Grazing Management: Pasture rotation combined with acaricide application is one economical method for controlling ticks on beef cattle and it reduces tick densities on large scale. Pasture burning can also be used to control tick application.

Vaccination: There may be alternative tick control measures, immunization against ticks at present seems both practical and sustainable due to their cost effectiveness, reduction of environmental contamination and prevention of drug resistant ticks caused by repeated acaricide application.

Table 2: Zoonotic viruses transmitted by ticks around the world.

Powassanencephalitis	Flavivirus	Ixodes spp. U- cookei, l. mono, I. sptnipalpus, I. persulactus), Dermacentor spp. (D. andersoni, D. silvarum), y Haemaphysalis sp (H. longkomis)
Tide-borneencephalitis	Flavi virus	Ixodes spp. (/. ricinus; I. persukatus)
Kyasanur forest disease	Flavivirus	Haemaphysalis spinigera
Colorado tick fever	Coltivirus	Dermacentor andersoni
Omsk hemorrhagic fever	Flavivirus	Dermacencor marginatus,D. retkulatus, Ixodes persulcatus
Crimean-Congo haemorrhagic fever	Nairovirus	Hyalomma marginatum
Thrombocytopenia syndrome with severe fever	Flebovirus	Haemaphysalis longkomis
Langat Virus	Flavivirus	Ixodes granulatus. I persulcatus; Haemaphysalis papuana
Tyuleniy Virus	Flavivirus	Ixodes uriae

4.3. Mites

Mites have the abdomen broadly joined to the thorax with little or no evidence of segmentation. Adults and nymphs generally have 8 legs, and the larval stage has 6. Itch and mange mites (Psoroptes, Sarcoptes, and Chorioptes) feed on the surface or burrow just beneath the skin, making very slender, winding tunnels from 0.1 to 1 inch long. The fluid discharged at the tunnel openings dries to form nodules. A toxin is also secreted that causes intense irritation and itching. Infested animals rub and scratch continuously, often producing inflamed areas with only scattered hairs remaining, which is called as mange. All stages of the life cycle are found within the hair follicle. The mites cause nodular lesions in the skin that sometimes break, producing holes in the hide and opening the skin to secondary infection.

Irritation from mites is usually seen on the head, neck and legs. It is associated with crowded conditions and poor husbandry. Infestations of mites cause dermatitis in all species. The mites cause intense itching and discomfort which is associated with decreased feed intake and production. Scratching and rubbing caused by mites result in extensive damage to hides and fleece.

Mites are able to cause mange on different species of livestock but are somewhat host specific, thus infecting some species more severely than others.

Mange	Etiology	Animals affected
Sarcoptic mange	*Sarcoptes scabiei*	All species
Psoroptes mange	*Psoroptes ovis*	Sheep, Cattle and Horses
Chorioptic mange	*Chorioptes bovis*	Cattle, Horses, Goats and Sheep
Demodectic mange	*Demodex bovis, D. ovis, D. caprae, D. equi and D. Phylloides*	Cattle, Sheep, Goats, Horses, and Pigs

Control and treatment of mites

Use of various chemicals for control and management of parasites is very important to ensure optimal production and supply of high quality dairy produce.These are:

Organophosphorus compounds- Diazinon

Synthetic pyrethroids- Cypermethrin

Amidines- Amitraz

Macrocyclic Lactones- Ivermectin and Doramectin

CYTHRIN 10% (Cypermethrin)

It is a synthetic pyrethroid, indicated for the treatment and control of ectoparasites like ticks, mites, midges, all type of flies and lice in livestock. It acts on sodium channels in insect nerve membranes and cause a nonlethal knockdown effect by peripheral nerve intoxication and a lethal effect that is thought to be associated with both peripheral and central neuronal toxicity in the insects.

Cythrin is recommended to be applied as spray or dip in following dilutions.

Animals	Dilutions
Cattle, Buffaloes, horses and camels	1.5 ml/liter of water
Sheep and Goats	0.75ml/liter of water
Animal sheds	5 ml/liter of water

DIAZIN 600 (Diazinon 60%)

It is an organophosphate and used topically to control ticks, lice, mites, flies, screw worms, stable fly and blow fly larvae. The mode of action is by inhibition of insect acetylcholinesterase and, thus, ultimate block of nerve function (neuromuscular paralysis).

Animals	Spray Dilution		Dip Dilution	
	Diazin 15%	Diazin 60%	Diazin 15%	Diazin 60%
Cattle, Camels	1:250	1: 1000	1:250	1: 1000
Sheep, Goats	1:250	1: 1000	1:600	1:2400
Animal Houses	1:6	1: 25	-	-

ECTRAZ (Amitraz 12.5%)

Amitraz is the only formamidine used topically to control the external parasites such as ticks, mites (mange), keds and lice on cattle, camels, sheep, and goats. It may act to inhibit the enzyme monoamine oxidase and as an agonist at octopamine receptors; monoamine oxidase metabolizes amine neurotransmitters in ticks and mites, and octopamine is thought to modify tonic contractions in parasite muscles. Amitraz has a relatively wide safety margin in mammals .

Recommended usage:

Cattle and Camels:

Dip and Spray: 1 liter ECTRAZ per 500 liters of water

Dip Replenish: 1 liter ECTRAZ per 250 liters of water

Sheep and Goats:

Spray: Mix 1litre of ECTRAZ in 250 liters of water (0.05). Spray on the animals uniformly, with special emphasis in skin folds.

Dip: Mix 1 liter of ECTRAZ in 250 liters of water. Top-up the dip bath with 1.50 liters of ECTRAZ every time, when the volume of dip falls by 20.

Ivermic (Ivermectin)

Ivermectin is probably one of the most widely used antiparasitic drugs worldwide, and its efficacy is well established. Ivermectin was first marketed in 1981 by Merck Sharp and Dohme as an antiparasitic agent, and it remains the leading worldwide antiparasitic agent for livestock. It has exceptional potency against endo and ectoparasites (endectocide) at extremely low doses, this account for its large margin of safety. It is neurotoxic to parasites by potentiating glutamate-gated chloride ion channels in parasites. Paralysis and death of the parasite is caused by increased permeability to chloride ions and hyperpolarization of nerve cells. It also potentiates other chloride channels, including ones gated by GABA.

Ivermectin is highly effective against many arthropod parasites of domestic animals such as ticks, biting flies, and parasitic dipteran larvae.

Animal	Arthropods	Dose
Cattle	*Hypoderma* spp., *Sarcoptes bovis*, *Psoroptes ovis*, *Linognathus* spp. and *Haematopinus* spp.	200 µg/kg body wt. SC
Sheep	*Oestrus ovis, Sarcoptes scabiei, Psoroptes ovis* and *Melanophagus ovinus*	200 µg/kg body wt. SC
Goat	*Sarcoptes spp.* and *Psoroptes ovis*	200 µg/kg body wt. SC
Pig	*Sarcoptes scabiei* and *Haematopinus suis*	300 µg/kg body wt. SC

Ivermic Super (Ivermectin and Clorsulon)

This product has the advantage over ivermic as it has the active ingredient of Ivermic, with Clorsulon, an effective flukicide. Clorsulon is rapidly absorbed into the circulating blood. Erythrocytes with bound drug as well as plasma are ingested by liver flukes that lead to the destruction of the parasite, because of inhibition of enzymes in the glycolytic pathway, which is their primary source of energy.

Dosage and administration

Cattle and Sheep: 1ml/50 kg bodyweight (based on a dosage level of 200 µg Ivermectin and 2 mg Clorsulon per kg bodyweight) by subcutaneous injection.

Closectin (Ivermectin and Closantel)

It is indicated for the treatment of mixed trematode (fluke) and nematode or arthropod infestations due to gastrointestinal roundworms, lungworms, eyeworms, warbles, mites and lice of cattle.

Closectin offers all the benefits of Ivermic (Ivermectin) plus control of trematodes as it contains closantel along with Ivermectin. Closantel is a parasiticide with flukicide activity and efficacy against certain other helminths and arthropods. It is lipophilic and is known to shuttle protons across membranes, in particular the inner mitochondrial membrane. Closantel acts by uncoupling oxidative phosphorylation.

Dosage and administration

Cattle: 200 µg Ivermectin and 5 mg Closantel per kg bodyweight (1ml CLOSECTIN per 25 kg bodyweight), only by SC injection in the neck.

Doramec (Doramectin 1%)

Doramec is indicated for the treatment and control of gastrointestinal roundworms lungworms, sucking lice and mange mites in cattle, sheep and goats.

Recommended usage

200 µg/kg bodyweight (1 ml/50 kg bodyweight) as a single dose by SC or IM route.

Diminazine (Diminazine aceturate 7% RTU)

Diminazine aceturate is specially used for the treatment of Babesiosis, Trypanosomosis, Theileriosis and mixed haemoprotozoal infections. Its effect on the *Babesia* parasites seems to relate to interference with glycolysis, as well as with synthesis of DNA in the parasite while in others it intercalate with DNA and RNA (25).

Recommended usage:

Diseases	Dosage
Babesiosis and Trypanosomiasis	5-10 ml/100kg body weight
Theileriosis	5-10 ml/100kg body weight along with antibiotic
Mixed Haemoprotozoal infection	5-10 ml/100kg body weight

Imidol (Imidocarb dipropionate 12%)

Imidocarb is a carbanilide derivarive with antiprotozoal activity. It is usually administered as the dipropionate salt. It is indicated for the treatment and prevention of Babesiosis in cattle, sheep goat, horses, donkeys, mules and dogs, for the treatment of Anaplasmosis in cattle and Ehrlichiosis in dogs.

The mode of action of Imidocarb is uncertain though two mechanisms have been proposed: interference with the production and/or utilization of polyamines, or prevention of entry of inositol into the erythrocyte containing the parasite.

Animals	Dosage and administration
Cattle	1-2 ml/100 kg bwt by IM or SC route, single dose
Horses	2 ml/100 kg bwt by IM or SC route, 2 injections at 48 hrs interval may be required to treat *B. equi*
Sheep and Goats	0.2 ml/10 kg bwt by IM or SC route may be repeated not earlier than 7 days
Dogs	0.25-0.5 ml by SC route, single dose

Theilex (Buparvaquone 5%)

Buparvaquone is a second-generation hydroxynaphthoquinone related to parvaquone, with novel features that make it a promising compound for the therapy and prophylaxis of East Coast fever (*Theileria parva*) and Tropical theileriosis or Mediterranean theileriosis (*T. annulata*).

5. Internal Parasites

Internal parasites need to be properly managed so as to prevent the debilitating condition of the livestock, but it's a challenging task to control because of varied geo-climatic conditions. Various roundworms and flatworms can seriously affect the growth rate, scours, anaemia, decrease milk production and in severe conditions death also. The major action of most of nematodes is in stomach and intestine causing reduction in nutrient absorption by the host and increase amount of blood loss leading to Anaemia which further leads to debilitating condition of animal due to nutrient deprivation.

Survival

Moisture is essential for the worm survival. Moist pastures are the ideal environment for their growth, development, multiplication, survival. Young animal stock is more susceptible to the effects of worms and is maximal during one to two years of age.

Life cycle

Some parasites have direct life cycle and some have indirect life cycle.

Parasites with direct life cycle spend all their life in one host while parasites with indirect life cycle requires intermediate host for their transfer into the host.

Classification of Internal Parasites

Parasitism in cattle is divided into 5 main categories:

- Stomach worms
- Intestinal worms
- Liver flukes
- Lungworms
- Protozoa

Direct life cycle

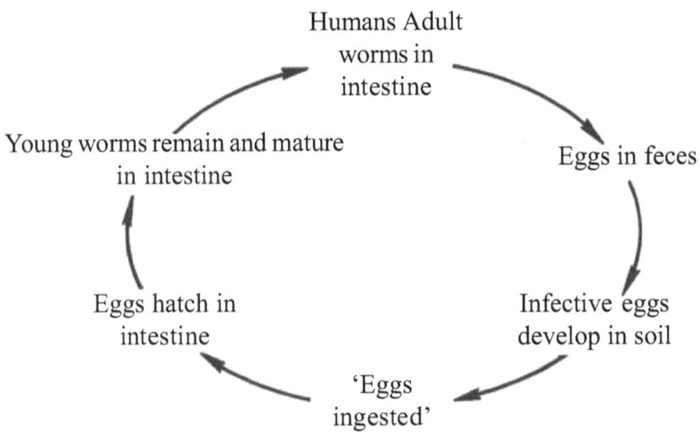

5.1. Stomach Worms

Haemonchus-the barber pole worm is a blood sucking parasite. This parasite causes great *economical damage in cattle and is one of the most important causes of death in the* animals. Larval stages can be found in rumen and abomasaal tissues and are very difficult to kill.

Ostertagia- brown stomach worm is the most prevalent parasite of cattle. Their larval stages invade and destroy the gastric glands which lead to reduction in digestion efficiency.

Trichostrongylus- bankrupt worm. These parasites suck fluids from gastric mucosa, causes necrosis of the mucosa. These parasites have kidney bean shaped eggs but very difficult to differentiate from Ostertagia and Haemonchus

Indirect life cycle

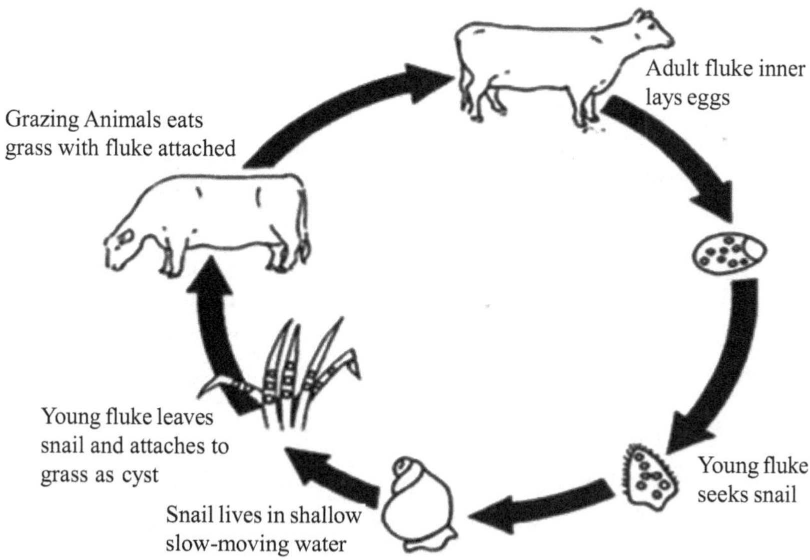

Intestinal Worms

Cooperia- It disrupts the digestive functions of intestine. Cooperia is considered as second most prevalent parasite of cattle. Eggs can be easily found in faecal sample and have elongated parallel sides.

Nematodirus- thread neck worm is most commonly found in young animals sometimes in adults. Larvae survive well in cold weather and can survive for two years on pasture. This parasite is common cause of diarrhoea and sometimes death in young stock. It is a very pathogenic parasite so older animals acquired very strong immunity against them.

Bunostomum- hookworms, they suck blood by feeding on plug of mucosa in the intestine. The larvae penetrate the skin and migrate through the lungs causing dermatitis and pneumonia.

Oesophagostomum- nodular worms, they form nodules on intestines causing decrease weight gain, diarrhoea, anorexia. Most commonly found in adult animals.

5.2. Intestinal cestode parasites

These tapeworms generally reside in small intestine and can grow up to 1inch wide and six feet long. They absorb nutrition through their cuticle. In large numbers these tapeworms can block the intestines.

5.3. Cattle Lung Worm (*Dictyocaulus viviparous*)

Lungworms are mostly acquired through grazing. Cattle on rotational and intensive grazing systems are often exposed to lungworms. Lungworms cannot be seen well in faecal sample but rather the faecal must be subject to a separate test called a "Baermann test" to find lungworm larvae.

5.4. Trematodes Parasites (Liver Flukes)

Fasciolosis- most common fluke found in India and also in RS Pura region of Jammu (*Fasciola hepatica*).Treatment in early summer or early fall is desirable to reduce contamination. Snails which act as intermediate host carries infection through the winter and cattle become infected in the spring when grazing wet areas where infected snail habitat is present.

5.5. Protozoan Parasites

Coccidia are single-cell protozoa that can wreak havoc in a sheep and goat herd. Young lambs and goats are especially susceptible to coccidia. They are very host specific. Coccidia are ingested through faecal contaminated feedstuff. Cattle become infected when they ingest oocyst containing sporozoites, which escapes the oocyst and penetrates intestinal wall. It generally occurs when coccidia number is high and the immune system is low. Cattle shedding high number of oocysts indicate that cell damage is going on.

Giardia: one of the common protozoan infecting at first week of life. It is very important parasite of cattle causing diarrhoea and ill health in calves and is a zoonotic threat to man from pasture runoff that can contaminate drinking water.

Symptoms

Loose foul-smelling stools, Diarrhoea, Mucous in stools, Abdominal cramps and gas, Loss of appetite, Distended abdomen, Coughing, Fever, Vomiting, Listlessness and generally feeling unwell.

Diagnosis

A faecal (stool) exam (an ova and parasite test) :

This test is for those parasites that cause diarrhoea, flatulence, cramping and other abdominal illness. Three to four faecal samples collected on separate days, be examined. This test looks for the ova (eggs) of the parasites.

Endoscopy/Colonoscopy

This test is also used to find parasites that cause diarrhoea, flatulence, lose and watery stools and other abdominal illness. This test is done when examination donot reveal the cause of diarrhoea stool. This test looks for parasites and other abnormalities that may be causing symptoms.

Blood tests

Some of the parasitic infections can be detected by testing blood. There are generally two kinds of blood tests;

Serology

This test is used to look for antibodies or for parasite antigens produced when the body is infected with a parasite and the immune system is trying to fight against invader.

Blood smear

This test is done for the parasites which are found in blood e.g., Theleriosis, Babesiosis, Filariasis can be diagnosed.

X-ray, Magnetic Resonance Imaging (MRI) scan, Computerized Axial Tomography (CAT) scan

These tests are performed for the parasites that may cause lesions in blood.

6. Prevention and Control

The various control measures with or without use of chemicals will be useful for sustainable production as per agro-climatic conditions.

6.1. Housing management

The animals having good living conditions resist or tolerate internal parasites very efficiently as compare to animals living in poor housing conditions. Animals should be kept in well ventilated areas and proper light management to maintain required humidity and air circulation. In high humidity and low light, parasite growth rate increases. Always keep optimum number of animals in the shed to prevent proliferation of certain parasites.

Animals should not be fed on ground instead proper feeders should be provided to avoid faecal and urine contamination.

Water should be clean and free from faecal matter. Facilities of proper drainage in the shed reduce the chances of survival of parasites. The newly introduced animal should be quarantined for at least 4-6 weeks to prevent infection.

Always keep manure by making heap so that eggs, larvae, cyst or other stages of parasites are killed due to heat generated during composting. The bedding material should be properly decomposed with manure as it act as important source of various parasitic infections like winter coccidiosis. Application of nitrogen fertilizers like urea to the manure surface also prevents some parasitic infections.

6.2. Nutritional management

Vitamin A, D and B complexes are essential in diet to prevent susceptibility of animals to parasites. Vitamins A, B, D are essential in developing immunity against parasites. Minerals like Zinc, iron, cobalt, sodium, potassium, phosphorus, etc are very essential for proper functioning of immunological phenomenon going inside the animal's body to develop functional immunity against parasites. Vitamin A is essential for intestinal epithelial integrity. Deficiency of Zinc shows impaired cell mediated cytotoxicity and T helper cell function, impaired NK cell function and phagocytosis by macrophages. Cobalt deficiency promotes parasitism as it is essential for vitamin B_{12} synthesis. Iron supplements are also very important in animals suffering from blood sucking parasites.

6.3. Pasture management

It is the most effective way to control internal parasites in grazing livestock. Ideally, animals are allowed to graze clean or new pasture to fetch maximum productivity from them. The clean or new pastures are those which have not been grazed since 6-12 months. Regular burning of old or grazed pasture should always be practiced to obtain parasite free pasture land. Overstocking in a small piece of land increases the concentration of parasites so allows only optimum number of animals to graze in a particular piece of land.

6.4. Biological control

This may be defined as the use of one living organism to achieve control over targeted organism like parasite, and thus reducing the population of pathogen below threshold level. For e.g.-*Duddingtonia flagrans* is relatively easy to culture and can be released in environment against targeted parasites in a controlled fashion. So it is widely used to control gastro-intestinal parasites of grazing animals by reducing pasture load.

6.5. Anti-parasitic drugs management strategies

Anti-parasitic drugs still plays a very important role in control of parasitic infections. In Indian conditions, it is necessary to dose the animal twice a year at the onset (May end) and offset (September end) of monsoon. However, strategic use of drugs is very important to prevent overdose and under dose of drugs.

Reduce use of anti-parasitic drugs-Injudicious use of anthelmintics leads to fast development of drug resistance. Drug use should be minimised to 2 or 3 times per year so as to prevent resistance. Frequent dosing of same anthelmintics must be avoided.

Use of full dose of anti-parasitic drugs- The anti-parasitic drug dose rate should be as per the species of animals, the same dose rate for different species must be avoided. For instance goat, has physiologically different metabolism from cattle and sheep, so require twice the drug dosage than sheep or cattle.

Alternate the type of anti-parasitic drugs- Drugs should always be given alternately on annual basis but frequent change is also not recommended which can cause resistance against group of anthelmintics.

Table 3: Deworming Program for Dairy Cows

Level of Contamination	Time of Treatment	Recommended Product Type
High to moderate	Freshening	Avermectin
Low	Freshening	Benzimidazole
Extremely low	No treatment	

7. Conclusion

The parasites are crucial in animal health and productivity management. They are the limiting factors for the profitable livestock farming by affecting the quantity and quality of produce and products. Most of the parasitic infections, not only cause reduction in productivity by 10-30%, but also lead to the death of animals in certain cases. Lower hide and meat quality, there by result into huge economic loss to the farmers. Proper management facilities like clean houses with proper ventilation and sunlight, manure removal with proper nitrogenous sprays leads to decrease in flies' movement and other parasitic growth. There must be judicial use of ecto- and endoparasitic drugs so as to prevent resistance of animals against diseases. Proper drug dosage at appropriate time period plays a very important role to achieve sustainable management of parasites and parasitic infections.

8. References

Bram RA .1983. Tick-borne livestock diseases and their vectors. 1. The global problem. *Wld. Anim. Rev.*, (FAO). 36:1-5.

Canga AG, Sahagu´n Prieto AM, Lie´bana MJ, Martý´nez, NF, Vega MS and Vieitez JJG .2009. The pharmacokinetics and metabolism of Ivermectin in domestic animal species. *The Vet Journal.* 179:25-37.

Colebrook E and Wall R .2004. Ectoparasites of livestock in Europe and the Mediterranean region. *Vet Parasitol.* 120: 251-274.

Curtis RJ. (1985) Amitraz in the control of non-ixodide ectoparasites of livestock. *Vet Parasitol.* 18(3):251-264.

Greenberg B .1973. Flies and diseases: Princeton University. Press, Princeton, New Jersey.

Petney TN., Kolonin GV. and Robbins RG. 2007. Southeast Asian ticks (Acari: Ixodida): a historical perspective. *Parasitol Res.* 101 (Suppl 2): S201-205.

Radostits OM, Gay CC, Blood DC and Hinchcliff KW .2003. Veterinary Medicine-A textbook of the diseases of cattle, sheep, pigs, goats and horses. 9th ed. Book Power (Formerly ELST).

9

Technological and Marketing Interventions for Doubling Farmers' Income

MH Wani*, Nallamilli Siddardha and Arshad Bhat

**Rajiv Gandhi Chair, SKUAST-K, Shalimar, Jammu & Kashmir, India*

1. Introduction
2. Doubling farmers' income - The concept
3. Status of Indian agriculture
4. Scenario of agricultural growth
5. Rising demand for food
6. National consultation on doubling the farmers' income
7. Measures for increasing farmers' income
8. Conclusion
9. *References*

Abstract

Doubling the farmers' income", implies a 100 per cent growth of the current level of income of the farmers within a specific time frame, through multifaceted efforts of technological advancements in agriculture, policy formulation/ implementation, and efficient market system. The idea of doubling the farmers' income during seven year period has by many experts been deemed impractical owing to the fact that a consistent annual growth rate of 14.86 per cent would be required in agricultural sector to double its GDP which has never had any history in the Indian agriculture. Some experts point out the possibility of success through appropriate technological intervention and viable government policies specific for each of the agro ecological zones of the nation. Increase in the farmer's income doesn't imply increase in nominal income through excessive production, but increase in real income, taking inflation into account. Production technologies, their use and impact are important factors to focus on doubling the farmers' income. These technologies are already available across all the regions of the country but their adoption remains a problem to discuss always and partial adoption of the technological package can never be expected to get the desired results on ground. The results are suggestive of the pent up need to focus on the extension support on end-to-end approach from production to marketing with appropriate facilitation for inputs, insurance, credit, storage, marketing facilities etc. However, it would need involvement of all the stakeholders to come up on board to pursue this goal.

Keywords: doubling farmers' income, concept, technological interventions

1. Introduction

Hon'ble Prime Minister Shri Narendra Modi while addressing a farmers rally in Bareily in Uttar Pradesh on 28th of February, 2015 mentioned about the idea of doubling the farmers' income, the idea was further taken up the by Hon'ble Finance Minister of India Shri Arun Jaitley ji during his 2016 Budget speech, that invited a lot of attention by the people in general and stakeholders in particular. The first question that strikes one's mind on hearing this was, 'Why specific focus on farmers alone?' The question found the answer in admitting the fact that 58 per cent of the population of the country is dependent on agricultural sector directly or indirectly, for both food and livelihood. It is one of the main sectors of the economy, contributing to around 14-15per cent of the total GDP of the country, even though its contribution has been gradually been declining since 1951. Though the number of cultivators nearly doubled from 1951 to 2011 (118.6 million in 2011), the percentage of cultivators of the total workforce of the nation declined from 49.9 per cent in 1951 to 24.6 per cent in 2011. The reason could be population growth and diversion of the nation's workforce towards the non-agricultural sectors. However, a healthy sign is that the productivity of the farms have increased over the years owing to consistent efforts made in agricultural sector, by the agricultural scientists who are trying their best to ensure sufficient food for nation. Despite these efforts we are observing a decline in the percentage of agricultural workforce, a technological fatigue which could harm the country's food security, also the fact that any rational person would continue to invest his time and resources in an activity, if it generates incremental income. So, the function of reinvestment in agriculture and farmer's income is bidirectional in nature, and the beginning of this must be made by increasing the farmer's income, which necessitated to propose the idea of doubling the farmers' income by the Government to accelerate agricultural development and improve farmers' livelihood.

This paper concentrates on some of the measures needed to be taken by the policy planners, farming community and those involved in the marketing of agricultural produce. The paper has been divided into eight different sections, each part giving a view into the aspect, means and methods that have the potential of doubling farmers' income as the study progresses. Beginning with an overview of what 'Doubling Farmers' Income' means, we progress towards the status of Indian Agriculture and the constraints in reaching its full potential, which need to be addressed by a wide range of scientific and economic solutions which are conceived after an in-depth study into the problems.

2. Doubling Farmers' Income – The Concept

The idea of doubling the farmers' income during seven year period has by many experts been deemed impractical owing to the fact that a consistent annual growth rate of 14.86 per cent would be required in agricultural sector to double its GDP which has never had any history in the Indian agriculture (Chand 2016). Some experts point out the possibility of success through appropriate technological intervention and viable government policies specific for each of the agro ecological zones of the nation. Increase in the farmer's income doesn't imply increase in nominal income through excessive production, but increase in real income, taking inflation into account. The notion of "More Output – More Income" is valid till the supply matches the demand, after which the glut brings about a decline in prices, resulting in low income. So, all the activities from decision making at farmers' level to the distribution of final product to the final consumer deserve due importance. Ultimately, demand-based production, resource use efficiency and market efficiency are said to have a positive impact on the farmers' income.

Therefore, the concept, "Doubling the farmers' income", implies a 100 per cent growth of the current level of income of the farmers within a specific time frame, through multifaceted efforts of technological advancements in agriculture, policy formulation/implementation, and efficient market system.

3. Status of Indian agriculture

Agricultural sector is a critical part of the Indian Economy as more than half of the India's population relies on it directly for livelihood and acts as an important source of raw material for a large number of industries. It meets the food requirements of 1.3 billion Indians, and contributes significantly to employment and demand generation through various backward and forward linkages (Anonymous, 2015). As of 2014, agricultural sector of India contributed to 18.03 per cent of India's GDP (USD 2035 billion), and its total production amounted to USD 366.92 billion (World Bank, 2014). It is the single largest private sector occupation, providing employment to 54.6per cent of workforce even a decade ago, which comprises about 263million farmers and agricultural labour (Census 2011) in contrast to its percentage of 58.24 in 2001, comprising 234.27 million farmers, implying that despite the level of increase in the population as well as workforce, the proportion of agricultural workforce has seen a decline due to the shifting of citizens towards non-agricultural sectors. Average holding size has been declining since the 1960s, as indicated by the sharp decline on large and medium holding size accompanied by the increase in number of marginal holdings over the years (Fig 1). Irrigation capacities for agriculture have not been fully utilized, owing to the reason that increase in net irrigated area has been at a slower pace to meet the requirements of net sown area in India (Fig 2). Technologies have been under-utilized, and many studies from India seem to suggest that the farm inputs like fertilizers, pesticides and high yielding varieties have been used sub-optimally (Narayanamoorthy *et al.* 2017).

Despite technological breakthroughs, mechanization hasn't been at its full scale of utilization, due to capital constraints with the farmers. Cost of production of crops is increasing at a rate of 4-7 per cent per annum (Table 1) and also increase in labour wages over the years, indicating an increase in per hectare investment. To support the farmers, the Government has taken several initiatives over the years. It has supplied inputs to the farmers on subsidy to support them to encourage farming. As of 2010, out of the per hectare agricultural subsidies in India amounting to Rs. 5565, a majority of 99.8 per cent (Rs.5556.13) comprises of fertilizer subsidies alone, but the farmers have been trapped in an illusion of 'More Fertilizer-More Yield' and the sub-optimal utilization of fertilizers led to increase in farm costs, but not a proportionate increase in yield.

Numerous lacunae in the marketing system, like less number of regulated markets, lack of sufficient market services & infrastructure and inefficient markets have resulted in decreased farm income and wastage of agricultural produce after harvest. The above mentioned facts therefore explain the factors responsible for the lower growth rate of Indian Agriculture, that need to be addressed efficiently to aid the Indian Agriculture to reach the targeted growth rate of 14.86 per cent by the set time frame if the farmers' incomes is to be doubled.

Table 1: Crop-wise Cost of Production* of some important crops in India (2012-13 to 2015-16)

(In Rs. per Quintal)

Crop	2012-13	2013-14	2014-15	2015-16
Rabi Crops				
Wheat	716	679	744	789
Barley	620	676	735	776
Gram	1696	1786	1902	2124
Kharif Crops				
Paddy	814	961	978	1020
Maize	814	860	914	941
Jowar	1240	1269	1370	1467
Cotton (Medium Staple)	1970	2485	2510	2753
Groundnut (In Shell)	2873	2720	3232	3314
Sunflower Seed	2955	3000	3129	3282
Sesamum	2893	2919	3765	4132

*Excluding rental value of owned land and interests on fixed capital

Source: https://www.indiaagristat.com/agriculture/2/costofcultivationproduction/32320/stats.aspx)

4. Scenario of agricultural growth and trade

The post-independence era has witnessed a rapid growth in agriculture, as indicated by the average growth rate of 2.51 per cent between1950-51 and 1964-65, during which yield increased, combined with horizontal expansion in agriculture. The advent of Green Revolution in 1966 boosted the yield, with the growth rate spiking to 3.07 per cent between 1980-81 and 1990-91 when the Green Revolution was in its full bloom cross the country. This prosperous era was followed by a decline in the growth rate owing to the agricultural reforms and neglecting the agricultural sector due to the society's interest in other sectors of the economy, with the lowest average annual growth rate of 1.6 per cent from 1997-98 to 2004-05. Government's focus on agriculture with increased scientific efforts revived agricultural growth to an average of 3.47 per cent from 2004-05 to 2010-11, however, the drought-hit 2015-16 which year recorded an annual growth rate of 1.2 per cent, an all-time low. Therefore, it was expected to rise again to 4.1 per cent in 2017,however, it seems beyond our perception to reach the targeted 14.86 per cent under the present status, more specifically due to the agricultural productive capacities that are under deep pressure of increasing demand of inelastic nature, owing to population growth and over exploitation of natural resources.

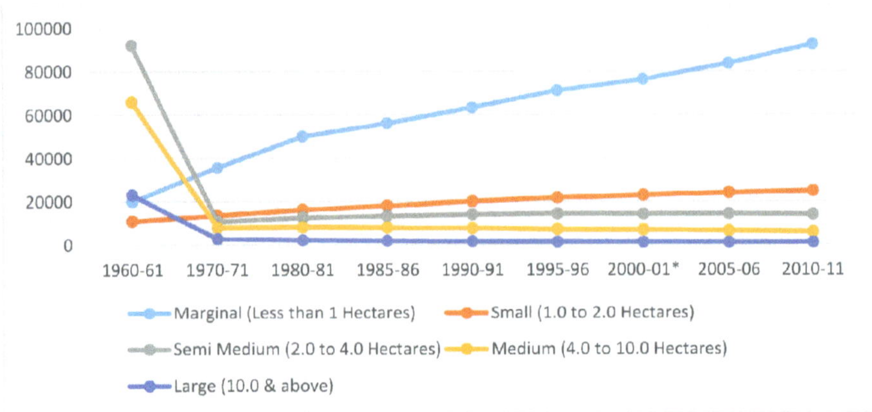

Fig. 1: Category-wise Distribution of Number of Land Holdings in India (*Source:* Based on the data by Ministry of Agriculture, Government of India, 2012)

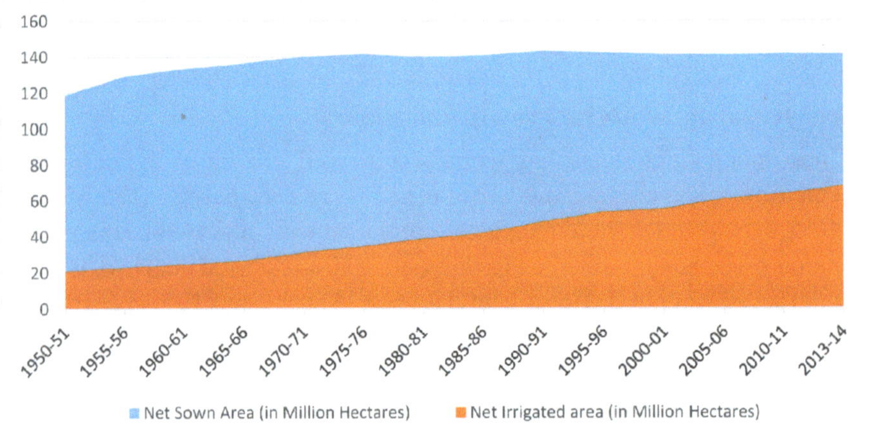

Fig. 2: Temporal Data of Net Sown and Net Irrigated area in India (*Source:* Based on the data by Directorate of Economics and Statistics, 2015, Government of India)

The heavy consumption requirements of the all time population growth led to the scenario of the quantum of imports surpassing that of exports, creating a trade deficit over the years(***Table 2***). In 2016, India's trade deficit was observed around $ 95.73 billion, amounting to 14.49 per cent which over the decade demonstrated decreased linear trend of Trade Deficit (***Figure 3***). This is a positive sign, but its further decline resulting from increased surplus from the agricultural sector suggests to ensure positive increased growth in agricultural GDP. The challenges that contain Indian Agriculture reach the desired growth are Capital inadequacy, Technology fatigue, degradation of natural resources, small size land holdings, reduced productivity of inputs and market inefficiencies, which need to be addressed on priority through R&D efforts and effective policies.

Table 2: India's Exports, Imports and Balance of Trade from 2000-01 to 2010-11

Year	Value (in Rs. Crores)			Percentage Growth		
	Exports	Imports	Balance of Trade	Exports	Imports	Trade Deficit
2000-01	203571	230873	-27302	n/a	n/a	n/a
2001-02	209018	245200	-36182	2.68	6.21	32.53
2002-03	255137	297206	-42069	22.06	21.21	16.27
2003-04	293367	359108	-65741	14.98	20.83	56.27
2004-05	375340	501065	-125725	27.94	39.53	91.24
2005-06	456418	660409	-203991	21.60	31.80	62.25
2006-07	571779	840506	-268727	25.28	27.27	31.73
2007-08	655864	1012312	-356448	14.71	20.44	32.64
2008-09	840755	1374436	-533681	28.19	35.77	49.72
2009-10	845534	1363736	-518202	0.57	-0.78	-2.90
2010-11	1142922	1683467	-540545	35.17	23.45	4.31

(*Source:* Foreign Trade performance of India, www.dgciskol.nic.in/annualreport/book_3e.pdf)

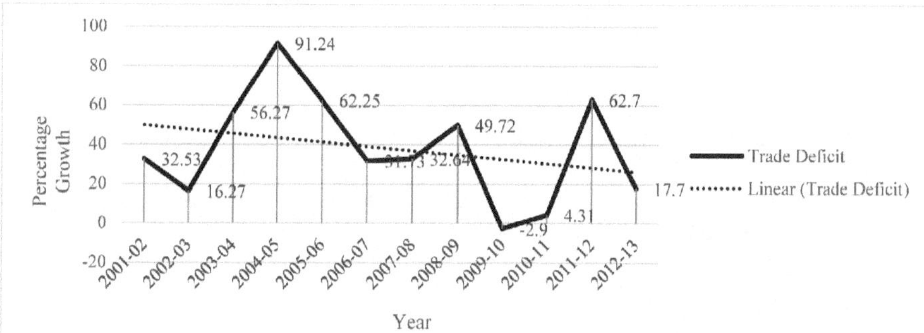

Fig. 3: Trade Deficit in India from 2001-02 to 2012-13
(*Source:* Foreign Trade performance of India
www.dgciskol.nic.in/annualreport/book_3e.pdf)

5. Rising demand for food

Ever increasing population of the country needs to be constantly fed to meet its nutritional requirements. Cereals, Oil seed crops and pulses which are consumed in greater quantities have a constant increase in demand, but the supply is projected to be lower than the demand, as shown in Table 3. Crops like Sugarcane and Coarse Cereals have greater supply than the demand, indicating a possibility of reduction in their market prices.

Table 3: Projected Demand and Supply of Food Commodities in India (2016-17 and 2020-21)

Crop/Group of Crops	Projected Demand (Million Tonnes)		Projected Supply (Million Tonnes)
	2016-2017	2020-2021	2016-2017
Rice	110	117	98-106
Wheat	89	98	93-104
Maize	19	22	-
Coarse Cereals	36	38	42-48
Cereals	235	253	240-251
Pulses	22	25	18-21
Food-grains	257	277	258-272
Oilseeds/Edible Oils	59	71	33-41
Sugarcane/ Sugar	279	312	365-411
Vegetables	161	189	-
Fruits	97	124	-
Milk	141	173	-
Fish	11	-	-
Meat, Other than Poultry	3.7	5	-
Poultry Meat	3.3	4.3	-

(*Source*: www.indiaagristat.com)

6. National consultation on doubling the farmers' income

Indian Council of Food and Agriculture (ICFA), on 30th April, 2016, organized a national consultation in New Delhi, consisting of the National Round Table chaired by Professor MS Swaminathan. The National Round Table gave about 40 recommendations for doubling farmers' income by 2022, which have been categorized into five major areas:

A. Increasing incomes by improving productivity

a. Biotechnological applications in crop and livestock production

b. Improving agricultural productivity in rain fed regions of India

c. Bridging yield gaps among the States and increasing budget on farmers' Inter-State Exposure Visits and Training Scheme of Ministry of Agriculture

B. Water and Agri-Input Policies

a. Fertilizer Subsidy and Rationalizing the NPK pricing

b. Provision of quality plant protection chemicals

c. Farm Mechanization

d. Integrated Water Use Policy

e. Educating farmers on water usage systems

C. Integrated Farming System

a. Promotion of Integrated farming system approach

b. Encouraging Dairy Husbandry among small farmers

c. Promotion of intensive vegetable production

D. Better market price realization

a. Revision of the APMC Act and monitoring its implementation in the states

b. Easing license norms to the launch of National Agricultural Markets (NAM)

c. Reforms to the APMC Acts to permit additional market services

d. Strengthening of market infrastructure

e. Reducing post-harvest losses by strengthening storage infrastructure

E. Special Policy Measures

7. Measures for increasing farmers' income

A. Rationalization of land resources based on the choice of the crops: Horizontal integration of agriculture with respect to land is a subject of debate, as it is difficult to bring the land utilized for non-agricultural purposes into cultivation. As of 2012-2013, the cultivated land in India was about 85.3 per cent of the total cultivable area, which implies that a potential of 26.7 mha could be made productive (DES, 2013). But many studies at national level indicates that the cultivable area had been declining in recent years due to improper utilization of resources. Also, over the generations, with increasing population, land got split into smaller holdings, resulting in smaller production from a single unit. As indicated in Figure 1, Marginal land holding numbers have increased inexplicably from 1960s, marked by a steep decline in the number of semi-medium, medium and large land holdings in just a decade. About 70 per cent farmers are marginal, and 77 per cent of them earn an average per capita income of Rs.6067, most of them were mostly spread in northern states of Rajasthan (5.8 per cent), Bihar (11.4 per cent), Uttar Pradesh (27.4 per cent), etc. (Birthal *et al.*, 2018) indicating that the overall production has split into smaller units, and the income from each of the units would be insufficient to the holder of such smaller portion of the land to improve his livelihood. So, the key to offset the disadvantages of declining farm size would be higher productivity per hectare of crop area operated by the farms.

An observation of share in Gross Cropped Areas of each type of crop in a seven year period from 2006-07 to 2012-13 (Table 4) points out a change in

Table 4: Share in Gross Cropped Area

Crop/ Crop Group	2006-07	2007-08	2008-09	2009-10	2010-11	2011-12	2012-13	SD (Standard Deviation)
Rice	22.77	22.49	23.31	22.17	21.69	22.49	21.99	0.533006
Wheat	14.55	14.36	14.2	15.05	14.71	15.26	15.43	0.464574
Maize	4.1	4.15	4.18	4.37	4.32	4.48	4.46	0.152737
All Cereals	***52.24***	***51.44***	***51.57***	***51.87***	***50.75***	***51.26***	***50.16***	***0.695167***
Chick Pea	3.89	3.86	4.04	4.32	4.64	4.24	4.38	0.282598
Pigeon Pea	1.8	1.9	1.72	1.83	2.21	2.04	2	0.166976
All Pulses	***12.05***	***12.1***	***11.31***	***12.31***	***13.36***	***12.5***	***11.96***	***0.622461***
Groundnut	2.9	3.22	3.15	2.89	2.96	2.69	2.42	0.271539
Rapeseed and Mustard	3.52	2.98	3.22	2.95	3.49	3.01	3.27	0.237547
All Oilseeds	***13.78***	***13.67***	***14.1***	***13.73***	***13.77***	***13.44***	***13.62***	***0.200333***
Cotton	4.7	4.82	4.81	5.36	5.67	6.22	6.16	0.645302
Other	0.5	0.49	0.46	0.47	0.44	0.46	0.44	0.022991
All Fibers	***5.2***	***5.31***	***5.27***	***5.84***	***6.11***	***6.68***	***6.6***	***0.628369***
Plantation	0.9	0.9	0.93	1	0.98	1	0.98	0.044668
Sugarcane	4.7	2.58	2.26	2.2	2.47	2.57	2.57	0.867542
Fruits, Vegetables, Spices and Condiments	11.5	14	14.56	13.05	12.56	12.55	14.11	1.084866
Total	**100**	**100**	**100**	**100**	**100**	**100**	**100**	-

(Calculated by authors based on land data from Directorate of Economics and Statistics, Government of India) distribution of area under various crops. The proportion of area under cereals has been declining and that of pulses, fibers and horticultural crops has increased, indicating the movement of agriculture from subsistence to commercial lines. A rational decision maker should have a combination of crops that best suits the agro-ecological setting of that region or area. The usage of inputs must be directed towards maximum efficiency, to increase the productivity with additional use of resources. Some of the major inputs with increased use over years have been identified to enhance their productivity, which are mentioned in Table 5.

Table 5: Some Major Inputs with Increased Use

S.No.	Factors	Year 2005-06	Year 2014-15	Increase
1.	Irrigated Area	58.78 Lakh Hectares	95.99 Lakh Hectares	63%
2.	Certified Seeds	23 Lakh Quintals	44 Lakh Quintals	91%
3.	Fertilizer Consumption	47.62 Kg/Ha	82.38 Kg/Ha	73%
4.	Farm Power	0.74 Kw/Ha	1.73 Kw/Ha	134%

B. Production Technologies under various crops: Increase in productivity could be brought alone by adoption of technically feasible and economically viable technologies, which comprise improved farm practices and inputs, some of which are described below:

a. Farm Mechanization

Improved farm implements and machinery contribute significantly to the income of the farmers by shortening the time duration required for certain farm activities. Development of fuel-efficient machinery is the ultimate milestone that augments the farm infrastructure, with the added advantage of reduced expenditure by utilizing them in place of obsolete technologies, which are considered "Gas guzzlers". Mechanization in some field practices and their benefits are suggested in Table 6.

b. Organic Farming

Reduction in usage of chemical inputs in cultivation and replacing them with organic substitutes not only increases farmers' real incomes by reduction of costs, but also ensure a high value of the produce through normal cultivation practices. Organic farming involves utilization of commonly found natural resources to enrich the soil and repel any crop pests involved, apart from creating a micro-environment within the field in which useful organisms like earthworms and pest-predators can thrive freely. For example, in West Godavari district of Andhra Pradesh, paddy farmers have been greatly benefitted by organic agriculture, that costs them about Rs.14000-15000 per acre in contrast to chemical agriculture that costs them more than Rs.25000 per acre. They use organic solutions like Jeevamrutham and Keetakanivarini as fertilizer and pesticide

Table 6: Notable Farm Mechanization Interventions

S.No.	Intervention	Effect	How Farm Income is affected
1.	Deep Ploughing	Increase in fertility, water absorption and retention capacity, weed control	15-20 % increase in productivity
2.	Better seedbed preparation by Rotavators	Better germination and plant growth	Increases productivity by 10%, reduction in cost of land preparation by 20-25%
3.	Improved sowing practices	• Better seed placement with control of plant population	Increase in productivity by 25-35 %
		• Raised bed and Ridge-furrow planting saves crop in adverse climatic conditions like excess or deficit rainfall. Aerobic planting improves plant health and vigour.	Rabi fallow after paddy can be brought under cultivation, helps in crop residue management.
		• Zero till and Happy seeder technology saves water, time and cost of land preparation	Increase in productivity by 25-45 %. Reduced cost of cultivation
		• Mechanized rice transplanting saves time and labour	
4.	Mechanized methods of weed and pest control	Reduced cost of labour and efficient use of inputs	Reduction in cost of cultivation by 10-20%
5.	Mechanized harvesting	Reduces Cost and Timely harvesting	Reduction in cost of cultivation by 10-20%
6.	Better crop residue management by machines.	Promotes Soil Health and Environment	Extra income of 10-15 % from residues.

respectively, prepared using inputs from the commonly available plants and weeds of the locality, in combination with urine of cattle. The output produced in their farms valued about 35-45 per cent more than that produced through inorganic means, which stands as the reason for their contentment in organic agriculture and have extended organic farming to Sugarcane production as well.

c. Soil Nutrient Application and Monitoring

Nutrient inputs may be in the form of Urea, DAP, Potash, Manure, etc. One must have a full knowledge of the nutrient status of his field in order to utilize the fertilizers more efficiently. Recently in these lines of thought, the Government has taken an initiative to measure the nutrient status of farmers' fields and produce documents containing the reports of their nutrient status and specific recommendations for the area crop-wise. A refined form of this scheme with more sample coverage and zonal specific fertilizer recommendations could be of greater advantage to the farmers. Also, application of fertilizers during the time of critical need is suggested, and practicing fertilizer application techniques such as fertigation could save time and resources.

d. Clean Energy

Efforts directed towards generating technologies fueled by renewable sources of energy such as Solar and Wind power are a necessity. The farm equipment like water pumps fueled by such technologies has a greater life period, and such technologies generate negligible wastes in comparison with those fueled by non-renewable energy sources. The application of the technologies must be location-specific, such as utilization of solar power in arid areas and wind power in coastal and hilly areas. India's per capita consumption of energy is only around 314 kWh, in contrast to that of developed countries, which is around 5000 kWh, and the lacuna of power requirement must be filled through utilization of green energy.

e. Improving Cropping Intensity

Increase in the number of crops per unit area to derive maximum yield is made possible by intensified cropping, without creating a vigorous competition for resources among the crops. Increase in yield due to cropping intensity is subject to the availability of inputs like irrigation, labour, fertilizers and plant protection chemicals and farm management skills. This lends support from the data of cropping intensities of last decade given in Table 7, in which growth rates of states like Orissa, Andhra Pradesh, Haryana, etc. are in positive figures compared to the resource poor states implying thereby that the resource availability combined with cropping intensity adopted in those states have a synergistic impact on the growth of agricultural income.

f. Diversification of Farm Components

A well performing enterprise mix within the farm and state boosts the agricultural income by assured returns and protection of the farm against the production risks and marketing risks arising out of monocropping. Diversification of crops with some of the high value crops among their elements and also with livestock through integrated farming system may result in incremental returns.

The observations above suggest technology and inputs that deliver maximum output with their application in minimum quantities with less possible wastage improves productivity. Recent studies have proved that the technologies used resulted in the rate of increase in the cost of cultivation surpassing that of growth in yield, implying a slow pace of technological improvement in Indian agriculture (Srivastava *et al* 2017), thus suggesting making significant efforts towards advancement of agricultural technologies, comprising of improved farm machinery, disease and pest resistant seed varieties, etc. Also, educating the farmers on resource-efficient cultivation methods and efforts to accelerate their level of adoption through efficient extension strategies.

C. Irrigation Facilities

Water has become one of the scarce natural resources used as agricultural input. Unsustainable use of ground water resulting from rapid extraction has resulted in the dual loss of resource depletion and increased cost of extraction per unit of ground water. As of pre-monsoon reports of ground water levels of 2017 released by Central Ground Water Board, out of 15078 analyzed wells, a majority of the wells (43%) have water levels at 5-10 m below ground level, which is a very drastic change as compared to the 27% of the wells at the same level of depth in the year 2012. A time series data comparing net sown area and net irrigated area of India shows us that increase in the irrigated area has been at a slower pace (Figure 2), and the problem of deficit irrigation must be answered by building additional infrastructure for water distribution to the farms. In case of drylands, conservative irrigating practices like as drip irrigation and sprinklers could be utilized in the farms so as to increase the water use efficiency, combined with water conservation practices like mulching, scooping, laying out proper bund structures, etc. Pebble mulch and straw mulch, which have low costs, could be an economical option for mulching. Also, check dams for controlling soil erosion is suggested.

Table 7: State Wise Cropping Intensity (2000-01 to 2008-09)

State/UnionTerritory	2000-01	2001-02	2002-03	2003-04	2004-05	2005-06	2006-07	2007-08	2008-09	Growthrate	CV	Total
Andhra Pradesh	121.9	122.5	120.2	122.2	121.2	124.4	126.3	126.1	127.3	4.43	2.05	123.57
Assam	146.5	143.6	143.8	143.7	141.5	143.4	136.7	139.4	144.7	– 1.23	2.08	143
Bihar	141.1	139.4	139.0	138.0	132.8	133.1	136.3	137.1	137.7	– 2.41	2.02	137
Chhattisgarh	111.8	116.6	114.5	119.4	119.8	120.6	121.4	121.6	120.7	7.96	2.90	118
Haryana	173.4	177.2	174.4	180.8	182.2	182.4	179.8	179.7	181.3	4.56	1.84	179
Himachal Pradesh	170.9	173.9	173.6	176.8	175.6	175.0	174.5	178.9	173.1	1.29	1.31	175
Jharkhand	161.1	140.4	121.6	136.4	105.0	126.2	107.0	109.1	112.3	– 30.29	147.52	235.46
Karnataka	118.0	116.3	117.2	116.3	122.0	124.0	123.1	123.7	121.6	3.05	2.70	120
Kerala	137.0	136.6	135.7	134.9	139.0	140.0	138.8	132.2	129.0	– 5.84	2.59	136
Manipur	100.0	100.0	100.0	100.0	100.0	100.0	100.0	100.0	100.0	0.00	0.00	100
Meghalaya	120.0	120.1	120.6	123.7	120.2	121.7	115.7	120.4	118.7	– 1.08	1.80	120
Mizoram	100.0	100.0	100.0	100.0	100.0	100.0	100.0	100.0	100.0	0.00	0.00	100
Orissa	135.2	150.5	138.2	149.0	151.9	156.9	158.5	160.3	161.9	19.75	6.24	151
Punjab	186.8	186.7	185.0	186.5	188.8	187.7	187.9	188.0	189.8	1.61	0.75	187
Rajasthan	121.2	124.1	122.3	124.5	127.3	128.9	128.5	129.9	129.7	7.01	2.61	126
Sikkim	109.8	109.8	109.8	109.8	109.8	109.8	109.8	109.8	109.8	0.00	0.00	110
Tamil Nadu	119.5	120.4	113.1	113.4	115.5	115.0	114.0	114.9	115.5	– 3.35	2.22	116
Uttar Pradesh	150.4	151.4	146.5	151.8	153.0	152.2	153.3	154.2	155.6	3.46	1.70	152
Uttarakhand	159.2	157.3	159.7	160.	161.0	157.9	158.1	157.3	157.7	– 0.94	0.84	159
West Bengal	168.3	177.1	177.6	178.0	177.2	180.0	181.9	184.1	185.1	9.98	2.77	179
Chandigarh	170.9	170.9	170.9	147.5	150.0	151.5	151.5	151.5	151.5	– 11.35	6.51	157
Puducherry	177.9	162.9	168.7	181.1	184.5	175.7	175.5	174.6	170.6	– 4.10	3.74	175
Total India	140.9	140.8	138.7	140.6	139.9	141.2	139.9	140.5	140.6	0.04	0.53	145.43

(*Source:* Kalaiselvi *et al.*, 2011)

Farm ponds and percolation tanks, lined internally with materials like tiles and slabs should be dug out to conserve percolating water and rain water that could be used whenever necessary in dry areas.

Recently, Indian Agricultural Research Institute (IARI) has designed a prefabricated concrete lining technology suitable for several irrigation projects for the sandy and sandy loam areas of Northern India, which has the potential to save 5 million ha-m of surface water, which will irrigate 10 mha of additional crop area and increase food grain production by 10 MT annually in the country.

D. Institutional Finance

Timely credit availability and insurance against unforeseen risks of production and market have a positive impact on the farmers' incomes. A banking system with thoroughly structured lending regulations could provide the farmer with requisite capital for cultivation purposes at reasonable rates of interest. Collective management of agricultural lending departments of all the nationalized banks, co-operative and regional rural banks could be suggested to ensure smooth flow of need-based credit from the institutions and farmers, which has added benefits of easy monitoring, follow-up and recovery of loans. The lending agencies should revise the purpose of loan and suggest alternatives to the farmers for efficient utilization of credit, providing the services of an agricultural advisor. Such services are still inaccessible to some of the remote rural and tribal areas, implying the need for the expansion of institutional framework for agricultural credit and requisite banking infrastructure. Government has initiated schemes such as Pradhan Mantri Fasal Bhima Yojana (PMFBY), aimed at strengthening the farmer financially and also providing an insurance to the farmers suffering crop loss/damage arising out of unforeseen events. Previously, institutions have estimated the total credit flow for agriculture and allied sectors during the ten year period (2010-2020) to be at Rs.48,12,250 crore (Table 8).

E. Agricultural Education

Agricultural Universities and institutes have been highly instrumental in imparting farm knowledge to the youth through a well-structured curriculum and to the farmers by organizing farm visits, training camps and other activities through their extension departments. They have the responsibility of answering the queries of the farming community and address any issues concerned with farm activities and information related to new farm technologies, credit availability and marketing activities. Students of Agricultural institutes should be directed to think in a farmer's point of view to come up with innovations that could be applied in the field for the farming community to realize increased returns.

Table 8: Perspective Credit Plan (both Investment Credit & Production Credit) for 2020

(Rs. Crore)

Periods	GDP Agrl. @ 4.1 %	GCF Agrl.ICO R =4.05	Pvt. Invt. (@ 77.8 % of GCF Agrl.)	Pvt. Invt + Induced Invt.	Invt Credit (@ 63.33% of Pvt. Invt)	Prodn. Credit (6)*3.2	Total Credit (6)+(7)	Total Credit #
(1)	(2)	(3)	(4)	(5)	(6)	(7)	(8)	(9)
2009-10	603743	122560	98048	128579	81429	260573	342002	362522
2010-11	628496	127585	102068	132599	83975	268719	352694	375619
2011-12	654264	132816	106253	136784	86625	277200	363825	389293
2012-13	681089	138261	110609	141140	89384	286028	375412	403568
2013-14	709014	143930	115144	145675	92256	295219	387475	418473
2014-15	738083	149831	119865	150396	95246	304786	400032	434034
2015-16	768345	155974	124779	155310	98358	314745	413103	450283
2016-17	799847	162369	129895	160426	101598	325113	426711	467249
2017-18	832641	169026	135221	165752	104971	335906	440877	484964
2018-19	866779	175956	140765	171296	108482	347141	455623	503464
2019-20	902317	183170	146536	177067	112137	358837	470974	522781
Total	8184618	1661478	1329183	1665024	1054461	3374267	4428728	4812250

- Total credit calculated after adjusting for inflation @6.0 per cent on a tapering basis.

F. Tilting Terms of Trade in favor of Farmers

Export prices per unit of a commodity are higher than the imports in the current state, but there is a decline in the terms of trade and is projected to go lower in 2018 (Figure 4). Export promotional policies should be formulated that could favour leads to increase in terms of trade of agricultural commodities.

ICOR – Incremental Capital Output Ratio (Samantara *et al.,* 2014)

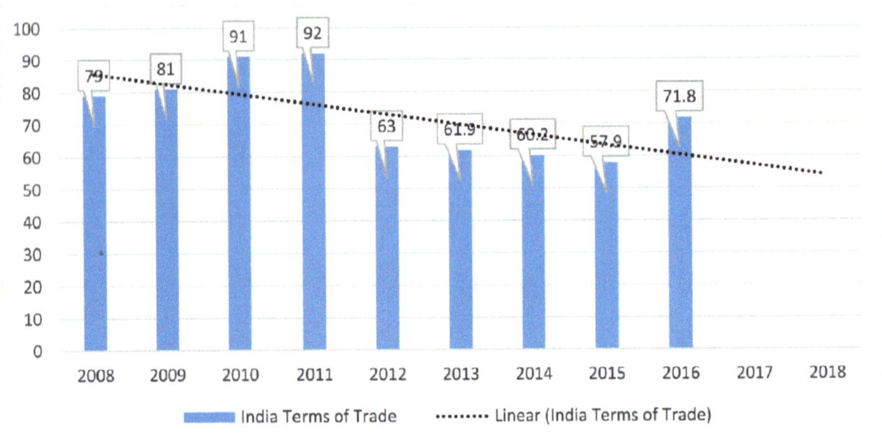

Fig. 4: Terms of Trade in India
(*Source:* https://tradingeconomics.com/india/terms-of-trade/forecast)

A. Subsidies

One of the main commodities the Government provides to the farmers on subsidies are Fertilizers. Between 2006-07 and 2014-15, the amount of subsidies for imported, high quality fertilizers has increased considerably than that of indigenous fertilizers (Table 9). This implies that farmers favor those fertilizers that are of highly qualitative than the indigenous ones, necessitating the need to probe into the indigenous fertilizer improvement. If granting subsidies for the imported fertilizers is continued and is deemed beneficial to the economy in the long run then obviously subsidies stand as a support for the farmers and provide room for improvement of the farming sector in the face of shortage of requisite capital required by the farmers for the procurement of inputs. Or if the financial burden on India is expected to be higher, R&D efforts towards qualitative development of indigenous fertilizers is required.

Table 9: Amount of Subsidy sanctioned for Fertilizers in India (2006-07 to 2014-15)(In Rs. Crore)

Fertilizer	2006-07	2014-15
Indigenous Urea	10410.37	10226.77
Imports of Urea	1093.54	1450.48
Indigenous P and K Fertilizers	4399.00	4132.49
Imported P and K Fertilizers	1350.00	3411.12

Source: www.indiaagristat.com/table/economy/8/subsidyonfertilisers19762016/485931/412462/data.aspx

B. Marketing: According to APMC, as on March 31, 2014, the Market capacity of India is as follows:

- Total Number of Wholesale Markets – 5964
- Total Number of Primary Rural Markets – 22759
- Total Number of Regulated Markets – 7114
- Total – 35837

And most of the markets (80.14 per cent) are unregulated. Increase in the number of well-regulated markets ensures that the farmers realize a greater share in consumer's rupee by a uniformity in prices for a grade of a commodity throughout the market. Focus on developing the market infrastructure and provision of market services on a single platform at reasonable rates must be given priority. Some avenues in which marketing system could be improved are stated below:

a) Warehouses and Cold Storages

Storage of Farm Produce contribute to the farmers' income by preserving the produce through the times of low market prices, ensuring remunerative returns for their produce. As of 2017, the combined storage capacity owned by Food Corporation of India (FCI) and Central Warehousing Corporation (CWC) is 309.14 lakh metric tons. CWC has created an additional storage capacity of 1.66 lakh metric tons in 2016. But that has not been sufficient to cater to the total production of agricultural produce (in 2015) of 714.57 lakh metric tons. Therefore, the number of warehouses and scientific storage godowns need to be increased on priority.

b) E-Marketing

Electronic Marketing initiatives such as e-NAM (Electronic National Agricultural Market) helps to create a national network of buyers and sellers, and exchange of agricultural produce between buyers and sellers becomes more efficient with the reduction of middlemen, and the farmers realize fair returns for their produce. Marketing activities aided by Information Communication Technology improves market coverage and will increase the sale of agricultural produce dramatically.

c) Market Linkages

Market linkages facilitate trade relationships between the target population or "clients," small producers, local firms and cooperatives, and the external market. The market linkage model can be either embedded or integrated. Market linkages have innate services of import-export, market research and broker service, facilitating smooth functioning of the market system.

d) Market Information System

A well-organized system of data recording and analysis, coupled with facilities for the ease and accessibility of information is required for the beneficiaries to market their produce at the right place and at right time, and also to make use of price trends to plan their farm activities. Electronic media has been a boon for rapid transmission of information, and need-based information for the farmers must be classified according to their requirements and must be made available on the electronic media through interactive mobile apps. Training sessions must be given to the farmers to enable them with the ability of making good use of information they obtain.

Apart from these measures, they could contribute to the incremental incomes of the farmers only when the farming community is in a state of well-being, and are in a position to invest their time and resources in agriculture. It can be said

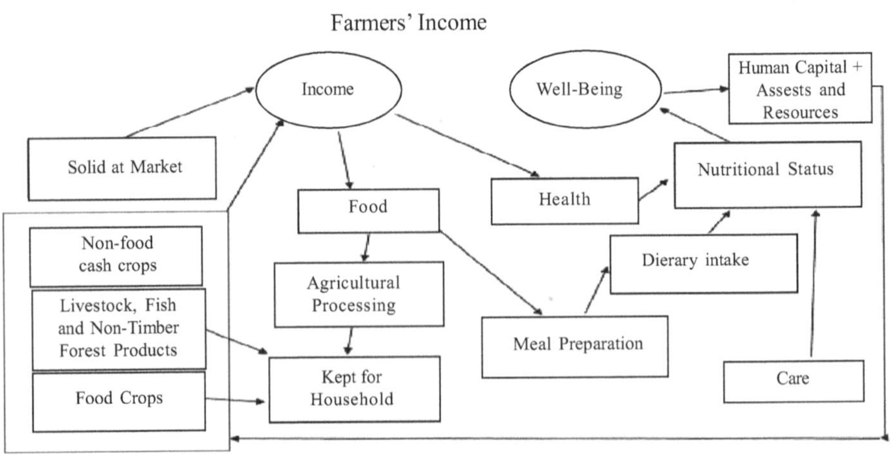

Fig. 4: Linkages between Agricultural Development, Nutrition Pathways and Doubling Farmers' Income
(*Source:* Publications of International Centre for Research on Women)

that earning of farm income and state of well-being of farmers have influence over one another. This statement could be illustrated better by the pathway as follows.

8. Conclusion

A multi-faceted approach involving the efforts from all the fields that could contribute to the comprehensive development of the farming community need to be followed for doubling the farmers' income. Production technologies, their use and impact is an important factor to focus on doubling the farmers' income. These technologies are already available across all the regions of the country but their adoption remains a problem to discuss always and partial adoption of the technological package can never be expected to get the desired results on ground. The results are suggestive of the pent up need to focus on the extension support on end-to-end approach from production to marketing with appropriate facilitation for inputs, insurance, credit, storage, marketing facilities etc. Acceleration of agricultural growth being a function of quality and optimum quantity of inputs and services involved, and execution of decisions formulated regarding optimum combination of such inputs could result in the increase in the farmers' income. This strategy could possibility help in doubling the farmers' income within the said timeframe and can become a reality. However, it would need involvement of all the stakeholders to come up on board to pursue this goal.

8. References

Anonymous .2012.Foreign Trade performance of India, www.dgciskol.nic.in/annualreport/book_3e.pdf

Anonymous .2016. Report on Doubling Farmer's Income by 2022: Farm Crisis and Farm Distress. Published by Indian Council of Food and Agriculture, New Delhi.

Anonymous .2017. Terms of Trade. : https://tradingeconomics.com/india/terms-of-trade/forecast

Birthal PS and Negi DS .2018. Budget 2018: How to double farmers' income. www.business-standard.com/article/printer-friendly-version?article_id=118011300781_1

Birthal PS, Joshi PK, Negi DS andAgarwal S.2013. IFPRI Discussion Paper on Changing Sources of Growth in Indian Agriculture: Implications for Regional Priorities for Accelerating Agricultural Growth.

Chand R .2016. Doubling Farmers' Income: Strategy and Prospects. Presidential Address of seventy sixth annual conference of The Indian Society of Agricultural Economics.

Kalaiselvi S and Sundar I .2011. Interstate Disparity in Cropping Intensity in India. *International Journal of Business Management, Economics and Information Technology*3 (2) : 269-273.

Narayanamoorthy A, Suresh R and Alli P .2017. Dynamics of Input Use Efficiency in Selected Crops Cultivation in India. *Indian Journal of Agricultural Economic,* 72 (3) : 215-229.

Samantara S and Badatya KC .2014. NABARD Paper on 'A Perspective on Indian Agriculture Credit for 2020'.

Srivastava SK, Ramesh C and Singh J .2017. Changing crop production cost in India: input prices, substitution and technological effects. *Agricultural Economics Research Review* 30: 171-182.

Statistical data by Directorate of Economics and Statistics, Government of India.
Statistical Data compiled from www. indiaagristat.com.
Other Online Sources:
https://data.worldbank.org/country/india?view=chart
https://www.businessinsider.in/Heres-why-we-need-to-focuson-agriculture-inIndia/articleshow/48468689.cms
http://censusindia.gov.in/Census_And_You/economic_activity.aspx
https://www.indiaagristat.com/agriculture/2/costofcultivationproduction/32320/stats.aspx
www.dgciskol.nic.in/annualreport/book_3e.pdf
www.indiaagristat.com
https://tradingeconomics.com/india/terms-of-trade/forecast
www.indiaagristat.com/table/economy/8/subsidyonfertilisers19762016/485931/412462/data.aspx

10

Seed Priming: Invigorating Seed, Seedling, and Crop for More Yield and Climate Resilience

FA Khan, S Narayan*, Narinder Panotra, Imtiyaz Murtaza, Ajaz Ahmad Malik*, K Stephen, Mansah Gul, M. Amir** and Satish Kumar*****

Division of Basic Sciences and Humanities
**Division of Vegetable Science, SKUAST of Kashmir, Shalimar-190025, India*
***NDUAT, Kumarganj, Faizabad, Uttar Pradesh, India*
****OFRC, SKUAST-Jammu, Jammu and Kashmir, India*
****Seed Production Farm, Chatha, SKUAST-Jammu, Jammu and Kashmir, India*

1. Introduction
2. Types of seed priming
3. Benefits of seed priming
4. Physic-chemical genesis of seed priming
5. Seed deterioration and accelerated ageing
6. Seed ageing and morpho-physiological attributes of seedling
7. Seed osmo-priming and biochemical attributes of seedling
8. Osmo-priming and reversal of ageing effects: Morpho-physiological attributes
9. Osmo-priming and reversal of ageing effects: Biochemical effects
10. *References*

Abstract

Seed priming is the innovative way of ensuring optimum germination and plant stand under moisture deficit situations. It enables the seed to tide over initial stress from biotic and abiotic factors. Higher yield with better quality seed are reported. The seeds of agronomic and horticultural crops are significantly affected by ageing and deterioration. Reversal or rejuvenation of aged seeds is therefore of primary interest. Experiments related to reversal of seed deterioration effects due to ageing relying heavily on accelerated ageing (AA) of seeds and their priming using various priming agents especially osmotic substances. Repair during germination is a hypothetical event supported by some investigators and questioned by others. Repair includes the spontaneous reorganization of plasma membrane phospholipids, which occurs during seed hydration. Alternatively or additionally, metabolic repair might occur. Experimental evidence for repair in imbibed seeds has been elusive. Priming reduced electrolyte leakage as well as lipid peroxidation in seeds implying the activation of membrane repair processes. Priming was also associated with increased levels of antioxidants like ascorbic acid and tocopherols particularly the latter and the activities of enzymes SOD, CAT POX involved in the mitigation of oxidative damage. In comparison with the priming of unaged seeds, the aged seeds experienced a diminution of response in terms of changes in the levels of antioxidants and scavenging enzymes. Thus, seed priming technique under climate extremities seems the best and economical means to sustain higher crop yields. The technique needs to be popularized among the farmers practicing agriculture and horticulture under rainfed situation so as to sustain production under climatic adversaries and enhance livelihood security and more profitability at the farm.

Keywords: seed priming, seed quality, germination, seedling emergence, reversal of ageing, resilience

1. Introduction

Slow emergence results in smaller plants and seedlings, which are more vulnerable to soil-borne diseases. Extended emergence periods predispose the planting bed to deterioration and increased soil compaction, particularly under adverse environmental conditions. Prevailing of stress conditions at the time seed maturation or occurrence of stresses at the of sowing lead to poor germination or uneven germination and poor crop stand consequently low yields at the farms. In the last two decades, seed priming has become a common seed treatment to increase the rate and uniformity of emergence in many field crops, vegetables and flower species. Seed priming or osmo-conditioning is a seed pretreatment where moisture is controlled, allowing the seed to activate the germination process to just before root and shoot emergence and seed coat remains intact. Priming allows some of the metabolic processes necessary for germination to begin without germination take place in complete. In priming, seeds are soaked in different solutions with high osmotic potential. This prevents the seeds from absorbing in enough water for radicle protrusion, thus suspending the seeds in the lag phase.

2. Types of seed priming

Seed priming is of six types depending on the type priming material used namely hydro-priming, halo-priming, osmo-priming, sand matrix priming, bio-priming and hormonal priming.

Hydro-priming

It involves soaking of seeds in water and drying back to storage moisture prior to sowing. Sometimes air-drying of the seeds may or may not be followed. It is a low cost approach, designated as on-farm seed priming involve merely soaking of seed in water before sowing. This pre sowing seed treatment, known as hydro-priming, allows the seed to imbibe water and go through the first phase of germination in which pre-germination metabolic activities are started while the latter two phases of germination are inhibited. In many agricultural areas, a major cause of poor stand establishment and low crop yield is unfavorable environmental conditions for seed germination and seedling emergence. However, hydro-priming favors rapid germination and seedlings emerge. Such seedlings produce deep roots before the upper layers of the soil are dried out and crusted, which may result in good crop establishment and higher crop yield. Hydro-priming reduces the effect of salinity on the morphological parameter of the plants. Any factor that facilitates rapid germination may contribute to establishment of a successful crop. Soaking seed in water and drying before sowing is the easiest way to achieve hydration.

Soaking is not suitable for some plant species, as rapid hydration may cause leakage of essential nutrients out of the seed, resulting in seed damage. To overcome these potential problems, various methods have been devised to deliver appropriate hydration to the seed. One method is seed humidification a pre sowing treatment in which seed are treated under conditions of high humidity. For example, in partially-aged mustard (*Brassica juncea*) seeds, humidification resulted in a significant improvement in germination and seedling vigor and a decrease in leakage of electrolytes from germinating seed. A second method of pre-sowing seed hydration is aerated hydration (AH), in which seed are hydrated in a column of aerated water to moisture content close to that required for radicle protrusion.

Halo-priming

Halo-priming is the soaking of seeds in solutions containing salt such as sodium chloride. A number of studies have shown a significant improvement in seed germination, seedling emergence and establishment, and final crop yield in salt affected soils in response to halopriming. Seed priming with NaCl has been found to be better treatment as compared to non-primed seeds in case of hot pepper for improving the seedling vigour and stand establishment under salt-stressed conditions. Priming with NaCl and KCl was helpful in removing the deleterious effects of salts. Rice seed treated with a mixed salt solution germinated more speedily than unprimed seed under salt-stress conditions. Seed germination is promoted by halopriming but also stimulate subsequent growth, thereby enhancing final crop yield. Under undesirable conditions such as salinity stress, priming with GA_3 and NaCl can prepare a suitable metabolic reaction in seeds and can improve seed germination performance and seedling establishment. Halo-priming has very important role in germination, seedling emergence, and plant growth at all developmental stage of the plants.

Osmo-priming

Osmo-priming is the use of osmotic solutions of chemicals for seed priming such as mannitol, potassium nitrate (KNO_3), potassium chloride (KCl), polyethylene glycol (PEG). Osmopriming is commercially used technique for improving seed germination and vigour. It involves controlled imbibition of seeds to start the initial events of germination followed by seed drying up to its original weight. Osmopriming has many advantages including rapid and uniform emergence, improved seedling growth and better stand establishment under any environmental and soil conditions (Chiu *et al.* 2002). Polyethylene glycol and KNO_3 solutions increased the fresh and dry weight of roots in maize at 2% and 5% concentration primed for 12 h and 18 h. Of these, changes in activity of enzymes involved in hydrolysis of storage products play important roles in the initial growth and development of the embryo. Grain yield was significantly increased in many crops subjected to priming as compared to non-primed crops. The increase in yield was 13% in case of hydro-priming alone and 26% when primed with $ZnSO_4$ solution. So, it can be concluded that both the treatments have contributed well to the total increase in yield. Final emergence, emergence index, plant height, leaf area, stover dry weight, total dry weight, individual cob weight, cob yield, cob number and number of grains per cob were observed to indicate almost same kind of response to priming treatments in increasing the final yield (Harris *et al.* 2007)

Priming seed with inorganic salts may significantly alter activity of enzymes in germinating seed. For example, seed of muskmelon soaked with KNO_3 solution showed enhanced activity of dehydrogenase and α-amylase under low temperature. In untreated wheat seed germinating under salt stress, amylase activity decreased with increasing salinity; in wheat seed pretreated with $CaCl_2$, the negative effect of salinity was diminished (Roy and Srivastava 1999). Similarly, in *Pennisetum americanum* and Sorghum bicolor seeds soaked in $CaCl_2$ or KNO_3 solution, activity of total amylase, α-amylase and proteases was increased in germinating seeds under salt stress (Kadiri and Hussaini, 1999). Seed primed with mixed-salt solution resulted in significant increase in activity of α-amylase, β-amylase, and root dehydrogenase, and moderate increase in the activity of shoot catalase under salt stress in rice (Chang-Zheng *et al.* 2002). Such increases in enzyme activity have direct or indirect effects on subsequent seed germination and seedling growth and development. Salinity interacts not only with organic substances but also with inorganic nutrients in the plant. Mobilization of seed food reserves to the developing embryo during germination is a ubiquitous process. Osmo-conditioning also enhanced the activity of ATPase in the germinating seed of peanut primed with PEG. Furthermore, acid phosphatase and RNA syntheses were significantly higher in embryonic axes and cotyledons of osmo-conditioned seed compared to control seed.

Solid matrix priming

Solid matrix priming (SMP) is a term used for a presowing seed treatment in which a solid-matrix instead of an osmotic solution is used to enhance germination. It is a process that uses solid matrix materials, water, and seed in combinations to control water, oxygen, and temperature effects on germination. The process controls the hydration of seed to a level that allows pre-germination activity but that prevents radicle emergence.

Solid matrix priming involves the incubation of seeds in a moist sand of insoluble solid matrix, such as vermiculite, diatomaceous earth, or mist sans another highly water absorbent polymer, with a limited amount of water, allowing for slow imbibition. Hu *et al* (2005) used sand matrix priming in rice. Seeds were mixed with sands that contained 3.8% (v/w) water and sealed in plastic box and then were primed at 18°C for 72 h. Four varieties of rice were used to investigate the effect of sand priming on germination of direct-sown rice (*Oryza sativa* L.) in the laboratory. The results showed that the energy of germination, germination percentage, germination index and vigor index were improved in four varieties. Meanwhile, seedling height, root length, number of root and root dry weight were significantly higher than the non-primed controls.

Bio-priming

Bio-priming is a new technique of *seed* treatment that integrates biological (inoculation of *seed* with beneficial organism to protect *seed*) and physiological aspects (*seed* hydration) of disease control. It is biological seed treatment that refers combination of seed hydration (physiological aspect of disease control) and inoculation (biological aspect of disease control) of seed with beneficial organism to protect seed. It is recently used as an alternative method for controlling many seed- and soil-borne pathogens. An ecological approach that uses selected fungal antagonists against the soil- and seed-borne pathogens. Biological seed treatments may provide an alternative to chemical control.

Biopriming pearl millet seeds with *Pseudomonas fluorescens* isolates resulted in improved growth of the plants and also induction of resistance against downy mildew disease caused by the fungus *Sclerospora graminicola.* Although all of the test isolates reduced disease severity and promoted growth both under greenhouse and field conditions, high variability was observed in their efficiency. Treatment due to *Pseudomonas fluorescens* resulted in enhancement of: germination, seedling vigour, plant height, leaf area, tillering capacity, seed weight (measured for 1000 seeds) and yield. The time required for flowering was advanced by 5 days. Isolate UOM SAR 14 registered higher levels of vegetative and reproductive growth; most importantly there was a 22% increase in grain yield. The isolates also effectively induced resistances against downy mildew disease both under greenhouse and field conditions. The isolates offered protection ranging from 20 to 75%. However, the level of disease control was less than that achieved by the systemic fungicide Apron. UOM SAR 14 offered 71 and 75% and remained consistent under all test conditions. Further studies showed that the resistance induced was systemic, required a minimum of 3 days to build up, and was sustained throughout the plant's life. Seeds primed with neem seed kernel extract and eucalyptus leaf extract have been also exhibited to positive effect.

Hormonal priming

Hormonal priming is soaking of seed in hormone solution is referred as hormonal priming. GA_3, Salicylic acid, Ascorbic acid, Cytokinins etc can be used as priming material. The primed seeds of carrot, onion and tomato showed that priming these seeds with GA_3 increased the germination percentage and rate. Afzal *et al* (2006) evaluated the effect of hormonal priming with ABA, salicylic acid, or ascorbic acid on Wheat germination and seedling growth under normal and saline conditions.

Hormonal priming has reduced the severity of the effect of salinity but the amelioration was better due to 50 ppm SA and 50 ppm ascorbic acid treatments as these showed best results on seedling growth, fresh and dry weights under non-saline and saline conditions whereas hormonal priming with ABA as not effective under present experimental material and conditions (Afzal *et al* 2006). Ashraf *et al* (2002) found that GA_3 treatment enhanced the vegetative growth of two wheat cultivars under but caused a slight reduction in their grain yield. GA_3 treatment enhanced the deposition of Na^+ and Cl^- in both root and shoots of wheat plants under prevailing field conditions. It also caused a significant increase in photosynthetic activity in both lines at the vegetative stage of the crop. Hussein *et al* (2007) evaluated the effect of salinity and salicylic acid on growth of maize plants. The beneficial aspects of SA are that it could be used for the improvement of salt bearing capacity of many crops.

3. Benefits of seed priming

- Higher rate of seed germination
- Faster bio-mass gathering and seedling emergence
- Better seed germination under adverse agro-climatic conditions
- Increased seedling vigour and better crop establishment
- Improves uniformity of crop at all stages so better field operations efficiency
- Increases resilience in plants against climatic stresses
- Higher input use efficiency
- Higher crop yields

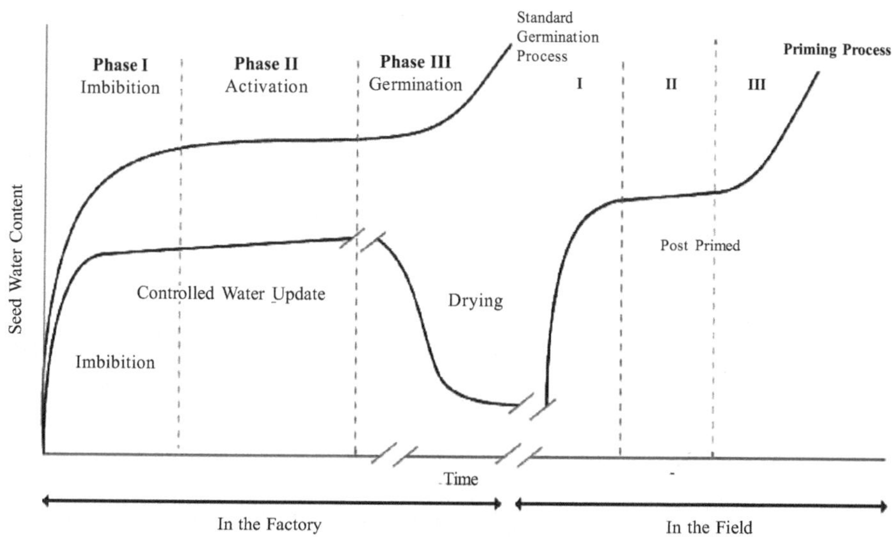

Fig. 1: Standard germination process vs. seed priming process

4. Physico-chemical genesis of seed priming

Seed is the most vital and crucial input for crop production as use of good quality seed is a basic qualification for the production of a good quality crop. However, seed quality loses after harvest due to ageing unless special precautions are taken during storage. Deterioration of seed quality and viability is a serious problem in developing countries where seeds are stored in places without a proper control of humidity and temperature. The main external factors causing seed deterioration during storage are the temperature, relative air humidity and oxygen/carbon dioxide concentration. High temperature, moisture content and O_2/CO_2 increase the respiration of seeds, causing seeds to deteriorate more rapidly. Possibility to regulate these factors makes the basis for longer seed storage. The detrimental effects of ageing may also be nullified (repaired) by exposing aged seeds to osmopriming treatments (Tilden and West 1985; Khan *et al* 2016) that may be described as a pre-sowing seed treatment in osmotic solution of low water potential followed by re-drying, which allows seeds pre-germinative metabolic activities to proceed (first stage of germination) but prevents radical protrusion through the seed coat. The process can improve the speed and uniformity of germination, especially under adverse conditions. The promotion of germination with seed priming may take place for several reasons, but changes in metabolite levels are important events during seed priming. It reduces the effects of ageing by reducing Malon dialdehyde (MDA) and free radicals production and maintenance of antioxidant activities. Improved seed performance after priming has been explained by completion of DNA repair, more favourable metabolic balance at initiation of germination process and changes in protein pattern (Osborne, 1983; Dell'Aquila *et al* 1978; Davison and Bray, 1991). The response of seeds to priming treatment can vary between crop species and dependent on the duration of the treatment and the osmotic potential of the solution rather than a specific salt. Various aspects of the reversal of the seed ageing by osmotic priming are discussed this article. The objective of the present article is to underline implication of seed quality, its deterioration mechanism (s) and possibility of the amelioration of deteriorative process.

5. Seed deterioration and accelerated ageing

Seed deterioration may be explained as the loss of seed quality (vigor and viability) due to ageing or adverse environmental factors particularly higher temperature, air relative humidity and oxygen/carbon dioxide ratio during pre-harvest, harvest and postharvest periods. Harrington (1972) suggested that within the normal range of moisture and temperature for stored seeds, each 1% reduction in seed moisture or each 5°C reduction in temperature doubles the storage life of the seeds. Deteriorative changes enhance when seed exposure to external challenges increases thus decrease the ability of the seed to survive. The process has been described as cumulative, irreversible, degenerative and inexorable that is separate event from seed development and germination. Progressive loss of seed quality due to impairment of the structure and functions of seed with passing of time which ultimately leads to the loss of seed viability is termed as seed ageing. Loss of seed quality due to ageing as well as adverse conditions has been attributed to a series of metabolic defects accumulated in embryonic and non-embryonic structures. At the cellular level, seed ageing is associated with various alterations including membrane disruption, solute leakage, reduced energy metabolism, impairment of RNA and protein synthesis, and DNA degradation resulting in several detrimental effects on seed. Deterioration caused by field weathering is directly related to seed exposure to adverse conditions. However, the seed quality and viability during storage depend upon the initial quality of seed and the manner in which it is stored (Jyoti and Malik 2013).

Assessment of seed quality is done through a technique known as accelerated ageing (AA) which was initially developed for testing the storage potential of seeds. The principle of the method is based on the artificial acceleration of the deterioration rate of the seeds, by exposing them to high temperature (40 - 45°C) and relative humidity (greater than 95%) levels which are considered as the most prominent environmental factors with respect to the intensity and velocity of deterioration. In this situation, low-quality seeds deteriorate more rapidly than more vigorous ones, presenting a differentiated decrease in viability. An environment of 41 to 43 °C of temperature for 24 to 72 h is considered to be applicable for a large number of species in AA. However, the most appropriate ageing environment needs to be determined for each species.

6. Seed ageing and morpho-physiological attributes of seedling

Controlled deterioration of pepper seed has been reported to reduce germination percent (GP) but increase mean germination time (MGT). The reduction in GP and the increase in MGT due to controlled ageing treatments were proportional to their duration. Decrease in seed vigour as affected by deterioration has also been proved in mungbean and chickpea seeds. The rate at which the seed aging process takes place depends on the ability of seed to resist degradation changes by protection mechanisms which are specific for each plant species. The accelerated aging has proved a very efficient resource to assess seed vigour, thus sorting seed lots according to their ability to germinate and establish in the field. In this test, the rate of seed deterioration is accelerated by their exposure to high levels of temperature and relative humidity. Balesevic-Tubic *et al* (2007) described that the seeds rich in lipids have limited longevity due to their specific chemical composition and lead to loss of germination ability and seed viability.

Accelerated aging of seed leads to a loss of vigour and eventually to a loss of viability. Working on water melon and cucumber Demir and Mavi (2008) concluded that accelerated ageing of seeds at 45°C significantly reduced the seed germinability in the laboratory. Kapoor *et al* (2010) reported seed quality in chickpea deteriorated following accelerated ageing treatment of 45 °C and

100% humidity for 24, 48, or 72 hours. With increasing time of ageing treatment, seed moisture content increased and all physiological parameters measured such as germination percentage, seedling root length, shoot length, and vigour index decreased in all varieties. Balesevic-Tubic *et al* (2010) stated that accelerated aging test can be used to predict the length of storage life of sunflower and soybean seed. In comparison to sunflower seed, soybean seed is more sensitive to damage and reduced germination during storage. Kapoor *et al* (2011) informd that prolongation of AA period in five rice varieties *viz*. Pusa-1, Sugandha-4, Sugandha-5, Saket-4 and Saket-370 led to deterioration of both germinability and seed viability. Biabani *et al.* (2011) reported that artificially deteriorated seeds of chick pea with 0 (control), 7, 14, 21 and 28 days of deterioration (DOD) in 40°C humid storage showed declined seed germination and growth in terms of radicle length, seedling length, root weight and seedling weight with increasing storage, and germination was zero after 21 or 28 days. They further elucidated that the percentage emergence of deteriorated seeds is less than healthy seeds. DeTune *et al* (2011) reported that the use of unsaturated and saturated solutions of NaCl reduced water absorption by onion seeds as compared to plane water and suggested that 48 hour treatment with unsaturated and saturated NaCl solutions is a better AA test because it promotes a better classification of the onion seed lots at different vigour levels.

Mohammadi *et al* (2011) showed that seed ageing in soybean results in reduced seedling growth and this is a consequence of decline in weight of mobilized seed reserve (seed reserve depletion percentage), not seed reserve utilization efficiency. Kaewnaree *et al* (2011) found that germination ability in terms of percentage of radicle emergence (ER%) decreased and exhibited significantly different levels (<0.01) due to different accelerated ageing times (42°C and 100% relative humidity). Experiments conducted on soybean explained that rapid ageing treatment has significant and adverse effects on GP, MDG, means time to germination (MTG), coefficient of velocity of germination (CVG) and germination index (GI). AA also decreased germination uniformity (GU), increased abnormal seedling (ABS) percentage (Rastegar *et al* 2011; Zahra *et al* 2011). Accelerate ageing treatments of soybean seed (41°C and 90-100 % RH) showed that increasing ageing duration caused significant reduction in germination characteristics with decreased germination percentage, means time to germination, germination index and normal seedling percentage (Yadollhhi Nooshabadi and Mashayekhi 2013). AA through use of saturated salt solution for 48 h or 72 h at 41ÚC decreased the percentage germination, first germination count and emergence percent in tomato. (Almeida *et al* 2014).

Seed ageing and biochemical attributes of seedling

Loss of seed germinability following deterioration has been reported several seed species and attributed to a series of metabolic defects. Studies have shown that seed deterioration is associated with reduced capacity for protein synthesis due to an excessive loss of RNA synthesis which could be a consequence of damage to nuclear DNA. Deterioration during accelerated aging of soybean seeds also involves an imbalance between Glycolysis and TCA cycle. Tilden and West (1985) explained that accelerated ageing pre-disposed seeds to imbibition injury and slowing the rate of hydration prevented the loss of seed electrolyte leakage and germinability which indicate that cell membrane permeability or rupture was a major factor contributing to the loss of germinability after ageing. There is a negative relationship between high oil content and seed longevity. Damage to the organization of cell membranes during seed ageing may constitute an important factor in explaining seed deterioration. Integrity of ribosomal RNA in seeds of *Allium porrum* has been found to correlate with germination performance (Bray *et al.,* 1989) and AA of onion seeds showed a marked variation in seed moisture content, ranging from 11.8 to 24.0% (germination after the aging period was inversely proportional to seed moisture content).

Membrane disruption is considered as one of the main reasons of seed deterioration and major causes of membrane disruption are increase in free fatty acid level and free radicals productivity by lipid peroxidation. AA resulted in increased lipid peroxidation, decreased levels of anti-oxidants and reduced activity of several enzymes involved in scavenging of free radicals and peroxides (Balesevic-Tubic *et al* 2005). The degree of cell membrane damage in response to ageing can be measured in terms of rate of seed electrolyte. Loss of membrane integrity may be responsible for the decreased germinability, vigour and ultimately viability. A comparable loss of seed viability, reserve mobilization and germination was recorded in natural and accelerated (Cortelazzo *et al* 2005). In addition, there were alterations in the arrangement of proteins, and many cell walls were ruptured. There was a decreased acid phosphatase activity in seeds after AA exposure (Balesevic-Tubic *et al* 2005) which suggests that enzymatic activity can be used as a bio-marker for seed viability and vigour. Studies also indicated that in sunflower seeds, loss of viability is associated with an accumulation of Malondialdehyde (MDA), suggesting that seed deterioration is accompanying with Lipid peroxidation related to a decline in the efficiency of the antioxidant defense system.

Seed deterioration is also associated with various cellular, metabolic and chemical alterations including chromosome aberrations and damage to the DNA, impairment of RNA and protein synthesis, changes in the enzymes and food reserves and loss of membrane integrity. Ageing induced deterioration increase the extent of protein oxidation thus inducing loss of functional properties of proteins and enzymes. Lipid content was found to decrease in wheat seeds after accelerated aging and it was linked to a loss in the germination and vigour of wheat seeds, thus AA is a good test to predict the longevity of the seeds. A decrease in the activities of CAT and SOD was observed in onion seeds due to ageing and a high level of correlation was found between the loss of seed viability and the decreases that occurred in CAT and SOD activities (Demirkaya *et al* 2010). Oxidative damages are responsible for the deteriora-tion changes observed in aged seeds and free radical oxida-tions, enzymic dehydrogenation and aldehyde oxidation of proteins might reasonably contribute to the progress of seed quality and causes of membrane disruption are enhancing in free fatty acid level and free radicals productivity by lipid peroxidation (Ghassemi-Golezani *et al* 2010). Free fatty acid can damage lipid bilayer particularly of mitochondria leading to reduce energy production and free radicals have potential to damage membrane, DNA, enzymes, protein and ultimately cellular repair mechanism. In order to inhi-bition of oxidative damage to tissues, the cells equipped with various enzymatic and non-enzymatic compounds for detoxify (Kibinza *et al.*, 2011). Kaewnaree *et al* (2011) found that EC, K^+, Na^+, CA_2^+ and Mg^{2+} concentrations were increased in soaked seed solution during ageing. They further described that Malondialdehyde (MDA) was the major product of lipid peroxidation. The decreased seed germination and viability in rice varieties due to AA were coinciding with the biochemical parameters with increased moisture content.

Osmopriming and morpho-physiological attributes of seedling

Quality of seeds in terms of germinability is increased through osmopriming of seeds. Seed priming has been successfully demonstrated to improve germination and emergence in many crops including seeds of vegetables and small seeded grasses but the response to a given priming treatment can vary between crop species (Bradford 1986). Onion seeds primed with manitol (-1.1 MPa) reduced the MGT and T_{50}. Osmotically primed tomato seeds germinated more rapidly as compared to unprimed seeds and showed improved stand establishment, early seedling growth and yield. Also, seedlings from primed seeds maintained greater mean plant dry weights, leaf areas and ground cover percentages than untreated seedlings throughout the pre-flowering period. In another experiment, it was found that salt solution primed tomato seeds was more beneficial to subsequent germination than PEG solution. Similarly, osmotically conditioned pepper seeds retained a high rate of germination and germinated to a high final percentage as compared to untreated seeds. Priming of seeds using higher water potential solution with shorter duration of time showed better germination ability as compared to seeds primed at lower water potential and for longer periods (Hardegree and Emmerich, 1992). Controlled hydration of tomato seeds followed by drying is used to break dormancy, speed germination, and improve uniformity of radicle emergence (Farooq *et al* 2005). It has alsobeen reported that sunflower seeds primed with osmotic solution of PEG 800 improved the seedling length and dry mass of both shoot and root.

Osmopriming of muskmelon in different solutions with and without aeration revealed that an osmotic potential around -1.30 MPa is most adequate for muskmelon priming. Controlled hydration of asparagus seed using PEG 6000 (-1.0 or -1.2 MPa) or sea water (-3.3 MPa) or hydropriming presented higher germination speed, independently of their initial physiological quality and beneficial effects of priming on germination and vigour were more expressive in the seed lot of low physiological quality (Bittencourt *et al* 2005). Osmopriming of sunflower seeds resulted in early 50% emergence, increased plant population, achene yield and achene proteins as compared to control. Likewise, seed priming of soybean resulted in faster and improved emergence and higher grain yield. Pereira *et al* (2009) explained that priming of carrot seeds (cv. Brasília) can be useful for improving carrot seedling emergence in the field and seed performance under supra and sub-optimal temperatures. Works on pearl millet indicated that osmoconditioning of seeds with PEG10000 were found effective in improving the germination percentage and plumule & radicle growth. Osmopriming of parsley seeds with PEG 6000 (–0.5 MPa, –1.0 MPa and –1.5 MPa), KNO_3 (0.30 mol/L and 0.35 mol/L), Mannitol (0.50 mol/L and 0.60 mol/L) for 2, 4, 6 and 8 days revealed significant increase in percentage of germination (Dursun and Ekinci 2010). Use of six levels of PEG6000 as priming media (0, 0.4, -0.8, -1.2, -1.6 and-2 MPa) clarified that different osmotic potential and priming duration had significant effect on germination percentage, mean germination time, germination index, and the time to get 50% germination of soybean seeds.

Matric priming (sand) of onion seeds with (24 h in 80% WHC of sand) recorded the highest germinability over control as compared to osmopriming or hydropriming. However, in case of carrot the highest germination attributes were recorded with 24 h hydropriming (Selvarani and Umarani 2011). Also, priming of alfalfa (*Medicago sativa* L.) (cvs. Hamedani and Yazdi) with water and mannitol (4%) for 12 h at 25 ± 1°C resulted in enhanced germination percent and seedling growth with respect to root and shoot length in comparison with seedlings obtained from non-primed seeds. Seed priming positively improved the germination potential in rice cultivars and different genotypes affected differently with respect to priming media. Kalpana *et al* (2013) studied that application of primers in wheat varieties (KRL 210 and HD 2733) brought a considerable increase in germination and growth parameters like plant height, tiller numbers and plant dry weight. An analysis of the available data across experiments carried out with different species under varying conditions showed an average 11% increase in percent germination and 36% shorter mean germination time (MGT) in primed vs unprimed seeds. Moreover, in primed seeds MGT was less dependent on temperature, which is consistent with the effects expected from the treatment. Works on seed priming in pepper (*Capsicum annuum* L.) cultivars indicated that effectiveness of priming depends on concentration, duration and cultivar. Seed priming studies on coriander revealed that seed priming with NaCl had diminished the negative impact of salt stress in all cultivars and primed plants showed better response to salinity compared to unprimed plants. Zhang *et al* (2015a) investigated that seed priming with PEG increased the environmental range suitable for sorghum germination and has potential to provide more uniform and synchronous emergence.

7. Seed osmopriming and biochemical attributes of seedling

The promotion of germination with seed priming may take place for several reasons, but completion of DNA repair during priming and onset of germination is associated with a rapid resumption of RNA and protein biosynthesis. It has been explained that application of osmopriming treatment in wheat through PEG 6000 indicated a relationship between the pattern of water absorption, the reactivation of mitotic activity lead to start and synchronization of germination. Primed lettuce seed (*Lactuca sativa* L. cv. Minetto) in aerated solutions of 1% K_3PO_4 and water at 15°C for various periods of time and reported that cell division occurred at 21 h in water and at 27 h in 1% K_3PO_4 prior to radicle protrusion. There was a considerable biochemical activity during priming and the significant benefits in germination performance of primed leek seeds is accompanied by marked increases in protein, DNA and nucleotide biosynthesis (Bray *et al* 1989). In contrast, other study revealed that the synthesis of a group of proteins associated with radicle emergence was reduced during imbibition of wheat seeds in NaCl.

The positive effects of priming on the germination performance of many species are attributed to the induction of biochemical mechanisms of cell repair: the resumption of metabolic activity can restore cellular integrity, through the synthesis of nucleic acids (DNA and RNA), proteins and the improvement of the antioxidant defence system. Studies also reported that improvement in germination by priming might be due to enhanced repair of membrane due to reduced leakage of electrolytes in primed watermelon seeds than in control. Priming treatments in PEG solutions might induce DNA replication in the embryo root tips of pepper seeds. Under the same osmotic condition the amount of induced DNA synthesis was proportional to the length of the treatment and its effectiveness in improving seed performance, as measured by the reduction in MGT.

It has been seen that primed sunflower seeds diverted a greater part of the cotyledonary resources towards the shoot which was crucial to its earlier establishment and photosynthesis for vigourous growth. It also reprogrammed the gene expression leading to *de novo* protein synthesis, a membrane repair mechanism and other substrates available for improved and synchronized germination (Cruz-Garcia *et al* 2003). It is also evidenced that improved germinability of tomato seeds due to osmopriming with PEG or K_2HPO_4 was associated with increased CAT and POX enzymes and decreased MDA concentration. Osmopriming of tomato seeds (Nagina, Pakit, Riogrande improved and Roma) resulted in lower electrical conductivity of seed leachates than untreated seeds. Experiments on six varieties of wheat (Tatara-96, Ghaznavi-98, Fakhri Sarhad, Bakhtawar-92, Pirsabaq-2004 and Auqab- 2000) concluded that seed priming with NaCl significantly increased seed germination potential with high shoot chlorophyll.

Hydro- and osmo- primed (manitol 4%) seeds of two alfalfa (*Medicago sativa* L.) varieties (Hamedani and Yazdi) showed enhanced activities of CAT, POD, SOD) and proline content and reduced the MDA accumulation and electrolyte leakage. Osmoconditioning of sorghum seeds induced an increase in CAT and POX activities and these enzymes protected the seedlings against oxidative damage caused by seed accelerated aging and salinity in nutrient solutions. Kalpana *et al* (2013) described that seed priming in wheat varieties (KRL 210 and HD 2733) brought a considerable change in biochemical parameters *viz*., total chlorophyll content and starch content. Likewise, seed priming with PEG significantly increased the chlorophyll (a and b) contents in shorghum seedlings (Zhang *et al* 2015a). However, there are reports that chlorophyll and carotenoid content did not affect by seed priming treatments in calendula. Zhang *et al* (2015b) investigated that osmopriming of sorghum seeds with PEG resulted an increased environmental range suitable for germination and strengthened the antioxidant activities of APX, CAT, POD, and SOD, as well as compatible solutes including free amino acid, reducing sugar, proline, soluble sugar, and soluble protein contents. As a result, seed priming reduced lipid peroxidation and stabilized the cell membrane, resulting in increased stress tolerance under drought or excessive soil moisture environments.

8. Osmopriming and reversal of ageing effects – morpho-physiological attributes

Slowing the rate of hydration prevents the loss of germinability due to imbibition injury caused by AA treatments. Germinability of accelerated aged seeds was increased from 10 to 90% by controlling the rate of imbibitions (Tilden and West 1985). Osmo-conditioning prior to storage, in addition to the acceleration of germination, results in a dramatic delay of the ageing rate, thus increasing considerably the longevity of seeds and enhanced the germination rate. These results were consistent with the hypothesis that age related deterioration was reversed by pre-germination metabolism. Research revealed that osmopriming treatments reduced both the mean time to germination and the speed of germination for two leek seed-lots of high viability but differing vigour. In addition, the differences in germination performance between these two seed-lots, was abolished by the priming treatments. Effect of priming in sunflower seeds was found to help the previously aged seeds to regain their initial ability. McDonald (2005) concluded that artificial ageing of tomato seeds increased the percentage of aberrant anaphases in seedling root tips while osmopriming partially counteracts the detrimental effects of artificial ageing on germination rate, uniformity and normal seedling and it did not influenced the frequency of aberrant anaphases in seedling root tips. Priming of low vigour seeds in sunflower hybrids (Hysun 33, Hysun 38, Hysun 44 & F-330) was found effective in reducing the T_{50} and MGT and increase in GP. Priming of normal/low-vigour seeds improved the vigour of seedling in term of radicle length, plumule length and their root/shoot fresh weight. Many seed priming treatments have been used to reduce the damage of aging and invigorate their performance in many crops (Farooq *et al* 2009). Priming of aged sunflower (*Helianthus annuus* L.) seeds showed that deprived germination potential due to ageing was found to revive in osmoprimed seeds (Kibinza *et al.*, 2011). Reversal of ageing effects due to hydropriming chickpea seeds has also been recorded in the studies.

Osmopriming (PEG-10% for two days in dark) of aged tomato (ZZ1 hybrid) seeds enhanced GP, GI and MGR with a substantial increase in the radicle length (RL), shoot length (SL) and total fresh weight (FW) compared with unprimed aged seeds (Zhang *et al.*, 2012). Parmoon *et al* (2013) found that accelerated aging caused to reduce the germination rate and seedling growth while as osmopriming treatments induced perking up of germination percentage, seed vigour and seedling growth. Priming of aged French bean (*Phaseolus vulgaris* L.) seed improved the seed quality and showed improved seedling length, seedling dry weight which in turn improved SVI, germination speed and MGT. Sibande *et al* (2015) observed that priming of soybean seed lots of different ageing level using water, KNO_3, *Moringa oleifera* leaf powder (MLP), custard apple (*Annona reticulata* L.) leaf powder (CALP) against a control has significant effects on the rate of germination, germination percentage and other seedling vigour traits. The unprimed (control) soybean seed had the highest germination results. There was significant reduction in germination percentage with increase in ageing level. The results therefore showed that soybean seed priming may not always lead to beneficial effect on the rate of germination, germination percentage and other seedling vigour traits but seed storage duration.

9. Osmopriming and reversal of ageing effects - biochemical attributes

Slow hydration of germinating seeds prevented seed electrolyte leakage (Tilden and West 1985) which indicates that cell membrane permeability or rupture was a major factor contributing to the loss of germinability after aging. The mechanism of this reversal was probably metabolic because it depended on temperature, seed moisture, and treatment duration. The 'rejuvenation' was accepted as evidence for metabolic repair. Since the vigour of seeds was increased by priming, metabolic repair probably included other sub-cellular components as well as the plasma membrane. Reversal of chromosomal damage (induced during seed ageing) achieved through partial hydration of lettuce seeds by osmopriming to 33 to 44%. Reversal by priming of deteriorated seed generally occurs in the meristematic axis or the radicle tip.

Germination and initiation of incorporation of S-methionine into radicle tips of cauliflower is delayed by controlled deterioration but osmopriming accelerated these processes and also alleviated the delays. There are proteins whose expression is correlated with the rate of germination which is reduced by controlled deterioration but enhanced by osmopriming. In certain seeds osmopriming reversed the effect of controlled deterioration and even caused an enhancement up to the level of un-aged osmoprimed seeds. There are reports that osmotic priming of aged onion seeds with 25% PEG-8000 for 5 d resulted in a marked reduction of electrolyte leakage as well as lipid peroxidation and increased levels of antioxidants (ascorbic acid & tocopherols and catalase & peroxidase) involved in the mitigation of oxidative damage. In comparison with the priming of un-aged seeds, the aged seeds experienced a diminution of response in terms of changes in the levels of antioxidants and scavenging enzymes. Research revealed that priming is responsible to repair the age related cellular and sub-cellular damage of low vigour seeds that may accumulate during seed development. It has also been found that effects of ageing in pepper (*Capsicum annuum* L.) seeds may be partly reversed by priming and part of priming effects is related to the induction of nuclear replication. The induction of DNA replication in aged seeds may thus serve as an indicator for the resumption of metabolic activities in the seed during imbibition in water or PEG. It has been explained that priming can reverse some of the aging-induced deteriorative events and thus improve seed performance. Further, the effect of priming in sunflower seeds was associated with a decrease in the level of lipid peroxidation and restoration of antioxidant defense systems. This treatment also helps the previously aged seeds to regain their initial ability to germinate by repairing the lipid peroxidation induced membrane damage. Priming appears to reverse the detrimental effects of seed deterioration by increasing the free radical scavenging enzymes and counteracting the effects of lipid peroxidation and reduce leakage of metabolites (McDonald 2000).

Kibinza *et al* (2011) informed that accelerated ageing affected seed germination and priming treatment reversed partially the ageing effect. The inhibition of CAT by the addition of aminotriazol during priming treatment reduced seed repair indicating that CAT plays a key role in protection and repair systems during ageing. These results clearly indicate that priming induce the synthesis of CAT which is involved in seed recovery during priming. Increased ageing duration in maize (*Zea mays* L.) seeds resulted in reduced antioxidant activity and germination behaviour while as priming of aged seeds with KNO_3 had positive effects on antioxidant activity as well as on seed germination. The improved germination attributes due to priming of aged seeds was associated with increased CAT and POX activity. Osmopriming of artificially aged pepper seeds (42°C and 100%RH) resulted in an improved germination with decreased levels of MDA and total peroxide concentration. Research on bitter gourd (*Momordica charantia* L.) seeds revealed that improvement in germination attributes of healthy and aged seeds due to seed priming was mediated through initiation of cell cycle, metabolic repair and reduction in the deleterious effects of ageing.

10. References

Almeida AD, Deuner C, Borges CT, Meneghello GE, De-Tunes LM and Villela FA .2014. Accelerated Aging in Tomato Seeds. *American Journal of Plant Sciences* 5: 1651-1656.

Balesevic-Tubic S, Malenèiae D, Tatiae M and Miladinovic J .2005. Influence of aging process on biochemical changes in sunflower seed. *Helia* 28 (42): 107-114.

Balesevic-Tubic S, Tatic M, Đorðevic V, Nikolic Z and Đukic V .2010. Seed viability of pil crops depending on storage conditions. *Helia* 33(52): 153-160.

Balesevic-Tubic S, Tatic M, Miladinovic J and Pucarevic M .2007. Changes of fatty acids content and vigour of sunflower seed during natural aging. *Helia,* 30(47): 61-67.

Biabani A, Boggs LC, Katozi M and Sabouri H .2011. Effects of seed deterioration and inoculation with *Mesorhizobium cicerion* yield and plant performance of chickpea. *Australian Journal of Crop Science*, 5(1): 66-70.

Bittencourt MIC, Dias DCFS, Dias LAS and Araújo EF .2005. Germination and vigour of primed asparagus seeds. *Scientia Agricola (Piracicaba, Braz.)*62 (4): 319-324.

Bradford KJ .1986. Manipulation of seed water relations via osmotic priming to improve germination under stress condition. *Horticultural Science* 21: 1105-1112.

Bray CM, Davison PA, Ashraf M and Taylor RM .1989. Biochemical changes during osmo-priming of leek seeds. *Annals of Botany*, 63(1): 185-193.

Chiu KY, Sung JM .2002. Effect of priming temperature on storability of primed sh-2sweet corn seed. *Crop Sci.* 42 1996-2003

Cortelazzo AL, Coutinho J and Granjeiro PA .2005. Storage and ageing of French beans (*Phaseolus vulgaris* L.): effect on seed viability and vigour. *Brazilian Journal of Morphological Sciences* 22(2): 121-128.

Cruz-Garcia F, Gomez A, Zuniga, JJ, Plasencia J and Vazquez-Ramos JM .2003. Cloning and characterization of a COBRA-like gene expressed *de novo* during maize germination. *Seed Science Research*13: 209-217.

Davidson PA and Bray CM .1991. Protein synthesis during osmopriming of leek (*Allium porrum* L.) seeds. *Seed Science Research,* 1: 29-35.

Dell'Aquila A, Savino G and De-Leo P .1978. Metabolic changes induced by hydration-dehydration presowing treatment in wheat embryos. *Plant and Cell Physiology* 19: 348-354.

Demir I and Mavi K .2008. Seed vigour evaluation of cucumber (*Cucumis sativus* L.) seeds in relation to seedling emergence. *Research Journal of Seed Science*1: 19-25.

Demirkaya M, Dietz KJ and Sivritepe HO .2010. Changes in Antioxidant Enzymes during Ageing of Onion Seeds. *Notulae Botanicae Horti AgrobotaniciCluj-Napoca* 38(1): 49-52.

DeTunes, L.M., Tavares, L.C., Rufino, C.D., Vieira, J.F., Acunha, T.S., Barros, A.C.S.A. and Muniz, M.B. 2011. Accelerated aging of onion seeds (*Allium cepa* L.) submitted to saturated salt solution. Rev. Colomb. Cienc. Hortic. *Revisita Colombiana De Ciencias Horticolos* 5(2): 244-250.

Dursun, A. and Ekinci, M. 2010. Effects of different priming treatments and priming durations on germination percentage of parsley (*Petroselinum crispum* L.) seeds. *Agricultural Sciences*1(1): 17-23.

Farooq, M., Basra, S.M.A., Saleem, B.A., Nafees, M. and Chishti, S.A. 2005. Enhancement of tomato seed germination and seedling vigour by osmopriming. *Pakistan Journal of Agricultural Sciences* 42(3-4): 36-41.

Farooq, M., Basra, S.M.A., Wahid, A., Ahmad, N. and Saleem, B.A. 2009. Improving the drought tolerance in rice (*Oryza sativa* L.) by exogenous application of salicylic acid. *Journal of Agronomy Crop Science* 195:237-246.

Ghassemi-Golezani, K., Bakhshy, J., Raey, Y. and Hossainzadeh-Mahootchy, A. 2010. Seed vigour and field performance of winter oilseed rape (*Brassica napus* L.) cultivars. *Notulae Botanicae Horti. Agrobotanici Cluj*. 38(3): 146-150.

Hardegree, S.P. and Emmerich, W.E. 1992. Effect of Matric-Primlng Duration and Priming Water Potential on Germination of Four Grasses. *Journal of Experimental Botany*43(247): 233-238.

Harris D, Rashid A, Miraj G, Arif M, Shah H. 2007. 'On-farm' seed priming with zinc sulphate solution-A cost-effective way to increase the maize yields of resource poor farmers. Field Crops Res. 102 119-127.

Hu, J.; Zhu, Z.Y.; Song, W.J.; Wang, J.C.; Hu, W.M .2005. Effects of sand priming on germination and field performance in direct-sown rice (*Oryza sativa* L.) Seed Science and Technology, 33(1): 243-248.

Jyoti and Malik, C.P. 2013. Seed deterioration: a review. *International Journal of Life Science Botany and Pharmacy Research* 2: 3.

Kaewnaree, P., Vichitphan, S., Klarnit, P., Siri, B. and Vichitphan, K. 2011. Effect of accelerated ageing process on seed quality and biochemical changes in sweet pepper (*Capsicum annum* Linn.) seeds. *Biotechnology*10(2): 175-182.

Kalpana, Khan AH, Singh AK, Maurya KN, Mubeen, Yadava RK, Singh U and Gautam AR .2013. Effect of different seed priming treatments on germination, growth, biochemical changes and yield of wheat varieties under sodic soil. *International Journal of Science and Research (IJSR)* 6(14): 306-310.

Kapoor N, Arya A, Siddiqui MA, Amir A and Kumar H .2010. Seed deterioration in chickpea (*Cicer arietinum* L.) under accelerated aging. *Asian Journal of Plant Science* 9(3): 158-162.

Kapoor N, Arya A, Siddiqui MA, Kumar H and Amir A .2011. "Physiology and biochemical changes during seed deterioration in aged seeds of rice (*Oryza sativa* L.)", *America Journal of Plant Physiology* 6(1): 28-35.

Khan FA, Bhat SA, Narayan S, Maqbool R, Murtuza I and Khan FU (2017). Seed Deterioration and Priming - An Overview. *SKUAST Journal of Research* 19 (1): 12-21.

Khan FA, Narayan S, Bhat SA and Maqbool R. 2016. Vermipriming - A Noble Technology for Seed Invigouration in Rice (*Oryza sativa* L.) *SKUAST Journal of Research* 18(2): 124-129.

Kibinza S, Bazina J, Baillya C, Farrant CF and El-Maarouf-Bouteaua H .2011. Catalase is a key enzyme in seed recovery from ageing during priming. *Plant Science,*181: 309-315.

Mc-Donald MB .2000. Seed priming. In: *Seed Technology and its Biological Basis,* (Eds. M.Black and J.D.Bewley). Sheffield Academic Press, Sheffield, UK, pp. 287-325.

Mc-Donald MB .2005. Flower seed longevity and deterioration. In: *Flower Seeds: Biology and Technology,* (Eds. M.B. Mc-Donald and F.Y.Kwong). CABI Publishing, CAB International, Wallingford, Oxfordshire, OX10 8DE, UK. pp. 187-205.

Mohammadi H, Soltani A, Sadeghipour HR and Zeinali E .2011. Effects of seed aging on subsequent seed reserve utilization and seedling growth in soybean. *International Journal of Plant Production*5(1): 65-70.

Osborne DJ .1983. Biochemical control of system operating in the early hours of germination. *Can. Journal of Botany* 61: 3568-3577.

Parmoon G, Ebadi A, Jahanbakhsh S and Davari MI .2013. The effect of seed priming and accelerated aging on germination and physiochemical changes in milk thistle (*Silybum marianum*). *Notulae Scientia Biologicae* 5(2): 204-221.

Pereira MD, Denise-Dias CFS, Dias LAS and Araújo EF .2009. Primed carrot seeds performance under water and temperature stress.*Scientia Agricola*(*Piracicaba, Braz.*) 66(2): 174-179.

Rastegar, Z., Sedgi, M. and Khomari, S. 2011. Effects of accelerated aging on soybean seed germination indexes at laboratory conditions. *Notulae Scientia Biologicae*3(3):126-129.

Selvarani, K. and Umarani, R. 2011. Evaluation of seed priming methods to improve seed vigour of onion (*Allium cepa cv. aggregatum*) and carrot (*Daucus carota*). *Journal of Agricultural Technology*7(3): 857-867.

Sibande GAK, Kabambe VH, Maliro MFA and Karoshi V .2015. Effect of priming techniques and seed storage period on soybean (*Glycine max* L.) germination. *Journal of Dynamics in Agricultural Research* 2(5): 46-53.

Tilden RL and West SH. .1985. Reversal of the effects of aging in soybean seeds. *Plant Physiology* 77: 584-586.

Yadollhhi NSJ and Mashayekhi F .2013. Enzyme activity and seedling growth of soybean seeds under accelerated aging. *Journal of Stress Physiology and Biochemistry* 9(4): 65-72.

Zhang F, Yu J, Christopher RJ, Wang Y, Zhu K, Lu F, Zhang Z and Zou J .2015a. Effect of seed priming with PEG and soil moisture stress on chlorophyll content in sorghum seedlings. https://dx.doi.org/10.1371.journal.one.0140620.t003.

Zhang F, Yu J, Christopher RJ, Wang Y, Zhu K, Lu F, Zhang Z and Zou J .2015b. Seed priming with polyethylene glycol induces physiological changes in sorghum (*Sorghum bicolor* L. Moench) Seedlings under suboptimal soil moisture Environments. *PLos One*. 10(10): e 0140620.doi:10.1371/Journal.pone.0140620.ecollection 2015

Zhang M, Wang Z, Yuan L, Yin C, Cheng J, Wang L, Huang J and Zhang H .2012. Osmopriming improves tomato seed vigour under aging and salinity stress. *African Journal of Biotechnology*11(23): 6305-6311.

11

Meadow Orchard System: A Step Towards Transformation in Horticulture

Akash Sharma, Vikas Sharma, Anil Bhat**, Satish Sharma, Amitesh Sharma and SK Singh

Organic Farming Research Centre, SKUAST-J, Chatha, J&K, India
***Division of Agril economics & Agribusiness, SKUAST-J, Chatha Jammu & Kashmir, India*

Abstract

Worldwide trend in fruit crops has shifted to high density or meadow orcharding to manage tree size for desired architecture to allow better light interception and easy in operations such as pruning, pest control and harvesting. The meadow orcharding facilitates increase production as well as quality of fruits. High density planting (HDP) is one of the recent and novel concepts of increasing the productivity without affecting the quality of fruits. The HDP has been successfully demonstrated in fruit crops such as apple, mango, citrus, banana, pineapple and guava. However, for more location specific benefit research must continue on appropriate plant canopy, integrated nutrient management suitable varieties, ageing of orchard and tree replacement. HDP accommodates more number of trees per unit area ranging from 500-10,000 plants/ha depending on the type of fruit crop and the level of density such as medium high density 500-1500 plants/ha, optimum high density 1,500-10,000 plants/ha ultra-high density 10,000-1,00,000 plants/ha. High density orcharding is a highly technical entrepreneurship where nutrient management, irrigation and canopy management practices widely vary from traditional orchards hence growers must have full execution knowledge of this technology in present as well as future perspective. Post harvest, storage and marketing are closely associated with the success of HDP technology. Fruit yield increases 2 to 4 times vertically enhancing income of fruit growers.

Keywords: fruit crops, high density planting, technology, constraints, cost benefit ratio

1. Introduction

The horticultural fruit crops put together cover approximately 11.35% of the total cropped area with an annual production of about 114million ton, making an overall contribution of more than18% in terms of the gross agricultural output of the country. Horticultural sector can play a pivotal role in diversifying agriculture in terms of increasing production and productivity providing food assortments, nutrition, income and employment.

Horticulture despite the deficit monsoon, unseasonal rains and hailstorm or other constraints has outpaced the production of food grains since 2012-13 (Table 1). Innovative technologies of orchard establishment have still a long way to go as the traditional system of cultivation has often posed problems in attaining desired levels of productivity due to large tree canopy. Currently, worldwide trend in fruit trees has shifted in favour of high density or meadow orcharding to control tree size and maintain desired architecture for better light interception and easy in operations such as pruning, pest control and harvesting. The meadow orcharding facilitates enhance production and quality of fruits. High density planting (HDP) is one of the recent and novel concepts of increasing the productivity without affecting the quality of fruits. The HDP has been successfully important in fruit crop such as apple, mango, citrus, banana, pineapple and guava.

Table 1: Comparative production trends in food grain and horticultural crops

Year	Horticulture (Million tons)*	Food grains (Million tons)**
2012-13	268.85	257.13
2013-14	277.35	265.04
2014-15	280.99	252.02

Source: * Horticulture Statistics Division, DAC&FW

** Directorate of Economics and Statistics

It is well known that the diversity in soil and climatic conditions in India permits growing of a large variety of tropical, sub-tropical and temperate fruits in different regions, due to which India is regarded as a horticultural paradise. In recent year, the concept of fruit production is undergoing a change where emphasis is being given to higher production per unit area. "High density planting technique is a modern method of fruit cultivation involving planting of fruit trees densely, allowing small or dwarf trees with modified canopy for better light interception and distribution and ease of mechanized field operation". HDP and meadow orcharding gives higher yield as well as returns/unit area due to increasing the no. of trees/unit area. It is possible by regular pruning and use of bio regulators for maintaining the size and shape of the tree. High density planting or meadow orchard system is the fastest way of reducing the gestation period and increasing the productivity of the orchards. The choice of the system of planting in the orchard depends on topography, crop, variety, plant density, production technology to be followed.

2. Concept of high density planting and meadow orcharding in fruit crops

Accommodation of the maximum possible number of the plants per unit area to get the maximum possible profit per unit of the tree volume without impairing the soil fertility status is called the high density planting. High density orchards were first planted in Europe at the end of the 19th century and since then these are a decline in traditional orchards with low densities. The underlying principle of a HDP is to make the best use of vertical and horizontal space per unit time and to harness maximum possible return per unit of inputs. In other words, it is the planting of more number of plants than optimum through manipulation of tree size. Meadow Orchard System is a new concept of planting. Meadow orchard: When ultra closer planting of apple is done accommodating about 70,000 trees per hectare and harvesting is done by moving around the orchard, the planting is often referred as meadow orchard or meadow-grassland or ultra high-density orchard or meadow system which has been developed in guava for the first time in India at CISH, Lucknow. The Meadow Orchard is a modern method of fruit cultivation using small or dwarf tree with modified canopy. Better light distribution within tree canopy increases the number of well illuminated leaves. Fertilizer dose, spacing, growth regulation by the training and pruning, use of the mechanical devices etc. may also be tried either singly or coupled with other crop management practices for a successful adaptation of these concept. It also promotes rate of photosynthesis that leads to high yield per unit area. Basically, the availability of a dwarf plant is the first and foremost prerequisite for establishing any high density or meadow orchard.

3. Types of Planting system

Low density planting

Non intensive system, age old planting system, trees planted at wider spacing, accommodating about 100-250 plants/ha. Dwarfing root stocks are not used. Trees acquire commercial production potential after 10-15 years of planting. Output from orchard during early 10-15 years is less. Less input and care intensive, holds popularity among growers.

Medium density planting

Highly minimized distance covering 250-500 plants/ha.Proper pruning undertaken to manage tree in desirable shape. More care intensive, labour requirement is more, obtained yield is also more. Lead in output reliable growers to produce amenable fruit crops like pomegranate, citrus, guava, papaya, banana, etc.

High density planting

- Very condensing planting with 500-10,000 plants/ha depending on fruit crop.
- Medium high density: – 500-1500 plants/ha.
- Optimum high density: – 1,500-10,000 plants/ha.
- Ultra-high density: – 10,000-1, 00,000 plants/ha.

It relies heavily on rigorous training and pruning. Maintenance of pruning is very heavy. Dwarfing rootstock and chemicals also used in this system. Yield as well as expenses per unit area is high.

Meadow orcharding

Meadow-grassland, also known as Ultra-high density planting. 10,000-1, 00,000 plants/ha in order to maintain tree form, severe top pruning is practiced similar to mowing of grassland. Plants intended to produce yield after 2 years age. Heavy use of growth regulators as well as pruning.

Table 1: Spacing in different planting system of fruit crops

S.No.	Crop	Normal Spacing(m)	HDP Spacing (m)	Meadow Spacing (m)
1.	Mango	7.5 x7.5 - 12.5 x 12.5	3 x 2.5 – 4.5 x 4.5	2.5 x 2.5 - 3 x 1
2.	Banana	2 x 2 - 2 x 3	1.5 x 1.5 - 1.8 x 1.8	1.2 x1.2 - 3 x 0.5
3.	Citrus	6 x 6 – 8 x 8	3 -6 x 3 -4.5	
4.	Papaya	2 x 2 – 3 x 3	1.8 x 1.8	1.2x1.2 – 1x1
5.	Guava	6 x 6 – 8 x 8	6 x 3 - 3 X 3 – 3 x 1.5	2 x 2 – 2 x 1
6.	Sapota	10 x 10	5 x 5	
7.	Aonla	10 x 10	5 x 5	
8.	Apple	10 x 10	3 x 0.75	3 X 0.37 - 0.60

4. High density mango orchard

Ultra-high density plantation (UHDP) is a new and proven technology, commonly practiced for mango cultivation worldwide and combined with other sustainable agricultural techniques, has the potential to yield 200% more produce than that of the traditional method. The ultra-high density mango plantation is a technique which has utilised all the resources optimally and thus, increased the production per unit area as well as raises profit margin of mango farmers. Now-a-days, mango is cultivated through this technique by the farmers for their consumption as well as for export purpose which includes mango fruits of uniform shape, colour, flavour and freshness. In the conventional planting technique of mango cultivation, it is very difficult to maintain uniformity, but the adoption of new technology called "Ultra-High Density Mango or Meadow Orcharding" planting ensures export quality of mango fruits.

Hi-density mango cultivation involves spacing of 3 M by 1 M row to row and plant to plant spacing. The success of hi tech mango fruit cultivation depends on the canopy management that involves removing diseased and insect damaged, weak, criss cross , very old and unproductive branches and maintaining standard number of productive branches to produce quality fruits. The canopy management involves periodical light pruning and occasional heavy pruning to facilitate easy penetration of air and sun light through entire canopy that trigger more flowerings and conversion of most of the flowers into fruits. Mango tree under meadow orchard needs 30-50 litre of water per tree per day/ week. Pre flowering irrigation is avoided to induce spurting of more flower buds in mango. To increase the fruit set and retention of fruits spray 2% Potassium nitrate (20 grams in 1 lit water) or 20 PPM NAA at flowering stage to retain fruits. The yielding potential of Meadow orchard mango cultivation is 12-15 MT per acre.

5. High density guava

Meadow orchard system is a new concept of fruit plantation in guava. It was introduced for the first time in India at Central Institute for Subtropical Horticulture, Lucknow. The meadow orchard system of guava accommodates 5000 plants ha^{-1}, when planted at 2.0 x 1.0 m spacing when managed with regular topping and hedging, especially during initial stage of growth. Topping and hedging in guava are helpful for controlling tree vigour, which leads to better light interception within tree canopy by increasing the number of well illuminated leaves. It also promotes rate of photosynthesis which directly increase the yield per unit area.

Fig. 1: Meadow orchard system in guava

6. High Density Litchi

Litchi cultivation under high density involves planting of litchi trees densely, allowing small or dwarf trees with modified canopy for better light interception and distribution and ease of mechanised field operations.

The normal planting distance in litchi has been 9-10 m. Such orchard takes 10-15 years to provide economic returns depending upon the cultivar, and cultural practices whereas in high density spacing is reduced to 2-4m.

Four steps in high density litchi

Planting Density

Depending on the planting system, tree density under different system of high density planting in litchi ranges from as low as 400-700 plants per hectare. Optimum light interception is ensured by maintaining appropriate level of tree density and canopy modification.

Planting Geometry

Planting system is a combination of tree arrangement and plant form. Tree arrangement in HDP system must have sufficient alley ways for movement of farm machinery. The way trees are arranged also determines the light distribution pattern and light interception level. In litchi, single hedge row and double hedge row system and or square system with 4-5 m apart having enough alley space is in practice in some developed countries for HDP (Fig. 2).

Pruning System

The tree growth of litchi in high density planting remains similar as in low density upto eight years. The training begins when the tree is first planted and continues throughout its productive life. Proper tree forms, branch angle and limb spacing in itself aids in growth control. First training is done after one growing season. Each plant is allowed to maintain single stem (main stem) with upward growth upto 60-80 cm and then four scaffold branches are allowed in four directions to make the tree frame. Thereafter, 2 shoots arising from each primary branch at a distance of 60-75 cm from main stem is allowed to form secondary and likewise the tertiary branches. After start of bearing in plants, shoots arising from secondary and tertiary branches are given 15-20 cm deep pruning soon after fruit harvest. Spray of 1% urea combined with 0.2% Blitox-50 or any other copper fungicide should be done soon after pruning.

Regular pruning induces new shoot production within 45-60 days during July-August. In general, every pruned shoot produces more than one shoot. After harvest of crop, about 50% branches of the tree canopy should be dehorned in high density orchard when the plant starts intermingling of canopies and the remaining 50% branches should be dehorned in next July after crop harvest to have a proper balance. In single hedge row or double hedge row system, the orchard is developed with a concept of single canopy with multiple roots and therefore, only side branches are pruned to develop alley of space. Good light distribution within tree canopy increases the number of well illuminated leaves. This condition induces a high rate of canopy photosynthesis that leads to high yield/ tree. Small and compact canopy plant form is desired for high density which can be achieved by constant pruning and dehorning.

Mechanization

- High density litchi planting favours the system of automation which contributes to high production efficiency
- Farm operations that needed to be automated are irrigation and fertigation
- Irrigation and fertigation have been identified as one of the key factors for the success of high density orchards in case of litchi.

- Plant should not be kept under stress after pruning therefore, assured irrigation coupled with fertigation is essential after pruning and during fruit development in high density litchi orchards.

Fig. 2: High Density Planting at National Research Centre for Litchi with a spacing of 2x2 m and 4x4 m66 A Manual for Litchi Production

Management of High Density Orchards

- Soil application of full doses of P and K should be done in July; whereas N may be given in two equal doses in March after fruit set and after crop harvest in July.
- The standard schedule of fertigation should be followed during vegetative and reproductive growth phase and fruit development stage.
- Leaf litter should be allowed to decompose in the orchard soil.
- High density litchi orchard should be irrigated as and when required particularly soon after paclobutrazol application during September-October, and from panicle emergence to crop harvest at15-20 days interval.
- No irrigation is applied from first shower of the rains in June to February-end.
- Tillage operations should be done in October-November to keep the orchard free from weeds and to mix fertilizers and leaf litter into the orchard soil.
- to control the pests and disease, the recommended practices should be followed.
- Weed cause some problems in initial stage of orchard. These should be removed and mulching may be done.

Benefits

- Litchi plants under high density planting system start fruiting after 4-5 years.
- These orchards have more number of tertiaries per unit area, hence, orchard become economical earlier than normal planting.
- There is also better light interception and distribution thus improved fruit quality.
- The increase in yield, early and maximized return,
- Reduced cost of production and improved fruit quality result in greater orchard profitability
- Provide better competitive advantage of local litchi growers.
- An estimated yield of 14-16 tons/ha can be obtained from High Density litchi orchard

7. Basics of high density planting in fruits

Main components of HDP and Meadow orcharding are

1. Dwarf scion varicties 2. Dwarf rootstock varieties 3. Training and pruning 4. Suitable crop management practices 5. Use of bio-regulators 6.Planting Density 7. Planting Geometry 8. Mechanization

The HDP can be with one species (mono-species) or with different species (multi-species, multi-storied) of crops. The mono-species HDP basically comprise the planting of small tree densely, restricting their vegetative growth by using dwarfing rootstocks, bio regulators or other horticultural technique such as pruning thereby, diverting much of the plant energy to the economical parts. In the multi-species HDP, the interception of incident solar radiation at different tiers by canopies of various species based on their light transmission characteristics and shade tolerance are exploited. Beside, ramification of their root system at different soil depths ensures effective nutrient and water uptake.

7.1. Training and Pruning

Training and pruning are effective tools in HDP and meadow orcharding by virtue of their impact on shape and size control of the tree. The training begins when the tree is first planted and continues throughout its productive life. Proper tree forms, branch angle and limb spacing in itself aids in growth control. First training is done after one growing season. Each plant is allowed to maintain single stem (main stem) with upward growth upto 60- 80 cm and then four scaffold branches are allowed in four directions to make the tree frame.

Thereafter, 2 shoots arising from each primary branch at a distance of 60-75cm from main stem is allowed to form secondary and likewise the tertiary branches. After start of bearing in plants, shoots arising from secondary and tertiary branches are given 15-20 cm deep pruning soon after fruit harvest. Spray of 1% urea combined with 0.2% Blitox-50 or any other copper fungicide should be done soon after pruning.

7.2. Use of bio-regulators

1. Prolonging dormancy 2. Reducing vegetative growth 3. Flowering 4. Reducing fruit drop

7.3 Adoption of suitable crop management practices

Mulching, Fertigation, Organic farming, INM, IPM

7.4 Planting Density

Even though a small canopy with a high number of well-illuminated leaves is efficient in photosynthesis but it is very poor in light interception, which leads to low potential yield per hectare. Light interception could be improved by increasing tree density. An optimum tree density is the level of density which is required to facilitate optimum light distribution and interception leading to high photosynthesis. As a result, yield per hectare is maximized. An optimum light interception is a factor of plant form, planting density, tree arrangement and leaf response to light for photosynthesis. Optimum light interception can be defined as a level of light intercepted by an orchard system above or below which, the economic yield will be reduced.

7.5. Planting Geometry

Planting system is a combination of tree arrangement and plant form. Tree arrangement in HDP system must have sufficient for movement of farm machinery. The way trees are arranged also determines the light distribution pattern and light interception level. Single hedge row and double hedge row system and square system having enough alley space is being practiced in developed countries for HDP.

7.6. Mechanization

Another component in high density fruit planting is the system automation which contributes to high production. One of the important farm operations that can be automated is irrigation and fertigation vis-à-vis indiscriminate mechanical. In fact, irrigation and fertigation have been identified as one of the key factors for the success of high density orchards. Plant should not be kept under stress after pruning therefore, assured irrigation coupled with fertigation is essential during fruit development in high density orchards.

Table 2: Comparison between Traditional system and HDP/Meadow system of fruit growing

S.No.	Attributes	Traditional System	HDP/Meadow System
1.	Tree numbers	Few large trees/ha (150- 200 trees/ha)	Many small trees/ha (500-1,00,000 trees/ha)
2.	Bearing	After two years	From first year
3.	Production	Lower yield	Higher yield
4.	Management	Difficult to manage due to large tree size	Easy to manage due to small tree size
5.	Labour requirement	Requires more labour	Requires less labour
6.	Production cost	Higher cost of production	Lower cost of production
7.	Harvesting	Difficult	Easy
8.	Quality	Large canopy, poor sunlight penetration and Poor quality fruits.	Small canopy, better air and Sunlight penetration, mini disease incidence and high quality fruits with good colour development

Table 3: Comparison between Traditional System and HDP System of Mango Growing

Attributes	Traditional System	HDP System
Plant Spacing	10x10 meter	4.5x4.5 meter
Tree numbers	100 plants/hectare	495 plants/hectare
Bearing	After third years	After second year
Production	Lower yield	Higher yield

Table 4: Per hectare Maintenance cost and returns from mango orchard under Jammu Sub-tropics

Year	At 10 x 10m spacing					At 4.5 x 4.5 spacing				
	Total Expenditure	Prod (tons)	Gross Return (Rs. Th)	Net Income (Rs. Th)	C:B Ratio	Total Expenditure	Prod. (tons)	Gross Return (Rs. Th)	NetIncome (Rs. Th)	C:BRatio
, st	40236	0	0	0	0	75365	0	0	0	0.00
2nd	39165	0	0	0	0	65870	0	0	0	0.00
3rd	39240	3	45	5.76	1.15	66450	8	120	53.5	1.81
4th	42578	4	60	17.4	1.41	66532	12	180	113.5	2.71
5th	50588	5	75	24.4	1.48	78950	15	225	146.1	2.85

Table 5: Comparison between traditional and high density guava orchard

Attributes	Traditional system	High density orcharding
Plant Spacing	6 x 6m	6 x 3, 3 x 3m &3 x 1.5m
Tree numbers	277 plants/hectare	555, 1111& 2222plants/hectare
Bearing	After Two years	After first year
Production	Average yield is 12-20t ha^{-1}	Average yield is 40-60 t ha^{-1}

Table 6: Per hectare Maintenance cost and returns from high density guava orchard under Jammu Sub-tropics.

Year	At 6 x 6m spacing					At 6 x 3 spacing				
	Total Expenditure	Prod. (tons)	Gross Return (Rs.)	NetIncome (Rs.)	C:BRatio	Total Expenditure	Prod. (tons)	Gross Return (Rs.)	Net Income (Rs.)	C:BRatio
1st	37175	0	0	0	0	40245	0	0	0	0.00
2nd	35350	1.11	12210	-23140	0.35	38055	1.67	18370	-19685	0.48
3rd	35845	6.0	66000	30155	1.84	39145	11	121000	81855	3.09
4th	36487	12.0	132000	95513	3.62	40305	17	187000	146695	4.64
5th	38250	15.0	165000	126750	4.13	44765	24	246400	201635	5.50

Table 7: Per hectare maintenance cost and returns from high density guava orchard under Jammu Sub-tropics.

Year	At 3 x 3m spacing					At 3 x 1.5 spacing				
	Total Expenditure	Prod (tons)	Gross Return (Rs.)	Net Income (Rs.)	C:B Ratio	Total Expenditure	Prod. (tons)	Gross Return (Rs.)	Net Income (Rs.)	C:BRatio
1st	48565	0	0	0	0	65250	0	0	0	0.00
2nd	44576	2.78	30580	-13996	0.69	58248	4.44	48840	-9408	0.84
3rd	45650	18	198000	152350	4.34	59324	26	286000	226676	4.82
4th	46855	26	286000	239145	6.10	60789	38	418000	357211	6.88
5th	49230	30	330000	280770	6.70	66280	47	517000	450720	7.80

8. Merit of HDP over Normal Planting

The high density planting has certain definite advantages as well as limitations compared to the conventional low density planting. It is worth mentioning here that under high density planting system the yield per plant is low as compared to low density planting. However, the total yield per unit area of land is several times higher than low density planting. Increasing pressure on land owing to diversion of farm field to various other obvious reasons as well as rising energy and land – costs, together with increased demand for fruits have made it necessary to achieve higher productivity from limited space.

- High density orcharding appears to be the most appropriate answer and need of the hour to overcome low productivity and long gestation period for early returns and export quality fruits.
- High density planting facilitates better utilization of solar radiation and increase in bearing surface per unit land area.
- HDP plants are precocious, easily manageable and fetch higher return per unit area.
- High density orchards have better amenability to modern, input saving horticultural techniques such as drip irrigation, mechanical harvest etc.
- The use of dwarf trees and managing excessive vegetative growth gives higher productivity and harvest index as well as early economic returns.
- High density planting system is more amenable to horticultural operations such as pruning, plant protection measures and harvesting which reduces the labour cost involved.

9. Constraints in adopting high density planting systems

- Poor availability of planting material in dwarf varieties as well as vegetatively propagated rootstocks in different horticultural crops.
- Lack of standardization of production technology in HDP of various fruit crops.
- High density planting needs higher initial establishment cost as compare to traditional system of planting.
- Least possibility of inter and mixed cropping system.
- Need for a more professional and scientific approach for management compared to the conventional planting at wider spacing

- Crowding and intermingling of branches may occur in coming years which can result in poor performance of trees.
- Non availability of complete package for HDP and use of mechanization

High yield and high fruit quality can be achieved with a high density orchard when the orchard has good light distribution throughout the tree canopy and there is a balance between vegetative growth and cropping. Planting density is one of the most important factors which determine the yield of an orchard. After the first year, fertigation regime should be maintained with a balance between fruiting and cropping. Excess fertility often results in excessive vegetative growth, delayed cropping and soft and poorly unmarketable fruit. The goal of HDP is to get the trees into cropping as soon as possible from a limited space. This is best accomplished by following proper pruning and training regime combined with a precocious rootstock to obtained significant production.

10. Points of note and contention in adaptation of HDP

Low rate of variety development and replacement

Development of varieties in fruit crops is time taking and a few scientists take up this challenging field. Breeding varieties in fruit crops is rare event and less attended area. Consequently development and replacement rates are quite lower in fruit crops compared to field and vegetable crops.

Poor Cultivation Practices

General neglect and non-adoption of scientific cultivation practices are the major constraints for poor return from most of the horticultural crops in the state. Despite conducive environment, the productivity and growth of most of the horticultural crops are lower than the all India average. This tendency leads to poor response to innovative technologies like high density orchards where scientific interventions are mandatory.

Lack of Quality Planting Material

It is imperative to generate disease free & healthy planting materials & screening of planting materials before its distribution is of utmost importance. Roping of private sectors is highly wanted to overcome this problem.

Lack of Marketing Facilities

Organized marketing structure is still rare and needs prior consideration. The middlemen usually amass a large chunk of profit at the expenses of the farmers. Due to perishable nature of the products and absence of adequate market support, the farmers sell their produce at throwaway prices to the middleman without even getting the opportunity to display them. Transportation and storage are perhaps the most serious constraints in the horticultural development of this region. Due to this farmers are getting low return and show low interest to adopt innovative technologies like HDP.

Trained manpower

Dearth of trained manpower is major hurdle in development of horticulture. Where trained manpower and the extension services are working in tandem, very efficient, the pace of progress is seen horticulture.

Long Gestation Period

Since horticultural crops, more specifically, plantation crops have long gestation period and initial cost of establishment of orchard or plantation is high, it becomes almost impossible for the marginal/ small farmers to go for such ventures without long-term credits from financial institutions.

Problems of Processing

The processing industry can help to a certain extent in mitigating the problem of proper disposal of perishable commodities. In the state of Assam, the storage facilities are inadequate and only available; few processing unit sexist but are not functioning up to the desired capacity and this is deemed to be one of the weakest areas in the entire region.

Inadequate Investment on Research

Investments on research in horticulture have always remained low when compared to the large number of crops it covers. As a result, many more researchable issues remain unattended to for years together. There is an urgent need to increase the level of investment on research front.

Absence of Adequate Insurance Coverage

Risk management in horticultural crops is almost nonexistent although the crops like onion and potato are covered under the National Agriculture Insurance Scheme. There is a need to cover the risk in case of other horticultural crops as well, perhaps on the basis of potential production coverage instead of average yield. This would encourage higher investment to achieve higher productivity. Other bottlenecks of horticultural development in the region are as follows: -

i. Inadequate thrust on conservation and exploitation of horticultural germplasm.

ii. High rainfall, soil erosion and high rate of leaching of nutrients.

iii. Heavy infestation of weeds, insect-pests and diseases.

11. Researchable issues

- There is need to do more research on time and intensity of pruning on each fruit crop.
- Screen the varieties having less canopy area and erect growth.
- Research on PGR for increasing yield and improving quality under HDP as well as meadow orchard system.
- Needs more research on development of meadow orchard system applicable to all the major fruit crops.

12. Conclusion

HDP and meadow orcharding gives higher yield as well as returns/unit area due to increasing the no. of trees/unit area. It is possible by regular pruning and use of bio-regulators for maintaining the size and shape of the tree. Mango planted at spacing of 4.5m x 4.5m (Dashehari and Alphonso) and 3m x 4m (Dashehari) gives higher yield under High density orcharding. Guava planted at spacing 3.0m x 1.5m and 6m x 3m under HDP and 2m x 1m under meadow gives higher production as well as more income in L-49 and Shweta. Citrus gives higher production when planted at 6m x 3m spacing under HDP. For HDP in banana is planted at 1.0 x 1.2m spacing gives better yield in cv. Rajapuri. High density orchards are highly technical, time and resource demanding but competent to provide full time employment. As an entrepreneurship of commercial magnitude in fruit crops, high density planting or meadow orcharding is indispensable for high profit per unit of land.

13. References

Anonymous .2006. Study on development of plant canopy and fruit yield of Kagzi lime as influenced by planting density. Horticulture Research Report of JAU. Junagadh: pp 41-43.

Athani SI, Revanappa, Dharmatti PR .2009. Effect of plant density on bunch weight and yield of banana cv. Rajapuri. Karnataka. *Journal Agricultural Sciences*, 2 (1): 143-146.

Dalvi NV, Salvi BR, Chavan SA and Kandalkar MP .2010. High density planting in mango cv. Alphanso. *Hort. Science*. 5(2): 117.119.

Kerutagi MG, Mallu B, Deshetti and Abhilash K .2017. Comparative economics of traditional *viz*. High Density Mango cultivation in Karnataka. *Asian Journal of Agricultural Extension, Economics & Sociology*. 18(3): 1-12.

Kundu S .2007. Effect of high density planting on growth, flowering and fruiting of guava (*Psidium guajava*). *Acta Horticulturae*. 735: 267-270.

Sharma A, Wali VK, Bakshi P and Sambyal S .2014. High density orcharding of guava. *Extension Bulletin* pp. 36.

Sharma A, Wali VK, Bakshi P and Sambyal S .2014. High density orcharding of mango. *Extension Bulletin* pp. 24.

Sharma A, Wali VK and Bakshi M .2015. Calendar of Operations for High density Orcharding of guava. Division of Fruit Science, FoA, SKUAST-J, Chatha Jammu, *Extension Folder*.

Singh G .2009. High density and Meadow Orcharding of Guava. *Extension Bulletin CISH*. Pp.20.

12

Innovative Technological Strategies to Transform Horticulture in Jammu & Kashmir State

DB Singh, MY Zargar*, JI Mir and Pradeep K Sharma**

ICAR-Central Institute of Temperate Horticulture, Old Air Field Rangreth Srinagar, (J&K), India
**Sher-e-Kashmir University of Agricultural Sciences and Technology, Kashmir Shalimar, Srinagar, (J&K), India*
***Sher-e-Kashmir University of Agricultural Sciences and Technology, Jammu Jammu & Kashmir, India*

1. Introduction
2. Weaknesses of horticulture in J&K
3. Horticulture as potential candidate for doubling farmers' income
4. Technological interventions required
5. Strategic approaches

Abstract

The J&K state, like other Himalayan states, is endowed with varied climates and agro-climatic situations and has the potential for improvement in a horticulture sector. Focus on selective issues based on the niches of the areas , strengthening the on-going programs of different developmental departments, site specific issues, backed up with latest technologies need to be identified which can have tangible and immediate impact on the farm economy. The horticulture section is doing well in Jammu and Kashmir state when compared with others food crops, since it fetches good price because of its nature of seasonality. The estimation of the potential profits can be drawn by the fact that a farmer producing wheat of 1 kg gets 10 times higher prices for the same produce in horticulture section. Considering this high potential, the concept of doubling farmer's income can work magically with horticultural crops. There is a need of shift from traditional crops and cropping patterns. Technological interventions are required to strengthen the conditions of cold storage, adoption of farming system approach, instead of cropping system approach, incorporating element of diversification, promotion of cultivation of high value crops, efficient post-harvest management, value addition etc. popularization of technologies and schemes to achieve targeted growth in horticulture. Strengthening water resources through rainwater harvesting, soil moisture conservation and efficient utilization of stored/conserved rain water (micro-irrigation, fertigation). Promotion of niche commodities based on agro-ecological situations will benefit promotional efforts in horticulture development with increased benefit cost ratio.

1. Introduction

Jammu and Kashmir (J&K) is a hill state, situated between 32.17" and 36.58" North altitude and East to West, and 73.26" and 80.30" longitude, and constitutes the northernmost extremity of India. The total area of Jammu and Kashmir is 2, 22,236 sq km, of which 78,114 sq km is under illegal occupation of Pakistan and 37,555 sq km under China. In addition, 5,180 sq km area of J&K was illegally ceded to China by Pakistan. The J&K is the 6th largest state of India occupying 6.8% of the country's total geographical area. J&K is a multi-lingual, multi-religious and multi-racial state and each group has its own distinct and peculiar cultural ethos, further deepened by geographical divisions created by formidable mountain ranges. The state comprises three main regions, namely, Jammu, Kashmir and Ladakh. The State is further divided into 22 districts, two in Ladakh, 10 each in Jammu and Kashmir. The number of Tehsils and CD Blocks are 82 & 142, respectively. There are as many as 6,652 villages and 68 urban areas besides 7 urban agglomerations. The sector contributes immensely to strengthen the financial condition of the State, poverty alleviation, employment generation and is a core sector of Jammu and Kashmir horticulture. The variety of horticultural products of the State has earned world-wide fame because of its good quality and taste. The fruit crops grown in the state are apple, almonds, walnuts, pears, cherries and apricots in temperate areas and mango, citrus, litchi, papaya, guava etc. in subtropical areas. Saffron cultivation in Jammu and Kashmir is unique in the world.

Table 1: Climatic zone classification based on fruit crop adaptation

Zones	Areas	Suitable Fruit Kinds
Temperate Zone	Entire Kashmir Valley, Parts of Poonch, Rajouri, Doda, Kathua and Udhampur Districts of Jammu Division	Apple, Pears, Cherry, Walnut, Almond, Chestnut, Strawberry, Stone fruits and Grapes etc.
Sub- Temperate (Mid Zone)	Parts of Kathua District, Parts of Poonch District (Surankote), parts of Rajouri District (Rajouri and Kalakote), parts of Udhampur District parts of Reasi, some portion of Doda District, Ramban and Kishtwar), besides minor locations in Uri Tehsil of Baramulla District and Karnah Tehsil of Kupwara district.	Stone fruits (like Peach, Plum,Apricot) Almond, Pears, PecanNut, Olive and Kiwi.
Sub– Tropical Zone	Jammu District , parts of Kathua district, parts of Rajouri district, parts of Udhampur district and lower areas of Reasi) , parts of Doda District (Ramban)	Mango, Citrus, Guava, Litchi, Ber, Aonla and Grapes.
Arid Temperate Zone	Districts of Leh and Kargil	Grapes (Resin type), Prunes and drying varieties of Apricots. Seabuck thorn besides cultivation of Apple, Walnut, Currants in certain areas of the region.

2. Weaknesses of horticulture in J&K

Predominance of old and senile orchards

In mango, ber, apple etc. there is predominance of old and senile orchards. Their productivity has declined drastically. Rejuvenation of old and declining mango orchards standardized recently has shown a ray of hope. However, serious efforts in this direction are still lacking.

Low density of plantation

In general, mango and aonla are planted 10-12 meters apart and area in between remains vacant for a long time. This is because of non-availability of precocious variety, dwarfing root stock and other growth contributing factors. Identification of precocious, prolific varieties rootstock, canopy management (training, pruning) growing of intercrops, possibility of use of growth retarding chemicals, have not been thoroughly worked out for most of the fruit crops which needs due attention.

Lack of efficient use of irrigation water

Water is the critical input in fruit crop production. Its efficient use is inevitable for achieving higher production from shrinking ground water resources. Micro-irrigation, popularly known as drip irrigation is an efficient way of irrigation with high frequency applications of water close to feeder roots. It economizes water use by 40-60 percent, added with enhanced yield, reduces weed population and quality production. Such techniques have not been fully exploited by orchardists.

Inadequate adoption of plant protection measures

The plant protection measures in terms of pest and disease management are not being adopted seriously which also contributes to the low productivity in the region.

Post harvest losses

The development of horticulture is closely associated with the growth of post harvest technology as unmarketable surplus horticulture produce during glut periods have to be properly preserved. There is very high degree of wastage due to improper handling, storage, marketing, processing and distribution system.

Lack of transfer of improved technology to field

No doubt in recent years, new techniques have developed but selection and use of appropriate channels in transmitting the information to orchardists have received little attention. Use of print media has limited scope due to high level of illiteracy in the rural areas. The farmer, the last link in the transfer of technology is the ultimate user of the technology. His attitude, knowledge about the technology, skill to adopt it and host of other factors make him to think several times before making the final decision.

3. Horticulture as potential candidate for doubling farmers' income

The Government of India has set up a target of doubling farmers' income by 2022-23. Horticulture sector has proved beyond doubt its potentiality for gainful economy especially in most fragile ecosystems. Hence there has seen a dynamic shift from sustenance production to commercial production in many horticultural commodities. Moreover, the horticulture sector is one of the most vital sector for providing stability and sustainability in economic productivity and profitability. Technological change has been the major driving force for increasing productivity and promoting horticulture development. In the past, the choice of technologies and their adoption was to increase production, productivity and farm incomes. Over many decades, policies for agriculture, horticulture, trade, research and development, education, training and advice have strong influences on the choice of technology, the level of production and farm practices. Horticulture is becoming more integrated in the food chain and the global market, while environmental, food safety and quality, and welfare regulations are also increasingly impacting on the sector. It is faced with new challenges to meet growing demands for fruit/vegetables, to be internationally competitive and to produce horticultural products of high quality. At the same time, it must meet sustainability goals in the context of on-going policy reform, further trade liberalization and the implementation of multilateral environmental agreements.

The farmers in Jammu and Kashmir State need an immediate support of technologies for increasing the farm income to double their income. The J&K state, like other Himalayan states, is endowed with varied climates and agro-climatic situations, which has the greatest potential for improvement in a horticulture sector. Focus on selective issues based on the niches of the areas, strengthening the on-going programs of different developmental departments, site specific issues, backed up with latest technologies need to be identified which can have tangible and immediate impact on the farm economy.

Table 2: Comparative productivity potential of different fruit crops

S.No.	Crop	Productivity (MT/ha) of Jammu province	Productivity (MT/ha) of J&K	Productivity (MT/ha) of India	Productivity (MT/ha) of World
	Fresh Fruits				
1.	Apple	2.11	10.60	8.09	16.75
2.	Pear	3.98	6.08	7.80	16.38
3.	Apricot	1.45	2.22	2.79	6.61
4.	Peach	1.53	2.38	5.94	15.25
5.	Plum	1.59	2.50	3.45	
6.	Cherry	-	2.92	2.92	5.57
7.	Grapes	1.64	2.02	19.72	10.45
8.	Litchi	2.46	2.46	6.33	-
9.	Citrus	2.35	2.35	12.08	9.16
10.	Olive	0.10	0.65	-	1.499
11.	Mango	1.89	1.90	8.70	8.015
12.	Ber	2.00	2.01	9.81	-
13.	Aonla	1.75	1.76	10.86	-
14.	Guava	3.69	3.69	13.92	-
15.	Kiwi	-	-	2.75	15.73
16.	Strawberry	-	2.23	5.00	21.72
17.	Pomegranate	-	0.15	11.68	
18.	Other fresh	1.75	2.15		
	Dry Fruits				
1.	Walnut	2.41	2.98	2.47	3.48
2.	Pecan nut	0.21	0.20	1.00	
3.	Almond	0.04	0.89	0.66	1.55

Technological developments in IFS and post harvest management will play an important role in doubling the farmers income in the state as the state being a hill state, where land holdings are relatively small and scattered, and majority of the farmers fall in the marginal to small category, integrated farming system is the best model suited for the state and post-harvest management of the farm produce, especially of perishable commodities, like fresh fruits and vegetables, which are the major products of J&K state, is another important aspect of farm economy. Due to high speed of technological developments farmers, advisors and policy makers are faced by complex choices.

4. Technological interventions required

Interventions that are categorized as new technologies/innovations emphasize the introduction of a 'new' farming method, product, or service. These new technologies and innovations can include: fertilizers; new crops; more nutritious crops; and new industries and incorporate these technical developments into new farming systems.

Table 4: Status of horticultural crops in J&K.

Crop	Area (000 ha)	Production (000 MT)
Apple	141.71	1852.41
Pear	12.53	62.50
Apricot Cherry Other fresh	5.853.4653.50	130.64
Total fresh fruits	217.05	2045.55
Walnut	89.78	163.74
Almond	17.65	12.50
Other Dry fruits	0.58	0.19
Total Dry fruits	108.01	176.43
Total fruits	325.06	2221.98

(*Source:* Indian Horticulture Database, 2013-14)

In India scientific technologies are being implemented on ground for increasing productivity and quality of the produce to obtain maximum value out of it and the same need to be done at State level. Technological interventions are required for doubling the farmer's income but all the interventions have analytical aspects like:

- The adoption of technologies for sustainable farming systems is a challenging and dynamic issue for farmers, extension services, agri-business and policy-makers.
- Demand is driving the adoption of technologies for doubling the farmers income
- The ways in which technologies are developed and adopted differ across countries

- Research efforts, farmer education and training, advice and information are shifting towards balancing economic efficiency with environmental and social sustainability
- Technologies are increasingly being developed in a global market, applied at the farm level but impacting on sustainability beyond the farm
- Adopting technologies for sustainable farming systems and for doubling income is multi-disciplinary
- Adopting technologies for sustainable farming systems and doubling income involves uncertainty and tradeoffs.
- Several factors are facilitating the adoption of technologies for sustainable farming systems and farming systems required for doubling the income of farmers.
- Other factors are constraining the adoption of technologies
- Farmers need to face the right signals for the adoption of appropriate technologies
- Assessing technologies for farming systems from a sustainability/profitable perspective is in its infancy

There are three basic principles to make horticulture sector as a whole profitable and sustainable:

i. Increasing the productivity and quality of produce, and reducing the cost of production
ii. Linking farming community with assured market
iii. Policy support for creating conducive environment

5. Strategic approaches

Strategies and approaches which need implementation for doubling farmer's income in horticulture are:

- Enhancing production and productivity of produce with low cost of production using efficient input-use technologies
- Use of modern production technologies, such as resource conservation technologies, micro-irrigation techniques, high density plantations, quality planting/seed materials, mechanization, protected cultivation, precision farming etc.
- Adoption of farming system approach, instead of cropping system approach, incorporating element of diversification.

- Promotion of cultivation of high value crops, efficient post-harvest management, value addition etc.
- Popularization of technologies and schemes to achieve targeted growth in horticulture
- Strengthening water resources through rainwater harvesting, soil moisture conservation and efficient utilization of stored/conserved rain water (micro-irrigation, fertigation)
- Promotion of niche commodities based on agro-ecological situations
- Production of safe food using technologies aiming at reduced use of agro-chemicals, such as organic farming, integrated nutrient use, integrated disease and pest management, use of biopesticides etc.
- Establishment of rural business and services hubs at each focal point, and strengthening of input supply through rural business and service hubs.
- Promotion of commodity groups/FPOs/SHGs etc.; however, such promotions need very strong local leader/progressive farmer who can act as nucleus to sensitize local people and organize such cooperative movement in rural areas on commodity/region basis.
- Promotion of contract, corporate and precision farming in order to take care of small and fragmented land holdings
- Establishment and development of linkages between government agencies, research institutions and farmers to achieve higher growth trajectory in agriculture/allied sectors
- Establishing strong linkages between farmers and assured market to enable the farming community to realize desired net profit from their produce; assured market is in fact the main driver for sensitizing farming community towards adoption of modern farming techniques, and maximizing net profits.
- Increased emphasis on awareness/trainings of the farmers, traders and other stake-holders on use of modern production, post-harvest management and marketing technologies.
- Strong legislation against conversion of agricultural land for non-agricultural purposes.
- Implementation of all government schemes immediately in letter and spirit.

The horticulture is diversified to cover 6 subsectors namely vegetables, fruit crops, spices, ornamentals, plantation crops and mushrooms. The horticulture section is doing well in Jammu and Kashmir State when compared with others food crops, since it fetches good price because of its nature of seasonality. Though sections like movement of the produce and post harvest practices are few areas where the lion's share of problems persists. The estimation of the potential profits can be drawn by the fact that a farmer producing wheat of 1 kg gets 10 times higher prices for the same produce in horticulture section. Considering this high potential, the concept of doubling farmer's income can work magically with horticultural crops. There is a need of shift from traditional crops and cropping pattern.

Total Export of fresh fruits	10.87 lakh MT
Total Export of Dry fruits	0.27 lakh MT
Export of Almond outside the country	91 MT
- Foreign exchange earned	1.64 crore
Export of walnut outside the country	9524.55 MT
- In-shell	382.72 MT
- Kernel	9141.83 MT
- Foreign exchange earned	206.85 Crore

(Source: Indian Horticulture Database, 2013-14)

Technological interventions are required to strengthen the conditions of cold storage. Every other fruit/vegetable type uses different process/method for the protection and preservation of produce. We are falling short of various components of cold storage like packed houses, ripening chambers and cold vans etc. Horticultural produce can be stored from 20 days to 6 months using these advancements. The advancements also face gaps when we talk of storage houses for potato, tomato and onion, which are considered to be game changer crops. The first and foremost thing for doubling farmer's income is to create market for farmers and provide market access and links for growing their business. Alternative sources of income along with horticultural crops should be looked into, like Apiculture, where-in the bees also helps in the pollination and also draws extra income for the farmers. The govt. is also promoting Mission for Integrated Development of Horticulture (MIDH) scheme to support the various components of horticultural crops. Starting with nursery development, covering sustainable irrigation practices, emphasizing on subsidies for storage structures till market linkages, all the prospects are taken care of, under MIDH.

The Horticulture Sector in Jammu and Kashmir needs a focused attention for its development and the short and long term initiatives to be adopted to achieve the targeted goals are given below:

Sr.No	Strategy	Interventions
1.	*Production of quality planting material, bud-wood and rootstocks for high density planting*	
	• Selection and introduction of the planting material/rootstocks of outstanding value • Creation of bud wood/rootstock banks • Propagation and multiplication of quality planting material/ rootstocks • Screening and monitoring of planting material against disease and pests	• Introduction of rootstocks/varieties from horticultural advanced countries • Mass multiplication of disease free planting material at different Research Stations/Development Department farms/KVKs • Establishment of bud-wood /rootstock bank at public and private sector • Demonstration of technologies for production of planting material of walnut, kiwi etc. • Establishment of virus indexing/plant protection measures • Establishment of mobile soil and leaf testing labs • Establishment of green house/mist chambers for propagation • Human Resource Development in Horticulturally Advanced Countries for training of master trainers • Establishment of Crop Insurance facilities for orchardists
2.	*Improving productivity, quality and shift towards high density*	
	• Validation of package of practices for high density orchards (Performance Study & Compilation) • Organic farming and precise nutrient scheduling • INM in high density orchards • Standardization of Leaf nutrient standards • Training and pruning of high density orchards (Validation, extension, capacity building and compilation)	• Establishment of demonstration modules of high density orchards • Establishment of precise nutrient scheduling models • Demonstration of efficient training and pruning techniques in high density orchards • Demonstration of orchard management techniques up to district level to provide skill input to the farmers. • Human resource development of officials of line departments • Zonalization and suitability of various zones for high-density orchards.
3.	*Canopy Management and Plant Architecture*	
	• Developing suitable plant modules (Plant Architecture) • Canopy management of traditional orchards	• Establishment of plant architecture modules for high density orchards. • Establishment of ideal canopy modules in traditional orchards • Human Resource Development • Establishment of modules for inter-cropping in existing orchards • Demonstration of various canopy management modules

Contd.

4. *Hi-Tech Horticulture*	
• Use of PGR and biotech tools • Value added and micro-propagation • IWM, INM, IPM and IDM • Protected cultivation • Organic and precision farming • Canopy management of high/ultra density orchards • Use of diagnostics	• Nutritional security (Protein energy malnutrition) • Breeding for health traits • Nutritional and antioxidants • High altitude research • Value added plant propagation. • Aeroponics, hydroponics etc. • Providing soil health cards to identify suitability of soil for production capability of soil
5. *Rejuvenation & Revival of old and Senile Orchards*	
• Phasing-out of old orchards/senile with improved varieties • Revival and registration of Ambri through geographical indications	• Establishment of demonstration orchards of new and improved varieties. • Phasing-out of old and senile orchards • Revival of traditional apple variety Ambri through breeding, selection and orchard management.
6. *Modernization and Establishment of Hi-Tech Nurseries*	
• Accreditation/registration of nurseries • Establishment of hi-tech nurseries. • Establishment of hi-tech nurseries.	• Establishment of hi-tech nurseries • Establishment of virus indexing facility • Establishment of green house/mist chambers for propagation • Mass multiplication of disease free planting material at different Research Stations/Development Department farms/ KVK's • Establishment of bud-wood/rootstock bank at public and private sector.
7. *Creation of Irrigation Network/systems through CSS like PMKSY*	
• Micro-irrigation scheduling • Individual Ponds/ water storage tanks • Community water tanks • Micro irrigation – (a) sprinkler and (b) drip	• Establishment of Micro irrigation models • Modals for reducing risk in case of bad monsoons • Augmentation of irrigation assets over 65% land area that is at the mercy of monsoon and sporadic rainfall • To identify best nearby water resources to the area for ensuring the irrigation benefit to every farmer • Help of Satellite imagery and 3D photography to guide best possible sources of irrigation
8. *Establishment of Centre of Excellence*	
• Production of Quality planting material. • Establishment of Clonal rootstock bank • Crop Improvement and molecular characterization of varieties • Standardization of production technologies (INM and IPM)	• Production of quality planting material of elite varieties • Import of planting material and rootstocks of outstanding merit • Shift of fruit farming system in Kashmir from conventional to high density

Contd.

• Gene Bank establishment • Standardization of post harvest, processing techniques and development of value added products. • Standardization of quality parameters in order to improve export. • Human Resource Development	plantation • Phasing out of old and senile orchards with high density orchards • Promotion of high density plantation by using size controlling rootstocks and improved spur varieties • Crop Improvement and molecular characterization • of varieties • Standardization of production technologies (INM and IPM) • Standardization of post harvest, processing techniques and development of value added products.· Standardization of quality parameters in order to improve export· Gene bank establishment· Promote good horticultural practices for harnessing high productivity potential· Human resource development
9. *Pollination Management for various plant densities*	
• Pollinators, pollinizers and managed pollination for high density and conventional orchards. • Standardization of suitable pollinizers and rootstocks under different planting densities • Raising of Pollinizers for mass distribution • Awareness for pollination management.	• Awareness of orchardists regarding pollination management • Imparting training to farmers and other stakeholders • Demonstration of pollination techniques
10. *Natural Resource Management*	
• Development of orchard based cropping systems (Horti-pastoral system) • GIS based temperate resource maps for land use planning vis-à-vis climate change • Management of physiological disorders (Technology validation only)	• Establishment of Horti-pastoral systems with thrust on use of wind breaks and wild pollinizers. • Establishment of climate resilient varieties of various fruit crops. • Technology validation for management of physiological disorders
11. *Crop Improvement and Micro-Propagation*	
• Strategic approach for improvement of quality and disease resistance • Assessment & Refinement of protocols for mass multiplication of clonal rootstocks.	• Development of disease/pest resistant varieties of major fruit crops • Establishment of climate resilient varieties of various fruit crops • Establishment of suitable perils for efficient production • Establishment of protocols for mass multiplication of rootstocks • Establishment of tissue culture lab.
12. *Disease & Pest Management*	
• Monitoring and Surveillance	• Establishment of monitoring and

Contd.

• High-Tech Immuno-diagnosis • Revisiting of Spray Schedule • Non-chemical remediation for disease and insect/pests • Pesticide residues • Insect and disease map	surveillance group for early detection of farm problems. • Establishment of bio-pesticide lab • Establishment of Quality control and residue analysis lab • Establishment of mechanism for vibrant spray schedule' • Establishment of disease forecasting
13. *Hort-Net Facility and State Coordination Cell* • Develop R&D website highlighting proven technologies.	• Development of Hort Net facility for the State • Development of efficient marketing channels. • Development of efficient coordination between University and various Line departments • Use of IT and remote sensing in the method of data collection • Establishment of uniformity in data collection • Human resource development of all • levels in line departments
14. *Zonalization* • Zone specific horticulture practices	• Zonalization for area specific crops· Development of fruit specific areas (Fruit villages) in line with zonalization and diversification strategies.

13

Biochar – A Strategic Approach for Carbon Sequestration and Higher Crop Productivity

Peeyush Sharma, Vikas Abrol, Vikas Sharma, Vivak Arya and Sandeep Sharma*

Division of Soil Science, SKUAST-Jammu, Jammu and Kashmir, India
[*]Division of soil Science, PAU- Ludhiana, Punjab, India

Abstract

Biochar is the product of thermal degradation of organic materials in the absence of air (pyrolysis), and is distinguished from charcoal by its use as a soil amendment. Biochar is generally alkaline in pH and may increase soil pH with greater increase observed in sandy and loamy soils than in clayey soils. Biochar addition can increase cation exchange capacity, base saturation, exchangeable bases and organic carbon content as well as decreases in Al saturation in acid soils. Biochar enhances soil productivity by improving the physical, chemical and biological soil conditions. Improvement in soil structure increase soil water retention. A comparative study of soil fertility and leaching losses of nutrients between an Anthrosol and an adjacent unamended Ferralsols revealed that the Anthrasol had significantly higher P, Ca, Mn and Zn availability than the Ferralsol, and an increased biomass of both cowpea and rice by 38–45% without fertilization. More experimentation is needed to substantiate multiple benefits of biochar application in relevant soil-environment-climate-management factors and minimize any possible drawbacks in Indian perspective. Efficient use of biochar in agricultural system is one viable option that can enhance natural rates of carbon sequestration in the soil, reduce farm waste, enhance crop yield with concomitant improvement in soil quality.

1. Introduction

In India, about 93 million tons of crop residues are burned each year primarily to clear the fields in the form of straw and stubble after the harvest of preceding crop. The problem is severe in irrigated agriculture, particularly in the mechanized rice-wheat system in the Northern India due to unavailability of labour, high cost in removing the residues, use of combine-harvester in rice-wheat cropping system and less time for sowing of wheat after harvesting rice. Besides atmospheric pollution, burning of residues lead to loss of entire amount of C, 80% of N, 25% of P, 50% of S and 20% of K present in straw, adversely affecting soil fertility (Mandal *et al* 2004). In addition, burning of agricultural residues releases ozone depleting gases such as carbon dioxide, methane, carbon monoxide, nitrogen oxide, sulphur dioxide and very small particles in the air (aerosols) which adversely affect the atmospheric composition. Biochar has the unique ability to indirectly enhance soil fertility by encouraging the growth of soil microbial population and retain soil water and plant nutrients. The world population is currently increasing at a fast rate and is expected to reach 9 billion by 2050. To meet a growing demand for food from a growing population, we need to increase agricultural productivity upto 70%, and food production in the developing world will need to double by 2050 (FAO). There is increasing demand of organic inputs in agriculture with the objectives of increasing soil health and crop yields due to increasing cost of fertilizers. The major crop residues produced in India are straws of paddy, wheat, millet, sorghum, pulses (pigeon pea), oilseed crops (castor, mustard), maize stover and cobs, cotton and jute sticks, sugarcane trash, leaves, fibrous materials, roots, branches and twigs of varying sizes, shapes, forms and densities. Direct incorporation of crop residues into agricultural soil to conserve soil nutrients and organic carbon content can cause considerable crop management problems. However, long-term field research has confirmed that adding crop residues to agricultural soils leads to large increases in soil C stocks in the short term but minimal increases in the long term due to natural decay. Soil organic matter is the key to soil health and in wet tropical condition, organic matter is easily subjected to decomposition and mineralization. Mineralization produces CO_2 in just a few seasons and causes nutrient content to be low. Biochar significantly improve soil tilth, productivity, nutrient retention and availability to plants via both direct slow- nutrient release fertilizing properties and indirect effects on improved water holding capacity, nutrient holding ability and soil aggregate stability, when used as a soil conditioner along with organic and inorganic fertilizers. Biochar production converts labile molecules in the feedstock to complex, stable organic molecules which contribute to its recalcitrance to microbial degradation and higher residence time in soil (Glaser *et al* 2001).

2. What is Biochar

"Biochar" is a relatively new term, yet not a new substance. It actually comes from the study of very old soils in the Amazon Basin (Terra preta de Indio) formed by indigenous peoples centuries to thousands of years ago when they accumulated charcoal and other fire residues and also nutrient-rich waste such as animal and fish bones, in waste piles near dwellings. Over the time these wastes resulted in black colored humus-modified soils which were up to two meters deep, while the surrounding soils were reddish to yellowish. Charcoal amalgamated soils are more fertile than surrounding, unmodified soils.

3. Properties of biochar

- Biochar is very stable: sustains for thousands of years
- Biochar identified as a vital soil amendment for carbon sequestration
- A sustainable solution for waste management and water saving
- One ton of biochar is equivalent to 2.7 tons of carbon dioxide removed from the atmosphere
- Minimize pollution and protect the environment,
- Check soil degradation and erosion,
- Maintain long-term soil fertility by optimizing conditions for biological activity in the soil
- Maintain biological diversity within the system
- Recycle materials and resources within the enterprise

The World Bank has identified biochar as the most effective system of greenhouse gas abatement in soil compared to all other sustainable management practices.

4. Principles of biochar production

Biochar is the product of thermal degradation of organic materials in the absence of air (pyrolysis), and is distinguished from charcoal by its use as a soil amendment. Production of biochar generally releases more energy than it consumes, depending on the moisture content of the feedstock. Heat, oil and gas that are released can be recovered for other uses, including the production of electricity. After pyrolysis, the solid byproduct is a porous network of carbonates and aromatic carbon. Different feed stocks used lead to different properties (Table 1). Biochar is not a pure carbon, but rather mix of carbon (C), hydrogen (H), oxygen (O), nitrogen (N), sulphur (S) and ash in different proportions (Masek, 2009). The central quality of biochar that makes it attractive as a soil amendment is its highly porous structure, potentially responsible for improved water retention, high cation exchange capacity, that ultimately favours the retention of nutrients and prevention in their loss; direct nutrient supply and the capacity of being a habitat for beneficial microorganisms, which can promote the release and uptake of nutrients by plants (Sohi *et al* 2010).

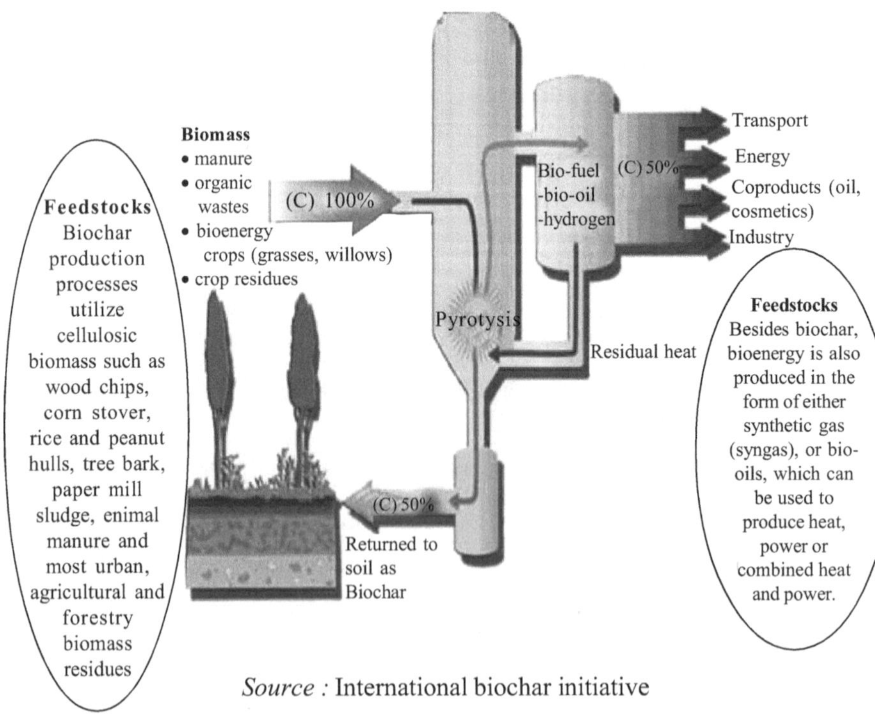

Source : International biochar initiative

Table 1: Characteristics of biochar used in different experiment

Materials used for producing biochar	pH	Total C (%)	Total N	C:N	Ca	Mg	P (cmol/kg)	K	CEC	Reference
Paper mill waste 1- (waste wood chip)	9.4	50.0	0.48	104	6.2	1.20	-	0.22	9.00	. . . . *et al.* (2010)
Paper mill waste 2- (waste wood chip)	8.2	52.0	0.31	168	11.0	2.60	-	1.00	18.00	Van Zwieten *et al.* (2010)
Green waste (grass clippings, cotton trash, and plant prunings)	9.4	36.0	0.18	200	0.4	0.56	-	21.00	24.00	Chan *et al.* (2007)
Eucalyptus biochar	-	82.4	0.57	145	-	-	1.87	-	4.69	Novak *et al.* (2009)
Cooking biochar	-	72.9	0.76	96	-	-	0.42	-	11.19	Novak *et al.* (2009)
Poultry litter (450°C)	9.9	38.0	2.00	19	-	-	37.42	-	-	Chan *et al.* (2008)
Poultry litter (550°C)	13	33.0	0.85	39	-	-	5.81	-	-	Chan *et al.* (2008)
Hardwood sawdust	-	66.5	0.3	221	-	-	-	-	-	Singh *et al.* (2010)
Mixed wood	8.13	88.9			50.9			14		Abrol et al. (2016)

5. How can biochar be carbon negative?

Fossil fuels are carbon positive; they add more carbon dioxide (CO_2) and other greenhouse gasses to the air and thus exacerbate global warming. Ordinary biomass fuels are carbon neutral; the carbon captured in the biomass by photosynthesis would have eventually returned to the atmosphere through natural processes like decomposition. Biochar systems are carbon negative by transforming the carbon in biomass into stable carbon structures in biochar which can remain sequestered in soils for hundreds and even thousands of years. The result is a net reduction of CO_2 in the atmosphere as shown below

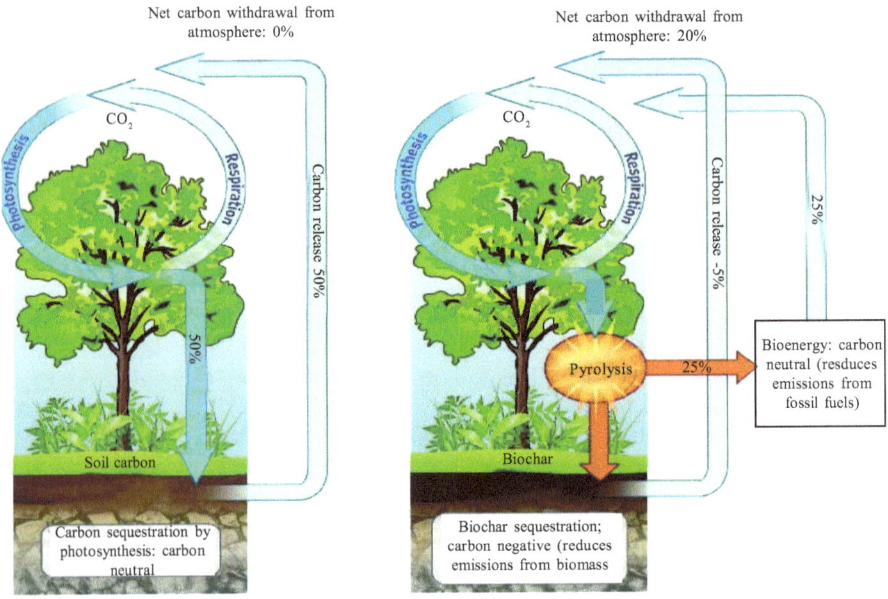

Source: International biochar initiative

6. Biochar application

The application of biochar depends on many factors including the type of biomass used, the degree of metal contamination in the biomass, the types and proportions of various nutrients (N, P, etc.) and also on edaphic, climatic and topographic factors of the land where the biochar is to be applied. Research revealed that even low rates of biochar application @ 1 t ha^{-1} significantly increase crop productivity assuming that the biochar is rich in nutrients which that soil lacks. Studies suggested that biochar is applied in variety of methods ranging from broadcasting, soil incorporation, band placement and can be applied in sole or in combination with organic manures and inorganic fertilizers.

Biochar application during land preparation

7. Biochar as a waste management technique

The availability of biomass in India (2010-2011) is estimated at about 500 million tons/year. Studies by the Ministry of New and Renewable Energy (MNRE), Govt. of India have estimated surplus biomass availability at about 120-150 million tons/annum (MNRE, 2009). Of this, about 93 million tons of crop residues are burned in each year (IARI 2012). Conversion of organic waste to produce biochar using the pyrolysis process is one viable option that can enhance natural rates of carbon sequestration in the soil, reduce farm waste and improve the soil quality (Srinivasarao *et al* 2012). Since raw material required is locally available with beneficiary, the activity holds promise of becoming self-sustainable after completion of project and excess produce can be sold with proper packaging and marketing for augmenting farm income as well. There is evidence that suggests that biochar application into soil may increase the overall net soil surface area (Chan *et al* 2007) and consequently, may improve soil water retention (Downie *et al* 2009). An increased soil-specific surface area may also benefit native microbial communities and the overall sorption capacity of soils. Biochar composition is highly heterogeneous, containing both stable and labile components (Sohi *et al* 2009). Carbon, volatile matter, mineral matter (ash) and moisture are generally regarded as its major constituents (Antal and Gronli 2003). Total carbon content in biochar was found to range between 172 to 905 g kg^{-1}, although

OC often accounts for < 500 g kg^{-1}, as reviewed by Chan and Xu (2009) for a variety of source materials. Total N varied between 1.8 and 56.4 g kg^{-1}, depending on the feedstock (Chan and Xu, 2009). Total P and total K in biochar were found to range broadly according to feedstock, with values between 2.7 - 480 and 1.0 - 58.0 g kg^{-1}, respectively (Chan and Xu, 2009). The recent studies on biochar have proved biochar as indispensible input for nutrient supplying source, carbon sequestration to mitigate climate change aberrations effectively. Nutrient supplying capacity of biochar will reduce the dependence on inorganic fertilizers in one hand with economic saving for farmers and sustainable soil health with carbon aggradations thereby protecting environment.

8. Effect of biochar application on soil chemical properties

Biochar is generally alkaline in pH and may increase soil pH (Chan and Xu, 2009) with greater increase observed in sandy and loamy soils than in clayey soils (Tyron *et al* 1948). Biochar addition can increase cation exchange capacity, base saturation, exchangeable bases and organic carbon content as well as decreases in Al saturation in acid soils (Glaser *et al* 2002). Widowati *et al* (2012) observed that incorporation of biochar increased organic carbon and decreased nitrogenous fertilizer requirement. Rondon *et al* 2007; Novak *et al.*,2009 and Laird *et al.*, 2010 also reported similar observations with different type of feedstock and soil. Lehmann *et al* (2003) and Steiner *et al* (2008) reported that the use of biochar can improve the efficiency of nitrogen fertilizer as biochar can reduce the loss of nitrogen and potassium that occurs through leaching (Widowati *et al* 2011). Glaser *et al* (2002a) concluded that the charcoal may be more than just a soil conditioner, and act as a fertilizer itself, as seen also in the results of Chan *et al* (2008). Sukartono *et al* (2011) reported that application of biochar increased aromatic carbon which improved soil properties as soil organic carbon, cation exchange capacity, available phosphorus, exchangeable potassium, calcium and magnesium of the sandy soils in Lombok, Indonesia. Biochar is highly porous and has a large specific surface area, its impact on soil cation exchange capacity and other nutrients that have correlation with cation exchange capacity is very important. Biochar amendment significantly decreased extracted Cd in the soil by 17 to 47 per cent. Some types of biochar also appear to reduce the mobility of heavy metals such as Cu and Zn (Hua *et al* 2009).

9. Effect of biochar application on soil physical properties

Studies showed biochar effects on soil physical parameters such as bulk density, porosity, water holding capacity and aggregate stability (Table 2). Tyron (1948) reported that in a sandy soil, there was a monotonic increase in the percent of available moisture as a function of charcoal volumetric proportion with an increase of about 6 per cent available moisture per cent under any amendment amount, while the available moisture per cent in the clay soil decreased by nearly 7 per cent under a 15 volume per cent load of charcoal has been argued to enhance soil physical properties including soil water retention and aggregation both of which may improve water availability to crops as well as decrease erosion (Glaser *et al* 2002a). Glaser *et al* (2002b) observed that charcoal rich Anthrosols from the Amazon region whose surface area was 3 times greater than that of surrounding soils which have 18 per cent greater field capacity. Further charcoal has also been reported to form complexes with minerals as a result of interactions between oxidized carboxylic acid groups at the surface of the charcoal particles and mineral grains soil aggregate stability (Glaser *et al* 2002b). Chan *et al* (2007) observed improvement in texture and behavior of a hard setting soil with significant reduction in tensile strength at higher rates of biochar application. Many studies showed enhanced soil water holding capacity (Asai *et al* 2009, Karhu *et al* 2011), improved soil water permeability (Asai *et al* 2009), improved saturated hydraulic conductivity, reduced soil strength, modification in soil bulk density (Laird *et al* 2010), modified aggregate stability (Busscher *et al* 2010; Peng *et al* 2011). Soil amendment with biochar can result in decreased bulk density and soil penetration resistance and increased water holding capacity (Abrol *et al* 2016). Research findings indicated lower bulk density with biochar application (Karhu *et al* 2011) due to high porosity which allows high water holding capacity. However it is hydrophobic as it is dry due to its high porosity and light bulk density.

10. Effect of biochar application on soil biological properties

The addition of biochar to the soil is reported to have different effects on the soil biological properties. Quilliam *et al* (2012) observed that the activity of soil microorganisms by soil respiration and assessed that repeated application of biochar significantly increased the level of basal soil respiration with the highest rate of 50 t/ha soil application at the beginning and 40 t/ha soil reapplication 13DAS. In addition, Graber *et al* (2010) reported that with increasing rate of biochar application resulted in maximum number of culturable colonies of general bacteria, bacillus spp., yeasts and *Trichoderma* spp., whereas minimum number of culturable colonies of filamentous fungi *Pseudomonas* spp and *Actinomycetes* spp were found in the soil. The positive effects have been reported to enhanced biological nitrogen fixation (Rondon *et al.,* 2007), improved colonization of *mycorrhizal* fungi, earthworms showed preference to biochar amended soils (Van Zwieten *et al*, 2010), increased methane uptake (Karhu *et al* 2011), potential catalyst in reducing nitrous oxide to nitrogen (Van Zwieten *et al* 2009). Integrated use of 50% N through FYM +50% N through vermicompost + 2 t ha^{-1} biochar gave higher value of soil moisture (1.5 times), decreased bulk density (1.1 times) and crack volume (1.8 times) in rice crop (Sharma *et al* 2018) as shown in Fig. 1 (a, b and c).

Table 2: Effect of biochar addition on soil properties

Property	Effect	Biochar property	Mechanism	Reference
Soil organic matter	Increased	High C content	Increased carbon concentration	Zhang *et al*. (2012)
Water-holding capacity	Increased	Porous structure	Increased macro porosity and hydrophilicity	Herath *et al*.(2012), Atkinson *et al*.(2010)
Porosity	Increased	Porous structure	Dilution effect and formation of macro aggregates	Herath *et al*. (2013)
Plant crop yield	Increased	Soil organic matter, pH, bulk density, CEC, high porosity	Due to the positive effect of soil quality; chemical, physical, microbial and nutrient availability	Zhang et al. (2012)
Environment CH_4 emissions	Decrease	Porous structure, pH	Abundance of methanotrophic proteobacterial, methenogenic bacteria reduced at too high or toolow pH	Feng *et al*.(2012)
N_2O emissions	Decreased	Recalcitrant, porous structure	Enhanced aeration and stable carbon, increased microbial activity and immobilization of N	Zhang *et al* (2012)
Carbon sequestration	Increased	Recalcitrant or stable C; Recalcitrant or stable C;	Long-term storage of stable carbon in soil	Kameyama *et al*.(2010), Matovic,(2011)
Nutrient leaching	Decreased	Porous structure, surface area and negative surface charge	Enhanced CEC facilitates retention of nutrients	Biederma and Harpole (2012)
Bulk density, Cracking volume	Decreased	Porous structure	Improved aggregation	Peeyush (Project report, NABARD)
Infiltration rate	Decreased	Porous structure	Improved aggregation	Sharma et al 2018

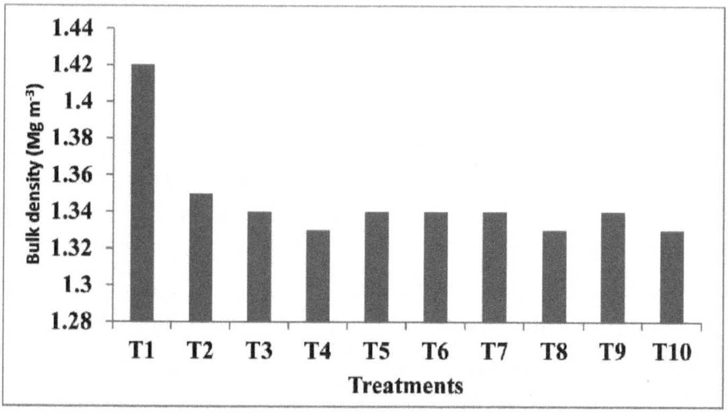

T1. Control,T2. 100% N through FYM,T3.100% N through vermicompost,T4. 50% N through FYM +50% N through vermicompost ,T5.1t/ha biochar (rice husk) +T2 ,T6.1t/ha biochar + T3, T7.1t/ha biochar + T4 ,T8.2t/ha biochar + T2,T9 2t/ha biochar + T3,T10 2t/ha biochar + T4

Fig 1: (a) Effect of biochar application in conjunction with organic manures on bulk density

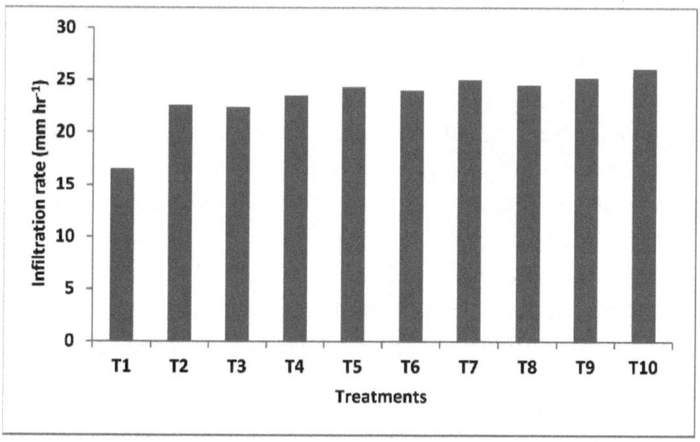

Fig 1:(b) Effect of biochar application in conjunction with organic manures on infiltration rate

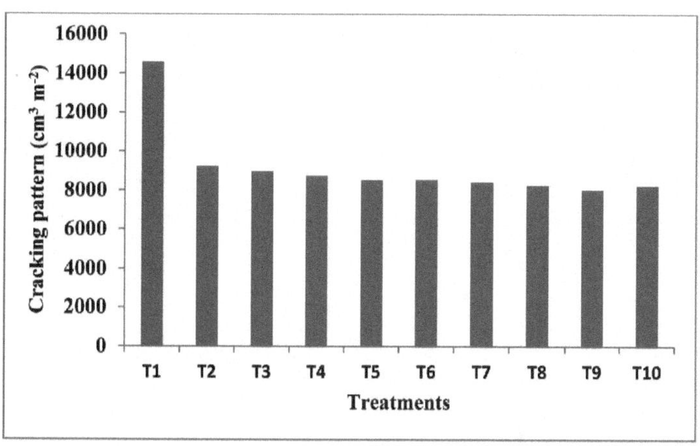

Fig. 1: (c) Effect of biochar application in conjunction with organic manures on cracking volume

11. Influence of biochar application on crop performance

The response of different crops to various biochar application levels is summarized in table (Table 3). Application of biochar can enhance soil productivity by improving the physical, chemical and biological soil conditions (Glaser *et al* 2007, Lehmann *et al* 2003, Chan *et al* 2007). Improvement in soil structure increase in soil water retention and decrease in soil strength have been reported by Chan *et al* (2007) conducted a study on Australian soil. Lehmann *et al* (2003) compared soil fertility and leaching losses of nutrients between an Anthrosol and an adjacent unamended Ferralsols. The Anthrasol showed significantly higher P, Ca, Mn and Zn availability than the Ferralsol, and an increased biomass of both cowpea and rice by 38–45% without fertilization. Conjunctive use of paper mill waste biochar with inorganic fertilizer, showed higher soybean and radish biomass compared with sole application of inorganic fertilizer (Van Zwieten *et al* 2010). Similarly, Widowati *et al*., 2012 reported that application of chicken manure and city waste biochar increased maize biomass which was attributed increase in soil pH and CEC (Liang *et al*., 2006) with the addition of biochar. Crop yields of soybeans were also reported to increase by a factor of 1.5 after an application of 0.5 Mg charcoal/ha (Kishimoto and Sugiura 1985). Asai *et al*. (2009) studied the effect of biochar application on grain yields of upland rice (*Oryza sativa* L.) in northern Laos. Three different experiments conducted under upland conditions at 10 sites, combining variations in application amounts (0-16 t ha^{-1}), fertilizer application rates (N and P) with different rice cultivars (improved and traditional) revealed that biochar application resulted in higher grain yields at sites with low P availability and improved the response to N and NP chemical fertilizer treatments. They concluded that biochar application has the potential to improve soil productivity of upland rice production in Laos, but the effect is highly dependent on soil fertility and fertilizer management. Studies conducted on integrated use of biochar with organic manures (50% N through FYM +50% N through vermicompost + 2 t/ha biochar) in irrigated sandy clay loam soil of Jammu resulted the highest grain yield of cultivar Basmati-370 and was about 83% higher over the control (Sharma *et al* 2018).

Table 3: Effect of biochar application on crop yield in different soil types

Crops	Soil type	Biochar treatment (t ha^{-1})	Fertilizer treatment (kg ha^{-1})	Yield increase over control a (%)	Reference
Wheat	Ferrosol	0 & 10	1.25g Nutricote® per 250g soil b	+ 250	Van Zwietenet *al.* (2010)
Radish	Alfisol	0, 10, 25 & 50	N (100)	+ 320	Chan *et al.* (2008)
Radish	Alfisol	0, 10, 50 & 100	N (100)	+ 95 to + 266	Chan *et al.* (2007)
Wheat	Silt loam	0 & 9	Nil	No effect	Karhu *et al.* (2011)
Maize	Oxisol	0, 8 & 20	Lime (dolomite) (2.2); N (156 – 170; P (30 – 43); K (84 – 138)	+ 28 (2004) + 30 (2005) + 140 (2006)	Major *et al.* (2010)
Maize	Ultisol	0 & 2.4	N (150); P_2O_5 (100); K_2O (150)	+ 146	Peng *et al.* (2011)
Beans	Oxisol	0, 30, 60 & 90[c]	Lime (300); N (20); P (20)	+ 39	Rondon *et al.* (2007)

a Control indicates that no biochar was used and + and – signs indicates if yields increased or decreased.
b Nutricote® contains 15.2% N, 4.7% P, 8.9% K, 3.3% Ca, 1.1% S, and micronutrients.
c Fertilizer applied was in g·kg^{-1} (pot trial).

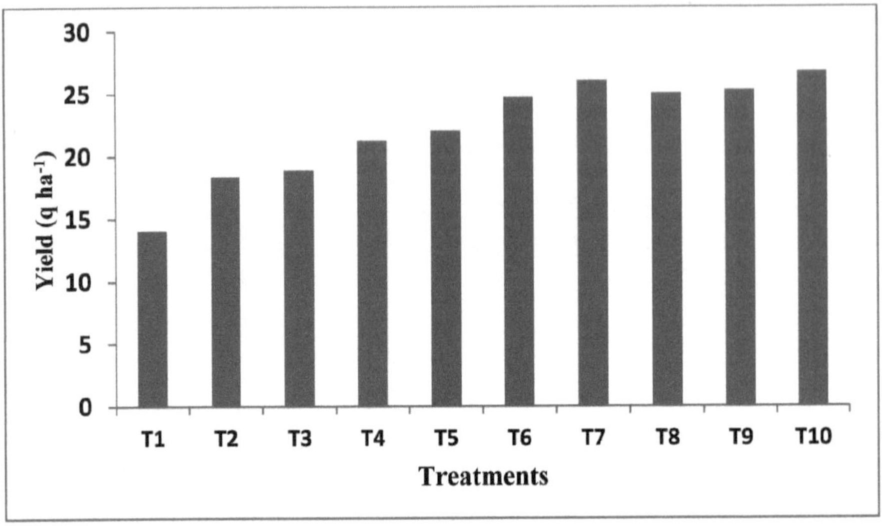

Fig. 2: Effect of biochar application in conjunction with organic manures on rice grain yield

T1. Control, T2. 100% N through FYM, T3.100% N through vermicompost, T4. 50% N through FYM +50% N through vermicompost, T5.1t/ha biochar (rice husk) +T2, T6.1t/ha biochar + T3, T7.1t/ha biochar + T4 , T8.2t/ha biochar + T2, T9 2t/ha biochar + T3, T10 2t/ha biochar + T4

12. Conclusion

Biochar as soil amendment for improving soil quality and soil-carbon sequestration has attracted global attention but further research is required in order to maximize the possible advantages of biochar applications. More experimentation is needed to substantiate multiple benefits of biochar application in relevant soil-environment-climate-management factors and minimize any possible drawbacks in Indian perspective. Efficient use of biochar in agricultural system is one viable option that can enhance natural rates of carbon sequestration in the soil, reduce farm waste, enhance crop yield with concomitant improvement in soil quality parameters.

13. References

Abrol Vikas, Meni BenHur, Frank GA Verheijen, Jacob J Keizer, Martinho AS, Martins Haim Tenaw, Ludmilla Tchehansky, Ellen R Graber E. 2016. Biochar effects on soil water infiltration and erosion under seal formation conditions: rainfall simulation experiment. *Journal of Soils and Sediments*, 16 (12): 2709-2719.

Antal MJ and Gronli M (2003) The art, science, and technology of charcoal production. *Industr Engineer Chem Res.* 42(8):1619-40.

Asai H, Samson BK, Stephan HM, Songyikhangsuthor K, Homma K, Kiyono Y, Inoue Y, Shiraiwa T and Horie T .2009. Biochar amendment techniques for upland rice reduction in Northern Laos 1. Soil physical properties, leaf SPAD and grain yield. *Field Crop Res.* 111: 81 – 84.

Busscher WJ, Novak JM, Evans DE, Watts DW, Niandou MAS and Ahmedna M .2010. Influence of pecan biochar on physical properties of a Norfolk loamy sand. *Soil Science.*175: 10 – 14.

Chan KY, Van Zwieten L, Meszaros I, Downie A, Joseph S .2007. Agronomic values of green waste biochar as a soil amendment. *Aus. J. of Soil Res.* 45 (8): 629-634.

Chan KY, Van Zwieten L, Meszaros I, Downie A, Joseph S .2008. Using poultry litter biochar as soil amendments. *Aus. J. of Soil Res.* 46 (5): 437-444.

Chan KY and Xu Z .2009. Biochar: nutrient properties and their enhancement. In: Biochar for environmental management (J. Lehmann and S. Joseph eds.), Science and Technology, Earthscan, London. pp 67-84.

Chan KY, Van Zwieten L, Meszaros I, Downie A and Joseph S .2007. Assessing the agronomic values of contrasting char materials on an Australian hard setting soil. Paper presented in International Agrichar Initiative (IAI) .2007. Conference, 27 April–2 May 2007, Terrigal, New South Wales, Australia.

Downie A, Crosky A and Munroe P .2009. Physical properties of biochar. In: Lehmann J and Joseph S (ed) Biochar for Environmental Management: Science and Technology. Pp.13-32. Earthscan, London

Glaser B, Haumaier L, Guggenberger G and Zech W .2001. The 'Terra Preta' phenomenon: a model for sustainable agriculture in the humid tropics. Naturwissenschaften, 88: 37-41.

Glaser B, Guggenberger G and Zech W .2002. Past anthropogenic influence on the present soil properties of anthropogenic dark earths (Terra Preta) in Amazonia (Brazil). *Geoarcheology.* 45:68-78.

Glaser B, Lehmann J and Zech W .2002. Ameliorating physical and chemical properties of highly weathered soils in the tropics with charcoal - a review. *Biology and Fertility of Soils.* 35 (4): 219- 230.

Glaser B .2007. Prehistorically modified soils of central Amazonia: a model for sustainable agriculture in the twenty-first century. *Phil Trans R Soc B.* 362:187–196.

Graber E R *et al* .2010. Biochar impact on development and productivity of pepper and tomato grown in fertigated soilless media. *Plant Soil.* 337:481–496

Herath HMSK, Camps-Arbestain M and Hedley M .2013. Effect of biochar on soil physical properties in two contrasting soils: an Alfisol and an Andisol. *Geoderma,* 209–210: 188–197.

Hua L, Wu W, Liu Y, McBride MB, Chen Y .2009. Reduction of nitrogen loss and Cu and Zn mobility during sludge composting with bamboo charcoal amendment. *Environ. Sci. Pollut. Res.* 16: 1–9.

Huang M, Yang L, Qin H, Jiang L and Zou Y. 2013. Quantifying the effect of biochar amendment on soil quality and crop productivity in Chinese rice paddies. *Field Crops Res.*154: 172–177.

IARI, 2012. Crop residues management with conservation agriculture: Potential, constraints and policy needs. Indian Agricultural Research Institute, New Delhi, 32 p.

Karhu K, Mattila T, Bergström I, and Regina K. 2011. Biochar addition to agricultural soil increased CH4 uptake and water holding capacity – Results from a short-termpilot field study. *Agricultural, Ecosystems and Environment,* 140: 309 -313.

Kishimoto S and Sugiura G .1985. Charcoal as a soil conditioner. *Int. Achieve. Future* 5: 12-23.

Laird DA, Fleming P, Davis DD, Horton R, Wang B and Karlen D .2010. Impact of biochar amendments on the quality of typical Midwestern agricultural soil. *Geoderma.* 158: 443 – 449.

Lehmann J and Rondon M .2006. Bio Char soil management on highly weathered soils in the humid tropics. In: N Uphoff *et al* (ed) *Biological approaches to sustainable soil systems.* Pp.517–30. Florida: CRC Press, Taylor and Francis Group.

Lehmann J. 2007. 'A handful of carbon'. *Nature*. 447: 143-144.

Lehmann J, Pereira da Silva Jr J, Steiner C, Nehls T, Zec W and Glaser B .2003. Nutrient availability and leaching in an archaeological Anthrosol and a Ferralsol of the Central Amazon basin: fertilizer, manure and charcoal amendments. *Plant and Soil* 249: 343-357.

Liang B, Lehmann J, Solomon D, Kinyargi J, Grossman J, O'Neill B, Skemjstad Major J .2013. Practical aspects of biochar application to tree crops. IBI Technical Bulletin #102, International Biochar Initiative. (Accessed online at http://www.biocharinternational.org/sites/default/files/Technical%20Bulletin%20Biochar%20Tree%20 Planting.pdf).

Major J .2013. Practical aspects of biochar application to tree crops. IBI Technical Bulletin #102, International Biochar Initiative. (Accessed online at http://www.biocharinternational/org/sites/default/files/Technical%20Bulletin%20Biochar%20Tree%20 Planting.pdf).

Mandal KG, Misra AK, Hati KM, Bandyopadhya KK, Ghosh PK and Mohanty M .2004. Rice residue management options and effects on soil properties and crop productivity. *Food Agric Environ*. 2:224-31.

Masek O .2009. Biochar production technologies, http://www.geos.ed.ac.uk/sccs/ biochar/documents/BiocharLaunch-OMasek.pdf.

MNRE .2009. Ministry of New and Renewable Energy Resources, Govt. of India, New Delhi. www.mnre.gov.in/biomassrsources.

Novak JM, Busscher WJ, Laird DL, Ahmedna M, Watts DW and Niandou MAS .2009. Impact of biochar amendment on fertility of a southeastern coastal plan soil. *Soil Science*. 174: 105 – 112

Peng X, Ye LL, Wang CH, Zhou H and Sun B .2011. Temperature and duration dependent rice straw-derived biochar: Characteristics and its effects on soil properties of an Ultisol in southern China. *Soil and Tillage Res*. 112:159 – 166.

Rondon MA, Lehmann J, Ramirez J. and Hurtado M .2007. Biological nitrogen fixation by common beans (*Phaseolus vulgaris* L.) increases with biochar additions. *Biology and Fertility of Soil*. 43: 699 – 708.

Sharma Peeyush, Abrol Vikas, Gupta NK, Singh Brinder .2018. Project Completion Report. On-farm training and demonstration of biochar and climate change mitigation in kandi belt of Jammu: 19-29.

Singh BP, Hatton BJ, Singh B, Cowie AL and Kathuria .2010. Influence of biochars on nitrous oxide emission and nitrogen leaching from two contrasting soils. *J. Environ. Qual.*, 39:1224–1235.

Sohi S, Lopez-Capel E, Krull E and Bol R .2009. Biochar's roles in soil and climate change: A review of research needs. *CSIRO Land and Water Science Report* 05/09, p 64.

Srinivasarao Ch, Vankateswarlu B, Lal R, Singh AK, Kundu Sumanta, Vittal, KPR, Balaguruvaiah G, Vijaya Shankar Babu M, Ravindra Chary G, Prasadbabu MBB and Yellamanda Reddy T .2012. Soil carbon sequestration and agronomic productivity of an Alfisol for a groundnut-based system in a semiarid environment in southern India. *Eur. J. of Agronomy*. 43: 40-48.

Steiner C, Glaser B, Teixera WG, Lehmann J, Blum WEH and Zech W .2008. Nitrogen retention and plant uptake on a highly weathered central Amazonian Ferralsol amended with compost and charcoal. *Journal of Plant Nutrition and Soil Science*. 171: 893 – 899.

Sukartono Utomo WH, Kusuma Z and Nugroho WH. 2011. Soil fertility status, nutrient uptake, and maize (*Zea mays* L.) yield following biochar application on sandy soils of Lombok, Indonesia. *J. Trop. Agric*. 49: 47–52

Quilliam RS, Marsden K, Gertler C, Rousk J, DeLuca TH and Jones DL .2012. Nutrient dynamics, microbial growth and weed emergence in biochar amended soil are influenced by time since application and reapplication rate. *Agriculture, Ecosystems & Environment*.158: 192e199.

Tyron, EH .1948. Effect of charcoal on certain physical, chemical and biological properties of forest soils. *Ecol Monograph*. 18: 81-115.

Van Zwieten, L., Kimber, S., Morris, S., Chan, K.Y., Downie, A., Rust, J., Joseph, S. & Cowie, A., 2010. Effects of biochar from slow pyrolysis of papermill waste on agronomic performance and soil fertility. *Plant and Soil*. 327: 235 – 246.

Van Zwieten L, Sigh B, Joseph S, Kimber S, Cowie A and Chan KY .2009. Biochar and emissions of non-CO_2 greenhouse gases from soil. In: Lehmann, J. & Joseph, S. (Eds.), *Biochar for Environmental Management – Science and Technology*. Earthscan, London: 227-247.

Widowati and Asnah Sutoyo. 2012. The effects of biochar and potassium fertilizer on the absorption and potassium leaching. *Buana Sains*. 12: 83-90.

Widowati, Utomo WH, Soehono LA, Guritno B. 2011. Effect of biochar on the release and loss of nitrogen from urea fertilization. *J. Agric. Food Technol*. 1: 127–132.

14

Organic Agriculture: Export, Entrepreneurship and Employment Opportunities

Ravikant Avasthe, JP Saini* and Shahid Ahamad**

ICAR-National Organic Farming Research Institute, Tadong, Gangtok, Sikkim
**CSK, HPKV, Palampur, Himachal Pradesh, India*
***PME Cell, Directorate of Research, SKUAST Jammu, Jammu & Kashmir, India*

1. Introduction
2. Current status of organic farming in India
3. Organic farming and socio-economic dimensions
4. Productivity and profitability: A review
5. Economic benefits
6. Constraints in adoption of organic farming
7. Challenges for developments
8. Recommendations for promotion of organic farming
9. Certification
10. Infrastructure for organic products development & supply chain
11. Employment opportunities
12. Conclusion
13. *References*

Abstract

Organic farming has proved to be effective technology for socio-economic empowerment of Indian farmers as it imposes positive changes in social factors in the local communities. There is tremendous scope of export, entrepreneurship and employment opportunities in organic farming in India. Local, regional, national and global markets are developing sinks for organic products. Organic crop production is sustainable and has positive impact on the ecology and socio-economic status of the peoples. Various socio-economic factors influence the farmers' choice to adopt organic cultivation. Several threats and weaknesses exist. Hence, there is a need to address the weaknesses of the organic system by integrating it with innovative tools of marketing and ICTs so that there is alignment in demand- production-supply so concerted efforts are needed to establish production-consumption linkages through PPP mode. It will offset threats of organic farming thereby making it more remunerative and promising. The existing evidences suggest greater research efforts in this area are required. There is need to identify the gaps between the adoption of techniques of organic farming and remove them by strengthening production-consumption and marketing linkages. Moreover, it is important to assess and analyze the status of organic farming and feasibility to different sustainable practices in different production systems and farming situations across the country for promotion of this value added entrepreneurship.

Keywords: organic farming, status, constraints, entrepreneurship and socio-economic dynamics

1. Introduction

Organic agriculture is, economically sound, socially acceptable and environmentally safe than conventional agriculture (Scialabba 2007, Rahmann 2011). Organic farming is centered on ecological processes; knowledge of the agro-ecosystem is thus a pre-requisite to any organic farm. In this regard, farmers with a traditional knowledge base are potentially capable to develop ecological processes. Traditional farming systems have been described as a "reservoir of adaptations" (FAO 2008).

In other words, organic farming to be a form of sustainable agriculture that reduces reliance on external inputs while increasing farm derived resources, which improves environmental protection, natural ecological processes, food quality, and economic viability (Rigby and Caceres 2001, Lockie *et al* 2006). It is observed that organic manure based farming systems increases the buildup of soil organic matter, which reduces the erosion, runoff and transport of organic and inorganic matter to streams and rivers, besides improving the physical, chemical and biological properties of soil from fertility point of view (Bhutia *et al* 2012). Pimentel and his associates (2005) reported that organic production systems are more energy efficient.

Table 1: Energy Used in Different Corn Production Systems Expressed in Litres of Diesel per ha (Pimentel *et al* 2005)

Conventional Tillage:	231 litres per hectare
Conventional No-till:	199 litres per hectare
Organic Tillage:	121 litres per hectare
Organic No-till:	77 litres per hectare

Organic farming has proved an effective entrepreneurship for socio-economic changes in social factors in the local community. These factors include age, gender, land holdings, educational status, farm size, personal income, membership of cooperatives, access to credit, extension, poverty, policy problems and prospects, proximity to markets infrastructural facilities provided such as electricity, roads, housing, schools, clinics (FAO 2008). All these are also important factors for adoption of organic farming practices. Organic farming systems impose a positive impact on the community's economic as well as social status.

Organic farming facilitates many opportunities *viz.,* a vast regional, national and global organic market, promoting healthy life style, sustainable use of resources, lowering dependence on food and input imports, creating seed availability, development of local organic manure suppliers, conserving local crops, building soil fertility, introducing premium price for organic products, and addressing unemployment (Tashi and Wangchuk 2016). Apart from that, it also promotes the traditional local landraces which are resistant against diseases and insect- pests.

Table 2: Global Organic Food Market (USD)

2020: 102.0 billion US dollars (projected)
2017: 80.0 billion US Dollars
2012: 69.0 billion US Dollars
2010 : 59.1 billion US dollars
2009 : 54.1 billion US dollars
1999 : 15.2 billion US dollars

In India, various conventional farming regions are slowly transforming towards the sustainable farming. There is considerable latent interest among farmers in conversion to organic farming in India. Despite the attention which has been paid to organic farming over the last few years, very little information actually exists on the costs and returns of organic farming and its impact on social development in India.

2. Current status of organic farming in India

India has tremendous potential, largely untapped; for a major breakthrough in organic agriculture. India has the largest number of organic producers in the world most with small holdings. Sikkim has become India's first fully organic state by implementing organic farming systems. Government of India has initiated programs like National Program for Organic Production (NPOP) and National Project on Organic Farming (NPOF) for systematic promotion of organic farming in the country in project mode different states (Anonymous 2017). Several forms of organic farming are successfully practiced in diverse agro-climates, particularly in rainfed, mountains and hilly and tribal areas of the country (Mitra and Devi 2016). Many of the forest products of economic importance, such as herbs and medicinal plants are in this category by default. As per the available statistics, the total area under organic certification is 648617 ha and 3009449 ha area is under forest and wild harvest in 2016-17 (Table 1). India produced various certified organic products which includes all varieties of food products namely oilseeds, sugarcane, cereals and millet, cotton, pulses, tea, spices & condiments, medicinal and aromatic plants, fruits, vegetables, dry fruits, coffee, ornamental plants and flowers *etc.* (Table 2, 3). The production is not limited to the edible sector but also produces organic cotton fiber, functional food products *etc.*

Table 3: Area under organic certification process (2016-17)

S. No.	State name	Organic Area (ha)	In Conversion area (ha)	Total Farm area (ha)	Wild harvest area (WH) (ha)	Total WH + Farm
1.	Andhra Pradesh	9812.8	7871.0	17683.8	155099.1	172783.0
2.	Arunachal Pradesh	21.4	3989.7	4011.2	68300.0	72311.2
3.	Assam	2544.0	21326.3	23870.3	60.0	23930.3
4.	Bihar	-	1.2	1.2	678.0	679.2
5.	Chhattisgarh	2339.7	10372.3	12712.1	167040.0	179752.1
6.	Goa	14116.7	1645.6	15762.4	-	15762.4
7.	Gujarat	36034.2	28206.8	64241.0	6253.9	70495.0
8.	Haryana	4482.7	528.8	5011.5	20.1	5031.7
9.	Himachal Pradesh	5903.7	6473.0	12376.7	2000.0	14376.7
10.	J & K	9550.0	13058.2	22608.3	159000.0	181608.3
11.	Jharkhand	88.4	26725.4	26813.9	10000.0	36813.9
12.	Karnataka	22478.2	58610.8	81089.0	859.7	81948.8
13.	Kerala	13809.2	11003.4	24812.7	18889.1	43701.8
14.	Lakshadweep	895.5	-	895.5	-	895.5
15.	Madhya Pradesh	213968.1	250891.2	464859.4	1827837.9	2292697.3
16.	Maharashtra	84338.7	139668.7	224007.5	68384.2	292391.7
17.	Manipur	-	241.4	241.4	-	241.4
18.	Meghalaya	1414.8	8214.7	9629.5	-	9629.5
19.	Mizoram	-	210.0	210.0	-	210.0

Contd.

20.	Nagaland	1508.6	3191.2	4699.9	-	4699.9
21.	New Delhi	9.2	-	9.2	-	9.2
22.	Odisha	36710.3	55479.7	92190.1	7546.0	99736.1
23.	Pondicherry	2.8	-	2.8	-	2.8
24.	Punjab	434.5	598.0	1032.5	16616.0	17648.5
25.	Rajasthan	46088.7	105521.1	151609.9	387912.2	539522.1
26.	Sikkim	72145.4	3072.8	75218.2	-	75218.2
27.	Tamil Nadu	2058.2	3654.5	5712.7	5062.8	10775.6
28.	Telangana	4457.4	5230.3	9687.8	-	9687.8
29.	Tripura	203.5	-	203.5	-	203.5
30.	Uttar Pradesh	39929.4	16319.8	56249.3	45210.5	101459.9
31.	Uttrakhand	18510.3	12397.0	30907.4	62679.0	93586.4
32.	West Bengal	4759.8	416.1	5176.0	-	5176.0
	Total	648617	794920	1443538	3009449	4452987

(Yadav 2017)

Table 4: State-wise production during 2016-2017 (farm production)

S.No.	State	Organic Production (Mt)	In Conversion Production (Mt)	Total Production (Mt)
1.	Andhra Pradesh	8367.6	5.3	8372.9
2.	Arunachal Pradesh	37. 7	—	37.7
3.	Assam	32395.8	—	32395.8
4.	Chhattisgarh	3108.4	—	3108.3
5.	Goa	4758.7	—	4758.7
6.	Gujarat	41510.9	100.0	41610.9
7.	Haryana	8192.8	—	8192.8
8.	Himachal Pradesh	1836.8	—	1836.8
9.	Jammu & Kashmir	9407792.0	—	9407.8
10.	Karnataka	164047.5	117.3	164164.8
11.	Kerala	14623.2	1.8	14624.9
12.	Madhya Pradesh	382799.9	8798.4	391598.4
13.	Maharashtra	254309.7	1625.1	255934.7
14.	Meghalaya	1111.4	—	1111.4
15.	Nagaland	878.1	—	878.1
16.	Odisha	26537.5	4124.1	30661.5
17.	Pondicherry	2.5	—	2.5
18.	Punjab	711.5	—	711.5
19.	Rajasthan	64244.8	—	64244.8
20.	Sikkim	184.4	1.1	185.4
21.	Tamil Nadu	11019.5	65.5	11084.9
22.	Telangana	468.2	52.9	520.9
23.	Tripura	338.8	—	338.8
24.	Uttar Pradesh	87760.6	422.5	88138.0
25.	Uttrakhand	28155.4	5.900	28161.237
26.	West Bengal	17977.4	—	17977.4
	Total	1164786.2	15319.7	1180105.8

(Yadav 2017)

Table 5: State-wise area and production under wild harvest collection (2016-2017)

S.No.	State	Area (ha)	Production (MT)
1.	Andhra Pradesh	155099.1	6.3
2.	Arunachal Pradesh	68300.0	0.4
3.	Assam	60.0	-
4.	Bihar	678.0	9.0
5.	Chhattisgarh	167040.0	421.6
6.	Gujarat	6253.9	-
7.	Haryana	20.2	-
8.	Himachal Pradesh	2000.0	49.9
9.	J & K	159000.0	5176.5
10.	Jharkhand	10000.0	122217.0
11.	Karnataka	859.7	17.1
12.	Kerala	18889.1	-
13.	Madhya Pradesh	1827837.9	1523.4
14.	Maharashtra	68384.3	11.1
15.	Odisha	7546.1	536.1
16.	Punjab	16616.0	-
17.	Rajasthan	387912.2	1009.9
18.	Tamil Nadu	5062.9	435.3
19.	Uttar Pradesh	45210.6	18.9
20.	Uttarakhand	62679.0	179.3
	Total	3009449.1	21611.7

(Yadav 2017)

3. Organic farming and socioeconomic dimensions

Evaluation of the benefits and limitations of organic agriculture on food security is complex. The effect of the transition to organic practices will depend on the farmer and farming society, their skills, and the resources accessible to them. Organic agriculture can increase productivity, especially in situations where farmers are vulnerable to food shortages; it can increase income through higher financial value, and lower prices paid for inputs, or the combinations of these three. The variety of production in organic agriculture decreases the risk of crop failure and relevant food security and economic problems. Organic agriculture is a sustainable and environmentally friendly production system that offers developing countries a wide range of economic, environmental, and social benefits. Although organic farming systems under some circumstances may produce yields less than conventional agriculture but they are more profitable to farmers because consumers are willing to pay more. Organic agriculture has three dimensions—social, economic, and environmental—and these three dimensions can improve food security.

3.1. Social dimension

Organic farming requires more field and post harvest work and thus, is the potential entrepreneurship to contribute to long-term employment in rural areas. It plays an important role in employment in rural areas because of the hiring of more seasonal workers and, given the increases in organic food sales, however, opportunities are relatively more in the occupations related to value added organic foods. Organic farming promotes entrepreneurship and promising activity that decreases immigration in rural areas, thus, it enables new and different groups in the society to be involved in agricultural activities and will help to improve employment. Additionally, organic farming recognizes the value of indigenous and traditional knowledge and combines indigenous knowledge with production procedures which enhances social capacity while empowering farmers and local communities, which is consistent with achieving food security.

3.2. Economic dimension

Organic farming is a sustainable option for small farmers to improve food security and to enhance the overall performance of farm income. Organic farming is cost-effective for farmers due to the lack of usage of chemicals (due to its expensive price), turning to inexpensive methods, such as biological resources rather than chemical fertilizers and pesticides. Other reasons that persuade farmers towards organic farming is the raising of product prices and consequently increased profits from the sale of these products and the lack of intermediaries to sell them. Organic farming uses existing local assets rather than consuming capital resources intensively, so poor farmers can improve their farm productivity and fertility while avoiding dependence on expensive external inputs. Organic farming can increase productivity and income, thus helping to improve food security. There are a large number of economic opportunities that lead to the increase of added value of organic products through processing and marketing activities and the improvement of food security in the long-term.

3.3. Environmental dimension

Organic farming improves soil quality, secures farm future, and offers environmental protection. The fertile soil leads to stability and is effective in the production cycle. More nutrients given to the soil result in less soil erosion and increase soil biodiversity, which improves food security in the long-term. Additionally, in organic farming with minimum tillage, biological fertilizers, proper crop rotation and cover crops, green manure, etc., an increase in soil fertility occurs. Organic farming enhances food security by improving resistance to diseases and pests, combating desertification by reducing soil erosion and protecting water resources, and maintaining and improving environmental services. Avoiding chemical residues and pesticides and consuming fresh products, acquiring healthy diets, and taking advantage of the nutritional value of organic products are among other motivations that improve food and nutritional security.

Organic Agriculture Perspectives and Progress in India

In India, organic farming was started first by the agribusiness entrepreneurs around 2000, supported by the Ministry of Commerce. Initially, organs of the Ministry of Commerce, APEDA, Spices Board and Coffee Board were in a way directed to promote organic production of export commodities for two reasons, one because of new trade regime of Non-Tariff Barriers linked to residue contaminations and unsafe agri-products; and two because of premium prices organic enterprises could enjoy. Tremendous progress in promoting organic agriculture in India has been made during last fifteen years. Eleventh plan document on Organic sector and National Commission on farmers has recommended organic farming as a tool for 2nd Green Revolution. FAO with the help of IFOAM and other International Agencies recommended Organic Farming as a tool to address Millennium Development Goals (MDG) 1&7. The first MDG is the eradication of extreme poverty and hunger, whereas, the seventh MDG is to ensure environmental sustainability.

4. Productivity and profitability: A review

With the advent of organic farming in the recent years there had been concerns on the production potential of the system. But the results of long term experiments released during the last 10 years from world over have eliminated all fears. Under irrigated conditions organic farming may be yielding 5-12% less than their conventional counterparts but under rain-fed and water deficit conditions organic system yields 7 to 15% more. Review of 154 growing seasons' worth of data (Halwell 2006) reveals that organic corn yields were 94 percent of conventional yields, organic wheat yields were 97 percent, and organic soybean yields were 94 percent. Organic tomatoes showed no yield difference. A seven-year study from Maikaal project in Khargone District in central India (Eyehorn *et al* 2009) found that average yields for cotton, wheat, chili, and soybean were as much as 20 percent higher on the organic farms than on nearby conventionally managed ones. The study carried out in the Central Valley of California (Drinkwater *et al* 1995) showed that tomato yields were quite similar in organic and conventional farms. However, significant differences were found in soil health indicators such as nitrogen mineralization potential and microbial abundance and diversity which were higher in the organic farms. Nitrogen mineralization potential was three times greater in organic compared to conventional fields. The organic fields also had 28% more organic carbon.

Another trial's result from Sustainable Agriculture Farming Systems project (SFAS) at University of California, Davis (Clark *et al* 1999) showed that organic and low-input systems had yields comparable to the conventional systems in all crops which were tested - tomato, safflower, corn and bean, and in some instances yielding higher than conventional systems. In one such study at South Dakota in Midwestern United States shows the higher average yields of soybeans (3.5%) and wheat (4.8%) in the organic compared to conventional farming system (Welsh 1999). 21 year study compared plots of cropland grown according to both organic and conventional methods at Institute of Organic Agriculture and the Swiss Federal Research Station for Agro-ecology and Agriculture found that Organic yields were less by about 20% but Fertilizer, Energy and Pesticide use were less by 34%, 53% and 97% respectively as compared to conventional (Maeder *et al* 2002). Also organic soils housed a larger and more diverse community of organisms.

The study at Iowa State University assessed (Delate and Cambardella 2004) the agro ecosystem performance of farms which found initially the yield was slightly lower (Organic corn & soybean yield averaged 91.8% & 99.6% of conventional respectively) in organic plots but in fourth year organic yield exceeded conventional for both corn and soybean crops (Delate *et al* 2002). 30 Years Farming System Trial (FST) at Rodale Institute showed organic corn yields 31% higher than conventional in years of drought (Pimentel *et al*, 2005). The study conducted by ETC Organic Cotton Program in Andrha Pradesh showed that the organic cotton yielded 232 Kg seed cotton /acre vs. conventional cotton at 105 Kg/acre. The pest control expenses were observed about Rs. 220 and Rs. 1624 per acre for organic and in conventional cotton, respectively (Daniel *et al* 2005).

Research findings released from UAS, Dharwad, Karnataka under Network Project on Organic Farming (ICAR) reported results from six year long experiment comparing yields and net returns from organic cultivation, chemical farming and integrated nutrient management (INM). The results for three crop combinations are as follows:

Crop combination	Yield kg/ha	Yield kg/ha	Returns Rs/ha
Groundnut-sorghum	Groundnut yield	Sorghum yield	Net returns
Organic	2975	1166	48345
Chemical	2604	1043	40790
INM	2842	1155	46090
Soybean-Wheat	Soybean yield	Wheat yield	
Organic	1769	1081	21120
Chemical	1521	933	16313

INM	1733	1062	19929
Chilli-Cotton	Chilli yield	Cotton yield	
Organic	447	662	19502
Chemical	427	559	14176
INM	445	681	19540

Source: UAS Dharwad 2011

Kshirsagar (2007) conducted a study in Maharashtra to find out the impact of organic farming on economics of sugarcane cultivation. The study was based on primary data collected from two districts covering 142 farmers, 72 growing Organic Sugarcane and 70 growing Inorganic Sugarcane. It was observed that in organic crops cost of cultivation was lower by 14.24 per cent than conventional farming. Although the yield from organic was 6.79 per cent lower than the conventional crop, it was more than compensated by the lower cost and price premium received and yield stability observed on organic farms. The organic farming gave 15.63 per cent higher profits and profits were also more stable on organic farms than the conventional farms. Tej Pratap and Vaidya (2009) in a nationwide survey of organic farmers suggest that "The cost-benefit analysis indicates favourable economics of organic farming in India. Farmers in 5 out of 7 states are better placed, so far as organic farming is concerned. The returns are higher in Himachal Pradesh, Uttaranchal, Karnataka, Maharashtra and Rajasthan. In Karnataka organic farmers had 4-35% higher returns than inorganic farmers. In Kerala the differentials ranged between 4-37% in favour of inorganic farmers. In Maharashtra the difference in net profit was more than 100% in case of organic soybean. Organic cotton farmers were enjoying comfortable profit margin. The profit differential in Rajasthan ranged from 12-59% in favour of organic farmers. In Tamil Nadu organic farmers were better placed with two crops, while inorganic farmers were at slight advantage in other two crops.

In another study by Ramesh *et al* (2010), it has been reported that on an average, the productivity of crops in organic farming is although lower by 9.2% compared to conventional farming. There was a reduction in the average cost of cultivation by 11.7% compared to conventional farming. However, due to the availability of premium price (20–40%) for organic produce in most cases, the average net profit was 22.0% higher in organic compared to the conventional farming. In traditional rainfed agriculture (with low external inputs), organic agriculture has shown the potential to increase yields and profits. The economics of organic cotton cultivation over a period of six years indicated that there is a reduction in cost of cultivation and increased gross and net returns compared to conventional cotton cultivation in India.

A field experiment was conducted during the *kharif* 2012, 2013, 2014,& 2015 and *rabi* seasons of 2012-13, 2013-14 and 2014-15 in factorial RBD at the Model Organic Farm of Department of Organic Agriculture, CSKHPKV, Palampur. During *kharif* season mash and okra and in *rabi* season gram and wheat+gram were sown in alternate years. In the organic treatment, the seed of pulses was treated with the biofertilizers (*Rhizobium*+PSB) and of okra and wheat with *Azospirillum* + PSB. Vermicompost 5.0 t/ha was applied as the basal dose at the time of sowing during all the years of study. Three applications of the liquid manure (vermiwash) were given at 15 days interval commencing from 20 days after sowing. In inorganic treatment, recommended doses of NPK were applied. In integrated, 50% of the recommended NPK along with 50% of vermicompost were applied. In farmers practice, $1/4^{th}$ of the recommended NPK and vermicompost were applied. Recommended plant protection practices were adopted both for organic and inorganic farming. Data presented in the tables revealed that though irrigated conditions recorded comparatively higher yields over the rainfed situation during the *kharif* seasons but the differences were not significant. However, during *rabi* seasons irrigation resulted in significantly higher yields over the rainfed conditions except during 2013-14 when the difference was non-significant. As a result the average gram equivalent yield and net returns were significantly higher in irrigated treatments to the tune of 10.4 & 9.1 %, respectively over the rainfed treatments. Among the nutrient sources, organic treatments being at par with the integrated source resulted in significantly higher gram equivalent yield over other treatments. Whereas, mash equivalent yield in organic treatments was significantly higher over other treatments during all the years of experimentation except during *kharif* 2013, where it was also at par with the integrated treatments. Application of inorganic sources of nutrients resulted in significantly lower yield during the first year of study however, during the second and third years it was at par with that obtained in farmers practice. The pooled gram equivalent yield and net returns were significantly highet in organic treatment to the tune of 37.4 & 52.8 %, respectively over the inorganic treatment.

Table 6: Effect of different treatments on crop yield

Treatments	Pooled Gram equivalent yield of the system (q/ha) 2012-15	Economics	
		Net return (Rs/ha)	B:C ratio
Irrigated	27.31	162342.1	2.90
Rainfed	24.74	148777.9	3.03
LSD (P=0.05)	2.54	12250.0	NS
Source of nutrients			
*Organic	31.86	200857.1	3.72
Inorganic	23.18	131368.6	2.43
Integrated	27.45	165570.0	3.06
*Farmers practice	21.56	124457.1	2.60
LSD (P=0.05)	2.25	12070.0	0.25

**Organic: VC 5t/ha+Bifertilizers(Rhiz.+PSB)+Vermiwash (Liquid manure)*
**Farmers practice: 1/4th of the recommended NPKalongwith 1.25 tones/ha of vermicompost*

Table 7: Effect of treatments on soil physical, chemical& biological properties

Treatments	Physical properties		Chemical properties	Biological properties	
	Bulk Density (Mg m^{-3})	Water holding capacity (%)	Organic Carbon (%)	DHA (MgTPF$g^{-1}hr^{-1}$)	SMBC (μg g^{-1} soil)
Irrigated	1.20	55.68	1.43	4.85	125.4
Rainfed	1.30	56.25	1.39	4.65	118.6
LSD (P=0.05)	NS	NS	NS	0.17	6.2
Organic	1.24	59.42	1.48	5.11	138.7
Inorganic	1.30	55.51	1.34	4.06	105.0
Integrated	1.24	58.62	1.42	4.99	128.9
Farmer's practices	1.28	55.0	1.40	4.84	115.4
LSD (P=0.05)	NS	NS	0.05	0.18	8.4
Initial	1.28	50.0	1.20	1.75	86.0

*Organic: VC 5t/ha+Bifertilizers(Rhiz.+PSB)+Vermiwash (Liquid manure)
*Farmers practice: 1/4th of the recommended NPKalongwith 1.25 tones/ha of vermicompost

Comparative performance of organic *vis-à-vis* inorganic management practices in potential vegetable based cropping sequences

A field experiment was conducted in split plot design with three replications and twelve treatment combinations at Research Farm of Department of Organic Agriculture, CSKHPKV, Palampur (H.P) India *w.e.f. kharif* 2012 to *kharif* 2015 to find out the most economical cropping sequence and the best management practice among organic, integrated, chemical and farmer's practice. Pooled Okra equivalent yield (2012-15) of the system in organic treatment was significantly higher over all other nutrient management practices which ultimately resulted in higher net returns in organic management over the other management practices. The studies on soil health showed that the available N, P & K contents were comparatively higher in integrated nutrient management practice, however, it was at par with chemical and organic treatment. The dehydrogenase activity in organic and integrated practice was at par with each other but significantly higher than chemical practice. Organic practice resulted in significantly highest soil microbial biomass carbon (SMBC) over all other treatments which was followed by integrated practice of management.

Table 8: Effect of different crop rotation and management practices on equivalent yield of different crops

Treatments	Pooled okra equivalent yield of the system (q ha^{-1}) 2012-2015	Economics	
		Net return (Rs/ha)	B:C ratio
Crop rotations			
Okra-Cauliflower- French bean	211.21	358728.6	5.63
Tomato-Radish- Pea	187.11	318528.6	5.72
Brinjal-Cabbage- French bean	188.63	319557.1	5.54
CD (P=0.05)	**18.50**	**25024**	**NS**
Management practices			
Organic	232.86	392309.3	5.30
Integrated practices	218.13	377866.1	6.41
Chemical practices	212.33	369080.1	6.57
Farmers practice	111.53	181652.1	4.63
CD (P=0.05)	**20.12**	**26058**	**0.50**
Crop rotations			
Okra-Cauliflower- French bean	211.21	358728.6	5.63
Tomato-Radish- Pea	187.11	318528.6	5.72
Brinjal-Cabbage- French bean	188.63	319557.1	5.54
CD (P=0.05)	**18.50**	**25024**	**NS**
Management practices			
Organic	232.86	392309.3	5.30
Integrated practices	218.13	377866.1	6.41
Chemical practices	212.33	369080.1	6.57
Farmers practice	111.53	181652.1	4.63
CD (P=0.05)	**20.12**	**26058**	**0.50**

*Organic: Vermicompost 5t/ha in pulses & Vermicopost 10t/ha in other crops+Bifertilizers (Rhiz.+PSB)+Vermiwash (Liquid manure)

Table 9: Effect of different crop rotation and management practices on physical, chemical and biological properties of soil

Treatments	Organic carbon (%)		N (kg ha^{-1})	SMBC (µg g^{-1} soil)	
Crop rotations	0-15 cm	15-30 cm	0-15 cm	0-15 cm	15-30 cm
Okra- Cauliflower- French bean	1.41	1.36	117.5	117.5	106.5
Tomato- Radish- Pea	1.44	1.40	121.4	121.4	111.4
Brinjal- Cabbage- French bean	1.41	1.37	119.7	119.7	109.6
CD (P=0.05)	0.03	0.03	NS	NS	NS
Management practices					
Organic	1.58	1.54	328.3	140.7	129.3
Integrated practices	1.41	1.37	335.7	116.9	107.5
Chemical practices	1.34	1.30	333.0	106.5	94.8
Control	1.29	1.25	321.7	102.9	92.6
CD (P=0.05)	0.07	0.07	9.93	11.33	11.17
Initial	1.22	295		88.0	

5. Economic benefits

Organic farming systems not only fulfill the family food requirement but also give reasonable amount of profitable income and reduction in the cost of production with sustainability of the agro-ecosystem. There is emerging evidence that organic farming can improve farm finances, potentially reduce payouts to some farm financial safety nets, and contribute to rural community vitality following more widespread adoption (Mac Rae *et al* 2007). In Europe, most farm comparisons show profits for organic farms between ± 20% of conventional (Nieberg and Oppermann 2003).

Nazeer Udin (2014) indicated that there was a wide choice of diversification of farming practices such as manure, water and biological pest management and also rural employment generation, provides food security at the household level where maximum utilization of naturally available inputs may offer the greatest prospects for poverty reduction and sustainable livelihood outcomes.

However, there is considerable latent interest among farmers in conversion to organic farming in India. But, some farmers are reluctant to convert because of the perceived high costs of cultivation. Those who have converted earn equal incomes to their conventional counterparts, if premium markets exist for organic produce (Mac Donald 2004). Organic farming provides higher net profitable income to the producer by 22% as compared to conventional farming, mainly due to the reduction in cost of cultivation and availability of premium price (20-40%) for the certified organic produce (Ramesh *et al* 2010).

Several studies reported that if all the outputs and all the inputs are taken into account, organic farming which relies on internal inputs has higher productivity than external input chemical agriculture (Mac Donald 2004; Chhetri 2015). The importance of exchange of labour among organic farmers in the form of non-monetary support as the outcome of a survey among the organic farmers in Shimoga District of Karnataka, India has been reported (Nazeer Udin 2014).

Social benefits and impact on rural community

Organic farming practices have high social value of general suitability, are compatible with their own cultural systems, are inexpensive, are natural form of farming, and are eco-friendly (Adesope *et al* 2012). The shift to organic farming had a positive impact on the socio economic status of farming in all the agro-climatic zones of Northern Karnataka, India. The score of variable component revealed that organic farming families were slightly better in all the aspects *viz.,* socio-economic status, expenditure pattern, saving and investment, family health status. Hence, organic farming was significantly superior as compared to conventional farming families (Desai 2013).

Organic agriculture also develops positive and happy attitude among the farmers towards family and satisfactory form of life (Nazeer Udin 2014). The organic farmers were more aware of the internet and they participated in different events such as conferences, congresses, and workshops (Tuncer and Boz 2017). Socio-economic conditions improved after adopting conservation agricultural practices (Uddin and Dhar 2017).

Relationship between socio-economic characters of farmers and adoption of organic farming practices

Rapid increase in the market demand for organic products presents a remarkable opportunity for expansion of organic agriculture. Various socio-economic factors influence the farmers' choice to adopt organic or conventional farming systems. Organic farmers have greater tendency to join various organizations such as cooperatives and unions, carry social security mostly given to government workers and medium level state officers, and use fewer loans for the farming investments as compared to the conventional farmers (Tuncer and Boz 2017). Gender also plays a role in organic farming practices (FAO 2008, This vol.).

The size of the household, total annual income and education were said to influence use of organic manure; then they deserve particular attention in developing plans and implementation (Nyengere 2017). In one of the survey in Nimar valley of Madhya Pradesh state in central India among cotton growers observed that organic farmers with larger land holdings were more concerned about reducing their reliance on external inputs whereas medium and small holding organic farmers were evidently motivated by the premium price of organically produced cotton (Riar *et al* 2017).

In a survey from Pudukottai district in Tamil Nadu, India the majority of the respondents fell under the medium level category when they were classified for variables *viz*., farming experience, livestock possession, farm power, social participation, extension agency contact, mass media exposure and information source utilization (Ramesh and Govind 2005).

6. Constraints in adoption of Organic Farming

- Farmers' anxiety lies in non-availability of sufficient amount of organic supplements, biopesticides, bio-fertilizers and local market for organic produce.
- Marketing of organic produce is the main problem for organic farmers especially from remote areas.
- Organic farmers cannot find consumers who are willing to pay premium prices and are after forced to sell their produce as conventional farmers.
- Inability of the government to take a firm decision regarding the policies and promotion of organic agriculture.
- Additionally, lack of access to proper technology, lack of market information and vocational training, and risk of low yield, unawareness about the certification process are important limitations.

7. Challenges for future developments

- To increase and enhance government policy initiatives and assistance, especially for and during the conversion process.
- To create organic agricultural faculties at the most important agricultural universities.
- To introduce organic extension services and training for farmers' field schools
- To build up adequate infrastructure for transport, storage, processing and market facilities.
- To create a guarantee system for the domestic market.
- To increase consumer awareness about the safe and environmentally friendly production of food.
- To add organic information to the existing oversees reports on markets.

- To spur production and supply of organic seeds, organic manure, organic bio-fertilizers and bio-pesticides
- To provide funds for proper scientific studies on income generation, household income and food security, yields and soil improvement from organic agriculture

8. Recommendations for promotion of organic farming

The Ministres of Agriculture and Commerce should introduce favorable government policies and strategies for the promotion of organic agriculture. These should include:

- A program of assistance to farmers who want to convert their lands to organic farming.
- An increase in investment and research in organic agriculture and a scale-up of projects that have already proven successful. There should be an emphasis on comparative research of the costs of production, productivity and other benefits accruing from organic farming as compared to conventional agriculture. To this end, the Indian Council of Agricultural Research could initiate organic faculties in key agricultural universities.
- A strengthening of links and cooperation between the government, the private sector and NGOs on the national level.
- Government assistance in micro-credit and micro-enterprises to self-help groups of landless agricultural families, particularly women, for organic compost, bio-pesticides and bio-fertilizers (accessing usufruct rights of common property resources, such as waste land, exclusively for resource poor)
- Awareness campaigns on the benefits of organic agriculture products.
- Support structures should be introduced for small farmers' group certification.
- The establishment of a monthly information bulletin for organic farmers on local and international prices of the most common food items should be supported.
- There should be special emphasis placed on supporting the implementation of the IFOAM Accreditation system as a basis to enable reciprocity of guarantees, and to reduce overlapping certification work, bureaucracy and costs.

9. Certification

Why is Organic Certification Needed?

The consumer requests healthy and environmentally sound products and is willing to pay a higher price for them

Trust

The farmer produces according to defined organic standards and can sell his products at a higher price. Any agricultural produce can be designated as organic only after it is certified as organic. Organic certification is a process vides which organic food producers and processors are certified to have produced various products by following fixed standards and under fixed regulations. Organic certification is basically an auditing process that assures that the organic growers and product manufactures abide by the fixed standards and regulations. In general any vocation which is directly involved in the production and marketing of organic produce can be certified and this includes seed suppliers, organic food producers, food processors, retailers and even restaurants which serve organic food to its client.

Third Party Certification

India already has policies and mechanisms in place for maintaining standards and trust of certified organic products. National Program on Organic Production being operated under FTDR Act and APGMC Act meet the requirements of quality assurance in organic for export, import and domestic markets. Even though there are 16 certifying agencies across the country but keeping in view the Mission 2020 goals, their number will prove inadequate. Therefore Mission 2020 should include a program on expanding the number of certifying agencies in the country.

- Financial assistance be allocated for setting up of new certification bodies, especially in states with at least one agency in each state.
- Supporting ICS management and certification by the grower group certification system through service providers and data management for thorough traceability. Support may be provided for setting up of National/ Regional web hosted data base system to develop repository of organic farmers and organic products.
- Funding establishment of 20 new residual testing laboratories across the country, preferably under PPP mode.

Farmers' Participatory Guarantee System (PGS)

To ensure low cost farmer guaranteed alternative quality assurance system, there is need to promote PGS or any other form of system. It will encourage farmers to understand the benefits of quality assurance and it should encourage them to use it as a precursor to certification by third party. The PGS system should be based on National Standards of Organic Production. Further PGS system developed for the country should ideally be based on peer evaluation system rather than individual farmers' record maintenance.

10. Infrastructure for organic products development & supply chain

Promotion of organic farming is directly linked with the market development. Therefore, efforts are needed to ensure adequate support to strengthen supply chains. The mission strategies should therefore include provision for providing financial support to develop dedicated organic supply chain components, namely, grading, cleaning, primary processing units for dal making and flour making etc, packing units and storage units with organically compatible fumigation/ protection during storage.

Organic Farmers should be encouraged to form producer companies or SHG (self help group) or FIG (Farmers integrated group) for creating value addition, storage infrastructure development and for direct marketing. Organic Farming Mission should support such dedicated farmer group owned producer companies. Farmers must be well convinced that individual adoption of such activity may not be commercial sustainable. Individual approach will certainly be trouble shooter.

11. Employment opportunities

Organic farming is expanding fast both in the domestic as well as international markets. Further employment opportunities are enhanced because of possible diverse entrepreneurships (Table 12).

Table 12: Entrepreneurship in organic agriculture

Organic crop production
Organic fruit crop production
Organic seed /planting material production
Organic composts
Biofertilizers
Bio-pesticides
Organic dairying
Organic poultry
Organic mushrooms
Processing and value addition
Organic grocery store
Organic inputs enterprise
Apiculture
Consultancy, inspection and certification services

12. Conclusion

India provides considerable scope and opportunities in organic farming. However, there are several threats and weaknesses. Various socio-economic factors influence the farmers' choice to adopt organic cultivation. Sustainable crop production has positive impact on the socio-economic status of the peoples. However, there is a need to address the weaknesses and implement effective mechanisms to offset threats of organic farming. The existing evidence suggests greater research efforts in this area are required. There is need to identify the gaps between the adaptation of techniques of sustainable production. Additionally, it is important to examine the status of organic farming and feasibility to different sustainable practices in different production systems and farming situations across the country for promotion of organic farming.

13. References

Adesope OM, Matthews-Njoku EC, Oguzor NS and Ugwuja VC .2012. Effect of socio-economic characteristics of farmers on their adoption of organic farming practices. *In*: *Crop Production Technologies*, Book edited by Sharma P. and Abrol V., Intech publication, London, pp. 211-220.

Anonymous .2017. National Project on Organic Farming. National Centre of Organic Farming.Department of Agriculture, Cooperation and Farmers Welfare Ministry of Agriculture and Farmers Welfare Government of India, http://ncof.dacnet.nic.in.

Bhutia K, Pradhan Y, Avasthe RK, Bhutia PT .2012. Agriculture in Sikkim: Transition from traditional to organic Farming. *In*: *Handbook of organic crop production in Sikkim*. Edited by Avasthe R., Pradhan Y. and Bhutia K., published by Sikkim organic mission, GOI of Sikkim, Gangtok, Sikkim, India in collaboration with ICAR Research complex for NEH region, Sikkim center, Tadong , Gangtok, Sikkim, 1-20.

Chhetri M. 2015. Empowering Farmers through Organic Farming in the Himalayan State of Sikkim. *American International Journal of Research in Humanities, Arts and Social Sciences* 11(2): 97-101.

Clark S., Klonsky K., Livingston P., Temple S. (1999), Crop-yield and economic comparisons of organic, low-input, and conventional farming systems in California's Sacramento Valley, *American Journal of Alternative Agriculture*, 14(3), pp 109-121

Daniel A. R., Sridhar K., Ambatipudi A., Lanting H., Brenchandran S. (2005) Case Study on Organic Versus Conventional Cotton in Karimnagar, Andhira Pradesh, India. Second International Symposium on Biological Control of Arthropods, pp 302-317.

Desai, R. M. 2013. Role of Women in organic farming and their family quality index in the selected agro-climatic zones of northern Karnataka. Ph.D. thesis submitted to University of Agricultural Sciences, Dharwad, pp. 192.

FAO, 2008. Organic agriculture and climate change. Food and Agriculture Organization, Rome.

FAO, 1999. Guidelines for the production, processing, labeling and marketing of organically produced foods. Joint FAO/WHO Food Standards Program Codex Alimentarious Commission, Rome, CAC/GL 32, p. 49.

Delate K., Cambardella C., Karlen D. (2002), Transition strategies for post-CRP certified organic grain production. Crop Management doi: 10.1094/CM-2002-0828.

Delate K and Cambardella CA.(2004) Organic production: Agroecosystem performance during transition to certified organic grain production. *Agronomy Journal* 2004, 96, 1288-98.

Drinkwater L. E., Letourneau D. K., Workneh F., Bruggen A. H., Shennan C (1995), Fundamental Differences between Conventional and Organic Tomato Agroecosystems in California, Ecological Applications, 5(4), pp 1098-1112.

Eyhorn F, Paul Mäder, Mahesh Ramakrishnan 2009, The Impact of Organic Cotton Farming on the Livelihoods of Smallholders - Evidence from the MaikaalbioRe project in Central India, Organic Farming Newsletter, 5(1): 19-21

Gill, M.S. and Kamta Prasad 2009, Network Project on Organic Farming – Research Highlights, *Organic Farming Newsletter* 5(2) : 3-10.

Halwell, B. 2006. Can Organic Farming Feed Us All. World Watch Magazine Vol. 19 (3): 18-24.

Kshirsagar, 2007,Gokhale Institute of Politics and Economics, Pune 411 004, Maharashtra, India

Lockie, S., Lyons, K. Lawrence, G and Halpin. D. 2006. Going organic: Mobilizing networks for environmentally responsible food production. CABI Publishing, Wallingford, UK.

MacRae, R. J., Frick, B. and Martin, R. C. 2007.Economic and social impacts of organic production systems.*Canadian journal of plant science* 87:1037-1044.

MacDonald DM .2004. Agri Impact Assessment study for organic cotton farmers of Kutch &Surendranagar, Agrocel Industries Ltd, September 2004, India.

Maeder, P., Fliessbach, A., Dubois, D., Gunst, L., Fried, P. and Niggli, U. 2002. Soil fertility and biodiversity in Organic Farming. Science 296, 1694-1697.

Mitra, S. and Devi, I. 2016. Organic Horticulture in India. *Horticulturae* 2:17, doi:10.3390/horticulturae2040017.

Nazeer Udin, 2014. Organic farming impact on sustainable livelihoods of marginal farmers in Shimoga district of Karnataka. *American Journal of Rural Development*2(4): 81-88.

Nieberg, H. and Oppermann, N. 2003. The profitability of organic farming in Europe. *In*: OECD, ed. Organic agriculture. Sustainability, markets and policies. CABI Publishing, Wallingford, UK, pp. 141-152.

Nyengere, 2017. Socioeconomic factors affecting adoption of use of organic manure as climate smart agriculture technology in Malawi. *International Journal of Science and Research* 6(2): 496-498.

Ramesh P *et al* 2010, Status of organic farming in India, Productivity vs Profitability Current Science 2010, Vol98: 1190-1194

Pimentel D *et al* .2005. Environmental, Energetic and Economic Comparisons of Organic and Conventional Farming Systems. *Bioscience*. 55:7.

Rahmann G .2011. Biodiversity and organic farming: what do we know? *Applied Agricultural and Forestry* Research. 61(3):189-208.

Ramesh P and Govind S .2005. Personal and Socio- economic characteristics of organic farmers. *Karnataka Journal of Agricultural Sciences*18(1):192-195.

Ramesh P, Panwar NR., Singh AB, Ramana S, Yadav S K, Shrivastava,R and Subba Rao A. 2010. Status of organic farming in India. *Current Science* 98(9):1190-1194.

Riar A, Mandloi LS, Poswal RS, Messmer MM and Bhullar GS. 2017. A diagnosis of biophysical and socio-economic factors influencing farmers' choice to adopt organic or conventional farming systems for cotton production. *Frontiers in Plant Science* 8:1289. Doi: 10.3389/fpls.2017.01289.

Rigby D and Caceres D. 2001. Organic farming and the sustainability of agricultural systems. *Agricultural Systems* 68:21-40. Doi:10.1016/S0308-521X(00)00060-3.

Scialabba NEH .2007.Organic agriculture and food security. *In*: *Proceedings of the International Conference on Organic Agriculture and Food Security*, FAO, Rome, Italy, May 2007.

Tashi S and Wangchuk K .2016. Prospects of organic farming in Bhutan: A SWOT Analysis. *Advances in Agriculture*, http://dx.doi.org/10.1155/2016/1717352.

TejPratap and CS Vaidya 2009 Organic Farmers Speak on Economics and Beyond, Westville Publishing House, New Delhi p 160.

Tuncer AG and Boz I. 2017. Comparison of conventional and organic farmers on their socioeconomic characteristics and communication behaviors. *International Journal of Scientific Research and Management* 5(6): 5354-5262.

UAS Dharwad .2011. Research Accomplishments. ICAR Network Project on Organic Farming, Institute of Organic Farming. Directorate of Research. UAS Dharwad.

Uddin TU and Dhar AR .2017. Conservation Agriculture practice in Bangladesh: Farmer's socioeconomic status and soil environment perspective. *International Scholarly and Scientific Research and Innovations* 11(5):1251-1259.

Welsh R. (1999). The Economics of Organic Grain and Soybean Production in the Midwestern United States. Henry A. Wallace Institute for Alternative Agriculture, available at http://www.hawiaa.org/pspr13.htm, accessed during May 2012.

Yadav AK. 2017. Organic Agriculture in India: An Overview. *In: Proceedings of 'National Conference on Organic farming for Sustainable Agriculture and live hood Security under changing climatic condition'* December 12-13, pp. 1-9.

15

Dairy Farming: An Entrepreneurship for Socio-economic Transformation

Neelesh Sharma[1*], Zul-I-Huma[1], Sabhyata Sharma[2] and SK Gupta[1]

[1]Division of Veterinary Medicine, FVSc & AH SKUAST-J, RS Pura, Jammu, Jammu and Kashmir, India
[2]Department of Veterinary Parasitology, NVC, MAFSU, Nagpur, Maharashtra, India

Abstract

Over the years, India has emerged as one of the world's biggest producers of milk, with the total milk production rising from 122 Million Metric Tons in 2010 to 171 Million Metric Tons in 2017 with dairy market in India touching a value of INR 7,916 Billion. An average livestock contributes about 12 % of farmer's income and the same for small and marginal farmers and landless laborers' is 36 %. While farmer's income in agriculture is growing at 3.5 % annually, income from livestock is growing at about 14.5 %. Despite this, the majority of the dairy industry in India is still highly unorganized and dominated by small and marginal dairy farmers. Of all the major rural enterprises, dairy is an important profession of economic and social transformation to supplement the income and employment to the rural sector in general and rural women in particular. The process of dairy development would be incomplete and lop sided, unless farm women are fully involved in it. Indian dairy industry also offers good opportunities to both domestic and foreign investors for entry and expansion. Low yielding breeds, costly animal feeds, inadequate market linkage and predominance of handling dairy through indigenous technologies mar the Indian dairy industry. It is imperative to develop proper production, processing and marketing infrastructure if India has to emerge as an exporting country which is capable of meeting international quality requirements. It is anticipated that milk production in India will further grow at a CAGR of around 15% between 2018 and 2023. A comprehensive plan for producing quality and safe dairy products should be formulated with suitable legal backup. Dairy products' consumption has been growing exponentially in the country owing to their rich nutritional qualities. Thus, it has enormous scope for women empowerment and socio-economic transformation of rural India and must rank top in our developmental agenda.

1. Introduction

Livestock farming plays an important role in socio-economic status of India. Out of this dairy farming has emerged as one of the potent enterprise supporting livelihood and nutritional security. Government is progressively taking initiatives to promote the dairy industry in India, in which inclination towards cattle breeding, clean milk production, dairy development, and feed fodder management are included. The importance of dairy farming in a country like India hardly needs emphasis but in terms of dung and urine management certainly deserves innovative perception. India has vast resources of livestock and proper disposal of dung and urine is boon for sustainable agriculture, can play an important role in the national economy and also in the socio-economic development of millions of rural households being entrepreneurial in nature like that of dairying. The Indian dairy sector contributes a large share of the agricultural gross domestic product (GDP). Although the contribution of agriculture and allied sectors to the national GDP has declined during the past few decades, but the contribution of the livestock sector has increased from less than 5 % in the early 1980s to 8% in 2009 (FAO corporate document repository; Haleem, 2009).

For rural households, dairy's contribution is around third of their gross income whereas it is around half in those without land inferring a promise enterprise for landless farmers. Dairying in India is an integral part of total farming system, India ranks first in terms of milk production, accounting for 18.5 % of world production, achieving an annual output of 146.3 million tons during 2014-15 as compared to 137.69 million tons during 2013-14 recording a growth of 6.26 %. Over the years, India has emerged as one of the world's biggest producers of milk, with the total milk production rising from 122 Million Metric Tons in 2010 to 171 Million Metric Tons in 2017 with dairy market in India touching a value of INR 7,916 Billion.

The private participation in the Indian dairy sector has also increased over the past few years. Both national and international players are entering the dairy industry, attracted by the size and potential of the Indian market. The focus is being given to value-added products such as cheese, yogurt, probiotic drinks, etc. Private players are also introducing innovative products keeping in mind the specific requirements of the Indian consumers. These players are also improving their milk procurement network which is further facilitating the development of the dairy industry in India. Looking forward, the market is expected to reach a value of INR 18,599 Billion by 2023, exhibiting a CAGR of around 15% during 2018-2023.

Comparing other sectors of agriculture as was estimated by CSO (Central Statistical Organization) in 2005-06 it was seen that the total output was around Rs 1,73,350 out of which milk alone accounted for 68% which was certainly higher than paddy and wheat. It is estimated that over 60 million rural households of which three fourth are landless, marginal or small farmers are engaged in milk production which is a major source of their livelihood. Besides, it is also providing livelihood to the people living in drought areas like Rajasthan and Gujarat, etc.

2. Status of livestock and dairy in India

We can make an estimate of importance of livestock in India's economy by the fact that nearly 90 million milch animals are reared by the farming families. In India it was seen on an average livestock contributes about 12 % of farmer's income and the same for small and marginal farmers and landless laborers' is 36 %. While farmer's income is growing at 3.5 % annually, income from livestock is growing at about 14.5 %.

This livestock population serves as a vital asset for our country which will help in sustaining and propelling of Indian economy in future. India is the world's largest producer and consumer of milk and has the world's largest dairy herd, comprised of water buffalo and indigenous and crossbred cattle. India vast resource of livestock and poultry and the species wise population during the last three Censuses is given below:

S.No.	Species	17th Livestock Census 2003 (no.in millions)	18th Livestock Census 2007 (no.in millions)	19th Livestock Census 2012 (no. in millions)	Growth Rate (%) 2007-12
1.	Cattle	185.2	199.1	190.9	-4.10
2.	Buffalo	97.9	105.3	108.7	3.19
3.	Yaks	0.1	0.1	0.1	-7.64
4.	Mithuns	0.3	0.3	0.3	12.88
	Total Bovines	283.4	304.8	300.0	-1.57
5.	Sheep	61.5	71.6	65.07	-9.07
6.	Goat	124.4	140.5	135.2	-3.82
7.	Pigs	13.5	11.1	10.3	-7.54
8.	Other animals	2.2	1.7	1.48	-12.94
	Total Livestock	485	529.7	512.05	-3.33
9.	Poultry	489	648.8	729.2	12.39

The average yield of milk per day per animal at National level from different species during 2015-16 is given below:

Exotic cows (kg/day)	Cross-bred cows (kg/day)	Indigenous cows (kg/day)	Non-descript cows (kg/day)	Indigenous buffaloes (kg/day)	Non-descript buffalo (kg/day)	Goat (kg/day)
11.21	7.33	3.41	2.16	5.76	3.80	0.45

Despite this, the majority of the dairy industry in India is still highly unorganized and dominated by small and marginal dairy farmers. As the industry possesses huge untapped opportunities, it has attracted a number of private companies and investors. In addition, the Indian government has also been taking initiatives towards the development of the dairy sector by providing support to the milk cooperatives and rural milk producers.

Moreover, the sustained growth of the Indian economy has led to a rise in the spending power of consumers, rapid urbanization as well as changes in the dietary patterns. With an increase in the working population, hectic lifestyles and increasing health consciousness among the consumers, there has been a shift towards healthy and ready-to-eat dairy products. Apart from this, a large number of affluent consumers who prefer value-added and premium dairy products have further facilitated the growth of the organized dairy sector.

3. Breeds and productivity

India continues to be the largest producer of milk in the world. It has been achieved only because of huge number of livestock whereas an average milk production per animal is still less both in International as well as domestic standards. Several measures have been initiated by the government in order to increase the productivity one being, by introduction of new high yielding breeds. Consequently, a tremendous growth has been seen over the years, production has increased right from 102.6 million tons at the end of 2006-07 to 127.9 million tons in 2011-12. There has been an annual growth of 6.72% with per capita availability being around 337g/day in 2015-16.

Various cattle breed in India enlisted belows

Breed	Characteristics	Milk yield/ lactation
Indigenous breeds		
Gir	Originated in Gir forests of South Kathiawar in Gujarat Horns are peculiarly curved, giving a 'half moon' appearance. This breed is known for its hardiness and disease resistance	1200-1800 Kg
Red Sindhi	Originated in Karachi and Hyderabad (Pakistan) regions of undivided IndiaBullocks despite lethargic and slow can be used for road and field work	1250-1800 Kg
Sahiwal	Originated in Montgomery region of undivided India Best indigenous dairy breed Heavy breed with symmetrical body having loose skin	1400-2500 Kg
Deoni	Originated in Western Andra Pradesh Bullocks are suitable for heavy cultivation	638-1229 Kg
Indigenous draught breeds		
Hallikar	Originated from Karnataka. The breed is best known for its draught capacity and especially for its trotting ability	227-1134 Kg
Amrit mahal	The breed is best known for its draught capacity and especially for its trotting ability Horns are long and end in sharp black points	542 Kg
Khillari	Originated from Sholapur and Sitapur districts of Maharashtra Long horns turn forwards in a peculiar fashion Bullocks are fast and powerful	240 - 515 Kg
Kangayam	Originated in Kangayam The horns are spread apart, nearly straight with a slight curve backwards Moderate size with compact bodies	540 Kg
Bargur	Found around Bargur hills in Tamil Nadu Developed for work in uneven hilly terrains. Known for their speed and endurance in trotting	250 - 1300 Kg

Contd.

	Cautious in behaviour and tends to remain away from strangers.	
Umblacherry	Originated in Thanjavur of Tamil Nadu Suitable for wet ploughing and known for their strength and sturdiness	1200-1800 Kg
Pullikulam/ Alambadi	Commonly seen in cumbum valley of Madurai district in Tamil Nadu Mainly used for penning in the field and ploughing Dual Purpose	547 - 730 Kg
Tharparkar	Originated in Tharparkar district (Pakistan) of undivided India The bullocks are quite suitable for ploughing and casting	1800-2600 Kg
Hariana	Originated from Rohtak, Hisar, Jind and Gurgaon districts of Haryana The bullocks are powerful work animals	600 - 800 Kg
Kankrej	Originated from Southeast Rann of Kutch of Gujarat and adjoining Rajasthan The horns are lyre-shaped The gait of Kankrej is peculiar called as 1 ¼ paces (sawai chal) Kankrej is valued for fast, powerful, draught cattle. Useful in ploughing and carting	1738 Kg
Ongole	Home tract is Ongole taluk in Guntur district of Andhra Pradesh Large muscular breed with a well developed hump. Suitable for heavy draught work.	1000 Kg
Krishna Valley	Originated from black cotton soil of Karnataka Animals are large, having a massive frame with deep, loosely built short body	900 Kg
Exotic breeds		
Jersey	Originated from Jersey Island, U.K Smallest of the dairy types of cattle Dished forehead; compact and angular body. Economical producers of milk with 4.5% fat	5000 - 8000 Kg
Holestein Friesian	Originated from the northern parts of Netherlands Largest dairy breed and ruggedly built is shape and possess large udder	7200 - 9000 Kg
Brown Swiss	The mountainous region of Switzerland Breeds are rugged in nature and good milk production The Karan Swiss is the excellent crossbred cattle obtained by crossing this breed with Sahiwal cattle at NDRI, Karnal	5000 Kg
Red Dane	Originated in DenmarkIt is also a heavy breed	3000 - 4000 Kg
Ayrshire	Origin is Ayrshire in Scotland and considered asmost beautiful dairy breed. These are very active animals but hard to manage They do not produce as much milk or butter fat (only 4%) as some of the other dairy breeds	7000 - 8000 Kg
Guernsey	Originated from Small island of Guernsey in France The milk has a golden colour due to an exceptionally high content of beta carotene	6000 Kg

Contd.

	The Guernsey cow has many notable advantages for the dairy farmer over other breeds includes high efficiency of milk production, low incidence of calving difficulty and longevity.	
Buffalo indigenous breeds		
Murrah	Tightly curved horn is an important character of this breed. Most efficient milk and butter fat producers in India. Butter fat content is 7.83% Also used for the grading up of inferior local buffaloes	1500 to 2500 kgs
Surti	The horns are sickle shaped, moderately long and flat. The peculiarity of this breed is very high fat percentage in milk (8-12per cent)	1000 to 1300 kgs
Jaffrabadi	This is the heaviest Indian breed of buffalo The horns are heavy, inclined to droop at each side of the neck and then turning up at point (drooping horns) The udder is well developed with funnel shaped teats	1000 - 1200 kgs
Bhadawari	Medium sized buffalo The body is usually light or copper coloured is a peculiarity of this breed. Eye lids are generally copper or light brown colour. The fat content of milk varies from 6 to 12.5 per cent. This breed is an efficient converter of coarse feed into butterfat and is known for its high butter fat content.	800 - 1000 kgs
Nili Ravi	The peculiarity of the breed is the wall eyes Horns are very small and tightly coiled. Bullocks are good for heavy trotting work.	1500 - 1850 kgs
Mehsana	The breed is evolved out of crossbreeding between the Surti and the Murrah	1200 - 1500 kgs
Nagpuri	Sword shaped horns	700 - 1200 kgs
Toda	They are gregarious in natureHigh fat content of 8% Characteristic crescent shape of horns	500 kgs

4. Key challenging issues

For a profitable dairy farming, three key factors are (a) animal health management through balanced rationing and control of production diseases, (b) high milk yielding animals and (c) effective marketing linkage. Misfortunately all the three points need to be resolved for implementation so far dairy profession is concerned. High cost animal feed, low productivity of animals, improper marketing linkage and predominance of indigenous technologies continue to haunt the prospects of dairy farming in India.

To focus on the low milk production we need to look into the basic etiologies which usually vary from any infectious as well as production diseases to an imbalance in nutrition and genetic makeup. It has been estimated that the annual economic loss due to mastitis, an infectious disease of udder has been calculated to be Rs. 7165.51 crore; with equal figure both for cows (3649.56 crore) and buffaloes (3515.95 crore). Amongst the various challenges faced by the dairy farmers, low milk production which is also a main cause for India's dairy deficit will be topping the list followed by the others as low market price and low extension services. Besides this the treatment cost, managemental cost also are burden to farmers (PDADMAS 2011). Similarly, for ketosis which is a metabolic disease leading to sudden drop in milk yield the total estimated annual loss due to treatment, prevention, and others approaches is around $150 million for US dairymen (Littledike *et al* 1981). To discuss the role of dairy in enhancing farmers a meeting was organized by CII National Committee on Dairy in New Delhi under the chairmanship of Dr H Rahman, Deputy Director General – Animal Sciences, ICAR. It was discussed and brought into highlights that the indigenous breeds were versatile, produced quality milk and were not likely impacted by the climate change. Of the 118 million milch animals that we have in the country, around 19 million are crossbreeds, about 48 million are indigenous and 51 million are buffaloes. On an average the crossbreds give 10.7 kg (milk) per day, the indigenous give around 2.3 to 2.4 kg, and buffaloes, yield about 4.8kg of milk with much higher fat content.

Similarly, proceedings in meeting of ICAR-Agricultural Technology Application Research Institute, Kolkata emphasized on breed improvement through the production of superior quality bulls, production of superior quality semen along with the conservation of high valued animal genetic resources.

In order to double farmer's income, there is a need to increase farm productivity, replace the low yielding animals, improve market access, and also to develop the industrial and service sectors, where the surplus farmers can find work. Fundamentally, there are three ways in which income of farmers may be enhanced, viz., increasing the gross income, reducing the costs and stabilizing the income.

4.1. Cold chain maintenance

In order to keep milk and its products which are highly perishable, fresh and maintain their shelf life, they are to be maintained at an optimum temperature of 4°C. This temperature is to be maintained right from the farmer's stage, during transportation and storage. Studies have shown that for every 2°C increase in the storage temperature of milk reduces its shelf life by 50% and adversely affects the quality causing problems such as sourness, unpleasant taste and odor etc. A cold chain is a temperature-controlled supply chain. An unbroken cold chain refers to maintenance of optimum temperature with an uninterrupted series of storage and distribution activities. On national average milk chilling is delayed by an hour at different collection and chilling centre's. Any break in the cold chain will lead to huge economic losses to dairy industry due to which dairy farmer's move away from dairy occupation looking out towards any alternative source of occupation. So in order to prevent that Apex body and other Dairy governing institutions have been investing money with the help of World Bank and other prestigious financial institutions for strengthening the cold chain level of Dairy Industry in India.

Bulk Milk Cooler (BMC) is one of cold chain equipment which can help farmer in maintaining the optimum temperature. BMC level set up requires on an average twenty-five lakhs including all milk chilling equipment, site readiness, DG, cleaning equipment and other accessories. Nearly 26,000 BMCs are being used by different dairy companies in our country. In dairy industry, altogether this technology is still in nascent stage and not being actively deployed. With remote monitoring cold chain solutions, the working capability of entire dairy supply chain can be completely revolutionized to modernize and digitally uplift the rural dairy economy. It will serve as the crucial aspect in making rural India active digitally and will also help in strengthening of dairy supply chain. Cold chain monitoring solution has the capability to turn around of looking at cold chain logistics domain as well.

4.2. Skill development of farmers

'Skill upgradation to help build a better India and if we ought to move towards development then skill development should be our mission' as stated by Indian Prime Minister Mr Narendra Modi. Dairy farming is much more complex and needs to be managed scientifically. Farmers involved in dairy management require broad knowledge, wide variety of multi-tasking skills and keen business acumen ranging from dairy herd improvement to hygienic milking. Few of the considerable points that dairy owners need to keep in mind while milking is as follows:

- Preparing milking equipments and bulk tank for milking,
- Ensuring proper cleaning of equipments before milking
- Wearing gloves while milking to help prevent spread of mass-causing organisms.
- Following recommended pre-milking preparation of cattle before milking.
- Milking cows in an orderly, proper and consistent manner.
- Farmers should make sure to check on to the treatment records in order to keep that milk separate from the bulk.
- Noticing any illness whether in mass or individually, and referring to treatment regimen as soon as possible.

- Cleaning of milking parlor, holding area and bulk tank room in order to maintain the sanitation and prevent any possible loci of infection.
- Besides this farmer should also keep fair knowledge of feed, timely feeding of animals, treatment of sick, proper care of calf etc

4.3. Unorganization

170 million matric tons milk produced in India as of now, 90% comes from rural area and of this almost 80% comes from unorganized and backyard farms. For the backyard farms, the main challenge is the reluctance in acceptance of balanced nutrition for their animals. Most of them still feed their animals in the traditional way with unbalanced feed, forage and supplements and this leads to less than expected milk output from the animals. The answer towards improvement lies in educating the farmers on the importance of balanced nutrition as per DMI / Protein /Energy needs. The industry players are adding a lot of focus on such extension activities but still lot more is needed to be done.

For semi-organized dairy farms, the key challenge is the improvement in the herd efficiency and maintaining the consistent milk production round the year. The solution lies in having a robust transition management and reproduction efficiency management. Also using quality and branded feed as per the life cycle need of the animals will also help.

For organized dairy farms, the key challenge is the economic availability of forage and maximizing the Income over Feed Cost on day to day basis. The solution lies in having a robust silage and TMR facility. Also, it is critical to have an excellent forward integration with the market, for being able to sell the output as value added milk and milk products with better realization price of the produce.

4.4. Women Empowerment

Of all the major rural enterprises, dairy is considered as an important instrument of economic and social change to supplement the income and employment to the rural sector in general and rural women in particular. Women are the prime decision makers in dairy production activities such as utilization of milk, care of pregnant animals and calves, bringing of fodder and feeding of concentrates (Veeranna and Singh 2004). Various micro level studies highlight women's significant role in dairy production. Nearly 50% of rural population constitutes of Women, who play an active role in all spheres of economic life and contribute richly towards national income.

Mrs. Ela Bhatt, well renowned and winner of prestigious Magsaysay Award highlighted the need for ensuring a place for women in the dairy development. For their empowerment and economic well being, women's access to training in modern dairy farming and cooperative management is essential. The employment of women is an index of their economic and social status in society. The Operation Flood Program (OFP), one of the world's largest and most successful dairy development program which was launched in 1970, has been playing an important role in dairy marketing in different parts of the country. This program recognizes that dairy farming at the household level is largely the domain of women, the products and income from dairy farming can be controlled by women and that dairy farming can be practiced on a small scale as well.

The process of dairy development would be incomplete and lop sided, unless farm women are fully involved in it. "Just as a bird cannot fly with its one wing only, a nation will not march forward if the women are left behind - *Swami Vivekanand*.

Unless constraints faced by farm women in dairy are identified and overcome, developmental programs cannot be implemented successfully. In 2012-13, it was estimated that around 2476 women (Dairy Co-operative Societies) DCS were functioning in the country in selected states. Out of 9.2 million, total membership in DCS, 18 per cent were of women (1.63 million).

5. Clean milk production

The need for clean milk production not only refers to production of quantum milk but should also be free from debris, microbes and must remain so, till it is consumed. Traditionally, villages were the prime locus of milk production in country. Even today the bulk of country's milk supply comes from the rural areas. The import of milk products has necessitated the production of quality milk by our farmers. Hygienic environment was not a priority back in those days, rather farmers used to utilize the milk for their own household; they didn't even sell the surplus production. Clean milk can be produced by good animal Husbandry practices in villages, small farms with the help of Dairy Development Boards and different Cooperative Dairy Federations. Raw milk quickly becomes sour when it is stored for long periods at high ambient temperatures because of the inherent lactic acid bacteria and contaminating microorganisms from milk vessels or the environment break down the lactose in milk to lactic acid. When sufficient lactic acid has accumulated, the milk becomes sour and coagulates. Raw milk that contains too much lactic acid, even if it does not appear to be curdled, will coagulate when heated. This makes the milk unfit for sale. The first and foremost step to clean milk production should be education and training of milk producers on hygiene, housekeeping, sanitation, milking methods and good animal husbandry practices.

5.1. Awareness and training

Extension programs including educational aids should be organized inorder to make farmers aware about the hygienic conditions and above all the importance of clean milk production. They should be made aware of proper handling of raw milk from udder to further processing, maintenance of hygienic environment while milking etc.

5.2. Feeding practices

Procurement of feed and fodder from a clean reliable source so as to ensure no direct or indirect contamination in the milk.

5.3. Housing management

Animal shed should be properly cleaned before milking. Besides keeping proper supply of electricity and light, there should be proper disposal of dung, urine or any other waste product.

5.4. Handling of milking vessels

Vessels should be preferably made of stainless steel and should be washed before and after milking with hot water and detergent. A milker should maintain their personal hygiene as well for proper disposal of milk.

5.4. Udder Hygiene

Surface of udder is known to carry micro-organisms, which may be due to contact with the dirty bedding stuff, splashing urine etc. After milking the teat canal is open for 2 hrs and it is during these hours that micro-organisms penetrate and multiply within the canal leading to mastitis. So, keeping udder clean and healthy is as important as other hygienic conditions which are to be kept during milking. There are many procedures for udder hygiene prior to milking such as:

- Washing by spraying water and wiping of teats
- Washing of teats with a cloth immersed in warm disinfectant solution and drying with a dry cloth
- Immersing of teats in disinfectant and wiping with a paper cloth.
- Cleaning of udder post milking with disinfectant is also important so as to remove the milk residues which can serve as the breeding ground for the environmental pathogens.

5.6. Health management

Regular monitoring of sick animals, so as to separate their milk from the healthy ones. Milking of healthy ones should be done first. Sick animals should be kept in a separate shed away from milking parlor.

5.7. Milk collection and transportation

Provision of cooling tanks so as to reduce the bacteriological load in the milk immediately after collection will be of great help. Excessive agitation while transportation should be avoided. When milk is agitated, the milk fat is destabilized which becomes easily oxidized.

6. Antibiotic residues in milk and milk products

Antibiotics have been in use in animal husbandry from last 3 decades, and an unprecedented use of antibiotic has not only lead to the development of resistance, but also lead to the presence of antibiotic residues in edible items and milk and its products are no different to it. Proper withdrawal time of antibiotics if not followed leads to presence of antibiotic residues in milk which eventually leads to adverse allergic reactions and also development of resistant strains. Because of the public health significance, milk and milk products contaminated with antibiotics beyond a given residue levels, are considered unfit for human consumption (Plumb 2005). The presence of even minute quantities of residues has lead to many problems in dairy industry including:

- Inadequate curdling of milk and improper ripening of cheeses during their manufacture
- Decreased acid and flavor production during the manufacture of buttermilk and similar products
- Diminished starter culture growth when propagated in reconstituted skim milk
- Resulting into inferior quality products often leading to breakdown of machines and huge cost of repair as well

The hazards can be categorized in to two types as direct - short term hazards and indirect - long term hazards, according to duration of exposure to residues and the time onset of health effects. The direct health hazards includes the health effects caused due to excretion of drug in milk, as an example the beta-lactam group of antibiotics regardless of their low concentration in milk causes allergic hypersensitive reaction in sensitized individual immediately after consumption whereas chronic toxic effects occurring with prolonged exposure to low levels of antibiotics include carcinogenicity, teratogenicity, reproductive effects, development of antibiotic resistance bacteria in treated animals and disruption of normal human flora in the intestine. Antibacterial agents like tetracyclines, nitrofurans and sulfonamides are used as feed additives in cattle feed which may excrete in milk and sometimes associated with toxicological effects in human (Vragovic *et al.*, 2012),. Many organizations are involved in monitoring of this residue menace and they have set a maximum residue levels (MRLs) for livestock products based on regular monitoring, control and surveillance programs, and following high concentrations products are certified illegal for sale in order to prevent public health menace.

Over the last few decades, efforts have been directed towards improving treatment efficacy, owing to the high frequency of clinical mastitis and the demand for high quality milk. Maximum use of antibiotics is in the food animals and for the treatment of mastitis in dairy animals. Mastitis directly affects the quality of milk and major cause of antibiotics residue in milk.

Acute clinical mastitis affects dairy cows throughout the world and has a substantial impact on farm economics, milk quality and cow welfare. Dairy producers and veterinarians must undertake, clinical mastitis treatment decisions or recommendations on a frequent basis. Despite more than a century of research and tremendous amount of field experience, clinical mastitis remains a frustrating disease to treat. Some cows die, become agalactic, or fail to return to profitable milk production despite aggressive and expensive treatment. The outcome of clinical mastitis is influenced by a variety of factors, including the effectiveness of the cow's immune response, the severity of mastitis at the onset of treatment, the duration of infections at the onset of treatment, the causative pathogen, and the drug regimens and ancillary measures used.

The choice of a suitable antibiotic is very difficult task for veterinary practitioner. There are numerous factors to consider when selecting an antimicrobial agent, and the route (parenteral or intramammary) to use, for the treatment of mastitis. The site of infection needs to be located and the type of microbe established. Then the *in-vitro* antimicrobial sensitivity of the organism and the minimal inhibitory concentration need to be determined. The likely ability to penetrate the area, the action of the antibiotic in the local environment and the maintenance of an effective concentration at the area must be considered. The selection also has to include the possibility of any potential toxic side effects as well as meat and milk withholding times (Andrews 2004). Once all these factors have been taken into consideration, the drug to be used, its dosage, route and frequency of administration can be determined.

7. Control of production diseases

Production diseases like mastitis, ketosis, milk fever, FMD etc lead to huge economic losses as they have their direct effect on milk production. In India the annual economic loss due to mastitis has been calculated to be Rs. 7165.51 crores; losses being almost same for cows (3649.56 crores) and buffaloes (3515.95 crores). Besides this the treatment cost, management cost also are burden to farmers. Financial losses in ketosis are from decreased milk, decreased body weight, cost of treatment, disposal of cows that have recurring cases, and possibly death. If treatment, prevention, and other costs could be determined, an annual loss in ketosis is approaching $150 million for US dairymen is probable. The average cost per case of milk fever has been estimated at $334, based on direct treatment cost and estimated production losses. Control of Production Diseases often involves various disciplines and therefore calls for a "multivariate approach". A routine monitoring and causal analysis of periparturient traits and diseases, production, fertility and abortions are carried out, relevant data are processed, and monitoring reports are issued routinely. Disease control programs should be developed in parallel with the increase in animal production in order to improve animal health, animal welfare and the production of healthy foods. Improvements are carried out, the emphasis being on:

- Reduction of the probability of an introduction of exotic livestock diseases in India.
- Minimization of the risk of national spread of a disease by restricting hazardous animal trade practices and improving biosecurity measures in peacetime.
- Effective disease surveillance and early detection of diseases.
- Appropriate and effective actions for the control of disease outbreaks.

8. Value addition of milk

India serves as the oyster for the global dairy industry, with lot more left unfolded and yet to be explored. Our dairy industry can serve for various entrepreneurs with opportunities galore for them. Value addition in agriculture predominantly offers a means to increase, rejuvenate and stabilize farm income. There is a phenomenal scope for innovations in product development, packaging and presentation.

Some of the points are enlisted below:

- Steps should be taken to introduce value-added products like shrikhand, ice cream, paneer, khoa, flavored milk, dairy sweets, etc. This will lead to a greater presence and flexibility in the market place along with opportunities in the field of brand building.

- Addition of cultured products like yogurt and cheese lend further strength – both in terms of utilization of resources and presence in the market place.
- Opening up of the opportunities in milk proteins through casein, caseinates and other dietary proteins, further opening up of export opportunities.
- Addition of infant foods, geriatric foods and nutritionals can help in adding another aspect.

9. Top 5 dairy brands of India

- Gujarat Co-Operative Milk Marketing Federation – AMUL
- Karnataka Milk Federation – NANDINI
- Rajasthan Co-Operative Dairy Federation – SARAS
- Bihar Milk Federation - SUDHA
- Tamil Nadu Co-operative Milk Producers' Federation Limited – Aavin

10. Indian policy

Rashtriya Gokul Mission was started by the government in December 2014 for the purpose of conserving and developing indigenous breeds. Under this scheme, so far proposals worth Rs.1,348 crore from 28 states have been approved and Rs.503 crore has been released. Among other initiatives, Rashritya Gokul Mission also includes setting up of Gokul Gram. These will act as centre for development of indigenous breeds and a dependable source for supply of high genetic breeding. Setting up of Dairy Infrastructure Development Fund (DIDF) by National Dairy Development Board (NDDB) for the implementation of National Dairy Plan (NDP) is another initiative, with basic aim being to increase the milk production, decrease the calving interval, age at first calving, decrease the load of diseases for better output, improving the genetic makeup etc. Enlisting the opportunities that still lie ahead of us in the dairy industry is as follows:

- Expanding market will create enormous job and self employment opportunities.
- Increase in investment opportunities as economy is growing at the rate of 8% of GDP
- Increased export potential for indigenous milk products.
- Increasing demand for dairy products becomes income elastic.
- Transform the quality of life in rural India where a lot needs to be done.

- Utilization of byproducts of the dairy industry for manufacturing value added products (VAP) for world market.

11. Opportunities and challenges in the Indian dairy industry

Dairy products are a major source of cheap and nutritious food to millions of people in India and the only acceptable source of animal protein for a large vegetarian segment of the Indian population, particularly among the landless, small and marginal farmers and women. Dairying has been considered as one of the activities aimed at alleviating the poverty and unemployment, especially in the rural areas in the rain-fed and drought-prone regions. In India, about three-fourth of the population live in rural areas and about 38% of them are poor. In 1986-87, about 73% of rural households own livestock. Small and marginal farmers account for three-quarters of these households owning livestock, raising 56% of the bovine and 66% of the sheep population. According to the National Sample Survey of 1993-94, livestock sector produces regular employment to about 9.8 million persons in principal status and 8.6 million in subsidiary status, which constitute about 5% of the total work force. The progress in this sector will result in a more balanced development of the rural economy.

11.1. Milk Processing

The milk processing industry is small compared to the huge amount of milk produced every year. Only 10% of all the milk is delivered to some 400 dairy plants. An issue of economic significance is the unorganized sector of milkmen, vendors who collects the milk from local producers and sell the milk in both, urban and non-urban areas, which handles around 65-70% of the national milk production. In the organized dairy industry, the cooperative milk processors have a 60% market share. The cooperative dairies process 90% of the collected milk as liquid milk, whereas the private dairies process and sell only 20% of the milk collected as liquid milk and 80% for other dairy products with a focus on value-added products.

11.2. Domestic Consumption

The huge volume of milk produced in India is consumed almost entirely by the Indian population itself, in a 50-50 division between urban and nonurban areas. Increasingly, important consumers of the dairy industry are fast-food chains and food and non-food industries using dairy ingredients in a wide range of products.

11.3. Trade

In spite of having largest milk production, India is a very minor player in the world market. India was primarily an import dependent country till early seventies. Most of the demand-supply gaps of liquid milk requirements for urban consumers were met by importing anhydrous milk fat / butter and dry milk powders. But with the onset of Operation Flood Program, the scenario dramatically changed and commercial imports of dairy products came to a halt except occasional imports of very small quantities. In the 1990s, India started exporting surplus dairy commodities, such as SMP, WMP, butter and ghee. The Agricultural and Processed Food Products Export Development Authority (APEDA) regulated the export and import of dairy products till early 1990s. However, in the new EXIM Policy announced in April 2000, the Union Government has allowed the free import and export of most dairy products.

The major destinations for Indian dairy products are Bangladesh (23.1%), UAE (15.4%), US (15.6%) and Philippines (8.9%). In terms of products, SMP is the most important product accounting for about 63% of total export volume, followed by ghee and butter (11.7%) and WMP. Export figures clearly demonstrate that the Indian dairy export is still in its infancy and the surpluses are occasional. Indigenous milk products and desserts are becoming popular with the ethnic population spread all over the world. Therefore, the export demand for these products will increase and hence, there is a great potential for export.

On the other hand, there has been a sharp increase in import of dairy products (especially milk powders) after trade liberalization. As per the latest report of Foreign Trade Statistics of December 2004, the imports of dairy products (milk and cream) has reached a cumulative total of 22.145 million tons for the period April – March 2004, as compared to only 14.73 million tons for the same period during the previous year. The main reasons for sharp rise in imports are huge export subsidies given by developed countries (mainly the US and EU).

12. Initiatives required

The demand for quality dairy products is rising globally and the countries which are expected to benefit most from any increase in world demand for dairy products are those which have low cost of production. Therefore, in order to increase the competitiveness of Indian dairy industry, efforts should be made to reduce cost of production *via* increasing productivity of animals, better health care and breeding facilities and management of dairy animals.

It is imperative to develop proper production, processing and marketing infrastructure if India has to emerge as an exporting country which is capable of meeting international quality requirements. A comprehensive strategy for producing quality and safe dairy products should be formulated with suitable legal backup.

Focus on buffalo milk based specialty Dairy industry in India is also unique with regard to availability of a large proportion of buffalo milk. Thus, India can focus on buffalo milk based specialty products, like Mozzarella cheese, tailored to meet the needs of the target consumers. There has been import of value-added products and export of lower value products with the trade liberalization, despite the attempts of Indian companies to develop their product range, it could well be that in the future, more value-added products will be imported and lower value products will be exported. The dairy industry has to prepare itself to meet this challenge.

13. New challenges of globalization and trade

The Indian cooperatives are expected to play a predominant role in the dairy industry in future. India is attaining its past glory and is once again becoming *Doodh Ka Sagar*. But, what percentage of this *Doodh Ka Sagar* is handled by the cooperatives just a little over 7%. Since liberalization of the dairy sector in 1991, a very large number of private sector companies / firms have, despite MMPO, established dairy factories in the country. The share of the total milk processing capacity by private sector is 44% of total installed capacity of 73 MLPD (Million Litres Per Day) in the country. Therefore, the total share of the organized sector, both cooperatives as well as the private sector is barely 12%. What is more concern is that as much as 88% share of the total milk production is contributed by the unorganized sector which is mainly selling sub-standard, unpasteurized milk more often than not adulterated with harmful chemicals. Besides, growth in milk production is likely to continue at the present rate of 4.4% in the near future. Demand for milk, at current rate of income growth is estimated to grow at 7% per annum. Interestingly, demand for milk is expected to grow steadily over the next two decades as the low income rural and urban families who have higher expenditure elasticity would also increase their income due to new economic environment.

14. Potential of the dairy enterprise

India has progressed from being deficient in milk production at 20 million MT in 1970 to becoming the world's largest milk producer at 160 million MT, accounting for 18.5 per cent of global milk production. India's dairy industry is expected to maintain 15 per cent compounded annual growth (CAGR) over 2016-20, and attain value of Rs 9.4 trillion on rising consumerism, a report said. "India's dairy industry is worth Rs 5.4 trillion by value, having grown at 15 per cent CAGR during 2010-16. Going ahead, the dairy industry is expected to maintain

15 per cent CAGR over 2016-20, and attain value of Rs 9.4 trillion on rising consumerism.

The Union government implemented the Central Scheme National Dairy Plan - Phase 1 during 2012-17 to improve productivity of dairy cooperatives through several input activities. Investments by private players in the domestic dairy sector is also expected to further augment milk productivity, it explained. India's milk production is expected to outperform global production and grow at a similar 4.2 per cent CAGR to 185 million MT per annum, and surpass EU to emerge the largest dairy producer by 2020. India has a potential of 15-30 per cent plus growth in VADP like cheese, whey, UHT milk over next few years. Led by rising disposable income, and growing consumer preference for branded and value-added milk and milk products, investments by organized players also in the sector has been on the rise.

Indian Dairy Industry holds an inimitable space in the country for its high employment potential and for ensuring the availability of nutritious yet affordable food for India's ever increasing population. Getting the tag of largest milk producer was made possible by Operation Flood and the historic dairy cooperative movement; and as production increased, dairy industry started showing promising growth potential. Rising disposable incomes and growing demand for dairy products are likely to fuel the Indian dairy industry's growth over the next few years. According to latest research report, "Indian Dairy Industry Outlook 2022", with an annual output of 138 Million Tons, India is the largest producer of milk in the world.

Indian dairy industry also offers good opportunities to both domestic and foreign investors for entry and expansion. Due to their rich nutritional qualities, dairy products' consumption has been growing exponentially in the country; and considering various facts and figures, it is anticipated that milk production in India will further grow at a CAGR of around 15% between 2018 and 2023. Thus it has enormous scope for women empowerment and socio-economic transformation of rural India.

15. References

Andrew AH .2004. Antimicrobial agents. In: Bovine mastitis: Diseases and husbandry of cattle edited by Andrew AH, Blowey RW, Boyd H and Eddy RG, 2nd ed., Blackwel publishing Co., pp. 1035-1044.

Annual report .2016-17. Department of Animal Husbandry, Dairying & Fisheries, Ministry of Agriculture & Farmers Welfare Government of India

Belhekar S and Dash S 2016. Role of Dairy Industry in Rural Development in India. *Indian Journal of Research*. 5(11): 509-510.

Bishop JR and White CH. 1984. Antibiotic residue detection in milk-a review. *Journal of Food Protection*, 47(8), pp.647-652

Bureau, F.P.J. 2016. Significance of dairy industry. *The Free Press Journal.*

Chennakrishnan P .2011. Dairy farming the rural cash cow. *Market survey.* 10-13

FAO. 2003. Project on Livestock Industrialization, Trade and Social-Health-Environment Impacts in Developing Countries by L.D. Christopher, A.N. Clare, M.T. Marites, FAO corporate document repository.

IDC .2013. The Economic Importance of Dairying. *International Dairy Federation.*

Madhusudhan, L. 2015. Agriculture role on Indian Economy. *Business and Economic Journal,* 6:176.

Marth EH and Ellickson BE .1959. Problems created by the presence of antibiotics in milk and milk products - A review. *Journal of Milk Food Technology,* 22: 266-272.

Maurice L, Jerry C, Lindsay K. and Keithly J. 2017. India's Dairy Sector: Structure, Performance, and Prospects. A Report from the Economic Research Service .

Nargunde AS. 2013. Role of Dairy Industry in Rural Development. *International Journal of Advanced Research in Engineering and Technology.* 4(2): 8-16.

Plumb DC. 2005. Veterinary drug handbook. 5th edn, Black well publishing professional, Ames, USA, 826- 862.

Vragoviæ N, Bažuliæ D and Zdolec N. 2012. Dietary exposure assessment of ß-lactam antibiotic residues in milk on Croatian market. *Croatian Journal of Food Science and Technology, 4*(1): 81-84.

16

Weather Forecasting and Advisory: An Aid for Sustainable Agricultural Transformation

Mahender Singh, Rohit Sharma* Charu Sharma and Bharat Singh Ghanghas**

Agrometeorology Section, SKUASU-J, Chatha, Jammu, Jammu and Kashmir, India
**Gramin Krishi Mousam Seva, AMFU, RARS, Rajouri, Jammu and Kashmir, India*
*** CCSHAU, Hisar-125004, Haryana, India*

1. Introduction
2. Need of weather forecasting for agriculture
3. Weather forecasting system in India
4. Agro-meteorological field units and agro-advisory
5. System of agro-meteorological advisory dissemination
6. Use of satellite data to derive new products and alerts
7. Seamless weather forecast
8. Climate risk management through agro-met advisory services
9. Crop yield forecasting
10. Adoption of climate smart agriculture
11. Future needs and strategies
12. Conclusion
13. *References*

ABSTRACT

Losses and benefits in agricultural production are associated with various weather parameters. So prediction of weather systems in different spatial and temporal scale over the Indian region therefore assumes considerable socio-economic importance. Meteorological information also plays an important role in the following operations in agriculture. The meteorological services can help the farmers & the planners exploit the potential of good weather and minimize the impact of bad weather as there exist tremendous opportunities for applications of meteorology in both day to day and long term planning in agriculture and such applications could contribute substantially to promote sustainable agriculture and poverty alleviation and the management of agrometeorological data is the key to these applications. Therefore, the area and input intensive agriculture is leading us into an era of unsustainable agricultural growth as the crucial components of sustainable agricultural production and distribution system such as integration of natural biological cycles and controls; protection and renewal of soil fertility and the natural resource base; optimization of the use of nonrenewable resources and of on-farm & off- farm inputs; ensuring dependable farm income. Hence, the meteorological information may help the farmer make the most efficient use of natural resources, with the aim of improving agricultural production both in quantity and quality. It becomes more and more important to supply meteorological information blended with weather sensitive management operations before the start of cropping season in order to adapt the agricultural system to increased weather variability. Subsequent to this, weather forecast based Agro-meteorological advisories become vital to stabilize their yields through management of agro-climatic resources as well as other inputs such as irrigation, fertilizer and pesticides. The main emphasis of the existing AAS system is to collect and organize climate/weather, soil and crop information, and to amalgamate them with weather forecast to assist farmers in taking management decisions. This has helped to develop and apply operational tools to manage weather related uncertainties through agro-meteorological applications for efficient agriculture in rapidly changing environments. Hence, weather information and advisories have assumed greater significance under the increased variability in the changing climate. Thus, Weather forecasting and advisory has become an indispensable aid for sustainable agro-transformation

Keywords: Weather forecasting, crop yield, climate change, agro-advisory

1. Introduction

Agricultural production depends upon many factors, of which weather is one of the major components. Weather varies with space and time, hence, its forecast can help to minimize the farm losses through proper management of agricultural operations. The complete avoidance of all farm losses due to weather factor is not possible but it can be minimized to some extent by making adjustments through timely and accurate information of weather forecast. Weather forecast and weather based agromet advisories help in increasing the economic benefit to the farmers by suggesting them the suitable management practices according to the weather conditions. Weather forecast also provides guidelines for selection of crops best suited to the anticipated climatic conditions. The objective of the weather forecasting is to advice the farmers on the actual and expected weather and its impact on the various day-to-day farming operations i.e. sowing, weeding, time of pesticides spray, irrigation scheduling, fertilizer application etc. and overall crop management. Weather forecast helps to increase agriculture production, reduce losses, risks, reduce costs of inputs, improve quality of yield, increase efficiency in the use of water, labor, and energy and reduce pollution with judicious use of agricultural chemicals.

2. Need of Weather Forecasting for Agriculture

Weather is one of the most important factors determining success or failure of agricultural production. It has a profound influence on the growth, development and yields of a crop, incidence of pests and diseases, water needs and fertilizer requirements in terms of differences in nutrient mobilization due to water stresses and timeliness and effectiveness of prophylactic and cultural operations on crops. From sowing to harvesting the entire life cycle of a crop is dependent on weather. Any variability in the weather during the cropping season, such as delay in the monsoon, excessive rains, flood, droughts, spells of too-high or too-low temperatures would affect the crop growth and finally the quality and quantity of the yield. Weather and climatic information plays a major role before and during the cropping season and if provided in advance can be helpful in inspiring the farmer to organize and activate their own resources in order to reap benefits. The sensitiveness of crops to weather depends upon the stage and state of the crop, its variety, the season, the climatic zone etc. So the type of weather information and advisories needed by users is area, season and crop specific (De 1992). Rathore *et al* (2001) discussed the weather forecasting scheme operational at National Centre for Medium Range Weather Forecast for issuing location specific weather forecast five days in advance. The effect of climate on agriculture is related to variability in local climates rather than in global climate patterns. The challenges facing agriculture in the country are ever increasing. In the first place agriculture is highly weather dependent and hence subject to its variability. Secondly, the possible impacts of climate change may pose major challenges. Finally, the very sustainability of intensive agriculture using present technologies is being questioned in the context of Global Climate Change debate. Hence it is imperative that weather and climate variability aspects are well understood so as to formulate more sustainable policies and strategies to promote food production and food security. The importance of forecasting for different weather parameters in various agricultural operations management are as:

a) Rainfall

In irrigated areas the advisory helps to decide whether to irrigate or not to irrigate at critical/moisture sensitive stages of the crop at which the irrigation is essential which by and large helps in optimizing the plant growth, development and ultimately the crop yields in consonance with other input factors. Rainfall forecasts help in deciding the irrigation frequency, sowing time, inter culture operations like weeding and hoeing, harvesting and post harvest operations. Rainfall forecasts also help the farmers by providing information regarding water availability period for the crops based on moisture adequacy index (MAI) and proper times of fertilizer application, so as to have judicious and efficient use of inputs (fertilizers) by the crop.

In the rainfed areas, rainfall and no rainfall forecasts help in formulating contingency measures for expected adverse weather conditions by suggesting farmers suitable technology like sprinkler or drip irrigation, use of hormones and mulching to avoid heat load, conserve soil moisture etc. All this will help the farmers to plan before hand the various activities to be under taken to counter the effect of adverse eventualities arising out of the expected probabilities of abnormal rainfall.

b) Maximum and Minimum Temperatures

Forecasting of air temperatures also help the farmers to take necessary measures before hand to save their field and fruit crops against cold or heat injury. Maximum temperature forecasts also help the farmers to take care of their cattle, sheep, goat, poultry birds and bee hives with regard to their proper feeding, watering and maintaining ventilation during summer season. However, forecasting of minimum temperature helps in adoption of requisite plant protection options in advance to shield crops from frost injury during winter season. The mean temperature helps in the forecasting of various insect pests in different crops.

c) Relative humidity

The prediction of relative humidity with temperature helps in providing forewarning of insect pests occurrences enabling the farmers to take up prophylactic cares against such warnings in advance and this may help to avoid the yield losses which otherwise are likely to occur in various crops viz; 50% in vegetables sand 20-25 % in mustard crop etc.

d) Wind speed and Direction

The wind speed and direction forecast is highly useful in deciding the direction of movement while taking plant protection measures, broadcasting of fertilizers and insecticide applications so as to have their judicious use and better efficacy etc.

3. Weather Forecasting System in India

India experiences large spectra of weather events having spatial scale of less than 1 km to more than 1000 km and temporal range of less than an hour to more than a week. Different parts of the country experience different kinds of weather conditions influence by different weather elements in various seasons such as:

Winter season (Jan- Feb) is characterized by Western Disturbances, Cold Wave, Fog;

Pre-Monsoon (Mar-May) by Cyclonic Disturbances, Heat Wave, Thunder Storms, Squalls, Hail Storm, Tornado;

Monsoon (Jun-Sep) by Southwest Monsoon Circulation, Monsoon Disturbances;

Post-Monsoon (Oct- Dec) by Northeast Monsoon, Cyclonic Disturbances.

Indian monsoon is a field of active research all over the world as it is a unique weather event which covers several oceans and continents but depicts its characteristic phase over Indian sub-continent. The monsoon rains are crucial for agricultural production in the country as most parts of the country depend on this rain for day-to-day agricultural operations. Meteorological Department in the country was one of first scientific departments which started scientific research on weather systems as early as in 18th century.

Prediction of weather systems in different spatial and temporal scale over the Indian region assumes considerable importance. Several organizations are engaged in developing techniques for prediction of these systems. In the recent past, IMD has made enormous improvement in the accuracy and lead time of forecasts for various usages including AAS. IMD has made Global Forecast System (GFS T574/L64, based on NCEP) operational in December 2009, implemented on IBM based High Power Computing Systems (HPCS). This incorporates Global Statistical Interpolation (GSI) scheme as the global data assimilation for the forecast up to 7 days. In horizontal, it resolves 574 waves (> 22 km in the tropics) in spectral triangular truncation. The model has 64 vertical levels (hybrid; sigma and pressure). Currently, it runs twice in a day (00 UTC and 12 UTC). In addition to this, the meso-scale forecast system WRF (ARW) with 3DVAR data assimilation is being operated daily twice, at 27, 9 and 3 km horizontal resolutions for the forecast up to 3 days using initial and boundary conditions from the IMD GFS-574/L64 (horizontal resolution over the tropics ~ 22 km). At ten other regional centres of IMD, very high resolution mesoscale models (WRF at 3 km resolution) are made operational. NWP based objective forecast products are prepared to support cyclone warning service. Doppler weather and mesoscale dynamical model based now cast system was made operational for the National Capital of Delhi. IMD has started issuing quantitative district level (about 640 districts) weather forecast of up to 5 days from 1st June, 2008. A full range of NWP products at different spatial and temporal scale are routinely made available on the IMD web site www.imd.gov.in. These offices undertake value addition to these products twice a week on Tuesday and Friday and communicate to 130 Agro Met Field Units (AMFUs) located with State Agriculture Universities (SAUs), ICAR etc.

Next generation model will target more accurate ways to initialize forecasts by improving data assimilation techniques, more accurate parameterizations and improved estimates of uncertainty in the modeling system and in forecasts. Coupling of the atmosphere to the underlying surface – land and ocean – is important and also critical for forecast lead times extending into fortnightly and monthly timescales. To adequately resolve the transient systems responsible for rainfall during monsoon and their movement, it is important to use models with high resolutions both in the horizontal and vertical.

By 2020, plan is to run global models of about 10 km resolution with about 100 levels in vertical (high-resolution GFS such as T1148-L64 (16 km) to T1500-L128 (13 km), and regional models with about one km resolution. The physical parameterizations need to be improved/ optimized for higher resolution models. As the model grid size approaches the horizontal scales of moist deep convection, special attention will be given to the parameterization of moist processes. Cloud resolving models are required to be embedded in the global and meso-scale models as clouds are the major cause of uncertainty in present day models. All current and future global NWP system will have to address the uncertainty inherent in the prediction over all temporal and spatial scales. The challenge is to increase the number of ensemble members which will further improve its value for all applications. The products are disseminated to Regional Meteorological Centres and Meteorological Centres of IMD located in different states.

Recent studies suggest that an interactive upper-ocean in a high resolution coupled general circulation model significantly enhance the prediction skill of weather in medium range.

Experiments at ECMWF and other centers have started showing the benefits of coupling in improving the skill in medium and 2 weeks to 1month monsoon forecasts. Therefore, ocean model with very high vertical resolution (1 m) in the upper ocean has to be coupled with a higher frequency (1 hour) of interaction with atmosphere model. Ocean data assimilation will be required to initialize the ocean model properly. Similarly a land surface model with its assimilation has to be also coupled to form the full 'Coupled Earth System Model'.

3.1. Weather Forecasting

Weather forecasting is the application of current technology and science to predict the state of the atmosphere for a future time and for a specific location or in other words it is the prediction of what the atmosphere will be like in a particular place in coming days by using technology and scientific knowledge to make weather observations.

Weather Forecasting Types

India Meteorological Department (IMD) classified weather forecasting in a wide range of operational products that traditionally are in the following groups:

Now-casting (NC)

Short Range Forecast (SRF)

Medium Range Forecast (MRF)

Long Range Forecast (LRF)

The general and qualitative description of different types of weather forecasts and their applications in agricultural operations are as below:

i. Now-casting (NC): A weather forecast in which the details about the current weather and forecasts up to a few hours ahead are given.

Validity: Less than 24 hours

Accuracy: Very high (> 90 percent)

Time and space resolution: 1 hour; typical space resolution is of the order of gamma mesocale (20-2 km).

Weather parameters covered: Precipitation amount and type, Cold and heat wave, High wind speed etc.

Agricultural Applications

Improved efficiency and saving for agricultural product transportation

Saving of harvested products of fruits and vegetables to safer places

Usefulness: Very low on real basis and low on potential basis

Main limitations: Unsuitability of broadcasting system; insufficient flexibility in agricultural technology.

ii. Short Range Forecast (SRF): Short range weather forecasts are weather forecasts valid up to 72 hours ahead. This forecast range is mainly concerned with the weather systems observed in the latest weather charts and also by considering the generation of new systems within the time period.

Validity: up to 72 hours (2-3 days)

Accuracy: High (70-80 percent)

Time and space resolution: Typical time resolution is 6 hours; typical space resolution is of the order of alfa or beta mesocale (200-20 km).

Weather parameters covered: Air temperature, relative humidity, wind speed and direction, solar radiation, precipitation amount and type, cloud amount and type, etc.

Agricultural Applications

- Irrigation scheduling
- Timing of field operations
- Protection of plants from frost
- Efficiency of chemicals
- Spray applications
- Labour efficiency
- Insect-disease effects
- Soil workability
- Livestock protection from cold and heat
- Animal production rate
- Drying rate of straw
- Drying rate of soil

Usefulness: Moderate on real basis and high on potential basis

Main limitations: Further adaptation of forecasts to farmer's requirements needed; farmer's doesn't know how to make the most use of available forecasts.

iii. Medium Range Forecast (MRF): These are weather forecasts valid for a period of 3 to 10 days. In this, the average weather conditions and the weather on each day will be prescribed with progressively lesser details and accuracy than that of the short range forecasts.

Validity: Beyond 72 hours and up to 240 hours (3-10 days)

Accuracy: High or moderate until 5 days; lower after (60-70 percent)

Time and space resolution: Typical time resolution is 12-24 hours; typical space resolution is of the order of alfa mesocale (2000-200 km).

Weather parameters covered: Air temperature, relative humidity, wind speed and direction, solar radiation, precipitation amount and type, cloud amount and type, etc.

Agricultural Applications

- To determine the depth at which seed be sown to achieve an optimal rate of seedling emergence
- To determine whether or not to sow a crop in this period
- To take account of expected rainfall to plan irrigation
- To decide whether or not to harvest a crop in this period
- To ensure maximum efficiency of spray program
- To prepare in time for the protection of crops against frost
- To the management of labour and equipment
- To animal feed requirements

Usefulness: High on real basis and very high on potential basis

Main limitations: Further adaptation of forecasts to farmer's requirements needed; farmer's doesn't know how to make the most use of available forecasts.

iv. Long range forecast (LRF): As per the World Meteorological Organization (WMO) definition, long range forecast is defined as the forecast from 30 days up to one season's description of averaged weather parameters. The monthly and seasonal forecast comes under long range forecast.

Validity: From 12-30 days up to one season

Accuracy: Low (60 percent)

Time and space resolution: Typical time resolution is 1 month; typically space resolution is of the order of the beta macroscale (10000 – 2000 km).

Weather parameters covered: Air temperature, precipitation amount and type, cloud amount and type, etc.

Agricultural Applications

- In soil moisture management
- In pasture management
- In determining irrigation frequency
- In harvesting crops for short term storage where adverse conditions are likely to interfere
- To decide whether to put perishable products into short term storage to even out supplies to market
- In avoiding chemical sprays when diseases or pests are unlikely to be troublesome

Usefulness: High in warning of delays in arrival of weather systems. Very low otherwise on real basis and poor on potential basis

Main limitations: Reliability (the reliability of LRF is higher for the tropics mid - latitudes. This is because tropical areas have a moderate amount of predictable signal, whereas in the mid-latitudes random weather fluctuations are usually larger than the predictable component of the weather).

• Special Weather Forecast for Extreme Events

Special weather forecast for agriculture provides the necessary meteorological input to assist farmers in making decisions. The requirements for these special forecasts will vary from season to season and crop to crop. Special forecast issued are as follows:

Tropical storms (cyclones, hurricanes, typhoons, etc.) associated with high winds, flooding and storm surges

Floods (other than those related to tropical storms) heavy rains due to monsoons, water logging and landslides

Severe thunderstorms, hail storms, tornadoes and squalls

Drought and heat waves

Cold spells, low temperature, frost, snow and ice-storms

Dust storms and sand storms

Pest and diseases of crop and livestock

vi. Early Warning Systems

IMD has developed early warning systems for extreme weather events like drought, flood, tropical cyclone, heat and cold wave, fog, hail. For drought monitoring and assessment, IMD has established system for real-time monitoring of rainfall on daily, weekly, monthly and seasonal basis for the districts/ meteorological subdivisions/ state in the country. IMD is preparing indices based aridity anomaly maps on weekly basis that gives information about the moisture stress experienced by growing plant. This analysis would indicate qualitatively retardation in the plants growth and so poor yields. Indirectly, this may also be helpful for irrigation scheduling, the amount and the time at which the water is badly needed by the plant. IMD is also preparing Standard Precipitation Index maps which describe dry and wet periods in the same way. SPI is an appropriate tool for monitoring agricultural drought but in combination with other information: water balance, crop condition, etc. Computation of SPI is done at a monthly time scale.

vii. Weather based Agromet Advisory Bulletin for Farm Management

Agromet Advisory Services is the entire set of organizations that support and facilitate people engaged in agricultural production to solve the weather related problems and to obtain information, skills and technologies to improve their livelihoods and it is well recognized as an important factor in promoting agricultural development. Weather based farm advisories as support system has been organized after characterization of agro-climate, including length of crop growing period, moisture availability period, distribution of rainfall and evaporative demand of the regions, weather requirements of cultivars and weather sensitivity of farm input applications. All this knowledge is used as background information. Following are the ingredients of a typical Agromet Advisory Bulletin to reap benefits of benevolent weather and minimize or mitigate the impacts of adverse weather; District specific weather forecast, in quantitative terms, for next 5 days for rainfall, cloud, max/min temperature, wind speed/direction and relative humidity, including forewarning of hazardous weather events likely to cause stress on standing crop and suggestions to protect the crop from them are as follows:

- Weather forecast based information on soil moisture status and guidance for application of irrigation, fertilizer and herbicides etc.
- The advisories on dates of sowing/planting and suitability of carrying out intercultural operations covering the entire crop spectrum from pre-sowing to post harvest to guide farmer in his day–to-day cultural operations.
- Weather forecast based forewarning system for major pests and diseases of principal crops and advises on plant protection measures.

- Propagation of techniques for manipulation of crop's microclimate e.g. shading, mulching, other surface modification, shelter belt, frost protection etc. to protect crops under stressed conditions.
- Advisory on contingency plan under extreme weather situations.
- Reducing contribution of agricultural production system to global warming and environment degradation through judicious particularly pesticides, herbicides and fertilizers.

viii. Advisory for livestock on health, shelter and nutrition

The support on above is rendered through preparing district specific Agrometeorological advisory bulletins by Agro-Meteorological Field Units (AMFUs). Inter-disciplinary group of agricultural and extension specialists at AMFUs formulates weather based farm advisory bulletin. These bulletins contain location specific and crop specific farm level advisories tailored to meet the farmers' need. The bulletins are encoded in a format and language which is easy to comprehend by the farmer in his decision making processes. The Agrometeorologists play a vital role in the encoding and decoding of the messages from the meteorologists to the agricultural sector. Crop weather calendars initially developed by IMD are used in preparation of weather based advisory bulletin. Recently All India Coordinated Research Project on Agrometeorology (AICRPAM) units in different states coordinated by CRIDA, Hyderabad have refined these calendars including pest & disease component which is very useful in crop specific advisory preparation.

4. Agro-meteorological Field Units (AMFUs) and Agro-advisory

Weather service to farmers is one of the most important operational services rendered by the India Meteorological Department (IMD), Ministry of Earth Sciences (MoES), New Delhi. It is a small step in this direction, aimed at "weather proofing" farm production. Among the services, the IMD, GKMS (Indian Meteorological Department, Gramin Krishi Mausam Seva) formerly known as AAS (Agrometeorological Advisory Service) is the largest public service sector. It is based on cooperation between the IMD (headquarter in New Delhi, with six regional and one in every state capital meteorological centers in India) and State Agricultural Universities (SAUs), Indian Council of Agricultural Research institutions (ICAR) and Indian Institute of Technology (IIT) which exist around the country. For disseminating forecasts and building forecast based agricultural advisories, GKMS works with 130 Agro-Meteorological Field Units (AMFUs), distributed across the agro-climatic zones of India. Based on forecasts provided by IMD, the AMFUs prepare weather-based agro-advisory bulletins in consultation with a team of experts from different sectors of agriculture. These units are responsible for recording agro-meteorological observations, preparing Agromet advisories for the districts falling under precinct of concerned agroclimatic zone and dissemination of the same. Concerned universities/ institutes have appointed Nodal Officer and Technical Officers, who prepare the advisory bulletins in consultation with the panel of experts already created at these units. The Agromet bulletins include specific advice on field crops, horticultural crops and livestock etc., which farmers need to act upon. Its frequency is twice a week i.e. Tuesday and Friday. Also in case of untimely development of weather, these units prepare the weather based advisory and warnings and issue to different users in a timely manner. At present bulletins are being issued from three levels as mentioned below.

4.1. National Agromet Advisory Bulletin

The bulletin is prepared for national level agricultural-planning & management and is being issued by National Agromet Advisory Service Centre, Agricultural Meteorology Division, India Meteorological Department, Pune, using inputs from various states. This bulletin helps identify stress on various crops for different regions of the country and suitably incorporate advisories. Ministry of Agriculture is prime user of these bulletins, which help take important decisions in Crop Weather Watch Group (CWWG) meetings at national level. The bulletins are also used by a large number of other agencies including fertilizer, pesticide industries Prime users of this bulletin are Crop Weather Watch Group, (CWWG), Ministry of agriculture. Bulletin is also communicated to all the related Ministries (State & Central), Organizations, NGOs for their use.

4.2. State Agromet Advisory Bulletin

This bulletin is prepared for State level agricultural planning & management. These bulletins are issued from regional meteorological centre/ meteorological centre units particularly at different State capitals. The State Level bulletin is a composite of district bulletins helping to identify the distressed district of the state as well as plan the supply of appropriate farm inputs such as seeds, irrigation water, fertilizer, pesticides etc. These bulletins are jointly prepared by State Meteorological Centre of IMD and AMFUs and mainly used by State Government functionaries. Prime user of this bulletin is State ACWWG. This is also meant for other users like Fertilizer industry, Pesticide industry, Irrigation Department, Seed Corporation, Transport and other organizations which provide inputs in agriculture.

4.3. District Agromet Advisory Bulletin

This is prepared for the farmers of the districts. These bulletins are being issued from 130 AMFUs functioning at State Agricultural Universities, ICAR centres and IITs. This contains advisories for all the weather sensitive agricultural operations form sowing to harvest. It also includes advisories for horticultural crops and livestock. Agricultural scientists at Agrometeorological Field Units have started using water balance, crop simulation models as a decision support tool for helping with weather forecast based farm management decision making. Agrometeorological Field unit can objectively assess the impact of skipping irrigation at a particular phenophase of a crop on its dry matter yield though with some uncertainties. Agrometeorologists can consider many of the factors involved and answer the question with a reasonable estimate. The crop models are also being used as technique for prediction of different phenophases and final yield. These weather based advisories are disseminated to the farmers through mass media dissemination, Internet etc as well as through district level intermediaries. The advisories are also communicated through multi-channel dissemination system.

4.4. Agromet Advisory Service in India

Agrometeorological Advisory Service (AAS) rendered by India Meteorological Department (IMD), Ministry of Earth Sciences (MoES) in active collaboration with ICAR, State Agriculture Universities, State Department of Agriculture etc. is a step to contribute to weather information based crop/livestock management strategies and operations dedicated to enhancing crop production and food security. The main emphasis of the existing AAS system is to collect and organize climate/weather, soil and crop information, and to amalgamate them with weather forecast to assist farmers in taking management decisions. This has helped to develop and apply operational tools to manage weather related uncertainties through agro-meteorological applications for efficient agriculture in rapidly changing environments. The information support systems under AAS include:

- Provision of weather, climate, crop/soil and pest disease data to identify biotic and abiotic stress for on-farm strategic and tactical decisions.
- Provide district specific (Pan India) weather forecast (rainfall, cloudiness, maximum/ minimum temperature, wind speed, wind direction, maximum/ minimum relative humidity) up to 5 days with outlook for rainfall for remaining two days of a week.
- Translate weather and climate information into farm advisories using existing research knowledge on making more efficient use of climate and soil resources through applications of medium range weather forecast.
- A broad spectrum of advisories include weather sensitive farm operations such as sowing/ transplanting of crops, fertilizer application based on wind

condition & intensity of rain, pest and disease control, intercultural operations, quantum and timing of irrigation using meteorological threshold and advisories for timely harvest of crops.

- Introduction of the state-of-art technologies such as remote sensing, GIS and crop simulation model based decision support system for agro-meteorologists to adapt agricultural production systems to weather & climate variability and to the increasing scarcity of input such as water, seed, fertilizer, pesticide etc.
- Develop effective mechanism for on time dissemination of agromet advisories to farmers,
- Effective training, education and extension on all aspects of agricultural meteorology

Being a multidisciplinary and multi institutional project, AAS project is being implemented through five tier structures to set up different components of the service spectrum. It includes meteorological (weather observing & forecasting), agricultural (identifying weather sensitive stress & preparing suitable advisory using weather forecast), extension (two way communication with user) and information dissemination (Media, Information Technology, Telecom) agencies.

5. System of Agrometeorological Advisory Dissemination

The task is to provide information to help farmers make the best possible use of weather and climate information. Critical factors for successful dissemination include relevance of information to weather and climate sensitive decision making in agriculture, followed by good outreach and uptake at grass root level. To ensure delivery of information to the farming community, a multi-mode dissemination system for agro-meteorological advisories is essential in which besides the conventional modes (radio, television & print media), the emerging modes of communication such as mobile phones and internet are also deployed. To smarten the service through continuous up-gradation of service one needs back flow of information on quality and relevant of information or demand for specific product, hence two way communication has to be the integral part of the dissemination system. AAS has considered different aspects pertinent to the flow and content of information and accordingly evolved a strategy for dissemination of agro-meteorological information. Although concerted efforts are being made to set up two way communications, but as of now the information flow is largely one-way. Although, Agro-meteorological Field Units (AMFUs) have direct contact with the farmers, good communication and working relationships have been set up with the agricultural extension, Krishi Vigyan Kendra (Agriculture Science Centres), Kisan (Farmer) Call Centre etc. to promote participatory methods for interactions with farmers. Information is disseminated through multi-modes of delivery including mass and electronic media. It includes, All India Radio, Television, Print Media (local news paper in different vernacular languages), internet (Web Pages) as well as group and individual relationships through email, telephone etc. The agrometeorological bulletins always contain dynamic information and hence, repetitive dissemination is being made. This reiterative process also helps to address large temporal and spatial variability having significant influence of weather & climate on agriculture. The use of electronic media such as e-mail or the Internet depend on the availability and access of these methods to the users, which is picking up in India particularly through initiative of Department of Information technology, who is in the process of setting up a very strong net work of common service centers (CSC). AAS is a scalable system, which can be incrementally developed and extended to cover all the farmers (crops) of India in a cost-effective manner. It enables the farmer to receive both crop and location-specific expert advice in a timely manner. With the advent of computers and Internet, emphasis is often being given to electronic communication systems. However, TV and radio services are still the best ways of communicating advisories among rural people as these are not only fast methods, but also large and illiterate masses can be contacted by these methods. Broadcasting of advisories in vernacular language provides an edge on other means of communication. Under Integrated Agromet Advisory Service (IAAS) scheme at IMD/MoES efforts are being made to strengthen the outreach of the agromet advisory as per the need of the farmers. Under this project, advisories are primarily disseminated to the farmers by mass mode, outreach at village level and human face for advisory dissemination.

Advisories are being disseminated to farmers through the following multi-channel systems;

- All India Radio (AIR) and Doordarshan
- Private TV and radio channels
- Newspaper
- Mobile phone /SMS
- Internet
- Virtual Academy / Virtual Universities /NGOs
- Kisan Call Centres / ICAR and other related Institutes / Agricultural Universities /Extension network of State
- Krishi Vigyan Kendra (KVKs)

The mobile telephony (with or without internet) is the most potent and omnipresent tool of agricultural extension in the present era. For dissemination through SMS on mobile phone, an information platform has been created by Ministry of Agriculture Cooperation and Farmer Welfare, Government of India by introducing mKisan Portal; Mobile Based Services for Farmers which allows the existing State Agriculture Universities, Krishi Vigyan Kendras, Agromet Field Units (AMFUs), ICAR Institutes, Organization in Animal Husbandry, Dairying & Fisheries etc. to provide the information in a convenient and timely manner. The advisories are crop and location specific and delivered within actionable time to the farmers in their vernacular language in a real time agricultural practices within the specific locations. Under IVR system the information from AMFUs for each state are collected and then stored, and converted into voice where the farmer would be calling and receiving the desired information. IMD is sending these SMS to farmers with the help of many private and government companies. IMD has so far partnered with Reuter Market Light (RML), Handygo, NOKIA, IFFCO Kisan Sanchar Ltd.(IKSL), National Bank for Agriculture and Rural development (NABARD), Maharashtra State Agriculture Department (Government of Maharashtra) and KISAAN SMS portal. The total number of farmers covered under SMS is presently 4.7 million.

5.1. Smart Dissemination System

IMD in collaboration with National Remote Sensing Centre (NRSC) is planning to use geo portal BHUVAN' to establish direct (virtual) interaction between farmers and the scientists to solve the field specific problems on real time basis by generating customized advisory and thus to minimize risk factor at farm level. Registered farmers raise queries and upload the crop images on operational farm activities to get specific advice. As geo portal is GPS enabled, this will help to get the location specific feedback from the farmers as well as status of the crops, which will enhance the ability of the scientists to prepare agromet advisories more customized to individual's need. Also BHUVAN portal will provide a platform for the dissemination of the existing and proposed agrometeorological products over a wide area and for a large number of users.

5.2. New dimensions in dissemination technology

There is very fast technological advancement in information technology. It has been well claimed that the present century will be of information technology. Easily available fast Internet facilities, supercomputers, high capacity servers, efficient linking between information points have added the much needed boost in the information technology. While in the last century the communication systems were mostly one-way communications, in the present century interactive communication systems are being discussed more profoundly. There are some examples of interactive communication systems for agricultural advisory dissemination, which are being adopted commercially by the most advanced providers and users in USA, Japan and some European countries. However, the choice of technology must be carried out at a very local level and farmers have to be reached and exposed to services information.

5.3. eAgromet System

As there is a need to develop a computer based decision support system and to automate the process of advisory bulletin preparation and dissemination, IMD in collaboration with IIIT, Hyderabad is generating a software for preparation of advisory bulletin under the scheme "IT-based eAgromet software for automated AAS bulletin preparation" to prepare district/block level AAS bulletins. It simplifies the preparation of district level AAS bulletin as it acts as an organizing tool for weather forecasts and Agromet advisories with the help of repository of past AAS bulletins. A server has been launched by IIIT for the said purpose. Number of AMFU scientists has already been trained and remaining AMFU scientists will be trained in utilization of the software and it will be implemented in GKMS.

6. Use of Satellite Data to Derive New Product Including Alerts

The regular and national scale Agrometeorological monitoring of the physiological processes and growth indicators require retrieval of basic land surface variables using spatial observations from the suit of current and future Indian geostationary satellite sensors. Satellite based agrometeorological products and the interpretation of the same in terms of crop and soil moisture status will help the experts to address spatial variability in framing the advisories and ultimately improve the quality of the advisories at higher resolution. A number of new products for agromet services are being generated recently. IMD in collaboration with Space Application Centre (SAC), Ahmedabad is using the Normalised Difference Vegetation Index (NDVI), derived from INSAT 3A CCD data, for agromet advisories. IMD is developing the softwares "Operationalization of Satellite Data Based Soil Moisture Monitoring System in India"in collaboration with IIT, Roorkee and "Determination of Soil Moisture over India using Space Borne Passive Microwave Sensors on board SMOS" in collaboration with ICRS, Jodhpur. Soil moisture data generated using this software will be used in water balance, irrigation scheduling and determination of sowing dates etc. for AAS. Besides, it is proposed to generate a number of satellite products in preparation of Agromet advisories including alerts to the farmers with respects to extreme weather.

7. Seamless Weather Forecast

a. Block level forecast

Though district level medium range weather forecast is being prepared for agromet services, there is an urgent need to prepare and issue high resolution (9 km × 9 km or finer using WRF model) accurate weather forecast at sub-district level. Thus it is proposed to generate block level forecast during XIIth Five Year Plan. On pilot mode block level weather forecast for the parameters like rainfall, maximum and minimum temperature, cloud amount, maximum and minimum relative humidity, wind speed and wind direction for 342 blocks in the country considering one district per state is being developed. This procedure would be followed until the bias removal techniques and high resolution (10-12 km) GCM becomes operational. Neural networks would be tried for MME forecasts and Kalman filter would be tried for maximum and minimum temperature as the bias removal techniques. As such, this forecast has been started for 37 selected districts in the country. By the end of XIIth FYP, block level forecast along with advisories will be scaled to cover the maximum districts in the country.

b. Extended range forecast

1. Under National Monsoon Mission set up by Ministry of Earth Sciences, Indian Institute of Tropical Meteorology (IITM), Pune in collaboration with IMD and National Centre for Medium Range Weather Forecasting (NCMRWF) has started experimental forecast for monsoon rainfall during next four pentads (up to 20 days) issued every week. IMD has started National Agromet Advisory bulletins based on Extended Range Weather Forecast during southwest monsoon 2013 to fulfill the needs of farmers and other users. Bulletin was prepared and issued for the next fortnight with update on every Friday. Successful implementation of this initiative would help the farmer to get more lead time to manage his weather based farm management.

2. In another effort entitled "Development and Application of Extended Range Forecast System (ERFS) for Climate Risk Management in Agriculture" supported by Ministry of Agriculture, Government of India, the key objectives to develop the experimental extended range test forecast from month to season scale for Indian region and its application for the development of climate risk management tools to address these risks with the involvement of agricultural scientists, farmers and service support agencies at field levels. This project integrates risk management and climate science research, involving leading institutions of India and abroad. The

project adopts a very strong demonstration approach, focusing on select districts in nine states that face significant livelihood impacts due to variability in the southwest monsoon: Andhra Pradesh, Gujarat, Maharashtra, Madhya Pradesh, Orissa, Himachal Pradesh, Rajasthan, Tamil Nadu, and Uttarakhand.

These forecast products include both type of forecasts *viz*., deterministic as well as probabilistic forecasts. Methods used to generate the deterministic rainfall and mean temperature forecast include Singular Value Decomposition (SVD) based Regression, Supervised Principal Component Regression, Canonical Correlation Analyses. In these regression techniques, predictors (independent variables) are different general circulation models' rainfall and temperature products while the predictand (dependent variables) is IMD rainfall and temperature. All these above stated forecasts were combined using some statistical techniques and has been converted in probabilistic forecast to see the chance of occurrence of particular event.

Probabilistic forecast is made in three categories *viz*., Below Normal, Near Normal and Above Normal. These categories are based on the previous year's observed data set (IMD's gridded data). The experimental forecast products thus generated since monsoon 2009 were disseminated to all the selected demonstration sites through IMD for its verification and application purposes. The performance of experimental test forecast products were evaluated at each selected pilot demonstration sites with the observed data of temperature and rainfall during the month.

8. Climatic Risk Management through Agromet Advisory Services

The idea of informed decision making at farm/ farming system level gains more reality during the crop season. Crop simulation models and DSS are being increasingly used in decision making for risk minimization in agriculture. These models need daily weather data for crop season. The major challenge in linking seasonal forecast to crop model is mismatch between spatiotemporal scale of forecast and crop model. On the one hand, these forecasts are available at bigger spatial domain for a month or season and on the other, crop simulation models can be run at point scale or smaller grid space. Forecast needs to be downscaled spatially and temporally. Crop model based generated viable management options against a given forecast require frequent validation through farmers participatory meetings. In order to make use of extended range forecast for decision making on strategic agriculture planning and risk management and integrate with ongoing advisory service system, a range of climatic risk management tools were developed.

1. Extended/ seasonal climate forecast.
2. Climatic risk matrices: Climate risk analysis for crop under various farming situations showing the impact of soil (type and depth), time of planting and weather requirement and extremes at various phenopahese.
3. Stochastic Weather generator: Downscaling can be achieved by linking a seasonal forecast with a weather generator. Non homogeneous hidden Markov model (NHMM) or HMM are used as a promising approach to constructing multi-station weather generators.
4. Crop simulation model and Decision support system: Crop models embedded in Decision Support System for Agro-technology Transfer (DSSAT), InfoCrop, APSIM etc. are process oriented, management-level model of crop growth and development and can be linked to daily sequence of desegregated weather data to generate crop growth performance against a number of weather realizations.
5. Farmers participatory meeting: A very critical process to validate/refine the above findings as viable options for farm management. Pilot study demonstrated use of monthly forecast on rainfall and temperature by establishing an end-to-end information generation and application. This was implemented with participation of agricultural universities/research centres, service support agencies at field levels and farmers for better crop planning and management in the following areas:

- Land preparation
- Nursery raising
- Irrigation scheduling
- Urea application to rainfed crops in normal rain forecast
- Frequent intercultural operation to conserve soil moisture
- Contingency plan under delayed monsoon onset rains
- Temperate apple crops- Chilling hours to help skip hormonal spray for bud breaking/ flower setting
- Nomadic farming hills- sheep, goat
- Livestock- malnutrition and disease infection under deficit rainfall

Future plan includes the integration of Extended Range Forecasting System (ERFS) experimental system in IMD for its operationalization, generation of seamless weather forecast for agriculture risk management expand to all parts of the country and R&D for continuous improvement in weather forecast products at fortnightly to monthly scale.

9. Crop Yield Forecasting

Reliable and timely forecast of agricultural commodity provides important and useful inputs for proper planning. This enables planners and decision makers to predict how much to import in case of shortfall or optionally, to export in case of surplus. It also enables government to put in place strategic contingency plans for redistribution of food during times of famine. In India, there is also growing need for micro level planning and particularly the demand for crop insurance, which increases the need for field level yield statistics. Forecasting Agricultural Output using Space, Agrometeorology and Land based observations (FASAL) involves developing econometric, remote sensing and agromet based model to generate multiple crop yield forecasts at national, state and district level starting with crop sowing to end of season for 11 major *kharif* and *rabi* crops *viz.,* Rice, Jowar, Maize, Bajra, Jute, Ragi, Cotton, Sugarcane, Groundnut, Rapeseed & Mustard and Wheat. IMD is implementing Agromet component of the scheme in coordination with 23 State Agromet Centres (SAMCs), 46 principal Agro-Met Field Units (AMFUs) and IASRI in the country to develop agromet models and issue in-season crop yield forecast based on statistical and crop simulation models. This information is shared with Mahalanobis National Crop Forecast Centre (NCFC), New Delhi.

10. Adoption of Climate smart Agriculture

At a global scale, both intensification and extensification of agriculture is responsible for a negative impact on environment by high level of greenhouse gas emission, promoting climate change through depletion of natural resources. According to FAO (2011) report, the world's population is going to reach 9 billion by 2050.Total food production will have to increase by approximately 70% to feed this growing population. About 870 million people are already estimated to be undernourished. Climate change is an added hurdle on the way to this goal, it causes rise in temperature and changes in rainfall pattern, pest and diseases find new ranges and more weather extremes lead to reduced global food production. According to 2015 United Nations Climate Change Conference, COP 21 Paris agreement has recognized the fundamental priority of safeguarding food security and ending hunger, particularly concentrating on vulnerabilities of food production systems to the adverse impacts of climate change.

Climate-Smart Agriculture (CSA) has the potential to increase sustainable productivity based on scale such as at local level, it increases productivity by using improved management techniques such as targeted use of fertilizers and increasing the resilience of farming systems to climate impacts consistent with CSA in smallholder systems which is applicable to all regions and climates of the tropics and subtropics. It is recommended that the following practices can be applied based on the topographical conditions such as rice management for humid conditions, grassland restoration and drip irrigation for dry land, terraces practices and contour planting for slopes. One of the most popular success story of CSA is from Sahel (West Africa), over 5 million hectare of degraded land in the Sahel have been restored through a practice known as 'farmer-managed natural regeneration' thus increasing the food security of millions of people and enhancing their resilience in the face of climate change.

CSA, however, is not a generic agricultural technology or practice that can be universally applied, but it is location specific and knowledge intensive approach which requires site-specific assessments to identify suitable agricultural technologies and practices. However, the good news is that, climate analogues (finding future climate for potential adaptation) already exist and it is estimated that 70% of expected future climatic conditions already exist somewhere location on the earth. It is essential to identify those analogues and adopt them for environmental sustainability.

For CSA, it is essential to converges other sectors like energy and water that are essential for capitalizing on potential synergies with agriculture, livestock, forestry and fisheries. CSA also help in enhancing over all prosperity by developing villages in to "Climate Smart Villages" that are Weather Smart, Water Smart, Carbon Smart, Nitrogen Smart, Energy Smart and Knowledge Smart. The CSA provides appropriate climate change solutions through government – private sector intervention in policies and financial investments. Agromet Advisory Services is an example of such alignment which at present is accessible to over 2.5 million farmers in India and Weather Based Crop Insurance adopted more than 9 million farmers. These interventions will help in breaking barriers for adoption, especially among farmers. This is just the beginning and more number of interventions shall be staged in the near future.

Climate smart agriculture is not a new agricultural system or a set of practices, but is a new approach, a way to guide the needed changes of agricultural systems, given the necessity to jointly address food security and climate change (Fig. 1).

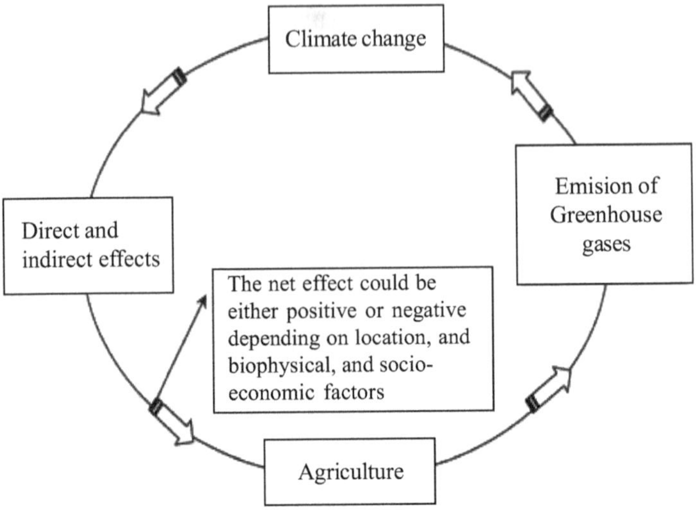

Fig. 1: Interrelationship between climate change and agriculture

11. Future Needs and Strategies

Though Agro met Advisory service is being provided efficiently at district level in the country, still there is need to strengthen in terms of observation, seamless weather forecast, manpower, real time information flow, research and development (R&D), dissemination etc. There is need to develop methodologies for remote sensing and conventional data merging. Concerted efforts are needed for ground based data collection, satellite data collection, GIS software applications, operational applications of meteorological satellite data, weather radars and the monitoring of cropping season by meteorological and remote sensing data to equip AAS units to generate better advisories. Though district level medium range weather forecast is being prepared for agromet services, there is an urgent need to develop and issue high resolution accurate weather forecasts to help tailor crop plan for the farmers at village level. Thus there is a need to scale up the service from district to block level with dissemination up to village level across the country to meet the end user's requirement. Such idea leads to take up the new concept of establishing the Gramin Krishi Mausam Sewa (GKMS) scheme under Integrated Agromet Advisory Services in the country during the XIIth Five Year Plan.

12. Conclusion

With better and higher resolution forecasts in future, the farmers will definitely be very much pro-active to weather and weather based farming to enhance their capability towards climate smart agriculture. This approach is efficient and useful through ICT in taking the weather based advisories to the doorstep of the farmers and is the first of its kind in India, and upscaling it will benefit the farmers many fold. Farmers are willing to pay for advisory services as long as they recognize financial benefits and profits from the services. Due to judicious and timely utilization of inputs, production cost for the AAS farmers reduced. The increased yield level and reduced cost of cultivation leads to increased net returns.

The total eradication of agricultural development problems can be achieved through extension service approach if the role of Agromet Advisory Service is properly conceived and effectively administered. New approaches to ICT for agricultural development and natural resource management exist to overcome extension challenges and new concepts are emerging for anticipation, learning and problem solving between the key players. The availability of extension agents and the ability to exchange and validate new techniques and/or productions to introduce at the farm level by researchers and specialists are highly desired. The studies showed that the application of agromet advisory bulletin, based on current and forecasted weather is a useful tool for enhancing the production and income. AAS farmers received weather forecast based agro-advisories, including optimum use of inputs for different farm operations. Due to judicious and timely utilization of inputs, production cost for the AAS farmers reduced. The increased yield level and reduced cost of cultivation lead to increased net returns.

13. References/Suggested Reading

AMD & IMD .2016. Annual Progress Report 2015–2016. Agricultural Meteorology Division (AMD), India Meteorological Department (IMD): Pune, India. Available online: http://www.imdagrimet.gov.in/sites/default/ files/APR%202015-16_final_1.pdf (accessed on 11 August 2017).

De US .1992. Operational services for agricultural users in India. WMO Symposium on Public Weather Services during the 10th CBS, 2-13 November, 1992, Geneva.

Anderson JR and Feder G .2007. Agriculture Extension, In RE Evenson and P Pingali (eds.), Handbook of Agriculture Economics, Chapter 44, Volume 3. Agricutural Development: Farmers, Farm Production and Farm Markets, Elsevier, Amsterdam, 2343-78.

Dasgupta D .2017. Extreme Climate Warnings Save Farm Losses. Available online:http://indiaclimatedialogue.net/2016/08/22/extreme-climate-warnings-save-farm-losses/ (accessed on 11 August 2017).

International Conference on Capacity Building for Climate Change 21 October 2002. www.ficci.com/media-room/speeches-presentations/2002/oct/oct-climate aggarwal.ppt National Council of Applied Economic Research.

Kanamitsu M, Kumar A, Ming H, Jung H, Kyung J, Wang WI, Yang F, Hong S, Peng P, Chen W, Moorthi S and Ji M .2002. NCEP Dynamical Forecast System 2000. *Bull. Am.Meteorol. Soc.* 83: 1019-1037.

Maia, J., Castro Neto, M., Oliveira, J., 2005. Supporting irrigation management strategies through the web: an application to the Portuguese Alentejo region. Available at the INSAM web site (www.agrometeorology.org) under "Accounts of operational agrometeorology" [Second prize 2005 INSAM Contest on best examples of agrometeorological services].

Meinke H, Nelson R, Kokic P, Stone R, Selvaraju R and Baethgen W .2006. Actionable climate knowledge: from analysis to synthesis. *Clim. Res.*, 33: 101-110.

NCAER .2010. Impact assessment and economic benefits of weather and marine services. Supported by Ministry of Earth Sciences, New Delhi.

Onyewotu LOZ, Stigter CJ, Abdullahi AM, Ariyo JA, Oladipo EO and Owonub, JJ 2.003. Reclamation of desertified farmlands and consequences of its farmers in semiarid northern Nigeria: A case study of Yambawa rehabilitation scheme. Arid Land Res. and Managem., 17: 85-101.

Rathore LS and Maini P .2008. Report on Economic impact assessment of Agrometeorological advisory service of NCMRWF. Ministry of Earth Sciences, New Delhi.

Rathore LS, Parvinder M and Kaushik S .2006. Impact assessment of the agro-meteorological advisory service of the National Centre for Medium Range Weather Forecast (NCMRWF). Available on the INSAM website (www.agrometeorology.org) under "Accounts of operational agrometeorology".

Rathore LS, Gupta Akhilesh and Singh KK .2001. Medium range weather forecasting and agricultural production. Journal of Agric. Physics.1 (1): 43.

Rijks D and Baradas MW .2000. The clients for agrometeorological information. *Agric. For. Meteorol.*, 103: 27-42.

Roncoli C .2006. Ethnographic and participatory approaches to research on farmers' responses to climate predictions. *Clim. Res.*, 33: 81-99.

Vogel C, O'Brien K .2006. Who can eat information? Examining the effectiveness of seasonal climate forecasts and regional climate-risk management strategies. *Clim Res.*, 33: 111-122.

WMO .1992. La radio rurale et la diffusion des informations agrometeorologiques. Proceedings of an International Workshop, Bamako. WMO, Geneva and CTA, Ed (Netherlands).

Weiss A, Van Crowder L and Bernardi M .2000. Communicating agrometeorological information to farming communities. *Agric. For. Meteorol.*, 103: 185-196.

17

Integrated Farming System for Sustainable Agricultural Transformation

Dileep Kachroo

AICRP on IFS, Division of Agronomy, SKUAST Jammu, Jammu and Kashmir, India

1. Introduction
2. Overview of agriculture production scenario in J&K
3. Need for farming system approach
4. Adoption of integrated farming system
5. Implementation of integrated farming system and its basic guidelines
6. Broader guidelines for adoption of integrated farming system
7. Recommendations

Abstract

Agriculture is at a cross-road in J&K wherein the small holdings, profitability, livelihood security and sustainability issues are the factors adding to the existing agrarian crisis in the state in particular and the country in general. This requires a decisive direction shift at the policy level towards adoption of integrated farming system. There is a need of fundamental change from the unilateral, top-down, prescriptive "knowledge generation and transmission" models of agriculture development adopted in the country so far, which have in fact resulted in an ecological, economic and social crisis in the farming sector of the state during 40 years of adoption and that climate change is one more imperative for drastic change to address the situation. Climate change is already a reality for farming community and that conventional models of agricultural research and extension have failed to address the need of the hour unless some fundamental recasting in the form of diversified farming system is adopted. The immediate need for interventional action precludes traditional models of research and support systems and requires alternative but urgent programmatic interventions, led by farmers' institutions and their local resources, knowledge and innovations. Existing mainstream models of farming are GHG-inducing and are not conducive to adoption either given their high external-input dependency-models which increases the risk of vulnerable farmers. Integrated farming system a key to sustainable agriculture, on the other hand, holds immense mitigation and adaptation potential, specifically in the context of climate change even as it improves rural livelihoods and addresses the ecological crisis in farming of today under various climatic regions of Jammu in particular and state in general. Jammu region of the J&K state is bestowed with varying climate zones i.e. subtropical, intermediate and temperate zones, which is best suited for diversified farming,as the promotion of single enterprise is neither beneficial from economy point of view nor is sustainable under the given climate change crisis. The integration of Crops, Horticulture, Animal ,Fish cum Poultry, Mushroom, Vermicompost, Apairy, Biogas and Boundary plantation enterprises in Jammu region under integrating farming system is having the potential to improve the farm income to three folds besides will address the sustainability issues in the long run.

Keywords: integrated farming system, climate change, adoption guidelines, farm profitability

1. Introduction

Agriculture will have to be in the centre of the national priority for meeting our ever growing needs of food, nutrition and household security, which in India's context is an integral part of the national security. Agriculture will have to change for the best and if not attended immediately, it would aggravate hunger, poverty and disparity, leading to social unrest conflicts. Therefore, we have to prepare ourselves like a war to fight against hunger, poverty, malnutrition and unemployment and this war has to be won for peace, prosperity and tranquility with the much needed balanced and harmonized inclusive agriculture.

The country has started its journey from nearly 50 million tonnes of food grains during 1950-51 to a production of about 260 million tonnes during 2013-14 which is a record production till date which involves rice of more than 95 million tonnes, wheat 86 million tonnes and pulses 18 million tonnes. Similarly the production of oilseeds, fresh fruits, milk, eggs, fish which is also the highest production witnessed during the year. Globally, the country produces 25 per cent of total pulses, 22 per cent of sugarcane, 21 per cent of rice, 12 per cent of wheat and 16 per cent of milk. Rice and wheat together produces nearly 33 per cent of total global production which has brought in sense of self- respect, confidence, pride and honour to country. Globally, India ranks number one in production of pulses, tea, jute and milk; number two in production of rice, wheat, maize, sugarcane and cotton and number three in production of cereals. Also, the country ranks highest in population of cattle, buffalo, goat and sheep which is in chronological order of one, two and three among the world . This production is coming with the share of 2.3 per cent of global land, 4.2 per cent of water resources and 11 per cent of arable land which supports 18 per cent of world's population.

Future projections revealed that demand of food grains would increase to 345 million tonnes in 2030 with decreased arable land, costly inputs, less water, poor soil health with multi nutrients, deficiencies of N P K Zn B and many micro nutrients, costly labour with climate change and global warming. In India, water availability per capita will be reduced to 1500 m^3 by 2025 from 500 m^3 in 1950. It is projected that availability of water for agriculture use in India may be reduced by 21 per cent by 2020 in drop of yields of irrigated crops especially rice. Thus price rise and withdrawal of food from poor masses, policy reforms are needed from now to avoid the negative developments in the years to come. These reforms may include the establishment of secure water rights to users, decentralization and privatization of water, management functions, appropriate levels, rising reforms, markets in tradable property rights, introduction of appropriate water saving technologies. There is a need of paradigms in our approach and future strategy. Our major concern to be addressed will be water crises, soil degradation, fatigue, genetic erosion, increasing biotic and abiotic stresses (pressures), inefficient management practices, inadequate markets, unfavourable trade, increasing knowledge lag in management, production of farm produce, harvest and post-harvest losses. New technologies should be science based, technically feasible, economically viable and socially acceptable.

The state of J&K accounts for 3.20 per cent of total area of the country with a geographical area of 103187 sq. km situated at an altitude variation of 300-5400 meters above mean sea level constitutes about 67.5 per cent of North-Western Himalayan region. In the state, agriculture is the core sector of economy which contributes about 26.91 per cent in the Gross State Domestic Product with 70 per cent of the state population deriving their livelihood directly or indirectly from this sector. In spite of increase in food grain production from 4.52 lakh tonnes in 1950-51 to 15.70 lakh tonnes, the demand is still deficit by 38 per cent. The deficiency in cereals is nearly by 40 per cent, 70 per cent each in pulses and oil seeds and 30 per cent in vegetables. The State still meets its demand by procuring large quantities from other states even after 6 decades of our independence. Similarly in vegetable sector, there is a need to produce 14.2 lakh tonnes vegetables as against 9.85 lakh tonnes. In livestock sector, although the quantum of products and bio-products has increased but there is a deficit of 1.55, 20.20 and 57.0 per cent in case of milk, egg and meat/poultry production, respectively. The state is also confronted with negative production growth rates of -2.55, -0.48, -3.36 and -0.44 per cent in case of maize, wheat, cereals & millets; and food grains, respectively with negative productivity trends of -2.78, -4.86 and -0.35 per cent in case of rice, wheat and total food grains respectively (Economic Survey, 2008-09).

Horticulture forms an important sector in the economy of J&K State and is one of the key sector for employment and income generation because large scale industrialization suiting to ecosystem has not taken place. The sector is currently having an annual turnover of fruits worth Rs. 3000 crores and giving employment to over 25 lakhs people. Keeping this in view the state government has declared horticulture a thrust area and is taking a number of steps to boost it. Temperate zone of Jammu & Kashmir State is the fruit bowl and perhaps no state has greater ambience for horticulture; as indigenous apple, pear, vine, mulberry, walnut, hazel, peach, apricot, raspberry, gooseberry, currant and strawberry are the potential examples. Besides saffron and kaala zeera the temperate crops are the other very important crops that have a history of many centuries. The state of J&K has the monopoly for producing saffron and is placed second in the world after Iran. The productivity is half in comparison to that of Iran and Spain. Commercial floriculture and cultivation of medicinal and aromatic plants have great potential which need to be promoted on a large scale due to their tremendous biodiversity and climatic advantages.

These temperate fruits grown at elevation of 1000 to 3000 metres above sea level are important cash-fetching fruits of the state. These fruits not only supplement the diet of the people in the state and country but form an important item of our exports. From the stage of tree plantation to the point of its marketing, it has a good potential in employment creation. There is need to explore other options, that too in the field of value added agriculture under its diversified practice. However, the state is facing many problems with regard to the development of horticulture. It includes low productivity, great variability in important fruit crops like walnut and almond, higher percentage of offgrade fruits, poor connectivity with the market place and small and fragmented land holdings having marginal farmers, which has forced us to introduce high-density plantation of apples and soft fruits like strawberry and currants around cities and towns.

Therefore, horticulture sector continues to remain the important sector for socio-economic development of the people. With serious constrains on area expansion and declining scope of other sources of growth of agriculture output, the diversification of agriculture towards non-food grains and high value cash crops including fruits and vegetables, compatible with the comparative advantage of the region is suggested as a viable solution. These crops have potential of income augmentation, employment generation, poverty alleviation and export promotion.

According to a study, in the state of Jammu and Kashmir, the scope to raise output through diversification is highest in the country as one per cent shift in area from food grains to non-food grains entails more than 3 per cent growth rate in crop output.

During the last several years, diversification of Agriculture in State towards high value commodities, i.e. fruits, vegetables and livestock products is taking place at a faster pace and is reflected in the high share of High Value Commodities (HVCs) in agricultural production in a number of districts. Sustained economic and income growth, urbanization and globalization are fuelling, rapid growth in demand for high value commodities in the State, high value horticulture has a comparative advantage in production and labour absorption over staple food items and thus is reckoned as an important activity for small orchard holders equally important, the consumption of high value commodities (HVCs) is on rise, the evidence shows that by 2025, demand for fruits, vegetables, milk, egg, meat and fish would almost be doubled than that was in 2000.This sector is most vibrant sector for economic development in state. The per capita income of Jammu and Kashmir is 324 US dollar which is more than the national average. The monthly expenditure of J&K is also higher than normal average. The urban/ rural difference is lesser due to horticulture earning of the farmers. Keeping this gap in production and requirement in view there is vast scope for boosting the agriculture in the state and simultaneously going for the diversification of agriculture which besides horticulture and crop sector includes mushroom cultivation, bee keeping, medicinal and aromatic plants and various animal products as the state has to invest more than Rs.1400 crores in procurement of meat, poultry and animal products including fodder, feed etc.

2. Overview of Agriculture production Scenario in J&K

In the state of Jammu and Kashmir, 58 per cent of the area under agriculture is rainfed and remaining 42% is irrigated (Fig-1). Agro-climatically the state is divided into four zones: Sub-tropical zone (2.53 lakh ha), intermediate zone (3.56 lakh ha), temperate zone (4.04 lakh ha) and cold arid zone (0.29 lakh ha). About 64%, 90% and 44 % of the area in sub-tropical, intermediate and temperate zone respectively is rainfed (Fig-2).

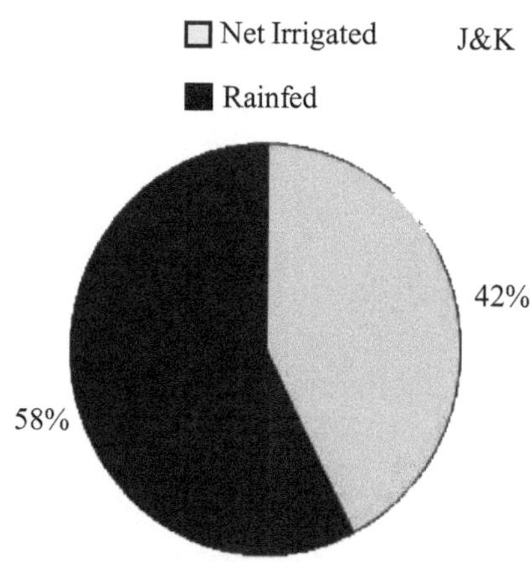

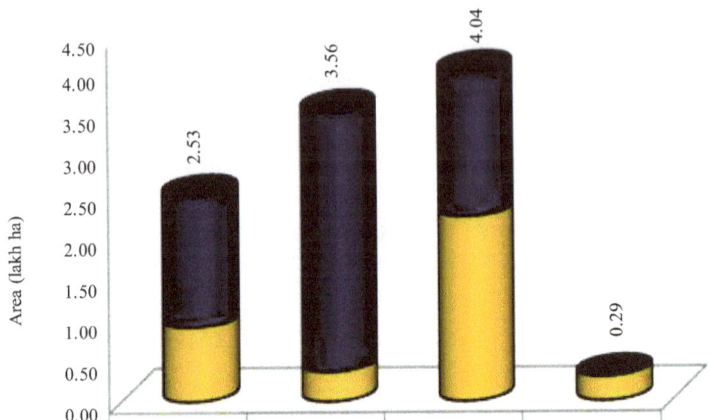

	Sub-tropical	Intermediate	Temperate	Cold arid
Rainfed	1.62	3.20	1.78	0.00
Irrigated	0.91	0.36	2.26	0.29

Fig. 2: Agroclimatic zones of J&K

The mean annual rainfall in these agro-climatic zones is 1069 mm (Sub-tropical zone), 1478 mm (intermediate zone), 680 mm (temperate zone) and 83 mm (Cold arid zone). Socio-economically the biggest constraint of the agriculture in the state is small land holding size of 0.66 ha with more than 77.97 % farmers having less than one hectare of land against 1.33 hectare holding size on National basis.

In J&K state, 11.28 per cent, 92.72 per cent, 56.99 per cent and 96.15 per cent area under rice, maize, wheat and barley, respectively is cultivated as rainfed crop which attributes to low productivity and production in comparison to national yields. The productivity of various crops including rice, maize, wheat, pulses and oilseeds in the State is 21.83 q/ha, 20.05 q/ha, 17.35 q/ha, 5.10 q/ha and 8.5 q/ha, respectively compared to 22.03 q/ha, 27.85 q/ha, 19.21 q/ha, 6.38 q/ha and 10.86 q/ha on national average.

The cultivated apple (Malus borkh) is considered as one of the most important and widely grown fruit in temperate zones of the world with regard to its acreage, production, economic returns and nutritive, value and popularity. The tree is small and deciduous reaching 3 to 12 meter tall with broad, often density twiggy crown blossoms are produced in spring simultaneously with the budding of the leaves. The fruit matures in autumn and is typically 5 to 9 cm's in diameter enriched with nutrients; the apple is fourth widely produced fruit in the world after banana, orange & grapes. In spite of certain problems the comparative feasibility and profitability in apple production has proved to be better as compared to the other farm enterprise during the last one and a half decades or so. The area under apples has increased significantly and resulted to higher production (Table 1), which clearly indicates its potential in Integrated Farming System in temperate fruits.

Table 1: Comparative productivity of Apple and Rice cultivation in J&K state

Year	Area under Apple (000 Hac)	Apple Production (000 Mt)	Productivity	Area under Rice (000 Hac)	Rice Production (000 Qunt)	Productivity
2004-05	107.93	1093.33	10.12	250.04	4928	19.70
2005-06	111.88	1151.34	9.01	259.01	5574	21.52
2006-07	119.04	1222.18	9.51	252.52	5546	21.96
2007-08	127.80	1311.85	10.54	263.25	5620	21.34
2008-09	133.10	1332.81	8.99	257.63	5637	21.88
2009-10	138.19	1373.00	9.16	259.89	5011	19.28
2010-11	141.17	1852.41	10.15	261.35	5077	19.42
2011-12	154.72	1747.22	10.46	262.54	5045	19.21
2012-13	173.63	1500.25	9.5	262.56	5078	19.34

Source: Digest of statistics Jammu Kashmir, Financial Commission (Rev), J&K

Socio economic status of farming community is one of the most important issue that needs a special attention. Smaller and fragmented holding size as small and marginal farmers constitutes 94 per cent of the total land holdings in J&K state, higher population growth rate, illiteracy, unorganized marketing and distribution, poor infrastructure etc. are the socio-economic constraints of temperate zone in particular and other zones of the state in general. As per the 8th Agriculture census (2005-06) of the State, the total number of operational holders has been worked out to be 1377808 and average size of operational holding was found out to be 0.67 ha. About 94% of the operational holders fall in the category of marginal and small farmers. About 5% of the operational holders fall in semi-medium category holding, only 1% of the operational holders fall in the medium category holding and only 0.04% of the operational holders fall in the large category holding. Adoption of Integrated Farming System is the only solution for uplift of the socio-economic status of the farming community of the state, which is having fragmented small and medium land holdings.

Paradigm shift towords Apple Cultivation

The state has the largest potential for production of quality temperate horticulture crops. It has created niche production of apple, pears & dry fruits, among temperate fruits Apple ranks first in terms of production and productivity. The annual production of apple in the state is about 9.09 lacks tone at an average yield of 10.09 tons per hectare. However the production & productivity of apple crop has been fluctuating during last two decades this is due to drought or some other conditions. In spite of this apple production has increased from just 6000 metric tons in 1950-51 to more than 9 lakh tones, area increased from 7000 hectares to more than 90 thousand hectors and yield per hectare in Jammu & Kashmir State is highest in the country, which is much higher than national average of 6.86 ton/ha. It is also compared well with the world average of 10.82 tone/ha or China (9.93 tone/ha) which is world's highest producer of apple.

3. Need for farming system approach

Integrated Farming System (IFS) is an interdependent, interrelated often interlocking production *system* based on few crops, animals and related subsidiary enterprises in such a way that maximize the utilization of nutrients of each *system* and minimize the negative effect of these enterprises on environment. Adoption of horticulture based Integrated Farming System approach in the state is having vast potential for taping the natural resources and increaseing the productivity, profitability and sustainability. Expanding population, urbanization and industrialization, are leading to decline in per capita availability of vital agricultural resources and also fragmentation of farm holdings, making them operationally uneconomic. The process of marginalization of land holdings is likely to continue due to various demographic reasons. As discussed above, it is evident that per capita arable land is continuously decreasing and is expected to shrink further. Such farm families have certain basic needs including food (cereal, pulses, oilseeds, milk, fruit, honey, fish, meat, egg etc.) feed, fodder, fibre, employment, etc. To fulfill these, farmers have been doing their own farming system for a long time.

At SKUAST-Jammu level, efforts have been made aiming at increasing the productivity of different components of farming system like crop, dairy, livestock, poultry, apiculture, vegetables production, horticulture, mushroom cultivation, sericulture, etc. have been made. But, our national scenario is clearly indicative of the fact that normally, a farming family maintains multi-enterprise systems, depending upon his/her family requirements, knowledge base, socioeconomic setup, agro-climatic conditions and available farm resources. However, to have a systematic integration of multi-enterprise systems in a scientific manner, components needs to be chosen in such a manner that product or by-product of one component becomes the input for other, becoming complementary and are organically well interlinked to each other without wastage. For example, by-product and waste material generated from cultivation of many crops is used as raw material for many industrial uses or as fuel or as feed/ fodder to the cattle of the farm. The animal dung may also be used as fuel or a mix of dung, urine and crop residues may be used for production of compost/ farmyard manure that is applied to crops and fish pond. The silt deposited at bottom of a fish pond can again be utilized as manure to crops. The FYM can substitute about 25% of recommended NPK for crops. Crops like mustard serve as a good source of nectar for honeybees, besides providing edible oil for human and cake for animal feed. The crop residues can substitute 12% of recommended NPK. If fish pond embankment is used for cultivating fodder/flower/fruit/vegetable crops, it provides extra output either for human or animal.

Farming systems approach of agricultural research is one venture to harness the complementarities and synergies among different enterprises and augment the total productivity, profitability and gainful rural employment. Unlike commodity research, where the focus is on increasing productivity/profitability of individual crop/ animal, under farming system approach it is the farm household that remains the focus of the research programme.

The university has developed a model of Integrated Farming System which includes multiple enterprises mainly Crop + Horticulture + Animal unit + Fish cum Poultry + Apiculture + Vermi-composting+ Biogas + Mushroom unit coupled with boundary plantation targeting small and marginal farmers. The model is having the potential to revolutionize the farming practices and the approach will not only boost the vertical productivity and sustainability but also will improve the livelihood security of the farmer to many folds. Therefore, the state govt. has to emphasize on launching of mega project on Integrated Farming System on the lines of the SKUAST-Jammu model with the intervention of including potential temperate crops.

Potential of Farming System towards Sustainable Agriculture (as LOW-GHG) and improving Livelihood Security

Integrated Farming System leads towards sustainable agriculture (with crops, trees, livestock etc.) which is based on locally adapted agro-diverse cropping patterns and use of local resources (natural resources and natural processes), based on local knowledge, skills and innovations. The integrated farming system approach would also like to highlight the potential of sustainable agriculture, in terms of mitigation of GHG emissions as well as adaptation to climate change. Further, it holds great potential for meeting global and national food security requirements even as it leads to improvement of farmers' livelihoods through enhancing their net incomes and improving the productivity of their resources in the long run.

Food security

A question that is often posed with regard to sustainable agriculture is whether it will be able to feed the growing population. We respond by saying that sustainable agriculture does not imply lowered yields, as experience of successful farmers' bears out on the ground. This is reinforced by an FAO report (2007) which says that "conversion of global agriculture to organic management, without converting wild lands to agriculture and without using N-fertilisers would result in a global agricultural supply of 2640 to 4380 Kcal/person/day". Sustainable intensification in developing countries through organic practices would increase production by 56 per cent. A meta-analysis of 133 scientific papers concluded that organics was particularly competitive under lower yield environments, a feature that is common in developing countries. Organic yields on an average are comparable to conventional yields although yields do decline initially when converting from high-input systems and almost double when converting from low-input systems. In India, it should be remembered that a majority of land is rainfed and continues to be low-input by default.

Improvement in Rural Livelihoods

While macro-level food production and availability levels are likely to increase through sustainable agriculture, at the individual and community level too, there are bound to be improvements. It has been felt that access to food will increase by livelihood improvement both for farmers and agricultural workers through integrating the various components in a farming system mode. Recycling of farm waste through various composting methods will improve food access by increasing productivity, diversity and conservation of natural resources, by raising incomes, improving employment and by reducing risks. It has been recorded that shift to sustainable agriculture practices can reduce the outward migration from rural areas.

Reduction in GHG Emissions

Changes in farming models and practices towards sustainable agriculture offer a significant opportunity at reducing GHG emissions. Under Integrated Farming System there is a great potential to reduce its fossil fuel dependence in many ways. For instance, for soil productivity management, internal inputs and practices are used, which in the longer run minimizes the use of chemical fertilizers – for instance, creating the micro-climate required for increased soil (beneficial) microbial activity. This is done by returning bio-mass to the soil. Legume production, crop rotation, mixed cropping etc., are other ways of achieving this.

Shifting to organic agriculture instantly under Indian condition is a debatable issue but adopting the Integrated Farming System can lead us to move towards organics and as per the estimates it prevalent that the IFS approach is having the potential for avoidance of methane emission to considerable limits through the promotion of aerobic micro-organisms and high biological activity in soils, oxidation of methane can be increased. Through practices like System of Rice

Intensification, which is mostly based on principles of ecological farming, flooding in rice paddies can be reduced and thereby, methane emissions.

Nitrous oxide, result of overdoses and losses on nitrogen, can be effectively minimized through integrated farming practices. While production of chemical fertilizers is an energy-intensive process that emits carbondioxide and nitrous oxide, application of nitrogen fertilizers makes the soil emit nitrous oxide. These can be avoided through by using recycled inputs in the system i.e interdependence of waste output of one component to be used as input for the other component.

Integrated Farming System also increases the Soil Organic Carbon (SOC) by incorporating organic materials into the soil. Soil can be a major source of storage of carbon, about twice as much carbon as in the atmosphere. Minimizing fertiliser use replaces soil organic matter in intensive systems, which reduces potential sequestration. Crop, tree and livestock integration with a systematic recycling of organic wastes is an integral part, which can lead to sustainability. Long term studies have shown that compost application and cover crops in rotation were particularly adept at increasing soil organic matter even in comparison to no-tillage techniques. While conservation tillage is promoted elsewhere as a way of sequestration of carbon dioxide, this is often done by the use of chemical herbicides and GMOs which have their own ecological implications. In sustainable agriculture however, mitigation of climate change can be addressed both carbon sequestration and minimized emissions of GHGs. Agro-forestry as a boundary plantation is also a desired principle of integrated farming systems which further adds to the potential towards sustainability in carbon sequestration.

4. Adoption of Integrated Farming System

Integrated Farming System (ecological farming/sustainable agriculture /LEISA etc) approaches are now acknowledged for the wide set of ecological and economic benefits that accrue to the practitioners as well as consumers of agricultural products. These approaches which are based on low external inputs are also low energy intensive and less polluting hence mitigate and help in adapting to the climate change. However, the promotion of Integrated farming system on a large scale is often confronted about its potential as well as its practical limitations.

These successful experiences had three elements in common. First, all have made use of locally adapted resource conserving technologies. Second, in all there has been coordinated action by groups or communities at local level. Third, there have been supportive external (or non-local) government and/or non-governmental institutions working in partnership with farmers. Almost every one of the successes has been achieved despite existing policy environments which still strongly favor 'modern and established' approaches (technology and support systems) to agricultural development. Now the challenge is to create a policy environment to scale up across the temperate region of the J&K in particular. This needs a newer approach in terms of capacity building, horizontal learning, newer institutional systems and newer forms of financial support to be put in place.

The programmatic support to agriculture today favour only high external input based agriculture. As a result, none of the mainstream programs provide any support for promotion of these models. This needs the recasting of program guidelines or initiating newer program to provide support to more sustainable models in agriculture which can be easily accessible to small and marginal farmers.

4.1. Integrated Farming System can initiate a programmatic support to scale up sustainable agriculture and livelihood security with the objectives to

- Characterize existing farming systems to know the productivity, viability and constraints.
- Develop and validate region-specific Integrated Farming System Models for enhanced system productivity, profitability and sustainability and reduce the risks and vulnerabilities with uncertain weather conditions and degraded and limited natural resources in these regions, by adopting suitable cropping patterns and production practices, which can build livelihood security systems to cope up with the natural disasters like drought, floods and other climate uncertainties.
- Assess relative efficiencies of the IFS model in terms of economics, resource use and energy and diversify the assets and income sources to sustain the livelihoods by integrating livestock and horticulture into agriculture and promoting on-farm and off-farm employment opportunities
- Optimize individual components of IFS in regional perspective. Conserve and efficiently use the available natural resources like soil and water, and promote biomass generation.
- Capacity building of stakeholders in Integrated Farming Systems through appropriate trainings and organize farmers into institutions which can help them to have better planning, greater control over their production, help to access resources and support, improve food security and move up in the value chain.

5. Implementation of Integrated Farming System and its basic guidelines

5.1. Sustainable Agriculture

It can be defined as an integrated farming system which is based on locally adapted cropping patterns and local resource (natural resources and natural processes) use based on local knowledge, skills and innovations. The capacity of a farming system to adapt to changing climate and weather conditions is based on its natural resource endowment and associated economic, social, and cultural conditions. The viability of these elements also constitutes the basis for sustainable agriculture, understood as agricultural production that: ensures adequacy of food production; does not harm the resource base; is economically viable; and enhances quality of life. Many climate and weather risk management strategies fit squarely into sustainable agriculture practices and can, therefore, be promoted with several of the programs and policies targeting environmentally responsible production.

Strategies to be adopted

a. Change cropping patterns and cropping systems to suit the local resources and weather conditions. Multiple/mixed cropping, intercropping systems with legume components etc.

b. Ecological farming practices which can maximise the local resource use. Many of these practices are based on indigenous knowledge and focus on building soil biological productivity. Less dependence on chemical Pesticidal Management, Organic Soil Management, Community Seed Banks, System of Rice Intensification, soil moisture management etc have already proven to be useful.

c. Locally adopted crop varieties specially in saline and flood prone areas, drought prone areas, making suitable selections adopting Participatory Plant Breeding and Participatory Varietal Selection.

d. Developing suitable farming systems integrating agriculture, horticulture and livestock.

5.2. Farmers' Institutions

Organized communities have proven to be more effective in planning and managing their resources and livelihoods, lobbying for a policy change and securing their entitlements. Appropriate institutional systems for each of the purposes need be established.

Strategy to be adopted

- Integrated farming research model needs to be extended to dry land agriculture as the total area under the rainfed situation of the state is about 77 % and their will be the real breakthrough for food security and livelihood for the poor resource farmers.
- Capacity building programmes for farmers shall be mandatory in which the provision may be made for making and arranging the need based trainings and visits of the farmers to the Integrated farming system model developed at SKUAST-Jammu. It has been observed that the farmers of the temperate region in particular and J&K region in general are lacking in technical efficiency, which has been estimated about 45%.
- Demonstration of IFS models on the farmers field near the University vicinity/ research institutions shall be under taken, so that more and more farmers shall adopt.
- There is a great potential of value addition and marketing aspects shall be accorded priority under the IFS components.
- The farmers would be organised into common interest groups federated into producer collectives. Existing institutions like Women SHGs etc would be used to initially anchoring the program.
- These institutions would take the roles of planning, mobilising resources, organising production, and take up post harvest management and marketing activities.
- The producer collectives or orgamiazations will improve the collective bargaining power of the farmers, will internalize market activities like bulking, primary and secondary processing which improve the village economy.

5.3. Food and livelihood Security

Shift to Integrated Farming system is often seen as a compromise on food security. This is mainly because food is understood as only wheat and rice, few pulses, oilseeds and vegetables. The food basket can be increased if we can expand the scope to include millets, coarse cereals, dryland fruits, uncultivated greens etc which can also bring in nutrition security. Data from National Centre for Organic Farming (NCOF), ICRISAT and CMSA have proven that crop productivity can also be maintained with organic/ecological farming. Going beyond the current food security systems like PDS and mid-day meal schemes, systems need to be established to improve livelihood security in terms of sustaining food production in the village, improving income generation opportunities to the small farmers and agriculture labor is important in the rural areas especially in temperate regions. The frequent monsoon failures results in droughts and support systems needs to be build to help the farm families and livestock to tide over.

- Building house hold food security systems by adopting suitable cropping patterns.
- Village level management systems for alternative models like grain banks would be appropriate and attempted.
- Suitable off-farm and non-farm employment opportunities would be identified and promoted.

5.4. Financial Support Systems

Currently all the financial support systems to agriculture are given only for external inputs. We need to create proper support systems for farm internalized inputs, community based infrastructure, knowledge and skill building and sharing etc.

- Direct subsidies to farmers rather than input subsidies.
- Integrating NREGA with integrated farming system so that each farmer gets 100 labour days for farming can provide ample scope in this direction.
- Explore tools like Direct Income Support which exist in many developed/ developing countries need to be explored as decent living income cannot be explored only through pricing mechanism.

5.5. Partnerships

At the district/village/block level we need build partnerships between various governmental and non governmental agencies to implement the program. At the state level we need to build an alliance of Public sector research organisations, extension agencies, departments dealing with rural livelihoods, SKUAST-Jammu and NGOs which are working on sustainable agriculture/ organic/ natural/ ecological farming.

6. Broader guidelines for adoption of Integrated Farming System

1. **Selection of Area:** Select a contiguous piece of land measuring 1.0-1.5 ha, to represent small and marginal farmers of the region. The yardstick for defining small and marginal farmers may vary among the stake holders and accordingly area selected for the IFS may also vary.
2. **Selection of Enterprise (Module):** There is no thumb rule for selecting a specific number of enterprises and allocation of area to different enterprises. It would largely depend upon the common logic of household

requirements of an average farm-family of the region, especially in respect of food, feed, fodder, fuel, fiber and reasonable cash. In farming system approach we have to ensure that output from the individual farm unit (IFS Project Area in our case) fulfils aforementioned requirements for a normal size family (size to be specified) along with its farm animals/ fish etc. Moreover, general agro-ecological situations, infrastructure availability, government policies and social acceptability have to be duly considered. As far as possible, select the farming system enterprises, which may fit in a modular format, i.e., they may be developed as self-contained components of the farming system as a whole, with well-defined interface(s) so that they can easily be connected to or disconnected from the system. It should be further diversified with additional components with well-defined objectives and principles of farming systems approach.

3. **Selection of Crops/ Cropping Systems/ Animals:** Within each component, identify crops and their most suited varieties to be grown, cropping systems to be adopted, type and number of animals to be raised, species/ breeds of livestock/ fish/ honeybees to be raised. Allocate optimum area under each unit. This should also be taken care in accordance with abovementioned criteria. Since under temperate conditions the important cash crop are the fruits, hence Horticulture based cropping system will have much more relevance.

4. **Technologies to be adopted:** All the latest available production technologies for different production/ processing units have to be adopted with optimum levels and should be specified in technical programme.

An Overview of Integrated Farming System Model Developed at SKUAST- Jammu

The SKUAST-Jammu after characterizing the existing farming of the region including the temperate areas has developed the model of 1ha for small and marginal farmers on its farm to study the synergistic of various components of farming. The farming system module developed comprises of Horticulture (Fruit, Vegetable and Flowers)+ Crop + Animal + Fish cum poultry + Vermicomposting cum farm waste recycling + biogas + mushroom unit + Small poly house + Boundry tree plantation. The area distribution with regard to 05 family members for individual enterprise has been standardized as under (Table 02).

Table 2: Component wise summary of net returns per ha.

Component	Year of start	Net Area (ha)	Gross return	Total Cost (Rs./ha)	Net returns (Rs./ha)
Crop Unit					
Cropping systems	2011	0.3802	63650	38068	25582
Horticulture unit					
Fruit crops	2011	0.3	13328	17887	9094
Vegetable (intercrop)	2011	-	29649	4234	11762
Floriculture	2011	0.07	7800	2890	4910
Agro-forestry	2011	0.1	1315	597	718
Livestock Unit					
Dairy animals (including Vermicompost & biogas unit)	2011	0.08	318212	174599	143613
Fish cum Poultry Unit					
Poultry/ Ducks	2011	0.001	76578	31989	44589
Fisheries	2011	0.1	42958	12258	30700
Apiary unit (03 boxes)	2011	0.001	4500	3300	1200
Green fodder (Fodder-Fodder Cropping System and on bunds planted pereinial Fodder crops (Hybrid napier)	2011	0.07	14543	1763	12780
Mushroom unit (6 qts wheat straw)	2014	0.02	31034	9780	21254
Grand total	-	1.0	603567	297365	306202

The profit is high to existing Farming System, which works out to be more than 3.0 lakhs/ ha.

It is evident from the above study of integrated farming system that their is having the potential not only to increase the profit to Rs 3.062 lakhs/ha as compared to existing farming system were the farmer is realizes only Rs 0.80 - 0.90 lakhs but also increases the sustainability issues. About 150 kg N is being realized through farm waste composting.

Table 3: Distribution of food commodity production for meeting household nutritional security of five member farm family through adoption of IFS model verses existing farming system Household nutrition for farm family member

Commodity	Requirement as per ICMR standards	Production in existing farming system	Production in improved farming system
Cereals (kg)	1320	3895	1370
Pulses (kg)	150	0	78
Oilseeds (kg)	150	20	80
Potato (kg)		0	800
Vegetables (kg)	768	50	1157
Fruits (kg)	270	50	823
Milk (litres)	660	1200	5648
Meat & Fish (kg)	66	0	476
Egg (nos.)	900	0	92
Green fodder (t)	26.8	3.5	14.3
Dry fodder (t)	6.25	6.02	2.77
Mushroom (kg)		0	361
Turmeric (kg)		0	44
Agro forestry (kg)		0	500
Rice equivalent Yield (ton)	6.3	23.35	

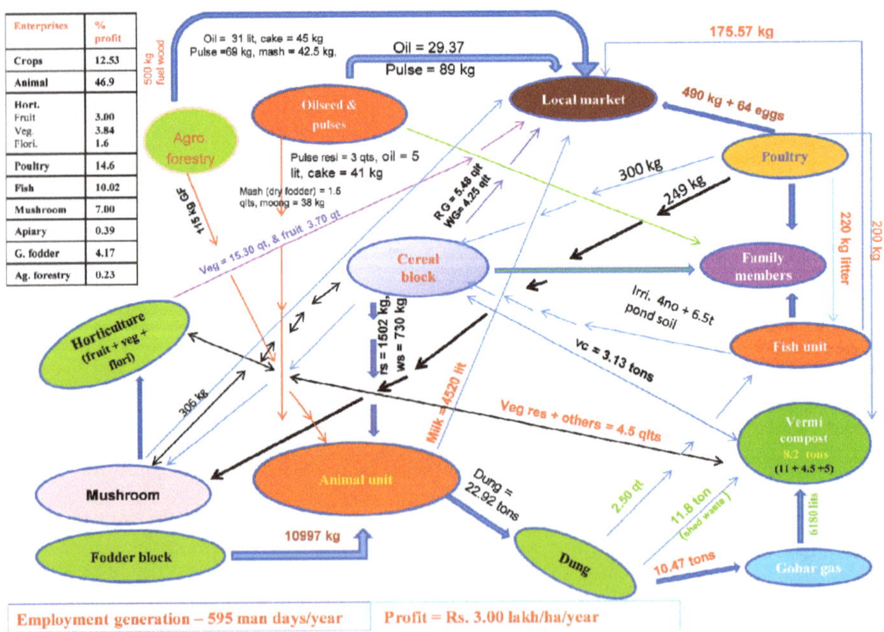

7. Recommendations

One ha Integrated Farming System Model comprising of cropping systems (rice-wheat-green manuring, rice-potato-blackgram, rice-mustard-greengram and berseem+oat-maize+sorghum with hybrid napier on bund) in 0.45 ha +

horticulture (Guava as main crop, Lemon & mango (Amarpali) as boundry crop and brocolii, KnolKhol, Cabbage, Cauliflower, okra and Marigold as intercrops) in 0.37 ha + dairy (2 cow, 1 buffalo heifer) including 2 m^3 bio-gas and vermicompost unit in 0.08 ha + fish cum poultry in 0.1 ha) + mushroom (button & dhingri) in 0.02 ha developed for the Mid to high altitude plain zone (JK-1) in Western Himalayas provides *round the year* average production (23.35 t REY/year), profit (Rs 3.05 lakhs/year) and employment (595 man days/year). Among all the enterprises the highest average net profit of Rs. 149875 (contributing 49.2 % share of profit) was realized from Animal Unit having two Cows and One Buffalo heifer including Vermicompost/farm waste recycling component then followed by crop block including green fodder (Rs. 348881), Poultry (Rs. 34343), Mushroom (Rs. 22681) and Fisheries (Rs. 20700) which contributes profit share of 11.5, 11.3, 7.4 and 6.8 % respectively. The overall average net profit Rs. 304713/year/ha was quite comparable to existing farming system which works out to be 0.80 to 0.90 lakh/ha (table 1).

The maximum average production and profit was realized in June (Table-3, Fig 1) while employment was in May month signifying the work even during lean period. The model also meets around 75 % of inputs required for different enterprises within the farm besides providing all the commodities (cereals, pulses, oilseeds, vegetables, fruits, mushroom, milk, egg, and fish) required for the farm family (Fig 2). The IFS Model of 1 ha contributed 60 kg Nitrogen, 20 kg P_2O_5 and 40 kg K_2O per year through recycling/vermicomposting besides bio gas unit of 2m^3 generated bio gas (@ 0.8 kg LPG/day/15 kg dung) equivalent to 17 LPG Cylinder of 14.5 kg capacity, respectively. Moreover this IFS model under sub-tropical condition of Jammu region is having the potential to improve the farm income to three folds besides will address sustainability issues in the long run.

Not withstanding with the doubling the farm income and generating employment through IFS it has been realized that model developed have the capacity to meet the household nutritional requirements of five farm family members. From the perusal of the data table-3, it was observed that a farm family on an average using IFS model generates different commodities which comparatively balanced and higher than the existing farming system. Therefore, farming system approach can play decisive role in transforming Indian agriculture towards sustainability and profitability and needs implementation on priority.

8. References

Kathiresan, R.M. (2007). Integration of elements of a farming system for a sustainable need and pest management in the tropics. *Crop Protection*, 26: 424-429.

Kathiresan, R.M. (2009). Integrated farm management for linking environment. *Indian Journal of Agronomy* 54(1): 9-14.

Greener Journal of Agronomy, Forestry and Horticulture ISSN: 2354-2306 Vol. 1 (1), pp. 001-011, September 2013.

www.gjournals.org 11

Research Article

Integrated Farming System - An Ecofriendly Approach for Sustainable Agricultural Environment – A Review

*S.S. Walia and Navdeep Kaur

18

Remote Sensing: A Vital Approach for Transforming Indian Agriculture

Veena Sharma, Mahender Singh, *Vikas Sharma, *Vishaw Vikas and **Narender Panotra

Agrometeorological Section, Division of Agronomy, FoA, SKUAST Jammu, India
**Division of Soil Science and Agril. Chemistry, FoA, SKUAST Jammu, India*
***Organic Farming Research centre, SKUAST Jammu, India*

1. Introduction
2. Satellites remote sensing
3. Uses of remote sensing in agriculture
4. Agro-met products
5. Normalized difference in vegetation index
6. Leaf area index
7. Evapotranspiration
8. Crop acreage estimation
9. Crop monitoring
10. Crop yield estimation
11. Crop simulation models
12. Crop condition/ stress assessment
13. Special advisories for extreme events
14. Drought prediction
15. *References*

Abstract

Remote sensing has wider applications in agriculture right from landscape mapping, soil moisture, planting dates, cropping systems to climate change effects. Growing uncertainties of weather and climate change pose a major threat to food security of the country and thus warrant for farmers empowerment of informed decision in agricultural risk management. The technology is competent to monitor crop growth, predict crop yield in terms of quantity and quality, assists in estimating crop acreage, its condition, disease and pest status. Over the last two decades, the development of space technology has led to a substantial increase in satellite earth observation systems. Simultaneously, the Information and Communication Technology (ICT) revolution has rendered increasingly effective the processing of data for specific uses and their instantaneous distribution on the World Wide Web (WWW). Satellite data provide better coverage in time and in area extent than any other alternative. It is important to make maximum use of this information to monitor our environment. Access to these Satellite data and products is only the beginning. In addition, the ability to interpret, combine, and make maximum use of this information is an integral part of weather and climate management at the national level. Production estimates, post harvest and quantity available for market enable the farmers and policy makers to chalk out sustainable strategy to match supply with market demand.

Keywords: Remote sensing, crop yield, stress assessment, agro-advisories.

1. Introduction

The term Remote Sensing means the sensing of the Earth's surface from space by making use of the properties of electromagnetic waves emitted, reflected or diffracted by the sensed objects, for the purpose of improving natural resources management, land use and the protection of the environment. It may be defined as "Group of techniques for collecting image or other forms of data about an object from measurements made at a distance from the object, and the processing and analysis of the data". Remote sensing has wider applications in agriculture right from landscape mapping, cropping systems to climate change effects. Growing uncertainties of weather and climate change pose a major threat to food security of the country and thus warrant for farmers empowerment of informed decision in agricultural risk management. Besides, the possible impacts of climate change also pose major challenges in agriculture sector in the country. The combination of long-term changes and the greater frequency of extreme weather events are also likely to have adverse impacts on the food production in the coming decades. Also increases in extreme weather such as floods and drought, as a result of climate change could have a negative impact on livelihoods that depend on climate-sensitive activities such as rain-fed agriculture and livestock rearing. Current concerns with the sustainability of agro ecosystems in different parts of the world have heightened the awareness for careful use of the natural resource base on which agriculture depends. For proper and efficient use of soils and plant/animal genetic material, knowledge of the role of climate is essential. Climate services are receiving increasing attention globally.

Meteorological Service in many cases is realigned, resourced and trained as providers of services for development and as participants in the development process. Climate information is tried to reach the last mile to create impact, enough information. There is a great need to convert the climate information into actionable information for farmers. Meteorological Services has great role to play to share climate information including the products with the small farmers. The agricultural meteorology is one of the most important components of applied meteorology. The operational consequences of this group play a key role to agricultural community which composes significant portion of population in India. All agro-meteorological and agro-climatological information that can be directly applied to try to improve and/or protect the livelihood of farmers in agricultural production may be considered to belong to agro-meteorological services.

India is transforming its traditional agriculture into modern agriculture, this brings many new requirements on agro meteorological services and which means transforming traditional agro meteorology into modern agro meteorology with automatic monitoring, accurate forecasting, quantitative evaluation, systematic services, and professional personnel. The climatic information is linked with the available technologies and best farming practices. To improve the information delivery system: a modern agrometeorological service platform and automatic information delivery systems are established; direct services for the farmer are strengthened; a public feedback mechanism has been established; current agrometeorological products are improved and updated as per needs and according to local characteristics and practicability for use among farmers;

There is more application of satellite remote sensing data and that agro-meteorological information to be delivered to farmers in a timely manner through multiple modern methods including TV, radio, network, cell phone text, community radio, agro-meteorological disaster alarming information receiver, etc. India has independent agro meteorological services. These services include the production of bulletins, daily forecasts, alerts, and special communications. Most agro meteorological services utilize GIS and satellite products in their operational work. Agro meteorological applications include agroclimatic modeling, interpretation of satellite images to agriculture, GIS, basic handling of agro-meteorological data; development of strategic alliances with organizations that have developed and using such tools; developed a program of regional exchange;

implementation of modern tools and technologies in agro meteorological services in order to improve the operational agro meteorological applications; and focus of agro-meteorológical applications on the current needs of the agricultural community.

2. Satellite Remote Sensing

Remote sensing provides spatial coverage by measurement of reflected and emitted electromagnetic radiation, across a wide range of wavebands, from the earth's surface and surrounding atmosphere. The improvement in technical tools of meteorological observation, during the last twenty years, has created a favorable substratum for research and monitoring in many applications of sciences of great economic relevance, such as agriculture and forestry. Each waveband provides different information about the atmosphere and land surface: surface temperature, clouds, solar radiation, processes of photosynthesis and evaporation, which can affect the reflected and emitted radiation, detected by satellites. The challenge for research therefore is to develop new systems extracting this information from remotely sensed data, giving to the final users, near-real-time information.

Over the last two decades, the development of space technology has led to a substantial increase in satellite earth observation systems. Simultaneously, the Information and Communication Technology (ICT) revolution has rendered increasingly effective the processing of data for specific uses and their instantaneous distribution on the World Wide Web (WWW).

The meteorological community and associated environmental disciplines such as climatology including global change, hydrology and oceanography all over the world are now able to take advantage of a wealth of observational data, products and services flowing from specially equipped and highly sophisticated environmental observation satellites. An environmental observation satellite is an artificial Earth satellite providing data on the Earth system and a Meteorological satellite is a type of environmental satellite providing meteorological observations. Several factors make environmental satellite data unique compared with data from other sources, and it is worthy to note a few of the most important:

- Because of its high vantage point and broad field of view, an environmental satellite can provide a regular supply of data from those areas of the globe yielding very few conventional observations;
- The atmosphere is broadly scanned from satellite altitude and enables large- scale environmental features to be seen in a single view;

- The ability of certain satellites to view a major portion of the atmosphere continually from space makes them particularly well suited for the monitoring and warning of short-lived meteorological phenomena; The advanced communication systems developed as an integral part of the satellite technology permit the rapid transmission of data from the satellite, or their relay from automatic stations on earth and in the atmosphere, to operational users. These factors are incorporated in the design of meteorological satellites to provide data, products and services through three major functions:

a. Remote sensing of spectral radiation which can be converted into meteorological measurements such as cloud cover, cloud motion vectors, surface temperature, vertical profiles of atmospheric temperature, humidity and atmospheric constituents such as ozone, snow and ice cover, ozone and various radiation measurements;

b. Collection of data from *in situ* sensors on remote fixed or mobile platforms located on the earth's surface or in the atmosphere; and

c. Direct broadcast to provide cloud-cover images and other meteorological information to users through a user-operated direct readout station.

- The Advanced Very High Resolution Radiometer (AVHRR) on board the National Oceanic and Atmospheric Administration (NOAA) series of satellites has been used for mapping vegetation cover and classification employing the Normalized Difference Vegetation Index (NDVI). Recently, this technique has been improved by converting NDVI with radiation measured in one of the thermal channels and converting brightness temperature into the Vegetation Condition Index (VCI) and Temperature Condition Index (TCI). These indices are being used for estimation of vegetation health and monitoring drought. The vegetation and temperature condition indices are used for drought monitoring in India.

3. Use of RS in Agro-Met Services

To gather information about

Crop Micro-climate (Canopy information)

Soil (moisture, temperature)

Vegetation/Crops (Vigor, Stress Type)

Pest & Diseases (Outbreak, Infestation Level-density & spread, Migration)

Water

Information compatibility to ICT, GIS and GPS

4. Agromet Products

At present many meteorological and agrometeorological variables are available at half hourly and daily scale such as insolation, vegetation index, land surface temperature, rainfall, hydro estimator, fog etc. these variables are further used to derive value added agrometeorological parameters/indicators such as in season crop area, sowing date, leaf area index, potential and actual evapotranspiration for regular monitoring of agriculture. This is further used for crop monitoring, yield estimation and improvement in high resolution weather forecast.

- Agrometeorological products are derived parameters from meteorological/ agrometeorological or other interdisciplinary information. It deals with application of weather and climate derived information in Agricultural Management.
- Timely availability and appropriate use of this information are vital for successful farming operations.
- These products serve as an important step for decision making to end users. The first and foremost consideration is user requirements. Thus Agromet products are crop and location specific.

Decision making using Agromet Products

These are useful for both strategical and tactical decision.

Strategical decisions

- Crop planning
- Management practices
- Marketing

Tactical decisions

- Sowing
- Cultivation
- Spraying
- Irrigation scheduling etc.

Various Agromet Products Used

Following are the Agromet Products in use for decision making to end users.

Rainfall

Only land based techniques of rainfall estimation are not sufficient for rainfall. Therefore meteorological satellites are used for their potential for improved identification and quantification of precipitation with the nature and development of precipitation processes. The primary scope of satellite rainfall monitoring is to provide information on rainfall occurrence, amount and distribution over the regional to national scales. At present, three algorithms are used to estimate rainfall from Indian geostationary satellite such as

a. GOES precipitation index (GPI)

b. INSAT multispectral rainfall Alogrithm (IMSRA)

c. Hydro estimator

Crop health

NDVI is very sensitive to background factors, such as the brightness and shade of the vegetation canopies and soil background brightness. Researchers have shown that when the background brightness is increased, NDVI also increases systematically. Given the effect of soil background, radiation increases significantly when the vegetation cover is sparse; conversely NIR radiation is reduced to make the relationship between vegetation and soil more sensible. Many VIs have been developed to adjust to the soil effect.. The Normalized Difference Vegetation Index (NDVI) has become one of the most successful tools to easily and quickly assess plant and crop health.

The amount of solar radiation flux or irradiance reaching at ground surface is known as surface insolation. One of the most important factors that influences plants development is the solar radiation intercepted by the crop. The solar radiation brings energy to the metabolic process of the plants. The principal process is the photosynthetic assimilation that makes synthesize vegetal components from water, CO2 and the light energy possible. A part of this, energy is used in the evaporation process inside the different organs of the plants, and also in the transpiration through the stomas. There are two main approaches Kondratyev-Kurbelka-Monk (KKM) (Rosema 1993) and Tanahashi physical model (TPM) (Tanahashi *et al* 2001) to retrieve insolation.

Land surface temperature

Canopy (or skin) temperature is more directly related to growth and evapo-transpiration than the air temperature. The difference between the two is a measure of crop stress. A single channel (SC) method is developed for LST (Land surface temperature) retrieval from K1-VHRR TIR data through a radiative transfer model (Pandya *et al* 2010). However, it is to be noted that the satellite derived skin temperature and canopy temperature are equivalent only when a satellite field of view is filled with vegetation, otherwise it is temperature of bare soil, crop *etc*.

Fog

Fog is disastrous weather phenomenon especially in terms of traffic safety and air quality. INSAT 3D data with improved spatial and temporal resolution is used for near and real time detection and mapping of fog. The general methodology of fog detection involves identification of some threshold radiances or brightness temperature at different wavelengths. Fog is formed when vapor in the lower atmosphere condensed in cold conditions. The fog droplets are much smaller than the cloud droplet. The presence of these droplets affects the atmospheric visibility. The radiation difference between cloud and fog is due to the spectral response differences of every channel. This provides the basis of fog detection. The difference of brightness temperature corresponding to two spectral channels (3.9 & 10.8μm) is used for the identification of fog.

Hail storm

Hail storm causes substantial damage to the standing crops as well as the horticultural crops within a very short time. Hail storm could be predicted from the data generated through Doppler Radar within 3 hours of the incidence.

Albedo

Land surface albedo, defined as the ratio of the surface reflected incoming and outgoing solar radiation, is one of the key geophysical variables controlling the surface radiation budget. Surface shortwave albedo is widely used to drive climate and hydrological models. During the last several decades, remotely sensed surface albedo products have been generated through satellite-acquired data. There are mainly 3 approaches to retrieve surface albedo using K1 VHRR

1. Kondratyev (Rosema, 1993)
2. B. Mossou (1989)
3. Gautier and Diak (1980)

Among all three approaches, Kondratyev is found to provide least bias.

Cold and heat wave

Impact of climate variability has assumed significance in recent years as warm winters have turned out to be a major impediment and cold wave conditions have significant positive impact on crop productivity in these areas. Thus the possible impact assessment of cold wave on crop productivity especially wheat can be done either by analyzing productivity data in relation to historical meteorological data or by using thermal infrared data from satellite.

5. Normalized Difference Vegetation Index (NDVI)

Vegetative index is a mathematical representation of spectral response of vegetation in different wavelength to know the vigor and health of vegetation. The Normalized Difference Vegetation Index (NDVI) is widely used for vegetation growth monitoring. Vegetation reflects more in green band (550nm) and less in red band (650nm) due to strong absorption by leaf pigments (chlorophyll) for photosynthesis. For land surfaces dominated by vegetation, the NDVI values being associate, is a calculation of vegetation or crop health. Mathematically comparing red and NIR light signals can help differentiate plant from non-plant and healthy plant from sick plant.

$$\text{NDVI} = \frac{(NIR - \text{Re}\,d)}{(NIR - \text{Re}\,d)}$$

Where red and NIR stand for the spectral reflectance measurements acquired in the red (visible) and near-infrared regions, respectively. When performing the calculation, NDVI values will range from -1 to 1. The higher the index value (more positive), the greater the crop health and vigor. NDVI values between -1 and 0 correspond to non-plant surfaces that have a reflectance in the Red that is greater than the reflectance in the NIR. These could be surfaces such as equipment, water, or soil. Soil's value is close to 0. Plant values range from 0.1 to nearly 1, and like stated earlier, the higher the NDVI value, the greater their density and health.

Applications

NDVI enables agronomists and farmers to see stressed crops in a field up to two weeks before the human eye would be able to detect. Crops stress sooner in the NIR than they do in the visual spectrum, so growers can identify diseases, pests, fungus, or arid conditions sooner, and then respond and make quicker decisions before the issues become an even bigger problem.

NDVI is a perfect tool for tracking plant health. Many agronomists and farmers capture a series of NDVI maps to track the health of their crops throughout the growing season and even from year to year. NDVI values can be averaged to establish the normal growing conditions for the crops in a given area for a given time of the year. NDVI gives powerful insights and makes it easier to visualize crop health that the naked eye can't see. It shows you where the problem is in advance so you can fix it faster.

6. Leaf area index

The productivity of a crop depends on the ability of plant cover to intercept the incident radiation, which is a function of leaf area available, the architecture of vegetation cover and conversion efficiency of the energy captured by the plant into biomass. Most production strategies are directed towards maximizing the interception of solar radiation. In the case of crops, this implies adapting agricultural practices in such a way as to obtain complete canopy cover as soon as possible.

Vegetative indices based on reflectance in broad wave bands have provided good estimates of radiation capture and yield in crop plants (Gallo *et al* 1985; Hatfield *et al* 1984). Vegetation indices have also provided good estimates of fractional groundcover (Boissard *et al* 1992; White *et al* 2000). More recently, spectroradiometers capable of measuring narrow band radiation have been used to monitor plant stress (Elvidge and Chen 1995). Radiometric satellite data are now available for the evaluation of large areas, and small portable radiometers are becoming less expensive as the technology progresses.

7. Evapotranspiration

Evapotranspiration is combined loss of water from soil as well as plants and it is also a crucial component of Hydrologic Cycle. But at the same time ET depends upon several factors and it is very difficult to calculate it precisely. Estimation of evapotranspiration is important for determining the agro-climatic potential of a particular region, water requirement of field crops, irrigation scheduling and suitability of crops or varieties, which can be grown successfully with the best economic returns. Evapotranspiration varies widely through both space and time, along with the biological and meteorological factors that drive it. Spatial and temporal heterogeneity of vegetation cover and function, as well as differences in available energy and water, all influence the rate at which ET occurs.

Plant growth processes and productivity of agroecosystems depend highly on evapotranspiration from the land (soil-crop cover complex) surface. Satellite observations supplemented with routine meteorological data provide a unique capability to estimate actual evapotranspiration over large areas needed for irrigation management and water balance.

8. Crop Acreage Estimation

The first step in using Remote Sensing for acreage estimation is to identify crop cover by Remote Sensing, For this reason, one must study the reflectance characteristics of green leaf. Remote Sensing based pre harvest acreage estimation methodology for major crops like paddy, wheat, cotton, soybean, sugarcane, sorghum etc. are well established.

9. Crop Monitoring

Burrough and McDonnell (1998) has defined GIS as a powerful set of tools for collecting, storing, retrieving at will, transforming and displaying spatial data from the real world for a particular set of purposes. The three major components of GIS are (i) computer hardware, (ii) computer software and (ii) digital geographic data. The information stored within a GIS is of two distinct categories. The spatially referenced information that can be represented by points, lines, and polygons, that are referenced to a geographic coordinate system and is usually stored in either raster (grid-cell) or vector (arc-node) digital format. The second category of information stored in a GIS is attribute data or information describing the characteristics of the spatial feature.

The use of GIS along with RS data for crop monitoring is an established approach in all phases of the activity, namely preparatory, analysis and output. In the preparatory phase, GIS is used for

(a) Stratification/zonation using one or more input layers (climate, soil, physiography, crop dominance etc.), or

(b) Preparing input data (weather, soil and collateral data) which is available in different formats to a common format. In the analysis phase use of GIS is mainly through operations on raster layers of NDVI or computing VI profiles within specified administrative boundaries. The final output phase also involves GIS for aggregation and display of outputs for defined regions (e.g., administrative regions) and creating map output products with required data integration through overlays.

10. Crop yield estimation

Crop yield is influenced by a large number of biotic factors and the remotely sensed spectral data of a crop is an integrated manifestation of the effects of all these factors on its growth. Several approaches are adopted for crop yield prediction using Remote Sensing data. Vegetation index of maximum vegetation growth phase of crop is directly related to crop yield and this can be determined by Remote Sensing. Remote Sensing data are used to estimate some of the crop biometric parameters like Leaf Area Index (LAI), crop cover, which in turn are input parameters to yield models.

Remote sensing technology has been proved as a useful application for natural resources evaluation and management. In the past, spectral data acquired via satellite has been extensively utilized for crop yield modeling in various parts of the world. The important assumption in use of remote sensing data for crop modeling is that the spectral data is strongly related with canopy parameters which are related to final yield at a critical stage of the crop growth.

Use of satellite spectral data in crop yield estimation surveys is examined. The satellite data at the time of maximum flowering/heading of the crop in the form of vegetation indices is used to stratify the crop area into vegetation vigor classes like high vegetation, average vegetation, poor vegetation etc. This is followed by developing certain post stratified estimator of crop yield based on yield data as obtained from crop cutting experiments. A substantial improvement in the efficiency of crop yield estimator as compared to the existing estimator. With the use of satellite spectral data along with the survey data based on crop cutting experiment either the number of crop cutting experiments can be reduced resulting in considerable reduction in the cost for obtaining district level estimate with the same precision or small area estimates at a lower level compared to the district (like tehsils or blocks) can be obtained with the existing crop cutting experiments in a district

11. Crop simulation models

Crop simulations models are based on physical plant processes and simulate the effects of change in growing environment on plant growth and development on a daily basis. A crop simulation model is a simple representation of a crop and is explanatory in nature. The processes essentially modeled are phenology, photosynthesis and dry matter production, dry matter partitioning, in simulation models aimed at potential production. Those aiming at crop-specific behaviour include modules for phyllochron, branching pattern and potential flowers/ grain filling sites. The response to water and nutrition limited environment is added by introducing models of soil water balance and uptake and transpiration by crop, and nitrogen transformations in soil, uptake and remobilization within plant, respectively. Models of effects of weeds and pests are being developed and could be available in new generation of crop simulation models. In dynamic crop simulation models, three categories of variables recognized are, state, rate and driving variables. The state variables are quantities like biomass, amount of nitrogen in soil, plant, soil water content, which can be measured at specific times. Driving variables, or forcing functions, characterize the effect of the environment on the system at its boundaries, and their values must be monitored continuously, e.g., meteorological variables. Each state variable is associated with rate variables that characterize their rate of change at a certain instant as a result of specific processes. These variables represent flow of material or biomass between state variables. Their value depends on the state and driving variables according to rules that are based on knowledge of the physical, chemical and biological processes that take place during crop growth. Under the International Benchmark Sites Network for Agrotechnology Transfer (IBSNAT) project a computer software package called the Decision Support System for Agrotechnology Transfer (DSSAT) was developed which integrates 11 crop simulation models (CERES cereal, CROPGRO legume and other models) with a standardized input and output (Jones, 1993) and has been evaluated/ used in a number of countries. Use of CERES-Wheat included in DSSAT for regional wheat yield prediction has been demonstrated recently in India (Nain *et al* 2004).

12. Crop Condition / Stress Assessment

Crop vigor / condition is affected by several factors such as supply of water and nutrients, insect and pest attack, disease outbreak and adverse weather conditions which cause physical / physiological changes and alter the spectral characteristics of crop canopy. Several Remote Sensing approach are developed for crop condition assessment. In optical Remote Sensing involving reflective spectral bands, crop condition assessment is done by studying Vegetation Index Anomaly.

Remote sensing technology can provide spatial distribution information of diseases and pests over a large area with relatively low cost. The presence of diseases or insect feedings on plants or canopy surface causes changes in pigment, chemical concentrations, cell structure, nutrient, water uptake, and gas exchange. These changes result in differences in color and temperature of the canopy, and affect canopy reflectance characteristics, which can be detectable by remote sensing (Raikes and Burpee 1998). Therefore, remote sensing provides a harmless, rapid, and cost-effective means of identifying and quantifying crop stress from differences in the spectral characteristics of canopy surfaces affected by biotic and abiotic stress agents.

13. Special advisories for extreme events

In India, around 26 Doppler weather radars are installed and also various types of satellite data is being used to provide information about extreme weather events like heavy rainfall to save the crops and also contingency planning is given to the farmers for taking appropriate crops in respect of expected climate variability during the monsoon season. Synoptic Methods, Statistical Methods and Numerical Weather Prediction models developed based on these observational network can be used for generation of rainfall, temperature, thunderstorm, dust storm, clouds, cyclonic storms (their courses and stages), heavy rainfall warnings, frost warning, squall warning, heat waves, cold waves etc. Digital and image information at 10 minutes interval from Doppler weather radar is very useful in addition to many other observed data in predicting thunderstorm activity.

Specialized products derived from satellites such as Normalised Difference Vegetation Index (NDVI), surface insulation, Leaf Surface Temperature (LST), Albedo, reference evapotranspiration, soil moisture, Aridity index, satellite-based rainfall etc. also play very significant role in disaster management in agriculture. Such generated agromet products are useful if they are promptly delivered to the end users to reduce disaster management risk for farmer community. Due to this information, farmers can tackle the situations under different extreme weather events and ultimately reduces the impact of bad weather. Efforts have also been made through automated advisory tools to develop a mechanism for generation of agromet advisories along with crop and its stages by using realized data recorded at surface observatories under Network of IMD.

14. Drought prediction

Remote Sensing (RS) and Geographic Information System (GIS) have played a remarkable role in assessment of various types of hazards either natural or man-made. RS and GIS are used in the field of drought risk evaluation. Data used for drought monitoring is acquired from the two sources, NDVI obtained from satellite sources and rainfall obtained from ground rainfall stations record. Drought risk areas are identified and extracted encountering agricultural and meteorological drought by using the Normalized Difference Vegetation Index (NDVI) obtained from the LANDSAT images. The NDVI images generated from LANDSAT data are used to examine large scale drought patterns and their climatic impact on vegetation. NDVI values reflect the different geographical conditions quite well. The NDVI and rainfall are highly correlated. Temporal variations of NDVI are convincingly associated with precipitation.

15. References

Boissard P, Pointel J and Tranchefort J .1992. Estimation of the ground cover ratio of a wheat canopy using radiometry. *International Journal Remote Sensing*. 13(9):1681-1692.

Burrough PA and McDonnell RA .1998. Principles of Geographical Information systems Oxford University press, New York, 333p.

Catherine Gautier, Georges Diak and Serge Masse .1980. A Simple Physical Model to Estimate Incident Solar Radiation at the Surface from GOES Satellite Data. *Journal of Applied Meteorology*. 19(8) 1005-1012.

Elvidge CD and Chen Z .1995, Comparison of broad-band and narrow-band red and near - infrared vegetation indices: *Remote Sensing of Environment*. 54: 38-48.

Gallo KP and Daughtry CST. 1986. Techniques for measuring intercepted and absorbed photosynthetically active radiation in corn canopies. *Agronomy Journal*. 78:752-756.

Jones JW .1993. Decision Support Systems for Agricultural Development, pages 459-471.

In: Systems Approaches for Agricultural Development, Vol. 2. (Penning de Vries FWT, Teng P and Metselaar K eds.), Kluwer Academic Publishers, Dordrecht, The Netherlands.

Moussu G, Diabate L, Obrecht D and Wald L .1989. A method for the mapping of the apparent ground brightness using visible images from geostationary satellites. *International Journal of Remote Sensing*. 10 (7).

Nain AS, Dadhwal VK and Singh TP .2004. Use of CERES-Wheat model for wheat yield forecast in central Indo-Gangetic plains of India. *J. Agricultural Science* (Camb.). 142: 59-70.

Pandya MR, Darji NP, Shah DB, Trivedi HJ, Ramakrishnan R, Panigrahy S, Parihar JS and Kirankumar AS .2010. Development of an algorithm to retrieve land land surface temperature from the INSAT- VHRR DATA. ISRS National Symposium 2010. Lonavala.

Raikes C and Burpee LL .1998. Use of multispectral radiometry for assessment of Rhizoctonia blight in creeping bentgrass. *Phytopathology*. 88: 446-449.

Rosema A .1993. Using METEOSAT for operational evapotranspiration and biomass monitoring in the Sahel region. *Remote Sensing of Environment*. 46: 27-44.

Tanahashi S, Kawamura H, Matsuura T, Takahashi T and Yusa H .2001. A system to distribute satellite incident solar radiation in real-time. *Remote Sensing of Environment*. 75(3): 412-422.

White MA, Asner GP, Nemani RR, Privette JL and Running SW .2000. Measuring fractional cover and leaf area index in arid ecosystems: digital camera; radiatuon transmittace and laser altimetry methods. *Remote Sensing Environment*. 74:45-57.

19

Krishi Vigyan Kendras: Hub of Technology Transfer & Agricultural Transformation

Shahid Ahamad, Banarsi Lal*, Akash Sharma**, Satish K Sharma

Directorate of Research
**Krishi Vigyan Kendras, Reasi, Jammu, Jammu and Kashmir, India*
***ACHR, SKUAST-Jammu, Jammu and Kashmir, Idnia*

1. Introduction
2. Mandates of KVK
3. Organization and functioning of KVK
4. Major responsibilities of KVK
5. Impact of specific skill imparted by KVK Reasi
6. Impact of FLDs in terms of Area expansion

Abstract

A Krishi Vigyan Kendra (KVK) is synonymous to farm science center with responsibilities of on-farm technological assessment, front line demonstrations, capacity building, advisory services and mulit-sector support to various private and public initiatives. The KVKs work under the ambit of ICAR, New Delhi with administrative support from local institutions or State Agricultural Universities. There were about 695 KVKs operational in India till October 2018. All KVKs fall under the jurisdiction of one of the 11 Agricultural Technology Application Research Institutes (ATARIs) spread throughout India. 21 KVKs are functioning in Jammu and Kashmir with seven of them in Jammu province namely KVK Jammu, Samba, Kathua, Reasi, Rajouri, Doda and Poonchh. The major thrust areas of hilly district Jammu and Kashmir are as integrated nutrient/pest/weed management in different crops, water management, promoting organic farming, protected cultivation of high value and low volume crops, promotion of aromatic and medicinal plants, increase in the productivity of livestock, drudgery reduction for farm women, promotion of loose flower cultivation, promotion of new single cross hybrids in maize, value addition of agricultural products and promotion of farming system approach. KVK Reasi has been able to motivate farmers of the district to adopt and practice organic farming, floriculture, backyard poultry farming and mushroom production at the commercial level.

Keywords: *KVK, technology tramsfer, Agro-entrepreurship*

1. Introduction

Jammu and Kashmir is a mountainous state in which about 30 per cent of the area is under cultivation. Agriculture is the mainstay of the people as it provides employment to about 75 per cent of the workforce. This sector contributes about 65 per cent of the state revenue which signifies the dependency of the state on agriculture. Agriculture is the major occupation of the people in Jammu & Kashmir where more than 75 per cent of the population is directly associated with agriculture. Thus, agricultural development harbingers the overall growth and development of the State. Judicious use of land is necessary to mitigate the growing needs of the increasing population by keeping the sustainability of soils, ecosystems and environment in view.

The Krishi Vigyan Kendras (KVKs) also known as Farm Science Centers, a gross root level scheme which was designed by the Indian Council of Agricultural Research (ICAR) in the country. In 1964-66, the Education Commission of Government of India under the chairmanship of Dr DS Kothari gave recommendations for the application of science to productive process including agricultural education. The Planning Commission of India and Inter-Ministerial Committee reviewed the recommendations. A committee under the chairmanship of Dr. Mohan Singh Mehta was constituted by the ICAR in 1973 which further gave the recommendations for the establishment of KVKs in the country. The first Krishi Vigyan Kendra (KVK) was established in 1974 at Pudducherry under Tamil Nadu Agricultural University, Coimbatore by the ICAR, New Delhi. Presently, the ICAR has established 641 KVKs all over the country under different organizations like State Agricultural Universities, the ICAR institutes, Deemed Universities, Central Institutes, State Governments and NGOs. In Jammu and Kashmir ICAR has established 19 KVKs under two agricultural universities SKUAST-Jammu, SKUAST-Kashmir. These KVKs are mitigating the scientific agricultural needs of the farmers of Jammu and Kashmir and are playing a pivotal role in transformation in rural areas of the state by updating the rural people about the latest agricultural technologies.

The KVKs have proved their worth to mitigate the agricultural needs of the farmers and empower them through need-based vocational trainings and helpful to change the socio-economic conditions of the farmers. Throughout the state the Krishi Vigyan Kendras conduct on- farm testing, identify the location specificity of agricultural technologies, lay out front line demonstrations to establish the production potential of various agricultural technologies at farmers fields, impart need-based and skill oriented training to the practicing farmers, in-service extensional personnel, to those who are interested for self-employment to update their knowledge and skills in new agricultural technologies, create awareness on improved technologies through various extension methods, produce and provide improved quality seeds, planting material, livestock, poultry, fisheries etc. to the farmers and work as agricultural knowledge centers for the public, private and voluntary organizations. These Kendras cater the needs of those who wish to be self-employed or those who are already employed. There is no particular syllabus for the Krishi Vigyan Kendras.

The programs and syllabus (action plan) of the Krishi Vigyan Kendras are tailored according to the needs, resources and potential for the agricultural growth in a particular area and is finally decided by involving the districts heads, Panches/Sarpanches and also progressive farmers of the district.

2. Mandates of KVK

- To conduct "On-farm testing" for identifying location specific sustainable production technologies.
- To organize trainings to update the Extension Personnel with emerging advances in agriculture research.
- To organize short and long-term vocational training courses in agriculture and allied vocations for the farmers and rural youths.
- To demonstrate efficacy of improved production technologies to farmers by laying Front-Line Demonstrations (FLDs) on various crops to generate production data and feedback information.

The prime objective of the Krishi Vigyan Kendras is agricultural growth. Priority is given to the weaker sections of the society like small, marginal, tribal farmers, agricultural labourers, drought prone areas, hilly areas, forest areas, coastal areas etc. and work-experience is the main method of imparting training. The first objective of the ICAR is to cover the entire country with one Krishi Vigyan Kendra in each district and priority is given to the backward areas. As there is a great demand for the improved agricultural technologies by the farmers so there is great demand of Krishi Vigyan Kendras throughout the state of Jammu and Kashmir. Farmers need not only the latest knowledge of the technologies but also more skills in the agricultural operations for adoption.

3. Organization and functioning of the KVKs

The KVK staff is comprised the sixteen members team. The Krishi Vigyan Kendra is headed by one Programme Co-ordinator (Senior Scientist-cum-head), six Subject Matter Specialists (Junior Scientists) from the different discipline like Agricultural Extension, Horticulture, Agronomy, Home Science, Animal Science and Fisheries, three Programme Assistants(trainings, farm and computer each), two administrative staff, two drivers and two OCCs. In the agricultural universities, KVKs are headed by the Director Extension (DE) and at zone level KVKs are monitored and guided by Zonal Project Director (ZPD).At central level KVKs are headed by Deputy Director General (DDG) Extension. The Indian Council of Agricultural Research (ICAR) provides guidelines to KVKs and conducts periodic supervision. In order to establish a KVK there is requirement of basic infrastructure. The KVK has its administrative building, farmers' hostel and six quarters for the staff. KVKs have rain water harvesting units, soil and water testing labs, e-connectivity, vermicompost units, polyhouse units, fish pond units, poultry farm units, beekeeping units, mushroom cultivation units etc. The KVKs also have a jeep, two wheelers and tractors facilities. The KVKs are also guided to establish crop cafeterias and technology parks for the demonstration purpose. KVK executes its activities with the help and guidance of local management committee. The KVKs need to constitute their Scientific Advisory Committees (SAC) involving the agricultural and allied departments' heads and is chaired by the head of the organization. In SAC meetings the progressive farmers are also involved. In order to get the technical and scientific guidelines to achieve the targets and also to present the action taken report, the KVKs need to conduct Scientific Advisory Committee (SAC) meeting twice in a year. The KVKs can spend their revolving funds for production of technological products.

Priority thrust areas

Crop/Enterprise	Thrust area
Cereals-Maize	Introduction of single cross commercial maize hybrids, Integrated Nutrient Management, weed management, common insect / pests management
Wheat	Introduction of new high yielding varieties of wheat, seed treatment, weed management, disease and pest management including termite control and rodents control. Seed production of new varieties.
Fodder	Promotion of new varieties, Increasing area under fodder crops. Round the year fodder production.
Oilseed	Introduction of new improved varieties, Promotion of insect pest management, control of Alternaria blight, Use of balanced nutrition. INM in oilseeds.

Contd.

Pulses	Promotion of improved varieties, Weed management, insect /pest and disease management.
Vegetables	Promotion of hybrids, introduction of new varieties. Diseases and pest management. Round the year vegetable cultivation, healthy nursery raising of vegetable crops, kitchen gardening.
Animal husbandry	To increase production potential of livestock by improved breeding, feeding and management practices. Promotion of backyard poultry
Mushroom cultivation	-Promotion of mushroom cultivation, growing of more species for year round cultivation.
Floriculture	Promotion of loose flower cultivation in the district, integrated nutrient management, introduction of new varieties. Disease management in marigold.
Agro-forestry	Fodder trees, Medicinal & Aromatic plants, Environment conservation.
SHGs/Farmers clubs	Formation, management and strengthening of SHGs/farmers clubs.
Fruits	Insect-pest and disease management in fruit plants.

Fig. 1. Skill upgradation programs for farmers by KVKs.

View of farmers training on and off campus

Formation of Farmers Clubs/Self Help Groups

KVK, Reasi has formed 24 farmers clubs and more than 80 SHGs in close co-ordination with the NABARD, SBI, PNB, NGOs etc. who are working excellently. The farmers clubs formed in the district are producing the organic vegetables at commercial level and fetching more prices. The SHGs on dairy farming, pickle making, food processing, vegetables etc. are generating extra income.

View of skill development/Vocational Training Programmes

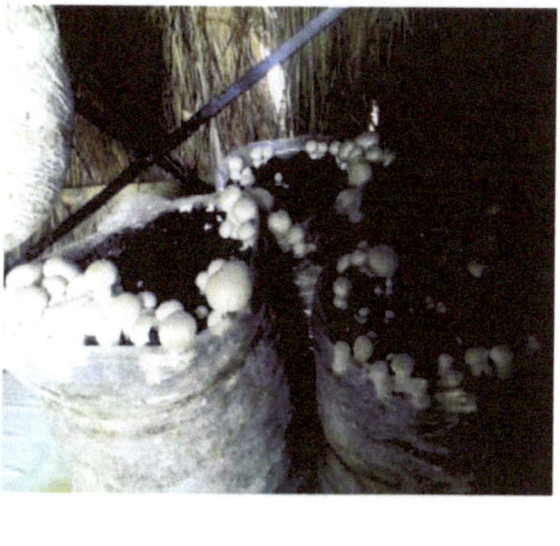

4. Major responsibilities of Krishi Vigyan Kendra

Every KVK in the country has four major responsibilities to take forward namely,

(i) To conduct on-farm tests, refinement, assessment and documentation of agricultural technologies. On farm testing of technologies is done to test already developed technologies in terms of location specific sustainable land use systems and it helps to solve farmers' problems in their fields through their participation. Thus, on farm testing of technologies is done to refine and modify the technology according to the location of a particular area. The farmers problems are identified through the Participatory Rural Appraisal (PRA) and on the basis of the problems faced by the farmers OFTs are conducted.

(ii) To layout front-line demonstrations at farmers' field to generate the production potential of new crop varieties and production technologies in crops, livestock, fisheries etc. to increase the production through improved methods at farmers fields in a given farming system and also to get feedback from the farmers.

(iii) To organize long-term vocational training for the rural youths in order to generate the self-employment. After trainings farmers can become agri-entrepreneurs.

(iv) To impart training to the farmers and extension functionaries to abreast them with the latest agricultural knowledge. Need based trainings are designed for different types of farmers. The training courses are designed on the basis of information received from village survey through Participatory Rural Appraisal (PRA) or Rapid Rural Appraisal (RRA) methods and characterize the human and physical resources.

The farming system of the farmers is taken into account while designing the courses of the programs. All methods and means to develop the skill among the farmers in their areas of interest are taken into account. Basically the trainings starts from the farmers production units such as farmers fields, dairy units, poultry units, goat units, sheep units etc. and terminates with discussion. No certificate or diploma is awarded to the farmers for the trainings. Follow-up extension programs are conducted after trainings in order to get the impact of the trainings on the trainees and proper documentation of the programs is done. The KVKs also aware the farmers, field functionaries and other stakeholders on the recent developments in agriculture and allied sectors through various extension methods. Also the KVKs take the help of mass media in timely dissemination of agricultural information to the farmers. Co-ordination of various development departments and private agencies plays a vital role for the success of extension programs of KVKs. The KVKs also conduct technology weeks to create awareness among the farmers about the latest technologies in agriculture and allied sectors. The KVKs also send information to the farmers of respective district through short message service (SMS) to solve their agricultural problems. The KVKs are also involved in production of quality seeds, planting materials, livestock material and bio-products and supply them to the farmers.

The Krishi Vigyan Kendra plans and conducts survey of the operational areas to identify the training needs of the farmers. It compiles all the recommendations for the district to utilize in the training programs. KVK conducts need-based, production oriented short and long-term training courses both on and off campus. KVK maintains the farm on the scientific basis for the demonstration purpose in order to provide the work experience to the farmers and also to disseminate the latest agricultural technologies. KVK also imparts some general training to the rural illiterates and school drop outs in order to convert them as the good farmers.

The KVKs decide certain thrust areas according to the agro-ecological, cropping pattern and farming system of the respective district.

The major thrust areas of hilly district Jammu and Kashmir are as

- Integrated nutrient/pest/weed management in different crops
- Water management
- Promoting organic farming
- Protected cultivation of high value and low volume crops
- Promotion of aromatic and medicinal plants
- Increase in the productivity of livestock
- Drudgery reduction for farm women
- Promotion of loose flower cultivation
- Promotion of new single cross hybrids in maize
- Value addition of agricultural products etc.

Follow-up of extension programs are conducted after trainings in order to get the impact of the trainings on the trainees and proper documentation of the programmes is done. The KVKs also take the help of mass media (electronic and print both) for timely dissemination of agricultural information even to the farmers of far-flung areas. Co-ordination of various development departments and private agencies plays a vital role for the success of extension programmes of KVKs. The KVKs also conduct technology weeks to create awareness among the farmers about the latest technologies in agriculture and allied sectors and disseminate the agricultural information to the farmers of respective districts through short message service (SMS). The KVKs are also involved in production of quality seeds, planting materials, livestock material and bio-products and supply them to the farmers. KVK maintains the farm on the scientific basis for the demonstration purpose in order to provide the work experience to the farmers and also to disseminate the latest agricultural technologies.

It has been observed that with the introduction of Krishi Vigyan Kendras in the state the adoption rate of new agricultural technologies has increased. Now, majority of the farmers of the state are using hybrid/improved/high yielding varieties of maize, paddy, wheat, pulses, oilseeds etc. KVKs are diverting the farmers from subsistence farming to commercial farming. Keeping in view the scope of floriculture in the state, floriculture industry in the state is spreading. Mushroom cultivation, sericulture, horticulture, dairy farming, vermicomposting, food processing, milk processing entrepreneurships are developed among the farmers in certain pockets of the state by the strenuous efforts of KVKs. KVKs are catering the agricultural needs of both the provinces of the state. These are the agricultural knowledge hubs in the respective districts.

5. Impact of specific skills imparted by KVK, Reasi

Disease and insect-pest management advisory to farmers by KVK expert

- From the last 3 years there has been heavy infestation of yellow rust of wheat in Reasi & Udhampur districts causing huge loss to the farmers.
- KVK, Reasi recommended Propiconazole (Tilt) @ 0.1% for the management of yellow rust of wheat which was heavily infested in the district. Infestation in more than 80% area was managed by advicing farmers for its control measures..
- There was heavy infestation of pod borer in chickpea in the district. KVK, Reasi managed the pest by recommending the Cypermetherin in more 30% area covered by Chickpea.

Title	Participants	%age Adoption	Annual Income(Rs.) Before Training	Annual Income(Rs.) After Training
Training programme on commercial organic farming	72	45	73,000/ha/unit	2,55,000
Training programme on commercial commercial floriculture	66	45	60,000/ha	1,10,000
Entrepreneurship development in agriculture	26	30	65,000/ha	1,75,000/ha
Training programme on backyard poultry as an entrepreneurship. .	40	20	40,000-50,000/per year/ per 1000bird unit	80,000-100000/ year/ 1000 bird unit (6-7 lots per year)
Processing of mango and other locally available fruits	26	30	For household use	54,000/unit/year
Processing of fruits and vegetables.	123	36	-	62,000
Training programme on scientific cultivation of mushroom/dhingri .	17	17	-	52,000/unit/year
Mushroom /dhingri cultivation as an entrepreneurship development among the rural youths.	28	25		65,000/unit

Views of Front Line Demonstrations

WELCOME
Dr.S.Ayyappan
HON'BLE DIRECTOR GENERAL, ICAR
KRISHI VIGYAN KENDRA, REASI

View of front line demonstrations laid by KVK, Reasi

6. Impact of FLDs in terms of Area expansion

S.No.	Intervention	Impact
1.	Single Cross Maize Hybrids (Maize var. Double Deklab, KH-517, Bioseed etc.)	More than 80% of area of the districts has been covered under single cross maize hybrids.
2.	Wheat Var. PBW-175	KVK, Reasi demonstrated FLDs on wheat var. PBW-175 in both the districts Reasi and Udhampur in the which gave encouraging results. As a result more than 1500 ha area of the districts has been covered by this variety.
3.	Mash var. Uttara	More than 25% area of the district under *Kharif* pulses has been covered by this variety.
4.	Mustard RSPR-01	More than 30% area of the district under *Rabi* Oilseed has been covered by this variety.
5.	Lentil L-4147	More than 15% area of the district under *Rabi* pulses has been covered by this variety.
6.	Backyard Poultry(Vanraja RIR, Chabro)	• A small but steady income of Rs 7680 per 10 birds/annum. • In year 2013-14, 83 HH & in 2014-15, 188 HH were given high egg laying birds(10 each HH). A survey of those HH revealed that • More no. of families have been rearing these birds and HH who were distributed have increased their birds' number to approx. 15-17 birds on an average. • Besides income, eggs and meat as protein rich food have also increased their overall health status. Success & awareness of above can be gauged from the fact that 22549 in 2013-14 and 31583 2014-15 birds of the same breeds has been purchased by farmers from the line department for backyard poultry

View of OFTs laid by KVK, Reasi

WELCOME

Table 4: Details of indigenous techniques practiced by the farmers which can be considered for technology development

S.No.	Crop / Enterprise	ITK Practiced	Purpose of ITK
1.	Vegetables	Use of ash to control red pumpkin beetle in cucurbits	to control red pumpkin beetle in cucurbits
2.	-do-	Use of ash to supply nutrients in cucurbits and vegetable crops to increase the yield	to supply nutrients in cucurbits and vegetable crops to increase the yield
3.	Maize	Control of weeds in maize crop by ploughing in between the plants of maize crop	Control of weeds
4.	Cucurbits	Sorghum and cucurbits are sown together to control the insects-pests	to control the insects-pests
5.	Cereals	Leaves of trees are used to increase the fertility in maize and wheat crop	to increase the fertility in maize and wheat crop
6.	Wheat	Leaves of Neem plant , Bana(Vytusnigundu) and Eucalyptus sp. plant are used to store the wheat grains and protect from stored grain pests	to store the wheat grains and protect from stored grain pests
7.	Cereals	Use of kerosene oil to protect the field crops from termite attack	to protect the field crops from termite attack
8.	Wheat	Protection of wheat crop from rabbits attack by using the white cloths and polythene sheets on sticks	Protection of wheat crop from rabbits attack
9.	Maize	Mixed cultivation of maize and cowpea to protect the maize crop from boars	to protect the maize crop from boars
10.	Vegetables	Staking of cucurbits, peas and tomato to increase the yield and also to get the good quality of crop	to get the good quality of crop
11.	Maize	Use of cow urine mix with the cow dung to control the insect-pests in maize crop	to control the insect-pests in maize crop
12.	Animals	Use of saunf, gur and mustard oil after boiling it and then filtering it to control bloating in animals	to control the insect-pests in maize crop
13.	livestock	Bleeding from certain parts of animals to control the bloating inanimals	animals to control the bloating in animals
14.	Livestock	Mixture of cotton and ghee to control the diarrhoea in animals	animals to control the bloating in animals
15.	Livestock	Use of Methi and gur mixture to control the diarrhoea in animals in winters	to control the diarrhoea in animals in winters

Contd.

16.	Livestock	Gur and saunf mixture to control the diarrhoea in animals in winters	to control the diarrhoea in animals in winters
17.	Livestock	17. Use of mixture of mustard oil and lassi to control the Diarrhoea in animals in summers	to control the Diarrhoea in animals in summers
18.	Livestock	Hooka (tobacco) water is used to save the animal if bitten by snake or any other poisonous organism	to save the animal if bitten by snake or any other poisonous organism
19.	Livestock	Use of kerosene oil to control the ticks and mites in animals	to control the ticks and mites in animals
20.	Livestock	Use of Dhaman plant leaves to increase the yield of milk in animals	to increase the yield of milk in animals
21.	Livestock	Use of mixture of salt, mustard oil and turmeric to control the foot and mouth disease in animals	to control the foot and mouth disease in animals
22.	Livestock	Black ink and ghee or oil to protect the animals from wounds infection	to protect the animals from wounds infection
23.	Fruits	Use of ripening of mango by using the wheat straw	Use of ripening of mango
24.	Livestock	Use of protein rich concentrate (mixture of wheat brawn, cotton cakes, mustard cakes, salt and chickpea bran) to increase the milk yield in animals	Use of ripening of mango
25.	Cereals	Protect wheat crop from rabbits attack by sowing lentil in fields	Protect wheat crop

20

Biotechnological Approaches in Agricultural Transformation

Manmohan Sharma*, RK Salgotra, Aarushi Singh and Jag Paul Sharma[1]

School of Biotechnology, SKUAST Jammu, Jammu & Kashmir, India
[1]Directorate of Research, SKUAST Jammu, Jammu & Kashmir, India

1. Introduction
2. Biotechnology applications in agriculture
3. Molecular marker technology in agriculture
4. Characterization, finger printing and identification
5. Genetic divergence and diversity study
6. Linkage map construction and gene tagging
7. Marker assisted selection (MAS)
8. QTL mapping and gene pyramiding
9. Genetic engineering in agriculture
10. Emerging biotechnological approaches for crop improvement
11. Biotechnology in livestock improvement
12. Microbial biotechnology in agriculture
13. *References*

Abstract

India with population of 1.30 billion in which 47 per cent is engaged in agriculture earnestly needs efficiently use of biotechnology and genetic engineering for transforming agriculture sector. Biotechnological tools offer great opportunities for increasing agricultural production and can play an important role towards the attainment of production sustainability of crops.

Biotechnological tools have the potential to release burgeoning pressure on agriculture and allied sectors; ecology and environment; plant, animal and microbial biodiversity; and allied resources such as land and water with improved and sustainable agricultural productivity which enhances food security. Agricultural biotechnology, including tissue culture, DNA-marker-assisted breeding and genetic engineering (GE) technology have potential to increase stress tolerant, selection efficiency, crop adaptation, crop productivity and food security in more efficiently manner through the development of improved varieties with increased yields, nutritional content and storage characteristics. Genetic engineering tools should continue to build capacity in this technology, giving priority to traits and crops that are of economic importance such as drought tolerance in maize, rice, beans; cold tolerance in rice; increased nutritional value and improved shelf life in fruits and vegetables. Crop varieties and livestock with improved characteristics have been developed using tools such as marker-assisted breeding and genetic engineering. Molecular pharming is one of the applications of genetically modified crops and livestock for the production of pharmaceutical proteins. Reproductive technologies are alternative ways for genetic improvement of livestock. The development of molecular diagnostics and vaccine technology as a tool improved the ability to detect and treat several diseases of livestock. The advancements in biotechnological tools such as protein engineering and metabolic engineering play a significant role in production of a large number of valuable and high quality industrial products.

Keywords: Biotechnology, genetic engineering, tissue culture, marker assisted breeding

1. Introduction

Indian agriculture is endowed with rich repository of biological diversity, valuable genetic resources of agricultural crops and plethora of natural resources. The agro-climatic conditions, in terms of seasons, rainfall, temperature regimes, soils and biological diversity that we have are probably unmatched elsewhere in the world. We have coexistence of tropical, temperate, semi-arid and conditions with wide range of soils and landforms. India is recognised as one of the mega-centres of biodiversity, accounts for 2.4% of the global land, 11.2% of arable land, 4.2% water and over 8,000 km of coastline. These resource endowments being unique to our country should be appreciated as our strengths and their potential needs to be harnessed to the advantage of agriculture sector.

Agriculture continues to be the biggest employer in the world with 40 per cent population engaged in this sector. India is projected to be the most populous country in the world with about 1.5 billion people by 2030 (FAO 2016). More importantly the country sustains 17.4% of the world population implying thereby that every 6th person in the world is an Indian. Hence, food security for all would be the most important challenge. The ever increasing demand for food, feed, nutrition and other basic needs has put a lot of pressure on agriculture and allied sectors. Agriculture is facing multifarious challenges such as shrinking land resources, unfavorable climate, limited water availability, crop losses due to biotic and abiotic stresses, increase in the input cost etc. These problems are becoming even more complicated in view of changing climatic scenario and ever increasing demand of feeding growing population. The impact of Green Revolution realized during the decades of 1960s and 1970s, which brought about exponential increase in production of major cereal crops to feed the growing population, could not be sustained for a longer time.

Need of the hour is to explore and exploit the potential of agricultural biotechnology to produce traits that reduce risk and unconditionaly increase yields; more efficiently grow crops from decreased or static land availability; mitigate risk of abiotic and biotic stresses; improving the nutritional quality of grains; decrease losses and increase output; and appropriately respond to impact of climate change. Biotechnological tools have the potential to release burgeoning pressure on agriculture and allied sectors; ecology and environment; plant, animal and microbial biodiversity; and allied resources such as such as land and water with improved and sustainable agricultural productivity which enhances the food security. Crop varieties and livestock with improved characteristics have been developed using tools such as marker-assisted breeding and genetic engineering. Molecular pharming is one of the applications of genetically modified crops and livestock for the production of pharmaceutical proteins. Reproductive technologies are alternative ways for genetic improvement of livestock. The development of molecular diagnostics and vaccine technology as a tool improved the ability to detect and treat several diseases of livestock. The advancements in biotechnological tools such as protein engineering and metabolic engineering play a significant role in production of a large number of valuable and high quality industrial products.

Adoption of biotechnology in agriculture has been the focus of controversy due to varied reasons, as questions have arisen regarding food and environmental safety of transgenic crops. The food safety assessment requires the evaluation of safety of newly added DNA and the safety of their gene products and overall safety of balance of food. The concept of substantial equivalence has been accepted as the cornerstone of the health hazard assessment of genetically modified (GM) foods. Therefore evaluation of such interventions necessitates establishing the reasonable likelihood of safety and that new varieties are as safe as or safer than the crops produced through traditional methods.

Biotechnology has played an important role towards the attainment of production sustainability of crops by using various biotechnological tools. The realistic utilization of biotechnology in agriculture has not only brought about profound changes in the crop productivity and quality, but has also opened up newer and hitherto unforeseen potential vistas including engineering novel traits, successful commercial micropropagation, manipulating plant architecture and molecular farming. The molecular techniques for plant diseases diagnosis and pathogen characterization, marker-assisted selection, parasitic diagnosis, development of transgenic crop, and gender friendly agri-entrepreneurship have found a stay in the economic development and prosperity of farmers in the hilly region. In this chapter, we are reviewing the development challenges facing in hill agriculture and try to elucidate how biotechnology can contribute to food security, poverty reduction and sustainable socioeconomic development.

Conventional and biotechnological research inputs have contributed in solving many of the barriers limiting crop productivity. However, limitations such as complex genome, narrow genetic base, poor fertility, susceptibility to biotic and abiotic stresses and long duration to breed elite cultivars, hinder crop improvement programmes. This article describes the developments in the *in vitro* culture systems and related biotechnologies tools such as marker-assisted selection (MAS), marker-assisted breeding (MAB), QTL mapping, genetic engineering etc that have evolved as novel strategies in the recent years for use in crop, livestock and microbe improvement. A critical but practical look at the prospects and constraints of various types of biotechnologies and their applications for transforming Indian agriculture has been attempted.

2. Biotechnology applications in Agriculture

Conventional and biotechnological research inputs have contributed in solving some of the constraints limiting crop productivity. However, limitations such as complex genome, narrow genetic base, poor fertility, susceptibility to biotic and abiotic stresses and long duration to breed elite cultivars, hinder crop improvement programmes. The following are the main biotechnological approaches that are being adopted with the aim of transforming agriculture sector

2.1. Micropropagation and cell culture

Plant Tissue Culture is the technique of growing various plant parts like cells, tissues, seeds or organs in a sterile environment provided by a medium of nutrients. The techniques include culture of cells, anthers, ovules and embryos on experimental to industrial scales; protoplast isolation and fusion, cell selection, meristem and bud culture. Plant tissue culture is one of the most important branches of biotechnology having tremendous applied value and thus may be considered as an important aid to modern agriculture. Plant tissue culture now has direct commercial applications which include:

Micropropagation using meristems, bud propagation, shoot culture and cell or protoplast culture to produce large number of identical individuals

- Somaclonal variation to select for disease resistance
- Large-scale growth of plant cells in liquid culture as a source of secondary products
- Interspecific/ wide hybridization for transfer of genes among distantly related individuals
- Production of doubled haploid plants from haploid cultures to achieve homozygous lines more rapidly in breeding programmes
- Virus free propagation from meristematic tissues
- As a tissue for transformation and regeneration of transgenic plants
- Micropropagation to produce large numbers of identical individuals
- Being indispensable for propagation of many plants, micropropagation is practiced for production of quality planting material.

Micropropagation

In a plant tissue culture laboratory micropropagation of economically important agricultural, horticultural, forest and medicinal plants *in vitro* is done with focus on cost minimization to make the technology commercially viable. Further, R& D efforts in introduction of new plants are pursued. The various applications of micropropagation technology are

Rapid multiplication: Micropropagation offers rapid multiplication of desired plant species.

Requirement of only limited number of explants: Small pieces of plant (explants)/tissue can be used to produce a large number of plants in a relatively small space.

Uniform or true to type plants: Micropropagation provides a high degree of phenotypic/physical uniformity. Since the production cycle takes place under controlled conditions, proper planning and scheduling based on the market demand is possible. The resulting product has very high degree of uniformity compared with traditionally propagated plants.

Germplasm storage: Plants can be stored *in vitro* in a small space under low or ultra low temperatures including cryopreservation and less labour is required for maintenance of stock plants.

Disease free planting material: Plantlets produced by tissue culture are usually disease free. With proper diagnosis and treatments, elimination of fungus, bacteria and virus prior to large scale propagation is possible. With the help of serological and molecular technique it is possible to index virus of mother plant/explant which is to be used for mass multiplication.

Growth manipulation: Nutrient levels, light, temperature and other factors can be more effectively controlled to manipulate the growth, multiplication and regeneration.

Round the year production: Micro-propagation is independent of season. As micro - propagation could be carried out throughout the year; production cycle can be scheduled to meet peak demands.

An alternate to conventional seeds: seed of species that have long generation time, low levels of seed production, or seeds that do not readily germinate, rapid propagation is possible through tissue culture.

Shorter life cycles: The time required is much shortened, no need to wait for the whole life cycle of seed development.

Plant Tissue Culture Technology has proved commercially viable in propagation of different types of crop plants to cater to the needs of farming community at large (Table 1).

Table 1: Commercially plants propagated through micro-propagation in India

Plant category	Plants
Fruits	Banana, Pineapple, Strawberry
Cash crops	Sugarcane, Potato
Spices	Turmeric, Ginger, Vanilla, Large cardamom, Small Cardamom
Medicinal plants	Aloe vera, Geranium, Stevia, Patchouli, Neem
Ornamentals	Gerbera, Carnation, Anthurium, Lily, Syngonium, Cymbidium
Woody plants	Teak, Bamboo, Eucalyptus, Populus
Bio fuel	Jatropha, Pongamia

2.2. Production of secondary metabolites

Plant cell cultures represent a potential source of valuable secondary metabolites which can be used as food additives, flavors, fragrances, pigments, dyes, pesticides nutraceuticals, and pharmaceuticals. The synthesis of phytochemicals by the cell cultures in contrast to these in plants is independent of environmental conditions and quality fluctuations. In many cases, the chemical synthesis of metabolites is not possible or economically feasible. Moreover, the natural food additives are better accepted by consumers in contrast to those which are artificially produced (Hussian *et al* 2012)

2.3. Production of doubled haploid plants to shorten breeding cycles of the crop varieties

Anther culture (androgenesis), to generate haploid plants from pollen microspores, is one way to shorten this process. It allows novel allele combinations, particularly ones involving recessive characters, to be assessed in intact plants. Useful individuals can then be developed into homozygous and fertile plants through chromosome doubling techniques, and brought into a breeding programme. There can be number of potential applications of doubled haploids (DH) in vegetable crops:

Incorporating DH in breeding programmes has the advantage of accelerating inbred line development by achieving homozygosity instantly within a generation. The production of pure lines using doubled haploids has several advantages over conventional methods as homozygosity is achieved in one generation, eliminating the need for several generations of self-pollination. The time saving is substantial, particularly in biennial vegetable crops.

DH technique can be used to transfer sterile cytoplasm of CMS lines into a desirable background in a single step avoiding many generations of backcrossing (Onion).

For self incompatible species, dioecious species and species that suffer from inbreeding depression due to self-pollination, haploidy may be the only way to develop inbred lines. The induction of DH lines in dioecious plants, in which sex is determined by a regulating gene, has an additional advantage. Such a case is well studied in asparagus, in which sex dimorphism is determined by a dominant gene *M*. Female plants are homozygous for the recessive alleles (*mm*), while male plants are heterozygous (*Mm*). Androgenically produced DH lines are therefore female (*mm*) or 'supermale' (*MM*). An advantage of supermales is that, when used as the pollinating line, all hybrid progeny are male.

DH can also be employed for studying inheritance of quantitative traits, QTL mapping, genomics, gene identification, as base material for Targeting Induced Local Lesions in Genomes (TILLING) populations, production of stable transgenic plants and reverse breeding.

2.4. Interspecific/ wide hybridization

Interspecific hybridization/wide crossing involves crossing plants belonging to two different species that are not normally sexually compatible. It is used to transfer useful characteristics from wild relatives to cultivated species or to combine favorable traits of two different species, but significant amounts of time and scientific expertise need to be invested. Biotechnology approaches such as *in vitro* embryo rescue and anther culture are crucial to overcome sexual incompatibility and to speed up the process. *In vitro* embryo rescue utilizes a sequence of tissue culture techniques to enable a fertilized immature embryo, resulting from an interspecific cross, to avoid abortion caused by unbalanced endosperms and to continue growth and development until it can be regenerated into an adult plant.

Embryo rescue has always remained very interesting for vegetable breeders in obtaining interspecific hybrids as some of the wild relatives of the common vegetables are endowed with genes for disease and insect resistance. The prominent examples include: *Solanum peruvianum* which shows resistance to virus, fungi and nematodes to which most varieties of the cultivated tomato (*Solanum lycopersicum*) are susceptible. The cross between cultivated and *S. peruvianum* results in the formation of fruits which contain underdeveloped embryos. These shriveled seeds do not germinate otherwise but hybrid plants have however, been obtained from this cross by rescuing hybrid embryos on an artificial medium (Lai *et al* 1990).

Solanum khasianum (wild species of brinjal) is known to be resistant to the attack of brinjal shoot and fruit borer (*Leucinodes arbonalis*), whereas the cultivated species *S. melongena* is highly susceptible to this insect. These species normally do not produce viable hybrids. With the application of embryo culture, however, hybrid plants could be obtained (Sharma *et al* 1980).

Resistance to potato leaf roll virus (PLRV) has successfully been introgressed from *Solanum etuberosum* to *S. tuberosum* through embryo rescue (Chavez *et al* 1988).

Interspecific hybrids have also been obtained making use of embryo rescue technique in leguminous crops namely Phaseolus (Kuboyama *et al.*,1991), cucurbits namely *Cucumis sativus, Cucumis melo,* and some wild species (*C. anguria, C. zeyheri and C. metuliferus*) (Skalova *et al* 2008),

Crosses of *Brassica napus* were made with an intergeneric hybrid Raphanobrassica (*Raphanus sativus* x *B. oleracea*) with the objective of transferring shattering resistance into *B. napus*.

2.5. Somaclonal variation to select for disease resistance

Plant tissue cultures isolated from even a single cell can show variation after repeated subculture. Distinct lines can be selected with their own particular morphology and physiology. It suggests that the tissue culture vessels contain a population of genotypes whose proportion can be altered by imposing an appropriate selection pressure. This variation can be transmitted to plants regenerated from the tissue cultures, and is called somaclonal variation. It provides an additional source of novel variation for exploitation by plant breeders. In plant tissue culture calli as well as their plants are regenerated. The cell cultures as well as plantlets can be successfully screened against culture filtrates of toxins of pathogenic bacteria and fungi; as well as abiotic stress factors for selection of resistant genotypes.

2.6. Virus free propagation from meristematic tissues

In vitro propagation of apical meristems is an important part of virus-elimination therapy for improving the health of plant collections. Failure of viruses to invade meristem is due to high auxin concentration in meristematic cells, competition for nutrients and enzymes for virus replication, active metabolic process which is not suitable for virus multiplication, action of growth regulators (cytokinins), presence of inhibitors (phenolamines), metabolic disruption of enzymes necessary for viral replication and RNA degradation. Virus free tissue culture raised plants have been produced in fruit crops like Banana, Papaya and Strawberry; spice crops like Black pepper, Small cardamom, large cardamom, Vanilla and Clove; cash crops like Sugarcane and Potato; forest plants like Teak, Eucalyptus, Poplar and Bamboo; and ornamentals like Aglaonema, Aistomeria, Alocacia, Anthurium, Asparagus, Begonia, Calathia, Carnation, Chrysanthemum, Orchids, Syngonium, Lilium, Ficus, Colocasia, Gerbera, Gladiolus, Fittonia, Freesia, Fittonia, Rose, Phylodendron, etc.

2.7. Reclamation of waste lands:

Many Govt., non Govt. and social organizations have large demand of tissue culture raised plantlets of teak, bamboo, eucalyptus and populus for reclaiming waste and forest lands.

3. Molecular marker technology in agriculture

Isozyme and molecular based research accelerate the conventional plant breeding. DNA markers are the most widely used type of marker predominantly due to their abundance. They arise from different classes of DNA mutations such as substitution mutations (point mutations), rearrangements (insertions or deletions) or errors in replication of tandemly repeated DNA (Paterson 1996). These markers are selectively neutral because they are usually located in non-coding regions of DNA. Unlike morphological and biochemical markers, DNA markers are practically unlimited in number and are not affected by environmental factors and/or the developmental stage of the plant (Winter and Kahl 1995). Increasingly, techniques are being developed to more precisely, quickly and cheaply assess genetic variation. In recent years different molecular markers include: (i) hybridization-based markers such as restriction fragment length polymorphism (RFLP), (ii) PCR-based markers: random amplification of polymorphic DNA (RAPD), amplified fragment length polymorphism (AFLP) and microsatellite or simple sequence repeat (SSR), and (iii) sequence-based markers: single nucleotide polymorphism (SNP) have been developed and applied to a large crop plant species. Now these molecular markers are being widely used to track loci and genome regions in several crop breeding programmes, as molecular markers tightly linked with a large number of agronomic and disease resistance traits are available in major crop species (Phillips and Vasil 2001; Jain *et al* 2002; Gupta and Varshney 2004). The majority of these molecular markers have been developed either from genomic DNA libraries (RFLPs and SSRs) or from random PCR amplification of genomic DNA (RAPDs) or both (AFLPs). These DNA markers can be generated in large numbers and can prove to be very useful for a variety of purposes relevant to crop improvement. Their association with genes/QTLs controlling the traits of economic importance has also been utilized in some cases for indirect MAS. Other uses of molecular markers include gene introgression through backcrossing, germplasm characterization, genetic diagnostics, characterization of transformants, study of genome organization and phylogenetic analysis (Gupta and Varshney 2004). Among vegetable crops, which act as a potential money spinner for the farmers, molecular markers have entered the scene of genetic improvement during one and a half decade ago. The major target traits for vegetable improvement in vegetable breeding include disease and insect pest resistance, fruit yield and quality, floral characteristics, cold, hardiness, and dormancy. The saturated genetic maps have also been developed for most of the important vegetable species, and a number of horticulturally important genes loci have been tagged. These advancements in biotechnology have leveraged the development of more efficient breeding tools substituting the conventional phenotype based selection procedures.

Molecular markers tagged with genes or quantitative trait loci (QTLs) of horticultural importance, could be/are being used as indirect selection criteria to improve breeding efficiency via marker-assisted selection (MAS) in many of the vegetable crops.

4. Characterization, fingerprinting and identification

Different crop species e.g. rice, winter wheat, buckwheat, pigeon pea, beans, barley etc are characterized using isozymes. DNA molecular markers (RAPD, SSR) can be used to characterize and fingerprint the varieties and landraces of rice, barley, beans and buckwheat. Isozyme profiles of pigeon pea; RAPD profiles of winter wheat and buckwheat and SSR profiles of rice and barley has been done successfully. Isozyme and DNA profiles of different accessions can be developed. For identification, similarity or dissimilarity bands, private alleles or standard genotyping can be used. These markers can also be used to identify variety, F1 hybrid and in plant variety protection. The techniques are highly relevant to determine evolutionary trends in crops, animals and microbes. These could be equally applicable to estimate effects of climate change on species stability and integrity.

5. Genetic divergence and diversity study

It is planned to use DNA markers (RAPD, SSR, SNP) to screen the accessions for particular trait e.g. blast resistance and susceptible rice accessions, drought tolerance accessions, cold tolerance accessions, high protein content accessions etc. Diversity is assessed among variety and landraces of rice, barely, buckwheat, winter wheat, beans, etc using morphological, isozymes, RAPD, SSR and SNP markers. Different diversity parameters are estimated. Clustering is the common method of showing relationship based on the genetic distance. These findings are very useful for parent selection and heterosis prediction.

6. Linkage map construction and gene tagging

Linkage maps based on either morphological, isozymes or DNA markers are prerequisite to identify and tag desired genes. Mapping and tagging agriculturally important genes with molecular markers is the foundation for markers assisted selection (MAS) and marker assisted backcrossing (MAB) in crop plants. Molecular tags, a prerequisite for MAS and MAB have been developed for many crop plants using different kinds of molecular markers elsewhere. Linkage map on common buckwheat using EST markers on F2 population has been constructed. It is planned to construct such map in other important crop species. Tagging blast resistance gene in rice landraces of hills is expected and it will be used for MAS.

7. Marker assisted selection (MAS)

MAS provides new solutions for selecting and maintaining desirable genotype. Once molecular markers closely linked to desirable traits are identified, MAS can be performed in early segregating population and at early stages of plant development. Marker assisted selection or identification can be used to pyramid the major genes including resistance genes with the ultimate goal of producing varieties with more desirable characters. With MAS it is now possible for breeder to conduct many rounds of selection in a year. Molecular marker technology is now integrated into existing plant breeding programmes all over the world in order to allow researchers to access, transfer and combine genes at a rate and with a precision not previously possible. The potential for accelerating backcross breeding is possible now after the advent of DNA markers. These markers can be used to select backcross progeny which had usually large portions of recurrent parent genotype reducing the number of backcross generation necessary to reconstitute a recurrent parent genotype. MAB has been very widely used by commercial firm savings of even 1-2 generations. From the beginning, the expectations about the potentials of MAS have been huge. Nevertheless, there is little systematic knowledge about the degree to which MAS is being used in modern plant breeding programs and for what purposes. MAS offered possibilities to plant breeders to overcome many of the problems faced during conventional breeding. Knowledge of the location of all genes in a genome extends molecular marker technology because it becomes possible to identify candidate genes controlling specific traits. The genes then become the markers and the process becomes more accurate and more efficient. The location and sequence of candidate genes makes it possible to design allele specific markers which readily lend themselves to automation. In biotechnology, marker-assisted selection (MAS) and marker-assisted breeding (MAB) have the potential to increase crop productivity in hill farming system in number of crops.

8. QTL mapping and gene pyramiding

Most of the important agronomic characters like yield and yield components, plant height and days to flowering are controlled by several genes. A number of methods for mapping quantitative trait loci (QTL) and estimating their effects have been suggested and investigated. Many QTL can be identified using DNA markers. The identified QTLs can be used in MAS or MAB programmes in crop improvement of rice for various traits like drought tolerance accessions, cold tolerance accessions, high protein content accessions etc.

9. Genetic engineering in agriculture

Genetic engineering offers plant breeders access to an infinitely wide array of novel genes and traits, which can be inserted through a single event into high-yielding and locally-adapted cultivars. This approach offers rapid introgression of novel genes and traits into elite agronomic backgrounds.

Future impacts of biotechnology in crop production will be in the areas of:

(i) developing new hybrid crops based on genetic male-sterility,

(ii) exploit transgenic apomixes to fix hybrid vigour in inbred crops,

(iii) increase resistance to insect pests, diseases, and abiotic stress factors,

(iv) improve effectiveness of bio-control agents,

(v) enhance nutritional value (vitamin A and iron) of crops and post-harvest quality,

(vi) increase efficiency of soil phosphorus uptake and nitrogen fixation,

(vii) improve adaptation to soil salinity and aluminium toxicity,

(viii) understanding nature of gene action and metabolic pathways,

(ix) increase photosynthetic activity, sugar and starch production, and

(x) production of pharmaceuticals and vaccines.

New crop cultivars with resistance to insect pests and diseases combined with bio-control agents should lead to a reduced reliance on pesticides, and thereby reduce farmers' crop protection costs, while benefiting both the environment and public health. Similarly, genetic modification for herbicide resistance to achieve efficient and cost effective weed control can increase farm incomes, while reducing the labour demand for weeding and herbicide application. Labour released from agriculture can then be used for other profitable endeavours. By increasing crop productivity, agricultural biotechnology can substitute for the need to cultivate new land and thereby conserve biodiversity in areas that are marginal for crop production. The potential of these technologies has been extensively tested in the model crop species of temperate and subtropical agriculture. However, there is an urgent need for an increased focus on crops relevant to the small farm holders and poor consumers in the developing countries of the humid and semi-arid tropics. The promise of biotechnology can be realized by utilizing the information and products generated through research on genomics and transgenics to increase the productivity of crops through enhanced resistance to biotic and abiotic stress factors and improved nutritional quality.

10. Emerging biotechnological approaches for crop improvement

The integration of biotechnologies into crop improvement is a very dynamic field of endeavour that is changing continually. A snapshot of the status of emerging technologies is provided by Lusser *et al* (2011) and reviewed by Mba *et al* (2012). The emerging biotechnologies in crop improvement include:

Zinc finger nuclease (ZFN): Single mutations or short indels are generated or new genes are introduced into pre-determined target sites of the genome.

CRISPR technology: Conventional plant breeding is unlikely to meet increasing food demands and other environmental challenges. By contrast, CRISPR/Cas technology is erasing barriers to genome editing and could revolutionize plant breeding. However, to fully benefit from the CRISPR revolution, we should focus on resolving its technical and regulatory uncertainties (Gao 2018)

Oligonucleotide directed mutagenesis (ODM): Targeted mutations of one or a few nucleotides are induced.

Cisgenesis and intragenesis: GMOs are produced by the insertion of hereditary materials derived from the species itself or from a cross-compatible species and are contiguous and unchanged (cisgenesis) or the inserted DNA may be a new combination of DNA fragments but must still be from the species itself or from a cross-compatible species

RNA-dependent DNA methylation (RdDM): Still being refined, modified gene expressions are epigenetic with the new phenotypes inherited only over a few generations

Grafting (on GM rootstock): Desired improvements are achieved by the grafting of non-transgenic scions onto GM rootstock

Reverse breeding: A combination of recombinant DNA techniques and cell biology procedures is used to generate suitable transgene-free homozygous parental lines rapidly for reconstituting elite heterozygous genotypes

Agro-infiltration: Used mostly in research settings, for example to study plant-pathogen interaction in living tissues, to select parental lines or to evaluate the efficacy of transgenes, a liquid suspension of *Agrobacterium* sp. containing the desired gene(s) is used to infiltrate plant tissues, mostly leaves, so that the genes are locally and transiently expressed at high levels

Synthetic genomics: Large functional DNA molecules that are synthesized without any natural templates are used for constructing viable minimal genomes which can serve as platforms for the biochemical production of chemicals such as biofuels and pharmaceuticals

10.1. Editing Genes for Adaptation through Targeted Mutagenesis

Plant breeders have been applying mutagenesis to induce genetic variation for increasing crop yield and later, the strategy has been used for improving the adaptability of crop plants. Initially, X-ray radiation was used as a mutagen since it was readily available to researchers. From recent times, chemical mutagenesis is being practiced since they are easy to use, do not require any specialized equipment, and can provide a very high mutation frequency. Compared to radiation methods, chemical mutagens tend to induce SNPs rather than chromosomal mutations. Currently, chemical mutagens, such as Ethyl methane sulfonate (EMS) are being used to induce random mutations into the genome and have become a useful complement to the isolation of nuclear DNA from mutated lines by TILLING (Targeting Induced Local Lesions in Genomes) technology and screening of the M2 population at the DNA level using advanced molecular techniques. Single mutations in specific genes for adaptation could be identified by cleavage of mismatched bases formed as a result of repeated melting and reannealing of PCR products amplified from a pool of alleles. NGS can efficiently accelerate the identification of mutations at the whole-genome level. Promotor mutations and mutation in other regulatory elements responsible for the downstream effect can be identified by qPCR, microarray and RNA-seq. Once a mutant allele is identified within gene(s) of interest, those mutations may be linked to a specific phenotype for stress resistance by backcrossing the mutant to the parental line. This TILLING approach is a reverse genetics procedure to associate a mutant allele to its phenotype. Of note, TILLING can also be used for a forward genetic approach by screening phenotypes for adaptation to stresses and then characterize the phenotype using a combination of whole-genome resequencing, linkage maps and microarrays, to gain a broad picture of gene expression changes due to the newly introduced SNPs compared to the original line. Other molecular tools and resources are now available for genome engineering and reverse genetics experiments in crop plants in order to implement precise manipulation of genetic building blocks and regulatory machinery that underlie yield improvement under stress condition and directly correct harmful mutations by genome editing.

Targeted genome engineering has emerged as an alternative to classical plant breeding and transgenic methods to improve crop plants and ensure sustainable food production. Currently, four types of engineered nucleases are used for genome editing: engineered homing endonucleases/meganucleases (EMNs), zinc finger nucleases (ZFNs), transcription activator-like effector nucleases (TALENs), and CRISPR (clustered regularly interspaced short palindromic repeats)/Cas (CRISPR-associated)9, Sequence-specific nucleases (SSN) enable precise genome engineering by introducing DNA double-strand breaks (DSB) that subsequently trigger endogenous DNA repair by non- homologous end joining (NHEJ) or homology directed repair (HDR) recombination mechanisms in different species.

Site- directed mutagenesis mediated via NHEJ can be achieved while HDR cause directed gene knock-in/correction at specific locations in the genome (HDR uses a DNA template to replace the DNA sequence at the break point). NHEJ functions throughout the entire cell cycle whereas HR is restricted to late S/G2 phases in the cell cycle. Therefore, NHEJ is the major DSB repair pathway in eukaryotes. A clear illustration of genome editing assays in model (*Arabidopsis thaliana* and *Nicotiana benthamiana*) and crop (*Oryza sativa,Triticum aestivum* and *Sorghum bicolor*) plant species has been drawn by Belhaj *et al.* (2013) and Osakabe and Osakabe (2015). These SSN effects generate targeted genome modifications including mutations, insertions, replacements and chromosome rearrangements and have been induced in a variety of important crops, such as rice, maize, wheat, barley, and soybean.

Major advantages of ZFNs are related to the acceptance of the technology as no transgenic is produced because viral vectors have been used for expressing transiently the nuclease, which do not integrate into the genome. However, it has disadvantages such as difficulties to design the experiments, limited number of target sites, and the regeneration of juvenile and chimeric mutated plants when custom-designed nucleases have been delivered in tree explants.

CRISPR was first discovered as an immune system of prokaryotes, which subsequently became a powerful tool for genome editing in eukaryotes. It has emerged as an alternative to classical plant breeding and transgenic methods to improve crop plants. Plant transformation and co- expression of the Cas9 with a chimeric guide-RNA (gRNA) targeting a GN19NGG motif in the gene of interest, results in a double-strand non-self DNA cleavage on both strands at a specific site near the protospacer adjacent motif (PAM). TheCas9 from *Streptococcus pyogenes* (SpCas9) recognizes 52 -NGG-32 as the PAM sequence (Hsu *et al.*, 2013). PAM plays an important role in target binding and cleavage by the Cas9–gRNA complex. CRISPR/Cas9 has greater number of advantages, including the straightforward construct design and assembly and the achievement of high mutation rates, matching or exceeding those obtained with ZFNs and TALENs. Only 20 nucleotides in the gRNA need to be modified to recognize a different target making unnecessary the sophisticated protein engineering for each target that is crucial for the other SSN approaches.

The CRISPR-Cas9 technology has been applied in *A. Thaliana*, Nicotiana *benthamiana*, *Oryza sativa*, *Solanum lycopersicum*, *Sorghum bicolor*, *Triticum aestivum*, *Citrus sinensis* and *Populus stremula* x *Populus alba*. Genes controlling traits of importance for adaptation have also been edited by CRISPR-Cas9 technology. gRNAs were designed to target three specific sites of the rice *OsMPK5* gene which encodes a stress-responsive rice mitogen-activated protein kinase and the targeted mutation of *OsMPK5* enhanced rice disease resistance(Xie and Yang 2013). Transgenic wheat plants carrying mutations in *TaMLO-A1* allele were susceptible to powdery mildew diseases (Wang *et al* 2014). The bacterial blight susceptibility genes, *OsSWEET14* and *OsSWEET11*, were targeted for mutation at the promoter region in Arabidopsis, tobacco, sorghum and rice (Jiang *et al* 2013). High CRISPR-Cas9 mutational efficiency was achieved for three 4-coumarate: CoA ligase (4CL) genes, *4CL1*, *4CL2* and *4CL5*, associated with lignin and flavonoid biosynthesis in *Populus tremula* x *alba*. Moreover, accelerated breeding of crop plants carrying targeted gene mutation(s) targeted gene mutation(s) without foreign DNA is possible using CRISPR genome editing. In fact, although transgene Cas9 and selectable marker integration is hemizygous, CRISPR editing at the target loci is biallelic. Therefore, in autogamous plants, self-fertilization of T1 plants will provide 25% of theT2 plants without the transgene but maintaining the edited gene in homozygosity. In self-incompatible or dioecius perennial woody trees, biparental hemizygous Cas9/sgRNA transformation and biallelic-edited gene can be produced. Controlled crosses between male and female primary transformants with confirmed biallelic mutations should produce transgene- free, biallelic mutants in 25% of the progeny (Zhou *et al* 2015). Taken together, genome engineering for targeted mutagenesis by editing genes serves as a potential strategy for generating elite cultivars of crop plants with durable climate resilience.

10.2. Increases the Efficiency of Selection

Conventional plant breeding that relies only on phenotypic selection has been historically effective. However, for some traits, phenotypic selection has made little progress due to challenges in measuring phenotypes or identifying individuals with the highest breeding value. The effects of environment, genotype by environment interaction, and measurement errors also contribute to observed differences. Evaluation of genotypes in multiple environments with replicated designs allows better estimation of breeding values, but requires additional time and expense. For some traits, it may be necessary to sacrifice the individual to measure phenotypes, or trait expression may depend on variable environmental conditions (e.g. disease pressure) and the stage of development (e.g. grain quality can only be assessed after flowering). Furthermore, plant breeders typically must simultaneously improve a suite of commercially valuable traits, which may limit gains from selection. Just as molecular plant breeding helps to expand genetic diversity, characterize genetic architecture, and modify gene action, its methods can also be applied to increasing the efficiency of selection.

Molecular marker genotypes that are either within genes or tightly linked to QTL influencing traits under selection can be employed as a supplement to phenotypic observations in a selection index. In cases where genetic correlations are high, further efficiencies can be gained by substituting genotypic for phenotypic selection during some selection cycles, which can reduce phenotyping efforts and cycle times by permitting the use of off-season nurseries. combining phenotypic data and molecular marker scores increase selection gains for maize grain yield and resistance to European corn borer (Johnson 2004). An effective strategy to simultaneously modify multiple traits is the use of selection indices that consider multiple factors in choosing the final improved genotype. Results obtained from the use of multiple trait indices and marker-assisted selection for nearly 250 unique corn breeding populations indicated that use of molecular markers increased breeding efficiency approximately 2-fold relative to phenotypic selection alone, with similar gains also observed in soybean (*Glycine max*) and sunflower (*Helianthus annuus*) populations.

Marker-assisted selection can also significantly enhance genetic gain for traits where the phenotype is difficult to evaluate because of its expense or its dependence on specific environmental conditions. Molecular markers may be used to increase the probability of identifying truly superior genotypes, by focusing testing resources on genotypes with the greatest potential (i.e. early elimination of inferior genotypes), by decreasing the number of progeny that must be screened to recover a given level of gain, and by enabling simultaneous improvement for traits that are negatively correlated. Successful examples include resistance to soybean cyst nematode, resistance to cereal diseases, and drought tolerance in maize.

The efficiency of phenotypic selection for some complex traits can be enhanced by including physiological or biochemical phenotypes as secondary traits, if these exhibit strong genetic correlations with the target trait and possess high heritability. Recent advances in functional genomics permit the population-scale profiling of RNA abundance, protein levels and activities, and metabolites that are associated with important traits. In addition to molecular markers that tag DNA sequence variation, such genetical genomics approaches may provide additional secondary phenotypes as selection targets particularly for traits defined by responses to environmental, developmental, or physiological cues.

Marker-assisted selection also accelerates the deployment of transgenes in commercial cultivars. Typically, this has been achieved through marker-assisted backcrossing. However, for future biotechnology improvements such as tolerance to drought or nutrient limitation, forward breeding may be required to cooptimize transgene expression and genetic background because endogenous genes and environmental factors may have the potential to influence the phenotypes resulting from transgenic modifications. Of course, use of molecular markers could aid forward breeding efforts as well. Alternatively, discovery efforts for additional genes or QTLs that are necessary for dependable trait performance may suggest design of new transgene constructs that stack primary transgenes with known genetic modifiers into second-generation transgenic events.

11. Biotechnology in livestock improvement

Many of the tools of animal breeding, genetics, and nutrition have played and will continue to play an important role in the selection, propagation, and management of desirable and economically important characteristics in livestock. However, in future, livestock production will rely even more on existing and emerging biotechnological advances to produce food products of animal origin. Genetically modified (transgenic) livestock, stem cells, and other emerging biotechnologies will have important roles in producing more and higher quality food derived from livestock.

Transgenic animals

The production of transgenics aims to introduce 'new' or modified genes and DNA sequences into livestock without crossbreeding or hybridizing. It is a more precise technique, but not fundamentally different from genetic selection or crossbreeding in its result. The transgenic livestock are produced to (1) study the genetic control of physiological systems, (2) build genetic disease models, (3) improve animal production traits, and (4) produce new animal products. Some of the common techniques for developing transgenic animals include:

- Recombinant Retroviruses,
- Pronuclear Injection,
- Sperm-Mediated DNA Transfer,
- Embryonic Stem Cells,
- Germ Cell Transplantation,
- Nuclear Transfer "Cloning

The genetic engineering as been used for improvement of nutrients in animal products, including their quantity, the quality of the whole food, and specific nutritional composition; to reduce the environmental footprint of animal agriculture; to change the composition of milk or to produce entirely novel proteins in milk; ; enhancing growth Rrates and carcass composition; improved disease resistance; improving reproductive performance and fecundity; improving hair and fiber (Golovan *et al* 2001; Wall *et al* 2005; Lai *et al* 2006; and Wheeler 2013).

12. Microbial biotechnology in agriculture

Microbial biotechnology, enabled by genome studies, will lead to breakthroughs such as improved vaccines and better disease-diagnostic tools, improved microbial agents for biological control of plant and animal pests, modifications of plant and animal pathogens for reduced virulence, development of new industrial catalysts and fermentation organisms, and development of new microbial agents for bioremediation of soil and water contaminated by agricultural runoff.

Microbial genomics and microbial biotechnology research is critical for advances in food safety, food security, biotechnology, value-added products, human nutrition and functional foods, plant and animal protection, and furthering fundamental research in the agricultural sciences. Microbial Biotechnology contributes to sustainable agriculture by reducing the dependence on agro-chemicals, particularly pesticides, through the deployment of genes conferring tolerance or resistance to biotic and abiotic stresses. Carefully selected genes from related or unrelated genetic resources are integrated in otherwise desirable genotypes. Microbial biotechnology has been used for developing bio-fertilizers, bio-pesticides, bio-herbicides, bio-insecticides and virus based bio-insecticides as alternatives to synthetic fertilizers and chemicals (Aruna and Sreekanth 2015). It will enhance sustainability of agriculture without having any adverse impact on soil, water, environment, animal and human health

13. References

Aruna KK and Sreekanth RM .2015. Microbial biotechnology: role of microbes in sustainable agriculture. In: *New Horizons in Biotechnology*. (Eds. Viswanath B and Indravathi G), Paramount Publishing House, India, pp. 051-052.

BICL .2008. National Certification system for tissue culture raised plants. *Plant Tissue Culture: Techno-Commercial Feasibility*. BICL and DBT, New-Delhi.

Food and Agriculture Organization .2016. The State of Food and Agriculture.

Gao C .2018. The future of CRISPR technologies in agriculture. *Nature Reviews Molecular Cell Biology*. 19:275–276.

Golovan SP *et al*.2001. Pigs expressing salivary phytase produce low-phosphorus manure. *Nature Biotechnology* 19:741-745

Gupta PK and Varshney RK .2004. Cereal genomics: an overview In: Gupta PK, Varshney RK (eds) *Cereal Genomics*. Kluwer Academic Press, Dordrecht, The Netherlands, p 639.

Hussain MS, Fareed S, Ansari S, Rahman MA, Ahmad ZI and Saeed M .2012. Current approaches toward production of secondary plant metabolites. *J. Pharm Bioallied Sci*. 4(1): 10-20

Jain SM, Brar DS, Ahloowalia BS .2002. Molecular techniques in crop improvement. Kluwer Academic Publishers, The Netherlands.

Lai L *et al* .2006. Generation of cloned transgenic pigs rich in omega-3 fatty acids. *Nature Biotechnology*. 24: 435-436.

Lusser M, Parisi C, Plan D, Rodríguez-Cerezo E .2011. New plant breeding techniques. State-of-the-art and prospects for commercial development. Luxembourg: Publications Office of the European Union.

Mba C, Guimaraes EP and Ghosh K .2012. Re-orienting crop improvement for the changing climatic conditions of the 21st century. *Agriculture & Food Security*. 1:7.

Paterson AH .1996. Making genetic maps. In: A.H. Paterson (Ed.), *Genome Mapping in Plants*, pp. 23-39. R.G. Landes Company, San Diego, California; Academic Press, Austin, Texas.

Phillips, R. L. and Vasil, I. K. (2001). DNA-based markers in plants. In: Phillips RL, Vasil IK (eds) *DNA-based markers in plants*. Kluwer Academic Publishers, Dordrecht, The Netherlands, p 497.

Wall RJ .2002. New gene transfer methods. *Theriogenology*. 57: 189-201.

Wheeler MB .2013. Transgenic Animals in Agriculture. *Nature Education Knowledge*. 4(11):1

Winter P and Kahl G .1995. Molecular marker technologies for plant improvement. *World J Microbiol Biotechnol* 11: 438-448.

21

Climate Change and its Impact on Parasitic Diseases of Livestock and Human

Anish Yadav, Shafiya Imtiaz Rafiqi, R Katoch, R Godara Pallavi Khajuria

Division of Veterinary Parasitology, FVSc, SKUAST-J, R.S. Pura Jammu-181102, Jammu and Kashmir, Idnia

1. Introduction
2. Effect of climate change on parasite-vector interaction
3. Effect of increasing temperature on parasite survival
4. Effect of rainfall pattern on parasite survival
5. Global-warming induced impact on trematodes
6. Schistosomiasis
7. Effect of climate change on nematodes
8. Effect of climate change on arthropod vector-borne diseases
9. Dirofilariasis
10. Climate change and its impact in Indian scenario
11. Conclusions and future strategies
12. *References*

Abstract

Climate models predict a global average increase of air temperatures in the range of 14°C by 2100 (IPCC 2014) - a pace exceeding that of past climatic modifications. Change in temperature is expected to influence species occurrence and distribution with up to 37% of all extant species "committed to extinction" due to climate change. These predictions, however, do not include species interactions and evolutionary change which will significantly alter the fate of species. It is therefore important to improve our understanding of host-parasite interactions and subsequent evolution in response to environmental changes in general and temperature changes in particular. Globally livestock production systems are estimated to account for around 18% of emissions. The need of hour is to draw on recent advances in climatology and epidemiology of various parasitic diseases to consider how environmental changes linked with urbanization and climate change can alter the biology of hosts, pathogens and vectors. Climate change is leading to unusual flare-up of diseases, outbreak recurrences, range expansions, or invasion into novel territories and ecosystems, concomitantly with vector or host range shifts. Higher temperatures increase the invertebrate metabolic rate, egg production amount, and feeding frequency, reducing the duration of the development periods and impacting on the number of generations per year and population abundance effecting livestock and human health and socio-economic transformation

Keywords: parasitic diseases, climate change, host-parasite interactions

1. Introduction

In recent years, research on environmental implications of parasites has seen a strong increase, leading to the establishment of 'Environmental Parasitology' (EP) as an accepted discipline covered in parasitology textbooks. EP in the sense of an ecologically based approach focuses on parasites as indicators of environmental health. The field of parasitism is broad, encompassing relationships between organisms where one benefits at the expense of another. Synergy among scientists and disciplines is identified as critical for the study of parasites and parasitic disease in context to changing environmental conditions. The global air temperature from the preindustrial era (1850-1899) to the present time has increased by 0.76 °C and the growth rate has progressively accelerated: the linear rate in the last 50 years is double the centennial rate, and 11 of the last 12 years rank among the warmest years since 1850. Among predictions for the 2020s, warming is not guaranteed at any one location, although in all locations the odds are high that warming will occur. It shall be noted that there is no perfect model of the climate system. Current climate models predict a global average increase of air temperatures in the range of 14°C by 2100 (IPCC 2014)- a pace exceeding that of past climatic modifications. Change in temperature is expected to influence species occurrence and distribution with up to 37% of all extant species "committed to extinction" due to climate change (Thomas *et al* 2004). Those predictions, however, do not include species interactions and evolutionary change which will significantly alter the fate of species (Dawson *et al* 2011; Moritz and Agudo 2013). It is therefore important to improve our understanding of host-parasite interactions and subsequent evolution in response to environmental changes in general and temperature changes in particular. Parasite and vector interactions would be changed under climate change.

The importance of parasitism for host populations depends on local parasite richness and prevalence: usually host individuals face higher infection risk in areas where parasites are most diverse, and host dispersal to or from these areas may have fitness consequences. Host-parasite interactions are an important component of community and food-web structure, and have been the focus of many recent ecological studies. Knowing how parasites are and will be distributed in space and time (in a context of global change) is thus crucial from both an ecological and a biological conservation perspective. Climate change can affect physical and biological processes differently and can have different effects on different species (Winder and Schindler 2004; Doi *et al* 2008). First is the shifting of the life cycles of host and parasite under climate change. Second is that the extinction of host and/or parasite. Extinction of host and/or parasites would alter their interactions, but the process of alteration would be different among parasite species, depending on their ability to switch host species if the host extinct. Global change affects individuals, e.g. by affecting the trade-offs for the host involving immunity and defense strategies or transmission pathways for the parasite (Lafferty and Kuris 2005); the interaction between hosts and parasites (Budria and Candolin 2014); and the ecological settings when host or parasite community composition or population structure change (Lafferty and Kuris 2005; IPCC 2014). The consequences of all these alterations depend on the specific characteristics of the "disease triangle" (Budria and Candolin, 2014) :(i) the host corner includes the variation of its life history traits, its immunity (innate and/or acquired) and its abundance; (ii) the parasite corner comprises its transmission rates, its ability to accomplish its life cycle and its virulence. Lastly, (iii) the environment corner represents the ecosystem in which the host and the parasite live.

2. Effect of climate change on parasite-vector interactions

Parasite and vector interactions would be changed under climate change. The human host-vector interaction of parasites, which are non-host-species suitable, could increase, because vectors would concentrate their bites on humans. Thus, climate change would increase infectious diseases for animals in the future and it might also be for human. The combined effects of environmentally detrimental changes in local land use and alterations in global climate disrupt the natural ecosystem and can increase the risk of transmission of parasitic diseases to the humans. Various climate models predict seasonal temperature and rainfall extremes to increase in severity and frequency over the coming century

(Wuebbles *et al* 2014). The observed changes in mean temperature and increased frequency of extreme climate events have already impacted the distributions, behaviors, and phenologies (Musolin Tougou and Fujisaki 2010) of various organisms, including insects (Yang and Rudolf 2010).

3. Effect of increasing temperatures on parasite survival

Concerning effects on population dynamics, life cycle and disease transmission, climate factors can have a direct impact on infectious diseases that have a development stage in the environment and/or in an invertebrate intermediate host or vector (De La Rocque *et al* 2008). Thus, most infectious agents do not replicate below a certain temperature threshold, and their growth rate is strongly modulated at temperatures above this level. Within an invertebrate vector, pathogen replication rate and dynamics may be affected by the invertebrate body temperature and, as a result, the infection process in the different organs of the invertebrate and the duration of the cycle will also be affected (Reiter 2001). Temperature increase is expected to bring a relaxation of the restricting effects of low temperatures on vector survival, dispersal and disease transmission in colder climates. A priori, this would make temperate environments more receptive to more tropical, mainly vector-borne, diseases. The effect may be more pronounced in areas where the abiotic conditions are near to the threshold prohibiting the disease development cycle, i.e., often around 14-18 ^{0}C at the lower end of the temperature scale and 35-40 ^{0}C for the maximum limit (Githeko *et al* 2000). When the development period of a pathogen exceed the life span of the invertebrate, its vector role becomes impossible and transmission does not occur. Moreover, vector competence, including capacity to attract infection, enable pathogen multiplication and ensure subsequent excretion, may be enhanced by higher temperatures (Purse *et al* 2008). Temperature directly impacts on the ecology, life cycle, behavior and survival of invertebrate vectors (Rodhain 2000), and therefore on vector population dynamics and disease transmission. Higher temperatures increase the invertebrate metabolic rate, egg production amount, and feeding frequency, reducing the duration of the development periods and impacting on the number of generations per year and population abundance (De La Rocque *et al* 2008).

4. Effect of rainfall on parasite survival

Disease transmission is modulated by the survival, reproduction rates and daily activity of the vector, as well as by the pathogen development rate inside the vector. For instance, changes in rainfall in (sub) tropical zones may render habitats more, or less, suitable for vectors. Moreover, the mosaic of local microclimates is also crucial for the distributions of vector and reservoir, similarly as for the potential impact of climatic parameter changes. This particularly concerns diseases transmitted by water-borne vectors as freshwater snails which present patchy distributions among the endemic areas (Mas-Coma *et al* 1999). The micro geographical fragmentation of such diseases may be locally modified by climate change, several transmission foci disappearing, moving or altering their transmission efficiency and new transmission foci appearing. Changes in precipitation and evapotranspiration rates may give rise to more standing water collections representing new habitats for vector hosts as mosquitoes and snails, while desiccation may reduce vector populations.

5. Global-warming-induced impact on trematodes

An increase of a few degrees in environmental temperatures should lead to marked increases in cercarial emergence from snail first intermediate hosts, with little if any reduction in their transmission efficiency. This may be taken into account as a common scenario for most host-trematode associations. Within the range of temperatures in which host and parasite can live, an increase in temperature is almost invariably coupled with an increase in cercarial output. This phenomenon results from two independent processes: higher temperatures not only trigger the emergence of cercariae from snails, but they also accelerate the production of cercariae within snails. The net outcome of increasing temperature will thus be a greater number of cercarial infective stages. This consequence of climate warming is not trivial: trematode parasitism is not only a major veterinary and health problem worldwide, but trematodes also play major roles in the structuring of animal communities. Any temperature- mediated increase in the extent of trematode infections may have measurable repercussions. Thus, global warming may also enhance the local impact of trematodes (Poulin, 2006).This is why fascioliasis has become the vector-borne disease presenting the widest latitudinal, longitudinal and altitudinal distribution known. Fascioliasis is unique in being capable to give rise to human endemic areas from below sea level (as besides the Caspian Sea) up to the very high altitude (as in Bolivia, Peru, Ecuador and Venezuela). No other vector borne disease presents such a wide altitudinal range (Mas-Coma *et al* 2003). The strong dependence of fascioliasis from weather factors indicate that climate change may have a marked influence on the future evolution of this disease Increasing drought and floods may also influence fascioliasis epidemiology. Drought may modify the spatial, typical patchy fragmentation of fascioliasis foci, and floods may facilitate lymnaeid survival and geographically expand their populations.

6. Schistosomiasis

It seems clear that climate change and global warming will result in changes in aquatic environments. The expansion of suitable habitats for invertebrate hosts of waterborne parasites could result in risk of waterborne infections in humans and animals and increased distribution of the disease. There are different environmental factors that impact on the distribution of schistosomiasis. Temperature, water body type, rainfall, water velocity and altitude can all have a significant effect on the schistosome life cycle and survival of the intermediate snail host (Fenwick *et al* 2007). Climatic changes are likely to affect the known geographical distribution of freshwater snails, such as *Biomphalaria* spp., the invertebrate hosts of *Schistosoma* spp. transmissible to humans, livestock and other animals (Morgan *et al* 2001).

Climate change has been related to another phenomenon giving rise to an increase of summer outbreaks of cercarial dermatitis. Global warming in recent years have had a mildering effect on areas presenting lakes used by migratory birds, as for instance anatids. This opens the possibility for the life cycle of the bird schistosomatids to expand their transmission in these lakes during months in which transmission was stopped in cold years. This larger seasonal window may originate higher infection prevalence in snails, whose population activity is in its turn also seasonally enlarged, as well as a higher number of schistosomatid generations per year and higher prevalence in the birds of the lake. All in all, when the human swimming summer period arrives, the water may have a pronouncedly higher density of cercariae able to give rise to a higher human infection both in space and time.

7. Effect of climate change on nematodes

The consequences of climate change are, therefore, particularly important in helminth parasites because of its potential to impact upon their free-living stages and/or their intermediate or paratenic hosts. The main economically important helminth parasites in sheep in the UK are the nematodes, *Nematodirus battus, Teladorsagia circumcincta,* and *Haemonchus contortus.* Cestodes and acanthocephalans may also be affected, but at a lower level and mainly indirectly through effects on their exothermic invertebrate or small endothermic vertebrate hosts (Mas-Coma *et al* 2008). The effects of rainfall and temperature on the population dynamics of nematode infections in sheep are well described and have been the subject of several modeling studies. The effects of climatic changes on sheep parasite populations are, therefore, theoretically predictable. Accumulation of infective L3 accelerates at higher temperatures, brought about by shorter generation intervals, leads to higher parasite abundance and increased risk of disease from midsummer onwards. Increases in temperature may also lead to an extension of transmission into the late autumn and winter and, conversely, appearances of more cold-tolerant species earlier in the season. There may be a decrease in spring disease, attributed to decreased larval survival over the winter and spring due to milder temperatures, the consequential effects of which are decreased exposure to infection early in the year, delays in acquisition of immunity and subsequent higher burdens building up later in the year.

8. Effect of climate change on arthropod vector borne diseases

Climate change, especially global warming, can also affect arthropod vector density, geographical distribution and vectorial capacity. In the last 10 years, "new" diseases have been reported in horses and carnivores, e.g. babesiosis in northern Germany and The Netherlands, canine monocytic ehrlichiosis (CME) in southern Europe, *Anaplasma platys* anaplasmosis in France, and *A. phagocytophilum* anaplasmosis in cattle, horses, dogs and cats in northern Europe. Various factors have been linked to the changing epidemiology of vector-borne disease. Altered geographical distribution, as well as density and period of activity of ticks, could underlie changes in vectorborne disease. The data suggest that *Rhipicephalus sanguineus* has tended to move north from its previously Mediterranean distribution, probably being transported on carnivores. This tick is now described all over France, in Belgium, Germany and The Netherlands. *Dermacentor reticulatus* is recorded in almost all European countries but formerly was relatively rare in cold continental climates (central and northern Europe). It is believed to be spreading now in these areas (Poland, northern Germany, The Netherlands, Denmark), enabling the establishment or increase of canine babesiosis. The spread of *Dermacentor* ticks is thought to be linked to importation and climate changes, notably the shortening of the winter period and increasing minimum temperatures. *Ixodes ricinus* is distributed all over Europe, except in the Mediterranean zone where it is too warm and dry except at altitude. The density of Ixodes ticks appears to have increased in some areas, which could lead to a higher risk of pathogen transmission. Changes in tick density may be related to increases in host populations, e.g. rodents, wild boars and wild ruminants, in European forests.

Chagas disease is a vector borne parasitic zoonosis caused by the protozoan *Trypanosoma cruzi*. It is estimated that over 7 million people are infected and 109 million individuals are at risk of infection in Latin America (OPS 2006). Control programs have greatly reduced the vectorial transmission of *T. cruzi* in Brazil and other Latin American countries (Coura and Vinas 2010). However, a recent study has demonstrated the existence of domestic populations of the triatomine bug *Panstrongylus megistus*, infected by *T. cruzi* in southeastern

Brazil (Villela *et al* 2010), which demonstrated the risk of vectorial transmission in this region. The presence of wild populations of *T. infestans* infected with *T. cruzi* in Chile (Bacigalupo *et al* 2010) shows that the risk of reintroduction of this vector into the domestic environment does exist in certain areas. Changes in land use, deforestation and movement of human populations can also bring people into contact with potential wild triatomine vectors (Guhl *et al* 2009) that might incidentally assume a primary role in *T. cruzi* transmission.

As with other vector borne disease, the leishmaniases are strongly influenced by global changes and by the dynamics of vectors, reservoirs and susceptible populations (González *et al* 2010). In particular, the ecology and distribution of phlebotomine sand flies are directly influenced by climate and other environmental variables (Peterson and Shaw 2003). Recent studies have highlighted the spreading of the leishmaniases, as they accompany the movement of the phlebotomine vectors into previously free areas as suggested for the spread of canine leishmaniasis from southern to northern Italy and from northern to southern Brazil (TomazSoccol *et al* 2009). Indeed, canine leishmaniasis is now well established in South America as far south as northern Argentina (DantasTorres 2009). Furthermore, global warming could prompt the establishment of canine leishmaniasis in areas such as the United Kingdom, where the vectors are currently absent, but where *Leishmania infantum* infected dogs that had travelled to endemic areas are present (Shaw *et al.,* 2009). In this regard, human cases of autochthonous visceral leishmaniasis have increasingly been diagnosed in Thailand and the existence of a suspected new species of *Leishmania* in this country has also been reported (Sukmee *et al* 2008). Interestingly, cases of cutaneous leishmaniasis by an undescribed species of *Leishmania* were diagnosed in Northern Australian macropods and dayfeeding midges have been incriminated as potential vectors (Dougall *et al* 2011). These findings are changing our understanding of the *Leishmania* spp. life cycles and may have practical implications on the epidemiology and control of the leishmaniases. Certainly, control measures have not been enough to stop the spread of visceral leishmaniasis and global changes are accelerating this process. The actual impact of global changes on the ecoepidemiology of the leishmaniases in both traditional and nontraditional endemic areas might be unpredictable.

9. Dirofilariasis

Currently, the mosquito's changing behavioural patterns (from mainly exophylic to partially endophylic), its generalistic feeding-behaviour (Romi and Majori 2008; Valerio *et al* 2008), the involvement in the recent outbreak of Chikungunya virus epidemics in Italy (Bonilauri *et al* 2008) and its urbanization (Valerio *et al*

2008) all increase the probability of transmission of canine, feline and human dirofilariosis in the urban environment, thus changing the epidemiological patterns of *Dirofilaria* infections (Pietrobelli 2008). Temperature, precipitation, and relative humidity are the three main factors that determine the abundance of mosquitoes and the prevalence of mosquito-borne diseases such as *Dirofilaria* infection. The optimum temperature for mosquito development of tropical/ temperate species is 25-27 ^{0}C (Monteiro *et al* 2007; Swain *et al* 2008), and there is a strong temperature dependence for the development of the parasites within the mosquito vectors (Kalluri *et al* 2007). Environmental factors that influence filarial worm distribution may affect the life cycle parameters of both the mosquito vector and the filarial species. Traditionally, attention in this area has focused primarily on temperature, humidity and altitude (Brooker and Michael 2000). The interplay of animal/ human, mosquito and nematode biology contributes to the clinical spectrum and geographic distribution of *Dirofilaria*. Each sphere influences and affects the others, all in the context of ecology and against the backdrop of climate and climate change.

10. Climate change and its impact in Indian scenario

India has a wide range of climatic zones, from mountain (cold, wet alpine) and semi-arid regions to the wet tropics, which make it suitable for a diverse range of vectors and pathogens of medical and veterinary importance, whose transmission and geographical distribution are closely linked to regional temperature, rainfall and humidity. Climatic conditions play important role in the distribution, degree of endemicity and epidemicity of diseases in an area. Some areas, which have most favourable conditions of temperature and rainfall, experience transmission of disease throughout the year, while in areas experiencing colder months, transmission is seasonal and does not take place throughout the year. Intergovernmental Panel on Climate Change's (IPCC) concludes that climate change is likely to expand the geographical distribution of several vector-borne diseases, including malaria, dengue and leishmaniasis to higher altitudes (high confidence) and higher latitudes with limited public health defenses and to extend the transmission seasons in some locations. In some locations, reduced rainfall or incremental temperature may cause decrease in transmission of some vector borne diseases. The role of climatic factors has been studied extensively in the epidemiology of malaria due to its global public health importance. In view of the projected rise in temperature, the future scenario by 2080 is likely to extend the transmission windows (TWs) in Punjab, Haryana, Jammu & Kashmir, Uttarakhand, Himachal Pradesh and northeastern states, while in Orissa, Andhra Pradesh and Tamil Nadu, it is expected that there may be reduction in number of months of TWs due to projected high temperatures. However, in such situations mosquitoes may adapt to micro niche as evidenced in Rajasthan (where adult mosquitoes prefer to rest in "tankas" to avoid high temperatures). Studies have been undertaken in Nanital district of Uttrakhand to find out the earlier evidence of climate change. Results have revealed very high densities of *An. fluviatilis* and presence of *P. falciparum* malaria cases in the month of March-April from the hilly parts which did not report malaria earlier.

In a preliminary study using A1B scenario of PRECIS model, transmission windows for dengue transmission (20-32°C temperature and >55% RH) were projected by the year 2030 which show increase in transmission months open for dengue transmission in northern areas and reduction in western part of southern India (Singh and Dhiman 2012). Also, Incidence of JE in India has increased in eastern Uttar Pradesh in the last five years. Inroad of JE into Delhi is also a matter of investigation to define the ecological/climatic and sociological changes which led to introduction of JE in Delhi. Modern approaches using Remote Sensing and Geographical Information System are required to map the ecological and environmental risks. The vectors of filariasis are widely distributed and may be less affected by climate change as compared to *Culex vishnui* (Diptera: Culicidae) group of vectors of Japanese encephalitis. However, there is scanty information about these diseases. Reporting of malaria and dengue in Nepal and Bhutan, chikungunya in India since 2005, and occurrence of kalaazar in Himachal Pradesh and reappearance in Asom are some of the examples which can be linked to climate change but need verification. With regard to the future scenario of VBD in India from the viewpoint of climate change impacts, there is a strong National Vector Borne Disease Control Programme (NVBDCP). In the field of malaria, under Global fund grant, hard core malarious states like Odisha and northeastern states are covered with Artemisinin-based combination therapy for the treatment of drug resistant malaria patients and long-lasting nets for personal protection, and the results are encouraging. No major outbreaks since 2006 have been witnessed except in a localized area at construction sites in Mumbai during 2010-11. The recent projections made for the year 2030 on transmission intensity of malaria show the possibility of a few new foci in Himalayan region (Dhiman *et al* 2011), increase in intensity of transmission in northeastern states while reduction in a few east coastal areas has also been projected. In tropical countries like India, most of the identified adverse health effects due to climate change are already experienced. The need of the hour is to undertake situation analysis for reasons of persistent disease burden and for identifying the operational gaps.

11. Conclusions and future strategies

Climate change is leading to unusual flare-up of diseases, outbreak recurrences, range expansions, or invasion into novel territories and ecosystems, concomitantly with vector or host range shifts. There are three main types of models, used to forecast future climatic influences on parasitic diseases, that include statistical, process-based mathematical, and landscape-based models. Statistical models require the derivation of an empirical statistical relationship between the current geographic distribution of the disease and the current location-specific climatic conditions. Process-based mathematical models use equations that express the scientifically documented relationship between climatic variables and biological parameters, e.g., vector breeding, survival and biting rates, and parasite incubation rates. In their simplest form, such models express, via a set of equations, how a given configuration of climate variables would affect vector and parasite biology and, therefore, disease transmission. The landscape-based modeling entails combining the climate-based models described above with the rapidly-developing use of spatial analytical methods, to study the effects of both climatic and other environmental factors, e.g., different vegetation types often measured, in the model development stage, by ground-based or remote sensors.

A novel system "FleaTick Risk"has been designed and can predict the abundance of parasites and the risk of disease transmission (i.e. animal and human infestations). The model can help establish the impact of the climate on parasite burdens and will also help veterinarians in their day-today activity of recommending suitable parasite treatment and prevention. It is not surprising, therefore, that prediction and attenuation of climate change and its likely effects preoccupies scientists in many areas. Perhaps more surprising is the sparse literature specifically addressing this problem in relation to parasites of veterinary importance, despite fears that a warming climate will favour parasites and lead to increased disease. Global efforts to mitigate anthropogenic climate changes have focussed largely on reducing emissions of greenhouse gases in an effort to reduce the rate of global warming. Globally livestock production systems are estimated to account for around 18% of emissions. The need of hour is to draw on recent advances in climatology and epidemiology of various parasitic diseases to consider how environmental changes linked with urbanization and climate change can alter the biology of hosts, pathogens and vectors. It would determine the success of sustainable socio-economic transformation.

12. References

Bacigalupo A, TorresPérez F, Segovia V, García A, Correa JP, Moreno L, Arroyo P and Cattan PE. 2010. Sylvatic foci of the Chagas disease vector Triatoma infestans in Chile: description of a new focus and challenges for control programs. *Mem. Inst. Oswaldo Cruz*. 105: 633–641.

Bonilauri P, Bellini R, Calzolari M, Angelici R, Venturi L, Fallacara F, Cordiolli P, Angelici P, Venturelli C, Merialdi G and Dottori M. 2008.Chikungunya virus in Aedes albopictus, Italy. *Emerg. Infect. Dis*. 14: 852–854.

Brooker S and Michael E. 2000. The potential of geographical information systems and remote sensing in the epidemiology and control of human helminth infections. *Adv. Parasitol*. 47: 246–279.

Budria A and Candolin U. 2014. How does human-induced environmental changeinfluence host–parasite interactions? *Parasitology*. 141: 462–474.

Coura JR and Vi˜nas PA. 2010. Chagas disease: a new worldwide challenge. *Nature*. 465: S6–S7.

DantasTorres, F., 2009. Canine leishmaniosis in South America. *Parasites Vectors*. 2: (Suppl. 1), S1.

Dawson TP, Jackson ST, House JI, Prentice IC and Mace GM. 2011. Beyond pre-dictions: biodiversity conservation in a changing climate. *Science*. 332: 53–58.

De La Rocque S, Rioux JA and Slingenbergh J. 2008. Climate change: effects on animal disease systems and implications for surveillance and control. In: De La Rocque, S., Hendrickx, G., Morand, S. (Eds.), Climate Change: Impact on the Epidemiology and Control of Animal Diseases. World Organization for Animal Health (OIE), *Paris. Sci. Tech. Rev.* 27(2): 309–317.

Dhiman RC, Chavan L, Pant M and Pahwa S. 2011. National and regional impacts of climate change on malaria by 2030. *Curr Sci*. 101(3): 372–83

Doi H, Gordo, O and Katano I. 2008. Heterogeneous intra-annual climatic changes drive different phenological responses in two trophic levels. *Climate Research*. 36: 181–190.

Dougall AM, Alexander B, Holt DC, Harris T, Sultan AH, Bates PA, Rose K and Walton SF. 2011. Evidence incriminating midges (Diptera: Ceratopogonidae) as potential vectors of Leishmania in Australia. *Int. J. Parasitol*. 41: 571–579.

Fenwick A, Rollinson D and Southgate V. 2007. Implementation of human schistosomiasis control: challenges and prospects. In: Molyneux, D.H. (Ed.), Control of Human Parasitic Diseases. Elsevier-Academic Press, London, pp. 567–622.

Githeko AK, Lindsay SW, Confalonieri UE and Patz JA. 2000. Climate change and vector-borne diseases: a regional analysis. Bull. WHO 78, 1136–1147.

González C, Wang O, Strutz SE, GonzálezSalazar C, SánchezCordero V and Sarkar S. 2010. Climate change and risk of leishmaniasis in North America: predictions from ecological niche models of vector and reservoir species. *PLoS Negl. Trop. Dis*. 4: e585.

Guhl F, Pinto N and Aguilera G. 2009. Sylvatic triatominae: a new challenge in vector control transmission. Mem. Inst. Oswaldo Cruz. 104: 71–75.

IPCC, 2014. Climate Change 2014: Synthesis Report Contributions of WorkingGroups I, II and III to the Fifth Assessment Report of the IPCC. Edited by CoreWriting Team, Pachauri R.K., Meyer L.A. Intergovernmental Panel on ClimateChange, Geneva.

Kalluri S, Gilruth P, Rogers D and Szczur M. 2007. Surveillance of arthropod vector-borne infectious diseases using remote sensing techniques: a review. *PLoS Pathog*. 26: 1361–1371.

Lafferty KD and Kuris AM. 2005. Parasitism and environmental disturbances. In:Thomas, F., Renaud, F., Guegan, J.-F. (Eds.), Parasitism and Ecosystems. OxfordUniversity Press, Oxford, pp. 113–123.

Mas-Coma S, Angles R, Esteban JG, Bargues MD, Buchon P, Franken M and Strauss W. 1999. The Northern Bolivian Altiplano: a region highly endemic for human fascioliasis. *Trop. Med. Int. Health* 4: 454–467.

Mas-Coma S, Bargues MD, Valero MA and Fuentes MV. 2003. Adaptation capacities of Fasciola hepatica and their relationships with human fascioliasis: from below sea level up to the very high altitude. In: Combes, C., Jourdane, J. (Eds.), Taxonomy, Ecology and Evolution of Metazoan Parasites, vol. 2. Presses Universitaires de Perpignan, Perpignan, pp. 81–123.

Mas-Coma S, Valero MA and Bargues MD. 2008. Effects of climate change on animal and zoonotic helminthiases. In: De La Rocque, S., Hendrickx, G., Morand, S. (Eds.), Climate Change: Impact on the Epidemiology and Control of Animal Diseases. World Organization for Animal Health (OIE), *Paris. Sci. Tech. Rev.* 27 (2): 443– 452.

Monteiro LCC, De Souza JRB and De Albuquerque CMR. 2007. Eclosion rate, development and survivorship of Aedes albopictus (Skuse) (Diptera: Culicidae) under different water temperatures. *Neotropical Entomol.* 36:966–971.

Morgan JAT, De Jong RJ, Snyder SD, Mkoji GM and Loker ES. 2001. Schistosoma mansoni and Biomphalaria: past history and future trends. *Parasitology*. 123: S211–S228.

Moritz C, and Agudo R. 2013. The future of species under climate change: resilience ordecline? *Science*. 341: 504–508.

Musolin DL, Tougou D and Fujisaki K. 2010. Too hot to handle? Phenological and life-history responses to simulated climate change of the southern green stink bug *Nezara viridula* (Heteroptera: Pentatomidae). *Global Change Biology*. 16: 73–87.

OPS. 2006. Estimacion cuantitativa de la enfermedad de Chagas en las Americas. Organizacion Panamericana de la Salud, Montevideo, Uruguay (in Spanish).

Peterson AT and Shaw J. 2003. Lutzomyia vectors for cutaneous leishmaniasis in Southern Brazil: ecological niche models, predicted geographic distributions, and climate change effects. *Int. J. Parasitol.* 33: 919–931.

Poulin R. 2006. Global warming and temperature-mediated increases in cercarial emergence in trematode parasites. *Parasitology* 132: 143– 151.

Purse BV, Brown E, Harrup L and Rogers DJ. 2008. Bluetongue and other orbivirus infections. In: De La Rocque, S., Hendrickx, G., Morand, S. (Eds.), Climate Change: Impact on the Epidemiology and Control of Animal Diseases. World Organization for Animal Health (OIE), *Paris. Sci. Tech. Rev.* 27 (2): 427–442.

Reiter P. 2001. Climate change and mosquito-borne disease. Environ. Health Perspect. 109 (Suppl. 1), 141–161.

Rodhain F. 2000. Modifications climatiques: impact potentiel sur la sante′, l'exemple des maladies a‘ vecteur. *Bull. Assoc. Anc. Ele'ves Inst. Pasteur* 162: 8–14.

Romi R and Majori G. 2008. An overview of the lesson learned in almost 20 years of fight against the "Tiger" mosquito. *Parassitologia*. 50, 117–119.

Shaw SE, Langton DA and Hillman TJ. 2009. Canine leishmaniosis in the United Kingdom: a zoonotic disease waiting for a vector? *Vet. Parasitol.* 163: 281–285.

Singh PK and Dhiman RC. 2012. Climate change and human health: Indian context. *J Vector Borne Dis* 49: 55–60.

Sukmee T, Siripattanapipong S, Mungthin M, Worapong J, Rangsin R, Samung Y, Kongkaew W, Bumrungsana K, Chanachai K, Apiwathanasorn C, Rujirojindakul P, Wattanasri S, Ungchusak K and Leelayoova S. 2008. A suspected new species of Leishmania, the causative agent of visceral leishmaniasis in a Thai patient. *Int. J. Parasitol.* 38, 617–622.

Swain V, Seth RK, Mohanty SS, and Raghavendra K. 2008. Effect of temperature on development, eclosion, longevity and survivorship of malathion-resistant and malathion-susceptible strain of Culex quinquefasciatus. *Parasitol. Res.* 103: 299–303.

Thomas CD, Cameron A, Green RE, Bakkenes M, Beaumont LJ, Collingham YC, Erasmus BFN, De Siqueira MF, Grainger A, Hannah L, Hughes L, Huntley B, Van Jaarsveld AS, Midgley GF, Miles L, Ortega-Huerta MA, Peterson AT, Townsend Peterson A, Phillips OL and Williams SE. 2004. Extinction risk from climate change. *Nature*. 427: 145–148.

TomazSoccol V, Castro EA, Navarro IT, de Farias MR, de Souza LM, Carvalho Y, Bispo S, Membrive NA, Minozzo JC, Truppel J, Bueno W and Luz E. 2009. Allochthonous cases of canine visceral leishmaniasis in Paraná, Brazil: epidemiological implications. *Rev. Bras. Parasitol. Vet.* 18: 46–51.

Valerio L, Marini F, Bongiorno G, Facchinelli L, Pombi M, Caputo B, Maroli M and della Torre A. 2008. Blood-feeding preferences of *Aedes albopictus* (Diptera: Culicidae) in urban and rural settings within the Province of Rome, Italy. *Parassitologia*. 50, 103–104.

Villela MM, Rodrigues VL, Casanova C and Dias JC. 2010. Analysis on the food source of Panstrongylus megistus (Hemiptera, Reduviidae, Triatominae) and its present importance as a vector for *Trypanosoma cruzi*, in the State of Minas Gerais. *Rev. Soc. Bras. Med. Trop*. 43, 125–128.

Winder M and Schindler DE. 2004. Climate change uncouples trophic interactions in an aquatic ecosystem. *Ecology*. 85: 2100–2106.

Wuebbles D, Meehl G, Hayhoe K, Karl TR, Kunkel K, Santer B and Sun L. 2014. CMIP5 climate model analyses: Climate extremes in the United States. *Bulletin of the American Meteorological Society*. *95*, 571–583.

Yang LH and Rudolf VHW. 2010. Phenology, ontogeny and the effects of climate change on the timing of species interactions. *Ecology Letters*. 13: 1–10.

22

High Intensity Cropping Systems to Transform Indian Agriculture

BC Sharma, Akhil Verma and Neetu Sharma Jag Paul Sharma*

*Division of Agronomy, *Directorate of Research*
SKUAST Jammu, 180 009, Jammu and Kashmir, India

Abstract

The future food grain demand in India is projected to increase beyond 300 million tons by 2025. There are only two ways to meet the increasing food and other agricultural demands of the country's rising population either expanding the net area under cultivation or intensifying cropping over the existing area. The net sown area of the country has risen by about 20 per cent since independence and has reached a point where it is not possible to make any appreciable increase. The option left is go for high cropping intensity for ahead of present of 137%. A major share of this increase is likely to come from increasing the number of crops produced per year on a given land using improved crop cultivars. Research indicates that maximum intensity of 400-500% is possible provided situation fulfills the requisite factors such as irrigation facilities, short duration varieties, mechanization and agrochemicals are available. The objective of increasing the cropping intensity will be achieved only by the inclusion of short duration varieties of cereals, identification of pulses and oilseed crops that can fit well in the cropping systems of different agro-ecologies that will ultimately improve crop productivity per unit of land making the efficient utilization of resources and will meet the objectives of crop diversification leading to food and economic security of the nation.

1. Introduction

The population of the world will reach 9 billion by 2050 which infers greater food security challenge in future. Studies indicate that the demand for food will be 60% higher than as it is today. To feed this vast growing human population, more food is to be produced available cropland that too shrinking because proliferation of human dwellings. The challenge to the food security for India is still higher than other countries of the world having only 2.3 per cent share in world's total land area which has to ensure food security to about 17.5 per cent of the world's population (Anonymous 2011).

The future food grain demand in India is projected to increase about 291 million tonnes by 2025 and to 377 million tonnes by 2050. There are only two ways to meet the increasing food and other agricultural demands of the country's rising population either expanding the net area under cultivation or intensifying cropping over the existing area. The net sown area of the country has risen by about 20 per cent since independence and has reached a point where it is not possible to make any appreciable increase. Thus, increasing the cropping intensity is the only viable option left. Cropping intensity refers to raising number of crops from the same field during one calendar year. Cropping intensity varies from 100 per cent in Mizoram to 194.43 percent in Punjab (1999-2000). Next to Punjab is West Bengal (174%), Himachal Pradesh (173%), followed by Haryana (169%), and Uttar Pradesh (151%). It is higher than the national average in Jammu and Kashmir, Assam, Manipur, Sikkim, Bihar and Orissa. It is low and very low in the states of peninsular plateau. It is imperative to increase the number of crops on existing arable lands to intensify the cropping systems. Cropping system usually refers to the combination of crops in time and space. Traditionally, increased food production has come from more land under cultivation. However, in large areas of the world, especially in Asia, all the land that can be economically cultivated is already in use. In future, most of the extra food needs must come from higher production from land already being cultivated.

In addition to yield increase, increasing cropping intensity may provide another promising opportunity to boost global crop production. A major share of this increase is likely to come from increasing the number of crops produced per year on a given land using improved crop cultivars. At the same time increasing number of crops per unit of land in the face of changing crop demands – brought about by increasing population, income and consumption pressures – have the potential to significantly increase the income opportunities of the agriculture dependent population. In India, the concept of cropping systems is as old as agriculture. Farmers preferred mixed cropping, especially under dry land conditions, to minimise the risk of total crop failure. Even in Vedas, there is a mention of first and second crops, indicating the existence of sequential cropping (Rana *et al* 2011). Rice based cropping systems belong to the most important food production systems on the earth, of which the rice-wheat cropping system is most prevalent one and is widely practiced in the Indo-Gangetic plains of the country on an area of about 13.5 million hectare (Singh *et al* 2012). These two crops have provided food security in India and has made the country self sufficient in food grains, but at the same time this has made the food security highly dependent on the performance of these two crops. Shrinking land resources coupled with increased demand for food to feed the burgeoning population has not only over exploited the cultivated lands and posed a serious challenge to the traditional resilience characteristics of these crop lands but has compelled the scientific community of agriculture to intensify the existing cropping systems.

Rice and wheat crops are the most promising crops of the irrigated ecology and we cannot eliminate both these crops from our agriculture production system with the intent to intensify the cropping systems and thus there is a need to look out for such a crop combinations wherein either rice or wheat forms one of the crops of the identified cropping systems. For instance, many agricultural scientists rightly pointed out that the main advantage is that vegetable crops grown on the soil columns can make effective use of the resources applied on the rice fields with reduced requirement of irrigation which makes it cost effective. Experts are of the opinion that crop diversification in rice field increases the cropping intensity with additional returns and generate more employment opportunities and will help to meet the objective of doubling farmers income.

The rainfed ecology, which currently encompasses about 60% of the total cultivated area in the country, contributes to the tune of 40% of the country's total food grain production comprising mainly of cereals (85%), pulses (83%), oilseeds (70%) and cotton (65%). It is further supplemented that even after attainment of full exploitable irrigation potential about half of the country's cultivated area would continue to lie under dryland ecosystem (Suresh *et al* 2014). The dryland/rainfed environments for agriculture are extremely fragile and have limitations for soil, water and crop management. Despite these limitations, this tract has enormous potential to contribute considerable magnitude of crop production to address the food safety issues of the country provided these are judiciously utilized as per their capabilities with the substitution of more crops which fit well in the existing agro-climatic ecosystem. Therefore, all cropping sequences that suit and sustain better on the natural resources of the rainfed ecosystems for a longer period of time needs to be explored to improve the cropping intensity of these drylands for more food and assured income.

2. Prevalent cropping systems in India

Owing to the diversified agro-ecologies, multiple cropping systems has been the main feature of Indian Agriculture. There are more than 30 types of cropping systems found in the country such as rice-wheat, rice-rice, rice-gram, rice-mustard, rice-groundnut, rice-sorghum, pearl millet-gram, pearl millet-mustard, pearl millet-sorghum, cotton-wheat, cotton-gram, cotton-sorghum, cotton-safflower, cotton-groundnut, maize-wheat, maize-gram, sugarcane-wheat, soybean-wheat, sorghum-sorghum, groundnut-wheat, sorghum-groundnut, groundnut-rice, sorghum-wheat, sorghum-gram, pigeon pea-sorghum, groundnut-groundnut, sorghum-rice, groundnut-sorghum, soybean-gram and so on.

However, there are 10 main cropping systems prevalent in India (Anonymous, 2018) are discussed below:

Rice-Wheat Cropping System

The Rice-wheat cropping system is India's most widely adopted cropping system practiced on an estimated area of around 11 million hectares.

Rice-Rice Cropping System

This type of the cropping system is found in irrigated lands and coastal regions of Odisha, Tamil Nadu, Andhra Pradesh, Karnataka and Kerala. Due to monocropping; these systems have suffered deterioration of the soil and micronutrient deficiency.

Rice-Groundnut Cropping system

Under this cropping system; groundnut is grown as *kharif* crop and rice is grown in fallows. Groundnut being a legume; the rice-groundnut cropping system is more sustainable and remunerative. This system is practiced in parts of Tamil Nadu, Odisha, Maharashtra, Andhra Pradesh and Gujarat.

Rice-Pulses Cropping System

This cropping system is followed in parts of Chhattisgarh, Odisha and Bihar. This has resulted in both high productivity of rice as well as pulses; but the problem is of erratic supply of irrigation in these areas.

Pearl millet-Wheat / Pearl millet-Mustard Cropping System

These are important cropping system in western part of the country, particularly semi arid regions of Gujarat, Rajasthan and Haryana. Wheat is grown as *Rab*i crop and Pearl Millet (Bajra) is grown in *Kharif* season. This system is also facing issue of decreased soil fertility and lowering of the groundwater table. Pearl millet can deplete the soil of essential nutrient system.

Maize-Wheat Cropping System

In this cropping system; maize is a principal crop of *Kharif* season while wheat is a principal crop in *Rabi* season. This system is practiced in Uttar Pradesh, Rajasthan, Madhya Pradesh, Bihar, Punjab, Jammu and Kashmir etc. Most of the area in the Maize-wheat system is rainfed area where uncertainty of rainfall is a major limitation.

Sorghum-Wheat Cropping System

This cropping system is prevalent in Rajasthan, Western Madhya Pradesh, and Western Maharashtra including Vidarbha, Southern Gujarat and Northern parts of Karnataka.

Sugarcane-Wheat Cropping System

Sugarcane-Wheat cropping system is prevalent in Uttar Pradesh, Punjab, Haryana and Bihar. This system also faces problem of imbalance of nutrients.

Cotton-Wheat Cropping System

In this system, short duration cotton is grown in sequence with wheat in Punjab, Haryana, Rajasthan, Western UP and some other parts of central India.

Soybean – Wheat Cropping System

This is relatively new cropping system emerged only after 1980s when Soyabean was introduced as a *Kharif* crop in several parts of the country. This system is prevalent in Madhya Pradesh, Rajasthan and some parts of southern Maharashtra.

3. Factors influencing cropping systems

Cropping systems of a region are by and large decided by number of soil and climatic factors which determine overall agro-ecological settings required for the cultivation of the crops suitable for the particular region. Nevertheless, potential productivity and monetary benefits act as guiding principles for a farmer to opt for a particular crop/cropping system. These decisions with respect to choice of crops and cropping systems are further narrowed down under influence of several other forces related to infrastructure facilities, socio-economic factors and technological developments, all operating interactively at micro-level.

a) **Infrastructure facilities**: Irrigation, transport, storage, trade and marketing, post-harvest handling and processing *etc.*

b) **Socio-economic factors**: Financial resource base, land ownership, size and type of land holding, household needs of food, fodder, fuel, fibre and finance, labour availability *etc.*

c) **Technological factors**: Improved varieties, cultural requirements, mechanization, plant protection, access to information, *etc.*

4. Essentials of higher cropping intensity

The cropping intensity shows great spatial variation in India, with higher levels in northern plains. Lower levels are found in dry, rain-fed regions of Rajasthan, Gujarat, Maharashtra and Karnataka. Various factors essential to raise cropping intensity are discussed below:

i) Irrigation

Assured water supply is necessary for increasing the cropping intensity of any area. Irrigation has played an important role in raising the cropping intensity in northern states where it has risen considerably. Irrigation helps raise the cropping intensity by enabling raising of crops during the dry season also thereby helping to enhance cropping intensity through temporal management.

ii) Proper nutrient management

Increasing number of crops from a unit area of land can exhaust vital nutrients from the soils of that area necessitating to leave the land fallow for some period to regain the lost nutrients but these can be dispensed by the addition of organic manures in combination with chemical fertilisers and following some other suitable cropping practices.

iii) Crop Rotation

It is the suitable arrangement of successive crops in such a way that the different crops draw nutrients in different proportions or from different layers of soil. For instance, if legumes (pulses, gram, *etc.*) or certain oilseeds are sown just before the cereals, they fix the atmospheric nitrogen in soil, which can be absorbed by the cereals.

iv) Mixed Cropping/Intercropping

This works on similar principles. In this case, wheat and barley or wheat and gram or barley and gram are grown together to maintain a balance of consumption between different nutrients.

v) Relay Cropping

Relay cropping refers to the sowing of succeeding crops prior to the harvesting of preceding crops. This means simultaneous sowing of different crops with different nurturing periods in the same field and harvesting them one after the other. For instance, highly fertiliser-intensive crops like sugarcane and tobacco can be followed by cereals, in order to utilise the residual nutrients. The practice of relay cropping helps to achieve higher cropping intensity through temporal and spatial management of crops.

vi) Farm mechanization

Use of tractors, tillers, harvsters, threshers, etc can save critical time between raising two crops, thus enabling the sowing of more than one crop.

vii) Use of short duration /early maturing varieties

Short duration varieties enable growing of more than one crop within a short span in growing season. Short duration varieties in rice, moong bean, urd bean are ready for harvest in 60-70 days after transplantation of seedlings/ sowing of seed. Short duration varieties in vegetable crops namely radish, coriander, spinach, methi and knolkhol are ready for market in just 30-40 days after sowing/ transplanting of seedling while cauliflower, broccoli and many cucurbits are ready for in 60-75 days after transplanting of seedlings.

viii) Appropriate Plant Protection

These measures include the use of pesticides and insecticides, seed treatment, weed control, rodent control measures etc. Appropriate plant protection measures are imperative to ensure that more and more crops can be taken up in cropping systems without suffering any crop failures. However, these measures are effective when all the farmers in an area take these up collectively.

ix) Sowing quality seed of improved cultivars

Sowing quality seed of improved varieties that fit well are most suitable in the cropping systems is the most important aspect determining the success of the high intensity crop sequences. Sowing of quality seed like certified seed ensures the good germination and good crop stand leading to higher crop productivity per unit of land, the real objective of the crop intensification.

A case study on "Real Time High Intensity Rice Based Cropping Systems for Enhancement of Farm Income in Irrigated Sub- tropics of Jammu Region" is under way in SKUAST-J at its main campus with objective of indentifying crop rotations of intensity upto 600% as against prevalent of 167%.

Different cropping sequences have been designed in order to intensify rice based cropping systems for enhancement of farm income in irrigated sub tropics of Jammu region by the Division of Agronomy, *Sher-e-Kashmir University of Agricultural Sciences and Technology –Jammu*. The key features of this project are raising rice crop in sequence with other short duration pulses and vegetable crops for maximising cropping intensity of irrigated sub-tropics to encourage the farmers to take more than three crops in a year thus raising average cropping intensity of this region. This will not only increase farmers income and employment generation round the year but also improve soil health. Based on the different crop combinations the cropping intensities of the different systems ranged from 300 to 600%. The project is in voyage and so far encouraging results are being recorded. The most practicable cropping systems with regard to their management, production potential and final economic returns will be standardized for the irrigated ecology of Jammu plains. The detail of the crops included in different rice based sequences have been given here under

A field view of crop intensification experiment of 300-600% cropping Intensity underway at Research Farm, SKUAST-Jammu

5. Specific strategies for increasing cropping intensity in rainfed ecosystems

Irrigation is very important factor to raise the cropping intensity by enabling raising of crops during the dry season. This is the reason that Northern irrigated plains have higher cropping intensities compared to the

Table 1: Real Time High Intensity Rice Based Cropping Systems for Enhancement of Farm Income in Irrigated Sub- tropics of Jammu Region

Cropping Systems						Cropping Intensity
Rice (Basmati-370)	Wheat (HD-3086)	Green gram (IPM -02-3)				300%
Rice (Pusa 1509)	Potato (Kufri Badshah)	Wheat (Raj 3765)	Green gram (IPM 02-3)			400%
Rice (IET-1410)	Fenugreek (JF-07)	Knol-khol (G-40) Relay cropping	Turnip (PTWG) Relay cropping	French bean (Anupama) Relay cropping	Green gram (IPM 02-3) Relay cropping	600%
Rice (SJR-129)	Knol-khol (G-40)	Potato (Kufri Sindhuri)	Green gram (IPM 02-3)			400%
Rice (NDR-97)	Radish (CR-45)	Spinach (JSB-07)	Knol-khol (G-40)			500%

Source: Division of Agronomy, SKUAST-J

lower levels that are found in dry, rain-fed regions of Rajasthan, Gujarat, Maharashtra Karnataka etc. But there is still some scope to increase cropping intensities in dryland ecosystems through various measures given under:

5.1. Crop substitution

Strategy has also been evolved for normal onset of rains, breaks in rains, early withdrawal, its uneven distribution; through selection of uneven crops/varieties which are to efficient to utilize the soil moisture, less responsive to production input and potentially low producers should be substituted by more efficient ones. Appropriate crops, suiting varying rainfall situations, have been identified for most of the dry land regions of India. For example, studies conducted in agro climatic conditions of Varanasi (eastern U.P.) revealed that under normal monsoon crops like short duration upland rice, maize, pearl millet, blackgram, greengram, sesame, pigeon pea etc. should be taken up on the basis of needs. These crops should be followed by chickpea, lentil, barley, mustard, safflower, linseed etc. on residual moisture during winter season. If monsoon sets in as late as second week of July, short duration upland rice (variety - NDR-97 and NDR-118) may be included in place of Akashi and Cauvery is recommended. If the rains are delayed beyond the period but start somewhere in last week of July or first week of August and growing season is reduced to 60-67- days, then cultivation of hybrid pearl millet (NHB 3-4, B.J. 104), blackgram (Type 9), greengram (var-Jagriti and Jyoti) may be included in place of T-44 and K-851 etc. should be grown. Yet another alternative could be to harvest a fodder of either pearl millet, maize, sorghum or a mixture of cowpea, blackgram and one of the above fodder crops. In case monsoon rains stop early towards the end of season, normal sowing of short duration upland rice, blackgarm and sesame may be taken up. If the rain stops very early, i.e. by the end of August or first week of September, only fodder crops or grain legumes could be harvested. Depending upon the soil moisture condition, relay sowing of crops like chickpea, lentil, mustard, linseed and barley could be done in *rabi* season (Yadav 2009)

5.2. Efficient Cropping System

Besides putting various measures to increase the productivity levels of dry land crops, efforts would also be needed to increase the cropping intensity in dry land areas which was generally 100%, implying that a single crop was taken during the year. Cropping intensities of dryland areas could be increased by practice of inter cropping and multi cropping (sequential) by way of more efficient utilization of resources. The cropping intensity would depend on the length of growing season which in turn depends on rainfall pattern and the soil moisture storage capacity of the soil. For example in Indore region, receiving 1000 mm annual rainfall, only single crop can be taken on shallow soils, inter cropping in medium depth soils and double cropping on deep soils. Similar crop combinations have been identified for different regions of the country. For instance, in dry land of Varanasi region upland rice-chickpea/lentil sequence can be practiced with advantage. Inter cropping of vegetables with grain crops can be pursued (Yadav 2009). Long duration pigeon pea can be inter cropped with vegetables such as okra, radish and chilli. Such inter-cropping systems would be very useful to get maximum returns from rainfed agriculture.

5.3. Proper utilization of rice fallows

Rice fallows basically imply to those lowland *kharif* sown rice areas which remain uncropped during *rabi* (winter) due to various reasons such as early withdrawal of monsoon rains leading to soil moisture stress at planting time of winter crops, waterlogging, lack of appropriate varieties of winter crops for late planting, and socio-economic problems. Rice fallows of South Asia accounts for 79% (11.65 m ha) of the total area (15.0 m ha) including India, Bangladesh and Pakistan. The rice fallows have a great potential for cultivation of short-duration pulses and oilseeds. Development and popularization of improved varieties of pulses and oilseeds suiting to rice fallows of different agro-ecological regions coupled with improved agro-technology will boost production, and thus improve income and livelihood security as well as nutritional security of farming community. Moreover, introduction of legumes can provide a sustainable production base to the continued rice mono-cropped system, which is otherwise leading to decline in total factor productivity. Most pronounced effect of climate change is a drastic change in the rainfall pattern in the form of delayed monsoon, early withdrawl or inadequate precipitation with poor distribution leading to either drought or waterlogged conditions, particularly in rainfed ecosystem. Therefore, timing of rice transplanting plays an important role in getting higher yield of rice and sowing of succeeding dry season crops mainly pulses or oilseeds. During *kharif* season, rice is grown with traditional practices and consequently land become unavailable for the sowing of second crop when sufficient residual moisture is available. The land can be brought under double cropping with proper utilization of carry-over residual soil moisture. For instance, dry season crops following short duration rice cultivars performed better in terms of grain yield. In the dry season, toria was profitable when sown earlier and if sowing was delayed green gram was suitable (Lal *et al* 2017).

5.4. Nutrient management and Fertilizer Use

Soils of dry lands in the country are not only thirsty but hungry also because these soils are severely eroded horizontally as well as vertically. Whenever efforts are made towards bunding and levelling of the fields in dry land areas, it is the surface soil which is removed. The resultant effect is that the fields are rendered shallow in depth and completely deprived of plant nutrients, particularly nitrogen, phosphorus and potassium. It is, therefore, necessary to apply all the three major nutrients in adequate amounts. Since soil moisture is limiting in dry lands, the availability of nutrients becomes limited, attempt should always be made to apply fertilizers in furrows below the seed. If seed-cum-fertilizer drills drawn by bullocks or tractors are available, this very objective can be fulfilled. Studies on the management of legumes in crop sequences for their residual effect indicated that in alluvial soils an advantage of 25-30 kg N/ha could be obtained in barley or mustard grown after black gram or green gram. In dry land areas, a proper mixing of organic and inorganic would be desirable. Organics have low nutrient content, but help to improve the moisture holding capacity of soils. In addition to yield advantage, nutrients like potassium help to increase drought tolerance by affecting plant-soil relationship. Transpiration losses are reduced and productivity per unit water increases.

5.5. Rain water management

Efficient management of rain water can boost agricultural production from dry lands. Water harvesting structures like ponds and wells can be of great use in bringing additional area under irrigation in the water deficit zone. Water harvesting techniques like capturing run off from rooftops and local catchments can also be used to collect excess water and then used for productive purposes. This in turn will increase the cropping intensity of the area ultimately leading to more output from the same area. Alternatively, application of compost and farm yard manure as well as raising legumes will add organic matter to the soil and increase the water holding capacity.

6. Conclusion

Cropping intensity plays an important role in the agricultural development of any region. Higher cropping intensity shows intensive use of land for agricultural purpose. The scope for expanding net sown area having already reached a saturation level and potential for raising for yield nearly exhausted in many crops and regions, stepping up of incidence multiple cropping will be necessary to augment agricultural production. Raising productivity per unit of land will need to be the main engine of agricultural growth as virtually all cultivable land is farmed. Water resources are also limited and water for irrigation must contend with increasing industrial and urban needs. All measures to increase productivity will need exploiting, amongst them: increasing yields, diversification to higher value crops, and developing value chains to reduce marketing losses. Although yields continue to increase in many areas, yields also never improve, stagnate, or collapse in other areas (accounting for about 25% of global croplands) (Ray *et al* 2012; Grassini *et al* 2013). Projections on future yields found that yield increase is obviously less than the expected annual growth rate required to double global production by 2050 (Ray *et al* 2013). Furthermore, how best to close the yield gap largely depends on the capacity of local farmers to access and use seeds, water, nutrients, pest management, soils, and knowledge, all of which face considerable technical and/or market constraints, such as high input costs or low returns from increased production. Closing yield gaps is also associated with uncertain impacts on the environment and the potential for negative feedback effects that could undermine future food production (Foley *et al* 2011). More intensive use of existing croplands by increasing cropping intensity may provide a possible alternative for increasing global food production (Dias *et al* 2016; Meng *et al* 2017). An increase in cropping intensity by increasing the number of crops per cropping cycle or intercropping with other crops can increase the frequency of harvests each year, resulting in increased food supplies without additional cropland expansion (Mauser *et al* 2015). Due to prevailing socio-economic situations (such as; dependency of large population on agriculture, small land-holding size, very high population pressure on land resource etc.), improving household food security has been an issue of supreme importance to many million farmers of India, who constitute 56.15 million marginal (<1.0 hectare), 17.92 million small (1.0-2.0 hectare) and 13.25 million (semi-medium) (2.0-4.0 hectare) farm holdings, making together 90 per cent of 97.15 million operational holdings. An important consequence of this has been that crop production in India is remained to be considered by and large, a subsistence rather than commercial activity. Under this scenario doubling real income of farmers till 2022-23 over the base year of 2015-16, requires annual growth of 10.41 per cent in farmers income. This implies that the on-going and previously achieved rate of growth in farm income has to be sharply accelerated. Therefore, strong measures will be needed to harness all possible sources of growth in farmers' income within as well as outside agriculture sector.

The major sources of growth operating within agriculture sector are:

1. Improvement in productivity
2. Resource use efficiency or saving in cost of production
3. Increase in cropping intensity of existing 138 % to 300 % or more
4. Diversification towards high value crops

The major sources of growth operating within agriculture sector that are aimed to uplift the farmers economic status *vis-a-vis* to tackle the food security issues are well inter related. The objective of increasing the cropping intensity will be achieved only by the inclusion of short duration varieties of cereals, identification of pulses and oilseed crops that can fit well in the cropping systems of different agro-ecologies that will ultimately improve crop productivity per unit of land making the efficient utilization of resources and will meet the objectives of crop diversification leading to food and economic security of the nation.

7. References

Anonymous, 2011. Department of Agriculture and Cooperation, Annual Report 2010-2011, Ministry of Agriculture, Government of India.

Anonymous, 2018. Integrated UPSC /IAS General Studies - Target 2018

Dias LCP, Pimenta FM, Santos AB, Costa MH, Ladle RJ .2016. Patterns of land use, extensification, and intensification of Brazilian agriculture. *Global Change Biology* 22 (8), 2887–2903.

Foley JA, Ramankutty N, Brauman KA, Cassidy ES, Gerber JS, Johnston M, Mueller ND, O'Connell C, Ray DK, West PC, Balzer C, Bennett EM, Carpenter SR, Hill J, Monfreda C, Polasky S, Rockstrom J, Sheehan J, Siebert S, Tilman, D., Zaks, D.M.P. 2011. Solutions for a cultivated planet. *Nature* .448: 337–342.

Grassini P, Eskridge KM, Cassman KG .2013. Distinguishing between yield advances and yield plateaus in historical crop production trends. *Nat. Commun.* 4: 2918. http://agropedia.iitk.ac.in/content/recent-advances-dryland-agriculture

Lal B, Gautam P, Panda BB, Raj R, Singh T, Tripathi R, Shahid M and Nayak AK .2017. *Crop and varietal diversification of rainfed rice based cropping systems for higher productivity and profitability in Eastern India.* PLOS (Public Library of Science) https://doi.org/10.1371/journal.pone.0175709

Mauser W, Klepper G, Zabel F, Delzeit R, Hank T, Putzenlechner B, Calzadilla A .2015. Global biomass production potentials exceed expected future demand without the need for cropland expansion. *Nat. Commun.* 6: 8946.

Meng Q, Wang H, Yan P, Pan J, Lu D, Cui Z, Zhang F, Chen X .2017. Designing a new cropping system for high productivity and sustainable water usage under climate change. *Sci. Rep.* 7: 41587.

Rana SS, Rana JC and SharmaTR .2011. A concept of diverse perennial cropping systems for integrated bioenergy production and ecological restoration of marginal lands in India. *Ecological Engineering,* 105:58-65.

Ray DK and Foley JA .2013. Increasing global crop harvest frequency: recent trends and future directions. *Environ. Res.* Lett. 8: 044041.

Ray, D.K., Ramankutty, N., Mueller, N.D., West, P.C., Foley, J.A., 2012. Recent patterns of crop yield growth and stagnation. *Nat. Commun.* 3, 1293.

Singh, A. K., Manibushan, Bhatt, B. P., Singh, K. M. and Upaadhaya, A. 2013. An Analysis of Oilseed and Pulses Scenario in Eastern India during 2050-51. *Journal of Agricultural Sciences,* 5(1): 241-249.

Singh A, Kour R, Kang JS and Singh G .2012. Weed dynamics in rice-wheat cropping system. *Global Journal of Biology, Agriculture and Health Sciences,* 1:7-16.

Suresh A, Raju SS, Chauhan S and Chaudhary KR .2014. Rainfed agriculture in India: An analysis of performance and implications. *Indian Journal of Agricultural Sciences*, 84(11): 1415-22.

Yadav K .2009. *Recent Advances in Dryland Agriculture.* GBPUAT, Pantnagar

23

Organic Agriculture: An Entrepreneurship for Women Empowerment and Socio-Economic Transformation

Jag Paul Sharma, Vikas Sharma, Narinder Panotra, Akash Sharma, SK Singh, Satesh Kumar, Ametesh Kumar, Manish Sharma, Balbir Dhotra, Anil Bhushan, Satish Kumar*

**Organic Farming Research Centre, Seed Production Farm, India*
Directorate of Research, SKUAST Jammu, Chatha, Jammu and Kashmir, India

"Just as a bird cannot fly with its one wing only, a nation will not march forward if the women are left behind - ***Swami Vivekanand***

1. Introduction
2. Socio-economic prospects
3. Concept of organic agriculture
4. Fundamentals of organic agriculture
5. Essentials for a beginner
6. Economic importance
7. Indian organic food industry
8. Entrepreneurship and employment generation
9. Drivers of organic growth and business in India
10. Organic sector: Challenges in India
11. Regulatory environment and government initiatives
12. Organic agriculture and women empowerment
13. Some attentions and actions for women empowerment
14. *References*

Abstract

Women empowerment is a buzz word of every platform starting from household issues to national politics. The best way to empower women is to make them economically self-reliant through entrepreneurial activities. In India agriculture is mainstay of the country and 70 percent women are farmers, so the best measure to empower them is through entrepreneurship in agriculture and allied sectors particularly organic agriculture as India currently holds a prominent position among 172 countries that actively practice it. At present, the country is home to more than 8, 50,000 organic producers, 699 processors, 669 exporters, and 7, 20,000 hectares under cultivation. Merely with 0.4 per cent of total agricultural land area under organic cultivation, India has attained global standing which infers that this industry still has a long way to go in terms of growth and opportunities for socio-economic development. Organic Food industry has been experiencing steadfast growth in past few years in India in spite of several challenges at producer, processor and consumer levels. With its annual turnover of Rs 4000 crore and annual growth rate of 25%, the country's budding organic food market is transforming into world's fastest growing organic food market with expected turnover of 10,000 crore by 2020. There is drastic change in consumer behavior and spending patterns in the country which has opened avenues for organic food industry at the national level besides export. This high-scale opportunity is driven by the fact that organic food consumption is not even 0.1 percent of India's $300 billion annual food consumption. Likewise, India's share in the $100 billion global organic food market is less than 0.2 percent. Further, the scope of the opportunity is also driven by the increasing variety of organic foods hitting the market and the emergence of e-commerce as a channel in which to sell the product. India today is on the threshold of organic revolution where women participation will act as booster but need to be supported by Govts and technical institutions. Barriers to improving women's agency include widespread deficiencies in policy support to women, and in fact to the organic farming sector as a whole. It is necessary to increase women's research presence in organic research institutions (including at the higher levels). To enable women to conduct research in the field, it is important to allow women to set research agendas, and to work with their research needs and priorities. Food security as a priority for organic agriculture involves women's empowerment since they hold a central role in providing nutrition for the household.

1. Introduction

World Conference on Human Rights, Vienna, 1993 advocated the full and equal participation of women in political, civil, economic, social and cultural life, at the national, regional and international levels and the eradication of all forms of discrimination on grounds of sex. The equal participation and partnership of both women and men is essential for balanced development of human society contrary to this, in all parts of the world, women are facing threats to their lives, health and well- being. The empowerment of women and the improvement in political, social, economic and health status is a highly important achievement in itself. In addition, it is essential for sustainable development.

Women empowerment is a buzz word of every platform starting from household issues to national politics. The best way to empower women is to make them economically self-sufficient through entrepreneurial activities. Women Entrepreneurs may be defined as a group of women who initiate, organize and operate a business or enterprise. The Government of India has defined women owned enterprises as "an enterprise owned and controlled by women having a minimum financial interest of 51 percent of the capital and giving at least 51 per cent of the employment generated in the enterprise to women" (Goyal and Prakash 2012 and Sharma 2013). So women entrepreneurship directly empowers the entrepreneur so also to other women members of community. In India, agriculture is the mainstay of the country and 70 percent women are farmers, so the best measure to empower them is through entrepreneurship in agriculture and allied sectors. Therefore, agripreneurship is an effective and logical means for women empowerment. The women farmers need to be motivated by organizing them into cooperatives, FPOs (Farmer producers organization), village producers organization (VPO), Farmers Club, Self Help Groups (SHGs), providing them land ownership, attracting them towards Micro, Small and Medium sized enterprises (Jena et al 2018). It will make them self confident, economically stable, independent decision taking, better purchasing power, socio culturally more involved. There are various opportunities in agriculture and allied sectors which can be practiced to get a sound economic benefit. Prominent being vegetable production, backyard poultry farming, dairying, value added products, commercial horticulture nursery and organic agriculture.

In organic agriculture India currently holds a prominent position among 184 countries that actively practice it. At present, the country is home to more than 8,50,000 organic producers, 699 processors, 669 exporters, and 7, 20,000 hectares under cultivation. Merely with 0.4 per cent of total agricultural land area under organic cultivation, India has attained global standing which infers that this industry still has a long way to go in terms of growth. Moreover, since the organic food segment is still at a nascent stage in India, both the government and other private players will have to develop a strong policy framework that can benefit all involved. For now, it can be safely concluded that the organic farming industry in India holds immense potential to grow. The organic products market in India has been growing at a CAGR of 25 per cent and it is expected to touch 10,000-12,000 crore by 2020 from the current market size of 4,000 crore, according to a report produced by ASSOCHAM.

Even though India has the highest number of farmers 8,35,000 currently engaged in organic farming, the country accounts for less than 1 per cent the global organic market pie which is valued at $90 billion in 2016, the report said. In terms of total area under organic cultivation, India ranks at 9th position with 1.5 million hectares. Australia, which tops the list, has more than 27 million hectares under organic farming.

2. Socio-economic prospects

Current farming practices involving use of mineral fertilizers and chemical synthetic pesticides have huge negative side effects, both in terms of poisonous effects on living organisms and of long term effects on ecosystems (Pretty 2005). Through the stimulation of systems relying on mono-cropping, which cause land degradation through decreasing humus layer, severe long terms negative health effects are created. Bad side effects for the current generations of high-chemical-input farming were clearly demonstrated through the so-called Green Revolution in India, where the country reached a point of productivity where they could export food, but where severe negative side-effects on the ecosystems were created, and where many smallholder farmers were bypassed, while the number of hungry people remained over 200 million. The bad side effects are, if possible, even more critical to a number of 'silent actors': the eco-systems, biodiversity, and the yet-unborn future generations, who must suffer from irreversible poisonings of the environment. Vaarst (2010) suggested for a global development strategy that explicitly includes future generations, gender equality, ecosystems, biodiversity and plant and animal species threatened by eradication and proposed that organic agriculture as being a relevant strategy to meet many millennium development goals (MDGs).

Table 1: The potential contributions and challenges of organic agriculture in relation to the MDGs 2015

Millenium Development Goals 2015 (MDG 2015)	Potential contributions and challenges related to Organic agriculture (OA)
1. Eradicate extreme poverty and hunger	OA increases productivity based on available resources, with minimum external inputs
2. Achieve universal primary education	OA is knowledge intensive; knowledge isowned by users, not connected to products.
3. Promote gender equality and empower women	Majority of smallholders are female farmers– emphasis on gender equity
4. Reduce child mortality	Diverse and well-balanced food rations.
5. Improve maternal health	Conscious gender equality and social capital building
6. Combat HIV/AIDS, malaria and other diseases	Being green agriculture approach has positive effects to combat the diseases

7. Ensure environmental sustainability	
A: Integrate the principles of sustainable development into country policies and programs and reverse the loss of environmental resources, B: Reduce biodiversity loss, achieving, by 2010, a significant reduction in the rate of loss, C: Halve, by 2015, the proportion of people without sustainable access to safe drinking water and basic sanitation, D: By 2020, to have achieved a significant improvement in the lives of at least 100 million slum dwellers.	OA builds on biodiversity maintenance, improvement of soil fertility through improved humus layer, recycling, planning and use of intercropping and crop rotation systems, interaction with natural environments and ecosystems.
8. Develop a global partnership for development	Fair conditions for development, trade and knowledge exchange

The Indian state of Sikkim has been officially named the first fully organic state in the country in 2015. The Organic foods market in India is estimated to be over USD 0.50 Billion. It is further projected to treble in the upcoming years, reaching up to USD 1.36 Billion within the next four years, i.e. by 2020. Overall, the organic foods segment in the country witnessed an estimated 25 per cent to 30 per cent growth, which is quite encouraging. India's progress in the organic sector has been remarkable. In the 1990s, the sector was limited to the export of tea to European markets. Currently, India is emerging as a key player in the global arena, exporting over 300 products in 20 different categories to over 20 countries. Additionally, India is the largest exporter of organic cotton and houses the largest number of organic producers in the world. Alongside the developments pertaining to the global markets, the domestic markets are growing at a rate higher than the global average and are expected to keep growing at a 25% CAGR through 2023. This high-scale opportunity is driven by the fact that organic food consumption is not even 0.1 percent of India's $300 billion annual food consumption. Likewise, India's share in the $100 billion global organic food market is less than 0.2 percent. As mentioned above, the scale of the opportunity is also driven by the increasing variety of organic foods hitting the market and the emergence of ecommerce as a channel in which to sell the product.

In a recent report by the UNCTAD-UNEP Capacity-Building Task Force on Trade, Environment and Development (CBTF), it was stated that 'the evidence presented in this study supports the argument that organic agriculture can be more conducive to food security in Africa than most conventional production systems, and that it is more likely to be sustainable in the long term. This is in line with the findings of the Food and Agricultural Organization of the United

Nations (FAO) International Conference on Organic Agriculture and Food Security, held in May 2007. Therefore, we encourage policymakers and development cooperation partners in Africa and around the world to take a new look at this promising production system with fresh eyes. It offers not only improved food security, but also an array of other economic, environmental, health and social benefits. However, Agro-ecological methods build primarily on local resources and rely on interactions with natural systems, and there are no patents or major trade systems involved. Since these methods do not use industrially produced inputs, they are not connected to economic interests. No patent rights exist on 'working with nature' methods of farming. Very often, they are quite labour-intensive farming systems, managing many types of crops and products. Noticeably, the organic agriculture requires knowledge of the concept, essentials, awareness and an ability to reflect and be innovative.

3. Concept of organic agriculture

Organic agriculture (OA) is a specialized production management technology that boosts ecological harmony by taking care of health of interdependent comminutes namely plants, soils, animals and human beings. OA is emerging most reliable alternative system that has competence to provide diverse eco-biological services. Moreover, it has gained global acceptance for commerce, ecological contributions and sustainability of the planet mother earth. Lower greenhouse gas emissions for crop production and enhanced carbon sequestration, coupled with additional benefits of biodiversity and other environmental services, makes organic agriculture a farming method with many advantages and considerable potential for mitigating and adapting to climate change. The definition of organic varies from place to place but may include things such as a minimum time period that a field is free of chemical use before being used for organic farming.

According to Sharma (2018) commercial viable definition of OA is "A competitively safe agricultural production management system that has capability to yield better qualitatively and quantitatively avoiding the application of synthetic fertilizers and pesticides". IFOAM (2000) has defined organic agriculture as "a process that develops a viable and sustainable agro ecosystem".

US Department of Agriculture defined Organic Farming as, "A system that is designed and mailed to produce to agricultural products by the use of methods, and substances that maintain the integrity of organic agricultural products until they reach the consumer". This is accomplished by using, where possible, cultural, biological and mechanical methods, as oppose to use substances to fulfill any specific fluctuations within the system so as to maintain long term biological activity, ensure effective management, recycle waste to return nutrients to the land, provides attentive cares for farm animals and handle the agricultural products without the use of extraneous synthetic additives or processing in accordance with the act and regulations in this part.

Description offered by Lampkin (1990) has been found to be the most comprehensive one covering all essential features of Organic Farming. According to Lampkin, "Organic Farming is a production system which avoids or largely excludes the use of synthetically compounded fertilizers, growth regulators and live stock feed additives, to the maximum extent, feasible. According to him the aim of organic farming is: "to create integrated, humane, environmentally and economically sustainable production systems, which maximize reliance on farm-derived renewable resources and the management of ecological and biological processes and interactions, so as to provide acceptable levels of crop, livestock and human nutrition, protection from pests and disease, and an appropriate return to the human and other resources".

Therefore, one should know the relationship among soil, water, plant and micro flora and overall relationship between plants animal kingdom. It is the totality of these relationships, which is the backbone of the Organic Farming. Above all, the success of organic farming depends to a great extent on the efficiency of agronomic management adopted to stimulate and augment the underlying productivity of the soil resources. All the management practices followed in organic farming are governed by the principles of ecology and are within the ecological means.

4. Fundamentals of organic agriculture

Organic agriculture by principles takes care of ecology, believes in maximization of nutrient cycling and shun away from use of synthetic fertilizers and other agrochemicals that play havoc with biotic communities. The word 'organic' has been given protection by many countries to assure the quality of the product that it supposed to fulfill as per specifications. However both certified and non-certified organic production systems are existing but certain steps mandatory to follow are.

- **Conversion period**: it varies from 2 to 3 years depending on the cultivation status of the field.
- **Crop rotation:** A single crop cannot be cultivated as organic. One or more potential crop sequences have to be identified for a region so that once the field is converted to organic phase, yield levels are maintained.
- **Buffer zone:** it is important when both organic and non-organic crops are grown at the farm. It may vary from 5 metres to 10 metres.

- **Integrated farming production system**: organic farming is an integrated production system where use of synthetic fertilizers and agrochemicals is prohibited. In other words, growers have to undertake crop production, rearing of animals, organic manure production and green manuring etc simultaneously.
- **Authentication or certification of products:** certification is mandatory when produce is intended for export. Certification is carried by some accreditated agencies or it may be through internal control system (ICS) or through participatory guaranteed system (PGS). Simple authentication may do for local market.
- **Record keeping of products and inputs:** certified organic agriculture demands for maintaining record of generation and sale of products as well as inputs. Complete protocols should be available if asked to provide.
- **Traceability:** this is required to know the origin of the product and purpose is that one can know the technical history of a product if desired.
- **Growers association and or marketing net work:** organic produce is usually intended for special market which accepts produce at premium price. 20-30% premium price is recommended for the organic enterprise to become a successful venture.

5. Essentials for a beginner

- Basics of organic agriculture
- What is the best for the location?
- Consumers' preference or choice
- Organic inputs for soil and crop management
- A mentor
- Market linkage

6. Economic importance

Organic agriculture is a multi-facet enterprise encompassing socio-economic as well as eco-biological dimensions. The approach is well acknowledged by IFAOM as biological safe and ecological promotive. Economical dimension gained momentum when organic products received a worldwide acceptability with bonanza of premium price. Now the organic agriculture is coming up as separate discipline in agricultural education. Keeping in view its commercial importance ICAR recently recommended commencement of postgraduate program in organic farming /agriculture.

Export/Commercial dimension

Organic farming is practiced with varying levels of success in 178 countries. However, the North American and European Union regions (as single markets) generate the bulk of the global sales. The global sales increased to US$89.7 billion in 2016 from US$7.9 billion in 2000. Country wise, the top consumers of organic products are the US (US$43.1 billion), followed by Germany (US$10.5 billion) and France (US$7.5 billion). The increase in demand has led to a considerable increase in the area subject to organic management techniques globally, surging from 11 million ha in 1999 to 57.8 million ha in 2016. The wild harvest and other non-agriculture organic collection area also increased to 39.9 million ha in 2016 from 4.1 million ha in 1999. The three countries with the largest area under organic cultivation are Australia (27.1 million ha), followed by Argentina (3.0 million ha) and China (2.3 million ha). 2 The three countries with the largest wild harvest area for organic products are Finland (11.6 million ha), followed by Zambia (6.7 million ha) and India (4.2 million ha). Organic agriculture movement has gained momentum globally encompassing 184 countries with 73 organic production systems recognized worldwide. The global market for organically produced foods in 2005 was US$ 30 billion and is estimated to grow to 102 billion US$ by 2020. It is growing with a pace of 20-30% annually revealing its commercial dimensions in international trade.

Table 2: Global Organic Food Market (USD)

2020 : 102.0 billion US $ (projected)
2016 : 89.7 billion US$
2012 : 69.0 billion US $
2010 : 59.1 billion US $
2009 : 54.1 billion US $
1999 : 15.2 billion US $

India is the member of IFOAM (International Federation of Organic Agriculture movement) and has maximum number of organic farmers in the world. Hence India must optimistically plan to venture into this area. Ranking third in wild harvest area, India also houses the highest number of organic producers globally with 835,000 organic farmers. It also ranks ninth in terms of area under organic cultivation with 1.49 million ha. Therefore, it occupies a robust position in producing organic products, having already exported 1.35 million MT of certified organic food products worth INR1,937 crore in 2015-16. The exports are largely concentrated around the US, Europe (EU), Canada, Japan and the West Asian markets. India is the largest exporter of organic cotton worldwide. In the food market segment, oilseeds comprised half of India's overall organic food export, followed by processed food products at 25%. The current Indian organic market is estimated at INR4000 crore and is likely to increase to INR10000–12000 crore by 2020 with a similar incremental trend in exports. Indian organic market has been progressing steadily with CAGR of 25% as compared to 16% global growth rates. However, despite the promising performance in terms of exports, the local consumption of organic produce is still at a nascent stage with a market share of less than 1% and per capita consumption at only EUR 0.1.

Table 3: Growth of Area under Organic Agriculture in India

S.No.	Year	Organic Area in India (ha.)
1.	2005	42,000
2.	2006	76,000
3.	2007	1,73,000
4.	2008	5,38,000
5.	2009	8,65,000
6.	2010	11,80,000
7.	2011	8,20,000
8.	2012	10,20,000

Source: Pant et al (2013), Pop. Kheti, 1(4):15-18

India exported 458 thousand tons of organic products worth $515 million in 2017-18 around 39 per cent higher from the previous year, said Agricultural and Processed Food Products Export Development Authority. Through more capacity building and bilateral agreements, India's organic exports is set to US$1 billion by 2020 as its produce receiving wide acceptance in many mature markets of the US and Europe. "Our vision is to make India the number one organic hub in the world over in the next 10 years" says Chairman of the Agricultural and Processed Food Export Development Authority (Hindu, 2010).

Organic Food industry has been experiencing steadfast growth in past few years in India. With its annual turnover of Rs 4000 and annual growth rate of 25%, the country's budding organic food market is transforming into world's fastest growing organic food market. There is drastic change in consumer behavior and spending patterns in the country which has opened avenues for organic food industry at the national level besides export. India today is on the threshold of organic revolution but need to be supported by Govts and technical institutions.

Table 4: Organic product- Export sale (Metric tons) from India

Oil Crops (except Sesame)	17966
Cotton & Textiles	17363
Processed Food	8752
Basmati Rice	5243
Tea	2928
Sesame	2409

Honey	2409
Rice	1634
Dry Fruits	1472
Cereals	1348
Spices-Condiments	1174
Medicinal & Herbal Plants/Products	627
Coffee	320
Vegetables	167

Govt of India constituted a Task Force on Organic Farming. One of the steering committees constituted by this Task Force under the Chairmanship of M. S. Swaminathan suggested taking up organic farming as a challenging task and as a thrust area. The steering committee advocated giving boost to organic farming in the rain fed areas and in the northeastern states, where there is limited use of agricultural chemicals. 50 districts comprising Orissa, Jharkhand, Uattrakhand, Himachal Pradesh, Jammu and Kashmir, Rajasthan, Gujarat, Madhya Pradesh and Chattisgarh use no to low fertilizers and thus could be target area to take up activity on organic farming in India. Local market for organic food is increasing whereas scope for export is expanding with rise in demand from the western world. Organic products available in global market are dried fruits and nuts, processed fruits and vegetables, cocoa, spices, herbs, oilseed crops and their products, sweeteners, dried leguminous products, meat, dairy products, alcoholic beverages and non-food items are cotton, cut flowers and pot plants etc.

Table 5: Organic product- Domestic sale (Metric tons)

Tea	1500
Coffee	750
Spices	500
Rice	5000
Jaggery, sugar	6000
Wheat & flour	3000
Pulses	2500
Fruits and vegetables	5000
Millets flour	2000
Oils & ghee	2000
Squashes, Jams	500
Snacks	500
Honey	2000
Others(essential seeds, etc)	500

Among the field crops, Basmati rice, cotton and sesame are exported from India. Cotton and sesame are mostly grown under rain fed / dry-land agriculture conditions, and it should not be difficult to grow those using organic manures. Basmati rice is grown in north India in the 'rice–wheat cropping system' belt, where large amount of fertilizers is not used, particularly in production of local basmati by farmers in Jammu region. Here again, areas need to be demarcated. Reasonable price guarantee with some incentives can be very supportive since yield levels in organic fields are likely to be low in the beginning. This area can also produce organic vegetables and wheat, the market for which is likely to grow in future. Perennial plantation crops can be easily grown with organic manures. Even today these crops are grown using organic manures.

7. Indian organic food industry: Emerging trends

Emerging trends are show that organics going to be vibrant industry in the 21st century globally. Thus it ensures more employment and increased investments in organic foods.

Demand for organic foods on rise

The current market size for organic food products is US$533 million, exhibiting 17% growth in 2015. According to ASSOCHAM, metropolitan cities have witnessed a 95% increase in demand in the last five years.

Online marketing channels

Many organic food companies are adopting the online route to expand their consumer base. The brick and mortar organic stores are usually located in metro and mini metro cities. These companies are reaching out to the rest of the consumers through online channels. Some of the players that have established their own online website include Farm2Kitchen, Organic Shop, Naturally Yours and Organic India. Premium food retail chains such as Godrej Nature's Basket also sell organic food brands such as Navdanya and 24 Mantra online. The online vegetable and fruit store I Say Organic sells five tons of vegetables and fruits a week and has a customer base of around 10,000 households in the National Capital Region (NCR).

More presence of Organic food restaurants and cafes

With increasing incidence of health problems such as diabetes, anxiety and stress plaguing urban India, many entrepreneurs are venturing into the area of organic café and marketplace. Some entrepreneurs organize the Organic Living Festival every fortnight and sell herbal lifestyle products like dental powder and digestive tonics and use natural and organic produce in its menu.

New product categories and varieties

Organic food companies are launching with new product categories and varieties to provide consumers with sufficient choice. Apart from fruits, vegetables, teas, pulses and spices, companies have also introduced ready-to-eat snacks, cookies, medicinal plants and herbs, and juices. Additionally, increased organic alternatives can be observed in established product categories are being enriched with alternatives.

8. Entrepreneurship and employment generation in organic agriculture

Organic agriculture offers much more entrepreneur opportunities than the conventional being a certified and guaranteed system. In the era of health consciousness, people want product of authenticity with traceability, the conditions which are met by organic agriculture. Right from the soil, seed to crop management and post harvest handling, organic agriculture has its own specific production package which involves many enterprises. Thus the approach has more income generating avenues than conventional one. (Table 6).

Table 6: Entrepreneurial areas for women empowerment

1. Organic vegetable production
   Organic farming by Farmer Producer Organizations (FPOs) and Village Producers' Organizations (VPOs) in large clusters, preferably of 1,000 hectares each, will be promoted by GoI. Women's Self Help Groups (SHGs) will also be encouraged to take up organic agriculture in clusters under the National Rural Livelihood Program.
2. Organic vegetable Shoppe
3. Organic fruit /juice corner
4. Organic dairying
   Rs100 billion has been allocated by Govt. of India to set up a Fisheries and Aquaculture Infrastructure Development Fund (FAIDF) for the fisheries sector and an Animal Husbandry Infrastructure Development Fund (AHIDF) for financing the infrastructure requirement of the animal husbandry sector. A Dairy Processing Infrastructure Development Fund (DPIDF) to help finance investment in dairying infrastructure had been announced last year.
5. Organic poultry
6. Organic seed production
7. Organic fish farming
8. Organic mushrooms
9. Organic grocery store
10. Organic tea/ coffee house
11. Organic feeds for cattle/ poultry
12. Herbal bath/ wash products
13. Herbal cosmetics and body products
14. Organic baby foods
15. Organic sweet shop
16. Organic bakery and confectionary
17. Organic food supplements
18. Organic root top gardening
19. Organic kitchen gardening
20. Organic indoor floriculture
21. Organic sericulture
22. Organic bee keeping
23. Organic horticulture nursery
24. Organic inputs store

Contd.

25. Commercial production of biocontrol agents and biofertilizers
26. Organic food restaurant.
27. Organic VAPs (Value Added Products) Shoppe
    With the food processing sector growing at an average rate of eight per cent per year, the government has decided to double the allocation to this sector, from Rs 7.15 billion in 2017-18 (revised estimates) to Rs 14 billion in 2018-19. The Pradhan Mantri Krishi Sampada Yojana is the flagship program for boosting investment in food processing.
28. Farm to food restaurant
    The government has allocated Rs 5 billion to launch Operation Green on the lines of Operation Flood. Operation Green will promote Farmer Producers Organizations' (FPOs), agri-logistics, processing facilities and professional management. Also, the government will set up state-of-the-art testing facilities in all the 42 Mega Food Parks to realize the potential of exports of agri-commodities

8.1. Employment generation

In two ways organic agriculture provides greater opportunities for employment. One it requires more mandays per unit of working area. Many farm operations and post harvest management of produce involve manual handling. Organic agriculture enterprises often require more labor input than conventional farming in order to replace external energy and capital inputs such as fertilizers and herbicides.

Crop diversification on organic farms, and related different planting and harvesting schedules, distributes labor demand through the season. This stabilizes employment, reduces turnover, alleviates problems related to labor migration, and helps to spread the overhead payroll costs per employee. For small and marginal organic farmers it is whole of the family employment source rather essential to make the organic farming more economical. Secondly being a specialized area, it opens avenue for a number of entrepreneurships (table 6) wherein one can establish income generating units.

9. Drivers of organic growth and business in India

Growth drivers of the organic business in India comprise both private and public sectors initiatives. The movement which began with ecological intentions now has established its creditability in commerce and trade. Therefore it has become the fastest growing area in global business. Key areas acting as drivers are enumerated below:

Health consciousness

With sharp rise of diabetes, cancer, arthritis and cardiovascular problems in human society, health concerns among Indian consumers or anywhere else are prime issues. Consumers have started giving importance to the nutrient content and the quality of the food they eat, thereby resulting in an increase in the consumption of organic food.

Rising purchasing power

Rising income and education levels are leading to an increase in the purchasing power and expenditure of people on healthcare products. The per capita income of Indians at current prices increased by 10.4% to INR1, 03,007 in 2016-17 as against INR 93,293 during 2015-16. Average household incomes are expected to triple in the next two decades, making India the world's third-largest consumer economy by 2025, up from the current seventh position.

Urbanization and working population

Increase in urban population implies growth in per capita purchasing power as well as a change in lifestyle and food habits. Urbanization is growing rapidly and 45% of the Indian population will be residing in urban areas by 2030. About 70% of the consumption growth in India in the next 15 years is expected to come from the working population (people aged 15-59 years). The urban consumers are open to paying increased prices for organic food products.

Increasing support from Government of India

The Government of India is promoting organic farming and the consumption of organic food in the country. Financial assistance is provided to farmers who are adopting organic farming under various central sector schemes such as Parampragit Krishi Vikas Yojana (PKVY), National Mission for Sustainable Agriculture (NMSA), Mission for Integrated Development of Horticulture (MIDH), National Food Security Mission (NFSM) and Rashtriya Krishi Vikas Yojana (RKVY). In the Union Budget of 2016, the GoI proposed to allocate 500,000 ha in the country under organic farming and develop value chains in the North-Estern Region (NER).

Technological developments

Noble efforts of R&D institutions such as organic crop production technologies, organic varieties and value added organic product developments are boosting the moral of the people involved in organic business. Ecozen Solutions, a Pune-based start-up, has developed solar-powered cold storage for fresh farm produce which can operate in remote areas with irregular power supply. Hyperspectral cameras are being promoted that use infrared rays to gauge the quality and shelf life of the product. Developments like these on a larger scale may help tackle various challenges faced by the organic sector. Finally, through IT and digital interventions, the traceability challenge of organic products has been resolved.

10. Organic Sector: Challenges in India

The organic agriculture in India has entered a transformation stage due to its multi-venture nature that has begun to attract the market with their one-of-a-kind offerings. In an effort to promote a healthier lifestyle, organic entrepreneurs are playing a pivotal role by providing consumers with wholesome organic products.

Organic food segment being at a nascent stage in India, both the Government and private players need to develop a strong policy framework that can benefit all involved. The organic farming industry in India holds immense potential to grow, provided it receives steady investment and benefits from both existing and new initiatives like incentivizing organic cultivation, food processing, certification and regulatory ease and tax benefits. Some of the challenges faced by the organic sector today can be grouped into three heads:

10.1. Producer-level challenges

Certification process

Issues like high certification costs, lengthy procedures, international validity, inadequate certifying agencies and inadequate supporting infrastructure facilities for verification are rampant in the certification process for pursuing organic farming. It costs between INR50 and INR500 per farmer per year for certification and the cost of internal audits and documentation is approximately INR2,500 per farmer. Although the cost of certification has reduced, it is still expensive for many small groups of farmers or individual farmers.

Certification standards

There is also a gap in the understanding of the certification standards and labeling requirements. Additionally, key trading partners have traditionally demonstrated a lack of willingness to sign equivalence arrangements.

Lack of market for the pre-certification produce

The harvest prior to certification or during the certification process of the farm or crop cannot be placed in the organic niche market due to the lack of an organic certificate. This harvest is sold as conventional crops, thereby causing the farmer to incur a loss.

Lack of standardization for the certification of different commodities

Dairy products have a different standard while meat has a different standard. The process of standardization of organic coconut will be different from that of the value- added products of coconut. Therefore, a company having multiple commodities needs to obtain multiple certifications and maintain multiple records as per the applicable standards.

High dependency on agriculture

India has the highest number of producers in the world yet they cultivate less than 1% of the organic area. The conventional production system is more lucrative given the land fragmentation.

Lack of special incentives for organic farmers

The transition from conventional to organic farming is accompanied by high input costs and low yields in the initial years. The cost of going completely organic is quite high, due to the high cost of organic manure. The commercially available bio-manure products may not be completely organic, and therefore the products sometimes get disqualified at the certification stage. This is one of the many reasons why farmers are skeptical when it comes to shifting from conventional to organic farming. In such cases, the farmers choose to play it safe by practicing conventional methods of farming.

Lack of standardized organic agriculture inputs and subsidy on organic inputs

Farmers also face an acute shortage of quality standardized organic agriculture inputs, which are often much more expensive than conventional agricultural inputs. There are no subsidies from the Government on agriculture inputs, especially biofertilizers and biopesticides, making the cost of cultivation for organic farming quite high. Unless the farmers use their own farm grown manure in large quantities, they are unable to meet the expenses. Lack of proper organic inputs often results in low yield making organic farming unsustainable for the farmers.

Lack of organic cultivation research and extension

The current research and extension on organic farming are much lesser than that on conventional farming. There is a lack of quality non-GMO seeds that are fit for organic cultivation. Strong government support for producing non-GMO high yielding varieties and niche crops for organic farming under different agro-ecological zones across India require investment in organic research and extension. The extension services are very limited for organic, for example, the ATMA scheme focuses more on conventional farming. There is no timely advisory available for organic pest and disease control measures.

10.2. Processor-level challenges

Supply chain issues

Many farmers are apprehensive of organic farming since it involves high production costs. The emphasis on collection, transportation and storage of fresh organic produce is very high. Due to relatively low volumes, the marketing and distribution chain of organic food products is relatively inefficient and the costs involved are very high. For example, organic produce cannot be stored in government warehouses that practice chemical treatment of storage areas. High demand and low supply further create inflationary pressure on organic food products. Therefore, these products have higher price markups than conventional products. Additionally, many sellers mix the produce from different geographical regions to help attain a competitive price, thus compromising the geographical origin norm. Lack of a proper organic supply chain is felt more acutely in hilly, tribal and remote areas that have a high potential for organic farming but have difficult terrain or underdeveloped infrastructure.

Global competitiveness

A major challenge India faces is that of increasing its share in the global organic food export market, in lieu of global competitiveness. There often exists a dichotomy between international quality and safety standards and Indian organic stands, which puts Indian produce at a disadvantage.

Lack of proper branding and packaging

Promotion and sale of organic products require separate packing material that is natural and requires distinctive branding that distinguishes organic from conventional products. At present, there is an absence of regulations on labeling standards. There is also lack of standards and clarifications regarding labeling and certification requirements for the domestic market and import market leading to malpractices such as mixing organic with conventional produce. The Indian certification agency plays an important role in branding. Since it requires financial assistance, the Government and private sector should come to a common understanding of organized export, brands development, and promotion with incentives from the Government.

10.3. Consumer-level challenges

Lack of awareness among consumers

Many consumers in India are still unaware of the health benefits of organic food products. The situation is worse in non-metro cities where consumers do not know the difference between conventional farming and organic farming.

They are buying products labeled as natural assuming them to be organic. Organic food products are produced, manufactured and handled using organic means defined by certifying bodies, whereas, natural food simply refers to food items that are not chemically altered or synthesized in any form. Therefore, companies can only expand their consumer base by increasing the awareness levels among consumers in non-metro cities.

The high cost of organic food products

The cost of organic food products in India is currently higher than that of conventional food items. Specialized farmer training cost, processing and inventory holding cost (without chemical additives), and increased packaging, logistics, and distribution cost (due to low volumes), contribute to the high price of organic food products. The switch to organic food is likely to cost an additional INR1, 200–1,500 per month for a family. Therefore, the purchase of organic food is restricted to the class of consumers residing in large cities.

Limited availability of organic food products

The limited availability of organic food products in the market is also posing a serious challenge to the growth of the Indian organic food industry. There are very few retail shops in India that store and sell organic food items. Many fake organic products are also available in the markets, which are diminishing the profits of genuine vendors. Therefore, the limited availability of organic food products is driving consumers to look for other options available in the market.

11. Regulatory environment and government initiatives

To address some of the challenges and increase competitiveness in organic Sector, the Government of India had taken several steps from a regulatory point of view to match the Global Standards of Organic Products, in an attempt to incentivize production for farmers and prompt companies to create consumer awareness.

Regulatory framework

1. Agricultural and Processed Food Products Export Development Authority (APEDA) for implementing the National Program on Organic Production (NPOP)

2. National Centre for Organic Farming (NCOF) for implementing the Participatory Guarantee System in India

3. Food Safety and Standards Authority of India (FSSAI) for regulation of food safety standards of organic packaged food and beverages products

APEDA: APEDA was established under the Agricultural and Processed Food Products Export Development Authority Act, passed by the Indian Parliament in December 1985. APEDA is the apex organization under the Ministry of Commerce and Industry, Government of India. It is mandated with the responsibility of promoting and developing the export of agro products from India. Its main functions include promoting the export-oriented production and development of scheduled products (including fruits, vegetables, cereals and rice), fixing of standards and specifications for the scheduled products for the purpose of exports.

NPOP: Since 2001, the Government has been promoting organic farming through third-party certification under NPOP. NPOP is implemented by APEDA to meet the stringent standards for exports. It provides information on standards for organic production, systems criteria and procedures for accreditation of Inspection and Certification Bodies. NPOP also lays down guidelines for the national organic logo and the regulations governing its use. The standards and procedures are formulated in relation to international standards such as those of Codex and International Federation of Organic Agriculture Movements (IFOAM). The NPOP standards for production and accreditation system are also recognized by the European Commission and Switzerland as equivalent to their country standards. The scope of NPOP includes:

- Policymaking for development and certification of organic products as notified by the Department of Commerce from time to time
- Creating national standards for organic products and processes
- Accreditation of certification programs to be operated by certification bodies

Certification of organic products

In 2006, India's organic certification process under NPOP had been granted equivalence with the European Union. It has also been recognized for conformity assessment by the National Organic Program (NOP) of the United States Department of Agriculture (USDA). The organic certification process set of standard and guiding principles laid down by NPOP are as follows.

The process of organic certification in India: Though organic certification can be obtained for all types of agricultural produce, including processed food and food served in restaurants, this section focuses on agricultural produce.

Large-scale farmers or small size landholder growers groups (minimum of 25 and maximum of 500 farmers who possess land in the same geographical area) can apply for organic certification of their produce. It is pertinent to note that the certification is provided to produce and not the land. APEDA offers an internet-based e-service called Tracenet to collect, record and report data on organic certification. It is also used to trace any organic produce all the way to the farm from anywhere in the supply chain.

Organic certification by APEDA

Certification agency: The organic certification process is carried out by accredited bodies under NPOP. There are 28 agencies accredited by APEDA. These certifying agencies verify farms, storages and processing units. Products certified organic by them carry the India organic logo.

Participatory Guarantee System-India (PGS-India)

The development of PGS in India began in 2006. It was only in 2015 that it was officially recognized. PGS-India is a process- based certification wherein a group certifies that its members are growing food organically. This certification process has been made free for the farmers, ensuring that they do not have to bear any cost other than a nominal cost as set by the farmer community. Currently, PGS-India is implemented by the National Centre of Organic Farming (NCOF) under the National Project on Organic Farming (NPOF), Department of Agriculture, Cooperation and Farmers' Welfare, Government of India.

PGS-India controls the quality system through internal QMS through Farmer Grower Group Certification (GGC) instead of a certifying agency. The role of GGC is as follows:

- Act as an internal quality control system for small farmer group and cooperatives
- Producers who share common products are organized under one management and marketing system
- Collective marketing of the organic products,
- Centralized processing, marketing, and distribution system,
- Internal control and supervision system to ensure compliance with organic certification.

PGS vs. third party

There is no connection between the two certification systems. For instance, exporters cannot process foods with PGS-certified ingredients because developed markets like the US, the biggest for organic products, and the European Union do not accept PGS yet.

In PGS the local farmers conduct their own appraisal and maintain the rules and standards of the group. It is simpler and cheaper and is controlled by the farming community itself. It's recommended for organic farmers who work as a group or who can come together as a group at village or district level. The design is best suited for small and marginal farmers where the community is supported by NGOs or any institution.

12. Organic agriculture and women empowerment

Gender relationships are fundamental to the way farm work is organized worldwide, and assets such as land, labour, seeds and machinery are managed, and to farm decision-making. Women worldwide have much less access to, or control over, privately-held resources such as land, machinery, or money, than do men. Women's economic empowerment refers to the ability for *women* to enjoy their right to control and benefit from the resources, assets, income and their own time, as well as the ability to manage risk and improve their economic status and well being. Few statistics from USA indicate that women are much more present in sustainable/ organic farming than in conventional farming. Women are primarily interested in producing for local markets, running small farms, and working with family labour. For women in particular, the boundaries between economic and non-economic activities are often fluid, as women seek to combine their roles as mothers and homemakers with community development and with income-generation. One message is clear: Women are much more likely than men to operate smaller scale farms. Barriers to improving women's agency include widespread deficiencies in policy support to women, and in fact to the organic farming sector as a whole. In a study paper of Farworth and Hutchings (2009) most respondents suggested strongly that external partners are part of the problem; they appear to consider working with male producers almost inevitable. With respect to developing countries, male farmers are often seen as innovative farmers interested in export production; women are seen as subsistence farmers.

Farworth and Hutchings (2009) indicated contribution of women scientists to developing organic paradigms has diminished over the past sixty years. The increasing institutionalization and professionalization of research has resulted in an ever-decreasing percentage of women scientists, particularly at the higher levels. As a consequence few women lead organic research institutes, and far fewer women than men publish research papers. Due to the different positioning of women in society, research domains in organic farming are narrowed and restricted by their absence. Their access to resources held in common may be restricted. Lack of access to resources can seriously limit the ability of women to put their values into practice. Improving the access of women (and disempowered men) to privately held resources, and to resources held in common, is thus fundamental to sustainable farming. Organic and sustainable farming has the potential to create new structures that actively work towards achieving women's empowerment and protecting the use of indigenous knowledge.

They suggested that most noteworthy enabling factor to improve women's participation in organic and sustainable farming is to make a concerted effort at increasing their agency. Women need to participate in all decision-making aspects of sustainable and organic agriculture, as farmers, as resear-chers and as leaders. Some observations of the report include:

- When women have the support of men their agency improves.
- Training in organic methods appears to be a critical support to enabling women to take on leadership functions, so they quite literally know and realize they know what they are talking about.
- The sustainable agricultural sector (including organic) has been quite successful in creating women-friendly spaces. This is important for the exchange of ideas, and marketing.
- It is necessary to increase women's research presence in organic research institutions (including at the higher levels). To enable women to conduct research in the field, wo-men in some cultures may need support. This might include providing chaperones or enabling them to work close to their homes. It is important to allow women the ability to set research agendas, and to work with their research needs and priorities as opposed to meeting the needs of what outsiders deem important and worthy of research for their communities.
- Food security as a priority for organics may also involve enabling women's empowerment since they hold, in most cultures, a central role in providing nutrition for the household.

13. Some attentions and actions for women empowerment

- Active choices have to be made for gender equality when working with partners. It is not enough to ensure that formal criteria are met, for example that women are members of committees and that separate washing and toilet facilities are provided.
- Attention needs to be paid to the strength of women's voice. Are women actually speaking in meetings? Are they taking decisions? Increasing women's agency will come when this is part of intentional project design, and when empowerment is a conscious part of an organization's agenda.

- Capacity development needs to be based upon an analysis of the constraints women face in organic and sustainable farming. For example, if women are to be stronger decision makers in the field (not just the office) there needs to be specific training for women on machinery operation and maintenance. We cannot assume men and women enter orga-nic and alternative farming with the same experience.
- Support for gender equality should not obscure the needs of the most poor, both men and women.
- Special organic initiatives can be developed to work with asset poor, even landless farmers.
- Widows and divorcees may form a special target group since they are the most likely to have no assets (including a lack of social capital and of land), but poor men should also be included.
- Diverse gender sensitive indicators, approaches and analyses appropriate to diverse situations and communities should be developed and used. These diverse approaches/solutions need to be shared amongst different global communities working towards in-creasing women's empowerment in organic farming and sustainable agriculture.

14. References

Farnworth Cathy and Hutchings Jessica .2009. Organic Agriculture and Womens' Empowerment. IFOAM, Germany. 100 Pp.

Goyal M and Prakash J .2011. Women entrepreneurship in India – problems and prospects. *Zenith International Journal of Multidisciplinary Research*. **1**(5): 195-207.

Jena Anupama, Mishra Prasanta Kumar K, Ojha Sadhna and Joshi Pragya .2018.Women empowerment through agripreneurship. *International Journal of Science, Environment and Technology*. 7 (4):1329 – 1333.

Lampkin NH. 1990. Estimating the impact of widespread conversion to organic farming on land use and physical output in the United Kingdom. *In Economics of Organic Farming* (Eds. Lampkin, N. H.and Padel, S.), CAB, Wallingford, UK, 1994, pp. 353–359.

Mette Vaarst. 2010. Organic Farming as A Development Strategy: Who are Interested and Who are not? *Journal of sustainable development*. 3(1): 38-50.

Pretty J (ed.) 2005. *The Pesticide Detox. Towards a more sustainable agriculture*. Earthscan, London, UK., pp. 294.

Sharma Y. 2013. Women entrepreneur in India. *IOSR Journal of Business andManagement*. (*IOSR-JBM*) 15(3): 09-14.

Sharma Jag Paul 2017. Understanding organic farming: Different facets and dimensions. In, Principles and Practices of Organic Crop Production Vol.I (Sharma, Jag Paul ed.). Kalyani Publishers, New Delhi. Pp 40-52.

Index

D

E

F

J

K

L

M

N

O

P

Q

R

S

T

U

V

W

Z

FSC
www.fsc.org
MIX
Papier | Fördert gute Waldnutzung
FSC® C083411

Kolibri 360 GmbH
Ferdinand-Jühlke-Straße 7
99095 Erfurt, Deutschland
produktsicherheit@kolibri360.de